Siege Warfare during the Crusades

Siege Warfare during the Crusades

Michael S. Fulton

Pen & Sword
MILITARY

For Elizabeth
(the best of moms)

First published in Great Britain in 2019 by
PEN & SWORD MILITARY
An imprint of Pen & Sword Books Ltd
Yorkshire – Philadelphia

ISBN 978-1-52671-865-5

A CIP catalogue record for this book is available from the British Library.

Typeset by Concept, Huddersfield, West Yorkshire, HD4 5JL
Printed and bound in India by Replika Press Pvt. Ltd.

Pen & Sword Books Ltd incorporates the imprints of Aviation, Atlas, Family History, Fiction, Maritime, Military, Discovery, Politics, History, Archaeology, Select, Wharncliffe Local History, Wharncliffe True Crime, Military Classics, Wharncliffe Transport, Leo Cooper, The Praetorian Press, Remember When, White Owl, Seaforth Publishing and Frontline Publishing.

For a complete list of Pen & Sword titles please contact
PEN & SWORD BOOKS LTD
47 Church Street, Barnsley, South Yorkshire, S70 2AS, England
E-mail: enquiries@pen-and-sword.co.uk
Website: www.pen-and-sword.co.uk
or
PEN & SWORD BOOKS
1950 Lawrence Rd, Havertown, PA 19083, USA
E-mail: uspen-and-sword@casematepublishers.com
Website: www.penandswordbooks.com

Contents

Lists of Illustrations vii

Preface xi

Regional Maps xiv

Introduction 1

1. Historical Context: the Period of the Crusades 3
   - Setting the Stage 3
   - The First Generations 8
   - The Age of Nūr al-Dīn and Saladin 19
   - The Ayyūbid Era 22
   - Early Mamlūk Rule 24
   - West vs. East, Christians vs. Muslims? 27

2. Strategy of Defence: Building and Using Fortifications 34
   - Before the Crusades 34
   - Administration 38
   - Location 59
   - Tactical Use 65
   - Defenders 88
   - Refuge 96
   - Planners 99

3. Strategy of Attack: Overcoming the Obstacle of Relief 105
   - Early Opportunism 105
   - Relief Forces 106
   - Distraction 115
   - Truces 120
   - Rapid Attack 124

4. Means of Attack: Siege Weapons 127
   - Armies 127
   - Action beyond the Walls 129
   - Siege Engines 132
   - Naval Support 169
   - Deception and Negotiation 174
   - Transfer of Knowledge 187

5. Means of Defence: the Design of Fortifications 190
   - Provisions 190
   - Walls and Towers 193

Entrances 214
Development 228
Shift in Design 235
Active Defence 252
Payoff 254
6. Influences and Trends 258
Fortifications 258
Trends: Distribution, Success and Duration 269
Conclusion: the Siege of Acre, 1291 281
List of Sieges 286
Rulers and their Reigns 300
Glossary 304
Notes 306
Select Bibliography by Site 308
Bibliography 316
Index 335

Lists of Illustrations

Maps

Regional Maps
Key . . . xiv
1. The Jazīra . . . xv
2. The Upper Euphrates . . . xvi
3. The Middle Euphrates . . . xvii
4. Cilicia and Western Syria . . . xviii
5. Western Syria and Northern Lebanon . . . xix
6. Lebanon and Northern Palestine . . . xx
7. Southern Palestine . . . xxi
8. Sinai . . . xxii
9. Egypt . . . xxiii
10. Cyprus . . . xxiv
The First Crusade . . . 7
The Frankish principalities at about their largest . . . 9
'Desert castles' . . . 35
Region around the Hula Valley . . . 43
Jabal 'Awf . . . 53
Reynald of Châtillon's Arabian campaigns, 1181, 1182–83 . . . 55
Templar towers on the road from Jaffa to Jericho . . . 67
Castles around Ascalon . . . 72
Strongholds slighted by Saladin (1190–91) and al-Mu'aẓẓam 'Īsā (1218–19) . . 86
Strongholds preserved and slighted by the Mamlūks, 1260–91 . . . 87
Major battles . . . 112
Baybars' campaign against Safed, 1266 . . . 118
Saladin's campaign in Palestine, 1187 . . . 184
Saladin's campaign in western Syria, 1188 . . . 185

Plans

'Desert castles' . . . 36
Damascus, citadel . . . 57
Bosra, theatre-citadel . . . 64
Kerak (with topography) . . . 74
Crac des Chevaliers and Jacob's Ford in the twelfth century . . . 79
Bānyās (with topography) . . . 108

Tyre (with topography) 110
Jerusalem, siege of 1099, final deployments (with topography) 146
Arsūf (with topography) 161
Antioch, town defences and siege forts of the First Crusade (with topography) 168
ʿAtlit, outer wall embrasure 195
ʿAjlūn, level 2 with exposed sections of level 1 199
Tortosa, keep 200
Caesarea, defences improved by Louis IX and earlier Roman wall (with topography) 203
Sidon, sea castle 204
Bent entrances 217
Cairo, Bāb al-Barqiyya 218
Aleppo, citadel gatehouse 221
Crac des Chevaliers (with topography) 227
Saone (with topography) 228
Twelfth-century quadriburgium enclosure castles 230
Belvoir 233
Cairo, citadel 237
Cairo, citadel towers Burj al-Ramla and Burj al-Ḥaddād 238
Ṣubayba 240
Montfort 243
ʿAtlit, second level of the outer defences, first level of the inner defences 245
Mamlūk towers with central pillars 247
Ṣubayba, outer southwestern tower 248
Edwardian castles 264
Acre, siege of 1291 283

Images

Jerusalem 5
Antioch, town walls as seen in the eighteenth century 11
Crac des Chevaliers 13
Apamea 16
Qaṣr al-Ḥayr al-Sharqī, entrance of the smaller enclosure 35
Montreal 41
Beaufort 43
Caesarea 46
ʿAjlūn 52
ʿAjlūn and region to the immediate south 54
Ṣubayba 56
Aleppo, citadel gatehouse 57
Castellum Regis, in the centre of Miʿilya 60
Montfort 61

Ṣubayba, from the east 61
Le Destroit 66
Kerak 73
Jacob's Ford, northeastern corner of the castle and the river to the right 78
Margat 93
Qalʿat Jaʿbar 99
Montfort, mine in the outer southwestern tower 141
Montfort, mine in the southern wall of the upper ward 141
Siege tower 144
Counterweight trebuchet, Cardiff castle 157
Traction trebuchet, Caerphilly castle 158
Al-Ṭarsūsī's Persian trebuchet 159
Arsūf, outer southern tower, featuring artillery damage inflicted during the siege of 1265 before the tower was destroyed by the Mamlūk sappers 162
Arsūf, artillery projectiles from the siege of 1265 162
Maṣyāf 178
Al-Ḥabis, from the great temple of Petra 191
Subayba, reservoir 192
Saone, cistern 192
Crac des Chevaliers, western end of the outer southern defences 194
Ṣubayba, casemates and embrasures of the southern rounded tower 196
Belvoir, embrasures of one of the inner towers 196
Belvoir, exterior of one of the embrasures of the inner enclosure 197
Saone, embrasures along the outer eastern wall 198
Kerak, line of casemates built by the Mamlūks along the outer western wall . . 198
Chastel Neuf, fosse 201
Kerak, northern fosse 202
Saone, eastern fosse 205
Caesarea, talus around the town defences 207
Shayzar, northern glacis 207
Kerak, eastern glacis 208
ʿAjlūn, slot machicolation over the inner gate of the outer gateway 210
Montfort, machicolation over the inner northwestern gate 211
Montfort, looking down through the machicolation over the outer northwestern gate 212
Crac des Chevaliers, Mamlūk box machicolations 212
Bānyās, through column 213
Arsūf, through column 214
Caesarea, outer gate of the eastern gateway, featuring a slot machicolation, portcullis groove, lower socket for a leaf door and pocket in the wall for a locking bar 216
ʿAjlūn, outer gate and barbican 219

'Ajlūn, inside the outer barbican 220
Safed, southwestern gate and barbican 221
Caesarea, closed postern in the northern town wall 223
Belvoir, staircase to the postern in the western mural tower 225
Belvoir, postern in the outer southwestern tower 224
Ṣubayba, postern in tower 11 226
Chastel Blanc 229
Belvoir 232
Crac des Chevaliers, eastern side of the outwork from the outer wall 235
Al-Raḥba 239
Montreal, inscription on the north tower 241
Le Destroit, with 'Atlit in the background 244
Ṣubayba, topmost northeastern shooting chamber of the outer southwestern tower 249
Montreal, from the west 263
Ṣubayba, upper castle from the outer southwestern tower 265
Fort Saint-André (Villeneuve-lès-Avignon), main gate 266
Chepstow, Marten's Tower and straight eastern entrance 268

Graphs and Tables

Use of siege towers, 1097–1200 149
Use of Frankish siege towers by decade 150
Maritime forces at twelfth-century Frankish sieges of coastal Mediterranean towns 173
Terms of surrender after the battle of Hattin 183
Belligerents of sieges 270
Distribution of sieges, before and after Hattin and Saladin's death 271
Sieges against coreligionists 271
Length of sieges 273
Distribution of twelfth-century sieges 277
Distribution of thirteenth-century sieges 278
Length and success rates of sieges by period 279

Preface

The study of siege warfare can be traced back to antiquity. Much as some Roman figures sought to learn from the engagements of the ancient Greeks, and certain medieval rulers looked to their Roman predecessors for inspiration, a number of early modern commanders tried to gain an advantage in battle by examining medieval, as well as ancient, sieges. As the modern discipline of historical study developed over the following centuries, armies grew to unprecedented sizes and the rate of technological innovation rapidly accelerated. In this context, which saw traditional fortifications become increasingly obsolete, most nineteenth- and early twentieth-century historians of medieval warfare focused naturally on the significance of battles rather than sieges. In the wake of the Second World War, guerrilla warfare became more prevalent and, consciously or not, historians began to shift their focus beyond the great battles. Today it is widely acknowledged that there were simply too few battles to decide the many wars and campaigns that raged across medieval Europe and the Middle East. Sieges tended to be more significant on a year-to-year, decade-to-decade basis, while raids, including small skirmishes, were by far the most common military actions.

In the medieval Levant, certain battles had dramatic consequences. The crusaders' victories at the battles of Dorylaeum (1097), Antioch (1098) and Ascalon (1099) allowed them to gain a foothold in the East, while the battles of the Field of Blood (1119) and Hattin (1187) saw the near eradication of Frankish armies and almost led to the collapse of the principality of Antioch and kingdom of Jerusalem respectively. The second battle of Ramla (1102) and battle of Forbie (1244) were decisive defeats for the Franks, but had few territorial consequences. By comparison, the Mamlūks' victory over the Mongols at ʿAyn Jālūt (1260) provided them with the opportunity to spread their authority across western Syria. Aside from these rather exceptional events, battles were rare and most campaigns were fought without one. Rather than battles, sieges and the possession of strongholds were the primary means of holding and expanding territorial power and influence.

Our understanding of siege warfare and the significance of castles and other fortifications has developed dramatically over the past 200 years. In the nineteenth century, theories regarding the fortifications built by the Franks in the Levant were influenced by the ways that forts had been used to defend Europe over the past few hundred years. Ideas that rings of castles were built along frontiers and borders, with interior strongholds to secure road networks and provide depth if an enemy broke past the outer ring, are reminiscent of the thinking that guided Vauban in the late seventeenth century and Séré de Rivières in the late nineteenth.

In the mid-twentieth century, R.C. Smail's seminal work, *Crusading Warfare*, redefined the role of medieval castles, critically pointing out that these were not simply early forts and those within could do little to obstruct the movement of large armies. Rather than searching for some overarching grand defensive design, which did not exist, Smail pointed to the more immediate motives that often influenced the construction and placement of castles. As he put it, 'The process of Latin settlement at the time of the First Crusade was not the result of a conquest ordered and organized by a single authority, but was extended by the boldness and greed of individuals.'[1] But even today, our appreciation of modern warfare influences our understanding of past conflicts.

In perhaps the most important contribution to the study of crusader siege warfare since that of Smail, Randall Rogers, writing at the start of the 1990s, despaired at what little attention was still devoted to the study of sieges. While Rogers wrote this highlighting the disproportionate attention given to battles, the same sentiment might just as easily apply to the study of castles. These great structures, which have captured the imaginations of tourists for centuries, came to attract more serious scholarly attention beginning with a line of scholars in the late nineteenth century and early twentieth, including Emmanuel Guillaume Rey, Max Van Berchem and T.E. Lawrence (of Arabia).[2] But what remains the defining study of Frankish castles is the three-part work of Paul Deschamps, beginning with his masterful examination of Crac des Chevaliers and concluding with a posthumously published survey of castles in northwestern Syria.[3] A number of studies have followed in the wake of Deschamps', including those of Robin Fedden and John Thomson, Wolfgang Müller-Wiener, and Hugh Kennedy, while two new studies of Crac have also been published.[4] Attention, traditionally devoted to 'crusader castles', has also begun to shift to more evenly include Muslim strongholds. This can be seen clearly in three excellent edited volumes published in the first decade of the twenty-first century, one in French, one in English and one in German, to which Cyril Yovitchitch's study of Ayyūbid fortifications might be added.[5]

Our ever-improving understanding of medieval fortifications is due in large part to the ongoing efforts of archaeologists. Thanks to C.N. Johns' work in the 1930s, some of the earliest scientific excavations in the region, we have a careful study of ʿAtlit, now off-limits as part of an Israeli military base.[6] Denys Pringle's surveys of smaller structures are perhaps the most comprehensive, and have provided an important record as urban sprawl and neglect threaten some of these less imposing structures.[7] Presently, Israeli-led excavations are under way at Arsūf and Montfort, French teams have recently worked at a number of Syrian strongholds, the crusader town of Caesarea and are now excavating at Belvoir, and a Syro-Hungarian team has been working at Margat for a number of years.[8] Elsewhere, excavations were conducted at Jacob's Ford and Montreal, but we still await the publication of their finds. Excavations in Syria, most of which have been interrupted by the current conflict, will hopefully continue and improve our understanding of the citadels of Aleppo and Damascus, and countless other strongholds, such as Qalʿat Jaʿbar and Qalʿat Najm. Christina Tonghini's thorough examination of Shayzar has proven an excellent start.[9] Outside of Syria, the mighty castles of Kerak, Safed, Ṣubayba, Toron, Beaufort and numerous others still await comprehensive excavation and analysis. Some strongholds, including Gaza and Jaffa, have already been lost to history, while Beaufort,

Crac, Aleppo and others have been damaged during the course of wars in just the last fifty years, adding urgency in what is still a volatile region prone to conflict.

Despite the attention dedicated to castles, siege warfare is often given little more than a token chapter in books on these strongholds or medieval warfare more generally. Perhaps the most important works on the topic, since that of Smail, are those of Randall Rogers and Christopher Marshall, both published in 1992.[10] Dealing with the twelfth and thirteenth centuries respectively, each is laudable in its own right, although both authors would no doubt have benefited from the opportunity to read the other's work before his own went to press. Both works are written from a primarily Frankish perspective and siege warfare, at least in the context of the Levant, is only a part of each. A generation later, it seems an updated synthesis and refinement might be in order.

* * *

To make this study more accessible to students and a general audience, few references have been included other than where direct quotations are given. European names have been anglicized, while those of Eastern figures have been transcribed using their most common forms when employed by historians and archaeologists of the period. Muslim names have also been abbreviated according to custom – for example, Saladin's brother is identified as *al-ʿĀdil* [Sayf al-Dīn], while his uncle appears as [Asad al-Dīn] *Shīrkūh*. To assist with pronunciation, most Arabic names and terms have been transliterated with diacritical marks. A short glossary and lists of rulers by region have also been included and, for anyone looking for more information related to a particular site, a brief list of the principal strongholds and studies relating to them can be found near the end of the book, as can a bibliography of primary and secondary sources.

* * *

This book would not have been possible without the help of a number of people, to whom thanks are in order. First, to John France, this generation's great authority on crusader warfare, who directed this project to me in October 2016, and to Denys Pringle, under whom I had the pleasure of working while in Cardiff, where much of my early research was conducted. Next, to the numerous archaeologists working on medieval sites in the Levant, many of whom have enthusiastically shared their experiences and insights with me over the years. Denys Pringle, Ross Burns, Michael Eisenberg, Jean Yasmine, Fraser Reed and Steve Tibble have generously provided some of the images that have been included. I am also indebted to Christopher Marshall, Steve Tibble, Niall Christie and Adam LeRoux, who read and commented on the first draft of this book; it is immeasurably better thanks to their input. Finally, I am grateful for the support of the History Department at the University of British Columbia, with whom I served as a Visiting Scholar while writing this book. To everyone mentioned above and countless others, a big thanks!

M.S.F
Vancouver, B.C.
December 2018

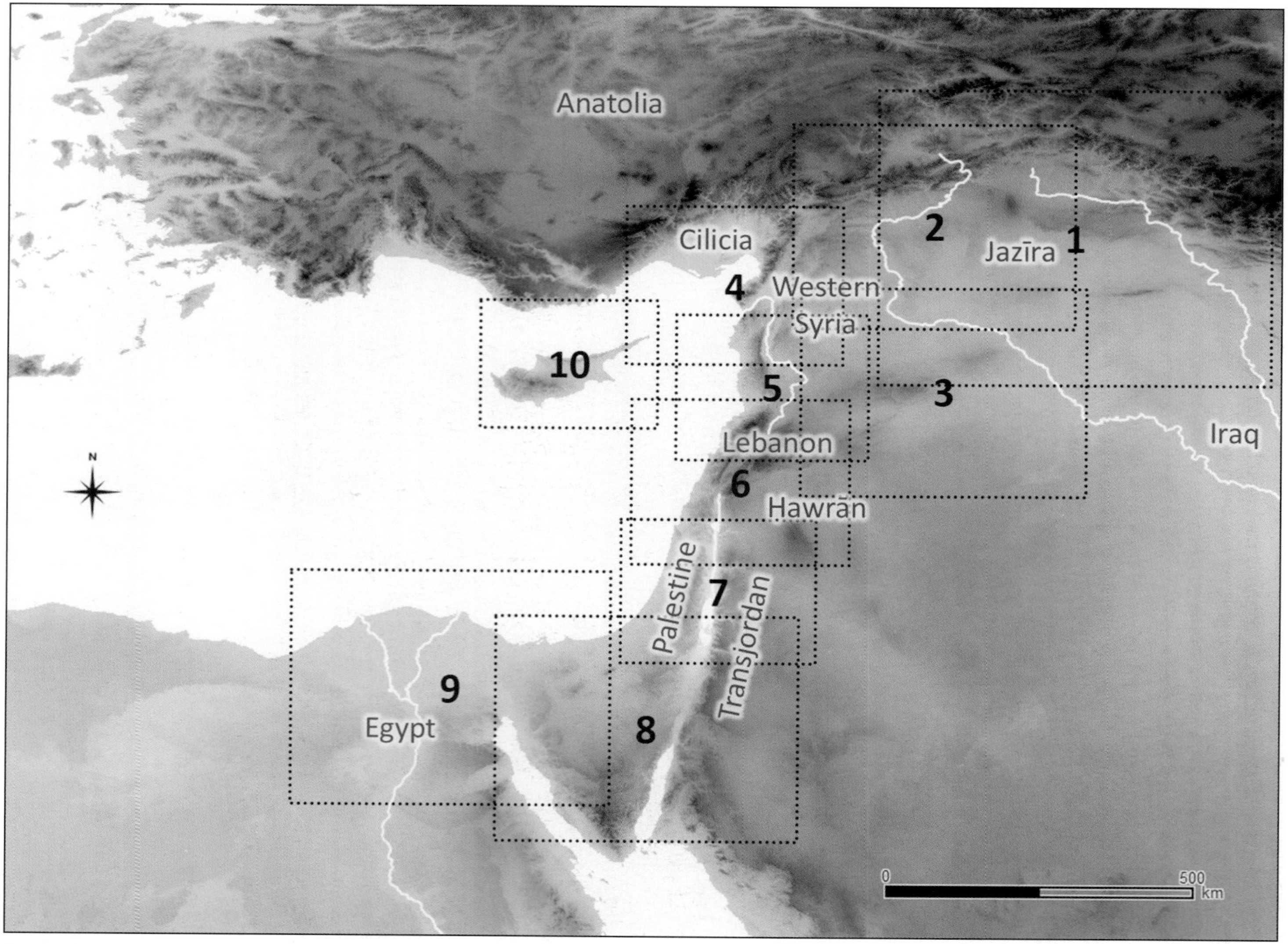

Regional Map Key

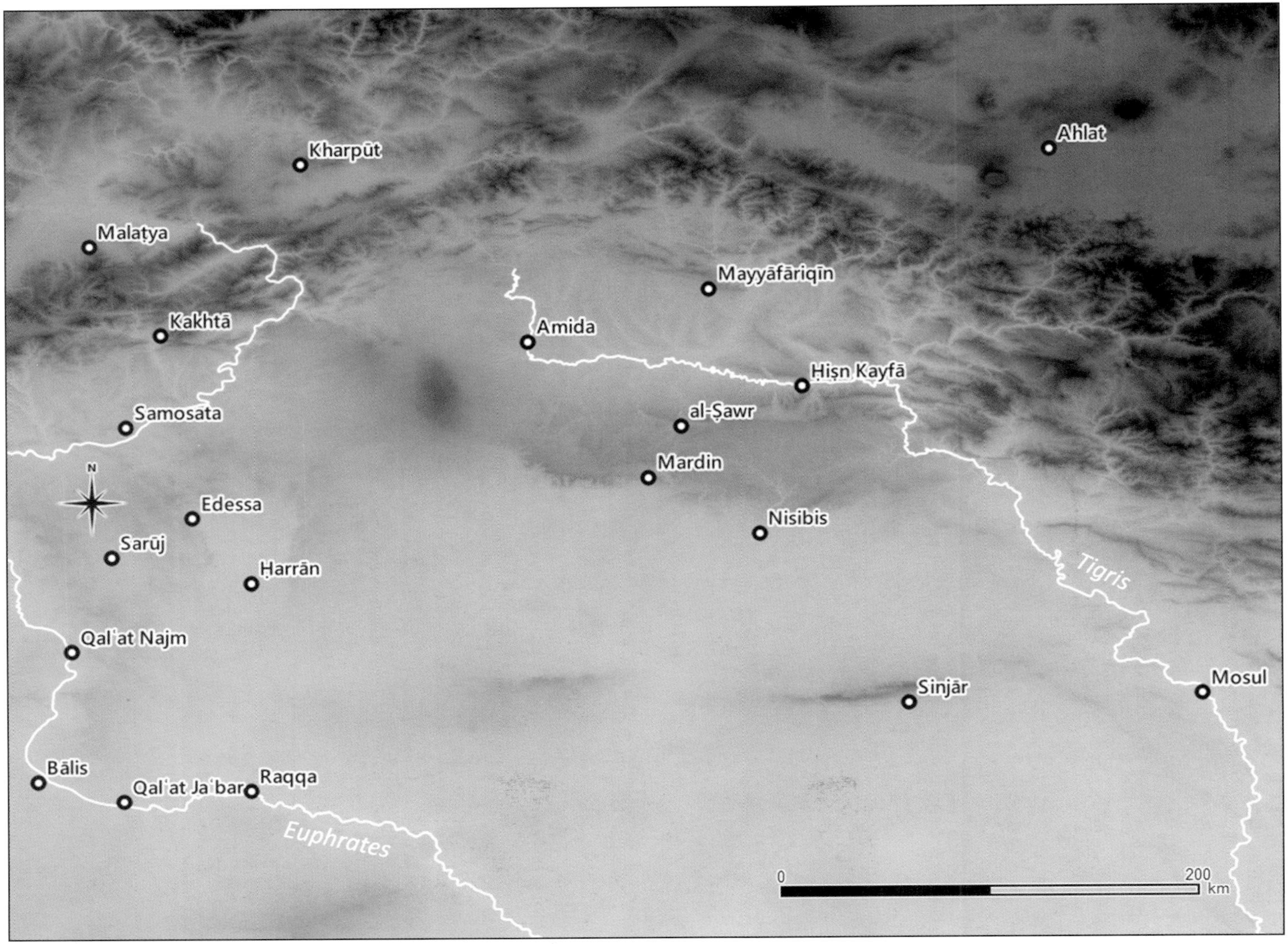

Regional Map 1. The Jazīra.

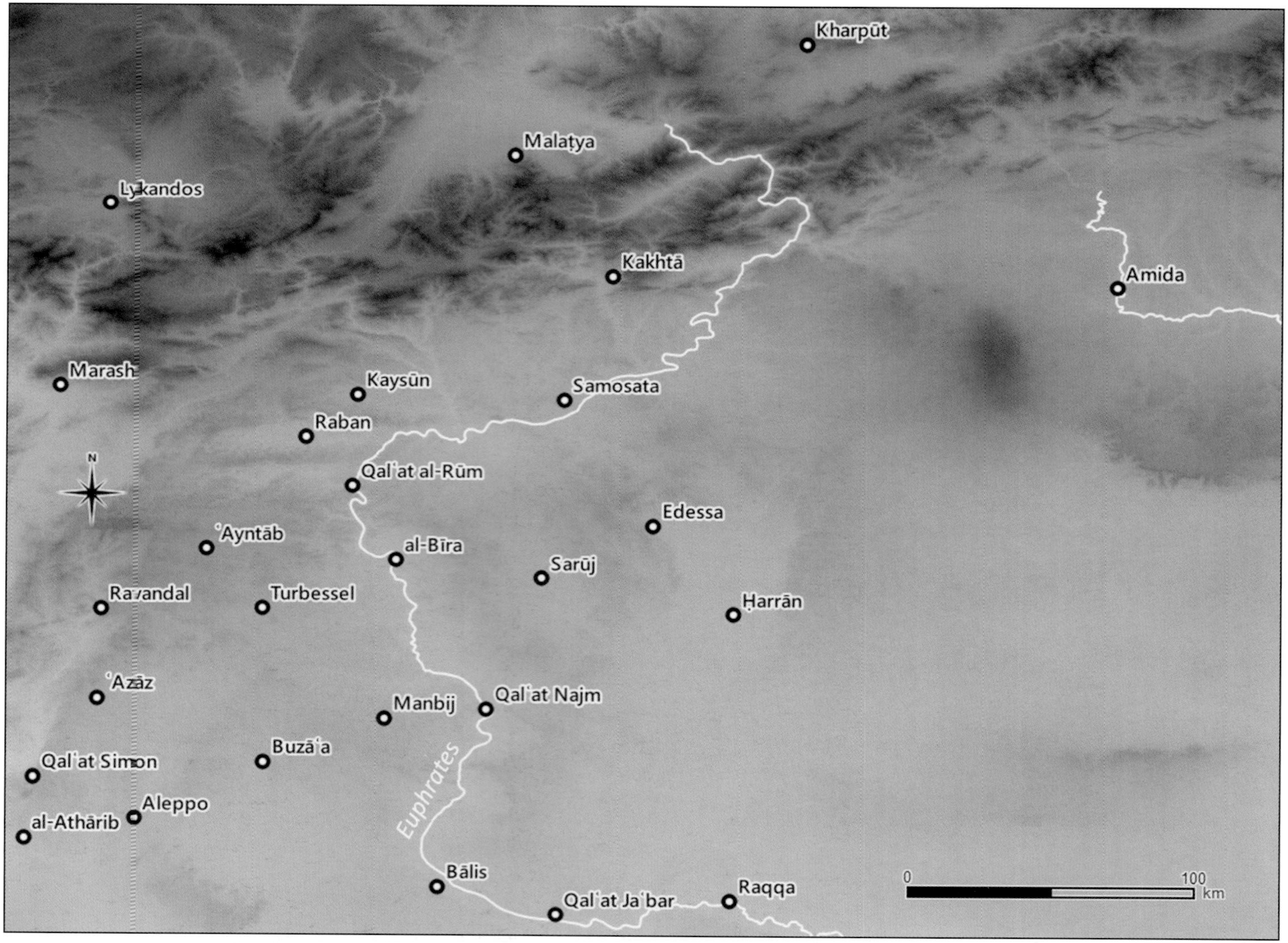

Regional Map 2. The Upper Euphrates.

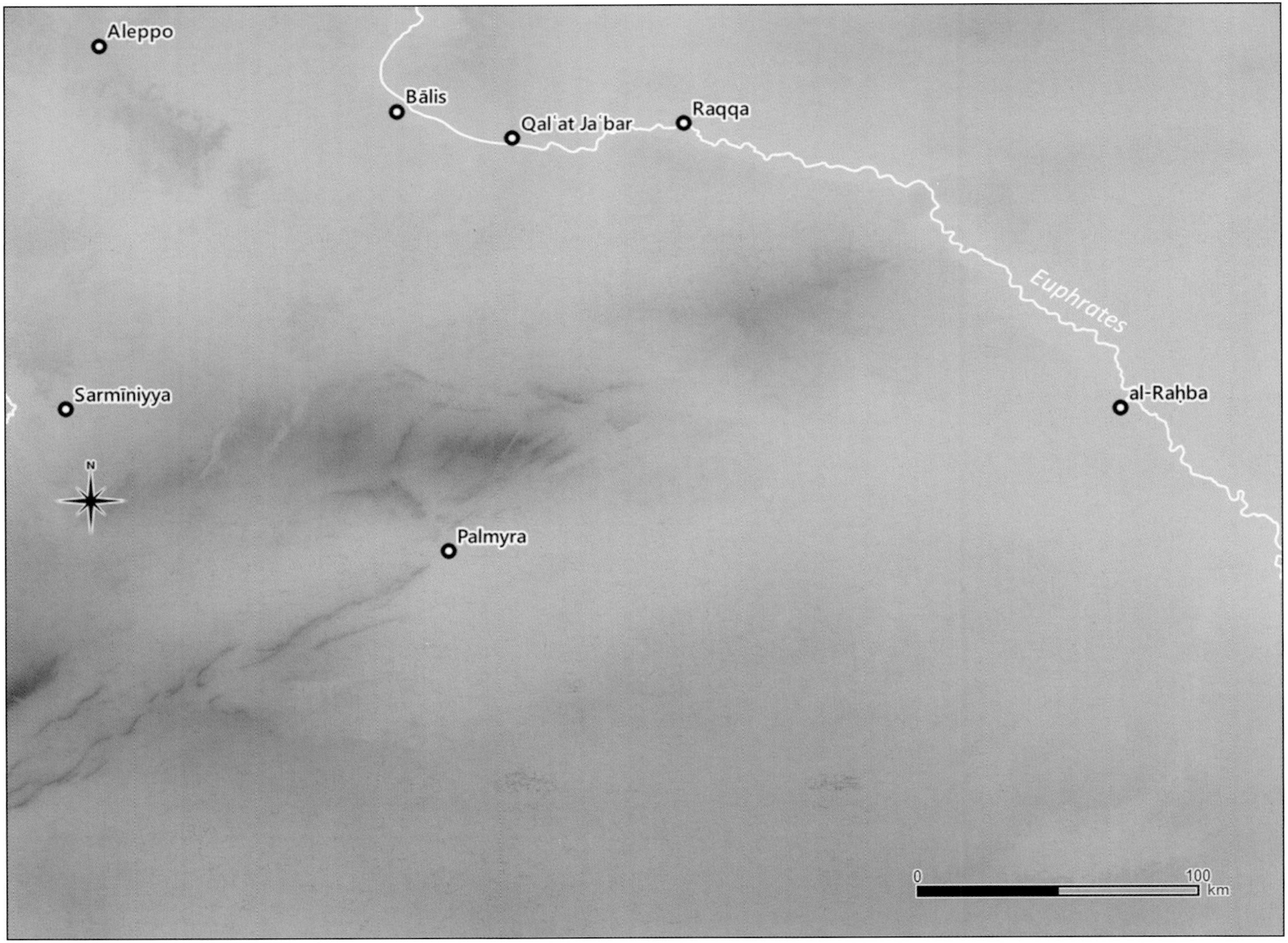

Regional Map 3. The Middle Euphrates.

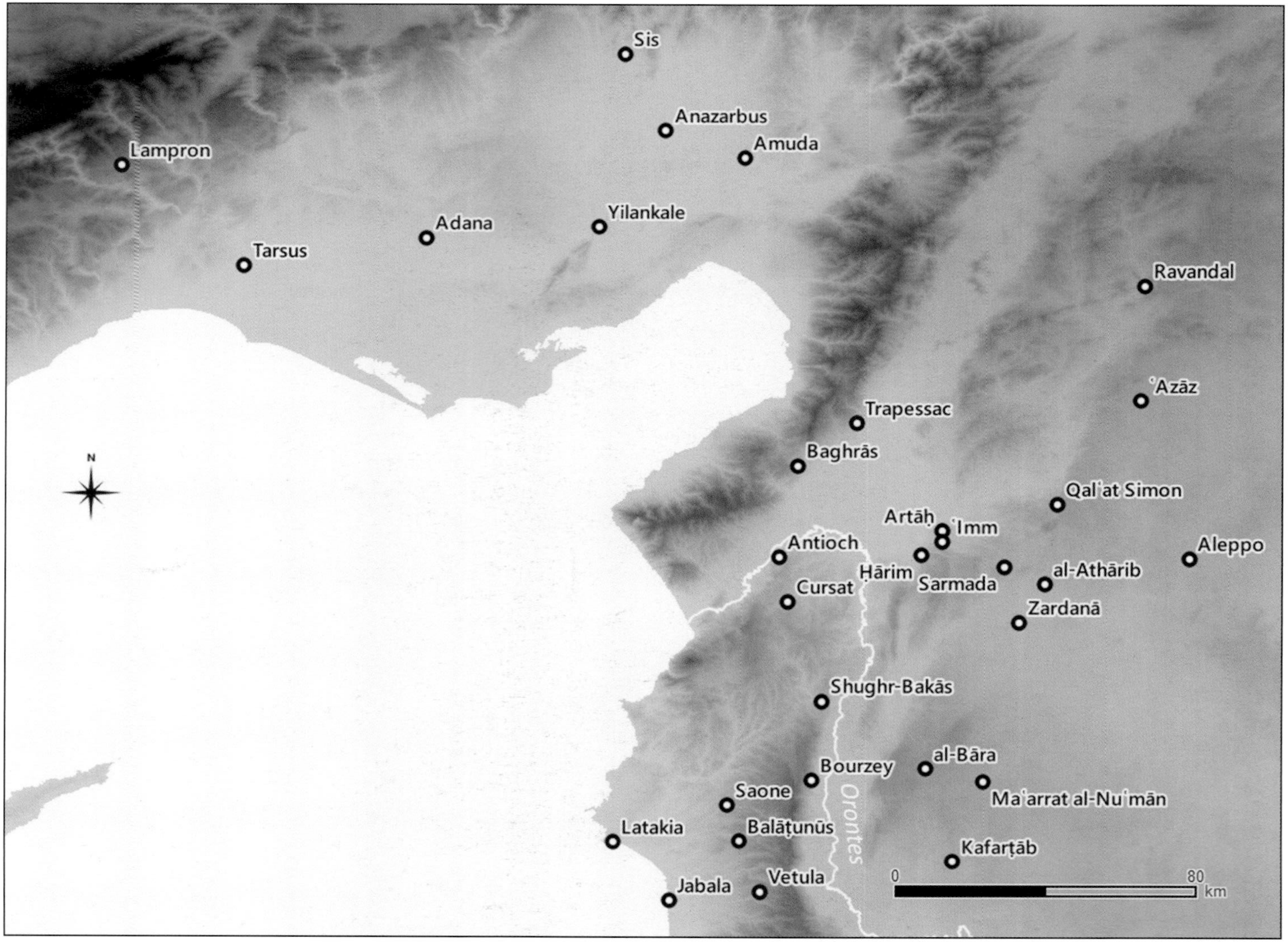

Regional Map 4. Cilicia and Western Syria.

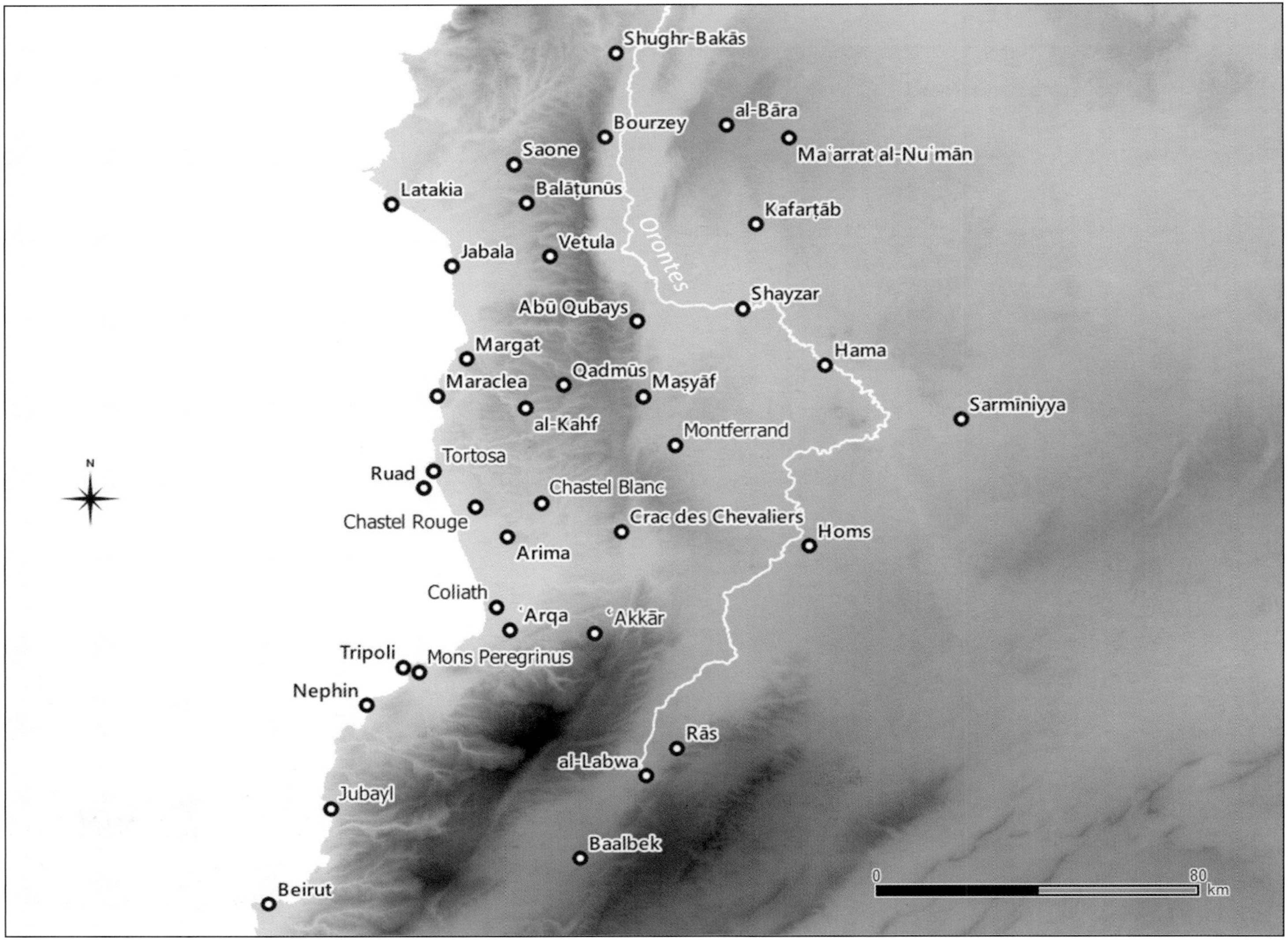

Regional Map 5. Western Syria and Northern Lebanon.

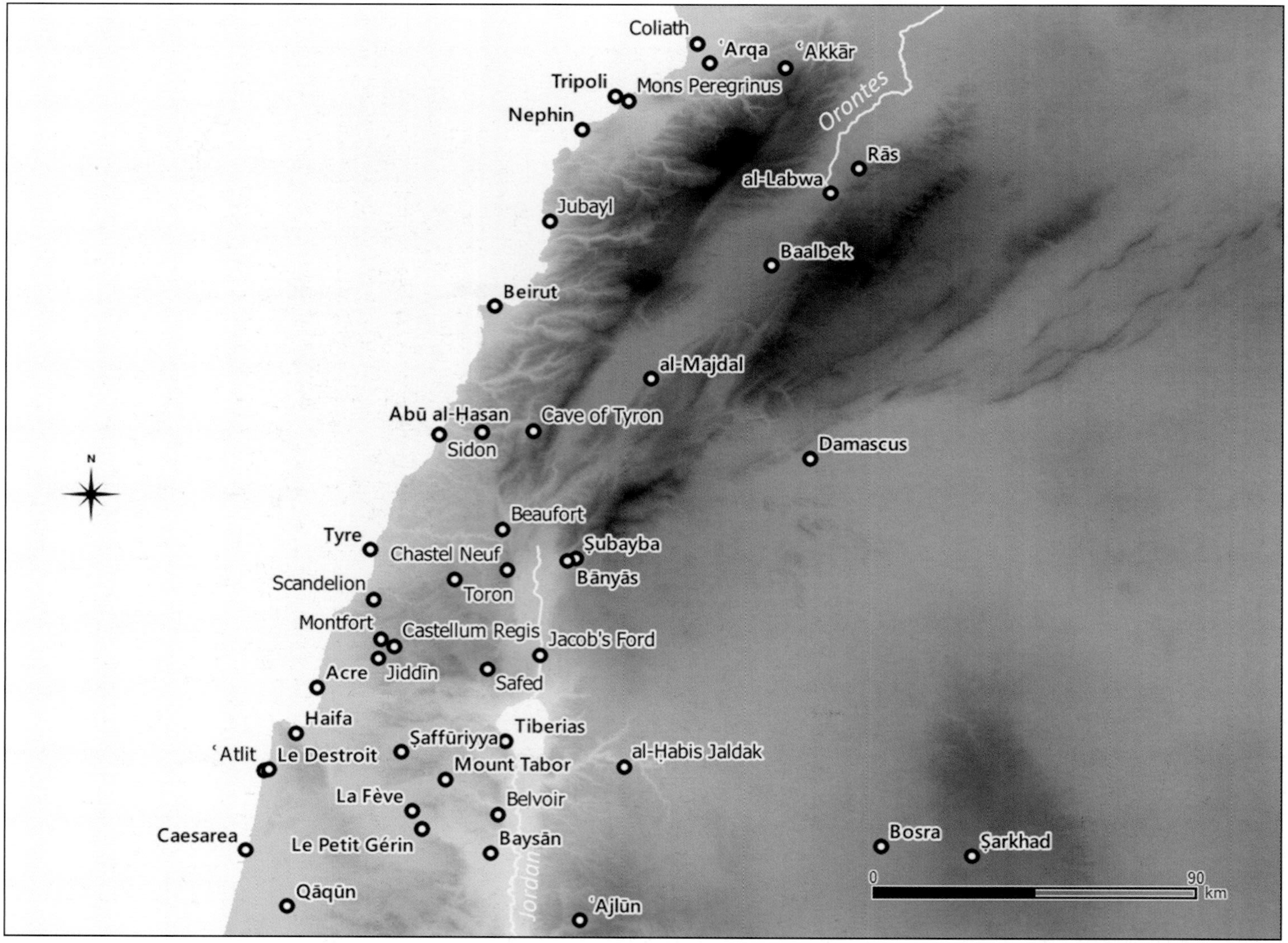

Regional Map 6. Lebanon and Northern Palestine.

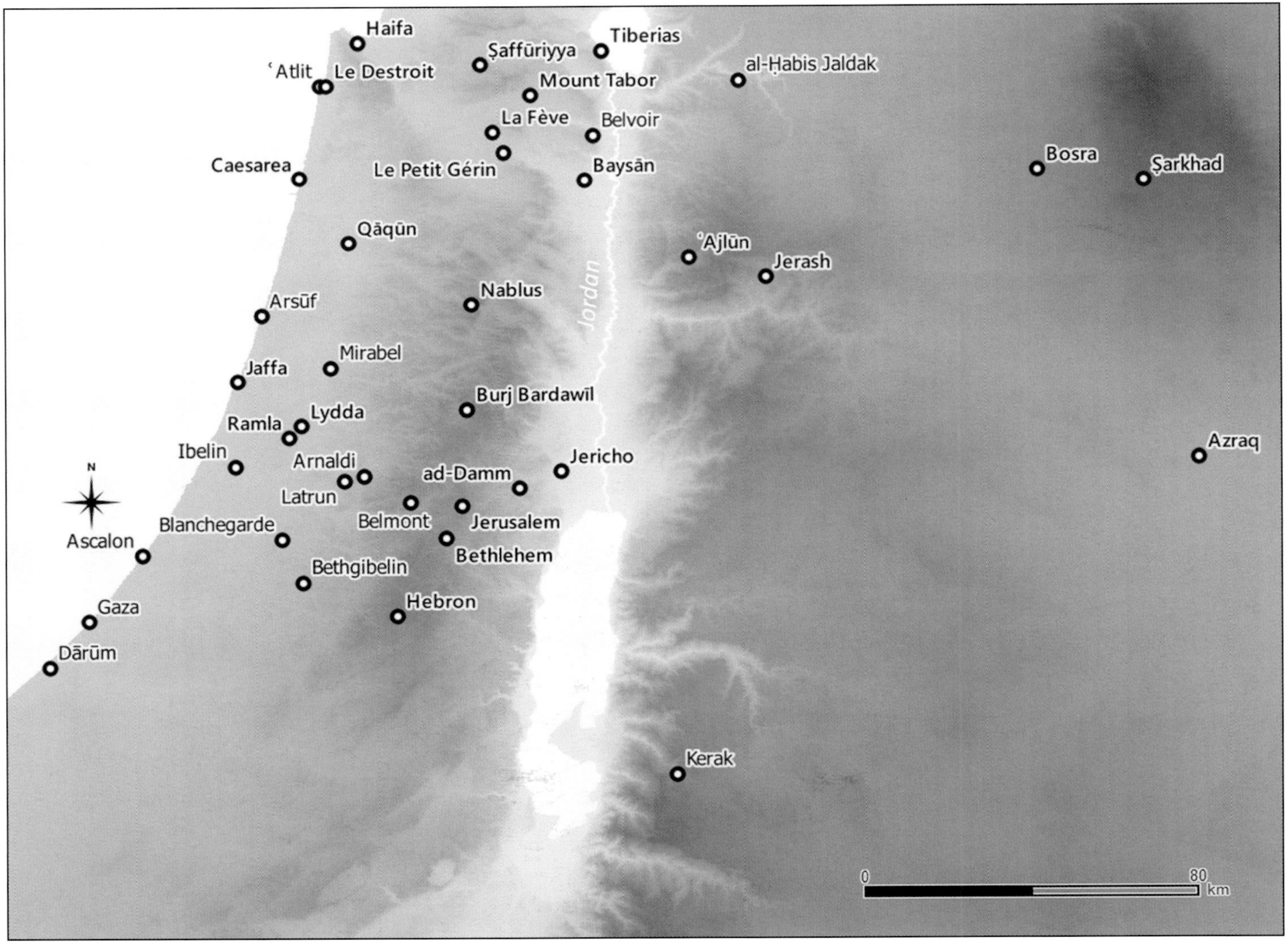

Regional Map 7. Southern Palestine.

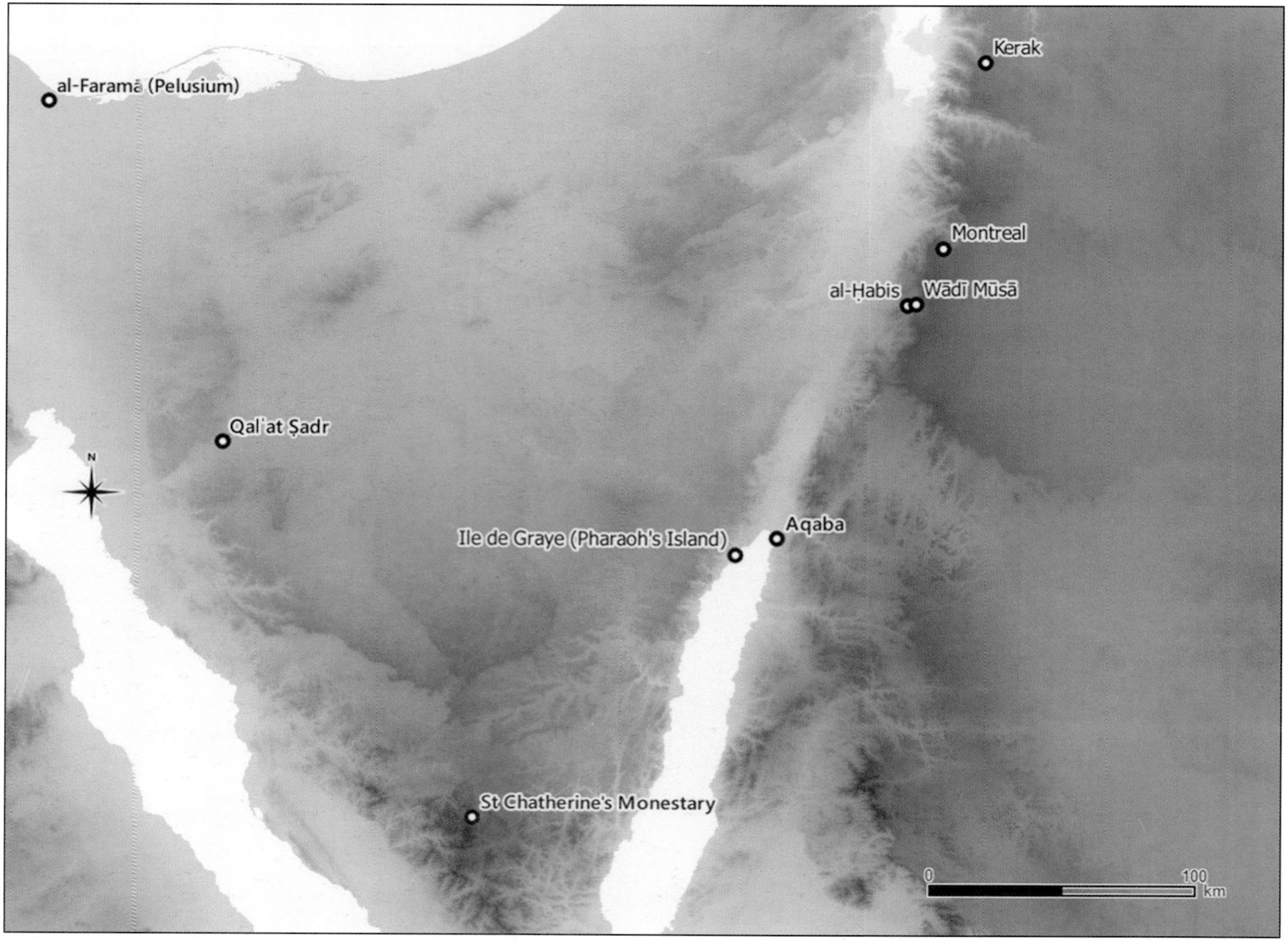

Regional Map 8. Sinai.

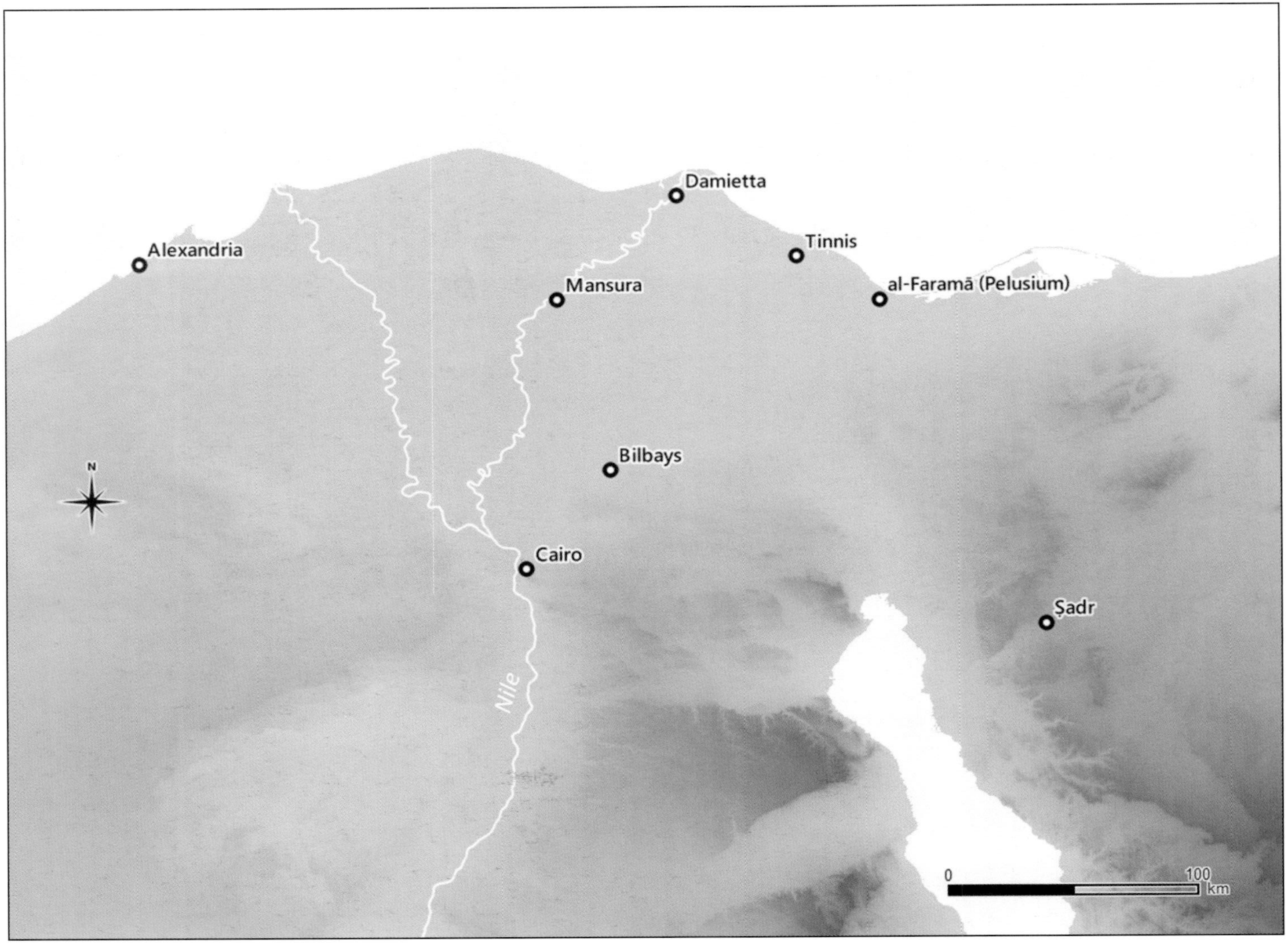

Regional Map 9. Egypt.

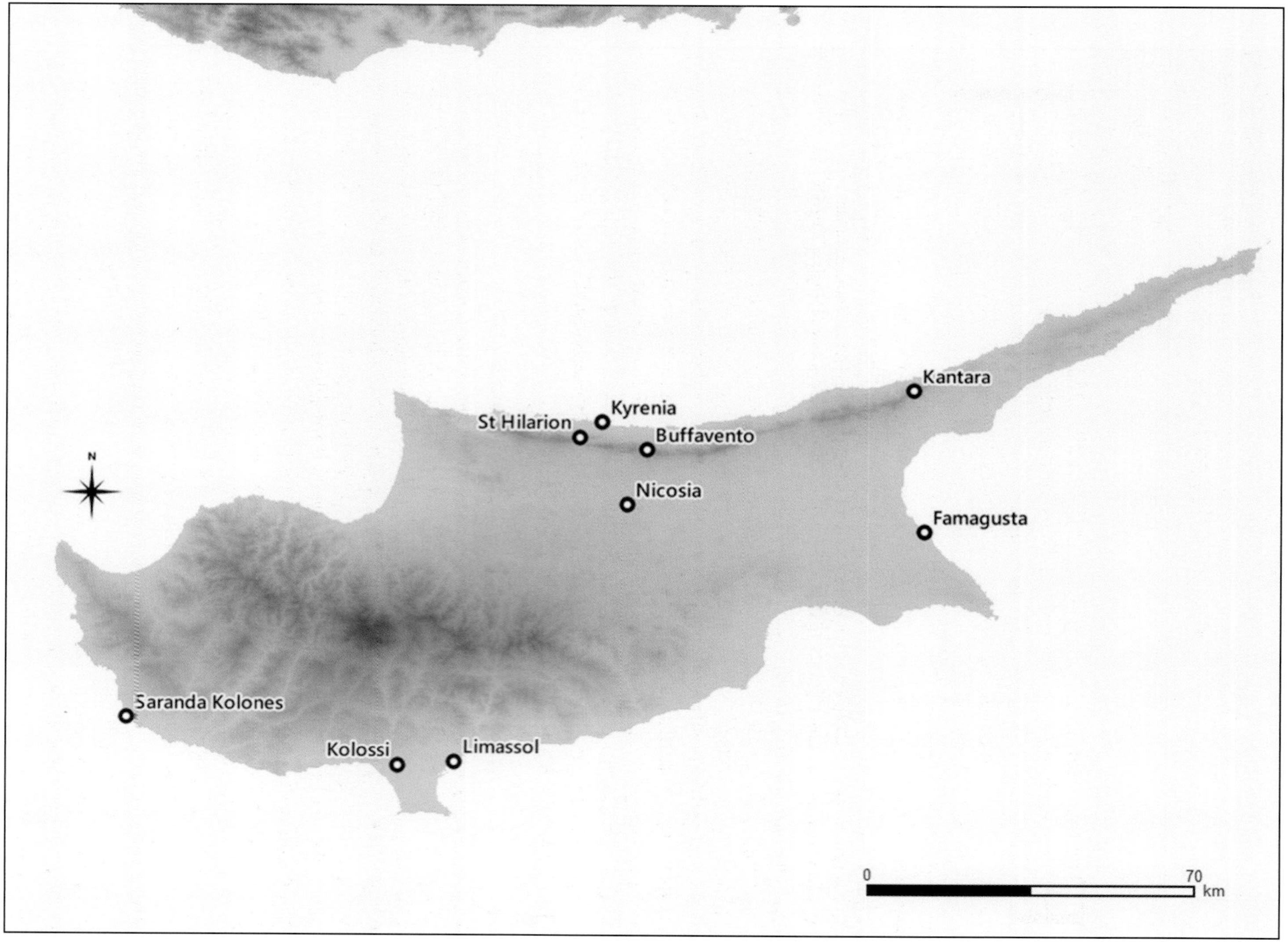

Regional Map 10. Cyprus.

Introduction

For two centuries, from about 1097 to 1291, Muslims and Christians fought with each other and with themselves for control of the Levant, its resources and holy places. This period, often referred to as 'the crusades', can be characterized by the involvement of Europeans in the Middle East; as such, it tends to be viewed from a Western perspective, framed as a binary struggle between Christians and Muslims. In reality, the conflicts of this period were far more complicated, with notions of 'crusade' and 'jihad' evoked for political advantage as well as religious piety. At the core of this contest for territory and influence was a series of sieges. Although a battle might precipitate or facilitate siege operations, it was the acquisition and possession of strongholds that allowed for the practical administration of territory and control of regional economics.

Strongholds (castles and fortified towns) were bases of influence from which local control was exercised, while sieges were simply the concerted attacks made against these defensible positions. Every siege was unique, influenced by an assortment of geographical, political, social, economic and other factors specific to each scenario; nevertheless, sets of conflicting strategic and tactical aims lay at the core of each: a desire to maintain control of a region and a desire to take it; the means of taking possession and the means of resisting. These fundamental principles will be used as the framework for most of the following chapters.

* * *

For almost as long as people have constructed dwellings, fortifications have been added around some individual residences and larger communities. By the Middle Ages, this desire for security led wealthy figures to commission impressive castles and town defences. The scale and strength of a given stronghold reflected a number of factors; foremost among these were the investment spent by its patron(s), the perceived value of the stronghold, and the threats it might be expected to resist. While a castle might be built to dominate a rural region, town walls provided protection for commercial centres. Every stronghold had an underlying military purpose, but most fulfilled a number of other functions. Many were seats of local or regional administration, while some were built as part of broader political strategies that aimed to weaken or counter the aggression of a neighbour – these were not just defensive structures.

To take a stronghold, a besieger had to first possess the resources to overcome its defences and defenders. There was then the threat of a relief force. It was difficult to predict when a hostile field army might arrive to help the defenders, and how large it would be; misjudging this could result not only in the failure of the siege, but in a crushing defeat from which the besiegers might struggle to recover. Accordingly, besiegers often struck at opportune moments, which might follow an adversary's defeat or his preoccupation elsewhere. Alternatively, besiegers might attempt to strike rapidly or at an unexpected time. Opportunity could also be created through peace agreements, which might isolate an opponent or provide security from the opportunistic attacks of others while conducting siege operations.

Once the aggressors had committed themselves to a siege, there was the matter of how to conclude it before a sufficient relief force arrived to drive them away. If besiegers decided on an aggressive tactical approach, they could endeavour to bring down a section of a stronghold's defences or to go over them. Alternatively, they might try to starve the defenders into submission or attempt to negotiate the fall of the stronghold, by persuading someone inside to help them in or by arranging a formal surrender. If an aggressive approach were taken, success might depend on the construction of siege engines, which could be as simple as ladders, or the work of sappers, who were relied upon to breach town and castle walls. Regardless of how they developed, most successful sieges ended with a negotiated surrender. If a stronghold fell instead by force, those within were entirely at the mercy of the besiegers.

With such high stakes, fortifications were constantly developing as their designers sought to confront new threats posed by besiegers and to create new challenges for them. In general, specific defensive elements and architectural features were arranged to allow defenders to resist potential besiegers for as long as possible. As besieging forces became stronger, fortifications became more elaborate, and an increasing emphasis was placed on facilitating an active defence.

The crusades were a nexus of interaction, drawing together people from as far away as Persia and Britain, but the extent to which the siege traditions of various parties influenced those of others is still hotly debated. Most siege technologies had spread prior to the arrival of the earliest crusaders, while those which would develop during the twelfth and thirteenth centuries, notably the counterweight trebuchet, had a far from dramatic genesis and were adopted and reproduced as soon as their potential value became apparent. Architecturally, the crusaders clearly imported certain features and designs with them, but so too were some Eastern elements brought back to Europe. Despite this environment of interaction and sharing, the structure of Frankish and Muslim armies remained distinct. Notwithstanding these differences, it seems inappropriate to suggest that any of the various parties possessed a superior siege tradition. Although clear patterns are evident in the frequency, success and length of this period's sieges, these trends were influenced primarily by broader political developments, rather than by the particular ability of certain individuals or the more advanced practices of any cultural group. Because these sieges are so intertwined with the broader historical context, it seems sensible to start with a brief overview of the period.

Chapter One

Historical Context: the Period of the Crusades

The era of the crusades is bookended by significant sieges, beginning with the siege of Nicaea in 1097, the first siege of the First Crusade, and ending with the Mamlūk siege of Acre in 1291, following which Frankish rule in the Levant effectively came to an end. For convenience, this period is often subdivided, split between events before and after the battle of Hattin in 1187 or Saladin's death in 1193, between which the Third Crusade (1189–92) took place.

From the perspective of the Franks – the Latin Christians who settled or were later born in the Levant – the first period is characterized by the establishment of the Latin principalities and the subsequent rise and then decline of Frankish influence. In 1187, the Franks were soundly defeated by Saladin at the battle of Hattin, leading to a considerable loss of territory. Although their presence was saved by the Third Crusade and Saladin's death shortly afterwards, the Franks were a side-line power through the following century. Crusades, essentially armed pilgrimages, would continue to bring periodic waves of large numbers of Europeans to the Holy Land, but the Franks were little more than a nuisance to their Muslim neighbours between these brief moments of greater influence.

From a Muslim point of view, the twelfth century saw the steady consolidation of power under the Zankids and then Saladin, under whom rule of Cairo, Damascus, Aleppo and Jerusalem was eventually united. From 1193, Saladin's successors struggled with each other for control of the empire left to them until Ayyūbid rule in Syria was brought to an end with the Mongol invasion of 1260. Mongol rule lasted less than a year and was supplanted by that of the Mamlūks, a dynasty of slave soldiers who had taken control of Egypt in the 1250s. The Mamlūks defeated the Mongols at the battle of ʿAyn Jālūt, which allowed them to spread their authority across western Syria thereafter. Although the Franks were able to maintain their presence in the Levant alongside the feuding Ayyūbids, the consolidation of regional power under the Mamlūks led to their steady expulsion.

Setting the Stage

The East

Of the roughly 7 billion people alive today, more than half identify themselves as Christian or Muslim. Much as it did a millennium ago, Jerusalem holds symbolic importance to members of both faiths: it is the holiest city in Christendom, where the crucifixion and resurrection of Jesus took place, and the most sacred city in Islam outside Arabia, the place traditionally associated with Muḥammad's Night Journey, during which he ascended to heaven. Jerusalem was part of a Roman client kingdom during the life of Jesus and had become a part of the Roman Empire by the time Christianity was legalized and officially embraced by the empire in the early fourth century. Although the western part of the Roman Empire collapsed in the fifth century, Jerusalem continued to thrive as a Christian city under the eastern component, now commonly known as the Byzantine Empire. Following the birth of Islam, Jerusalem was captured by the Arabs in 638, less than a decade after the death of the Prophet Muḥammad. The meteoric success of the Muslim conquests brought Egypt, Palestine, Syria and Mesopotamia all under Muslim control by the middle of the seventh century.

Jerusalem continued to prosper under Muslim rule, although local power was concentrated elsewhere. It was also a fairly tolerant city during this period: Christians were permitted to continue their practices and Jews, who had been banned from the city since a failed uprising against the Romans in the second century, were once more allowed in. Many living in Palestine gradually converted to Islam over the following centuries, although numerous Christian communities remained. Further north, in areas where Byzantine influence was more prevalent, Christianity remained the dominant religion.

The founding of the Fāṭimid caliphate in the early tenth century, and its conquest of Egypt in 969, placed Jerusalem between rival Muslim powers: the Shiite Fāṭimids, who controlled Egypt and the eastern portion of North Africa; and the Sunni ʿAbbāsids, whose influence spread across Mesopotamia and greater Syria. Over the following decades a war was waged over not just Palestine but the entire Levant. In 969, the Byzantines, who retained an interest in Anatolia and western Syria, captured Antioch, which had fallen to the Arabs in 637. While Fāṭimid armies swept northward from Egypt from 970, acquiring territory at the expense of the ʿAbbāsids, a Byzantine army invaded from the north in 975, failing to reach Jerusalem before it was compelled to retreat. Testament to the regional, rather than religious nature of the conflict, Byzantine forces came to the aid of the emir of Aleppo in 995, then besieged by a Fāṭimid army. A relatively rare moment of extreme religious intolerance accompanied the reign of Fāṭimid Caliph al-Hakim, who, in 1009, ordered the destruction of Christian holy places in Jerusalem and elsewhere.

The caliphs, both Sunni and Shiite, could trace their lineage back to the family of Muḥammad, and many regional rulers and officials were similarly of Arab ethnicity. It was not uncommon, however, to find Turks, Armenians and members of other groups who lived along the borders of the Muslim realm in positions of influence in both ʿAbbāsid and Fāṭimid administrations. Some of these figures were mamlūks, non-Muslims by birth who were bought as slaves and raised as Muslim soldiers. Through the patronage of certain rulers, such individuals who displayed particular abilities and loyalty might be elevated to significant administrative positions later in life. For example, Badr al-Jamālī, a mamlūk of Armenian heritage, became Fāṭimid vizier in the late eleventh century, effectively ruling Egypt on the caliph's behalf. He was followed in this paramount position of influence by a number of fellow ethnic Armenians, including his son, al-Afḍal Shāhinshāh, and grandson, al-Afḍal Kutayfāt, as well as Yānis and Bahrām, who was openly Christian.

To the east, the ʿAbbāsids had been the reigning caliphal dynasty since the eighth century, ruling from their capital of Baghdad. Through the tenth century, however, their authority over Syria began to decline. The northward migration of nomadic Bedouin communities upset the established agrarian administration, pitting farmers against herders for control of resources and trade, while pressure increased from both the Byzantines and Fāṭimids. The greatest threat to ʿAbbāsid power, however, was the Seljuk Turks, a conglomerate of semi-nomadic Turkish forces who loosely marched under the banner of the Seljuk family. Although they recognized the nominal authority of the ʿAbbāsid caliphate, the Turks came to assume practical control over most of greater Syria, Anatolia and Mesopotamia in the eleventh century.

From the steppes of western central Asia, the Seljuks had begun migrating into Persia in the tenth century, from where they continued to move westward. In 1055, Baghdad fell to the army of Ṭugril-Beg, grandson of Seljuk, the eponymous founder of the dynasty. Ṭugril took the title of sultan, thus becoming protector of the caliph and legitimizing his rule, which soon extended across much of Syria. Under Alp Arslān, Ṭugril's nephew and successor, Seljuk authority continued to spread. In 1071, Alp Arslān defeated a large Byzantine army under Emperor Romanos IV Diogenes outside the town of Manzikert. This victory encouraged opportunistic Turkish forces, often acting fairly independently, to spread further into Anatolia. As the Byzantines were pushed back, almost to the walls of Constantinople, Seljuk forces captured Antioch in 1084.

In the same year as the battle of Manzikert, another independent Turkish force, under the renegade Atsiz ibn Uvaq, who had served (and betrayed) both the Seljuks and Fāṭimids by this point, besieged and took Jerusalem. Atsiz carved out a lordship for himself in Palestine at the expense of the Fāṭimids, taking Acre (ʿAkkā) and

Jerusalem. (*Michael Fulton*)

Damascus, which became his seat of power, before his advances were checked when he was defeated attempting to invade Egypt in 1077. Facing a counterattack from the Fāṭimids, Atsiz summoned Tāj al-Dawla Tutush, the young son of the recently deceased Alp Arslān and brother of the current sultan, Malikshāh. Tutush, who became the principal power in western Syria, assumed control of Damascus and delegated authority over Jerusalem to one of his supporters, Artuq, who was succeeded in 1091 by his sons, Īlghāzī and Suqmān.

With the death of Malikshāh in 1092, the semblance of unified Seljuk authority in Syria collapsed as his family members subsequently fought over the succession. When Tutush was killed in 1095, his sons Riḍwān and Duqāq continued the family tradition. Riḍwān inherited northwestern Syria, ruling from Aleppo, and Duqāq set himself up in Damascus. In a bid for greater power and autonomy, many regional rulers sided with whichever brother's powerbase was further away: the Artuqid brothers in Jerusalem supported Riḍwān while Yaghī Siyān, who held Antioch, supported Duqāq; the allegiance of other regional powers was similarly divided between the brothers.

The fractured political landscape of regional rivalries meant that there was no unified or coordinated effort to confront the First Crusade, which crossed into Anatolia in the late spring of 1097 and arrived in northwestern Syria about five months later. One by one, forces sent from Aleppo, Damascus and Mosul were defeated or at least turned back by the Franks as they besieged Antioch through the autumn, winter and spring of 1097–98. Taking advantage of the situation and diversion of attentions caused by the arrival of the Franks, the Fāṭimids, under Vizier al-Afḍal, the son of Badr al-Jamālī, besieged and captured Jerusalem in August 1098. This victory, however, would be short lived, as the city fell to the crusaders less than a year later.

The West

In 1095, Pope Urban II delivered his famous sermon at Clermont, which set in motion the First Crusade. The pope's call for action had come in response to a request for help made by the Byzantine emperor, Alexius Comnenus. With the Turks on the doorstep of Anatolia, civil war had broken out among the Byzantines in the mid-eleventh century. Although Seljuk interests were focused elsewhere through much of the 1070s, the factional fighting between Byzantine parties, many of whom recruited Turkish fighters, increased the number of Turks and their influence in the region. Alexius seized the imperial throne in 1081 and consolidated Byzantine power, but this did little to stem the westward spread of the Seljuks.

A consequence of the Byzantine infighting had been the granting of lands in exchange for Turkish support. This led to the establishment of the Seljuk sultanate of Rūm, founded by Sulaymān ibn Qutlumush (father of Qilij Arslān), an opponent of Sultan Alp Arslān and his sons. By the time Alexius dispatched his appeal for help to the pope, the Byzantines retained only a small foothold east of the Bosporus.

There was little new in the request issued by Alexius – the Byzantines had a long tradition of using contingents of foreign fighters, regardless of their ethnicity. The elite Varangian Guard, for example, was composed of northern Europeans and it was not uncommon for political refugees and adventurers from Latin Europe to find fulltime employment with the Byzantines; others simply lent assistance while on pilgrimage, as did Count Robert I of Flanders a decade before the First Crusade. By all accounts, it was a similar body of experienced fighters or mercenaries that Alexius had in mind when he wrote to Urban.

The pope, however, appears to have taken this opportunity to press another initiative then circulating in Europe: the Peace of God. Directing Europe's necessarily militarized barons to fight non-Christians was seen as a way of reducing organized violence among Christians. In exchange for taking up this holy cause, the Church offered indulgences, granting forgiveness for sins and limiting the time that participants could expect to spend in purgatory when they died. This was not the first time that this had been attempted, but for some reason the combination of circumstances in this instance generated widespread popular support.

The accounts of Urban's speech, provided by figures who might have been at Clermont in 1095, were all composed after the capture of Jerusalem in 1099. Accordingly, it is unclear how Jerusalem might have figured in the pope's original plans. In the versions of the speech that have survived, the city is portrayed as suffering under Muslim rule; however, the last period of notable persecutions had taken place under Atsiz in the 1070s. Regardless of whether the 'liberation' of Jerusalem was part of Urban's original speech, he seems to have been playing on more general sentiments

The First Crusade.

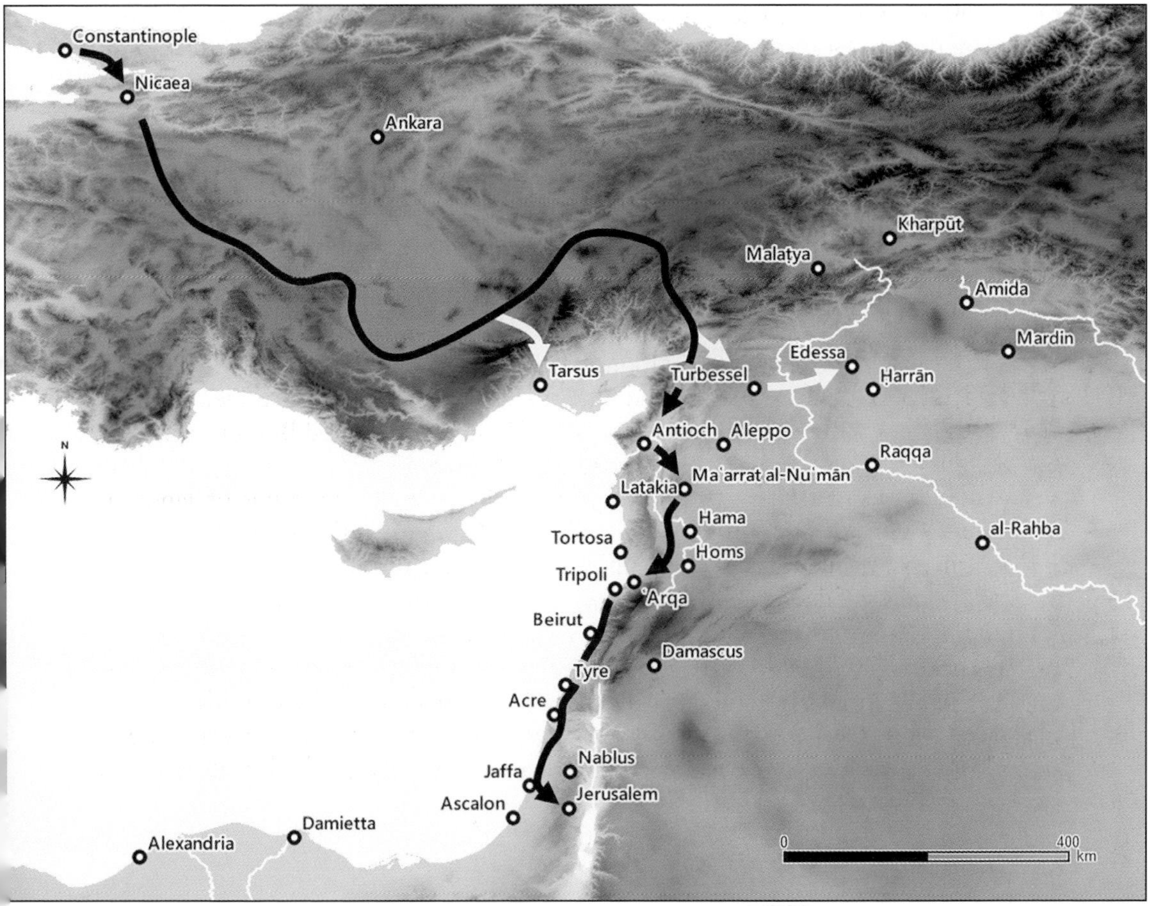

of perceived Turkish or Arab barbarity – using these stereotypes to stir his audience into action.

A popular movement, known as the Peasants' Crusade, set out in 1096 under the leadership of a charismatic figure known as Peter the Hermit. This first wave of crusaders, far from the military force that Alexius had desired, was soundly defeated later that year in western Anatolia by Qilij Arslān, the sultan of Rūm. The main crusade, which followed a few months later, was led by figures including Godfrey of Bouillon and his brother Baldwin of Boulogne, Raymond of St Gilles, count of Toulouse, Bohemond of Taranto and his nephew Tancred, Robert II of Flanders, and Robert II (Curthose) of Normandy. Although many of Europe's leading barons took part, none of its monarchs joined the crusade. After assembling at Constantinople, the crusaders set out and successfully besieged Nicaea, Antioch and Jerusalem in turn between 1097 and 1099. The success of the First Crusade was a relative anomaly, due largely to the division among the Muslim rulers of Syria and the resolve and singular objective of the rank and file of the crusader army. A similar expedition that followed soon afterwards, known as the Crusade of 1101, was soundly defeated as it made its way through Anatolia.

The First Generations

Two of the eventual four Latin principalities, sometimes referred to as the 'crusader states', were founded before Jerusalem's capture in 1099. A decade later, all four were established political powers. The Franks entrenched themselves in the region and, as one generation gave way to the next, their continued presence was noticeable – they were there to stay. What had been an expeditionary force that had taken up arms to recapture the Holy Land for Christendom, had turned into a significant political force. Although most participants of the First Crusade who had lived to see the fall of Jerusalem returned to Europe, others stayed and more followed, seeking religious, social or economic rewards in the East. The Franks carved up the landscape into a series of lordships, often following ancient boundary lines. Most local administrative structures were preserved, although a new ruling hierarchy was imposed and new laws governed the Latin ruling class. As Frankish rule became more established, so too did their influence increase at the expense of neighbouring Muslims. Although the balance of power shifted back and forth, most noticeably in the north, not until the establishment of Zankid rule in Aleppo can the tide be seen to turn gradually and consistently back against the Franks.

County of Edessa

There was a pre-existing tradition of fragmentary rule in the region of what became the county of Edessa. The predominantly Armenian lordships encountered by the Franks in the drainage basin of the upper Euphrates were based largely on kinship groups and centred on strongholds. Here, more than anywhere else, the Franks integrated themselves into the existing political system. Even before the county was established, the Franks benefited considerably from opportunistic alliances with some of these Eastern Christians, many of whom were relatively new to the region themselves. For example, a figure named Oshin, who had left the Armenian heartland in

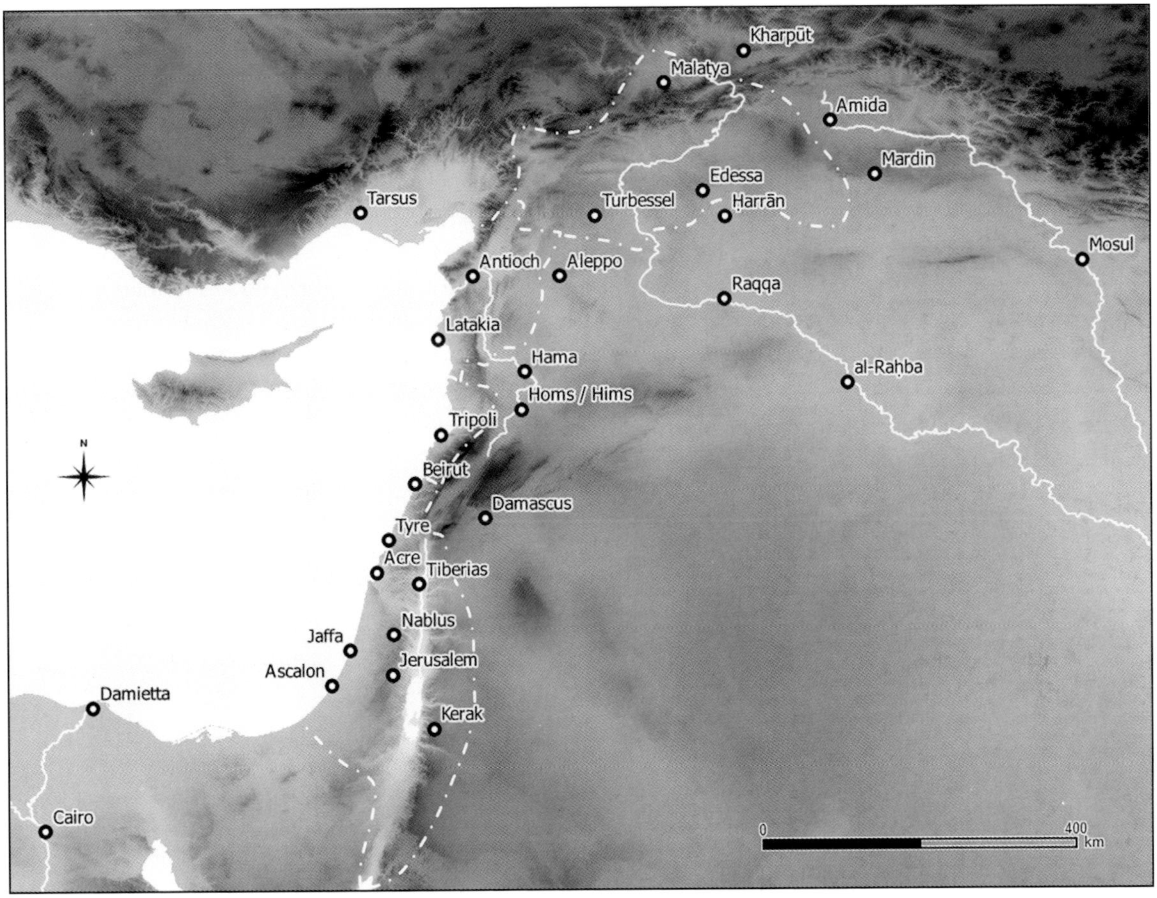

The Frankish principalities at about their largest.

the 1070s and migrated to Cilicia, where he captured Lampron, a castle in the Taurus Mountains that was held by a force of Turks at that time, was among those who later offered assistance to the First Crusade as it passed through Cilicia.

Before the siege of Antioch, Baldwin of Boulogne left the main army of the First Crusade and moved into the Armenian lands east of the Amanus (Nur) Mountains, where he began to accumulate territory. In early 1098, he travelled to the court of Toros, the Greek ruler of Edessa. In exchange for helping Toros against his Turkish neighbours, Baldwin was adopted as his son and successor, duly replacing Toros following his murder only weeks later. Under Baldwin I, the fledgling county of Edessa appears to have looked quite similar to those of his Armenian neighbours and Baldwin's direct authority may have been limited to only a few strongholds. Following the succession of his cousin, Baldwin II, Frankish authority was solidified and the county expanded across parts of southeastern Anatolia and the western Jazīra. Frankish rule developed on a fairly ad hoc basis, exploiting the divisions among the region's Armenian and Muslim rulers: allies were able to retain a significant degree of independence while opponents were typically replaced with Frankish supporters. Although Baldwin II was more aggressive than his predecessor, he was apparently a popular ruler.

Shortly after inheriting Edessa in 1100, Baldwin II created the county's largest lordship for another cousin, Joscelin of Courtenay (later Joscelin I of Edessa), a survivor of the Crusade of 1101. The lordship was centred on the castle of Turbessel (Tell Bāshir) and consisted of the earliest lands acquired by Baldwin I west of the Euphrates. Yet another of Baldwin's cousins, Galeran of Le Puiset, was given Sarūj (mod. Suruç) at some point after it was besieged in 1101.

Although Latin figures came to hold the most important positions, this remained a relatively Armenian polity, heavily dependent on the support of local communities. Most of the county's strongholds had been established before the First Crusade and their Frankish lords would have made use of considerable bodies of Armenian defenders. Similarly, the county's army almost certainly included more Armenians than Franks. Indicative of this, Usāma ibn Munqidh casually describes a group of hostages held at Shayzar by his father in the early twelfth century as 'some Frankish and Armenian knights'.[11] The apparent lack of a social divide is another indication that pragmatism trumped ethnic biases when it came to the county's 'feudal' structure.

The willingness of Franks and Armenians to seek alliances for mutual benefit is clearly seen in the intermarriage between influential Franks and powerful Armenian families. The first three counts (Baldwin I, Baldwin II and Joscelin I) all married daughters of important Armenian nobles. Galeran of Le Puiset's marriage, which probably took place in 1116, was a solution to a more immediate issue – it ended Baldwin II's year-long siege of al-Bīra. The marriage, which involved the daughter of al-Bīra's Armenian ruler, was essentially a term of the town's surrender: al-Bīra became part of Galeran's lordship, and thus the county of Edessa, while his new in-laws were able to retain a measure of their previous influence.

Principality of Antioch

Bohemond of Taranto, who had orchestrated the capture of Antioch in 1098, went on to establish a principality around the city. Like the Armenian regions to the north, this area also contained a significant Christian population, in addition to a number of Sunni Muslims and a considerable Shiite community. Many of the leaders of the First Crusade had begun amassing territory in this region as the expedition stalled in the second half of 1098. Bohemond, who remained in Antioch, acquired many of these lands when the others continued on towards Jerusalem in early 1099, although some regions fell back into Muslim and Byzantine hands.

Under the regency of Tancred, Bohemond's adventurous nephew, Frankish influence reached through the Sarmada Pass, towards Aleppo, and along the banks of the Orontes to the south. This set in motion the ebb and flow of a power struggle between Antioch and Aleppo as the frontier was contested and territory was traded back and forth over the following years. The strongholds on either side of the Sarmada Pass, which provided the easiest route through the Syrian Coastal Mountains between Antioch and Aleppo, were vital to controlling territory on the far side and securing lands on the near side from raids. Control of the Orontes Valley, south of Aleppo, and the plateau to the east, was similarly maintained through the possession of the region's fortified towns and castles, which were entrusted to Frankish vassals.

Most urban defences and castles in the region had been built by the Muslims or Byzantines before the Franks arrived. In the Syrian Coastal Mountains, strongholds such as Saone (Ṣahyūn), Bourzey (Barziyya) and Balāṭunūs had been founded by the

Antioch, town walls as seen in the eighteenth century (from *Voyage pittoresque*, ed. Cassas).

Byzantines, while Margat (Marqab) was first built under Muslim rule. Between Antioch and Aleppo, the defences of Ḥārim (Harrenc), al-Athārib, ʿAzāz and other strongholds, which were traded back and forth through the twelfth century, were almost certainly developed by both Frankish and Muslim rulers, as were those of Apamea (Qalʿat Muḍīq), Maʿarrat al-Nuʿmān and many of the fortified urban centres between the Orontes Valley and the Syrian Desert to the east.

Kingdom of Jerusalem

Jerusalem naturally formed the centre of the most prestigious of the Latin principalities. Following the capture of the city, Godfrey of Bouillon, brother of Baldwin of Boulogne, now Baldwin I of Edessa, was elected its first ruler. Godfrey declined the title of king – it was unclear at this point how the city and surrounding region would be administered: should it be a secular lordship or an ecclesiastical one? Godfrey remained protector of Jerusalem until his death in 1100, at which point he was succeeded by his brother Baldwin I of Edessa, who had no qualms about becoming King Baldwin I of Jerusalem.

Jerusalem, Ramla and Hebron, which had been captured in 1099, formed the southern heartland of the kingdom, while Tancred's acquisition of Tiberias provided a strong foothold in Galilee. Over the following decade, Frankish authority was extended along the Mediterranean coast through a series of successful sieges, often benefiting from Italian maritime support. By 1111, only Tyre, which was finally captured in 1124, and Ascalon, which did not fall until 1153, remained in Muslim hands. Further inland, the kingdom's nominal authority had spread across Palestine within a year or two after the capture of Jerusalem; however, it was a longer process to establish effective rule over this region, which was home to many Muslim communities and was largely devoid of significant fortifications. The gradual imposition of Frankish authority accompanied the construction of castles and smaller administrative towers; the former were financed by the monarchy and wealthy barons, while the latter were often commissioned by lesser lords who may have ruled over no more than a little village and its associated farmland.

Beyond the traditional limits of Palestine, the kingdom stretched up the coast north of Tyre and down the eastern side of the Great Rift, south of the Dead Sea. Both extensions were restricted by geographical factors. To the north, the kingdom's influence reached as far as Beirut but appears to have been restricted to the west side of Mount Lebanon, never seriously challenging the Muslim rulers of Baalbek for control of the Biqāʿ Valley. To the south, the Franks remained relatively confined to the arable land on the eastern side of Wādī ʿAraba. Beginning with the construction of Montreal (Shawbak) in 1115 and then Kerak (Petra Deserti) around 1142, these castles provided the Franks with a considerable degree of influence along this corridor between Syria to the north and Egypt and Arabia to the south.

The kingdom of Jerusalem had larger and somewhat more secure neighbours than the other Latin principalities. To the southwest, Fāṭimid Egypt launched a number of campaigns against the kingdom via Ascalon, the southernmost port on the Mediterranean coast of Palestine. To the east, Damascene lands beyond the Jordan became attractive targets for raids as Frankish control over Palestine increased. The Franks became such a threat, or nuisance, that a treaty signed in 1108 granted them two-thirds of the revenues of the Sawād and Jabal ʿAwf regions, east of the Jordan, south of Damascus. Compared to the principalities to the north, the borders of the kingdom of Jerusalem remained relatively fixed, having spread to incorporate the towns along the coast as they fell, and swaying at times over certain regions east of the Jordan.

County of Tripoli

The foundations of the fourth and smallest Latin principality were established by Raymond of St Gilles. Raymond had contested control of Antioch and built up considerable lands in the surrounding region in 1098. Eventually losing out to Bohemond, he seems to have set his sights on Jerusalem, although he found himself outmanoeuvred once more, this time by Godfrey of Bouillon. When he subsequently failed to gain a foothold along the Mediterranean coast, Raymond set off for Constantinople, where he joined the disastrous Crusade of 1101. Fortunate enough to survive, he returned south and his gaze eventually settled on the wealthy city of Tripoli. Although the city would not fall until 1109, four years after Raymond's death, his efforts to blockade Tripoli and conquer the surrounding area led him to be regarded as the county's founder.

The delayed establishment of the county of Tripoli probably contributed to its restricted size and influence. The county reached from Tortosa (Ṭarṭūs), which Raymond of St Gilles captured upon his return to Syria following the Crusade of 1101, down to Jubayl (Gibelet, anc. Byblos). Largely through the military orders, Frankish control was also extended through the Homs–Tripoli corridor, the natural gap between the Lebanon and Antilebanon Mountains to the south and the Syrian Coastal Mountains to the north. The Franks' ability to retain control of this region, which saw regular raiding back and forth throughout the twelfth century and much of

Crac des Chevaliers. *(Courtesy of Denys Pringle)*

the thirteenth, was due in large part to their acquisition, construction and retention of a number of castles. Although the Franks are most often associated with the great castles in this area, and much of what remains of them today was built by Frankish masons, the earliest phases of many were commissioned by Muslim or Byzantine figures. The region's most famous castle, Crac des Chevaliers (Ḥiṣn al-Akrād), was originally constructed in the eleventh century by a local Kurdish ruler, but was subsequently rebuilt by the Franks and developed further by the Mamlūks.

At times, the counts struggled to assert their autonomy from the kingdom of Jerusalem. When Raymond died in 1105, William-Jordan, who various sources claim was Raymond's cousin, nephew or illegitimate son, inherited his lands in the East and continued the blockade of Tripoli. William-Jordan's claim was challenged in 1109 when Bertrand of Toulouse, Raymond's son and successor in Europe, arrived in the Levant. Bertrand received the support of Baldwin I of Jerusalem, who helped him displace William-Jordan and capture Tripoli in July, from which point Baldwin claimed some sort of suzerainty over the county. When Baldwin II later assumed the regency of Antioch, following the death of Roger in 1119, he gained unprecedented power and authority – Joscelin of Courtenay, his vassal as lord of Turbessel and then Prince of Galilee, owed Baldwin his elevation to the county of Edessa, and Pons of Tripoli, Bertrand's son and successor, was compelled to openly pay homage to the king in 1122. Fears that the kingdom's hegemony would spread across the entire Latin East subsided in 1123 when Baldwin was captured and Bohemond II of Antioch came of age. Fears flared up again following the deaths of Bohemond II in 1130 and Baldwin II the following year. Fulk of Anjou succeeded Baldwin as king through his marriage to Melisende, Baldwin's daughter, but when he rode north to sort out the regency of Antioch, his interference was opposed by Pons of Tripoli and Joscelin I of Edessa, resulting in an open battle. It may have been in part a reluctance to call upon the king of Jerusalem for support that led Pons' son, Raymond II of Tripoli, to grant considerable lands to the military orders, choosing to rely on them rather than the kings to the south.

Military Orders

The military orders followed monastic rules that incorporated a militarized mandate. The Templars, established during the reign of Baldwin II with the mission of protecting Christian pilgrims in the Holy Land, were the first order to officially mix the roles of monk and knight. Not long after, the Hospitallers, an order centred on a hospital in Jerusalem, which had cared for pilgrims since the late eleventh century, also adopted a military function. Additional orders were subsequently created, but only the Teutonic Knights, a German order of hospitallers established during the Third Crusade and militarized in 1198, came to hold any sizeable castles.

The orders would become significant political forces in and of themselves. Brothers were born of the knightly class and raised in the tradition of arms, while people of lower ranks assumed lower positions. Kinship networks and the support they received from prominent secular and clerical figures, notably Bernard of Clairvaux, led to the rapid expansion of the orders' wealth and power through the twelfth century. Much of the wealth the orders came to command was acquired in Europe, donated by secular lords who hoped this would limit their time in purgatory, while land in the Levant was increasingly gifted or sold to them. With this wealth, the orders could finance the construction and maintenance of significant strongholds. Answerable only to the pope, the orders were technically immune from local taxes and authorities, giving them considerable autonomy.

Both the Templars and Hospitallers came to hold castles in the kingdom of Jerusalem and county of Tripoli, while the Templars also acquired a number in the Amanus Mountains, which divided the basin around Antioch from Cilicia. Following their establishment, the Teutonic Knights focused their resources on acquiring the lands once held by Joscelin III of Edessa in Galilee, which the titular count amassed thanks in large part to the patronage of his nephew, King Baldwin IV. Montfort was the order's greatest castle, but this was no match for the Templar strongholds of Safed (Saphet) and 'Atlit (Castrum Peregrinorum), or Belvoir (Kawkab), Crac and Margat of the Hospitallers.

Fāṭimids

Although rich, Egypt struggled internally and Fāṭimid authority declined steadily through the twelfth century. When al-Afḍal, who had captured Jerusalem in 1098, died in 1121, a half-century struggle for power ensued between figures who attempted to become or stay vizier, and the caliphs, who sought to assert their own authority.

Fāṭimid Egypt was separated from the kingdom of Jerusalem by the Sinai Peninsula, an overland journey of 250km from Tinnis, at the easternmost branch of the Nile Delta, to Ascalon on the Palestinian coast. The seat of Fāṭimid power was Cairo, which was at this time two cities: the old town of Fustat and new Cairo to the north (founded in 969). Cairo was the better fortified of the two; in 1168, the Fāṭimid vizier, Shāwar, was compelled to burn Fustat, lest it fall to the invading army of Franks led by Amalric. Under Saladin (al-Nāṣir Ṣalāḥ al-Dīn Yūsuf), a new citadel was built between the two, and the construction of new town walls to connect them continued through the reign of his nephew, al-Kāmil.

Cairo was linked to the coast by the two main branches of the Nile Delta. Near the mouth of the eastern branch was the fortified town of Damietta and its infamous Tower of the Chain, which controlled access up the river. To the west, at the end of the other main branch, Rosetta, which figures little in events of the crusades, was also fortified to some extent. At the very western end of the Delta, the classical city of Alexandria was defended by strong town walls and remained a significant port, although it was connected to the main shipping lane of the Rosetta branch by just a shallow canal. One of the few strongholds between Cairo and the coast was Bilbays, a fortified town one-third of the way from Cairo to Tinnis along a minor eastern branch of the Delta. Due to its position, Bilbays was besieged twice by invading Frankish armies in the 1160s.

The Fāṭimids maintained a presence in the Levant, through the towns along the coast, until Ascalon was lost in 1153. Egypt relied on its field army for protection, but the Levantine towns were so far away and the army took so long to assemble that they were dependent on the Egyptian fleet for relief when threatened. While raids might originate from these outposts, larger campaigns had to be organized in Egypt. The independence and vulnerability of these towns was revealed as most fell one by one through the first decade of the twelfth century; at the start of 1111, only Tyre and Ascalon remained. Tyre was secured by its legendary walls, while Ascalon benefited from its proximity to the Fāṭimid navy and its strategic value as a foothold on the far side of the Sinai Desert.

Damascus

In the early decades of the twelfth century, the Būrid rulers of Damascus were the most powerful figures between the Jordan and Orontes Rivers to the west and Euphrates to the east. The Būrids were the descendants of Ṭughtakīn, who overthrew the young son of Duqāq ibn Tutush shortly after Duqāq's death in 1104. Būrid rule was relatively stable and unchallenged until Zankī's capture of Aleppo in 1128.

The emirate was sandwiched between the Franks to the west and the Syrian Desert to the east. Within this corridor it ruled a considerable expanse of territory, from the Biqāʿ Valley in the north, between the Lebanon and Antilebanon Mountains, to the broad fertile region to the south known as the Ḥawrān. The most significant settlement in the north was Baalbek, from which the Biqāʿ was administered. The classical temple complex, which had been fortified following the Muslim conquest of the city in the 630s, was developed in a number of phases through to the early Mamlūk period. To the south, the traditional capital of the Ḥawrān was Bosra, while the eastern section appears to have been administered from Ṣarkhad. The citadels of both towns were later developed under the Ayyūbids.

Towns of the Orontes and Euphrates

East of the county of Tripoli, the southern stretch of the Orontes was dominated by Hama and Homs, at times independent emirates but often dominated by Aleppo or

Damascus. Between them were the fortified towns of Rafaniyya and Salamiyya, overlooked respectively by the hill of Baʿrīn, upon which the Franks developed the castle of Montferrand, and the ancient fortress of Shmemis, which was rebuilt by the Ayyūbid ruler of Homs in the late 1220s. Deep in the Syrian Desert, more than 140km east of Homs, Palmyra (Tadmor) remained a trading post for traffic moving through the desert. Originally a dependency of Damascus, Palmyra was transferred to Homs under the Zankids. It appears to have been Saladin's nephew, al-Mujāhid Shīrkūh of Homs, who later built the castle overlooking the ancient town, which replaced the temple of Bel, fortified by the Būrids, as the town's citadel.

North of Hama, a number of fortified towns, including Shayzar, Apamea and Maʿarrat al-Nuʿmān dominated the region east of the Syrian Coastal Mountains. When under Muslim control, these typically fell under the ruler of Aleppo, who claimed authority over a similar collection of towns, including ʿAzāz, Buzāʿa and Manbij, to the north. East of the Euphrates, Ḥarrān remained a base of Muslim influence south of Edessa. Although the town of Manbij and lands to the north of Qalʿat Najm were subject to periodic Frankish rule in the early twelfth century, Muslim forces maintained control of the major bases along the Euphrates between Aleppo and Ḥarrān. The fortified towns of al-Raḥba and Raqqa dominated the lower sections of the upper Euphrates, while a series of castles, including Qalʿat Jaʿbar, Bālis and Qalʿat Najm, did so further upriver. Even as many of these strongholds came more firmly under the authority of Aleppo, they retained their frontier significance along the Euphrates, the natural boundary between western Syria and Mesopotamia.

Aleppo

Aleppo was the main opponent of Antioch and a powerful adversary of the Frankish lords of Turbessel to the north. Riḍwān of Aleppo was a strong ruler who recognized

Apamea. (*monumentsofsyria.com*)

that Muslim rivals across the Euphrates posed a greater threat to his position and autonomy than did the princes of Antioch, leading him to decline offers of support from Mesopotamian figures. Although Riḍwān found himself in an uphill struggle against Tancred, order and stability were maintained until his death in 1113.

Rather than the Franks, it was Muslim rulers based in the Jazīra who ultimately captured Aleppo during the chaos that followed Riḍwān's death. Īlghāzī ibn Artuq, ruler of Jerusalem before the city was taken by the Fāṭimids in 1098, had returned to Mesopotamia and, after serving as prefect (*shiḥna*) of Iraq for a period, established himself at Mardin. A particularly radical figure, Īlghāzī fought alongside and against various Muslim and Frankish neighbours whenever it served his interests. In 1117, Īlghāzī gained control of Aleppo, and, after briefly turning his attention towards Mayyāfāriqīn, decisively defeated Roger of Salerno, regent of Antioch, in 1119 at the battle of the Field of Blood (Lat. *ager sanguinis*, known in Arabic as the battle of Balāṭ). The victory devastated the army of Antioch and left Roger among the dead, allowing Īlghāzī to gain considerable territory east of Antioch and relieve the pressure that had been mounting against Aleppo. Īlghāzī died in 1122 and his nephew, Balak ibn Bahrām, emerged as his eventual successor. Balak provided Aleppo with strong leadership until his own death in 1124.

In 1128, Aleppo once more came under the rule of a lord from the Jazīra. ʿImād al-Dīn Zankī, who had been raised by Karbughā of Mosul, himself became ruler of Mosul in 1127; he took control of Aleppo the following year. Zankī's ambitions towards Damascus quickly became clear, with both Hama and Homs falling under his authority during the 1130s. In 1144, Zankī did what many Muslim commanders before him had tried but failed to do: he took Edessa. Although remnants of the county would remain in Frankish control until the start of the 1150s, and Joscelin III would retain the title of count despite being born after the city's capture, the loss of Edessa essentially brought an end to the oldest, if shortest lived, of the Latin principalities in the Levant.

Assassins

Between the county of Tripoli and principality of Antioch, the Nizārī Assassins, an Ismāʿīlī group of Shiites, came to rule a region in the Syrian Coastal Mountains. The Nizārīs had their origins in Persia, where Ḥasan-i Ṣabbāḥ established the movement from the stronghold of Alamūt at the end of the eleventh century. They quickly faced opposition and persecutions were initiated by Sultan Barkyāruq in 1101; nevertheless, the movement spread and a faction took root in the region of Aleppo, where there was already a significant Shiite community. Despite failed attempts to capture Apamea in 1106 and Shayzar in 1109, the Assassins continued to flourish in the region around Aleppo, thanks in part to Riḍwān, who did little to inhibit their freedoms and in turn benefited from the disruption they caused among his neighbours. During the instability that followed Riḍwān's death in December 1113, a wave of persecutions was unleashed in the name of his young son and a new wave of intolerance was ushered in under Balak following his acquisition of Aleppo in 1123.

In late 1126, the Nizārī Assassins gained control of Bānyās. Their leader, Bahrām, had cultivated a relationship with Īlghāzī, who had recommended him to Ṭughtakīn of Damascus. Bahrām appears to have gained followers in Damascus but also the enmity of many locals, who were overwhelmingly Sunni. To both alleviate pressure in Damascus and provide Bahrām and his followers a safe base, Ṭughtakīn gave them Bānyās. Bahrām was killed in a raid shortly after and leadership passed to a certain Ismāʿīl, while Ṭughtakīn also died around this time and was succeeded by his son, Tāj al-Mulūk. As had happened in Aleppo, the new ruler of Damascus caved quickly to popular pressure and a violent wave of persecutions was unleashed from September 1129. The surge of opposition led Ismāʿīl to offer Bānyās to the Franks, receiving their protection in exchange. This allowed the Franks to use Bānyās as an assembly point and from it a large force marched up to the suburbs of Damascus before the end of 1129. A Damascene force was able to intercept the Franks before they could reach the city, forcing a standoff that eventually ended with the retreat of the Frankish army. Aside from the Second Crusade, this was the closest the Franks came to besieging Damascus. Meanwhile, the Assassins resettled themselves in the Syrian Coastal Mountains.

The Assassins had bought the castle of Qadmūs during their brief tenure at Bānyās. To this they added Maṣyāf, which they captured from a mamlūk of the Banū Munqidh ruler of Shayzar in 1140 or 1141. Similar to their brothers in Persia, as well as the Armenians and Franks, who ruled similar mountainous regions, the Assassins found comfort in their isolated strongholds. Although frequently forced to pay tribute to their Frankish neighbours, they earned the respect of most Christians and Muslims.

The community's trademark method of influencing political events around them through high-profile and often public murders has provided the modern term for someone who commits such an act: assassin. Over the years they killed a number of influential figures, including Janāḥ al-Dawla of Homs (1103), the Muslim ruler of Apamea (1106), Mawdūd of Mosul (1113), Aḥmadīl ibn Wahsūdān of Marāgha (1116), Āqsunqur al-Bursuqī of Mosul and Aleppo (1126), ʿAbbāsid Caliph al-Mustarshid (1135) and Raymond II of Tripoli (1152). An attempt to murder Tāj al-Mulūk Būrī of Damascus failed in 1131, although the wounds he sustained during this attack probably contributed to his death the following year. Assassins twice failed to kill Saladin, first in early 1175 during the siege of Aleppo and then the following year as he besieged ʿAzāz. Unsurprisingly, Saladin turned on the community, besieging Maṣyāf in August 1176. According to one version of events, the Assassins chose to threaten Saladin during the siege, perhaps to avoid another failed attempt to kill him. This, along with some persuasive words from one of his uncles, convinced Saladin to lift the siege. The Nizārī Assassins continued to rule in the mountains until they were subdued by Baybars in the thirteenth century, coinciding with the Mongols' suppression of the Nizārīs in Persia.

External Parties

In the early twelfth century, armies were occasionally organized in Iraq and sent west under the banner of jihad (*jihād*). Not unlike the efforts by the papacy to decrease violence in Europe by reorienting aggression towards the Middle East, these campaigns redirected hostilities towards the Franks, brought dissenting figures into line and enhanced the authority projected from Baghdad. It was not uncommon for the leaders of these armies, who included figures such as Mawdūd ibn Altūntakīn, Āqsunqur al-Bursuqī, Bursuq ibn Bursuq and Īlghāzī, to use these forces to suppress their own coreligionist rivals before engaging the Franks.

Unfortunately for the counts of Edessa, these armies frequently passed directly through their lands. Edessa and Turbessel were subjected to a number of sieges, but their ability to hold out, until 1144 and 1150 respectively, ensured the surrounding regions remained under Frankish rule after each army withdrew. Muslim rulers welcomed the arrival of these armies in different ways. Many, including Riḍwān of Aleppo, regarded them with particular suspicion and considered them a threat to their independence. For rulers of smaller territories, such as the Banū Munqidh of Shayzar, they posed less risk, as they were no more threatening than the other larger regional rulers, while good relations with these distant powers might provide support and economic opportunities. The Franks were compelled to muster their collective strength with the approach of these Mesopotamian armies, creating another unpredictable threat. In some instances, the Franks helped to protect the independence of local Muslim rulers; in others, they took advantage of their combined strength to undertake their own siege operations.

The Franks benefited more clearly from the waves of crusaders who arrived in the Holy Land seeking spiritual benefits and adventure. Although the largest waves of crusaders have been enumerated by historians, smaller armed pilgrimages were undertaken by many notable figures. Considering only the counts of Flanders: Robert I (r. 1071–93) visited Jerusalem a decade before the First Crusade and fought the Turks alongside Byzantine forces; Robert II (r. 1093–1111) led a contingent of the First Crusade; Thierry (r. 1128–68) made four armed visits to the Holy Land; and Philip I (1168–91) took up arms in the East twice, dying at Acre during the Third Crusade. The Franks also enjoyed the frequent support of Italian naval forces, who proved extremely helpful during sieges along the Mediterranean coast, and more generally secured the link between the Latin principalities and Europe.

The Age of Nūr al-Dīn and Saladin

Frankish influence stemming from Antioch was steadily checked as Aleppo fell under Artuqid and then Zankid rule, while the county of Edessa, the most exposed of the Frankish principalities, collapsed following Zankī's capture of its capital in 1144. When Zankī died in 1146, his lands in Syria and the Jazīra were divided between his successors: Mosul went to his eldest son, Sayf al-Dīn Ghāzī, and Aleppo passed to his younger son, Nūr al-Dīn. Relations between the brothers were amicable, allowing Nūr al-Dīn to continue his father's programme of expansion in western Syria. His eventual capture of Damascus in 1154, after a decade of applying unsubtle pressure, left him without any significant Muslim adversaries in the region, and for the first time the kingdom of Jerusalem became the main opponent of a major multi-regional power.

As power concentrated under Nūr al-Dīn, the Franks failed to keep stride. Fulk, a European outsider unpopular with some barons, died in 1143, leaving a minor to succeed him: his young son, Baldwin III. To the north, Raymond of Poitiers, prince-regent of Antioch, died in 1149, also leaving an infant son to succeed him.

More stable rule came to both regions following the Second Crusade (1147–49), when Baldwin III of Jerusalem came of age and a competent, if controversial, regent for Antioch was found in Reynald of Châtillon. When Reynald was captured and Baldwin died about two years later in February 1163, the transition was smooth for a change: Bohemond II of Antioch came of age just in time and Baldwin III was succeeded by his brother, Amalric. The ensuing face-off between Nūr al-Dīn and Amalric was not fought in Syria, but rather in Egypt.

At the urging of his Kurdish general Asad al-Dīn Shīrkūh, Nūr al-Dīn agreed to send forces into Egypt to ensure that the gasping Fāṭimid regime, crippled internally, did not fall to the Franks, to whom it had begun paying an annual tribute. The struggle between Zankid and Frankish forces in Egypt lasted from 1163 until the end of 1169, and eventually brought Egypt under Nūr al-Dīn's rule. Shīrkūh had established himself as vizier of Egypt after occupying Cairo in January 1169, but he died only weeks later, at which point he was succeeded by his nephew, Saladin. Tensions between Nūr al-Dīn and Saladin began to emerge as the latter showed signs of quietly asserting his autonomy. From Egypt, members of Saladin's family also conquered parts of North Africa, Nubia and Yemen. Nūr al-Dīn's death in 1174 prevented any chance of an open rift developing between Egypt and Syria, and allowed Saladin to step into the power vacuum – he took Damascus from Nūr al-Dīn's young son, al-Ṣāliḥ Ismāʿīl, before the year was out. Saladin then spent most of the following decade fighting Zankid and other Muslim rulers for control of western Syria and the Jazīra.

Only after subduing or considerably weakening most of his Muslim rivals and extending his control over much of greater Syria did Saladin finally devote significant attention to the Franks. In the south, unsuccessful attempts were made against Kerak in 1183 and 1184, part of an effort to remove Frankish influence from the vital desert road between Cairo and Damascus. He was also frustrated in Galilee. Despite his defeat of the army of Jerusalem in 1179, allowing him to take and destroy the incomplete Templar castle at Jacob's Ford (Chastellet, Qaṣr al-ʿAtra), subsequent invasions failed to draw the army of Jerusalem into the field. Although raiding forces inflicted economic damage, his inability to engage the main Frankish army directly denied him the opportunity to commit his forces to protracted siege efforts. In 1187, perhaps taking a page from Nūr al-Dīn's book, Saladin divided his forces, leading one contingent south and once more besieging Kerak, while another gathered east of the Sea of Galilee (Lake Tiberias) under his son, al-Afḍal. When a scouting party of the latter made contact with a force of Templars near the springs of Cresson, Saladin returned north, joined his armies and invaded Galilee in force. He knew that the army of Jerusalem would assemble to counter him but may have hoped that the Frankish defeat at Cresson would demand satisfaction, encouraging them to take a less conservative stance than they had in previous years. To further provoke the Franks, he invested Tiberias.

From about the 1150s, the Franks became increasingly reliant on the support of crusading Europeans to launch significant offensives, and by the time Saladin turned his attention towards the Latin principalities, Frankish military actions had become almost exclusively reactive. Part of this Frankish weakness was due to internal issues.

In 1174, Amalric had been succeeded by his teenage son, Baldwin IV, who suffered from leprosy, and who was succeeded in turn by his seven-year-old nephew, Baldwin V, who ruled for little more than a year between 1185 and 1186. Baldwin V was succeeded by Guy of Lusignan, who became king through his wife, Sibylla (daughter of Amalric, sister of Baldwin IV and mother of Baldwin V).

Since 1174, the kingdom, under young and sickly kings, had passed through numerous regencies. The lack of strong and stable rule had led to rivalries among the barons, who vied for influence. When Saladin invaded in 1187, Guy, whose reign was contested, faced pressure to act and demonstrate his strength. Having led the army and fractious baronage into Galilee, Guy bowed to pressure to relieve Tiberias and move away from Ṣaffūriyya (Saforie), where the Franks held a defensive position and were well provided with water from local springs. About 10km west of Tiberias, near an extinct volcanic hill known as the Horns of Hattin, the army of Jerusalem was soundly defeated by Saladin's forces on 4 July 1187.

With the Frankish army destroyed, Saladin was free to lay siege to the kingdom's strongholds. Most cities, with the exception of Tyre, were taken by the end of the year, and blockades were established around the kingdom's large inland castles. The following year, Saladin renewed his offensive, turning against the principality of Antioch. Having assembled his forces near Crac des Chevaliers, he led the army unopposed through the county of Tripoli. Reaching the coast, he turned north and carved a path to Latakia, capturing the Frankish strongholds along the way, with the exception of the Templar's tower at Tortosa and the Hospitallers' castle of Margat. From Latakia, Saladin turned inland, striking into the Syrian Coastal Mountains and the interior of the principality of Antioch. The Muslims captured a number of castles in the region and, having secured Jisr al-Shughr, one of the principal crossings over the Orontes, they moved north into the Antioch Basin. As a contingent of the army took up a shielding position facing the city, the strongholds around the Syrian Gates north of Antioch were captured. With the campaign season of 1188 nearing its end, Saladin compelled Bohemond III to accept a humbling truce. Meanwhile, further south, the strongholds of Safed, Belvoir, Kerak and Montreal, which had held out since the battle of Hattin, fell during the winter and following spring. Beaufort (Shaqīf Arnūn), the last of the kingdom's inland castles, surrendered in 1190.

Guy of Lusignan had been captured at Hattin, but was set free months later – his release had been a term of Ascalon's surrender. The king found himself shut out of Tyre by Conrad of Montferrat, an adventurous character who had arrived in the Levant only weeks after the battle of Hattin. Conrad, who had commanded the defence of Tyre through November and December of 1187, Saladin's only unsuccessful siege during his campaigns following the battle of Hattin, had no intention of turning the city over to the landless king. Left with few options, Guy made a daring move: taking what forces he had with him, he invested Acre in late the summer of 1189.

Acre had been one of the first cities to fall after the battle of Hattin, and Saladin subsequently commissioned some repairs, entrusting this work to Bahā' al-Dīn Qarāqūsh, who had recently overseen the construction of Cairo's new citadel. Saladin, who was then blockading Beaufort, was unprepared when news arrived that Guy was moving towards Acre. Although he reached Acre only days after Guy,

Saladin was unable to force the Franks to withdraw. After some initial engagements, both sides settled in for what would be the first of two winters, the Franks besieging the city and the Muslims besieging the Franks. The following year, Saladin's army swelled as forces returned from Mesopotamia, but so too was Guy aided by the arrival of crusaders responding to the Franks' defeat at Hattin and subsequent loss of Jerusalem. Another season of stalemate ensued and it was not until the early summer of 1191, and the arrival of Richard I of England and Philip II of France, that the balance was tipped and the city fell.

It was these waves of crusaders, collectively known as the Third Crusade, that were responsible for extending Latin rule along the coast of the Levant for another century. Had Guy been defeated at Acre in 1189, there would have been little to stop Saladin from investing Tyre and the remaining strongholds of the county of Tripoli during the following year. Although the Third Crusade failed to retake Jerusalem, it regained a stretch of the Palestinian coast and helped preserve what remained of the Latin principalities. The preoccupation of Saladin's heirs in the years that followed allowed for a measure of Frankish recovery, but the Franks would never regain the influence they had enjoyed in the mid-twelfth century.

The Ayyūbid Era

A new period followed the upheaval between 1187 and Saladin's death in 1193. Saladin had intended for his son, al-Afḍal, to succeed him as sultan, but had divided his realm among multiple family members, placing two of his other sons, al-ʿAzīz and al-Ẓāhir, as well as his brother, al-ʿĀdil, in influential subordinate positions. The arrangement quickly broke down and, after nearly a decade of infighting, al-ʿĀdil, who appears not to have initially sought to replace his nephews as leader of the Ayyūbid realm, emerged the ultimate victor.

For most of the first half of the thirteenth century, there was peace between the Franks and their Ayyūbid neighbours. This was in large part because there was a fairly even balance of power; although the sultan, based in Cairo, remained the wealthiest and most prestigious Ayyūbid figure, the rulers of Damascus and Aleppo, along with an assortment of secondary powers in Homs, Kerak and similar regional administrative centres, were able to hold him in check. The Franks emerged as another player in this system. Although their offensive capabilities were fairly limited, they invested heavily in their fortifications. These defences were rarely challenged, in part due to their strength but also because Muslim rulers were wary of encouraging another crusade, as had been precipitated by Saladin's victories in 1187.

The Franks twice regained Jerusalem in the first half of the thirteenth century and their authority reached as far as the Sea of Galilee in the early 1240s. Most of their significant territorial gains, however, came through treaties, and effective control over many interior lands, well beyond the walls of their principal strongholds, was similarly conditional on Muslim endorsement. The military orders, chief among them the Templars and Hospitallers, were the most professional and effective Frankish fighting forces in the Levant. Although they were able to extract tribute from some of their smaller Muslim neighbours north of Damascus, the orders' independent offensive capacities were limited to raiding.

Despite the relative peace between the Franks and their Muslim neighbours, there were plenty of hostilities. The contest for power and authority among the Ayyūbids continued after al-ʿĀdil's death, as his sons and their successors fought for supremacy or autonomy, while the Franks were equally divided. Frederick II, the Holy Roman Emperor, had shown an interest in the Latin principalities since the early thirteenth century. Frederick had pledged to go on crusade but repeatedly postponed his departure. This cost him papal favour and caused the Fifth Crusade to grind to a halt after taking Damietta in 1219; its participants refused to march on towards Cairo until the emperor, or a direct representative, arrived to lead them. In 1225, Frederick married Isabella (or Yolande) of Jerusalem, granddaughter of Conrad of Montferrat and his wife, another Isabella (daughter of King Amalric and half-sister of Baldwin IV). Isabella died in 1227, shortly after giving birth to a son, Conrad. Through his wife and then their infant son, Frederick claimed the throne of Jerusalem.

Frederick's repeated delays in fulfilling his vow to go on crusade led to his excommunication in 1227, which had not been lifted when he finally arrived in Palestine the following year. Officially outside the Catholic Church, Frederick received little support from the kingdom's baronage or the military orders, who reported directly to the pope. In a symbolic act of defiance, the Templars even denied him entrance to ʿAtlit. The Teutonic Knights, a predominantly German order, were among the few who supported the emperor. Although Frederick negotiated the return of Jerusalem to the Franks, this was overshadowed by opposition to his presence. Upon his departure, ending what is strangely known as the Sixth Crusade, open war quickly broke out on Cyprus, spilling over to the mainland, between imperialist figures loyal to Frederick and a local baronial faction championed by the Ibelin family.

Tensions continued through the following decades as the Italian merchant communities of Venice, Genoa and Pisa clashed, each supported by certain baronial parties. The Templars and Hospitallers, between whom there had been a rivalry since the late twelfth century, often used these feuds as proxy wars, managing to avoid direct clashes for the most part. Confined largely to the coast but relatively secure behind their impressive town and castle walls, the Franks were left to compete with each other. There was no longer the same sense of desperation and appreciation of their united strength, which had contributed to the success of the First Crusade, nor the strong leadership at the top which had harnessed these forces to march Frankish armies up to 1,000km to support a fellow Latin prince, as had happened on numerous occasions in the twelfth century.

The Mongol Invasion

The arrival of Mongol forces transformed the political landscape of western Syria. Eastern Persia had been subjugated by the Mongols in the early thirteenth century, during the life of Genghis Khan, but it was Möngke, a grandson and eventual successor of Genghis Khan, who looked towards the Middle East and sought the conquest of the ʿAbbāsid caliphate, in whose name the Ayyūbids continued to rule. Möngke entrusted this initiative to his brother, Hülagü, who captured Baghdad in 1258 and had led his forces across the Euphrates by the start of 1260. Although Mardin was subject to a long siege, Aleppo was the first and only stronghold to offer any significant resistance in western Syria. Mongol dominance was far from certain when Hülagü's forces arrived at Aleppo. Mayyāfāriqīn, east of the Euphrates, had been under siege since the autumn of 1258, but unbeknown to anyone at the time, the town's ruler would be cruelly executed for his opposition after the Mongols gained entry in April 1260, by which point Aleppo had fallen.

Aleppo was besieged for a week from 18 January and the citadel held out for another month before it too was taken. Strongholds to the south were then abandoned or captured after reasonably brief sieges. Although the Mongols relied on an army composed primarily of mounted archers – a light and mobile cavalry force with a nomadic tradition, not unlike the Turks – they were perfectly capable of mounting siege operations, employing both artillery and miners at Aleppo.

All of the Ayyūbid leaders had recognized the threat posed by the Mongols and reached out to them in some way before 1260. Some, notably al-Nāṣir Yūsuf of Aleppo and Damascus, fled at the approach of Hülagü's army, while others, including al-Manṣūr Muḥammad II of Hama and al-Mughīth 'Umar of Kerak, made sure to reiterate their submission before their lands could be overrun. Meanwhile, al-Ashraf Mūsā, who had been dispossessed of Homs, his patrimony, in 1248, had courted the Mongols more aggressively before their arrival, for which he was rewarded with the nominal title of 'sultan of Syria' in 1260. Bohemond VI of Antioch and Tripoli had also submitted to the Mongols before they arrived at Aleppo, following the lead of his father-in-law, Hethum I of Armenia, a strong Mongol supporter. Further south, the Franks of Palestine were less eager to recognize Mongol suzerainty.

Hülagü withdrew from western Syria only months after arriving, departing to address the Mongol succession following the death of Möngke. The small occupying force that was left under his leading general, Kitbugha, was decisively defeated by the Mamlūks at 'Ayn Jālūt on 3 September 1260. Al-Sa'īd Ḥasan, the son of al-'Azīz 'Uthmān ibn al-'Ādil, who had been dispossessed of Ṣubayba and imprisoned by al-Nāṣir Yūsuf, but subsequently freed by the Mongols, was among those who fought against the Mamlūks, for which he was executed after the battle. Conspicuously, al-Ashraf Mūsā of Homs abandoned his Mongol allies as the fighting commenced – the Mamlūks were the new source of power in the region and he knew it.

Fears of another Mongol invasion dominated Mamlūk foreign policy over the following decades. After withdrawing from 'Ayn Jālūt, the Mongols had regrouped but were again defeated in December 1260 at the first battle of Homs. A second significant invasion did not materialize until 1281. Although supported by Leo II of Armenia, son of Hethum I, the campaign was brought to an end when the Mongols were defeated by the Mamlūks at the second battle of Homs. In a third major battle, that of Wādī al-Khazindār (or the third battle of Homs), Mongol forces, under Maḥmūd Ghāzān, a great-grandson of Hülagü, supported by Armenians and Georgians, defeated a large Mamlūk army on 23 December 1299, by which point the Franks had been pushed out of the Levant.

Early Mamlūk Rule

In Egypt, the professional regiments of mamlūks, upon which the Ayyūbid princes had come to rely, had taken power for themselves in the 1250s. These regiments were typically loyal to a single prince or emir, leading to uncertainty and the potential loss or gain of influence when a ruler died, as the successor's mamlūks would expect to rise with their owner. The Mamlūk ascendency accompanied Louis IX of France's invasion of Egypt, an episode known as the Seventh Crusade, during which Sultan al-Ṣāliḥ Ayyūb of Egypt died. Facing the prospect of losing their influence, a group of al-Ṣāliḥ's mamlūks overthrew the new sultan, al-Muʿaẓẓam Tūrānshāh, seizing power for themselves. Authority was initially held in the name of a young Ayyūbid prince but eventually al-Muʿizz al-Dīn Aybak took power in his own name, establishing a new line of rulers that came to be known by their social origins.

The legitimacy of Mamlūk rule in Egypt was rejected by the Ayyūbid emirs of Syria, who recognized al-Nāṣir Yūsuf of Aleppo as the rightful Ayyūbid sultan. Al-Nāṣir, however, had attempted to stand against the Mongols and his inability to halt their advance led to the collapse of Ayyūbid rule in Syria. News of Aleppo's fall, which reached al-Nāṣir Yūsuf at Damascus, where he was assembling his forces, led to panic and the collapse of his army. Al-Nāṣir Yūsuf was captured during the following weeks and later executed after Hülagü learned of his army's defeat at ʿAyn Jālūt.

The victorious Mamlūk forces had been led by Sayf al-Dīn Quṭuz. Once a mamlūk of Aybak, Quṭuz had risen to a position of prominence by 1259; at this point, with the Mongols threatening to invade Egypt, he deposed Aybak's young son and successor. Following the battle of ʿAyn Jālūt, the Mongols were pushed back across the Euphrates, allowing the Mamlūks to step into the power vacuum left following the acute political disruption. For the first time since Saladin's death, Egypt and Syria were effectively united, bringing the considerable resources of this region under a single centralized administration. The Mamlūks also fielded a professional army, one trained in an institutionalized manner and with a degree of professionalism beyond the military traditions with which most Frankish, Turkish and Ayyūbid nobles were raised. In October 1260, less than two months after the battle of ʿAyn Jālūt, Quṭuz was usurped by Baybars, who, like Aybak, had been one of al-Ṣāliḥ Ayyūb's mamlūks. During Baybars' reign (1260–77), the Mongols, rather than the Franks, remained the greatest threat.

The Franks had been marginalized since the battle of Hattin and only with the arrival of large armies of European crusaders could they upset the status quo, as occurred during the Third, Fifth and Seventh Crusades, and to a lesser extent during the Barons' Crusade in 1239–41. The Seventh Crusade, however, was the last major crusade to reach the Levant. Louis IX planned a second crusade, the Eighth Crusade, but this ended in Tunisia, where the French king died in 1270. Prince Edward of England had planned to take part in this campaign but continued on to the Levant when he heard of its defeat, reaching Acre in 1271. The climax of the prince's crusade, sometimes called the Ninth Crusade, was a failed attack against Qāqūn (Caco), a tower that had formerly belonged to the lordship of Caesarea. Although none of these thirteenth-century crusades brought significant gains, the threat of triggering a major crusade from Europe, as Saladin had done in 1187, acted as leverage and a deterrent to pressuring the Franks too hard. This became a less significant threat following the spread and solidification of Mamlūk authority, and even less of a threat after the death of Louis IX of France.

Only when the Mongols were preoccupied with matters elsewhere did Baybars turn against the Franks. Aside from these opportune campaigns, Mamlūk policy typically sought to preserve peaceful relations with the Latin lordships, concluding these agreements from clear positions of strength. In 1265, the collapse of a Mongol assault against al-Bīra allowed Baybars, whose army had been mobilized, to besiege Frankish Caesarea (Qaysāriyya) and Arsūf (Arsur). He followed up the capture of these coastal strongholds the next year by seizing Safed, an important administrative centre in eastern Galilee at a crossroads along one of the main routes through Palestine from Cairo to Damascus. Beaufort and Antioch were taken in 1268. The fall of the latter

Ibn ʻAbd al-Ẓāhir: Baybars' siege of Caesarea, 1265

On Thursday, 9 Jumādā I 663 [27 February 1265], Baybars reached Caesarea and immediately surrounded its walls. The Muslim troops then assaulted it, throwing themselves into the fosse and ascending on every side, climbing up by means of iron horse-pegs, their shackle-ropes and halters on to which they hung; standards were raised, the gates of the city were burned and its guards slain, the occupants fled to the citadel ... Trebuchets were then erected against the citadel, which was one of the best and most strongly fortified ... The King of France [Louis IX] had brought flint [granite] columns for it and built it so effectively that in the coastal territories there had never been seen a stronger citadel or one better fortified or of loftier construction than this. The sea encircled it and kept its fosse full; its walls could not be sapped because of the columns built into them, so that they would not fall even if undermined ... Penthouses and siege machines were constructed and arrows brought from ʻAjlūn were distributed, four thousand arrows to each leader of one hundred horsemen and the same for the ḥalqa* and the soldiers. The Sultan issued orders for the transportation of firewood and of stones for the trebuchets, bestowing robes of honour on the amīr jāndār, ʻIzz al-Dīn al-Afram, for his zeal with the trebuchets, and on the men who were in charge of them ... Meanwhile, Baybars continued the siege and the fight, remaining in the church [of St Peter] with a group of archers, without visiting his tent, shooting and preventing the Franks from going to the top of the citadel. Occasionally he would mount one of the wheeled siege machines that were drawn up to the walls and on reaching them he would attack the breaches in person. One day he placed a shield on his arm and engaged in the fight, returning only when several arrows had become lodged in it.

On the night of Wednesday, 15 Jumādā I [5 March], the Franks fled, abandoning the citadel and its contents. The Muslims climbed the walls and burned the gates, entering from both its upper and lower parts, and the dawn prayer was called from its summit. The Sultan went up to the citadel and divided the town amongst his emirs, his attendants, his mamlūks and his ḥalqa, after which the citadel's destruction was begun. He went down and, taking a pickaxe in his hand, began to destroy it in person; seeing him thus, the officers followed his example and did the work themselves.

*A Mamlūk regiment of mostly free-born troops.

(Adapted from Ibn ʻAbd al-Ẓāhir, trans. al-Khowayter, 2:555–7.)

precipitated the collapse of the surrounding principality, leaving only a couple of outposts in the south. The next Mamlūk offensive against the Franks came in 1271 and targeted the major strongholds of the Homs–Tripoli corridor, the last significant inland projection of Frankish power. The capture of Crac des Chevaliers and ʻAkkār (Gibelacar) impaired the Franks' ability to raid into the plain around Homs and removed the remaining obstacles that might interfere with a direct assault against Tripoli. The seizure of Montfort later in the year extended Mamlūk authority across western Galilee.

Following the brief reigns of two of Baybars' sons, another of al-Ṣāliḥ Ayyūb's mamlūks, Qalāwūn, became sultan. Qalāwūn captured the last remaining strongholds of the principality of Antioch and county of Tripoli, with the exception of Tortosa, before his sudden death in 1290. He was succeeded by his son, al-Ashraf Khalīl, who lost no time executing the plan his father had been organizing at the time of his death, throwing the might of the Mamlūk war machine against Frankish Acre. Much as the Frankish siege of Acre in 1189–91 had extended Latin rule in the Levant, the Mamlūk siege in 1291 effectively ended the Franks' tenure in the region. With the fall of Acre, the remaining Frankish strongholds were abandoned.

West vs. East, Christians vs. Muslims?

The history of the crusades is often cast as a binary conflict between European Christians and Middle Eastern Muslims. While this might be true in a very general sense, at least from a distant European point of view, the reality on the ground was far more complex. Less than a decade after the conclusion of the First Crusade, Muslims and Franks were fighting alongside each other against rival coreligionists in significant pitched battles and concluding peace agreements that led to the formal sharing of important regions. Far from anomalies, such examples of opportunistic cross-faith alliances and land-sharing arrangements can be found throughout the twelfth and thirteenth centuries. Before his death around 1130, Fulcher of Chartres, one of the participants of the First Crusade who opted to remain in the Levant, summed up the Latin experience in the East:

> For we who were Occidentals have now become Orientals. He who was a Roman or a Frank has in this land been made into a Galilean or a Palestinean. He who was of Rheims or Chartres has now become a citizen of Tyre or Antioch. We have already forgotten the places of our birth; already these are unknown to many of us or not mentioned any more ...
>
> People use the eloquence and idioms of diverse languages in conversing back and forth. Words of different languages have become common property known to each nationality, and mutual faith unites those who are ignorant of their descent. Indeed it is written, 'The lion and the ox shall eat straw together'. He who was born a stranger is now as one born here; he who was born an alien has become as a native.[12]

To some extent, Fulcher's utopian remarks were part of an effort to attract more Europeans to settle in the Levant; however, the degree of cohabitation, coexistence and even cooperation among the different cultural groups of the region should not

Usāma ibn Munqidh: an encounter with Europeans in Jerusalem, mid-twelfth century

Anyone who is recently arrived from the Frankish lands is rougher in character than those who have become acclimated and have frequented the company of Muslims . . .

Whenever I went to visit the holy sites in Jerusalem, I would go in and make my way up to the al-Aqṣā Mosque, beside which stood a small mosque that the Franks had converted into a church. When I went into the al-Aqṣā Mosque – where the Templars, who are my friends, were – they would clear out the little mosque so that I could pray in it. One day, I went into the little mosque, recited the opening formula, 'God is great!' and stood up in prayer. At this, one of the Franks rushed at me and grabbed me and turned my face towards the east,* saying, 'Pray like *this*!' . . .

The Templars grabbed him and threw him out. They apologized to me, saying, 'This man is a stranger, just arrived from the Frankish lands sometime in the past few days. He has never before seen anyone who did not pray towards the east.'

* Whereas Latin Christians typically pray in an easterly direction, Muslims pray towards Mecca. In Jerusalem, this is an angle of about 157°, or 23° east of south.

(Adapted from Usāma ibn Munqidh, trans. Cobb, p. 147.)

be understated. The anecdotes of Usāma ibn Munqidh, which must also be taken with a grain of salt, speak to the level of interaction between Franks and Muslims through the twelfth century. When the Franks arrived and began to impose their rule over the areas they conquered, life probably changed little for most elements of society: farmers continued to farm; traders continued to trade.

Parallel calls for crusade and jihad were issued through the twelfth and thirteenth centuries. Following Urban II's sermon and the popular response and development of a broader crusading movement in Europe, similar polemics directed against the Franks gradually became more prevalent among Muslims of the Middle East. 'Alī ibn Ṭāhir al-Sulamī, a Damascene jurist who died in 1106, appears to have been the first to present the arrival of the crusaders as an act of religious warfare and to call for a jihad (in an armed sense) against them. The rhetoric of intolerance, then as now, was typically strongest amongst those with minimal daily interaction with the groups they targeted, and gained the support of individuals equally far from the fighting. This is among the themes highlighted by Usāma ibn Munqidh, who had regular contact with the Franks and crusaders during the twelfth century.

Intrafaith Conflict

Fighting among coreligionists is a theme that runs throughout the period of the crusades. Elements of the First Crusade came to blows with Byzantine forces, attacking Constantinople at one point, and Tancred and Baldwin of Boulogne (later Baldwin I of Edessa and then Jerusalem) clashed in Cilicia later in 1097. Meanwhile, the sons of Tutush were feuding in western Syria, Karbughā of Mosul was in conflict with the Dānishmands, and al-Afḍal's Egyptian forces took Jerusalem from Īlghāzī and his brother in 1098. This is perhaps less surprising when considering the broader context: the sons of Sultan Malikshāh were fighting with each other for control of the Seljuk Empire, and Europe's greatest monarchs, King Philip I of France and Emperor Henry IV, were both in conflict with the papacy at the time. Baronial warfare was common in Europe, while periods of civil war had only recently ended in Byzantium and Fāṭimid Egypt.

Through the following decades, Frankish infighting often stemmed from the infrequency at which the Latin princes were succeeded by adult sons. In 1132, King Fulk's efforts to interfere in the regency of Antioch led to an open battle with Count Pons of Tripoli, an event that did not escape the notice of neighbouring Muslims. A couple of years later, Fulk seems to have faced a revolt, led by the count of Jaffa, and, following Fulk's death, a brief civil war broke out when his son, King Baldwin III, came of age and attempted to assert his right to rule independent of his formidable mother, Melisende. Deeper discord accompanied the reign of Baldwin IV, whose leprosy fated him to an early death without a natural successor. The polarizing politics of the succession crisis that followed foreshadowed the nature of the intra-Frankish conflicts of the thirteenth century.

Meanwhile, Muslim rulers were far more regularly and obviously drawn into conflicts with coreligionist neighbours and subordinates. Although Nūr al-Dīn and Saladin both came to champion the cause of jihad against the Franks, this was at least in part a convenient means of building support and maintaining legitimacy while they dealt with rival Muslim powers – each spent the first decade of his reign fighting fellow Muslims more often than the Franks.

Intrafaith conflict became the norm through the first half of the thirteenth century: Saladin's heirs fought with each other for power and influence while Frankish factions did likewise. Damascus was besieged no fewer than nine times by Ayyūbid armies between Saladin's death in 1193 and 1246. Meanwhile, Frankish supporters and opponents of Frederick II fought openly at times and, as Louis IX was crusading in Egypt, the Pisans and Genoese turned Acre into a battlefield for a month in 1249. Tensions remained and the conflict among the Italian communities ultimately climaxed from 1256 in the War of St Sabas, pitting the Venetians and Templars against the Genoese and Hospitallers, each side drawing in supporters from the local baronage. By this point, the military orders had long been the Franks' most effective fighting forces and, although open fighting between the orders was rare, they regularly backed opposing parties. As willing as both the Franks and Muslims were to fight members of their own religion, many were almost as prepared to fight alongside neighbours who held different beliefs.

Interfaith Cooperation

Seven years after a Fāṭimid army had taken Jerusalem from the Seljuks, Shiite Egyptian forces were joined by Sunni Damascene troops at Ascalon and together they invaded the kingdom of Jerusalem in August 1105. A Damascene raid in late 1118 corresponded with another Fāṭimid invasion. As Frankish authority spread and significant populations of Muslims found themselves living peacefully under Frankish rule, Albert of Aachen claims that at least one group of Franks defected to the Muslims. At the siege of Sidon in 1107, he notes that a number of apostates originally from Provence, once part of Raymond of St Gilles' party, were found among the town's defenders.

The most famous and perhaps clearest episode of interfaith cooperation on the battlefield took place near the castle of Turbessel. In 1108, Tancred, as regent of Antioch, supported by Riḍwān of Aleppo, defeated Jāwulī Saqāo, who was joined by Baldwin II of Edessa, Joscelin of Courtenay and a force of Armenians. Rivalry and pragmatism were to blame for this peculiar episode. Jāwulī was tangled up in a broader conflict for control of the Jazīra and, having recently defeated Jokermish of Mosul and then Qilij Arslān, had gained possession of Baldwin II, a captive of Jokermish since 1104. Jāwulī ransomed Baldwin, gaining money and an ally in the process. In turn, Baldwin rallied the support of his cousin, Joscelin, and most of the local Armenians against Tancred, who had become regent of Edessa during Baldwin's captivity but now refused to return the county. Like each of the other parties, Riḍwān was an opportunistic figure. Although he was often an opponent of Antioch, an alliance in this instance placated Tancred and kept Jāwulī's influence out of western Syria. As one of the victors, Riḍwān was able to extend Aleppan authority over Qalʿat Jaʿbar.

The situation in the north was more conducive to alliances that cut across religious lines because there were more potential players: a collection of smaller powers who were often willing to set aside longstanding rivalries to confront a greater threat. The Franks were similarly able to look past rivalries and grievances to offer mutual support when required. Campaigns organized from Baghdad had a particular ability to unite both Franks and Muslims. When Bursuq ibn Bursuq led such an army into western Syria in 1115, he found Baldwin I of Jerusalem, Roger of Antioch, Ṭughtakīn of Damascus and other Muslim leaders united against him.

In the south, the number of parties was limited; nevertheless, it was not unheard of for disgruntled or dispossessed figures to look to a traditional enemy for support. When the Franks moved out to confront the joint Fāṭimid-Damascene invasion of 1105, they may have been joined by Baktāsh ibn Tutush, the dispossessed brother of Duqāq of Damascus. When the Franks besieged Aleppo in 1124–25, they were joined by the adventurer Dubays ibn Ṣadaqa, who afterwards returned to Mesopotamia and eventually found his way into Zankī's service. In 1111, fears in Egypt that Shams al-Khalīfa, the governor of Ascalon, might submit himself to Baldwin I were so great that it was deemed too risky to try to replace him. Similar fears among those in the town led to his murder within a few months. About twenty-three years later, when Hugh of Jaffa was accused of treason, he fled to Ascalon rather than meet his accuser, his stepson, Walter of Caesarea, in single combat. After gaining the support of the Muslim governor, he returned to Jaffa, where he was nearly besieged by Fulk before the patriarch intervened and organized a settlement that involved Hugh's exile.

The death of Ṭughtakīn and Zankī's acquisition of Aleppo in 1128 marked the beginning of a new dynamic in western Syria, one in which Aleppo would replace Damascus as the dominant power. In early 1135, Shams al-Mulūk, the grandson of Ṭughtakīn, attempted a coup against his own administration, threatening to surrender Damascus to the Franks unless Zankī took control of the city. This precipitated a revolt among his emirs and his murder. When Zankī moved against Damascus a few years later, following the succession of the young Mujīr al-Dīn in 1140, he was frustrated by the arrival of a Frankish force. Mujīr al-Dīn's regent, Mu'īn al-Dīn Unur, had struck an agreement with Baldwin II, offering to help the Franks take Bānyās in exchange for their support. The combined Frankish-Damascene force went on to successfully besiege Bānyās. As it turned out, the governor of Bānyās, who had recognized Zankī's suzerainty in late 1137, had been killed only days earlier during a raid towards Tyre, having encountered Raymond of Antioch as the prince marched south to join Baldwin II.

In 1148, Raymond II of Tripoli faced a threat to his authority when his cousin and rival claimant to the county, Bertrand of Toulouse, seized Arima (al-'Urayma). Lacking the strength to retake the castle himself, Raymond reached out to Nūr al-Dīn of Aleppo and Mu'īn al-Dīn of Damascus. Nūr al-Dīn seized the opportunity. He captured Arima, which he made no attempt to hold, and, to Raymond's delight, Bertrand was taken away into captivity, destined to remain a resident of the Aleppan dungeons until 1159. Raymond's son and namesake, Raymond III, would later engage in an equally scandalous alliance with neighbouring Muslims, permitting Saladin to send raiders through his lands on 1 May 1187.

In 1147, the ruler of Ṣarkhad, who had fallen out with Mujīr al-Dīn's administration, offered the Franks Ṣarkhad and Bosra in exchange for adequate compensation, precipitating a race for control of the Ḥawrān. Mu'īn al-Dīn placed both strongholds under siege and Nūr al-Dīn, with whom he had recently made peace, moved south to help. Using the topography to their advantage and cutting off the Franks from sources of water and pasture, the Muslims successfully shielded their besieging forces, ultimately enabling Mu'īn al-Dīn to secure both strongholds. Despite this episode and the Second Crusade's move against Damascus the following year, the relationship between Damascus and Jerusalem was not beyond salvaging.

Mu'īn al-Dīn died in 1149 and Mujīr al-Dīn took power in his own name. Although the young ruler had recognized Nūr al-Dīn's nominal suzerainty in 1150, he appealed to the Franks for help the following year. Like his father a decade before, Nūr al-Dīn, having marched against Damascus to apply unsubtle pressure, was compelled to withdraw with the arrival of Frankish forces. On this occasion, however, the Franks were unable to collect their promised compensation, Bosra, as they had Bānyās in 1140. Not long after, Nūr al-Dīn concluded a new peace with Damascus before laying siege to Bosra himself. The town's ruler had been able to govern fairly autonomously, using the balance of power between Jerusalem, Damascus and Aleppo to his benefit. But the era of small independent rulers was coming to an end, signalled by Nūr al-Dīn's acquisition of Damascus in 1154.

The contest for Egypt, which dominated the 1160s, was triggered when Shāwar, vizier of Egypt, was challenged and forced to flee by a rival, Ḍirghām. After regaining his position with the support of Nūr al-Dīn and forces under Shīrkūh, Shāwar called on Amalric for assistance, hoping to play the Franks and Zankids against each other. Although the Franks installed a garrison in Cairo for a short period from 1167, Shīrkūh successfully asserted control over Egypt around the start of 1169. In a strangely similar parallel, a source sympathetic to Raymond III of Tripoli states that a

Muslim force was stationed in Tiberias in 1186, ready to defend the count if attacked by Guy of Lusignan. Raymond was the leading opponent of Guy and an ally of Saladin, and it was his relationship with the latter that led Raymond to allow Saladin to send a party of raiders through the lordship of Tiberias (the principality of Galilee, which Raymond held in the name of his wife, Eschiva Bures) the following year. Although Raymond stipulated that the raiders should seize no property and return back across the Jordan the same day, he was nevertheless allowing a Muslim force to invade and scout the region, unknowingly setting in motion events that would lead to the battle of Hattin two months later.

Following their humbling in the late 1180s, the Franks were primarily observers of the Ayyūbid power contest. This changed in 1240, when the kingdom of Jerusalem joined an alliance led by al-Ṣāliḥ Ismāʿīl of Damascus against his nephew, al-Ṣāliḥ Ayyūb of Egypt. In return for their involvement, the Franks received considerable territory in northern Palestine, including the strongholds of Safed and Beaufort. The garrison of Beaufort, however, declined to give up the castle, compelling Ismāʿīl to besiege it himself. In the autumn of 1242, al-Jawād Yūnus, a one-time claimant to Damascus, joined the Franks on a raid around Nablus. Two years later, Frankish forces made up a significant component of the Syrian side at the battle of Forbie, where they were crushed by the Egyptian army. Aside from the Seventh Crusade, this defeat was effectively the last major field engagement involving Frankish forces.

In the second half of the thirteenth century, it was more often the Franks who sought the support of neighbours. Bohemond VI, as count of Tripoli, may have asked his Mongol allies for Baalbek following their capture of the city in 1260. In the years that followed, others called on the Mamlūks for support against their rivals. In the feud between Bohemond VII and his vassal Guy II of Gibelet, the latter is said to have offered to divide Tripoli with Qalāwūn in exchange for assistance taking the city. Guy's attempt to take Tripoli failed in January 1182 and he was later executed at Nephin.

Hospitality and Diplomacy

It takes only a quick glance at the anecdotes provided by Usāma ibn Munqidh or Ibn Jubayr to appreciate the regularity with which Muslims and Franks interacted: diplomats were exchanged; pilgrimages were made; trade flourished. Military leaders were even entertained through the course of certain conflicts. Following the siege of Alexandria in 1167, Saladin was hosted for a time in the Frankish siege camp outside the city. In 1244, al-Manṣūr Ibrāhīm, who led the Muslim forces alongside the Franks at the battle of Forbie, was entertained in Acre ahead of the battle. In the days leading up to the battle of ʿAyn Jālūt in 1260, Baybars may also have visited Acre, while refugees from Damascus, fleeing the advancing Mongols, were welcomed into Tyre from around the end of 1259. As allies of al-Sālih Ismāʿīl in the early 1240s, the Franks had a similar opportunity to visit Damascus, where they bought weapons and even siege engines. A decade later, Louis IX of France took advantage of a comparable peace, sending John the Armenian there to buy horn and glue for making crossbows. Diplomatic and intelligence networks had developed so quickly that, in 1126, ʿIzz al-Dīn Masʿūd learned about the death of his father, Āqsunqur al-Bursuqī, in whose name he was administering Aleppo, from a Frankish message sent from Antioch, which reached him before the official message, or even rumours, arrived from Mosul.

* * *

The period of the crusades was a dynamic one, in which parties from as far away as northwestern Europe and central Asia travelled to the Middle East to fight for control of the Levant. Although religion motivated many to take up the cause of crusade or jihad, driving them to travel hundreds if not thousands of kilometres, others fought to satisfy more worldly ambitions. For local figures, these conflicts were perhaps far less religiously motivated or dissimilar to those elsewhere than we might initially imagine – if we could peel away the religious rhetoric, the regional fighting between lords and emirs might look much like the patterns of conflict seen in other parts of the Middle East and Europe. To do so, however, seems impossible, because the religious rhetoric permeated contemporary language and considerations of faith influenced almost everyone to some degree.

Chapter Two

Strategy of Defence: Building and Using Fortifications

The castles and town defences built by the Franks and Muslims are some of the most iconic symbols of the crusader period. For centuries these impressive stone structures have attracted the attention of pilgrims, tourists and other travellers journeying through the Holy Land. The size and shape of these strongholds varies considerably, as each was designed and built with a different set of priorities and resources.

Although towers and castles may have fulfilled what might be termed an 'administrative function' more than anything else, the core of their purpose was to act as anchors of regional control. Expansionist neighbours were compelled to overcome these fortifications if they wanted to annex the surrounding area, while raiders were obliged to take these points of resistance or risk leaving the hostile force of defenders within to their rear. Although networks and patterns of strongholds developed over time, significant castles were far too expensive for a single ruler to undertake a grand fortification strategy akin to those commissioned by modern states. While rulers might add one or more strongholds to the existing landscape, this was a piecemeal process influenced by numerous factors. Whether built by a king or a minor lord, a sultan or an emir, each castle or tower was constructed with a particular set of strategic objectives in mind.

Before the Crusades

Fortifications have been built in the Near East since at least the Bronze Age. This has left a diverse landscape of defences as sites were developed, abandoned and rebuilt over the centuries. From the Muslim conquests in the seventh century until the arrival of the Franks at the end of the eleventh, most of the fortification efforts undertaken in the region can be divided into four categories: the Umayyad 'desert castles'; the development of town walls; the construction of isolated castles; and the redevelopment of urban citadels.

Desert Castles

The so-called 'desert castles', most of which are located east of the Dead Sea in modern Jordan, appear to have been rural palaces built under the Umayyads between the late seventh century and the early eighth. Many, including Qaṣr Kharana, Qaṣr al-Ḥallabāt, Qaṣr Qasṭal, Khirbat al-Minya and Khirbat al-Mafjar were built with a quadriburgium design. This type of square or rectangular plan resembles that of many Roman forts; however, of these sites, only Qaṣr al-Ḥallabāt appears to sit on earlier Roman foundations, which date to the second century. These are similar to

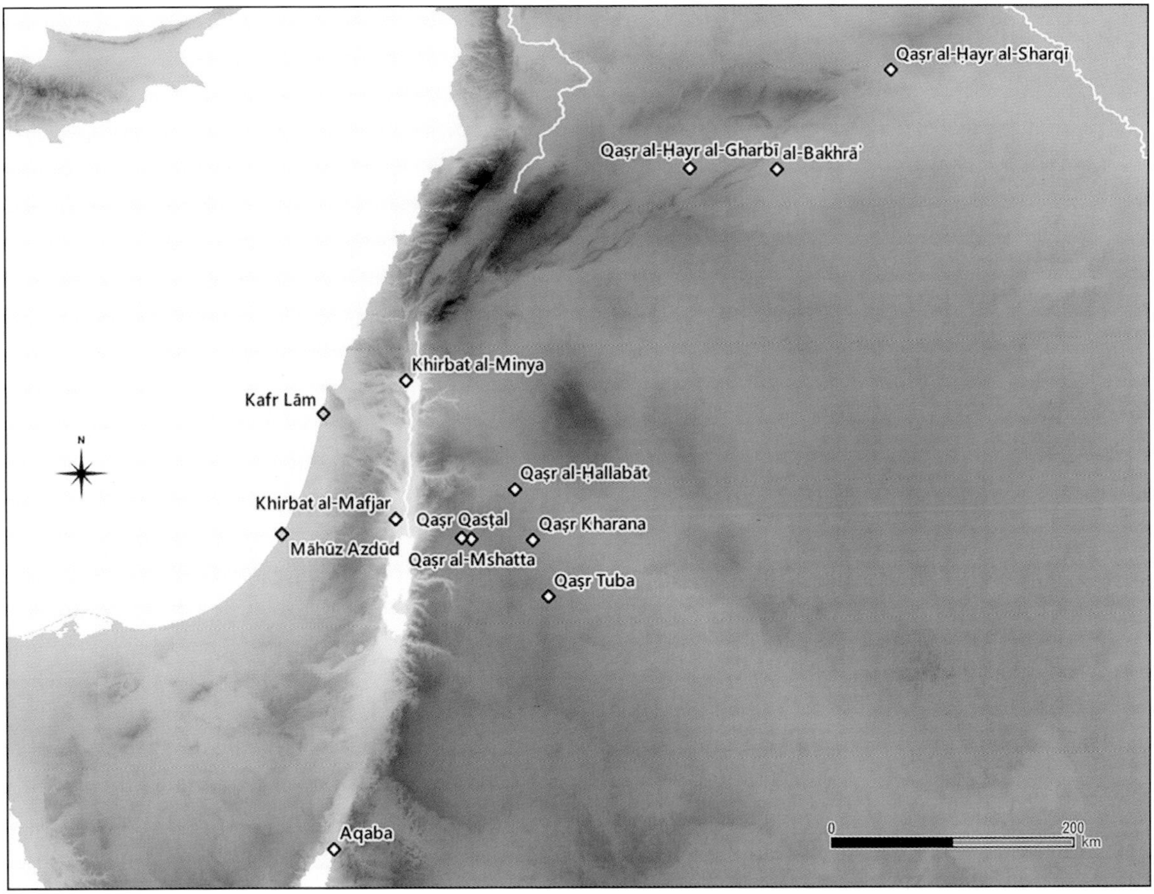

'Desert castles.'

Qaṣr al-Ḥayr al-Sharqī, entrance of the smaller enclosure. (*monumentsofsyria.com*)

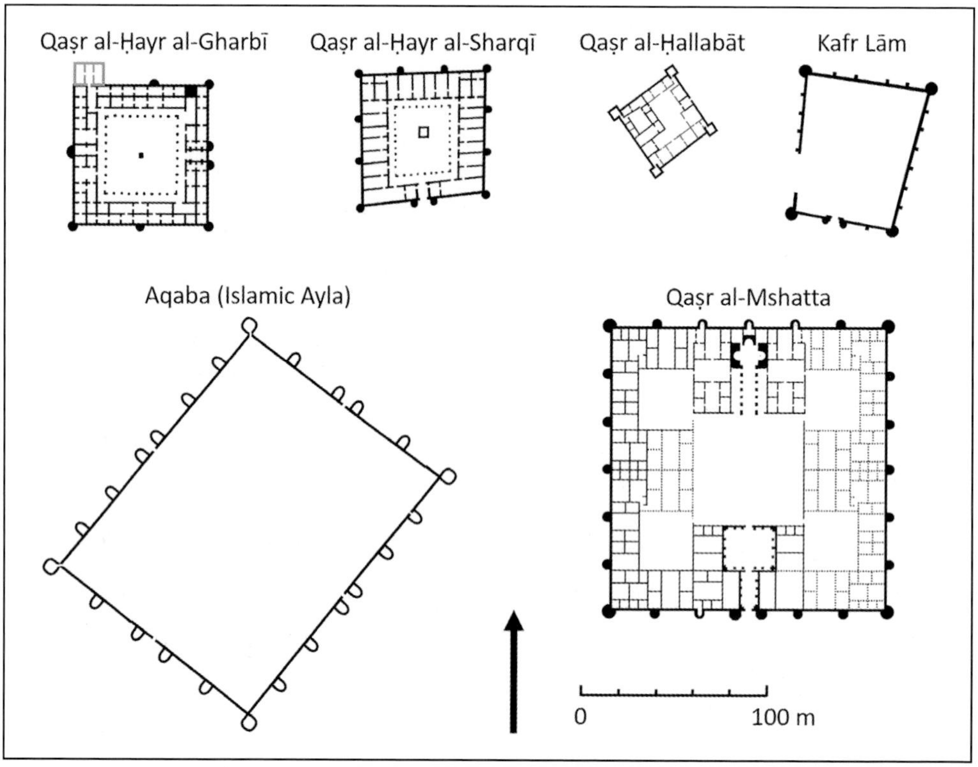

'Desert castles.'

Qaṣr al-Ḥayr al-Sharqī and al-Bakhrā' (Avatha): the former was a contemporary Umayyad palace with a pseudo-military plan constructed in the Syrian Desert to the north, between Palmyra, al-Raḥba and Raqqa; the latter, near Palmyra, sits on an earlier Roman fort, like Qaṣr al-Ḥallabāt. The size of these structures varied considerably and some, including Aqaba (Ayla), Qaṣr al-Mshatta, Qaṣr Tuba, al-Bakhrā' and the larger enclosure at Qaṣr al-Ḥayr al-Sharqī, are large enough to be classified as small towns, rather than simply palaces. Along the Mediterranean coast, Kafr Lām and Māhūz Azdūd were built with similar plans.

Urban Defences

Further west, urban defences, many predating the Muslim conquests, were maintained and developed under Muslim rule. Due to the periodic refortification of most cities, it can be hard to discern when certain walls were built, although Umayyad, 'Abbāsid and Fāṭimid work, especially along the coast, can all be found in various combinations. It was the Muslim defences of Jerusalem and many coastal towns, such as Ascalon, Caesarea, Arsūf and Tyre, that the Franks built upon or developed. This was also the case further north, where existing urban defences, whether constructed under the Muslims or Byzantines, were rebuilt or repaired at sites such as Antioch, Ma'arrat al-Nu'mān and al-Athārib. At some sites, such as Aqaba and Caesarea, a distinctly new line of Muslim walls was constructed, often within the larger trace of earlier Roman defences. One of the last refortification efforts completed before the arrival of the Franks was commissioned at Cairo by Badr al-Jamālī, adding the city's iconic late eleventh-century gates.

Isolated Strongholds

Isolated fortifications were more commonly built in the Syrian Coastal Mountains, Cilicia and the rougher terrain around the Taurus Mountains. In the sixth century, Justinian, the Byzantine emperor, carried out an extensive fortification programme across much of his empire, strengthening many town walls. In the seventh century, as considerable swathes of Byzantine territory in the East were lost, focus shifted from strengthening town defences to fortifying more inaccessible castles and citadels. The 'Abbāsid caliphs may have fortified a number of positions along their frontier with Byzantium, north of Antioch, in the eighth century, and another wave of Byzantine fortification efforts accompanied the successful campaigns launched across Anatolia and into Syria under Nikephoras II Phocas and his successors in the second half of the tenth century. Saone, Bourzey and many other Byzantine outposts in the Syrian Coastal Mountains south of Antioch were built during these initiatives. Bourzey, for example, appears to have been constructed by the mid-tenth century, at which point it was taken on behalf of Sayf al-Dawla of Aleppo. The stronghold was retaken under Emperor John I Tzimiskes around 975, but later fell to Seljuk forces following their capture of Antioch in 1085. In 1090, the castle was slighted on the orders of Qāsim al-Dawla Āqsunqur of Aleppo, Zankī's father, and it probably remained in a dilapidated state until it was occupied and refortified by the Franks in the early twelfth century.

Armenians had taken part in these Byzantine campaigns and a migration into southeastern Anatolia and northwestern Syria followed, encouraged further in the eleventh century by the Seljuk incursions into eastern and central Anatolia. As Byzantine influence waned, the Armenian lords of Cilicia and the Taurus Mountains asserted their autonomy and independence from the castles that they had captured or constructed, and it was from these that they continued to resist Turkish authority.

In the fractious political environment of northwestern Syria in the late eleventh century, a number of small Arab and Turkish lords similarly secured their regional authority through the possession and development of castles. Much like the Armenians, some Arab families, such as the Banū Numayr and Banū Munqidh, carved out and held on to regional authority, along the Euphrates and around Shayzar respectively, through the possession of castles rather than larger urban centres. In one of his anecdotes, Usāma ibn Munqidh (1095–1188) states that Shayzar had no town wall in the time of his father, the community relying entirely on the castle that dominated it.

Seljuk Citadels

A new focus was placed on urban defences with the arrival of the Seljuk Turks in the eleventh century. Whereas the 'Abbāsids and Fāṭimids, like the early Byzantines, had tended to develop town walls, the Seljuks focused instead on citadels. Unlike castles (often rural structures), the walls of which were the defenders' main line of defence (even if attached to a walled town), citadels were secondary strongholds along or behind the walls of what was often a significant urban community. These provided a place of refuge should the defences of the town beyond be overwhelmed by a hostile army, or if the urban population rose up in revolt.

For the Turks, who were relative outsiders, having only recently migrated to the region they came to dominate, these citadels served a military function but also symbolized the new socio-political hierarchy. The citadel of Damascus was likely commissioned in the 1070s while the Temple of Bel at Palmyra and theatre of Bosra were developed into citadels around the same time. Further north, many ancient tells were refortified under Seljuk rule, providing secure seats of local administration and positions from which the local communities below were dominated.

* * *

The Franks are most often associated with the fortifications built in the region during the two centuries that followed the First Crusade; however, they merely contributed to another chapter of what was already a long history. Many of the town walls they defended predated their arrival, while neighbouring Muslims continued to build and improve urban defences as well as a number of more isolated rural strongholds. Although broad trends can be identified, as different styles and systems of defences suited particular political and administrative structures, a unique set of circumstances, motivations and regional factors lay behind the construction, design and use of each stronghold.

Administration

The primary purpose of any fortified tower, castle or system of town walls was to provide a defensible position – an enclave of safety if the surrounding region were overrun. Although some strongholds were attacked on a near annual basis, most did not see action more than once per decade. During these extended periods of relative peace, most strongholds acted as important administrative centres: the seats of local authority and bases from which order was both protected and enforced. As Smail put it when addressing Frankish castles, 'as in Europe, so in Syria, castles had only occasionally to withstand a siege, but they continuously fulfilled their function as the physical basis of overlordship'.[13]

Frankish Power Structure

While Muslim rule was based primarily in the region's larger urban centres, Frankish authority was based upon a greater network of fortifications; the first of these they took from local Muslim and Armenian rulers, supplementing them with a number of new strongholds over the following years. This difference reflected the nature of the ruling political systems in Europe and the Near East at the time. Authority in much of Europe was structured according to a 'feudal' system: a varying concept whereby land and authority over the people who occupied it were held of a superior lord in exchange for military support. In the Frankish East, a firm system of feudal rights and obligations appears to have been slow to form and a more practical arrangement of support developed ad hoc. Even in the kingdom of Jerusalem, where a system of land-holding rights developed most clearly, the monarchy retained a considerable degree of influence in the twelfth century, shaping and reshaping the various lordships as vassals died without heirs or left only young successors, who were of little help on the battlefield. Unlike in Europe, most lords appear to have held their lands directly of the ruling prince, rather than an intermediary lord.

Following the initial spread of Frankish influence, the four Frankish princes (the king of Jerusalem, prince of Antioch, and counts of Edessa and Tripoli) retained large tracts of land for themselves; other areas were granted out as fiefs. In some instances, regions that adventurous figures had come to claim, such as Tancred's relatively independent acquisition of Galilee, were acknowledged as fiefs. The granting of land in this way was a means to provide members of the nobility (the military class) with a sustainable income and a stake in the collective venture that was the larger principality of which their fief was a part.

To administer their lands, lords typically built, developed or repaired some kind of stronghold, which served as a seat of local power and symbolized their authority. The seats of many significant lordships were in cities, occupying or building upon earlier citadels. Those whose power was based in a more rural setting often constructed a tower near the main source of the lordship's wealth, usually the main village or town, or developed a pre-existing stronghold, which often had a supporting community located nearby.

Large or small, the primary obligation of these lords, the price for the privilege of land ownership and the social and economic benefits that came with it, was military service. Each lord was expected to provide to his overlord a number of knights, or the equivalent sum to finance such, relative to the wealth of his lordship. In return, he could expect his overlord to defend his lands if they were threatened by a hostile power. During times of peace, some of these knights would have administered their lords' estates, acted as castellans of smaller strongholds and served as the leading members of the garrisons of larger castles and towns. Others would have served in baronial entourages.

In the Latin East, there are few mentions of the *corvée*, the system by which peasants were compelled to work a lord's lands for a certain number of days, and serfdom was far less prevalent than in Europe. Frankish lords appear to have sourced much of their rural incomes from the rents they gathered from tenant farmers, which replaced the need for forced labour to work the lands they retained. These rents were supplemented by fees to use communal service structures, such as the lord's mill, oven or baths, or those imposed on any sale of property. Some individuals were even given 'money fiefs' rather than lands: sometimes the revenue from a toll or urban tax, or a salary upon which the knight was expected to support himself.

Although power was expressed through the control of land, many significant seats of Frankish authority were located in the towns along the Mediterranean coast, which were both traditional bases of local power and centres of commerce. The largest interior lordships retained their importance; however, their source of revenue, the land, was more vulnerable to raids than the lands along the coast and the duties collected in the ports. As power became increasingly concentrated among certain baronial families, and the threat posed by Nūr al-Dīn became more apparent, smaller interior landholders sold or gave away their lands with increasing regularity to religious orders. But even after the collapse of the county of Edessa and the loss of

Knight-service in the kingdom of Jerusalem, 1170s or 1180s

Count of Jaffa and Ascalon	100
Jaffa (25), Ascalon (25), Ramla and Mirabel (40), Ibelin (10)	
Prince of Galilee	100
Lands to the Jordan (60), lands beyond the Jordan (40)	
Lord of Sidon	100
Sidon and Beaufort (50), Caesarea (25), Baysān (25)	
Lord of Transjordan and Hebron	60
Kerak (40), Hebron (20)	
Lordship of Joscelin of Courtenay	24
Castellum Regis (4), Saint George (10), lordship of Geoffrey le Tor (6), lordship of Philip Rufus (2), the chamberlain's lordship (2)	
Toron and the Maron	18
Toron (15), the Maron (3)	
Bānyās, Asebebe, Chastel Neuf	?
Ecclesiastical lands	16
Bishop of Lydda (10), Archbishop of Nazareth (6)	
Cities owed to the king	257
Jerusalem (41), Nablus (85), Acre (80), Tyre (28), Dārūm (2), Beirut (21)	
TOTAL	677

(Derived from John of Ibelin, ed. Edbury, pp. 607–14.)

inland territory that followed the battle of Hattin, which further concentrated Frankish rule in the coastal towns, Frankish authority was never as centralized nor as focused on urban centres as was that of their Muslim neighbours.

Twelfth-Century Building Trends

The earliest Frankish fortifications were occupied rather than built; they were the product of previous Byzantine and Muslim construction efforts, some acquired through conquest, others by treaty. We know little about the Franks' early castle-building efforts to the north, aside from the increased involvement of the military orders in the second half of the century. Although there are fewer significant castles in Palestine, the documentary evidence is better. Here, it is clear that the monarchy took a fairly proactive role in securing Frankish rule by commissioning a number of the kingdom of Jerusalem's most significant twelfth-century castles.

Montreal was commissioned by Baldwin I in 1115, during his expedition through Transjordan. The stronghold dominated a fertile area, wetter then than today, known to produce grain, wine and olives. The remains of sugar mills have also been found in the region. The original structure, built in just eighteen days, was probably rebuilt or enlarged soon after. William of Tyre described it as a castle defended by both natural and artificial defences, which included a wall and towers, an outer wall and a ditch, defended by a garrison of cavalry and infantry amply provided with arms, food and

Montreal. (*Courtesy of APAAME*)

machines. There was a settlement near the castle and a community of some size lived within the stronghold itself. Thietmar, who visited in 1217, similarly described the castle as very strong and defended by three lines of walls. Montreal still displays two lines of what appear to be Frankish walls, allowing for the possibility that the innermost structure (the third line of walls) viewed by Thietmar was the original structure built in 1115, which has since disappeared through the course of subsequent renovations by the Ayyūbids, Mamlūks and the later Arab community that occupied the castle until the 1980s.

Royal initiative was similarly responsible for the commissioning of strongholds such as Scandelion (Iskandarūna) in 1117, the castles built around Ascalon during the reign of Fulk, and Castellum Regis (or Castellum Novum). The latter is first mentioned in a document dating to 1160, suggesting it was constructed under Baldwin III or his father, Fulk. In 1178, Baldwin IV financed the castle at Jacob's Ford, with the understanding that it would be held by the Templars. Although castles were an important means of securing and administering the kingdom, they were expensive to maintain and defend, a cost the monarchy was increasingly willing to relinquish. Like the baronage, the kings of Jerusalem recognized that most commerce, and comforts, were in the cities and towns along the coast.

Castles are most often associated with baronial power and autonomy, so it is perhaps surprising how few significant Frankish castles were built by the nobility. This becomes understandable when considering the costs of constructing and maintaining these great structures. Toron (Tibnīn), among the baronial castles founded in the first decade of Frankish rule, would become an impressive stronghold, but it probably began as a simple keep tower. By comparison, Kerak, one of the kingdom of Jerusalem's most impressive castles, was planned as a monumental stronghold from the outset. Kerak was established a few decades after Toron, allowing its commissioner, Pagan the Butler, to draw upon the established and considerable revenue streams of his dominion, the lordship of Transjordan.

According to some Muslim sources, Safed was fortified prior to the arrival of the Franks, although a degree of confusion is evident as they suggest it was the Templars who rebuilt the castle in 1101–2. Although the Templar order had not yet been established, construction could have been overseen at this time by Hugh of St Omer, the commissioner of Toron. Marino Sanudo, writing at the start of the fourteenth century, confirms that Safed was built by the end of Fulk's reign and it was clearly in existence when Baldwin III fled there in 1157, having been defeated by Nūr al-Dīn after relieving Bānyās. The earliest twelfth-century record of the castle dates to 1168, when Amalric gave it to the Templars. The document reveals that Safed had been held by Fulk, constable of Tiberias, before it was acquired by Amalric, and suggests that the Templars may have held it of Fulk for some period before this, perhaps since the reign of King Fulk of Jerusalem. Refortification efforts had recently taken place and may have continued once the Templars received outright rule of the castle.

Beaufort, 18km northeast of Toron, predated the arrival of the Franks in some form. The castle was acquired by the Būrid dynasty of Damascus before it was surrendered to Fulk of Jerusalem in 1139. It was then allocated to the lordship of Sidon, rather than the closer but already quite influential lordship of Toron or principality of Galilee. If this represented an attempt to divide power in the north, it had limited success, as the three ruling families of these lordships were linked by marriage in the 1140s. It seems more likely that this was an effort to give a third major lord a stake in the affairs of the northeastern section of the kingdom. When justifying Baybars' siege of the castle in 1268, Ibn ʿAbd al-Ẓāhir calls Beaufort a threat to Ṣubayba, and implicitly Bānyās below, but this threat seems to have been symbolic. Beaufort, sitting high atop the western side of the steep valley carved by the Litani River, is visible from Ṣubayba, about 19km away, but these cliffs isolate it and deprive its garrison of the ability to strike rapidly into the Hula Valley, as those of Chastel Neuf (Hūnīn) to the south and Ṣubayba to the east could have done. A modern set of switchbacks, about 2.5km north of Beaufort, provide a route down to the Litani; however, it may have been necessary to travel a distance of 4km north of the castle to find a more natural path down to the river, from where both the Hula Valley to the south and Biqāʿ Valley to the north could be approached. It may have been this combination of isolation and access that allowed the castle to remain a part of a secular lordship until 1260 (although it was under Muslim rule from 1190 to 1240), while the lordship of Sidon's critical link to the sea and Europe beyond was probably another important factor.

Reynald of Sidon was one of the few Franks who survived the battle of Hattin. Although Sidon was abandoned less than a month after the battle, Reynald was less willing to give up Beaufort. When Saladin's army arrived at the castle in April 1189, Reynald, who could speak Arabic, went down to talk to him. In what turned out to be a ploy, Reynald offered to surrender Beaufort and join the Muslims if he were granted

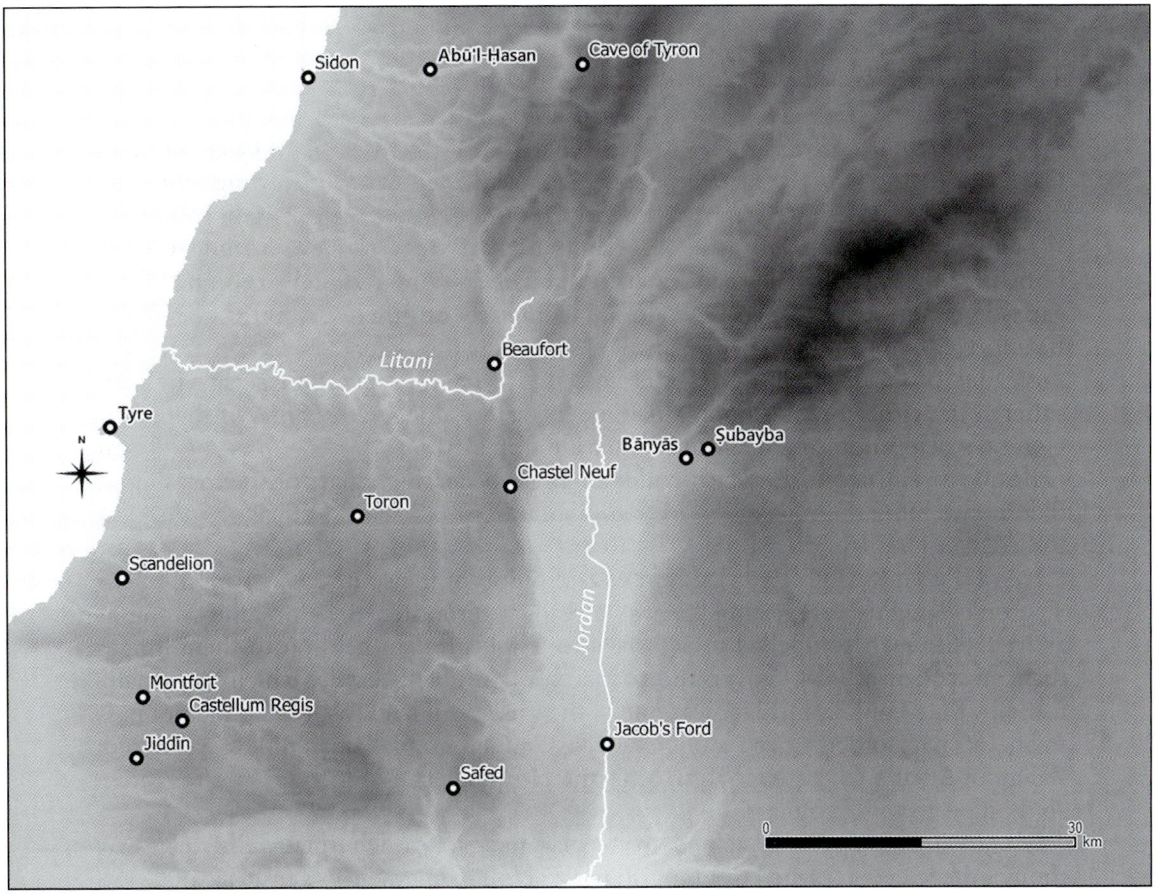

Region around the Hula Valley.

Beaufort. (*Courtesy of Jean Yasmine*)

three months to retrieve his family from Tyre. Saladin was eager to gain the castle without a fight, as Tyre, Tripoli and Antioch remained bastions of Frankish resistance and bases from which crusaders might quickly reverse his recent conquests. When Saladin returned, Reynald again visited his tent to play for more time. Growing impatient, Saladin had Reynald arrested and ordered him to command the garrison to surrender, which Reynald did, genuinely or otherwise, but they refused. Beaufort continued to hold out until 1190, when the defenders finally agreed to surrender provided their lord was released. Reynald's reputation seems to have suffered in neither Frankish nor Muslim eyes, as he, along with Balian of Ibelin, led Conrad's delegation to Saladin in the autumn of 1191.

Beaufort returned to Frankish hands in 1240, becoming a part of the lordship of Sidon once more. Following the Mongol raid on Sidon in 1260, Julian of Sidon was forced to sell both Sidon and Beaufort to the Templars. Julian had previously sold the Cave of Tyron (Shaqīf Tīrūn), 22km east of Sidon in the southern Lebanon, to the Teutonic Knights, suggesting he was already overburdened before the Mongols arrived. Although compelled to sell his strongholds, Julian held on to them longer than most. Cursat (al-Quṣayr), the patriarch of Antioch's castle, which was finally taken by the Mamlūks in 1275, was one of the very few inland castles that did not pass to the military orders. Even along the coast some baronial strongholds were sold: Balian of Arsur sold (or leased) Arsūf to the Hospitallers in 1261, a year after Julian sold Sidon to the Templars.

Montreal and Kerak remained in secular hands through the twelfth century, though they never returned to Frankish control following their loss in 1189 and 1188 respectively. Montreal had been expanded to essentially its present footprint by the 1150s, but whether most of this work was financed by the crown or the later lords of the castle is unclear. Kerak, founded in 1142 by Pagan the Butler, lord of Transjordan, came to replace Montreal as the lordship's seat of power. Kerak appears to have been planned as a mighty castle from the outset, as there is no sign of an early phase with a reduced footprint. Unsurprisingly, work on the castle is said to have continued under Pagan's successors. Even here, in these two bastions of baronial authority, the military orders had a presence by the reign of Maurice, nephew and successor of Pagan the Butler, who, in 1152, gave the Hospitallers property in both Kerak and Montreal.

The trend towards sharing the responsibility and costs of fortifications with the military orders can be seen easily in the case of Bānyās. The town had been given to the Franks by the Assassins during a period of persecution in Damascus, at which point Baldwin II bestowed it on Renier Brus. The town was retaken by Shams al-Mulūk of Damascus in December 1132, but it ended up back in Frankish hands from 1140, when the Damascenes exchanged it in return for support against Zankī. Bānyās came into the hands of Humphrey II of Toron through his marriage to Renier's daughter. Although Humphrey was constable of the kingdom and one of its leading barons, by 1157 the costs associated with Bānyās compelled him to give half of the town, and the burden of its defence, to the Hospitallers. The force of Hospitallers that was then marching to reprovision the town was ambushed on its way, leading the order to reconsider its decision to accept this offer.

Along what might be considered the Ascalon frontier, Bethgibelin (Bayt Jibrīn) and Gaza, completed around 1136 and 1150, were entrusted to the Hospitallers and Templars respectively. At the opposite end of the kingdom, the Hospitallers had established a presence in the region north of the Sea of Galilee by 1157, having acquired a portion of Chastel Neuf along with Bānyās. In 1168, the same year that outright ownership of Safed passed to the Templars, the Hospitallers acquired a new estate south of the Sea of Galilee, where the order would construct Belvoir. In addition to Safed, the Templars stood to gain Jacob's Ford, although construction was interrupted when Saladin seized and destroyed the incomplete castle in 1179.

Thirteenth-Century Building Trends

Around the time of the Fifth Crusade, James of Vitry, bishop of Acre from 1216, judged the success of a crusade by its actions to either besiege a stronghold or repair existing defences. Fortifications had become critical to preserving a Latin presence in the Levant, and as Muslim armies grew, so too was it necessary for Frankish strongholds to become more impressive. To build such elaborate fortifications, the assistance of crusaders was often required.

Crusaders had contributed to the construction of strongholds from at least the Third Crusade, when Richard I oversaw repairs to the defences of Acre and Jaffa and the rebuilding of Ascalon and Casel des Plains (Yāzūr). In the early phase of the Fifth Crusade, while the army waited in Palestine for the arrival of more forces from Europe, a group of crusaders helped strengthen Caesarea and another group assisted with the construction of 'Atlit, which was to become the Templars' great stronghold south of Acre. These defences were quickly put to the test. While the bulk of the kingdom's forces were campaigning in Egypt, al-Mu'aẓẓam 'Īsā sacked Caesarea, although not its citadel, in either 1218 or 1219, and besieged 'Atlit, without success, in 1220.

Before the worst of the partisan feuding that accompanied the arrival of Frederick II in 1228, participants of the Sixth Crusade helped construct and refortify certain strongholds. Duke Leopold VI of Austria, who participated in the early part of the Fifth Crusade, had made a significant donation to the Teutonic Knights, still a fairly new order. These and other funds were put towards acquiring lands in western Galilee, where the order was prepared to build a new castle, Montfort, by the time elements of the Sixth Crusade had begun to arrive. While German crusaders helped construct the first phase of Montfort in 1227, English, French and Spanish crusaders helped rebuild the defences of Sidon. In 1190, Sidon's town walls had been pulled down and its population moved to Beirut. It was reinhabited following the Third Crusade and shared between the Franks and Muslims for a period. By March 1228, the Franks had taken complete control and efforts were under way to refortify the town. It seems to have been at this point that a new castle was commissioned just offshore. Originally consisting of little more than two towers with a connecting wall between them, the sea castle of Sidon was developed over the following decades into an impressive stronghold.

As work at Montfort and Sidon progressed, Frederick seems to have been more concerned with refortifying the citadel of Jaffa, of which nothing now remains. The

Caesarea. *(Courtesy of Michael Eisenberg)*

citadel of Caesarea may also have been improved during this period, as permission to do so was secured in a treaty between the emperor and al-Kāmil of Egypt. In a letter to Henry III of England, his future brother-in-law, Frederick made a point of specifying that while the Franks were permitted to carry out these fortification efforts, al-Kāmil agreed not to build or repair any castles during the period of the ten-year truce they had arranged. Although Frederick could brag about this point, it had little real value considering al-Kāmil's strength was in his army and the manpower reserves he could raise, not in his fortifications.

Aside from Montfort and some work at Jerusalem, which had returned to Frankish hands under the peace negotiated by Frederick II, Frankish fortification efforts during the early thirteenth century focused on the port towns and their citadels in particular. Much as castles secured territory, these citadels held influence over key harbours, the critical portals to Europe. This policy continued during the Barons' Crusade with the fortification of Ascalon around 1240, overseen by Theobald I of Navarre and Richard of Cornwall. Rather than rebuild the town walls, in ruins since the Third Crusade, a castle was built at the north end of the town. The destroyed town defences provided plenty of stone and construction proceeded quickly. Although boats could anchor off Ascalon or moor on a stretch of beach, there was no natural harbour here and the castle appears to have been built as a forward base or buffer against Gaza, which had become the main staging point for Egyptian campaigns in Palestine and Syria, much as Ascalon had been under the Fāṭimids in the first half of the twelfth century.

While Richard of Cornwall was overseeing work at Ascalon, efforts began to rebuild the Templar castle of Safed. The castle had been destroyed by al-Muʿaẓẓam

ʿĪsā during the Fifth Crusade and it lay in ruins until al-Ṣāliḥ Ismāʿīl returned it to the Franks in 1240. Benoit of Alignan, bishop of Marseilles, led the initiative and the first stone was laid in December 1240. The bishop had made a pilgrimage to Damascus earlier in the year, having secured free passage to do so, and on his way back remarked that Ṣubayba was the only stronghold between Safed and Damascus. Although he calls Safed just a pile of stones, the fact that he was received there by Brother Rainhard of Caro suggests that some kind of structure was garrisoned before the rebuilding programme was launched. The castle was probably in its final Frankish form by the time the bishop returned to view it in 1260, six years before it was captured by the Mamlūks.

Refortification efforts shifted back to the coast during the Seventh Crusade, following Louis IX of France's ultimately disastrous campaign in Egypt. This fortification programme began with Acre in 1250 and expanded to include Haifa and then Caesarea from April 1251, at which point the town walls received their iconic continuous talus. From 1252 to 1253, attention shifted to Jaffa, its town walls, twenty-four towers and ditch, which extended around the town to the sea on either side.

De constructione castri Saphet: the rebuilding of Safed, 1240s

When it had been decided that Safed should be built, there was great joy in the House of the Temple and in the city of Acre and among the people of the Holy Land. Without delay, an impressive body of knights, sergeants, crossbowmen and other armed men were chosen with many pack animals to carry arms, supplies and other necessary materials. Granaries, cellars, treasuries and other offices were generously and happily opened to make payments. A great number of workers and slaves were sent there with the tools and materials they needed. The land rejoiced at their coming and the true Christianity of the Holy Land was exalted …

It is not easy to convey in writing or speech … what number, size and variety of construction of crossbows, quarrels, machines and every sort of arms, and what effort and amount of expense in making them; what number of guards every day, what number of the garrison of armed men to guard and defend and repel enemies who were continually required there; how many workmen with different trades, how much and what expenses are made to them daily …

In the first two and a half years, the Templars spent 1,100,000 Saracen bezants on building the castle of Safed, in addition to the revenues and income of the castle itself, and in each following year 40,000 Saracen bezants, more or less. Every day victuals are dispensed to 1,700 or more and in time of war, 2,200. For the daily establishment of the castle, 50 knights, 30 sergeant brothers and 50 turcopoles are required with their horses and arms, and 300 crossbowmen, for the works and other offices 820 and 400 slaves. There are used there every year, on average, more than 12,000 mule-loads of barley and wheat, apart from other victuals, in addition to payments to the paid soldiers and hired people, and in addition to the horses, patrols and arms and other necessities, which are not easy to account.

(Adapted from *De constructione castri Saphet*, trans. Kennedy, pp. 194–6.)

Here, Eudes of Châteauroux, a papal legate accompanying Louis, financed the reconstruction of one of the three town gates and a section of adjoining wall. Work extended to Sidon, where Simon of Montceliard, master of the king's crossbowmen, oversaw the development of the sea castle and town defences, including the old land castle at the southeast salient of the town, ahead of Louis' arrival in 1253. The French king's focus on coastal settlements is clear, but so too is his attention to town defences, rather than just citadels, reflecting his appreciation that the success of these communities, not just their survival, was critical to preserving Frankish rule in the Levant.

As Louis was seeing to the kingdom of Jerusalem's coastal fortifications, Muslim forces made a raid against the outskirts of Acre, destroying Doc (Da'uk) and Ricordane (Kurdāna), mills of the Templars and Hospitallers respectively. A more concerted attack was then made against Sidon, interrupting refortification efforts there and compelling the Franks to withdraw to the sea castle, allowing the Muslims to sack the town. While Louis marched north from Jaffa to Sidon, a contingent of the force he led attacked Bānyās. Although elements of the army were able to break into the town, they were quickly ejected and forced to content themselves with burning some of the surrounding fields. No attempt was made against Ṣubayba, which overlooked the town from the heights to the east.

There was value in occupying a crusading army with a physically demanding task, such as these refortification efforts. Pelagius, legate to the Fifth Crusade, encountered issues of idleness following the capture of Damietta, when the army refused to march out towards Cairo, and, in 1250, Louis IX had to scold one of his brothers who had already turned to dice and gambling as they sailed for Acre immediately after their defeat in Egypt. Beyond this pragmatic means of keeping discipline and avoiding rowdiness, there was the greater good: the defences that were built contributed to the Frankish principalities and there were spiritual benefits for the penitential service of completing these labours or financing them.

By the mid-thirteenth century, however, the inability of the Franks to re-establish Latin influence was becoming clear. John of Joinville provides an anecdote that in a way sums up European perceptions of the situation in the Levant in the 1250s. While John the Armenian was in Damascus sourcing crossbow materials for Louis IX, he encountered an old man who remarked to him: 'You Christians must be hating each other very much. For once, long ago, I saw King Baldwin [IV] of Jerusalem, who was a leper, defeating Saladin [at Montgisard, 1177], though he had only three hundred men-at-arms, while Saladin had three thousand. But now, through your sins, you have been brought so low that we take you in the fields just as if you were cattle.'[14]

Following the established trend of financing fortifications, Prince Edward of England commissioned a tower at Acre before leaving the Holy Land in 1272. This was probably the 'English Tower', which is labelled along a stretch of the town's outer walls near the northeastern salient on some early fourteenth-century maps of the city. A number of other improvements were made around this section of the city's defences between Louis IX's contributions in 1250 and the city's destruction in 1291. Ahead of the Accursed Tower, which anchored the apex of the inner line of walls, the round King's (or New) Tower stood at the corner of the outer line of walls. This was named after Henry II of Cyprus, who financed the reconstruction of the tower in the 1280s, improving the defences that had been built there by one of his predecessors in the mid-thirteenth century. Alice of Brittany, dowager countess of Blois, who arrived at Acre in 1287 and died the following year, financed another tower in this section of the town's defences. Nicholas of Hanapes, titular patriarch of Jerusalem, paid for another tower nearby, also in the 1280s. The attention devoted to this part of the city's defences was warranted: this was the same area where siege efforts had focused in 1191 and where Mamlūk forces would ultimately break into the city in 1291.

Muslim Power Structure

From the time of the First Crusade, the principal seats of power in western Syria were Damascus and Aleppo, while Cairo formed the third major Muslim power base in the region. Beyond these, a number of smaller administrative units were formed around the secondary towns and cities, such as Hama, Homs and Shayzar, which at times were able to exert their own authority and at others found themselves subject to the ruler of Damascus or his counterpart in Aleppo. Comparable, if quite different, from European feudal systems, was the Islamic *iqṭāʿ* system.

Whereas European fiefs were plots of land, the rights to which were typically granted in perpetuity and passed from one generation to the next so long as the reciprocal conditions of support were met, an *iqṭāʿ* was rather the right to collect taxes from a certain region. Although these sometimes carried administrative privileges, the land involved was not owned by the *muqṭaʿ* (he who held the *iqṭāʿ*). In the late eleventh century, Niẓām al-Mulk, a Persian scholar and Seljuk vizier under Alp Arslān and Malikshāh, provided the following advice in his treatise on governance:

> Officers who hold assignments [*iqṭāʿs*] must know that they have no authority over the peasants except to take from them – and that with courtesy – the due amount of revenue which has been assigned to them to collect; and when they have taken that, the peasants are to have security for their persons, property, wives and children, and their goods and farms are to be inviolable; the assignees [*muqṭaʿs*] are to have no further claim upon them.[15]

Although a feature of Muslim administrations across most of Egypt and Syria through the twelfth and thirteenth centuries, the nature of the *iqṭāʿ* system and the rights and responsibilities of the *muqṭaʿ* differed according to the political system, and ruling dynasty, of which they were a part. Whereas the Fāṭimid *iqṭāʿ* system appears to have been used to pay administrative officials, the Zankids expected *muqṭaʿs* to use their revenues to raise troops – Nūr al-Dīn was known to confiscate the *iqṭāʿ* of any *muqṭaʿ* who failed to meet his military obligations. When Saladin took power in Egypt, he preserved the existing structure of the Fāṭimid *iqṭāʿ* system, but reoriented it in order to bring it closer into line with the Zankid system of Syria. When the Mamlūks came to power, they developed the Ayyūbid system, which had evolved through the early thirteenth century, to better suit the slave-based nature of their political hierarchy.

Despite these differences, every *iqṭāʿ* was ultimately granted by the sultan and he retained the right to cancel or confiscate it at will. Accordingly, each *iqṭāʿ* would need to be confirmed, whether as a matter of routine or more elaborate ceremony, upon the accession of a new sultan. On the flip side, each *muqṭaʿ* was free to give up his *iqṭāʿ* at any time if he felt its revenues did not support the obligations expected of him.

The size of an *iqṭāʿ* could vary enormously. Some were essentially administrative regions, ruled by prominent figures from mighty seats of power; others were quite small and could even be shared. As Saladin came to rule Egypt and much of Syria, he placed his family members in critical positions, using the *iqṭāʿ* system to do so. He gave his father, Ayyūb, Alexandria and Damietta, the most important ports in Egypt; his brother, Tūrānshāh, was given significant districts in upper Egypt, from which he invaded Yemen; and Syria was similarly distributed among other family members and significant emirs, such as Ibn al-Muqaddam, who received Baalbek, and Saʿd al-Dīn Masʿūd, who received Safed. These grants became a part of the Ayyūbid power struggle that followed Saladin's death in 1193. For example, although al-ʿĀdil was recognized as ruler of Egypt in 1195, so too did he retain his *iqṭāʿs* in the Jazīra (Edessa, Ḥarrān and Mayyāfāriqīn). As the various parties manoeuvred for control of Syria, those who held *iqṭāʿs* in the area became influential, throwing their support behind the party who might best serve their interests or who would back their claim to their *iqṭāʿs*. Although mamlūks had been granted *iqṭāʿs* from the reign of Saladin, most of which were in Syria, such figures were typically not given significant positions until the reign of al-Ṣāliḥ Ayyūb, whose mamlūks would later murder his son and establish the Mamlūk dynasty.

While *muqṭaʿs* were relied upon to provide military support, it is easy to confuse these figures with a number of other administrative figures, as various titles tend to be translated in different ways. A *ṣāḥib* typically held his lands as a *muqṭaʿ* but ruled more independently. These figures could grant *iqṭāʿs* but were still required to provide the sultan with military support when summoned. It was in this capacity that Saladin's son, al-Ẓāhir Ghāzī of Aleppo, resisted his uncle, al-ʿĀdil, and al-Mughīth ʿUmar, *ṣāḥib* of Kerak, similarly refused to recognize the authority of the Mamlūks.

The *nāʾib* (provincial deputy) and *wālī* (governor), for example, were administrative positions. Although a significant town or castle was typically granted as an *iqṭāʿ*, a *wālī* was commonly entrusted with the citadel – Saladin gave Homs as an *iqṭāʿ* to his uncle, Shīrkūh, while governance of the citadel was given to a Kurdish emir, Badr al-Dīn Ibrāhīm al-Hakkārī. Saladin made Qarāqūsh, one of his most trusted emirs, *nāʾib* of Egypt, entrusting him with the region's administrative and political affairs. When Mamlūk influence spread across western Syria in the wake of the battle of ʿAyn Jālūt, the vacant seats of power left by Ayyūbid princes, most of whom had ruled as *ṣāḥibs*, were filled with *nāʾibs* and each was allocated an *iqṭāʿ* equal to the prestige of his position – the *nāʾib* of Kerak, for example, was assigned Hebron as an *iqṭāʿ*. As further conquests were made, a *nāʾib* was typically appointed to rule each district, although these lesser figures were not implicitly granted an *iqṭāʿ*.

Muslim Castles

Muslim strongholds were built and developed for many of the same reasons as those constructed by the Franks; however, Muslim authority was generally more centralized and regional seats of power were fewer. The Būrid rulers of Damascus, for

Al-ʿUmarī: the Mamlūk *iqṭāʿ*, 1337

The armies of the realm are partly resident at the Sultan's court and partly distributed around its provinces and throughout its lands. Some of them are nomads, such as the Arab tribesmen and the Turkomans. The regular troops are mixed in origin, being Turks, Circassians, *Rūmīs*,* Kurds and Turkomans. The majority are purchased mamlūks. They are ranked as follows. The greatest are those who hold an emirate of a hundred troopers together with a command of a thousand, from which category come the most important vicegerents. At times this figure may be increased for some by ten or twenty troopers. Next are the *ṭabl-khānah* emirs, the majority of whom have an emirate of forty, although there may be those for whom that figure is increased to seventy. The *ṭabl-khānah* rank is not held with fewer than forty.

Then follow the emirs of ten, consisting of those who hold an emirate of ten, and sometimes including individuals who have twenty troopers, but who are still only counted as emirs of ten. Next come the troopers of the *ḥalqa*, whose rights are issued from the Sultan, just as those of emirs are, while, on the other hand, the troops of emirs receive their rights from their emirs. For every forty of these *ḥalqa* troops there is an officer, one of their number, who has no authority over them except on active military service, when they muster with him and he is responsible for their dispositions.

In Egypt, the *iqṭāʿ* of some senior emirs of a hundred, close to the Sultan, may amount to 200,000 army dinars, sometimes more. For other emirs of this rank the figure progressively diminishes to around 80,000 dinars. The *ṭabl-khānah* emirates amount to 30,000 dinars with fluctuations above and below, with a minimum of 23,000 dinars. The emirs of ten have an upper limit of 7,000 dinars. Some *iqṭāʿs* of *ḥalqa* troopers reach 1,500 dinars, this amount and those that come near it being the *iqṭāʿs* of the senior members of the *ḥalqa*, the officers appointed over them. Then come lesser amounts down to 250 dinars. For the troops of emirs, the value of their *iqṭāʿ* is at the discretion of the emir.

Iqṭāʿs in Syria do not come near these figures, but are worth two-thirds of them, leaving aside what we have said about favoured senior emirs of a hundred, for this is unusual and without normal validity, and I am not aware of anything in Syria that comes anywhere near such a sum, except for what the Vicegerent of Damascus receives.

*This term, meaning 'Romans', usually refers to Byzantines; however, it may be used more generally to identify Anatolians, implying Armenians, in this instance.

(Adapted from al-ʿUmarī, *Masālik al-abṣār*, trans. Richards, pp. 20–1.)

example, relied on the support of the men they appointed to rule the secondary centres of Baalbek, Bosra, Ṣarkhad and, at times, Homs. Depending on the nature of the ruler's relationship with a secondary seat, it might be ruled by an appointed governor, as was Baalbek, or by a hereditary emir, as was Homs during much of this period. To the north, power was more fragmented, increasing the number of secondary seats, often corresponding with the larger urban communities and castles.

Although many of these secondary rulers enjoyed considerable autonomy in the early twelfth century, their independence declined steadily as power was consolidated by the Zankids and then Ayyūbids. Due to the urban focus of Muslim administrative structures, castles were comparatively rare.

Many Muslim castles, like those held by the Franks, had been built by the Byzantines; others were initially constructed by regional Muslim and Armenian powers. Castles such as Shayzar, Qalʿat Najm and Qalʿat Jaʿbar were among the region's most impressive and each rests on the remains of an earlier Roman or Byzantine settlement. These, as well as many town defences, were rebuilt or developed during the period of uncertainty from the late ninth century as various ʿAbbāsid, Byzantine, Fāṭimid and Turkish figures fought for control of the region. In the eleventh century, a number of smaller Arab rulers from Syria's tribal communities, who managed to carve out zones of influence for themselves, not unlike the Armenians in Cilicia, built castles to secure their rule – Shayzar was rebuilt by the Banū Munqidh while Qalʿat Jaʿbar was developed by the Banū Qushayr, and probably the Banū Numayr before them. Many castles and citadels were subsequently refortified in the second half of the twelfth century by Nūr al-Dīn, who used them as bases of power to secure his expanding realm. This work was apparently so significant at Qalʿat Najm that Ibn Jubayr, who spent a night there in 1184, described it as 'a new-built fortress'.[16] Few Muslim castles, aside from a selection constructed by the Assassins, completely post-date the arrival of the Franks. Three notable exceptions are ʿAjlūn, Qalʿat Ṣadr and Ṣubayba.

ʿAjlūn. (*Courtesy of APAAME*)

ʿAjlūn was built on the east side of the Jordan, about midway between the Sea of Galilee and the Dead Sea, possibly on the site of an earlier monastery. Commissioned by Saladin in 1184–85, construction was overseen by his nephew, ʿIzz al-Dīn Usāma. It is often suggested that the castle was constructed to check Hospitaller raids from Belvoir; however, its location, 16km from the Jordan and 36km southeast of Belvoir (as the crow flies), does not support this. A far more sensible position from which to mirror Belvoir would have been at least 25km to the north, due west of Adhriʿāt, from where it could observe Belvoir from the eastern side of the Jordan Valley. This would also have placed it in a position to dominate the main routes passing south of the Sea of Galilee to Bosra and the southern Ḥawrān, which had been raided by Raymond of Tripoli in December 1182. Instead, it was hoped that a castle at ʿAjlūn would provide greater influence in the affairs of the local Bedouins, who were known to ally with the Franks when it suited them, and to dominate the local iron industry. It also provided an administration hub in a region largely devoid of significant strongholds and with a history of Frankish influence dating back to the first decade of the twelfth century.

Qalʿat Ṣadr (al-Jundī) was built on a conical hill, about 200m above the surrounding landscape of western Sinai. The castle is around 58km east of Suez and about halfway between Bilbays and Aqaba. It was commissioned by Saladin in the 1170s and developed in 1182–83 under the supervision of his brother, al-ʿĀdil. The castle would have provided Saladin with greater control over the Sinai Peninsula and traffic

Jabal ʿAwf.

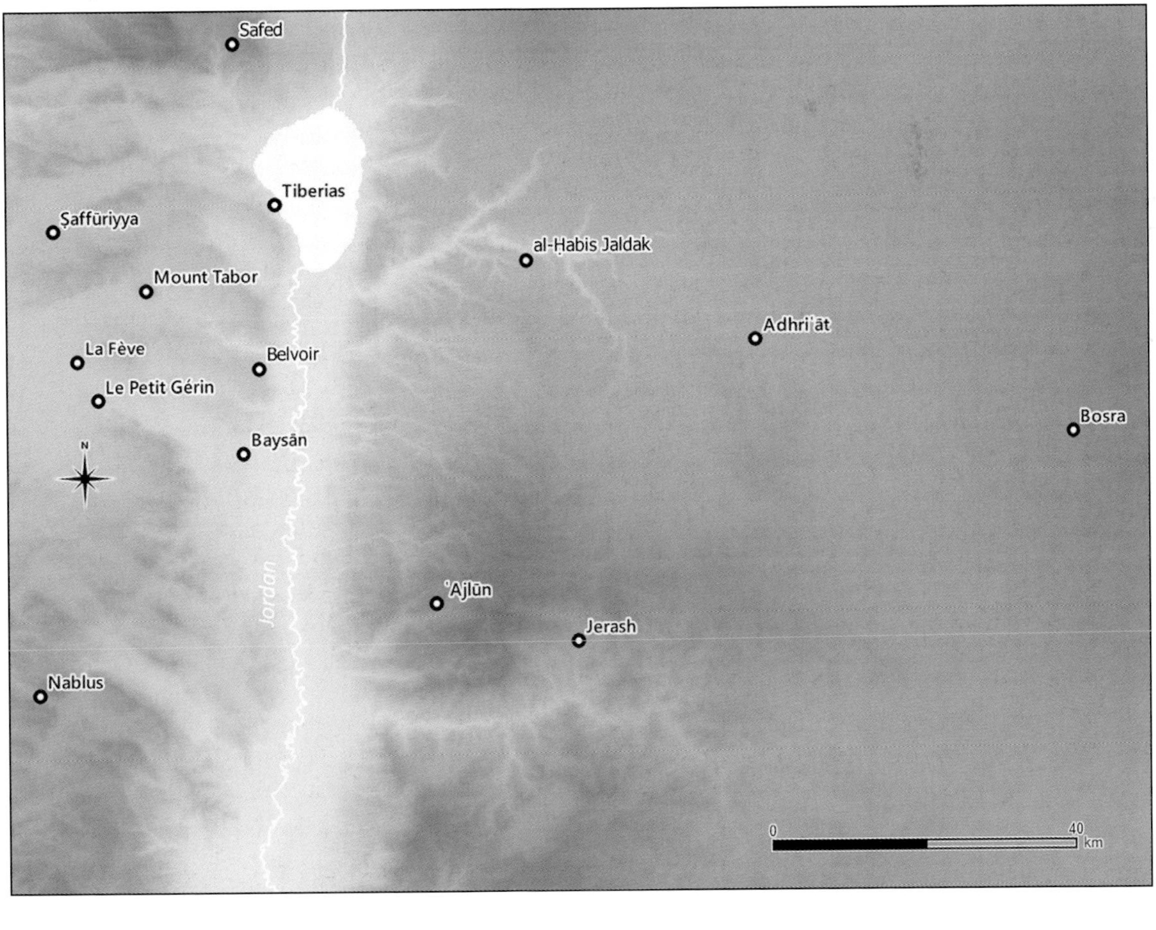

'Ajlūn and the region to the immediate south. (*Michael Fulton*)

moving across it, perhaps a comfort to Muslim pilgrims and merchants travelling between Egypt and Syria or Arabia. It was attacked by a party of Franks in 1178 and the timing of its refortification, five years later, suggests Saladin may have feared a new threat from the direction of Aqaba – Amalric's invasions of Egypt in the 1160s had instead proceeded along the Mediterranean coast. Although Saladin had captured Aqaba in December 1170, Reynald of Châtillon, the former prince-regent of Antioch, had become lord of Transjordan sometime around early 1177.

Already known for his aggression, it was quite possibly Reynald who had organized the attack on Qal'at Ṣadr in 1178. Reynald subsequently led an invasion into northern Arabia in late 1181 and orchestrated a daring and unprecedented maritime raid down the Red Sea around January 1183. Having carried boats overland from Kerak to Aqaba, his forces were able to threaten Mecca and Medina, the holiest cities of Islam. It would have been natural to fear that a raid into Egypt might be next. There are reports that in May 1183 a Muslim force heading for Dārūm intercepted a party of Franks, judged to be heading for Qal'at Ṣadr, on the road towards Aqaba. In September 1184, only months after more provisions had been sent to Qal'at Ṣadr, the inhabitants of Bilbays abandoned their homes and fled to Cairo after reports arrived that a party of Franks had reached Faqus, 40km to the northeast.

Ṣubayba was built from about 1227, during the uncertainty of Frederick II's visit to the Holy Land. Construction was undertaken by al-'Azīz 'Uthmān, a son of al-'Ādil, who ruled Bānyās for his brother al-Mu'aẓẓam 'Īsā of Damascus. Less than a decade earlier, al-Mu'aẓẓam 'Īsā had ordered the destruction of many castles west of the Jordan during the Fifth Crusade, but appears to have commissioned or approved of the construction of Ṣubayba before his death in 1227. The castle provided an

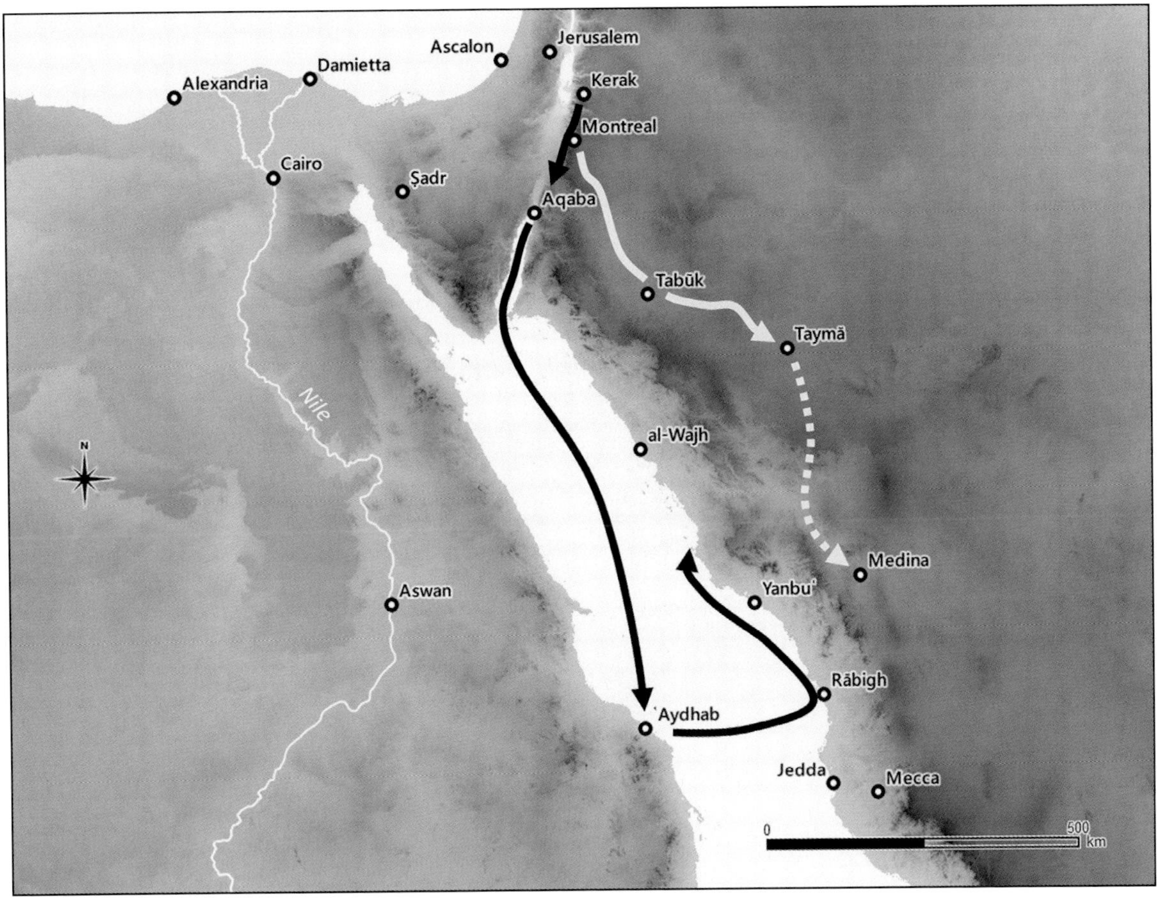

Reynald of Châtillon's Arabian campaigns, 1181, 1182–83.

advanced base for attacks into Palestine, should it fall back to the Franks, while also giving Bānyās, which it overlooked from the heights 2km to the east, a much stronger citadel. Regardless of the specific motivations for its construction, the castle was a significant stronghold on the main road between Damascus and northern Palestine.

To these might also be added Mount Tabor. Al-ʿĀdil ordered the iconic hill to be fortified in 1211 and a defensive perimeter, complete with towers, was built around the summit, enclosing the Christian monastic complex that had expanded there under the Franks during the twelfth century. The epigraphic evidence reveals that al-ʿĀdil's son, al-Muʿaẓẓam ʿĪsā, along with ʿIzz al-Dīn Aybak ibn ʿAbdullah and a few other emirs, helped oversee construction. Al-ʿĀdil's motivations to fortify Mount Tabor have been debated. Most interpretations hinge on a statement made by James of Vitry, who asserted that the stronghold was built to oppose Acre. Although possible, these fortification efforts may have been part of a more general effort to strengthen Ayyūbid authority over northern Palestine. The region had seen considerable action in the 1180s during Saladin's invasions of 1182 and 1183, and it was here that al-ʿĀdil had moved when elements of the Fourth Crusade arrived at Acre, preparing to counter a possible invasion. The garrison of Mount Tabor successfully repelled elements of the first wave of the Fifth Crusade when an attack was made in 1217, but al-Muʿaẓẓam ʿĪsā found himself doubting his ability to hold the newly built stronghold as the crusaders' focus shifted to Egypt. To prevent it from falling to the Franks,

Ṣubayba. (*Michael Fulton*)

he ordered it and many other castles slighted before the Fifth Crusade ultimately collapsed in Egypt.

Although these strongholds were significant, Muslim fortification efforts tended to focus more often on the citadels and town walls of the region's large urban centres. Such defences not only helped protect these centres of wealth and influence, but also acted as conspicuous instruments and symbols of authority.

Citadels and Symbolism

A by-product of any fortification was its symbolism – these were grand structures that typically inspired awe. For the Franks, their rural strongholds were statements of regional control, reminders to the local population of the ruling order and probably a reassuring sight for visiting European pilgrims. The relatively small strongholds first built by the Franks were eventually eclipsed by the great castles, now iconic symbols of the crusades, which were the result of considerable investment. Citadels presented a similar message.

Following the earthquakes of 1156–58 and 1170, Nūr al-Dīn commissioned the refortification of a number of Muslim strongholds across his growing realm. From the town walls of Damascus to castles on the Euphrates, these necessary repairs doubled as tangible statements of his authority. Al-ʿĀdil undertook a similar building programme in the early thirteenth century, adding to the defences of Jerusalem, the citadels of Cairo and Bosra, rebuilding the citadel of Damascus and fortifying the

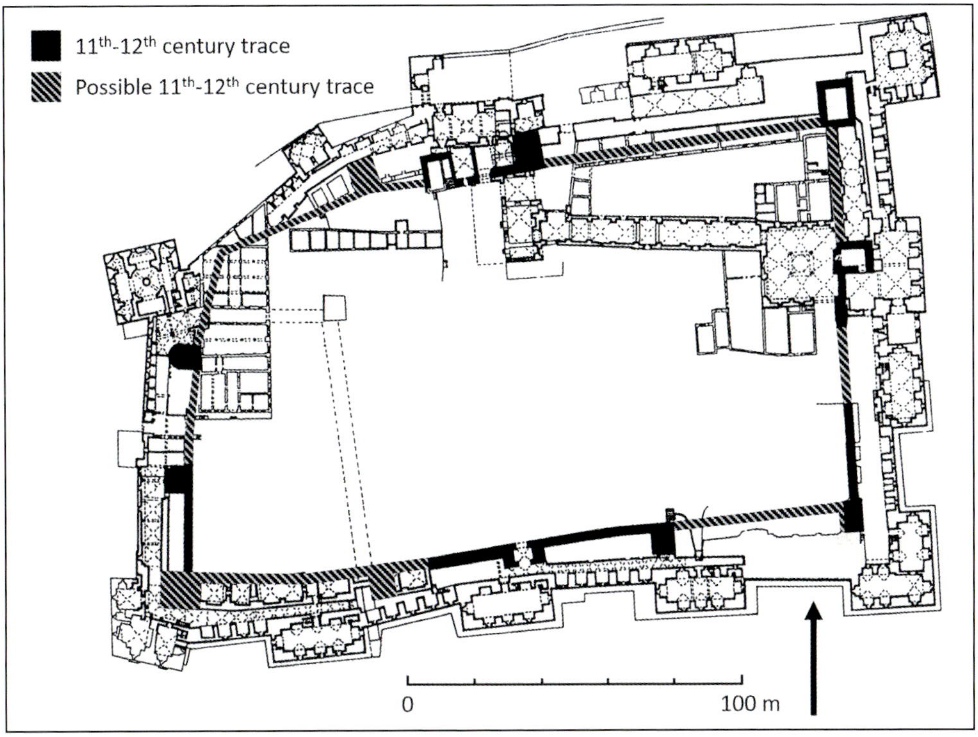

Damascus, citadel (after Hanisch and Berthier).

Aleppo, citadel gatehouse. *(monumentsofsyria.com)*

top of Mount Tabor. At each site, his consistent use of extremely large towers with a similar bossed masonry style – essentially his signature – left little doubt as to who built them and who was in control. At Damascus, he went so far as to enclose the citadel, originally built by the Seljuks, behind a new line of walls. While some Ayyūbids (including al-ʿĀdil) and later Mamlūks added bold inscriptions, prominently displaying who was responsible for constructing a certain tower or wall, al-ʿĀdil's signature building style could be understood by foreigners and the illiterate alike. For al-ʿĀdil, this was not only a way of strengthening important citadels and town defences but a statement of legitimacy – Saladin had intended his sons, not his brother, to succeed him.

Although citadels are perhaps associated more with Muslim fortification efforts, the Franks also built and developed urban strongholds. At some sites, such as Kerak, ʿAtlit and Arsūf, the castle was the focal point of the community's defences, although each also had town walls. Elsewhere, the Franks occupied and developed existing citadels, as at Jerusalem, Antioch and most other large urban centres.

Local Communities

Even the most isolated castle required some kind of a population centre to support it. The relationship between a stronghold and its supporting community was an important and mutually beneficial one, but the nature of this relationship could vary greatly. At Kerak, for example, the castle was built on a spur that extended south from the existing town, where a Byzantine monastery may once have stood, while the castle-turned-citadel at Shayzar dominated the town to the west. At Montreal, the local community was located to the southeast of the castle, roughly 300m away. Safed was built on a hill that was already occupied by a community of some size, while Beaufort, high above the Litani River, was neighboured by a small supporting settlement. Overlooking a tributary of the Orontes, Montferrand may have relied on the nearby sizeable town of Rafaniyya and Ṣubayba enjoyed the presence of nearby Bānyās. In the Syrian Coastal Mountains, some strongholds, such as Saone, Shughr-Bakās and Bourzey, had large outer enclosures, leaving it possible that a section of the local community may have had access to these areas, although the main population appears to have lived outside each castle.

These supporting communities carried out important day-to-day tasks: these were the farmers, tradespeople and small merchants who supplied the castle with goods and labour when required. In return, they benefited from the protection and consumer demand provided by the fighting men. Larger towns operated on the same principles, although the main commercial interests would have been in trade rather than agriculture.

Strongholds were also convenient places from which to extract and then store tax revenues. In both Frankish and Muslim lands, a variety of taxes were collected, but chief among them was a land tax, which was assessed based on the productivity of a region. Although at times levied on individual landholders, it seems villages were more often assessed as collectives. The rate varied by region, but was typically valued somewhere between a quarter and a half of a village's agricultural produce. In Muslim lands, the *jizya*, a head-tax, was levied on non-Muslims and the Franks adopted and imposed a similar tax on non-Christians, while tithes were similarly collected by both Frankish and Muslim rulers.

In areas where local populations were less amenable, strongholds provided secure bases from which revenue could be collected more forcefully. In 1125, Baldwin II commissioned the castle of Mount Glavianus, in the mountains inland from Beirut, because the Muslims of the area were reluctant to pay the local tax. Likewise, a motive behind the construction of ʿAjlūn was to impose greater control over the local Arabs, the Banū ʿAwf. Hand in hand with the ability to extract revenue was the need to protect it. Even small towers could safeguard from bandits the agricultural surplus gathered from a region, while larger strongholds might also provide a place of refuge during raids for the local population who worked the land – the same body of fighting men who were responsible for extracting wealth from the local community were typically its defenders.

Location

Whatever the motives behind the construction of a stronghold, a similarly unique set of considerations influenced where each was placed. First, there had to be something to defend. This could be as general as a desire to exercise and secure influence over a region, as may have been a significant motive behind the Hospitallers' construction of Belvoir. Alternatively, there may have been a specific commercial or administrative incentive. For example, the Templars' decision to commit considerable resources to fortify and defend Safed reflects the site's significance as a local administrative centre, while the citadel they constructed in Acre ensured they maintained an interest in the city and the wealth of its commercial activities. The foundation of Montreal seems to have combined both: in addition to extending general Frankish hegemony to the south, it came to dominate the caravan traffic along the desert road south of the Dead Sea and sugar production in the area. The fortified mills in the plain around Acre, including Doc and Ricordane, were foremost economic structures, while many towers built in and around the towns of Palestine would have been primarily seats of local administration.

With sufficient incentives to build a stronghold in a region and a nearby community to support its needs (either pre-existing or subsequently established), there remained the strategic considerations of whether the region could be effectively defended. Questions needed to be asked: How likely was it that the new stronghold might be besieged and how strong might the potential besieging force be? How quickly could relief forces be mustered and how likely was it that they would be able to break a siege? There was no point to building a castle if it could not be defended. This thought process can best be seen when figures opted not to garrison captured castles, although the costs of construction had already been paid. Accordingly, Baldwin II abandoned Jerash in 1121 and Nūr al-Dīn declined to hold Chastel Neuf in 1167. The slighting campaigns ordered by Saladin, al-Muʿaẓẓam ʿĪsā and Baybars similarly reflected fears that the strongholds they ordered destroyed might otherwise fall to large crusading armies and be used against them. By the same logic, the construction of Montreal, 120km from Hebron and more than 140km from Jerusalem (as the crow flies), speaks to the perceived lack of threats that it would face when it was initially founded in 1115.

Topography

Regardless of the region in which a stronghold was built, topography was always an important consideration. Castles were typically constructed on hills above the surrounding landscape, although the relative height of these hills varied considerably – most in the Syrian Coastal Mountains were sited on isolated spurs, while many in Palestine sat atop little more than a slight rise.

In Galilee, Castellum Regis was built in the town of Miʿilya on a hill that may have been the site of an earlier strongpoint. This was an ideal place for a mid-twelfth-century administrative centre, but when the Teutonic Knights sought to build a larger castle (Montfort) in the early thirteenth century they chose instead a spur along Wādī al-Qarn, almost 4km to the northwest, trading convenience for topographical strength. Further south, the Hospitallers used the topography between the Jezreel Valley (Marj Ibn ʿĀmir) and the Sea of Galilee as best they could, building Belvoir at the edge of the plateau overlooking the Jordan Valley to the east. Like many strongholds built along the coastal plain, Ibelin and Blanchegarde (Tell al-Ṣāfī) were built on small hills, the loftiest positions available.

Castellum Regis, in the centre of Miʿilya. (*Michael Fulton*)

Montfort. (*Michael Fulton*)

Ṣubayba, from the east. (*Michael Fulton*)

North of the kingdom of Jerusalem, strongholds such as 'Akkār, Crac, Saone, Bourzey, Shughr-Bakās, Margat and Baghrās (Gaston) were built on spurs or otherwise commanding positions. Even where the ground was flatter, as in the Homs–Tripoli corridor, east of the Syrian Coastal Mountains, and south of the Taurus Mountains, hills or old tells were often chosen, as was the case at Arima, Trapessac (Darbsāk), Turbessel and Ravandal. In the environs of Shayzar, the citadel of which was built on a natural spur that rises from the left bank of the Orontes, Abū Qubays (Bochebeis) was built on a hill at the edge of the plain, less than 22km to the west, and between them Tell Ibn Macher sat atop an ancient tell.

Along the coast, headlands and promontories could provide exceptionally strong positions. Seaward fortifications were harder to attack, as it was more difficult to undermine let alone approach them, allowing defences and defenders to be concentrated along landward sides. The city of Tyre, once an island connected to the mainland by a shallow tombolo, was synonymous with strength and impregnability since Alexander the Great's siege of 332 BC. According to William of Tyre, who was archdeacon of the city from 1167 and then archbishop from 1175, two lines of walls, complete with towers, ran along the city's seaward fronts and three lines of walls, studded with exceptionally large towers, guarded the narrow landward approach to

Oliver of Paderborn: construction of 'Atlit, 1218

Two towers of hewn and fitted stones, of such greatness that one stone is with difficulty drawn in a cart by two oxen, were built at the front of the castle. Both towers are 100 feet in length and 74 in width. Their thickness encloses two sheds to protect soldiers. Their height rising up much exceeds the height of the promontory. Between the two towers, a new and high wall was completed with ramparts; and by a wonderful artifice, armed horsemen can go up and down within. Likewise another wall slightly distant from the towers extends from one side of the sea to the other, having a spring of living water enclosed. The promontory is encircled on both sides by a high new wall, as far as the rocks. The castle contains an oratory with a palace and several houses. The primary advantage of this structure is that the assembly of Templars, having been led out of Acre, a sinful city and one filled with all uncleanness, will remain in the garrison of this castle up until the restoration of the walls of Jerusalem. The territory of this castle abounds in fisheries, salt mines, woods, pastures, fields, and grass; it charms its inhabitants with vines that have been or are to be planted, by gardens and orchards. Between Acre and Jerusalem there is no fortification which the Saracens hold, and therefore the unbelievers are harmed greatly by that new fortress; and with the fear of God pursuing them, they are forced to abandon these cultivated regions. This structure has a naturally good harbour which will be better when aided by artifice; it is 6 miles away from Mount Tabor. The construction of this castle is presumed to have been the cause of the destruction of the other, because in the long wide plain, which lies between the mountainous districts of this camp and of Mount Tabor, no one could safely plough or sow or reap because of fear of those who lived in it.

(Adapted from Oliver of Paderborn 6, trans. Gavigan, pp. 57–8.)

the east. A single gate controlled passage through the landward defences. A number of other cities, including Acre, Beirut and Tripoli, also made use of the sea for protection on multiple fronts.

Elsewhere, towns built against the sea might benefit from its protection on only one side. Some of these, however, had particularly strong citadels, which extended out into the Mediterranean, even if the town defences did not. The citadel of Caesarea and castles of ʿAtlit and Nephin were surrounded on three sides by the sea and water probably also filled the moat that separated each from the mainland to the east. When a new castle was built at Sidon in the early thirteenth century, it was sited on a shoal 120m offshore, connected to the town by only a narrow bridge. The stronghold of Maraclea (Maraqiyya) was similarly built on a shoal slightly further offshore.

Many Frankish strongholds built against the sea were among the last to fall to the Mamlūks: Bohemond VII agreed to destroy Maraclea in 1285; Tripoli fell in 1289; and Acre was famously taken in 1291. After the capture of Acre, Tyre, which had not fallen out of Frankish hands since it was taken in 1124, was abandoned, the townspeople of Sidon fled, and Beirut was seized in a ruse. During the following months, the last remaining Frankish strongholds along the coast – the Templar strongholds of ʿAtlit, the sea castle at Sidon and Tortosa – were all abandoned. The small fortified island of Ruad (Arwād), more than 2.5km off the coast of Tortosa, was the last remaining Frankish stronghold in Syria, its Templar garrison holding out until a Mamlūk marine force finally came against it in 1302.

Existing Structures and Building Materials

The availability of building materials was another significant factor that influenced where strongholds were constructed and what they looked like. Existing fortifications were typically occupied if available. This mitigated building costs and the incentives that had led to the initial construction of these structures often remained, while many continued to serve as symbols of regional authority. Some strongholds were left largely as they were found, merely repaired to ensure their defensibility. The majority, however, were developed or expanded over time.

Many of the Byzantine outposts built in western Syria were enlarged under Frankish rule, often through the construction of an outer bailey. Where outer defences already existed, as was likely the case at Saone, this is where further fortification efforts usually focused. In the coastal plain and other level regions, town defences were the most common fortifications at the end of the eleventh century. When town walls were strengthened, the line of the earlier walls was typically followed, allowing builders to incorporate new elements, such as additional towers or an outer wall, and rebuilding others on top of existing foundations.

Non-fortified structures might also be used as the core of a castle or citadel. The Roman theatres at Caesarea, Bosra and Sidon were all developed into significant strongholds. While that at Caesarea was fortified before the arrival of the Franks, the first work at Bosra appears to have taken place around the time of the First Crusade. Work continued later in the twelfth century under Muʿīn al-Dīn Unur, but it was under al-ʿĀdil and his Ayyūbid successors that Bosra's theatre-turned-citadel took its recognizable form, with final touches added by the Mamlūks. Although dilapidated, the plan of the original theatre at Sidon, which the Franks converted into a castle or citadel along the circuit of the town's walls, can still be discerned. At Baalbek, the Roman temple complex appears to have been made defensible to some degree before significant fortification efforts were undertaken in the twelfth century. It was further developed under the Ayyūbids and subsequently by the Mamlūks, converting the classical site into a formidable fortress. In the Syrian Desert to the east, the Temple of Bel was fortified and functioned as the citadel of Palmyra in the twelfth century, while a structure within the once-thriving Roman city of Jerash had been fortified by the time it was taken by Baldwin II in 1121. Like Kerak and 'Ajlūn, Dārūm, built on a slight rise at the eastern edge of the Sinai Desert, may have been built on top of an earlier Byzantine monastery.

The availability of stone and materials for mortar was a consideration whenever a new stronghold was built. At some sites, building materials were provided by existing structures. Scavenging pre-cut stone in particular saved both time and money. At Baysān, no effort was made to repair the expansive Byzantine walls; instead, a simple administrative tower was built among the ruins of the Hellenistic-Roman town. Likewise, Bethgibelin, Ibelin and Gaza were each built near or among the ruined remains of Byzantine settlements. From Kerak to Bānyās and sites further north, ancient column capitals are among the most conspicuous *spolia* integrated into

Bosra, theatre-citadel (after Yovitchitch).

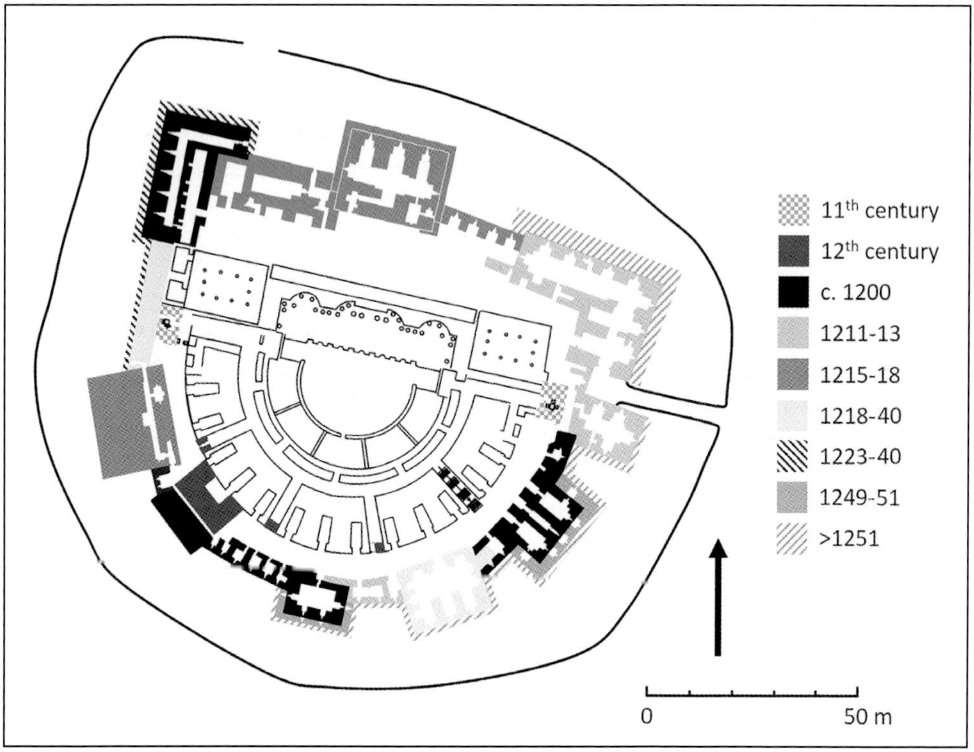

medieval walls. At sites without previous structures to incorporate or quarry, building materials had to be sourced elsewhere.

Unlike in contemporary Europe, suitable timber for wooden fortifications was rare in the Levant. This contributed to a different building tradition in the Near East, one far more reliant on stone. Particularly in the twelfth century, Frankish builders benefited from the involvement of local populations, who presumably provided most of the labour. In the north, friendly groups of Armenians and Syriac Christians may have been relied upon by the first generation of Frankish lords. In Palestine, where large building programmes were uncommon in the early twelfth century, the Franks would have become familiar with local practices over time, as they observed and worked with local communities of Christians and Muslims. European stylistic elements are most clear in the large castles and citadels of the thirteenth century, such as ʻAtlit, Montfort, Caesarea, Acre and Crac. These were financed by the military orders and visiting crusaders, and likely involved higher numbers of European masons, who often employed the gothic style to which they were accustomed.

Tactical Use

The availability of natural resources and the will to administer a region were not in themselves sufficient incentives to construct a stronghold; there also had to be a perceived threat. A tower was often sufficient to provide a base for a small policing force that had only to contend with bandits, while a great castle might be necessary to secure a claim over a broader frontier region. Although strongholds were fundamentally defensive structures, they were critical bases from which more offensive activities could also be launched.

Internal Security and Transportation Networks

Robbers had long plagued the roads of Palestine, preying on pilgrims and other bodies of poorly armed travellers. In 1065, a large group of German pilgrims, led by Bishop Gunther of Bamberg, was ambushed between Caesarea and Ramla. The pilgrims took refuge in a tower inside Kafr Salām until rescued by Fāṭimid forces from Ramla. The small towers built by the Franks, even when provided with an outer wall, were not meant to resist large invading armies, but rather smaller threats such as this. As more of these small strongholds were constructed, each serving the interests of its individual lord, Frankish rule expanded and banditry appears to have declined.

Similar to the administrative towers built by minor Frankish lords, the Templars constructed a number of towers along pilgrim routes and in areas particularly prone to banditry, reflecting the order's original mandate of protecting Christian pilgrims. Among these was the tower of Le Destroit. Built along the coastal road, 23km north of Caesarea and 11km south of where the Carmel juts out into the Mediterranean, the tower monitored a natural bottleneck between the heights to the east and the sea to the west. It was in this area that Baldwin I was wounded by bandits in 1103. In the words of Oliver of Paderborn, 'the tower was placed there originally because of bandits who threatened strangers ascending to Jerusalem along the narrow path, and descending from it; it was not far from the sea, and on account of the narrow path it was called Destroit'.[17]

The Templars constructed a string of similar towers along the pilgrim road from Jaffa to Jerusalem, and onwards to Jericho and the Jordan River. Elsewhere, the Templars showed a similar tendency to accumulate lands along critical roadways. Latrun (Toron des Chevaliers), Castellum Arnaldi (Yālu), Casel des Plains, La Fève (al-Fūla) and Le Petit Gérin (Zir'īn), as well as Safed and Jacob's Ford, all dominated a crossroads or important roadway and all came into Templar hands in the twelfth century.

Certain northern castles were similarly built in positions that overlooked critical mountain passes and restricted roadways. At the southern end of the Syrian Coastal Mountains, the Templar castle of Chastel Blanc (Ṣāfītā) was built on a secondary route between Homs and Tortosa, north of the main Homs–Tripoli corridor. Further north, Qadmūs, once a stronghold of the Nizārī Assassins, overlooks the road between Maṣyāf and the coastal town of Valenia (mod. Baniyas). Just south of Valenia, the Hospitaller stronghold of Margat sits 2km inland from the coastal road, leaving a satellite tower, the Tour du Garçon (Burj al-Ṣābi'), to police day-to-day traffic along the road. Al-Kahf, Malaicas (Manīqia), Vetula, Balāṭunūs and Saone were also positioned near or along routes across the Syrian Coastal Mountains, while Abū Qubays, Bourzey and Shughr-Bakās were near the eastern ends of roads through the mountains. Between the Iron Bridge and al-Athārib, Ḥārim and Artāḥ observed the western entrance to the Sarmada Pass, a chokepoint on the main route between Antioch and Aleppo, while Sarmada (Sarmadā) was fortified at the eastern end. North of Antioch, the eastern end of the Syrian Gates (Belen Pass), which connected Antioch and

Le Destroit. (*Michael Fulton*)

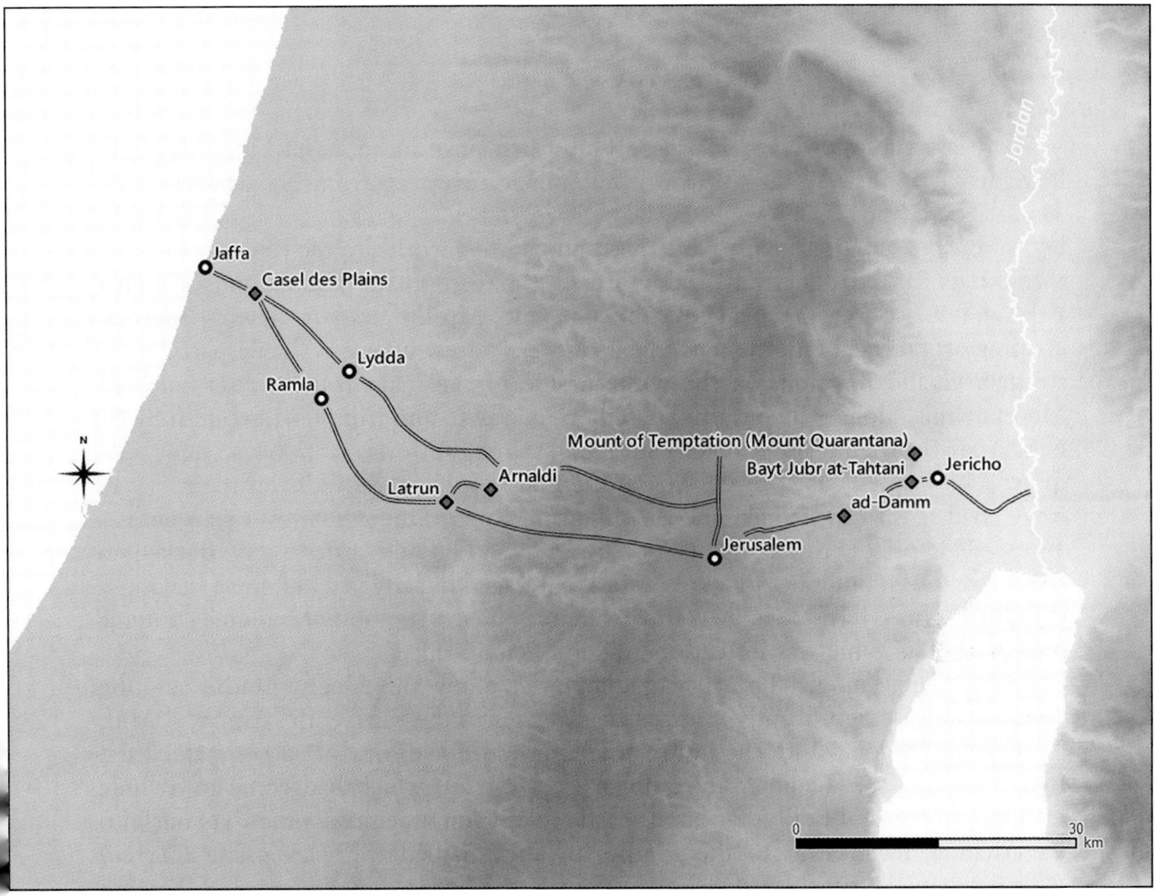

Templar towers on the road from Jaffa to Jericho

Alexandretta on either side of the Amanus Mountains, was observed from a distance by Baghrās and Trapessac, 6km to the south and 12km to the north respectively.

River crossings were also frequently defended. The fortified communities of Qal'at al-Rūm (Ranculat, Hṙomgla), al-Bīra, Qal'at Najm, Bālis, Qal'at Ja'bar, Raqqa and al-Raḥba each stood at a crossing over the upper Euphrates, while the Templar castle at Jacob's Ford was built at a natural crossing point over the upper Jordan. These strongholds and their garrisons could no more obstruct the crossing of a large army than could other castles block roads or mountain passes; however, in the absence of a hostile army, each could control traffic moving across the river. By occupying chokepoints, be they roads, passes or river crossings, the garrisons of these strongholds could intercept or block small raiding parties and launch reciprocal incursions into enemy territory.

Small strongholds might also be positioned to secure natural resources, most often water. Population centres usually developed naturally in areas where water was available, providing a number of incentives to fortify such sites. The springs at 'Ayn Jālūt and Ṣaffūriyya, rallying points for armies in the Jezreel Valley and lower Galilee, were both commanded by Frankish towers in the twelfth century. Neither of these strongholds would have been able to prevent a large army from accessing the springs, but their domination of these water sources was a practical and symbolic extension of Frankish influence over the surrounding area.

Many large cities owed their prosperity to their positions. Coastal cities like Acre, Tyre and Tripoli were major ports, while inland urban centres, such as Damascus, Homs, Hama and Aleppo were on the main inland road that ran north–south to the east of the coastal mountains. Each owed much of its wealth to the trade that moved through its gates. Collectively, these formed a transition area where goods from the East and West were exchanged, Christian and Muslim traders relying on their counterparts to facilitate the movement of their wares. Edessa was in a particularly strategic inland position, on the western side of the main route across northern Mesopotamia, along which traffic passed on its way to and from northwestern Syria, Cilicia and the Mediterranean. The advantages brought by its position also came with drawbacks: armies raised in the Jazīra often passed below its walls on their way to wage jihad against the Franks and the sultans of Rūm to the northwest regarded it as an appealing prize. From its acquisition by Baldwin I in 1098, Edessa was attacked no fewer than seven times before Zankī's forces besieged the city in 1144, finally taking it from the Franks. Jerusalem, by comparison, occupied a position of minimal strategic importance; its value was instead its religious significance.

The benefits enjoyed by urban communities along the Mediterranean saw the Templars invest significantly in three coastal sites in the thirteenth century – 'Atlit, Tortosa and Sidon. With the influx of labour and donations that accompanied the Fifth Crusade, the Templars tore down Le Destroit, which had come to include an outer bailey, and built a far larger castle ('Atlit) on a peninsula that juts out into the Mediterranean 1km to the southeast. They named this new castle *Castrum Perigrinorum* (Pilgrims' Castle). Further north, the order gained control of Tortosa in the 1150s. Here, they developed a tower into the heart of a much larger castle. The Templars did not acquire Sidon until 1260, from which point they developed the sea castle. The sea provided a measure of protection for each stronghold and direct access to Mediterranean trade networks. Although the Templars had no navy to speak of, they benefited from a close alliance with the Venetians through much of the thirteenth century. The only comparable coastal possession that the Hospitallers came to hold was Arsūf, which they acquired in 1261 and lost four years later.

Blockades

Some castles were built with the primary objective of isolating another stronghold. These were often employed like permanent siege forts, assisting with a distant blockade against a particular urban community. The fighters of the castle could both raid around the targeted town, depriving it of local resources and supplies, and intercept raiders who emerged from it, increasing security and promoting friendly economic activity to their rear. Castles were most often used in this way during the early twelfth century, when Frankish figures sought to apply pressure against cities they could not yet invest directly.

One of the first blockading castles was Mons Peregrinus (Sandjīl). Constructed by Raymond of St Gilles following the Crusade of 1101, the castle was built more than 2km from Tripoli, which Raymond hoped would eventually become his seat of power. Over time, a small town developed outside the castle, which was sacked in 1104 during a particularly successful sally led by Fakhr al-Mulk ibn 'Ammār, leader of the Tripolitans. Raymond was injured during the attack, possibly falling from a burning roof, and died the following year. Despite the success of this raid, the castle effectively isolated Tripoli from the interior of Syria, and the city enjoyed only sporadic Fāṭimid naval support. By 1108, the circumstances had become so desperate that Fakhr al-Mulk left to seek support from the caliph in Baghdad. In 1109, following the arrival of Raymond's son, Bertrand, the weakened city was attacked and taken by a combined Frankish force.

William of Tyre claims that Hugh of St Omer, who had succeeded Tancred as the second prince of Galilee, constructed Toron in order to apply additional pressure against Tyre. Hugh chose to build the castle at Tibnīn, about halfway along the main road between Tyre and Bānyās, the westernmost stretch of the route from Tyre to Damascus. The presence of the castle and its garrison would have been felt in Tyre as Frankish influence was more generally extended into the extreme north of Galilee. Hugh's choice of this position, conspicuously midway between the Jordan and the Mediterranean, may also have been a fairly open claim to this region, some distance from his seat of power at Tiberias. Something of a marcher lord in the European sense, Hugh died only months later fighting against a Damascene force in the summer of 1106. His successor, Gervais of Bazoches, was captured two years later and died a prisoner in Damascus. Galilee was then administered by royal officials until it passed to Joscelin of Courtenay in 1112.

When Baldwin I of Jerusalem led a force against Tyre in 1108, he ordered the construction of a small castle on Tell al-Maʿshūqa, probably 2–3km east of the city's walls. This castle is not mentioned thereafter, suggesting it was probably a siege fort rather than a permanent stronghold. The Franks spent a month outside the city before the Tyrians bought their withdrawal for 7,000 dinars, at which point the army moved on to attack Sidon. Baldwin led another unsuccessful siege of Tyre through the winter of 1111/12, before commissioning the castle of Scandelion in 1117. This stronghold was constructed about 14km to the south of Tyre and less than 4km inland from the Mediterranean, allowing the garrison to monitor traffic along the coastal road between Tyre and Acre. By the time Ibn Jubayr passed Scandelion in 1184, a walled town had developed around the castle. The construction of Toron and Scandelion contributed to the spread of Frankish influence, leading William of Tyre to observe that the Muslims of the city controlled little beyond its walls long before Tyre was taken in 1124.

With the fall of Tyre, Ascalon became the last Muslim foothold on the coast. It was reasonably cut off from the remainder of Palestine from the time of the First Crusade, during which the Franks occupied Jaffa (47km to the north), as well as Jerusalem and the settlements of the Judean hills to the east. Despite its relative isolation, Ascalon was regularly supplied by sea and raids from the city posed a significant threat to those living under Frankish rule in southern Palestine. In order to increase security between Jaffa and Jerusalem, a communal effort was undertaken to rebuild Castellum Arnaldi in the early 1130s. The small castle, which sat on a rise overlooking the road to Jerusalem as it leaves the coastal plain and enters the Judean hills, had been destroyed by a Fāṭimid force in 1106 or 1107. Once rebuilt, the stronghold and its garrison increased security in the area and made the journey from the coast to

Jerusalem much safer for pilgrims and merchants, as the Judean hills were a regular haunt for bandits. By 1179, the castle had passed to the Templars.

During the reign of Fulk, three castles were built to apply pressure against Ascalon and contain its raiders. Construction of Bethgibelin (Bayt Jibrīn) was undertaken by the patriarch and a group of nobles while Fulk was on campaign, and it was granted to the Hospitallers upon its completion in 1136. The site was a strategic one: well watered and at a crossroads on the edge of the Judean hills where roads reached out towards Hebron and Jerusalem to the east as well as Gaza and Ascalon to the west. Over the following years, a community developed around the castle. In 1141, Fulk, joined by the patriarch and notables of the kingdom, built a second castle at Ibelin. Whereas Bethgibelin was built to the east of Ascalon, on the main route to Hebron, Ibelin was built to the north, 7km from the coast, on the road to Jaffa where it forked and the eastern branch proceeded to Ramla and Lydda. The castle and land around it was granted to Balian the Elder, progenitor of what would become the influential Ibelin family, which took its name from the castle and accompanying lordship. The chosen site had an abundant supply of water and the small town nearby, which had been abandoned during the early twelfth century, saw new life following the establishment of the castle. The apparent success of the first two castles inspired the construction of a third. Blanchegarde was built the following spring (1142), and once more the leaders of the kingdom collectively set out to initiate the project. This time the king retained possession of the stronghold once it was complete. The castle was constructed between the other two and, like Bethgibelin, it was built at the edge of the Judean hills. Collectively, the three castles formed a line, Ibelin and Blanchegarde about 29km away from Ascalon and Bethgibelin a few kilometres further. By no means did they function as a wall that cut Ascalon off from the rest of Palestine; instead, they dominated the main roads running to and from the city, thus obstructing only the main arteries of travel.

There were considerable similarities between these castles. Scandelion, Arnaldi, Bethgibelin, Ibelin and Blanchegarde were all planned according to a quadrangular or quadriburgium design, typically with towers at each corner; all but Bethgibelin were positioned on a small hill; and a good water supply is noted near most. The quadrangular design was simple and efficient, providing a very functional internal space. It is often assumed that Fulk had a special affinity towards castles, as he is known to have commissioned some before travelling to the Levant and he hailed from Anjou, a region where some of the earliest known stone castles in Europe were built. However, eleventh- and early twelfth-century Angevin castles, often built around a central keep, were quite different from these quadrangular strongholds. Likewise, Fulk appears to have been present at the foundation of only two of the four castles built during his reign.

Raids from Ascalon were less frequent by the time Fulk came to the throne in 1131, owing to both issues in Egypt and the increasing strength of the Franks. Major raids aiming to take towns or create more general political instability had given way to minor profit-driven enterprises and small-scale efforts to ensure there remained a zone of Fāṭimid influence beyond the city's walls. Muslim raiders were forced to

William of Tyre: construction of Bethgibelin, Ibelin and Blanchegarde, *c.*1134–42

The Christians perceived that the bold incursions of the enemy showed no signs of ceasing; their forces were constantly renewed, and, like the hydra, they gained increased strength by the death of their citizens. Hence, after long deliberation, our people resolved to erect fortresses around [Ascalon]. These would serve as defences against this monster, which ever increased by the loss of its heads and, as often as it was destroyed, was reborn to our exceeding peril. Within these strongholds forces could be easily assembled which, from their very proximity, could more readily check the enemy's forays. Such fortresses would also serve as bases from which to make frequent attacks upon the city itself ...

This experiment convinced the nobles of the realm that by establishing the two strongholds, Bethgibelin and Ibelin, they had made decided progress in checking the audacious raids of the Ascalonites. In large measure through this course the insolence of the latter had been repressed, their attacks lessened, and their projects defeated. Accordingly, it was resolved to build another fortress the following spring. By increasing the number of fortified places, they could harass the people of Ascalon by more extensive attacks and more often cause them terror, attended by sudden danger as of siege ...

Accordingly, when winter was over and spring approached, the king and his nobles, together with the patriarch and the prelates of the church, well satisfied with the idea, assembled as with one accord at that place. Workmen were called, the people were furnished all necessary materials, and a stronghold of hewn stone, resting on solid foundations, was built. It was adorned with four towers of suitable height. From the top of this there was an unobstructed view as far as the enemy's city, and it proved to be a most troublesome obstacle and a veritable source of danger to the Ascalonites when they wished to go forth to ravage the country. It was called in the vernacular Blanchegarde ...

The result was that those who dwelt in the surrounding country began to place great reliance on this castle as well as on the other strongholds, and a great many suburban places grew up around it. Numerous families established themselves there, and tillers of the fields as well. The whole district became much more secure, because the locality was occupied and a more abundant supply of food for the surrounding country was made possible.

(Adapted from William of Tyre 14.22, 15.25, trans. Babcock and Krey, 2:81, 131–2.)

target the settlements closer to the blockading Frankish castles rather than the larger wealthier communities beyond, as they risked being surprised by the garrisons of these strongholds on their return, laden with booty. Usāma ibn Munqidh took part in these raids in the early 1150s, attacking the settlements around both Bethgibelin and Ibelin during the four months that he spent at Ascalon. He found himself there as part of a Fāṭimid delegation, which had recently solicited Nūr al-Dīn's help to disrupt Frankish efforts to fortify Gaza. After Usāma returned to Egypt, his brother was killed in a raid against this newest Frankish castle.

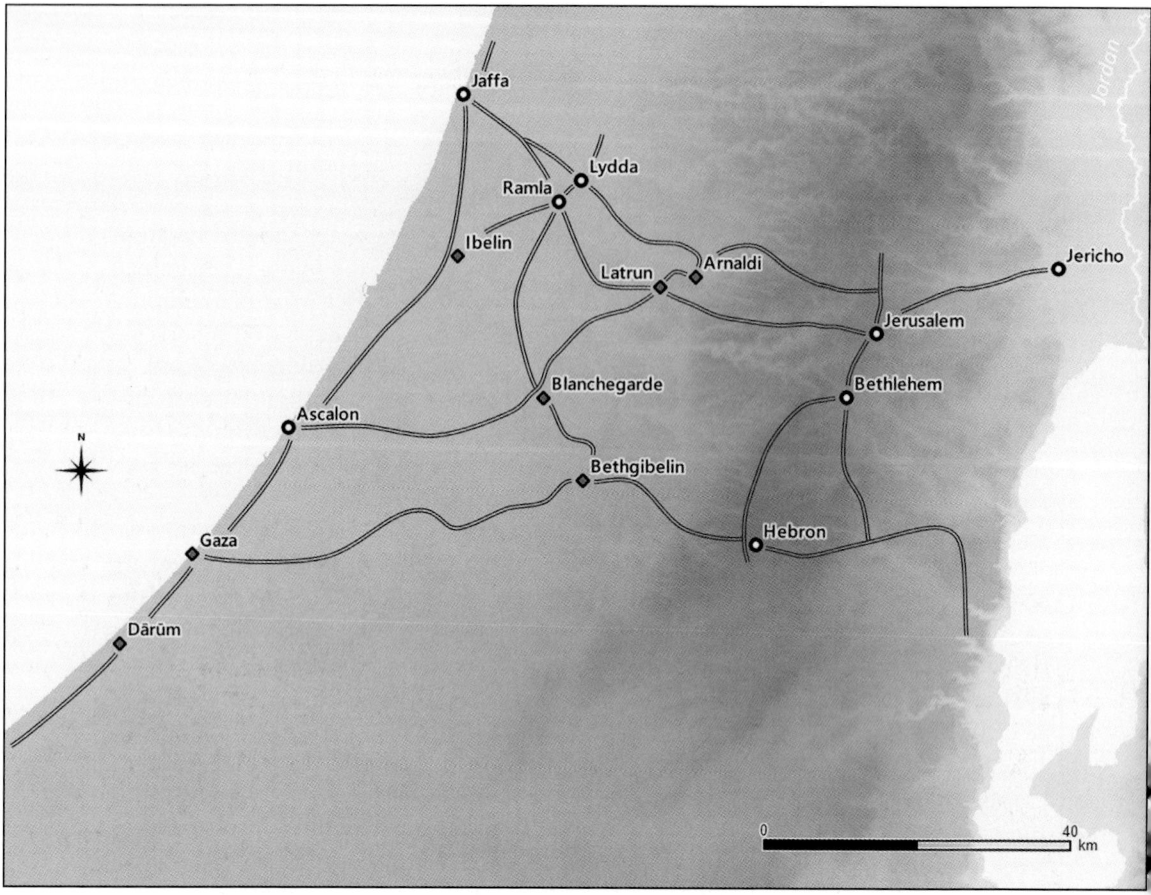

Castles around Ascalon.

Work at Gaza, 19km southwest of Ascalon, had begun in 1149 under the supervision of Baldwin III, the patriarch and a group of nobles. Rather than rebuild the abandoned town's old and derelict walls, a castle was built. Nothing remains of the Frankish stronghold, but it was probably designed with a quadrangular plan, similar to the others built against Ascalon. When complete, it was given to the Templars, who used it as a base to launch more aggressive raids against the Fāṭimid city and it in turn was attacked soon after its completion and again in 1152.

The fall of Ascalon in 1153 meant that Bethgibelin, Ibelin and Blanchegarde were no longer any more exposed to attack than most other settlements in southern Palestine. This added security allowed the communities around these castles to grow and, by 1160, thirty-two families lived in the settlement outside Bethgibelin, sufficient to encourage the construction of a parish church. South of Ascalon, Gaza also flourished and, by 1170, a town wall was built to surround the community that had developed next to the castle.

Sometime in the 1160s, Amalric commissioned another quadrangular castle at Dārūm, about 14km southwest of Gaza and less than 2km inland from the coast. It is unclear whether the primary motive behind the castle's construction was to facilitate Frankish actions in Egypt, to obstruct a potential Zankid attack from Egypt, or simply to push the frontier of Frankish control further south. Regardless, a prosperous town quickly grew up around the castle. Perhaps funded by revenues that were collected from traffic passing along the coast between Palestine and Egypt, town defences had been added by 1170, and these may have been strengthened by 1191, when Dārūm was besieged by Richard I during the Third Crusade.

Frontiers

The construction of a stronghold was a way of claiming authority over a region – it was a means through which rival challenges were resisted. While Muslim leaders reigned from their citadels, enforcing their rule through their sizeable armies, the Franks expanded their power and influence through the acquisition and construction of castles. Although common to all Frankish lands, this can be seen quite clearly in the southernmost and northernmost lordships of the kingdom of Jerusalem, and the regions that came under the military orders.

The lordship of Transjordan occupied the southernmost part of the kingdom. It extended from the Gulf of Aqaba up the east side of Wādī ʿAraba as far north as the Nahr al-Zarqāʾ (the Blue River), south of ʿAjlūn and Jerash, its frontiers extending into the deserts to the east and west. Montreal, commissioned by Baldwin I in 1115, was the first castle built in the region. It was originally retained by the monarchy, but appears to have become the seat of a large lordship during the reign of Baldwin II. From about 1142, the castle of Kerak was constructed under Pagan the Butler. Located 74km to the north of Montreal, Kerak became the new practical seat of power, bringing the influence of the lordship further north. While this might indicate a desire to be closer to the court at Jerusalem, it may also speak to the potential wealth and opportunity to be found east of the Dead Sea, rather than further south. With the

Kerak. (*Courtesy of APAAME*)

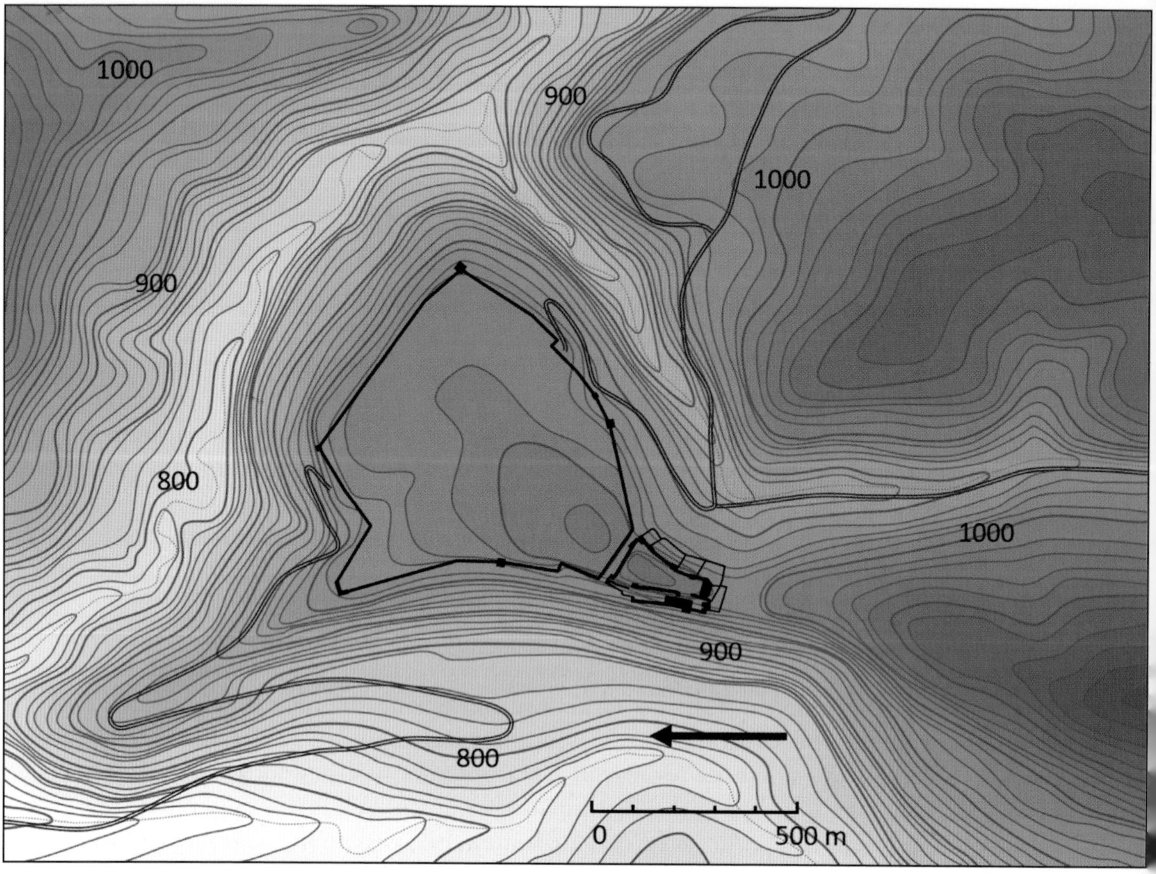

Kerak (with topography).

onset of the contest for Egypt in the 1160s, the importance of the lordship, and its dominance of the desert road between Damascus and Cairo, increased.

The lordship of Transjordan appears to have been enlarged when it passed to Philip of Milly in 1161. Philip was a proven and loyal knight who traded his rather modest lands around Nablus for the right to inherit the wealthy lordship. When Philip joined the Templars a few years later, the lordship passed to the successive husbands of his daughter, Stephanie. Reynald of Châtillon, the former prince-regent of Antioch and Stephanie's third husband from 1176, embraced his role as a marcher lord, dominating traffic along the desert road, claiming lordship over the Sinai Peninsula and threatening Arabia to the south. Kerak and Montreal anchored Frankish influence in the region and their strength – the result of successive refortification efforts over the years – was sufficient to resist multiple sieges launched by Saladin through the 1170s and 1180s. Besieged from 1187, both castles held out for more than a year and a half before they finally fell from Frankish hands.

To the north, the principality of Galilee was probably the kingdom's earliest and most prestigious lordship. It was created by Tancred and recognized by Godfrey in the immediate aftermath of the First Crusade. With its seat of power at Tiberias, the princes (or lords) of Galilee held the lands through which most invasions from Damascus passed as they entered the kingdom. The lords' authority reached across the Jordan to include areas east of the Sea of Galilee, where the Franks established a presence for periods during the twelfth century. When Tancred went north to assume the regency of Antioch, following Bohemond's capture in 1100, the principality was bestowed on Hugh of St Omer, who commissioned Toron and possibly also Chastel Neuf. When Hugh died without an heir in 1106, the principality passed to the monarchy. Baldwin I seems to have divided it around this point, detaching the northern part to create a distinct lordship centred on Toron. In so doing, Baldwin not only placed a second strong figure in the region, but ensured that the lordship of Galilee would not turn into a fifth independent Frankish principality – it was clearly a lordship of the kingdom but its lords continued to style themselves as 'princes'.

The capture of Sidon in 1110 led to the creation of another significant lordship, which was given to Eustace Garnier. During the reign of Fulk, Beaufort was added to this lordship, extending the reach, and interests, of the lords of Sidon inland and providing them with a strongpoint from which traffic moving between the Hula and Biqāʿ Valleys could be observed. As was done elsewhere, territory and strongholds were distributed to a number of strong figures, preventing any one from becoming too powerful but ensuring each was able to hold and defend his lands.

Despite the original ambitions of Hugh of St Omer, when Tyre was captured in 1124, it was not added to the lordship of Toron; the wealthy port was instead retained by the monarchy. In 1140, when Bānyās returned to Frankish hands, Fulk granted it not to the Bures family, which had inherited the principality of Galilee, but rather to Renier Brus, who appears to have held it of the lord of Beirut. When Renier died around the time of the Second Crusade, Bānyās passed to Humphrey II of Toron, who had married Renier's daughter. This seems to have been the point at which Humphrey also gained Chastel Neuf, which overlooks the north end of the Hula Valley from the west. It is possible that the castle had become, or remained, a part of the lordship of Toron before this point; however, it seems more likely that it came into the hands of Renier Brus, perhaps when he was granted Bānyās, and passed to Humphrey when he died.

The kingdom's northern lords ruled fairly large regions but probably also depended on wealth gathered from their Muslim neighbours to the east, either through tribute or raiding. Nūr al-Dīn's presence in the area and eventual acquisition of Damascus would have frustrated this revenue stream, while the greater threat posed by his army drove up the costs of maintaining the lordships' castles. With the lords unable to finance the defence of these strongholds, many were progressively given to the military orders, which came to replace the secular baronage as the primary guardians of this frontier of the kingdom. The Templars acquired Safed and stood to gain the castle at Jacob's Ford upon its completion, while the Hospitallers assumed shared ownership of Bānyās and constructed Belvoir to the south. Chastel Neuf and Beaufort remained in secular hands until they were lost following the battle of Hattin, but both would eventually be granted to military orders in the thirteenth century.

In the principality of Antioch, it seems a system of marcher lordships had been established by about 1130, each with its seat of power at a notable stronghold. The same probably took place on a smaller scale in the county of Tripoli and to an even looser degree in the county of Edessa, where Frankish rule was never as centralized nor as 'Frankish' as in the principalities to the south. These 'marcher' lords were capable of handling small threats, but their resources were insufficient to contend with the growing power of the Zankids on their own – the same forces that led to the collapse of the county of Edessa contributed to the rapid spread of the military orders' role and influence.

The princes of Antioch and Tripoli more actively sought the assistance of the military orders, by granting them lands and castles, than did the kings of Jerusalem. From 1135, Zankī began taking control of the Syrian plateau around Aleppo, up to the Coastal Mountains, and extending his authority southward until he took Baalbek in 1139. A significant part of the county of Tripoli was taken in 1137, leading Raymond II to donate considerable lands, most of which were now held by Zankī, to the Hospitallers in 1142, promising his dispossessed barons cash compensation. The donation included Rafaniyya, Montferrand and the originally Kurdish-built castle of Ḥiṣn al-Akrād, which the order would rebuild as Crac des Chevaliers. The donation, Raymond hoped, would essentially outsource the defence of the county's eastern frontier, while the relative autonomy he gave them, explicitly laid out in their grant, reveals his desperation. The Hospitallers proved to be ideal marcher lords: their resources allowed them to actively raid their Muslim neighbours until the region fell from their hands in 1271, while peace agreements concluded by the counts of Tripoli did not apply to them – the counts could enjoy peace while watching the Hospitallers continue to weaken their Muslim rivals.

In 1152, Nūr al-Dīn led an army through the Homs–Tripoli gap all the way to the coast, where he took Tortosa. Although the town was quickly reacquired, the estimated costs of refortifying it led Raymond II to offer the town to the bishop of Tortosa, who promptly passed it on to the Templars. Raymond's approval of this grant may have been part of a process of balancing the initial favour shown towards the Hospitallers. In addition to Tortosa, the Templars came to hold Chastel Blanc and Arima, while the Hospitallers, who also held Chastel Rouge (Yaḥmūr), Coliath (al-Qulayʿāt) and ʿAkkār, bought Margat from the Mazoir family in the months leading up to the battle of Hattin.

A similar trend is evident in the northern regions of the principality of Antioch. North of the Antioch Basin, the Templars acquired the castles of Baghrās and Trapessac, on the east side of the Belen Pass, and La Roche de Roussel (Chilvan Kale), deeper in the Amanus Mountains overlooking the secondary Hajar Shuglan Pass to the north. These strongholds gave the Templars conspicuous influence over the routes between Antioch and Cilicia. Further north, Baldwin of Marash appears to have solicited the support of the Hospitallers in the early 1140s, granting them a certain place provided they fortify it within a year; unfortunately, this place has not yet been identified.

Like the early blockading strongholds, frontier castles played an important role in both launching raids and intercepting hostile raiders. Strongholds that were captured, and could be held, deep in an opponent's territory were particularly useful in this capacity, as played out in the early twelfth century between Aleppo and Antioch. Following the battle of Hattin, certain captured Frankish castles became important Muslim frontier bases. Toron, for example, once more opposed a hostile Tyre: in July 1189, the garrison that Saladin had established there two years earlier attacked a group of Franks who had left Tyre to gather provisions. Almost eighty years later, in

October 1266, the garrison of Safed, which Baybars had installed after capturing the castle only a few months earlier, intercepted and defeated a small Frankish force that had set out on a retaliatory raid under Hugh of Lusignan, the future king of both Cyprus and Jerusalem.

Expansion

As a means of securing territory, fortifications were a critical part of conquest. When a ruler sought to expand his realm, he had to either capture or construct a stronghold, or field an army capable of removing any such obstacles that might be built by an opponent to challenge his authority. It is in the area around Palestine, a region with comparatively few significant strongholds, but detailed sources, that the use of castles as tools of expansion may be seen most clearly.

Almost immediately after the First Crusade's capture of Jerusalem, certain Franks set their sights on the lands east of the Jordan. Godfrey had joined Tancred at Tiberias and together they raided this region in 1100, exacting a tribute before withdrawing back across the river. The Golan Heights and the westernmost part of the Ḥawrān, known as the Sawād, were a particularly attractive region. Although the area has few trees, its volcanic soil is quite fertile, fed by numerous springs. The area was regularly raided by Frankish forces through the twelfth century, but gaining a permanent presence proved difficult.

In an early effort to annex the Golan, the Franks attempted to build a castle, which Ibn al-Qalānisī called ʿAlʿāl, east of the Sea of Galilee in 1105. Construction, however, was interrupted by Ṭughtakīn of Damascus, who arrived and defeated the Frankish force overseeing the castle's construction. This may have been the episode in which Hugh of St Omer, prince of Galilee, was killed. The engagement, which probably took place in 1106, may appear twice in Ibn al-Qalānisī's account. If so, a combination of luck and planning assisted the Muslims, as Baldwin I, who was then at Tiberias, was forced to confront a party of Tyrian raiders, who had invaded from the west and sacked the town outside the castle of Toron. Toron was one of Hugh's principal strongholds, but as the new castle beyond the Jordan would also become a part of his lordship, Baldwin left to address the raid, leaving Hugh to oversee activities east of the Jordan. With the Frankish army divided, Ṭughtakīn, who had assembled his army in the Sawād, was able to defeat Hugh and destroy the incomplete castle.

Baldwin I made another attempt to establish a fortified outpost east of the Jordan a few years later, developing a cave in a sheer section of wall along the canyon carved by the Yarmūk River. Known as al-Ḥabis Jaldak (Cava de Suet), the Frankish outpost was taken by Ṭughtakīn near the end of 1111 or start of 1112, while the army of Jerusalem was busy besieging Tyre. The stronghold was taken by the sword and the entire garrison executed. Around the time Joscelin of Courtenay became prince of Galilee, Ibn al-Qalānisī suggests that Baldwin I proposed Joscelin trade certain lands to Ṭughtakīn in return for al-Ḥabis and half of the Sawād – the implication being that these were the lands to be administered from the castle. Ṭughtakīn, however, declined. The cave castle returned to Frankish hands around the time of Baldwin I's death in 1118 and Frankish influence once more stretched into the Ḥawrān. A few years later, Baldwin II briefly considered occupying and garrisoning Jerash, 48km to the south of al-Ḥabis Jaldak. He had taken a stronghold there as part of a retaliatory raid in 1121, but decided it would be too isolated and expensive to defend.

Around 1139, Thierry of Flanders, who was then visiting the Holy Land, took part in an expedition that captured a cave stronghold east of the Jordan. It is unclear if this was al-Ḥabis Jaldak, but the stronghold had returned to Frankish hands by 1158, when Thierry, once more in the Levant, accompanied Baldwin III to relieve the castle. The Franks successfully interrupted Nūr al-Dīn's siege, forcing him to withdraw, although Shīrkūh brought the cave castle back under Muslim control in 1165. It was back in Frankish hands by 1182, when a contingent of Saladin's army captured the stronghold following a broader invasion of northern Palestine. According to William of Tyre, the castle fell after a siege of five days; either its defenders capitulated, after being bribed, or it was taken by force once Muslim sappers mined into the first level from the side. Later the same year, the Franks retook the cave castle on their return from a raid towards Damascus, taking advantage of Saladin's absence in the Jazīra. The Franks mined down towards the cavern from the top until, after about three weeks, the garrison sued for peace and were granted free passage to Bosra without their arms.

One of the more famous, if least impressive, castles built by the Franks was that at Jacob's Ford. In 1178, Baldwin IV commissioned the castle, alternatively known as Chastellet or Qaṣr al-ʿAtra, at the southern crossing over the northern stretch of the Jordan, between Bānyās and the Sea of Galilee. It was probably hoped that this would be a base from which the Templars could exert influence east of the Jordan and raid the environs of Damascus, 84km to the northeast. When Baldwin refused a large sum, perhaps 100,000 dinars, to cease construction, Saladin attacked the still-incomplete castle in August 1179, taking it before the relief force mustering at Tiberias was ready.

Later events have coloured many interpretations of this stronghold. There is little evidence that Jacob's Ford was originally planned as a much larger concentric castle.

Jacob's Ford, northeastern corner of the castle and the river to the right. (*Michael Fulton*)

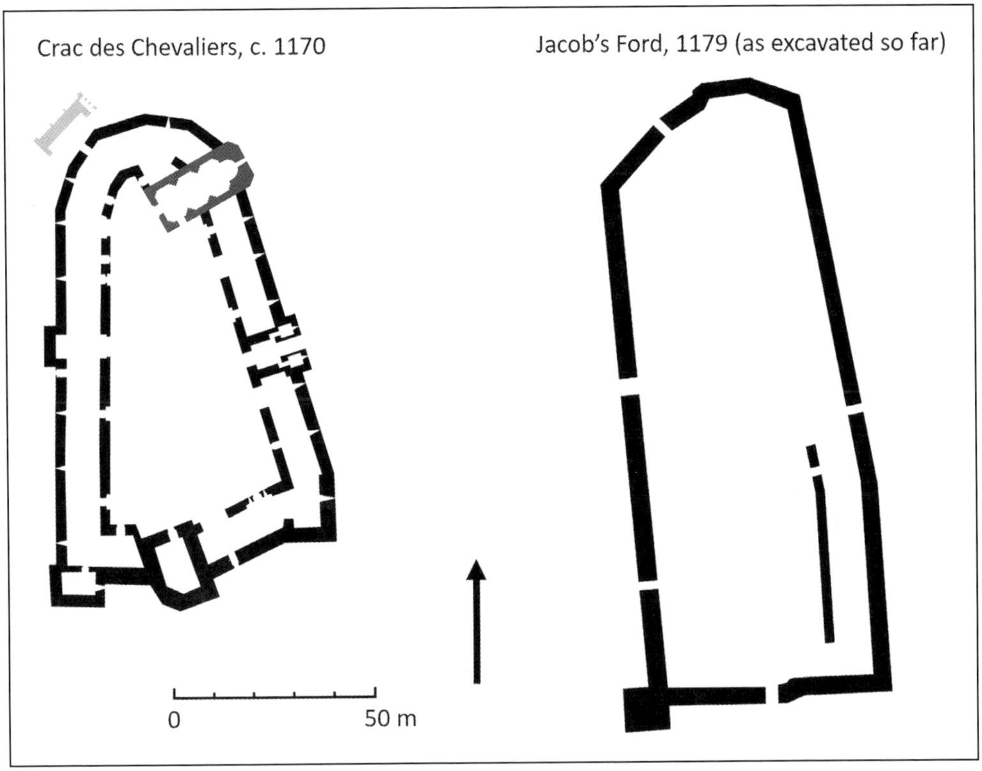

Crac des Chevaliers and Jacob's Ford in the twelfth century.

Instead, its design was fairly typical of its time: an elongated enclosure, following the shape of the hill, with a single tower. It is precisely because certain other castles that shared a similar plan in the late twelfth century, notably Crac, became much grander structures that there seems to be a desire for Jacob's Ford to have been something greater than it was. Unlike Crac or Belvoir, Jacob's Ford did not occupy a particularly strong position topographically: it sat on a small hill overlooked by the surrounding landscape on all sides. Despite certain suggestions to the contrary, the destruction of the castle was not the opening of a floodgate that precipitated the fall of the kingdom of Jerusalem. Aside from a raid a few months later, Saladin's forces opted to cross the Jordan to the south of the Sea of Galilee during their subsequent incursions into northern Palestine – although Jacob's Ford was unobstructed, Saladin evidently had little desire, or need, to use the crossing.

Built from about 1168, Belvoir had by far the most complex and developed plan of any single-phase castle built in the kingdom during the twelfth century. Despite the castle's strength, its garrison could do little as Saladin's forces repeatedly invaded the kingdom not far from its walls through the 1180s. Its presence, however, prevented Saladin from claiming and attempting to rule the surrounding region. Those in the castle were left to watch as Saladin's forces passed by once more in 1187, ahead of the battle of Hattin; however, they would exploit Saladin's decision to leave the castle to his rear following the battle. Although subject to a loose blockade, the garrison launched a raid in early January 1188, seizing two caravans, one of which contained arms and provisions from the captured Templar stronghold of La Fève.

Staging Points

Owing to the protection they provided and their geographical positioning, strongholds were often used as staging points for campaigns. The largest armies usually collected outside cities, including Cairo, Damascus and Acre, where there were markets large enough to support them. Moving out, they might pause at a secondary stronghold to wait for further reinforcements or to determine what the enemy was doing. When invading Galilee or the Jezreel Valley, Damascene forces often paused at Bānyās, the only significant town between Damascus and northern Palestine. This is where Ṭughtakīn based his efforts to disrupt the Frankish sieges of Tyre in 1111–12 and 1124, and Saladin similarly used Bānyās as his staging point in 1179 when moving against Jacob's Ford. During Baybars' campaign against Beaufort in 1268, he had Jamāl al-Dīn al-Najībī, his governor of Syria (*nā'ib al-Shām*), take the Damascene element of the Mamlūk army to Bānyās, from where it then proceeded to Beaufort.

When countering invasions into northern Palestine, the army of Jerusalem typically positioned itself at Ṣaffūriyya, where a tower dominated the community and nearby springs. It was the availability of water, the site's central location and the road networks leading away from the settlement, rather than the security provided by the tower, that made this an attractive position. When Ayyūbid forces assembled in the region in the thirteenth century, they preferred Nazareth, 6km to the south, which had more to offer their larger armies. When countering Fāṭimid invasions into southern Palestine in the early twelfth century, the Franks often assembled at Ramla, which, like Ṣaffūriyya, was defended by a tower, but was more importantly in a central position at a significant crossroads. Fāṭimid incursions from Egypt were naturally launched from Ascalon. More than most other sites, the defences of Ascalon were strategically important, given the stronghold's isolation and distance from support. While large armies often arrived after marching overland, smaller raids could be conducted by forces that arrived by sea. The defensibility of the site ensured it remained an effective Fāṭimid beachhead until 1153. Later in the thirteenth century, stronger Ayyūbid and Mamlūk forces moving into Palestine from Egypt preferred to pause at Gaza, which, like Nazareth, had no significant defences in the thirteenth century, but the larger community could better cater to these sizeable armies.

In 1137–38, the Byzantine emperor John Comnenus used Antioch as a staging point for his campaigns in Syria. His pretext for demanding free entrance into the city was that it was necessary to store his siege engines there over the winter. Intending to besiege Aleppo the following year, he claimed it was too far to store them in one of the towns of Cilicia. The emperor was effectively using the city's value as a staging point to reinforce his claim to suzerainty over it and the remainder of the Frankish principality.

Generating Wealth: Raids, Tribute, *Condominia* and Taxes

There were a number of ways in which strongholds could contribute to a lord's income. In addition to supporting his efforts to collect a share of the produce from the surrounding region, they might assist with the launching of raids and the exaction of tributes, taxes and tolls. The wealth accrued in these ways helped in turn to finance the upkeep, development and defence of these structures, as well as the costs of campaigning and the numerous other expenses incurred by the nobility and elites.

Raids were perhaps the most important, or at least most common, form of warfare during this period. Not only did they provide the figure who orchestrated them, as well as those who took part, with wealth (agricultural produce, animals, captives, precious metals, etc.), they impoverished the targeted adversary, inhibiting his ability to both defend his lands and launch similar raids. Particularly successful or regular raiding could often lead to an advantageous truce, in which the victimized party would agree to pay a tribute or share certain lands in exchange for peace. Strongholds also provided positions to which raiders could withdraw, as both defeated raiding forces and those weighed down by large quantities of booty were vulnerable.

It was not uncommon in Latin Europe at the time for lords to raid their neighbours, demonstrating their authority, extending their influence and acquiring wealth; however, this was extremely rare among the Latin lords of the Levant. Aside from the brief periods of open war between the princes of Antioch and Edessa in the early twelfth century, which were part of a broader network of alliances and rivalries, raids conducted by the Frankish baronage appear to have been limited to Muslim lands. This focus is rather exceptional when compared with the political landscape these men, or their ancestors, hailed from. Hostilities among local Muslim powers were more common, although these conflicts usually revolved around gaining territory or influence, often by acquiring strongholds – raiding between Muslim powers west of the Euphrates seems to have been almost as rare as it was between Christians. Most of the raids we know about were led by the Frankish princes or powerful lords, including those of Turbessel, Galilee and Transjordan, and their leading Muslim counterparts.

Raiding was an obvious way of acquiring immediate wealth, but so too could it be a powerful threat. The arrival of the First Crusade in Palestine led most towns along the coast to placate the crusaders by selling them provisions. In the decade that followed, many would offer an annual tribute to the kingdom of Jerusalem in exchange for peace. In 1285, almost two centuries later, Bohemond VII of Tripoli (and nominal prince of Antioch, the city having been lost in 1268) agreed to destroy the island stronghold of Maraclea when prompted to do so by Mamlūk Sultan Qalāwūn, who threatened to raid the lands around Tripoli if he did not.

From a defender's perspective, offering tribute was a way of avoiding potentially greater costs that might accompany raids, or a way of diverting a direct attack. For attackers, accepting tribute avoided the uncertainty and risks that were associated with raiding, or the costs and challenges that accompanied besieging a stronghold and then attempting to administer the surrounding region. But such a system of tributes, truces and taxes relied on an acknowledged network of regional borders – it had to be clear which areas would contribute to the tribute and would in turn be protected from further hostilities. A landscape of acknowledged landholding limits like this would have been foreign to most parts of Europe at the time.

Contemporary European boundaries were relatively fluid and frontiers shifted as the authority of one baron spread at the expense of his neighbour's. Perhaps owing to the higher population density and the continued use of many ancient administrative boundaries, borders were fairly well defined and agreed upon in the Levant. This did not inhibit frontier warfare and raiding, or otherwise imply that these borders were obstacles (they did not limit the movement of people or armies), only that it was widely appreciated where a certain regional power's authority, or that of a smaller landowner, ended and another's began. Likewise, borders could be shifted if necessary. For example, the archbishopric of Tyre traditionally fell under the patriarchate of Antioch; however, when Tyre became a part of the kingdom of Jerusalem, rather than the principality of Antioch or county of Tripoli, the archbishopric was transferred to the patriarchate of Jerusalem. The archbishopric had clearly defined and agreed upon limits, making its transfer, rather than the area of its extent, the matter of dispute. This episode, which was ultimately adjudicated by Pope Innocent II, speaks to the Franks' appreciation of the region's existing boundaries, even as relative newcomers to the area.

When passing from Damascus to Acre in 1183, the Andalusian pilgrim and traveller, Ibn Jubayr, noticed that there was a certain tree along the road that served as a border marker. He states that Frankish robbers would take captive anyone they found east of the tree but would set loose all those they found to the west of it. Although the tree was east of Bānyās, which had been held by a Muslim garrison since 1164, the Franks still lay claim to this region. Regardless of where the Muslims considered the border to have been, all acknowledged that the caravan was in Frankish territory by the time it crossed the Hula Valley, at which point it was compelled to take a detour to Toron, where each traveller was to pay one dinar and a twentieth. The caravan then set out for Acre, where the merchants would pay their customs dues.

Because regional boundaries were relatively agreed upon, land typically changed hands when a power centre was taken. Rarely was part of a region alienated and

Ibn al-Furāt: raiding and peace negotiations, 1261

The Sultan, al-Malik al-Ẓāhir Baybars, and a number of emirs sent a vast amount of barley and flour by sea from Damietta to Jaffa, which was in the hands of the Franks. When the Sultan went towards Syria, John of Ibelin, count of Jaffa, sent a messenger presenting his obedience and bringing gifts … When Baybars reached Damascus, a messenger came from the ruler of Acre asking for safe conduct for envoys from all the Frankish houses. The sultan wrote to the governor of Bānyās telling him to allow them to come, after which the Frankish leaders arrived and asked for peace. The sultan made many demands of them, and when they refused, he upbraided them and treated them with contempt. Muslim forces had set out to raid their lands from Baalbek, and the Franks asked that this force should be withdrawn. It happened that prices were high in Syria and the bulk of Muslim imports were coming from Frankish lands. So peace was agreed on the terms of the status quo at the end of the days of al-Malik al-Nāṣir … In the same way, a truce was agreed with the lord of Jaffa and the ruler of Beirut …

(Adapted from Ibn al-Furāt, trans. Lyons and Lyons, 2:43–4.)

absorbed by another; when it was, it was often done quite formally, by treaty rather than force. Unlike in Europe, where lordships often grew organically through force and intimidation, this was not the norm in the Levant. With more powerful figures in closer quarters, it was often wise to acknowledge boundaries, whether they were respected or not. The Franks' efforts in the early twelfth century to extend their influence into the Sawād through the construction of castles, as discussed above, was a relatively unique exception. The Franks recognized that they would need a stronghold to control this region, but pausing to build a castle in the lands of an opponent whose military structure was based on significant and mobile field forces was a risky endeavour, and it cost Hugh of St Omer his life.

If too weak to besiege a neighbouring power centre directly, the threat of doing so, or of conducting repeated raids into its lands, might result in an offer of tribute. This quickly became a formalized practice, as a way of expressing dominance and extracting wealth. In 1109, following the Franks' capture of Tripoli, Ṭughtakīn of Damascus agreed to give up the castle of 'Akkār and pay an annual tribute, which was to be gathered from the castles in the Syrian Coastal Mountains west of Homs, including Maṣyāf and Ḥiṣn al-Akrād (Crac des Chevaliers). In 1110, building on his success after taking Beirut, Baldwin I compelled Sidon to increase its annual tribute from 2,000 dinars to 6,000. In the same year, Tancred launched a raid against Shayzar, leading the city to agree to an immediate tribute of 10,000 dinars, a gift of horses and the release of prisoners in exchange for peace. When Tancred died in 1112, Roger of Antioch demanded that Aleppo and Shayzar continue to make their annual tribute payments of 20,000 and 10,000 dinars respectively.

Instability among the Muslims also played into Frankish hands. In 1117, the interim leader of Aleppo, fearing the approach of Īlghāzī, bought peace by surrendering the castle of al-Qubba to the Franks. By 1123, however, the balance of power had shifted and it was the Franks who were forced to give up al-Athārib in exchange for a truce. Issues in Damascus led the Būrids to pay the kingdom of Jerusalem an annual tribute in the mid-twelfth century. In 1149, a series of back-and-forth raids resulted in a two-year truce and tribute was once more to be paid to the Franks. When the kingdom's army moved to support the Damascenes against Nūr al-Dīn in 1151, the Franks made sure to collect their tribute before they withdrew. Even after taking Damascus, Nūr al-Dīn was inclined to buy peace with the Franks, which he did in 1155, in order to campaign in Anatolia. The following year, he arranged another truce with Jerusalem, which cost him 8,000 Tyrian dinars. Although substantial, these tributes may have been, to a degree, compensation paid by the Damascenes to the kingdom for acknowledgement of their right to the lands east of the Jordan, which the Franks had previously shared and at times still claimed.

Sometimes, rather than concluding an agreement of tribute, it was arranged for the lands of a certain region to be shared in *condominium* (*munāṣafa*). Whereas dividing territory might encourage further raiding, this was a means of promoting peace by sharing the produce and administration of an area. With both sides taking part of the total revenue, however, some of the highest tax rates are recorded for these areas.

In 1108, the first of these arrangements was concluded between the kingdom of Jerusalem and the emirate of Damascus. In return for a truce, the Franks were to receive two-thirds of the produce from the Sawād and Jabal ʿAwf, roughly the region from the Golan Heights to the mountains of ʿAjlūn. In 1109, a similar agreement saw the Franks receive one-third of the produce of the Biqāʿ. It may have been at this point that the Franks were also given ʿAkkār and Munayṭira, in return for not raiding the lands of Damascus, Maṣyāf, Ḥiṣn al-Akrād and Ḥiṣn al-Tūfān, from which a tribute would also be paid. The agreement was either confirmed later the same year or renewed the following year. In 1111, Baldwin I and Ṭughtakīn renegotiated their agreement and it was concluded they would each receive a half of the Sawād, Jabal ʿAwf and al-Jabāniyya. Although these arrangements were less common or infrequently documented in the north, the Franks were compelled to share Jabal al-Summāq (the mountainous region southeast of Ḥārim) with al-Bursuqī at one point in the 1120s. In this instance, the Franks, who retained most of the administration of the area, reportedly caused problems for the Muslim revenue collectors.

Following the Third Crusade, it was agreed that Sidon, Ramla and certain other regions would be shared. Al-ʿĀdil appears to have given up his rights to these places, along with Nazareth, in a subsequent peace that was concluded when elements of the Fourth Crusade began to land at Acre. According to al-Maqrīzī, half of Sidon still belonged to the Muslims in 1228, when the Ayyūbid administrators were thrown out by crusaders who had come to the Levant with Frederick II.

In the early thirteenth century, the Hospitallers, based in their castles in the northern part of the county of Tripoli and southern part of the principality of Antioch, found themselves in a particularly strong position. Having been bypassed by Saladin in 1188, they were able to launch pestering raids over the following decades into the lands of Homs and Hama, the rulers of which were often preoccupied with the greater threats posed by their fellow Ayyūbids. These Hospitaller castles also surrounded the Assassin enclave in the southern section of the Syrian Coastal Mountains. The order was probably extracting a tribute from the Assassins in the second half of the twelfth century and Wilbrand of Oldenburg valued this tribute at 2,000 marks when he visited in 1211. The burden was such that the Assassin legation sent to Louis IX at Acre, following the collapse of the Seventh Crusade, was willing to waive the customary tribute they demanded of rulers if Louis could release them from the payments they owed to the Templars and Hospitallers. The appeal failed and the Assassins found themselves the ones sending the king a tribute following the intervention of the orders, such was their influence.

With the rise of the Mamlūks, roles were reversed. After Baybars captured the Templar stronghold of Safed in 1266, the Hospitallers scrambled to extend their peace that was in place in the region of Homs. Baybars agreed to this provided the Hospitallers relinquish the tributes they were receiving from Hama (4,000 dinars), Abū Qubays (800 dinars) and the Nizārī Assassins (1,200 dinars), and pay further amounts of both wheat and barley. The treaty was ratified the following year, after Baybars had destroyed the order's mill outside Acre. The truce was to last for ten years, ten months and ten days and the final version saw the Hospitallers give up not only their tributes from Hama and the Assassins, but also Shayzar, Apamea and elsewhere. As it turned out, the Assassins simply paid Baybars the same tribute they had once paid the Hospitallers. This was not an insignificant development, as the

Assassins had previously exacted protection money from the distant Ayyūbid sultans of Egypt.

In addition to tributes, Baybars' treaties often included *condominia*. In his 1266–67 treaty with the Hospitallers, the region from the Orontes to a certain western boundary was to be held in *condominium*, as were the order's lands around Acre. Around the same time, Baybars negotiated a truce with Acre, which would have converted Sidon into a *condominium* once more had it been ratified. Another, negotiated in 1268 but also never ratified, would have turned considerable parts of the territory of Haifa, the Carmel and 'Atlit into *condominia*, while Sidon was to pass entirely to the Mamlūks. In 1271, the Hospitallers gave up their rights to previous *condominia*, while the lands around the castle of Margat were to be ruled as such. A later treaty between Qalāwūn and Lady Margaret of Tyre saw the ninety-three settlements of the lordship of Tyre divided between the two parties: five to Qalāwūn, ten to Margaret, and the remainder to be shared. This agreement seems to have been negotiated in 1271 between Baybars and John of Montfort, Margaret's husband, but it was not ratified until 1285, after both Baybars and John had died.

Besides controlling land, and the revenue drawn from it, fortifications could also dominate trade and impose tolls. While the Templars customarily built their towers and smaller strongholds along roads and Christian pilgrim routes, Roger of Antioch had evidently discovered how profitable the revenue from the *hajj* (the annual Muslim pilgrimage to Mecca) could be. In 1117, a clause in a treaty with Aleppo granted him not only a certain stronghold and tribute, but the right to collect the customary tax levied on those making the pilgrimage from Aleppo to Arabia. With an eye to similar revenue streams, Baldwin I had built the castle of Montreal two years earlier along the main caravan (and *hajj*) route through Transjordan. In the words of Albert of Aachen, 'he established a new fortress, so that in this way he might more powerfully subdue the land of the Arabians, and passage to and fro would no longer be available to merchants except by the king's favour and licence, nor would any ambushes or enemy forces suddenly appear, but would quickly be apparent to the king's faithful stationed in the citadel'.[18] Prior to this, the Franks had prevented a Turkish emir from fortifying Wādī Mūsā (near Petra) in 1107, and preyed on caravan traffic in the region in 1108 and again in 1112 or 1113. Accordingly, they would have been well aware of the profit to be gained by controlling this region.

Restriction

For powerful Muslim rulers, whose strength lay in the size of their large armies, exposed strongholds could be a liability. Rulers such as Īlghāzī, al-Bursuqī and Zankī, who brought forces from the Jazīra and made considerable use of seasonal Turkoman forces, showed a willingness to slight the fortifications of some smaller towns they captured in western Syria. The defences of more significant urban centres were typically retained and even developed, as these were often more defensible and protected wealthier communities. Nūr al-Dīn continued this policy to a degree even as his power grew. For example, when he took Chastel Neuf in 1167, he decided to destroy it, rather than attempt to hold it, much as his father had opted to do after capturing Arima in 1142. Both were relatively deep in Frankish territory and it would have been assumed that they would have come under immediate and concerted pressure after Muslim forces withdrew. This willingness to destroy fortifications, in order to deprive the Franks of them, was demonstrated by Saladin during the Third Crusade and by his nephews during the Fifth Crusade.

In 1190, as the siege of Acre dragged on and increasing numbers of European crusaders arrived in the Levant, Saladin issued orders to slight many of the fortifications he had captured along the coast, reissuing these orders in 1191 following Acre's capture. If left intact, these towns could serve as fortified bridgeheads for future crusaders. Less than three decades later, with large numbers of crusaders in Egypt, al-Muʿaẓẓam ʿĪsā similarly recognized that the Franks' ability to hold inland territory was based on their possession of strongholds. Fearing that his brother, al-Kāmil, might offer the crusaders Palestine in exchange for leaving Egypt, which he did, or that the Franks might attempt to recapture the Holy Land, he ordered an extensive slighting programme that included almost all castles in Palestine.

The group most opposed to the fortification of the Levant, however, may have been the Mongols. Relying on large armies of semi-nomadic fighters raised in Central Asia, strongholds were regarded as bases of potential resistance. When they invaded the Levant at the start of 1260, the Mongols pursued a policy of supporting local allies, who recognized their suzerainty, while destroying all strongholds held by those who had not submitted with sufficient zeal. Where there was resistance, as at Aleppo,

Strongholds slighted by Saladin (1190–91) and al-Muʿaẓẓam ʿĪsā (1218–19).

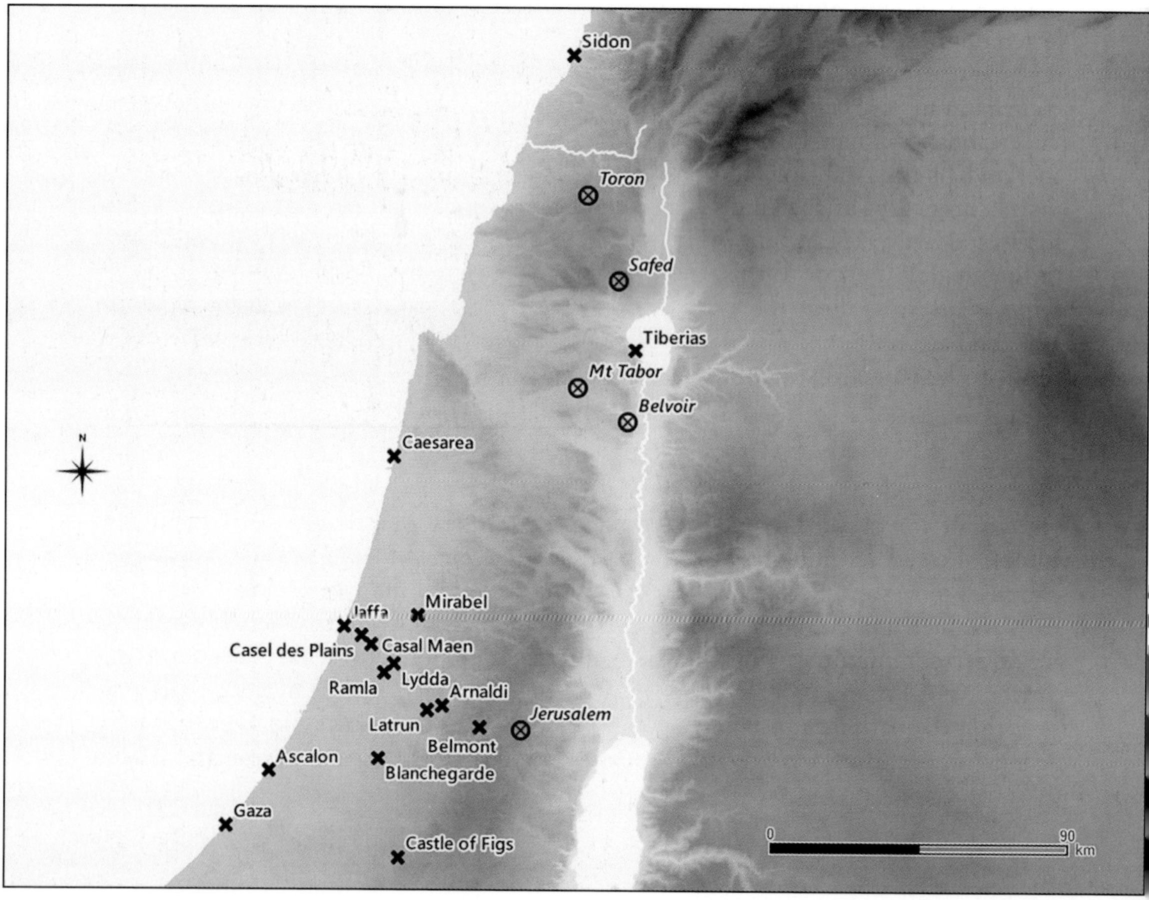

Ṣubayba, 'Ajlūn, Baalbek and Damascus, destruction followed. Hülagü may have intended to extend this destruction to the Assassins: in a letter sent to Louis IX of France in 1262, he asserted that he had charged Kitbugha with reducing their strongholds before leaving the region in 1260.

As the Mamlūks began to conquer Frankish lands in the 1260s, they instituted a policy of slighting coastal fortifications while retaining strategic inland castles. Like Saladin, Baybars and his successors recognized the threat posed by coastal strongholds and the protection they might offer European crusaders should they be captured. As defences were torn down, whole communities were disrupted, devastating certain industries and trade networks. Inland, large castles, such as Safed and Crac des Chevaliers, were developed and used as administrative centres, while the strategic value of others, such as Beaufort and Margat, ensured they too were preserved as secondary power bases. Both Baybars and Qalāwūn were aware of the benefits strongholds provided opponents in the region: al-Mughīth 'Umar, Baybars' final Ayyūbid opponent, was based in Kerak, while Qalāwūn was forced to confront Sunqur al-Ashqar, a rival to the Mamlūk throne, who held Saone. Both dissidents were overcome but neither stronghold was destroyed, as each was the administrative centre for the surrounding region.

In 1270, Baybars was alarmed by reports that Louis IX and other leading European nobles were sailing eastward. He had bridges built and the slighted defences of

Strongholds preserved and slighted by the Mamlūks, 1260–91.

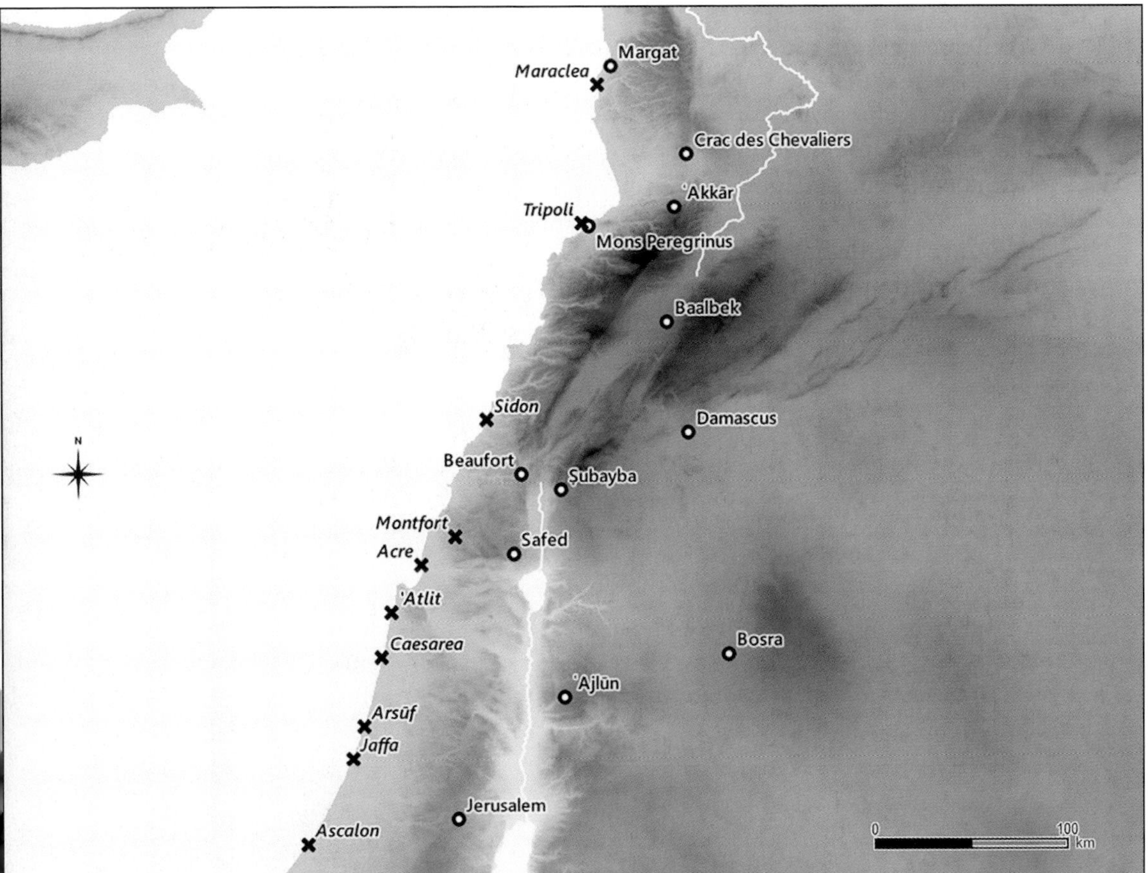

Ascalon reduced further, arranging for the stones of the stronghold to be thrown into the sea. The feared attack on Egypt never materialized, as the Eighth Crusade ended in disaster outside Tunis with Louis IX among the dead.

Back in 1250, Louis had been a prisoner in the Egyptian camp when al-Muʿaẓẓam Tūrānshāh was murdered by a group of mamlūks, including Baybars, initiating the ascent of the regime that followed. Fear of the French king's return had led Baybars to take preparatory measures shortly after assuming power in Cairo: he saw to the defences of Alexandria; ordered the mouth of the Nile narrowed at Damietta, to prevent any large ships from sailing up the river; and arranged for the construction of a watch tower at Rosetta, where the other main branch of the Nile emptied into the Mediterranean. In the years following, reports of planned crusades led Baybars to ensure that the Alexandrian fleet was in a good state of repair and that the city was provided with sufficient artillery around its walls, reportedly numbering a hundred engines.

While a crusade was feared in Egypt, the Mongols were instead the greatest threat to Mamlūk rule in Syria. Accordingly, while coastal fortifications were destroyed, Baybars rebuilt and developed not only the interior castles that he took from the Franks, but also those that the Mongols had slighted in 1260. It was hoped that these strongholds would counteract the numerical strength of the Mongols, tying up an invading army until Egyptian forces could be assembled and moved into Syria.

Defenders

As William of Tyre remarked in the twelfth century, it did not matter how strong defences were if there was no one to defend them. Garrisons were often composed of professional fighters, men whose social rank or occupational choice made war their profession. Because sieges were relatively rare, these experienced fighters were often relied upon to enforce local authority, take part in raids and even serve in the army at times.

A Frankish castle or citadel was ultimately the possession of a lord, who might rule from it directly or delegate command of the stronghold to a castellan, or viscount if it were a crown possession. This individual often received the support of a group

Ibn ʿAbd al-Ẓāhir: Mongol destruction, 1260

When the Mongols (may God defeat them) occupied Syria, they began to destroy the castles and walls. They demolished the walls of the citadel of Damascus, and the castles of Salt, ʿAjlūn, Ṣarkhad, Bosra, Baalbek, Ṣubayba, Shayzar and Shmemis. When the sultan [Baybars] took charge of affairs and God established him as the support of the Faith, he took an interest in the reconstruction of these castles and the completion of the destroyed buildings, because these were the strongholds of Islam. All these were repaired during his time; their fosses were cleared out, the flanks of their walls were broadened, equipment was transported to them, and he sent mamlūks and soldiers to [garrison] them.

(Adapted from Ibn ʿAbd al-Ẓāhir, trans. Sadaque, pp. 117–18.)

of retainers, a body of knights and sergeants drawn from the gentry, an entourage of capable fighting men who were supported for their services. Depending on the size of the stronghold, and various other factors, this well born body of fighters might make up 10–25 per cent of the total number of defenders, far fewer if townspeople were conscripted into the defence of a castle or town during a period of crisis. The remainder typically consisted of a semi-permanent fighting force, which had various other responsibilities, and perhaps a body of paid mercenaries, who fought purely for cash rather than any socio-political motivation.

As Frankish castles grew in the thirteenth century, mercenaries were increasingly used to defend them, funded from the same deep coffers with which the military orders had financed their great construction projects. Companies of crossbowmen were particularly valuable to the defence of strongholds. Although the number of mercenaries paid to provide garrison services probably increased in the thirteenth century, using paid soldiers in this way would not have been uncommon in the twelfth – mercenaries were among the Frankish defenders of Bānyās when it was taken in 1132.

Muslim defensive arrangements were similar. The smaller number of strongholds typically meant that, under the Seljuks and Ayyūbids, the ruler of an *iqṭāʿ*, or occasionally a deputy, was in command of a fairly professional body of defenders, with whose support rule was enforced. During the Mamlūk period, with more centralized rule, strongholds were entrusted to administrative governors, while a distinct garrison commander was also appointed by the sultan. Many of these garrison forces would have been mamlūks, raised from childhood to be soldiers.

In times of need, everyone inside a stronghold might be pulled into service – the consequences of defeat were death or slavery if the defences fell by force. Accordingly, it was typically in the interest of non-military figures, such as townspeople, to assist the garrison. In some rare instances, where a considerable portion of the general population supported the cause of the besiegers, assistance was minimal.

The environment of desperation that might accompany a siege provided an opportunity for women, generally excluded from both Frankish and Muslim military systems, to take a more active role, even if they were rarely involved in direct combat. Women played an instrumental role in retaking Shayzar following the Assassins' brief seizure of the citadel in 1109. The ruling Banū Munqidh had left to attend a festival hosted by the local Christians, permitting a group of Assassins to sneak into the citadel and surprise its remaining guards. Women in the barbican helped pull men up into the stronghold, allowing the Assassins in the citadel and town to be hunted down and slaughtered. During the Fāṭimid attack on Jaffa in May 1123, a portion of the garrison may have been absent, having gone north with Baldwin II, as the defenders are described as being few in number. However, 'the women of Jaffa were constantly ready with generous aid for the citizens who were struggling mightily. Some supplied stones, and others water to drink.'[19] Fifteen years later, in April 1138, an unnamed woman commanded Buzāʿa when it was besieged by Byzantine and Frankish forces.

In a less direct capacity, women played an important part in ensuring dynastic stability, which limited the vulnerability of strongholds in this period when male rulers often died young. Melisende, daughter of Baldwin II and widow of Fulk, served as regent for her son Baldwin III during his minority, fighting to retain her position even after her son came of age. Melisende's sister, Alice of Jerusalem, similarly sought to control the regency of her daughter, Constance of Antioch, following the death of her husband, Bohemond II. Like her mother, Constance would fight to assert her own rule later in life. Although all three were strong women and had an impact on the governance of their principality, the conduct of military matters, including sieges, remained the preserve of male councillors and deputies, as it was in Muslim spheres.

The marriage of Ḍayfa Khātūn, daughter of al-ʿĀdil, to al-Ẓāhir Ghāzī in 1212 ended the first phase of intra-Ayyūbid conflict. Her husband died in 1216 and their son followed him to the grave in 1236, at which point she assumed the regency of her grandson, al-Nāṣir Yūsuf, ruling through a council of men. Military actions were still undertaken by male figures, but Ḍayfa Khātūn was an influential figure in guiding policy. Although she initially sided with al-Ashraf against their brother al-Kāmil, she kept Aleppo relatively aloof of the continuing Ayyūbid power struggle following their deaths in 1236 and 1238 respectively.

Offensive Manpower

Town and castle garrisons were an important source of manpower for field armies. It was in the interest of rulers to retain experienced and capable fighting men, many of whom were used to garrison their strongholds when not otherwise needed. It was natural for a lord or *muqṭaʿ* to summon these forces when joining his prince's army, but doing so came with risks.

When Frankish Bānyās was besieged in December 1132, the town and citadel were captured after only a few days. As had been the case at Jaffa in 1123, the defenders of Bānyās are noted as being unprepared and without enough men, suggesting a portion of the garrison had gone north with Fulk to address the regency of Antioch. By comparison, the town resisted for around four weeks when besieged by Frankish and Damascene forces in 1140, but only for about a week when attacked by Nūr al-Dīn in 1164, when a number of its defenders were probably in Egypt with Amalric and the army of Jerusalem. The size of these forces that joined the army, or the proportion of Bānyās's defenders that they accounted for, is unclear. Later, on 30 September 1183, a force from Transjordan, almost certainly members of the garrisons of Kerak and Montreal, encountered a Muslim scouting party while heading north to join the army of Jerusalem at Ṣaffūriyya. If Bahāʾ al-Dīn is to be trusted, this was not a small force, as a hundred of the Franks found themselves prisoners after the engagement.

When garrison forces were similarly drawn into the kingdom's army in 1187, ahead of the battle of Hattin, the result was disastrous. As Smail remarked, 'The existence of Christian Syria depended ultimately on the simultaneous existence of an adequate field army and garrisons.'[20] It was reasonable to weaken the garrison of a strong castle or town provided the threat posed by the larger field army was sufficient to discourage or break a siege; however, this tactic relied entirely on the strength and survival of that army. This appears to have been impressed upon the Franks in 1179: defeated in the field, they were unable to muster sufficient numbers in time to relieve Jacob's Ford when Saladin invaded again months later. Over the following years, as demonstrated during Saladin's invasion of northern Palestine in 1183, the Franks declined to risk battle unless it was on their terms. With the army of Jerusalem intact, Saladin was unable to invest a significant stronghold, from which he could then make an attempt to hold the surrounding region. Although this was a prudent policy, it was not a popular one among certain influential figures.

In 1187, under mounting criticism and with the Frankish ruling elite bitterly divided, Guy of Lusignan made a series of decisions that led to the battle of Hattin. The resulting defeat decimated not only the Frankish army, and any potential relief force, but also significant components of many garrisons, contributing to the loss of many strongholds and the near-collapse of the kingdom of Jerusalem during the months that followed.

Garrison Numbers

It is difficult to determine the size of most garrisons, let alone the total number of defenders during a given siege. Aside from the challenges associated with estimating the number of people in any large group, some sources acknowledged the tendency of contemporaries to exaggerate. For instance, Ibn al-Athīr explicitly calls out ʿImād al-Dīn al-Iṣfahānī, Saladin's secretary and biographer, for misrepresenting Saladin's victory in 1176 over Sayf al-Dīn II of Mosul at Tell al-Sulṭān, about 45km south of Aleppo. Whereas ʿImād al-Dīn claims that Saladin's 6,000 cavalry triumphed over a force of 20,000 Mosuli cavalry, Ibn al-Athīr, who was in a position to review the Mosuli register, composed by no less a figure than his own brother, clarifies that the Mosuli force was instead between 6,000 and 6,500.

In the absence of detailed registers and financial records, we are left to rely on the remarks of contemporary observers and historians. For example, when al-Muʿaẓẓam ʿĪsā besieged the new Templar castle of ʿAtlit in 1220, it is said to have been defended by 4,000 men, including 300 crossbowmen. The bulk of the kingdom's fighting force, which probably included part of ʿAtlit's garrison, was in Egypt taking part in the Fifth Crusade, as was Oliver of Paderborn, who provided these figures. The threat to ʿAtlit was deemed sufficient that the master of the order returned to Palestine with a tested force of Templars and a number of barons. The regular strength of the garrison is unclear, as is how many Templar knights and sergeants may have been among the defenders, while the 300 crossbowmen were probably mercenaries. In a later episode, Baybars' secretary, Ibn ʿAbd al-Ẓāhir, noted that 480 fighting men defended the Templar castle of Beaufort when it was besieged in 1268. When the castle surrendered on 15 April, these men were led away into captivity, having arranged for the women and children in the castle to be escorted to Tyre as a term of their surrender. This would have provided an opportunity to count the male defenders, but there is no indication of their station. As at ʿAtlit, a minority of these fighters would have been knights; the majority were more likely professionals of a lower class, supplemented by every able-bodied man during such a time of emergency.

The size and make-up of Muslim garrisons is perhaps even less clear, although a small window is provided by the accounts that describe the garrisons installed by Qalāwūn in the 1280s. In 1285, after taking the Hospitaller castle of Margat, a considerable force was entrusted with its defence. This included 1,000 *aqjiyya* soldiers, 400 craftsmen, 150 emirs of the rank of *ṭablkāna*, and additional contingents of certain mamlūk corps. In 1290, a year after the capture and destruction of Tripoli, a force of 600 cavalry, under Sayf al-Dīn Ṭaqwī, was left to defend the new settlement that was established inland around the castle first built by Raymond of St Gilles. Although large, these figures align with those reported when Margat was under Frankish rule.

Wilbrand of Oldenburg visited Margat in 1211 and left a description of what he saw. He observed that it was guarded by 4 Hospitaller brothers (knights of the order), supplemented by twenty-eight watchmen. A force of 1,000 people, other than the general citizens of the castle and the attached castle-town, were retained in peacetime to defend the stronghold and presumably contribute to the Hospitallers' offensive capacity. Supplies were laid in to sustain the castle for five years. Elsewhere, charter evidence reveals that, by 1259, the Hospitallers had arranged to garrison Mount Tabor with forty knights and Crac des Chevaliers with sixty knights, although the number of others from lower stations is unknown.

The most detailed breakdown we have relates to Safed. Bishop Benedict of Marseilles, who led the effort to rebuild Safed when it returned to the Templars in 1240, claims that the defenders were provided with victuals for 1,700 people in times of peace and for 2,200 in times of war. The peacetime garrison consisted of fifty knights and twenty sergeant brothers, indicating that this was the Templars' main

Wilbrand of Oldenburg: Margat in the early thirteenth century, 1211

This is a large and very strong castle, fortified with a double wall, displaying in itself many towers, which seem more apt for sustaining heaven than for defence. For the mountain on which the castle is sited is extremely high, such that it holds up the high heaven on its shoulders like Atlas. Very broad at the base and rising gradually on high, it liberally furnishes to its masters each year 509 cartloads of render, which the efforts of its enemies cannot prevent, however often they have tried.

This castle belongs to the Hospitallers and is the greatest support of all that land. For it is opposed by many strong castles of the Old Man of the Mountains and the sultan of Aleppo, whose tyranny and assaults it has held in check to such an extent that it receives from them each year for keeping the peace the equivalent of the value of 2,000 marks. And because it is on guard lest any treason should occur, as can happen, each night it is guarded by 4 knights who are brothers of the Hospital, and by another 28 watchmen. For in time of peace in their outlay for defending the castle the Hospitallers maintain 1,000 people over and above the other citizens of the castle, in such a way that they provide them with every convenience and necessity, [sufficient to supply] the castle with the necessities of life for five years. At the foot of that mountain is a city called Valenia, which although it was at one time larger – so it is said and as may be seen – through divine punishment is now desolate and destroyed. Its episcopal seat has been translated into the castle of Margat, this being on account of fear of the Saracens. This castle is 6 short miles distant from Tortosa.

(Adapted from Wilbrand of Oldenburg 11, trans. Pringle, pp. 69–70.)

Margat. *(Courtesy of Denys Pringle)*

interior base south of the Lebanon. These men were joined by fifty turcopoles and 300 crossbowmen. A labour force of 820, augmented with 400 slaves (probably captured Muslims not valuable enough to ransom) fulfilled the day-to-day operations and construction work at the castle. Collectively, these individuals consumed 12,000 cartloads of barley and grain as well as other victuals each year. Besides people, animals were needed to help work the land and horses were required for the knights and other cavalry elements, as was specie to pay the mercenaries and labourers intrinsic to the castle's function.

In times of siege, the numbers of defenders would have swelled as more were hired, recruited or sent from elsewhere in support. According to the Templar of Tyre, more than a thousand Hospitaller and secular knights and sergeants defended Arsūf during Baybars' siege operations in 1265. Although this is almost certainly an exaggeration, Ibn ʿAbd al-Ẓāhir, who was present, wrote that thousands were taken away, bound with ropes, after the castle surrendered.

Castles like Margat, Safed and Arsūf were among the most impressive in the region – the Templars reportedly paid 1,100,000 Saracen bezants on building costs during the first two and a half years of Safed's reconstruction and around 40,000 bezants annually thereafter. We know less about the defenders of smaller strongholds. Baldwin, the castellan (and later lord) of Ramla, had eight knights under his command in the first decade of the twelfth century, a force sufficient to defend the town's tower; although it was an important administrative centre in the early twelfth century, Ramla lacked town walls. To the north, when Bohemond II joined Baldwin II's push against Damascus in 1129, he left 100 men to defend Kafarṭāb, a significant town between Maʿarrat al-Nuʿmān and Shayzar. This force marched out to confront a party of Muslim invaders and, although defeated, discouraged an attack on Kafarṭāb. Later, in the 1180s, the small Templar stronghold of La Fève seems to have been garrisoned by 80 knights, although this may be an estimate of the total number of defenders.

Ethnicity

The castellan and most other retainers who were entrusted with the defence of a large Frankish castle would have been drawn from the knightly class; however, the majority of defenders would have been of lower birth – mercenaries, Frankish burgesses or landowners, and members of the local Syrian population. Many Frankish strongholds were built in regions with a pre-existing Eastern Christian community, where a natural symbiotic relationship formed: the settlement provided goods and services needed by the stronghold, while the stronghold provided a market for such; likewise, a castle might discourage raids in the region, while it might in turn benefit from locals taking part in its defence.

Although Frankish castles are often regarded as enclaves of Latin Europe in an otherwise Muslim Middle East, this was hardly the case. When the kingdom of Jerusalem was established, a slight majority of people living in Palestine were probably adherents of Islam, although the cities along the coast would become predominantly Christian as they fell into Frankish hands. To the north, the princes of Antioch came to rule over diverse populations of Christians and Muslims of various sects, while the county of Edessa may have contained predominantly Armenian and Greek Christians.

Armenians probably made up the bulk of the defenders in the county of Edessa, some holding strongholds as lords and many more serving in garrisons, but local Christians also filled important positions to the south, at least in the twelfth century. In the kingdom of Jerusalem, Baras the Armenian is found in charters of the 1120s and George the Armenian appears in the service of the lord of Caesarea in 1145. The progenitors of most of these families probably accompanied Baldwin I or Baldwin II south when each assumed the kingship of Jerusalem, or came in the service of the Courtenay family, either when Joscelin I became prince of Galilee or following the collapse of the county of Edessa. To these can be added a number of Syrian Christians, such as Arnulf, son of Bertrand the Syrian, and David the Syrian, who held a cave in the Lebanon. In the principality of Antioch, the knights of Margat included the lords Zacharias, Georgius and Theodorus, whose names suggest they were Greeks. The post of marshal of Jerusalem, one of the kingdom's highest military appointments, may have been occupied by a local Christian during the second quarter of the twelfth century, a certain 'Sado', which might correspond with the Arabic Saʿd or Saʿīd. Although it seems unlikely that Sado was a Muslim, a charter from 1155 indicates that two Arab knights held villages in the kingdom.

If local Christians were able to hold lordships, it seems figures of lower rank would have been relied upon to provide some of the manpower required to garrison certain strongholds. Explicit references to garrisons of local Christians are rare south of the county of Edessa; however, one can be found in William of Tyre's history, where it is noted that the constable of Tiberias entrusted command and the defence of al-Ḥabis Jaldak to local Christian Syrians. This earned the constable of Tiberias William's criticism when the stronghold was taken in 1182.

In the far south, there were significant Christian populations in Transjordan. Both Montreal and Kerak were founded in areas occupied by local Christian communities, which, according to William of Tyre, meant that the locals could be relied upon. Local Christians helped Reynald of Châtillon transport his prefabricated fleet from Kerak to Aqaba in late 1182, and the townspeople of Kerak were permitted to seek refuge in the castle when Saladin besieged the stronghold the following summer. After the region fell under Muslim rule in the late 1180s, its Christian communities remained. The pilgrim Thietmar, who visited Montreal in 1217 on his way to St Catherine's Monastery in the Sinai, even encountered a Frankish widow still living in the community outside the castle.

Coreligionists were similarly relied upon to garrison most Muslim strongholds. Around the time of the First Crusade, Turks probably made up the core of most garrisons in Syria; however, a number of ethnic Armenians, who embraced Islam, are known to have been a part of some. For most Seljuk figures, their *'askar* probably consisted mostly of Turks, while the majority of the defenders of certain Arab strongholds, like Shayzar, may have been Arabs. Inevitably, there would have been a mix of ethnicities represented in many garrisons, which came to include growing numbers of men born around the Black Sea as Ayyūbid rulers became increasingly reliant on regiments of mamlūks.

Beliefs that coreligionists were more trustworthy inspired efforts to populate urban centres with such individuals. During the First Crusade, a portion of the Christian population living in Jerusalem may have been expelled ahead of the crusaders' arrival. This policy was reversed following the city's capture: Christian communities from Transjordan were transplanted to Jerusalem, in part to repopulate the city following the massacres that had accompanied its fall.

The populations of captured towns were treated in a range of ways; however, faith does not appear to have been a leading consideration. When cities were taken by force, as occurred at Jerusalem (1099), Caesarea (1101) and Beirut (1110), a sack typically followed and any survivors could expect to be enslaved. Where terms of surrender were arranged, different scenarios might play out. At Acre (1104), the townspeople were permitted to remain for a fee; at al-Athārib (1110), the local population was allowed to stay if it so chose; and at Tyre (1124), most of the population was escorted out of the city, although a significant number of locals probably chose to remain. Along the coast, cities came to be inhabited primarily by Franks, due in large part to the interest shown by the Italian merchant communities and other Europeans. Further inland, some towns that had surrendered on good terms probably remained predominantly Muslim.

Muslim policies were similar when taking over a town. The predominantly Christian population of Edessa was largely respected when the city fell to Zankī at the end of 1144; although he captured the town by force, the local population and captives were quickly set free. Nūr al-Dīn was less accommodating when he took the city in 1146, following its brief recapture by Joscelin II and Baldwin of Marash. During

Saladin's conquest of Palestine in 1187, Frankish urban populations were evicted, which seems to have suited those affected. While most appear to have been free to leave, the conditions of Jerusalem's surrender placed a small ransom on everyone who wished to depart: 10 dinars (or bezants according to Frankish sources) for a man, 5 for a woman and 1 or 2 for a child. The terms imply that those who could not afford the tax would be enslaved. The treatment of Syrian Christians and Muslims living under Frankish rule at this time was of less interest to both Frankish and Muslim commentators, so we know less about their fate.

From the payments made at Jerusalem, Ibn al-Athīr reports that 60,000 men had been in the city when it surrendered, its population having swelled as people from the countryside and refugees from other cities fled there in the weeks leading up to Saladin's arrival. These people then joined other refugees behind the walls of Tyre. This enormous body of potential defenders was a strength, so long as they could be fed, and probably contributed to Tyre's stiff resistance in December 1187. Critical to Tyre's defence, the Franks were able to maintain their dominance of the sea and a supply route remained open. Earlier, in 1183, Kerak was similarly swollen with extra people, guests at the wedding of Humphrey IV of Toron and Isabelle of Jerusalem. Although these were exceptional cases, involving larger groups of refugees than was the norm, providing asylum could be a critical function of many strongholds.

Refuge

The groups of people that strongholds were designed to shelter varied considerably, from town walls that secured whole urban communities to rural towers that were occupied by no more than their defenders. While farmers and burgesses might hope to find refuge in a local tower, large strongholds might provide security for defeated armies in times of need.

At the battle of Ascalon, fought to the north of the city on 12 August 1099, remnants of the First Crusade defeated a large Egyptian army. As the battle turned against the Fāṭimids, the city's defenders closed the northern Jaffa Gate, preventing the crusaders from entering the town but pinning hundreds between the town's walls and the Christian army. To the east, the right wing of the Muslim army was able to escape into the town through the eastern Jerusalem Gate. Despite their considerable losses, the Fāṭimids' ability to secure and then defend Ascalon, thanks in large part to the squabbling that broke out among the crusaders after the battle, ensured the city remained an Egyptian possession for another fifty-four years. Circumstances were reversed a few years later, when in May 1102, following the Franks' defeat at the second battle of Ramla, Baldwin I was saved by the network of fortifications that the Franks had recently acquired and begun to expand in southern Palestine. Fleeing the victorious Fāṭimid army, the king escaped first to Ramla, taking refuge in the tower that acted as the town's citadel, where he was briefly besieged before escaping and making his way across country to Arsūf and thence to Jaffa.

In 1133, Pons of Tripoli took refuge in Montferrand after he was defeated attempting to confront a large party of Turkoman raiders. The castle was besieged but held out long enough for Fulk to arrive with the army of Jerusalem. Four years later, Pons was again besieged in Montferrand, this time by Zankī, and Fulk mustered his forces once more and marched north to relieve the castle. On this occasion, however, the relief force was defeated. The loss would have been significantly greater had not Fulk and elements of his army been able to seek refuge in Montferrand, joining Pons and the besieged inside the castle. Although this provided the castle with numerous defenders, provisions were stretched extremely thin. Zankī rejected an initial offer of surrender, but was inclined to agree when a Frankish relief force approached, securing advantageous terms before the defenders learned help was at hand. In exchange for their freedom, a tribute of 50,000 dinars was arranged.

Safed played a critical secondary part in the defence of Bānyās in 1157. Nūr al-Dīn's siege was interrupted by the sudden arrival of a Frankish army led by Baldwin III of Jerusalem, which compelled the Muslims to withdraw and regroup. Baldwin then made a critical error: as he saw to the repair of the town's defences, he released his infantry and a number of knights, believing the main threat to have passed. Nūr al-Dīn, however, had kept his army together, allowing him to ambush what remained of Baldwin's force near Jacob's Ford, half way between Bānyās and Tiberias. The Franks were soundly defeated and many important nobles were taken prisoner. The Muslims searched for Baldwin III's body among the dead, not realizing the king had been among those to escape, having fled to the safety of Safed. Nūr al-Dīn then returned to Bānyās and besieged its citadel once more. He had not yet captured it when another Frankish relief force arrived, compelling him to abandon the siege.

Baldwin III's use of Safed as a point of refuge was not the first time he had taken advantage of a stronghold in this way. When evacuating the indefensible rump of the county of Edessa, around 1150, Baldwin skilfully moved between strongholds, frustrating Nūr al-Dīn's efforts to disrupt the marching order of the Frankish column before it reached the principality of Antioch. A generation later, in 1176, a Frankish force from the kingdom of Jerusalem benefited from the security provided by Tyre when raiding into the Biqāʿ Valley. Intending to join up with Raymond III of Tripoli, the raiding party was intercepted and forced to flee southward.

The importance of a stronghold to fall back on is perhaps most clearly seen in 1177, during Saladin's invasion of southern Palestine from Egypt. The episode corresponded with the absence of much of the kingdom's army, which had joined Philip of Flanders on campaign to the north. Baldwin IV, just sixteen at the time, held most of his remaining forces in Ascalon, while the Templars who had not gone north concentrated in Gaza. This left Saladin with a predicament: although his forces far outnumbered those of the Franks, to besiege either Ascalon or Gaza would leave a considerable hostile force within striking distance. Saladin decided to march past both, allowing elements of his army to raid the area west of Jerusalem. Ramla was evacuated and subsequently sacked, nearby Lydda was assaulted and many in Jerusalem, fearing a siege, fled to the Tower of David. As the Muslim army spread out, drawn by the prospect of plunder, the Franks recognized their opportunity. The Frankish army, led by Reynald of Châtillon, included Baldwin II of Ramla and his brother Balian of Ibelin, Reynald of Sidon, and the king's uncle, Joscelin III, titular count of Edessa and now seneschal of the kingdom, as well as Master Eudes of St Amant and his Templars. The Franks attacked the core of Saladin's army near Montgisard, soundly defeating it. Saladin had been unable to concentrate and organize his forces in time, but the Muslims' defeat was only the start of their troubles. With no stronghold to fall back to, the scattered Muslim army began a disorganized flight all the way to Egypt, a catastrophe made worse when local Bedouins, seeing their weakness, raided the baggage that had been left at al-Arish.

Saladin avenged this rout ten years later at the battle of Hattin. Few who fought on the Frankish side escaped following their defeat; however, a number of Templars and Hospitallers fled to Safed, 19km to the north, and Belvoir, 24km to the south, respectively. These men had a brief moment of respite to make last-minute preparations before contingents of Saladin's army arrived; the ensuing sieges of both castles lasted more than a year.

A similar situation played out following the battle of Forbie in October 1244. Having joined forces with the army of al-Ṣāliḥ Ismāʿīl of Damascus, which was led by al-Manṣūr Ibrāhīm of Homs, the Franks suffered particularly high losses in the ensuing battle against al-Ṣāliḥ Ayyūb of Egypt and his Khwārizmian allies. According to a letter sent to Europe after the battle, only thirty-three Templars, twenty-six Hospitallers and three Teutonic Knights survived the engagement; most nobles who had taken part were killed or captured and huge losses had been sustained by the Frankish infantry and crossbowmen. The patriarch of Jerusalem, who wrote the letter, along with Philip of Montfort and others who had managed to escape, took refuge in the new castle at Ascalon, work on which had begun a few years earlier during the Barons' Crusade. The castle was attacked a few weeks after the battle and was subjected to a loose siege that would continue in some form until 1247, when efforts were considerably intensified and it was finally taken.

While strongholds could provide shelter in the immediate aftermath of a defeat, they were also used as safe havens by figures on the run. Qalʿat Jaʿbar, for instance, was where Jāwulī Saqāo established himself around 1107, having been forced to flee Iraq. In 1121, Dubays ibn Ṣadaqa, former ruler of al-Ḥilla (96km south of Baghdad), was similarly welcomed at the castle when he fled the region. Both Jāwulī and Dubays lost little time looking to the Franks for further support.

Prisons

Although designed primarily to keep people out, the impressive strength of castles and citadels made them natural detention facilities. Following his capture by the Dānishmands in 1100, Bohemond was imprisoned in Neocaesarea (mod. Niksar), while Baldwin II, during his first captivity, was held in Mosul before Jāwulī moved him to Qalʿat Jaʿbar, where Joscelin I, Joscelin II and Yvette (daughter of Baldwin II) were also held captive at points in time. In a sensational episode, Joscelin I and his cousin Galeran found themselves the captives of Balak in Kharpūt, where they were later joined by Baldwin II, during his second stint in captivity from 1123. Aided by a party of Armenians, the Franks took control of the castle, sending out Joscelin to bring help. Balak returned and retook the castle, ordering the execution of all but the most senior figures. Baldwin II was moved to Ḥarrān and eventually released, but Galeran would later be executed.

The dungeons of Aleppo seem to have been particularly active, as notable figures defeated by Aleppan armies frequently found themselves its guests. Walter the

Qal'at Ja'bar. *(monumentsofsyria.com)*

Chancellor, who left a detailed account of the battle of the Field of Blood and his captivity thereafter, was among those taken to Aleppo following the Frankish defeat. Later, Joscelin II was blinded and would eventually die there, and Reynald of Châtillon spent about sixteen years in one of its cells. Further south, Gervais of Bazoches, third prince of Galilee, died a prisoner in Damascus and many notables taken captive by Nūr al-Dīn following the battle of Ḥārim in 1164 were held there for a period, as was Reynald of Sidon from 1189 to 1190. Although many castles served the function of prison at one time or another, it is perhaps important to remember that imprisonment, which was done with hopes of collecting a ransom, was reserved for the wealthy. In 1191, having captured the self-proclaimed emperor of Cyprus, Isaac Comnenus, Richard I is said to have promised him that he would never be forced to wear iron chains, so the English king had him clamped in silver shackles once he surrendered. Isaac was then given to the Hospitallers and held prisoner at Margat.

Those wealthy enough to be held for ransom could also prove useful during their captivity, occasionally acting as negotiators, a job some proved particularly effective at given their motivation to see a conclusion to hostilities that would bring about an exchange of prisoners. In 1167, Hugh of Caesarea, who had fallen prisoner to Shīrkūh in Egypt, was instrumental in negotiating the terms of Saladin's surrender of Alexandria to Amalric. Whether as a place of refuge for a defeated army, safe haven for citizens of a town, or place of incarceration, strongholds were dynamic structures.

Planners

We are fortunate that some sources record who commissioned certain strongholds and who subsequently added to them; however, we are left to infer who was responsible for the establishment and development of most. As little as we know about who paid for these works, we know even less about the individuals who were responsible for designing them and overseeing construction, let alone the hundreds of people that provided the various skills and labour that went into the building of any stronghold. We can assume that the commissioner of a castle, citadel or line of city walls had an influence on what the finished product would look like, but the extent to which this person was involved in choosing a layout or various design features is far from clear. In exceptional cases, we hear about an expert who was charged with overseeing refortification efforts. For example, Saladin placed Bahā' al-Dīn Qarāqūsh al-Asadī in charge of building his new citadel at Cairo, and later summoned him to refortify Acre after its capture in 1187.

Qarāqūsh was a manumitted mamlūk of Saladin's uncle, Shīrkūh, who went on to become one of Saladin's most capable emirs. Saladin tasked him with making repairs to Cairo's defences in 1170–71, before entrusting him with construction of the city's new citadel. The work was evidently satisfactory as he was relied on thereafter for Saladin's most important fortification works. When called to secure Acre, Qarāqūsh brought with him tools, supplies and manpower, indicating he had built up a logistical network through his work in Egypt. Qarāqūsh was part of the Turko-Kurdish military elite that had spearheaded the subjugation of Fāṭimid Egypt and his responsibilities at Acre included the city's defence – it was he who commanded the garrison through the Frankish siege of 1189–91, becoming one of the Franks' highest-ranking prisoners following the city's surrender.

Inscriptions on some Muslim strongholds identify the year that certain elements were added and the responsible patron. Although these reveal who oversaw or paid for building works, as will be addressed below, they provide a far from complete picture. For instance, inscriptions at Cairo, Jerusalem, Damascus, Bosra, 'Ajlūn and Mount Tabor credit the construction of towers to al-'Ādil, some of his sons and certain emirs; however, the similarities between these projects suggest a singular guiding policy was in place. Al-'Ādil appears to have arranged for all of these works to conform to his signature style, which included the use of large quadrangular towers and marginally drafted ashlars. Similar stylistic signatures can be seen in the works of Ayyūbid contemporaries, such as al-Ẓāhir Ghāzī of Aleppo and al-Mujāhid Asad al-Dīn Shīrkūh of Homs. While this gives a sense of how commissioners could influence the appearance of their strongholds, the role and input of the architects and master builders, who were probably used at multiple sites, remain less clear. Epigraphic and textual evidence from the Mamlūk period similarly provides the names of a number of emirs who oversaw significant refortification efforts; however, the same obscurities typically

Al-Maqrīzī: fortification of Mount Tabor, 1212

This year al-'Ādil encamped with his army around the citadel of Mount Tabor. He gathered artisans from all towns and employed all the emirs of the army in constructing this place and carrying the stones. Some 500 builders were employed in its erection, not counting the labourers and stone cutters. Al-'Ādil did not quit the site until the citadel was completed.

(Adapted from al-Maqrīzī, trans. Broadhurst, p. 156.)

remain, while the broader assortment of building styles evident in Mamlūk work complicates things even further.

At Ṣubayba, both round and square towers were added by the Mamlūks, but what is strange is the use of different masonry styles. Analyses of the surviving epigraphic evidence point to a single reconstruction campaign, overseen by Badr al-Dīn Bīlīk al-Khaznadār, one of Baybars' personal mamlūks. Whereas the quadrangular towers appear fairly functional, most of them built around earlier Ayyūbid towers, greater architectural grace is found in the rounded towers. The latter are quite similar to the southeast tower at Crac, which was also built under Baybars following the castle's capture in 1271.

Under the Mamlūks, when a castle was taken at the end of a siege, it was often granted to one emir while another was charged with overseeing its repair or expansion. Following the capture of Safed in 1266, Baybars made Majd al-Dīn al-Ṭawrī governor (*wālī*) of the stronghold and the surrounding region and placed 'Alā' al-Dīn Aidughdī in command of the castle's garrison. When he returned to inspect the castle the following year, the sultan took a more proactive role in developing its defences, dividing reconstruction tasks among the emirs of his army.

It was not uncommon for Muslim commanders, when building or destroying a stronghold, to assign sections or certain towers to their emirs. In 1191, Saladin had destroyed the defences of Ascalon in this way and went on to refortify Jerusalem in a likewise manner, as the Third Crusade threatened to besiege the city. Al-'Ādil distributed the task of destroying the citadel of Dārūm among the emirs of Egypt in 1196,

Al-Maqrīzī: slighting of Ascalon, 1191

On the nineteenth [of Sha'bān, 12 September] the Sultan [Saladin] arrived at Ascalon, which he wished to raze, being himself unable to hold it. He divided the towers among the emirs for demolition and great was the lamentation and weeping among the inhabitants in grief and sorrow at its razing. For it was one of the most beautifully constructed of towns, most strongly fortified in its walls, and most delightful to dwell in. The destruction and burning did not cease until the month of Sha'bān had ended [21 September].

The *Ḥāfiẓ* 'Abd al-'Aẓīm al-Mundhirī, in his book *al-Mu'jam al-Mutarjam*, says: 'I heard the illustrious Emir Iyāz ibn 'Abdallah – Abū al-Manṣūr al-Bānyāsī al-Nāṣirī – saying "When we razed Ascalon, I was given the Towers of the Templars. Khuṭluj demolished a tower on which we found inscribed 'Built by the hand of Khuṭluj' which was a most strange coincidence." Likewise, the illustrious Qadi Abū al-Ḥasan 'Alī ibn Yaḥyā al-Kātib told me: "I saw at Ascalon the Tower of the Blood while Khuṭluj al-Mu'izzī was demolishing it in the month of Sha'bān. And on it I saw this inscription: 'The construction of this tower was ordered by our illustrious master, the Emir of Armies – Badr al-Jamālī – and executed by his servant and lieutenant Khuṭluj in Sha'bān.'" I marvel at the coincidence, that it should be built in Sha'bān by a Khuṭluj and destroyed in Sha'bān by a Khuṭluj.'

(Adapted from al-Maqrīzī, trans. Broadhurst, pp. 93–4.)

and he may have leaned on the Ayyūbid princes of Syria, whom he had recently come to dominate, for assistance when he set about rebuilding the citadel of Damascus. When considering the former, this seems to have been a means of mobilizing labour, while circumstances surrounding the latter suggest it had more to do with procuring financing, as al-Manṣūr Muḥammad of Homs, who was more willing to help than others, is the only Ayyūbid prince named among the inscriptions marking the construction of the citadel's various towers. Half a century later, in 1265, Baybars distributed the work of dismantling Arsūf among his emirs in a similar fashion, forcing the defeated Hospitaller garrison to take part.

Returning to Safed, the task of rebuilding the towers of the castle was given to Sayf al-Dīn al-Zayni, though how much creative freedom the emir had is unclear. In 1268, following the capture of Beaufort, Ṣārim al-Dīn Qāymāz al-Kāfirī was made deputy (*nā'ib*), while rebuilding efforts were entrusted to Sayf al-Dīn Balabān al-Zaynī, presumably the same man who had overseen the construction of the towers at Safed. Three years later, following the surrender of Crac in 1271, Ṣārim al-Dīn Qāymāz al-Kāfirī was made governor, having received Safed earlier in 1266, while the rebuilding of the castle was delegated to 'Izz al-Dīn al-Afram and another emir. Al-Afram is again found with another 'restoring' the districts, or perhaps the castle, of al-'Ullaiqa, a recently surrendered Assassin stronghold, later the same year.

It is unclear whether these men were personally experienced or proven in the arts of fortification, or if this was rather part of their positions. 'Izz al-Dīn Aybak al-Afram was *amīr jāndār*, the emir of arms-bearers, which carried the rank of emir of a thousand and responsibility for the Mamlūk armoury and high-level executions. He was in charge of Baybars' artillery at the sieges of Caesarea, Arsūf and Safed and had been given the task of destroying the church of Nazareth in 1263. In 1275, he was among a small group charged with smoothing the banks of the Black River, the westernmost of three that flowed south into the Lake of Antioch, in order to help the army cross. He seems to have had some experience in such engineering projects as it was he who carried out the clearing and development work along the canals of the Nile during Baybars' reign. Sayf al-Dīn Balabān al-Zaynī was *amīr 'alam*, the emir of the banner, and another leading figure under Baybars. In 1264, he was sent to inspect the strongholds of Syria, to ensure they were sufficiently supplied, and to review the troops of Hama and Aleppo. It was also he who brought a trebuchet from Ṣubayba to Caesarea in 1265 and, in 1266, conveyed the artillery stored in Damascus to Safed. Ibn 'Abd al-Ẓāhir does not associate him with any other rebuilding efforts. While 'Izz al-Dīn al-Afram would appear to have had the experience to design or at least competently direct the construction of a castle, Sayf al-Dīn Balabān al-Zaynī seems to have acted in a more supervisory role, lacking direct engineering experience.

Turning to the epigraphic evidence, many Muslim building projects were commemorated with an inscription. These can be quite helpful when trying to date building phases, as they are often quite formulaic, typically including the name of the sultan, the emir who oversaw the work or whose lands the stronghold was in, and occasionally the person(s) who supervised the construction of the tower, wall or feature displaying the inscription. From these inscriptions we know that refortification efforts at Qal'at Ṣadr, which were overseen by al-'Ādil in 1182–83 on behalf of

Saladin, were coordinated by one of his emirs, Ṣārim al-Dīn Barghash al-ʿĀdilī, who appears later supervising building works at Kerak. Similarly, the name of ʿIzz al-Dīn Aybak, who carried out work on behalf of al-Muʿaẓẓam ʿĪsā, can be found on a number of strongholds, including Mount Tabor (1212) and ʿAjlūn (1214).

A number of inscriptions found at Ṣubayba also provide the names of lower figures. Among those dating to the early Ayyūbid building phase, which was completed under al-ʿAzīz ʿUthmān, some mention a figure named Abū Bakr, presumably the master builder or person who directly oversaw the work. A slightly later inscription on the large cistern in the southwestern part of the castle reveals that it was constructed in 1239–40, during the rule of al-Saʿīd Ḥasan (son of al-ʿAzīz ʿUthmān), under the supervision of Emir ʿAzīz al-Dawla Rayḥān al-ʿAzīzī, while an emir named Mubāriz al-Dīn was governor of the castle. A later Mamlūk inscription, which commemorates the reconstruction of a part of the castle during the reign of Baybars, notes that the work was carried out under Bīlīk, who held Ṣubayba as part of the *iqṭāʿ* of Bānyās. The governor of the castle at this time was a figure named Bektut, while building activities were directed by two civilians, ʿAbd al-Raḥmān and ʿAbd al-Wahhāb. These final figures were, respectively, the *muhandis* and *miʿmār*, which might, rather inaccurately, be translated as engineer and architect – the status of the latter was more akin to a repair person than a designer of buildings.

This kind of evidence can be found elsewhere. At Montreal, an inscription on one of the towers rebuilt at the end of the thirteenth century includes the names of Sultan Ḥusām al-Dīn Lādjīn (r. 1296–99), ʿAlāʾ al-Dīn Qubruṣ al-Manṣūrī, the emir who oversaw the tower's reconstruction, and a certain Muḥammad ibn ʿAbd al-Ḥamīd, the *muhandis*. Unfortunately, we know little more about this last figure or those who held this position elsewhere.

Despite the number and detail of the sources for this period, we still have few indications of who was ultimately responsible for determining the layouts of castles, the shapes of their towers and the siting of various elements. Although many lords and emirs probably provided significant input, the knowledge and experience to bring these visions to fruition was the responsibility of a master mason or *muhandis*, who combined the roles of architect, engineer and project coordinator. Below such experts were those who did more of the heavy lifting. There are references to the use of captive Franks during Saladin's construction of the citadel at Cairo and Muslim prisoners are said to have been used to help reconstruct Safed, but we know little else about the workforce used to build strongholds.

* * *

Fortifications were constructed for a number of reasons and fulfilled a plethora of functions; however, all strongholds shared a defining purpose: to keep the undesired out. Even if the surrounding countryside were suddenly flooded by a hostile army, a stronghold was an island of controllable land. Without taking a region's strongholds, an invader could hardly expect to maintain control once his army withdrew. Often built in strategic positions, in both political and geographical senses, strongholds were ideal places from which to project influence and launch raids or larger campaigns. Their garrisons could be used to boost the size of a field army and they might act as a secure place of refuge should a campaign fall subject to disaster. These capabilities, however, also made them potential bases of resistance, obstacles for powerful princes who relied more on large field armies to enforce their rule.

A vast number of factors went into the decision of where to build a stronghold. The availability of building materials and natural resources, sources of potential income and specific strategic objectives were just some of the most obvious. All strongholds, from the smallest tower to the largest castle, required the support of a local population. While many were built near existing communities, others were constructed in areas with obvious advantages, which then attracted the growth of new settlements. Local administration was often centred on these structures, as their defensibility was symbolic of the local ruler's authority – as true of the castles and towers in the countryside as of the citadels that dominated cities.

Chapter Three

Strategy of Attack: Overcoming the Obstacle of Relief

For any besieger, three fundamental questions dominated the decision to invest a stronghold or not. The first involved the relative strength of the attackers and defenders: did the besieger have sufficient forces and provisions, or access to such, to overcome the defenders and their defences, or to starve the garrison into surrender if necessary? The second was an assessment of value: how much time, money and manpower was the besieger willing to invest to take the stronghold and how aggressively was he willing to commit these resources? The third involved the probability of relief: what was the likelihood that a relief force would attempt to break the siege, how strong would it be, and when might it arrive? Even if a besieger could afford the material costs of a long siege, morale could be hard to maintain; calls to return home regularly arose during any lengthy campaign that failed or ceased to produce profitable plunder or wealth of another kind. On the defenders' side, there was an inverse equation to consider involving the same variables. How confident were they in their ability to defend their fortifications? How reliable was their potential source(s) of relief? And what terms of surrender were they willing to accept if necessary? While an attacker was often quite eager to offer generous terms at the start of a siege, this generosity typically decreased as investments of time and money mounted.

The threat posed by a potential relief army had a considerable influence on the strategy and tactics that an invading force might plan to employ. If they believed a considerable force could be assembled and brought forward quickly, the besiegers might execute a very aggressive siege, committing large numbers of men to frontal assaults or efforts to compromise the defenders' fortifications. If they believed the assembling force would be meagre, the besiegers might opt to divide their force, leaving a contingent to oppose the besieged stronghold while the remainder moved to engage the relieving army before it could break the siege or bring supplies to the defenders.

A siege undertaken with the expectation that relief would rapidly arrive carried significant risk. Alternatively, if relief was not expected to materialize quickly, besiegers had more freedom to design their approach to fit their strengths and resources. Despite the planning that went into any campaign, the unknown elements inherent in any estimation of an opponent's strength and willingness to commit to it allowed for a wide range of strategic options depending on what else was happening at the time.

Early Opportunism

The initial gains made by the Franks came about through expediency. In 1097, as the First Crusade moved through southern Anatolia, Baldwin of Boulogne and Tancred broke off from the main army and invaded Cilicia. The Muslim garrison of Tarsus surrendered, at least nominally, to Tancred and then to Baldwin, who followed with a larger force and compelled Tancred to move on. Tancred, however, found an ally in a local Armenian ruler, quite likely Oshin of Lampron, who encouraged him to capture Mamistra (al-Maṣṣīṣa), where a Latin garrison was then installed. This sideshow in Cilicia foreshadowed the way in which the Franks would take advantage of the fractious political environment over the following years, exploiting the isolation of Turkish garrisons and the rivalries among small Armenian lords.

In the autumn of 1097, while elements of the First Crusade besieged Antioch, Baldwin of Boulogne seized Turbessel and Ravandal. He then travelled to Edessa, where he became heir to the ruler of the city through an agreement of support. With the subsequent establishment of the county of Edessa, some Armenians were quick to accept Frankish suzerainty, recognizing the advantages of their support against rivals, be they Turks or fellow Armenians; others were more resistant, preferring to look elsewhere for assistance. This extended to smaller Turkish lords, such as Balduk, who sold Samosata to Baldwin and became a member of his household, though not a particularly trustworthy one, and Balak, the Artuqid ruler of Sarūj, who solicited Baldwin's help to take a Muslim town that was defying him. Before becoming king of Jerusalem in 1118, one of Baldwin II's last campaigns as count of Edessa was against the Armenian lords of northwestern Syria, which resulted in the capture of al-Bīra after a lengthy siege.

In some areas, where predominantly Turkish garrisons ruled over primarily Christian towns, some local populations, who probably interpreted the Franks as Byzantine mercenaries, rose up and expelled the Turks during the First Crusade. This took place at Turbessel in 1097 and Artāḥ the following year. Elsewhere, Muslim garrisons fled ahead of the crusaders' arrival, as took place at Marash, which the crusaders seem to have given to T'at'ul, an Armenian, who loosely held it in the name of the Byzantine emperor until he gave it to Joscelin of Courtenay years later. The garrison of Ḥārim abandoned the hilltop castle following Riḍwān's failed attempt to break the crusaders' siege of Antioch in early 1098; a few months later, the garrison of 'Imm fled when news arrived that Antioch had fallen. Both were turned over to the Franks by their Christian populations. Rather than uncalculated acts of cowardice, the Muslim garrisons appreciated their prospects of relief were dismal should the Franks turn against them – by fleeing, they secured what were essentially the best possible terms of surrender. Later in the summer of 1098, the ruler of 'Azāz took a different path, choosing to ally with the Franks against his lord, Riḍwān of Aleppo, and the town was duly relieved by Frankish forces when Riḍwān quickly moved to besiege it. Further south, power was more concentrated and Muslims outnumbered local Christians in many regions, limiting such opportunistic gains.

Relief Forces

Without the prospect of relief, there could be little hope for a besieged garrison. The norms of war placed a body of defenders entirely at the will of their captors if a stronghold fell by the sword, often resulting in death or enslavement for the defenders. Urban populations could expect the town to be thoroughly sacked, at the very least, while some degree of massacre was common and the complete enslavement of the population was not out of the question. Accordingly, a garrison was expected to hold out only as long as was reasonably possible and the vast majority of successful sieges ended with some kind of a negotiated surrender. Dying to the last man in defence of a stronghold might have been viewed by some as honourable or praiseworthy, but this was not an expectation – the stronghold was still lost and with it the lives of experienced fighters, who might otherwise have been able to help retake it.

Ultimately, it was up to a field force to break most sieges. Besiegers were typically obliged to take up vulnerable positions, focusing their attention towards the besieged stronghold and stretching their forces in order to surround or blockade it. The arrival of a sufficiently large hostile army usually compelled the besiegers to reorganize themselves, as they quickly faced threats not only from the besieged, who might launch a sally from the stronghold, but also from the field army to their rear. This pressure was often sufficient to compel the attackers to lift the siege, and either confront the relief force or withdraw so as to avoid an engagement.

In 1101, Suqmān ibn Artuq's siege of Sarūj was frustrated by the arrival of Frankish forces. Suqmān and his brother, Īlghāzī, had inherited the emirate of Jerusalem from their father, to whom it had been bestowed by Tāj al-Dawla Tutush, and it was they who had lost it to the Fāṭimids in 1098. Following their relocation to northern Syria, Suqmān had taken Sarūj and given it to his nephew Balak, who appears to have given the town to Baldwin I in 1098, at which point a Frankish garrison was installed under Fulcher of Chartres (not to be confused with the contemporary historian of the same name). Eastern Christian accounts note that Suqmān initially defeated the forces of the new count of Edessa, Baldwin II, allowing the Muslims to besiege Sarūj. The town appears to have been captured but resistance continued from the citadel. Although his initial victory had bought him time, Suqmān was unable to take the citadel before Baldwin returned with another relief force, which defeated Suqmān and effectively ended the siege. Afterwards, the sources agree that there was widespread slaughter within the city at the hands of the Franks, suggesting that a faction of the locals may have attempted to assert their independence or preferred the rule of the Artuqids, to whom the town had belonged less than three years earlier. This defiance may have been encouraged by the death of the town's Frankish lord, Fulcher, who had fallen in the first engagement between Baldwin and Suqmān. A similar siege played out in 1133 when Pons of Tripoli failed to defeat a large force of Turkoman raiders, who then besieged him in Montferrand. Pons was eventually able to slip out of the castle and make his way back to Tripoli, where he rallied a relief force and was joined by an additional contingent under King Fulk. This force then returned to Montferrand and defeated the Turkoman besiegers, compelling them to withdraw to nearby Rafaniyya.

In May 1157, Nūr al-Dīn undertook his second siege of Frankish Bānyās, having failed in his first attempt a few years earlier. The Muslims' ability to break into the town was in part due to Shīrkūh, one of Nūr al-Dīn's generals and Saladin's uncle, who defeated a small Frankish force outside Chastel Neuf, just 14km to the west on the other side of the Hula Valley, delaying relief efforts. Following his victory, Shīrkūh remained at Hūnīn (the town outside the castle), where he was able to

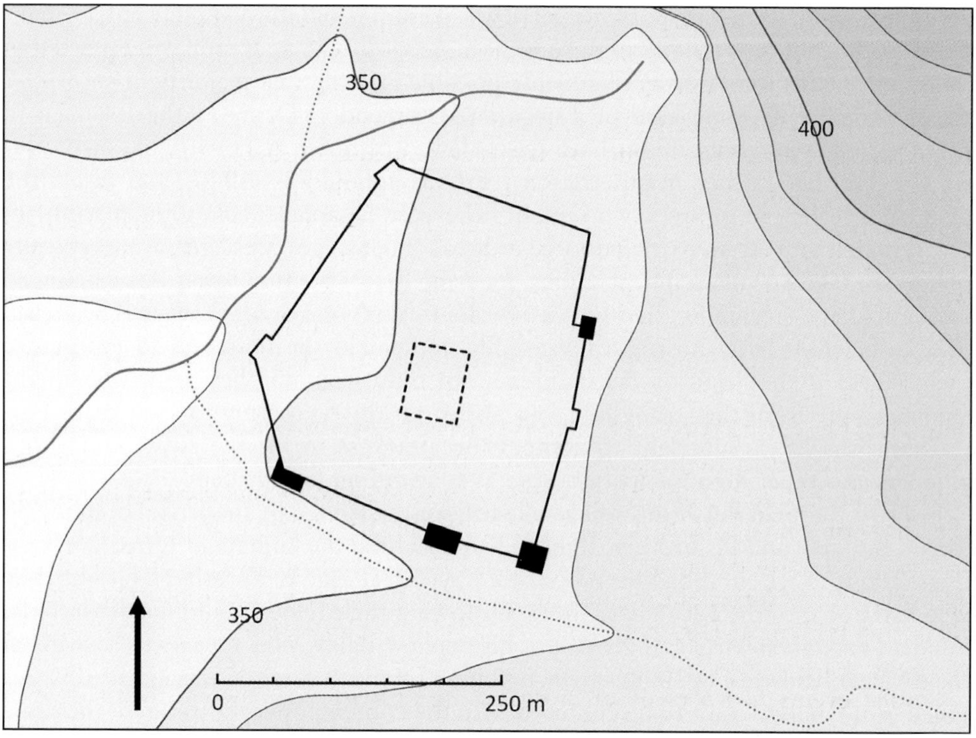

Bānyās (with topography).

monitor the crossroads leading away to Toron, Safed and Beaufort. According to Ibn al-Qalānisī, terms of surrender were offered by Humphrey II of Toron, who commanded the citadel's defence, but they were rejected by Nūr al-Dīn. This proved to be a costly error as Baldwin III soon arrived with the army of Jerusalem, surprising both Nūr al-Dīn and Shīrkūh. Although the Muslims were compelled to break the siege, Nūr al-Dīn was able to defeat Baldwin's force not long after at Jacob's Ford, allowing him to return to Bānyās and renew his siege efforts. Hugh of Scandelion, who led the defence of Bānyās after Humphrey II of Toron joined Baldwin's main army, opted not to defend the town but to concentrate on the citadel. This second siege was brief. Reynald of Châtillon, prince consort of Antioch, and Raymond III of Tripoli were already on their way with additional relief forces and Nūr al-Dīn withdrew as they approached Hūnīn, deciding not to try his luck in the field again.

The risks associated with opting to engage a relief force are revealed by events surrounding the struggle between al-Bursuqī and Baldwin II of Jerusalem for control of the region between Aleppo and Antioch. In 1125, al-Bursuqī and Ṭughtakīn besieged ʿAzaz, which dominated the plain north of Aleppo. They had undermined a section of its outer defences when a relief force arrived under Baldwin II. The Muslims turned to face the Franks but were defeated, compelling them to withdraw back to Aleppo. A year later, Baldwin II similarly broke al-Bursuqī's siege of al-Athārib, about 30km west of Aleppo near the eastern entrance of the Sarmada Pass. Rather than risk a defeat similar to that of the previous year, al-Bursuqī opted to withdraw before he could be forced into an engagement. Al-Bursuqī appreciated the risks associated with losing his army, one that may have been gathered largely from his base of support east of the Euphrates, and that defeating a relief army was no guarantee that the accompanying siege would end successfully. In 1138, the besiegers of Edessa defeated a Frankish relief force from Samosata, but they remained unable to take the city. As it turned out, Joscelin I of Edessa's final action was to relieve Kaysūn, which was besieged in 1131. The count was suffering from injuries sustained while undermining a tower months earlier, and died soon after receiving news that the Muslims had withdrawn upon the approach of his army.

The arrival of a relief force was the most common cause for a siege to be abandoned, but not all relief attempts were successful. Nūr al-Dīn's efforts to take Ḥārim in 1162 had been frustrated by a Frankish relief force; however, he was more fortunate when he returned two years later. A relief army, led by Bohemond III of Antioch, Raymond III of Tripoli, Joscelin III, titular count of Edessa, Hugh VIII of Lusignan, who was on crusade, Toros II of Armenia and Constantine Coloman (Kalamonos), the Byzantine governor of Cilicia, moved to break the siege, but this force was defeated at the battle of Ḥārim. Nūr al-Dīn had initially withdrawn to Artāḥ upon the approach of this force, but then rapidly turned on the Christians, capturing many of their leaders. Nūr al-Dīn then returned to Ḥārim and renewed his siege, taking the stronghold a few days later.

Similar events had played out in the spring of 1105, as Tancred, then regent of Antioch, competed with Riḍwān of Aleppo for control of Artāḥ. The town was a strategic stronghold at the western entrance to the Sarmada Pass, through which the road between Antioch and Aleppo ran as it crossed the Syrian Coastal Mountains. The Armenian garrison declared itself for Riḍwān, causing the forces of Antioch and Aleppo to race towards the town. Tancred arrived first and established a siege before turning the bulk of his force against Riḍwān. In the engagement that followed, Tancred emerged victorious, compelling Riḍwān to flee and allowing the Franks to take complete control of the Antioch Basin.

In 1109, 'Arqa, still in Muslim hands, requested aid from Damascus. The town was either in dire straits due to the pressure applied by the Franks loosely blockading Tripoli, or its governor, a mamlūk of the ruler of Tripoli, believed this to be an opportunity to gain greater independence from his master. In either case, the town offered its submission if Ṭughtakīn would come and take possession. Ṭughtakīn sent an officer ahead to take control of the town but the movement of his main army was hindered by winter rains and snow, delaying his arrival by two months. Sensing weakness, William-Jordan seized the moment to besiege the town. When Ṭughtakīn arrived, he declined to engage the superior Frankish force he found waiting for him, instead withdrawing to Homs as elements of William-Jordan's army harassed him along the way. 'Arqa continued to hold out, but without any prospect of relief, and its defenders ultimately surrendered when their provisions ran out.

With an army to their rear, besieging forces were typically compelled either to turn and fight or to withdraw. Very infrequently, besiegers were sufficiently strong to hold their position against the relief force that had come against them. This required exceptional focus and often considerable short-term losses: if the besiegers were not immediately distracted, it was not uncommon for the relief force to invade and plunder the besiegers' territory. The siege of Tyre in 1124 is one such rare example where the besiegers maintained their focus despite the assembly of a hostile force to their rear.

Having failed to take Tyre during an ambitious siege over the winter of 1111/12, the Franks returned at a time when Baldwin II was a prisoner of Balak. The Franks were prompted into action by the arrival of a Venetian fleet, which had come to the Levant with the intention of taking part in the siege of a significant port, for which they would expect commercial privileges once the city was taken. It was decided that they would attack Tyre rather than Ascalon, and preparations were made for a long siege. Upon their arrival, the besiegers dug two lines of defences: one cut across the isthmus to provide protection against sudden sallies by Tyre's garrison; the other, on the eastern side of the siege camp, sheltered them from the attacks of a potential relief army. The siege was indeed a long one, but the Frankish siege works proved sufficient. Attempting to pull the Franks away from Tyre, Fāṭimid raiders from Ascalon reached as far as Jerusalem. From the other direction, Ṭughtakīn moved a considerable force to Bānyās, sending raiders into Galilee and threatening to cross the Jordan and invade the kingdom in force. Neither, however, was prepared to attack the besiegers' fortified camp and the Franks were willing to endure the raids in order to continue the siege. When this became clear, and Tyre's provisions were exhausted,

Tyre (with topography).

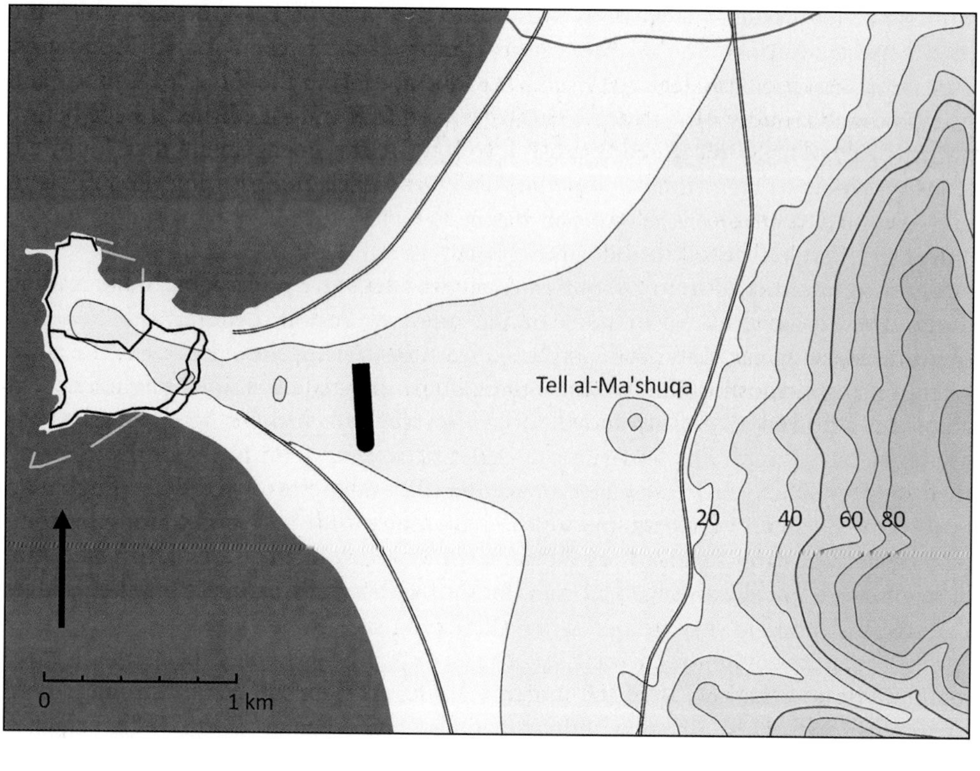

Ṭughtakīn stepped in and negotiated the city's surrender, although it was technically still under Fāṭimid rule.

The siege of Acre (1189–91) played out in a similar, if more prolonged and desperate, manner. Guy of Lusignan's inability to quickly take the city led to a protracted siege, in which the Franks, joined by successive elements of the Third Crusade, were in turn besieged by Saladin's field army. During the Fifth Crusade, the siege of Damietta was also executed with a considerable Muslim force in the region. Al-Kāmil kept the bulk of his army on the east side of the river through the first phase of the siege, pulling back to Manṣūra once the Franks gained the right bank in February 1219. Throughout both phases of the siege, the crusaders and their camps were subjected to frequent attacks.

Instances in which besiegers were not dislodged by the arrival of a relief force were rare, usually corresponding with Frankish sieges that were launched following the arrival of large groups of Europeans. The Mamlūks' dominance of the region in the years following 1260 provided them with the numbers to conduct similar operations; however, their strength was so significant that their sieges were seldom challenged by Frankish forces.

For an army unwilling to maintain a siege with a relief force to its rear, the decision whether to withdraw, cutting its losses, or to turn and fight, risking even greater losses if defeated, was critical. The defeat of a relief force typically dealt a devastating blow to the morale of the besieged, often leading the defenders to seek terms shortly thereafter, as was the case at Ḥārim in 1164. On the other hand, as came about at Bānyās in 1157, lifting a siege, even temporarily, provided the defenders with a brief respite and quite possibly the chance to bring in provisions – even if the relief force were defeated, the besiegers might be compelled to start their siege all over again.

Although the battle of Hattin drastically upset and reshaped the balance of power, the principle of relief remained the same through the thirteenth century. In 1199, the efforts of al-Ẓāhir and al-Afḍal to besiege Damascus and their uncle, al-ʿĀdil, were foiled with the arrival of a relief army led by al-Kāmil, al-ʿĀdil's son, bringing to an end a siege that had lasted six months. Ironically, the siege of Damascus had the effect of breaking another siege: al-Kāmil had been besieging Mardin until news arrived suggesting he needed to move to his father's aid. Al-ʿĀdil had initiated the siege of Mardin almost a year earlier, leaving it to al-Kāmil to complete when he returned to face brewing opposition in western Syria. The ultimately successful defence of Damascus allowed al-ʿĀdil to move on Cairo, from which point he emerged as the most powerful Ayyūbid ruler since the death of Saladin in 1193.

In January 1265, Baybars, who had become the most powerful man in the region little more than four years earlier, moved out of Cairo with his army to relieve al-Bīra. The important stronghold, which dominated a crossing of the upper Euphrates, had been invested by Mongol forces and their Armenian allies from late 1264. Moving with the main body of his army, Baybars sent an advance force ahead to support the besieged garrison and stiffen their resolve. Whether it was the size of this advance force or the foreshadowing of the larger Mamlūk army to come, the Mongols were persuaded to lift the siege and withdraw while Baybars was still at Gaza (700km away).

The Consequences of Battles

One of the ways a besieging force could avoid a relief army appearing to its rear was to engage that force before initiating a siege. Seeking an engagement in this way should not be considered in a Napoleonic sense, where annihilating an enemy's army was the key to victory; instead, it was a means of temporarily weakening an opponent to gain enough time and space to take a stronghold, and with it the surrounding region. This was the potential prize that an invading army stood to gain if it was willing to commit to battle, but seeking such an engagement was rarely planned from the outset of a campaign.

On 28 June 1119, the Franks suffered one of their greatest defeats in an engagement known as the battle of the Field of Blood. Roger of Antioch had mustered his forces in response to an invasion by Īlghāzī, taking up a position near Sarmada from which he could rapidly move to relieve al-Athārib or any other stronghold that might be invested. Although this spot allowed the Franks to shield the Antioch Basin and quickly relieve a besieged stronghold to the east, the topography limited their ability to withdraw rapidly if necessary and the surrounding hills screened the movements of some elements of the Muslim army. Rather than commit to a siege with a large force mustered against him, Īlghāzī seized the opportunity to confront the vulnerable Frankish army, surrounding it on three sides. The Franks were crushed in the battle that followed and Roger lay among the dead. Īlghāzī then sent a contingent to

Major battles.

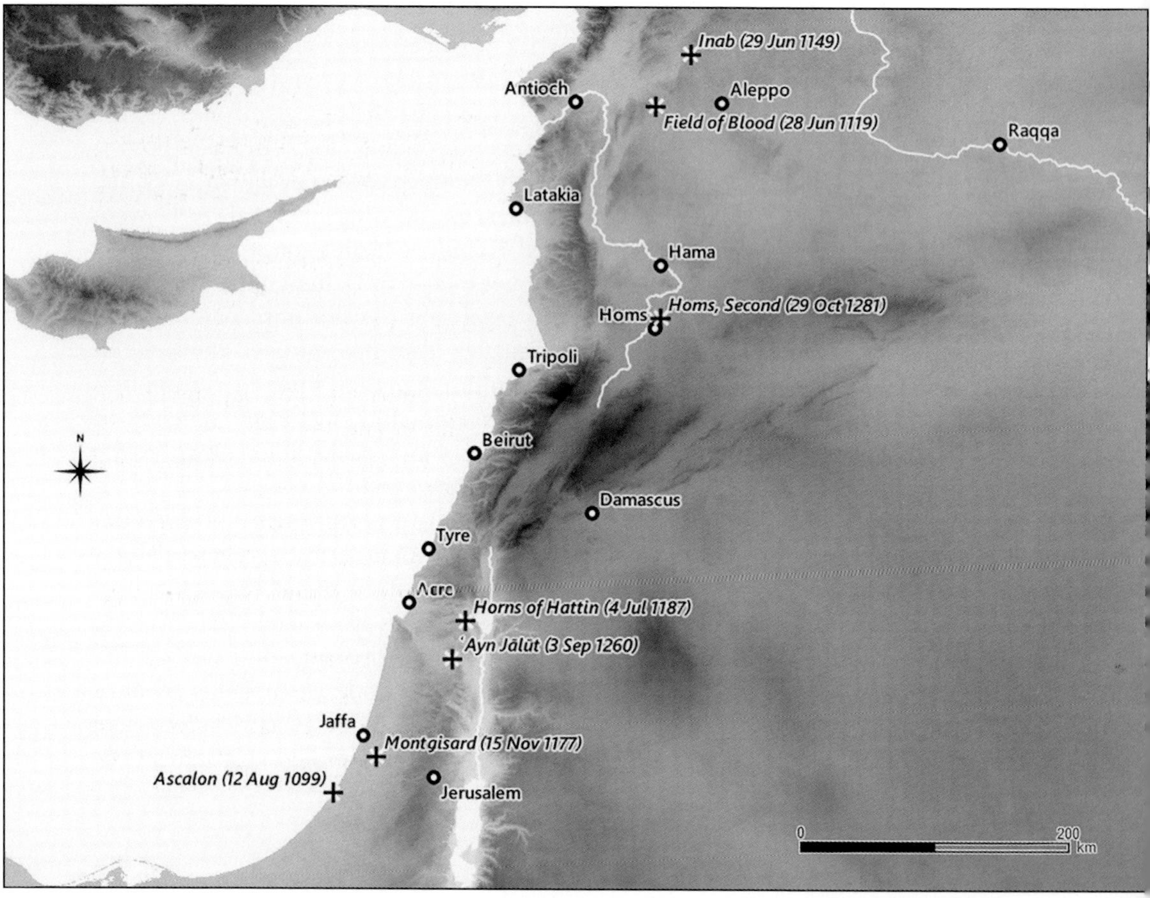

raid the region around Antioch, providing his Turkoman forces with plunder and tying down the remaining Franks in the city, while he took al-Athārib and Zardanā, which submitted with minimal opposition.

Īlghāzī's decision not to invest Antioch directly has been criticized, but it was probably quite sound. Had Antioch surrendered without much of a fight, he would then have faced the wrath of the Byzantines, who had never given up their claim to the city. If he were to be drawn into a more protracted siege, he risked the sudden arrival of another Frankish army – as would play out countless times, the defeat of one Frankish force precipitated the arrival of another soon after. As it turned out, Baldwin II soon appeared with the army of Jerusalem. Īlghāzī's measured reaction following his victory left his forces prepared to confront Baldwin's army, fighting it to a standstill on 14 August. Both sides then withdrew from the region, preventing Īlghāzī from making any further gains but securing those he had already made.

Similar events may have played out in January 1126 when Baldwin II of Jerusalem invaded the Ḥawrān. According to Ibn al-Qalānisī, the Franks planned to besiege Damascus but were prevented from doing so when Ṭughtakīn intercepted and defeated them on 25 January – Ṭughtakīn prevailing against Baldwin where Roger had failed against Īlghāzī. The reality, however, appears to have been somewhat different. When considering that forces from neither Antioch nor Edessa were involved in this campaign, nor was a significant body of crusaders, it is very unlikely that Baldwin had any intention of besieging Damascus. Revealingly, Baldwin made no attempt to garrison or defend any of the small strongholds that he captured leading up to the battle, indicating he did not intend to claim or otherwise hold the region he had invaded. The aims of this campaign were instead short-term wealth, which was gathered through raiding, and a show of force, perhaps something he hoped the Damascenes would recall when terms of a truce were next negotiated. The engagement that came about, like the battle of the Field of Blood, was probably the result of a series of circumstances rather than strategic planning: neither side had set out with the objective of drawing the other side into a major pitched battle.

One of Nūr al-Dīn's most decisive victories over the Franks took place before his power had expanded beyond the plain around Aleppo. On 29 June 1149, his army defeated Raymond of Antioch, Reynald of Marash and 'Alī ibn Wafā, the leader of the Assassins, at the battle of Inab. All three men were dead by the end of the day, allowing Nūr al-Dīn to quickly acquire Ḥārim, 'Imm and Artāḥ. His opponents had mustered against him after he had raided around Ḥārim and then settled down to besiege Inab. When the Franks approached to break the siege, Nūr al-Dīn pulled back his forces, but, learning they had made camp in the open ground around Inab, he opted to risk battle. Despite crushing his opponents in the engagement that followed, Nūr al-Dīn, like Īlghāzī thirty years earlier, opted not to attack Antioch. He decided instead to join elements of his army that had laid siege to Apamea, solidifying his control over the region north of Hama.

Many of Saladin's early campaigns against the Franks displayed greater restraint than those from 1182 onward, by which point he had humbled many of his Muslim rivals and his dominance of western Syria was near complete. In late 1178, while Saladin was busy subduing Shams al-Dīn Ibn al-Muqaddam, *muqṭaʿ* of Baalbek, the

Franks began construction of the castle at Jacob's Ford. The following May, just weeks after the death of Humphrey II of Toron, a capable northern lord and constable to the sickly Baldwin IV, Saladin took the first of a series of actions against the incomplete castle. The attack went on in some form for a week, but was probably limited to sacking the work site. Saladin returned to Bānyās in June, sending raiders towards Sidon. In response, Baldwin IV marched north to Toron and then east towards the Hula Valley, where he could observe Saladin's position, fortuitously intercepting the returning Muslim raiders on 15 June. Saladin, who had stored his baggage in Bānyās, saw his raiders fall in with the Franks and, noticing the disorganization of the latter, chose to commit his forces to a full attack. The Muslims emerged victorious and many prominent Franks were taken prisoner. Rather than push his advantage, Saladin withdrew and waited more than two months before returning to the area and finally taking the Templar castle at Jacob's Ford, overcoming its defenders while Baldwin IV was still assembling his forces at Tiberias.

The degree to which Saladin's victory in June facilitated his capture of Jacob's Ford is hard to determine, considering the castle was still incomplete and fell to the sword just six days after the Muslims arrived. However, he appears to have recognized the advantage he had gained by weakening the army of Jerusalem, which together with his consolidated power base, persuaded him to launch bolder campaigns against the Franks. It seems that he even sought to provoke the Franks into offering battle during his invasions of Galilee in 1182 and 1183. On their part, the Franks avoided a defeat by shadowing Saladin's movements, travelling between defensible positions. Small strongholds, including Baysān (Bethsan, Scythopolis), Forbelet (Afrabalā), Le Petit Gérin and others, were evacuated in 1183 ahead of the advancing Muslim army but, with the army of Jerusalem still intact, Saladin made no effort to hold them. He was finally able to bring his superior numbers to bear in 1187. Judging that the Templars' readiness to engage the raiders that had been sent across Raymond of Tripoli's lands was an indication that the Franks were more willing to fight, Saladin gave up his siege of Kerak and invaded Galilee, attacking Tiberias to further prompt the army of Jerusalem into action. This precipitated the battle of Hattin.

The consequences of the battle of Hattin were far more dramatic than those that had followed the Field of Blood or Inab, and they almost certainly exceeded any expectations Saladin may have had earlier that spring. His resources had enabled him to field an army great enough to overcome not only the army of Jerusalem but also forces from Tripoli, under Raymond III, and a contingent from Antioch that Bohemond III had sent under his son, Raymond. The weakening of all three remaining Frankish principalities removed the threat that a subsequent relief army might arrive and allowed Saladin to systematically reduce the kingdom's strongholds. The Mamlūks' victory at 'Ayn Jālūt had a similar outcome to Hattin: the defeat of the Mongol force left in Syria under Kitbugha, so far from support, essentially gifted western Syria to the Mamlūks.

Battles were fairly unpredictable and sometimes it was parties other than the principal participants that benefited most in their aftermath. In 1104, following the battle of Ḥarrān, during which the forces of Jokermish of Mosul and Suqmān ibn Artuq of Mardin bested those of Bohemond I of Antioch and Baldwin II of Edessa, it was

Riḍwān of Aleppo and the Byzantines, neither of whom had committed forces to the battle, who profited most. Riḍwān jumped on the moment of Frankish weakness and seized considerable territory in the Orontes Valley, while many towns in Cilicia, including Tarsus, Adana and Mamistra, turned away from the Franks and looked to the Byzantines for support. Ironically, although the battle had been fought east of the Euphrates and Baldwin II of Edessa, along with Joscelin of Courtney (later Joscelin I of Edessa), was taken prisoner after the battle, it was Bohemond who lost far more territory, losing it to two powers who had taken no part in the defeat of his army. Among the participants of the battle, Tancred might be considered the real victor, despite having been on the losing side. He had acted as regent of Antioch while Bohemond was a prisoner of the Dānishmands, but was left with little when he was released. With Baldwin II's capture, Tancred was quickly acknowledged as the regent of the county of Edessa and once more became regent of Antioch when Bohemond left for Europe before the end of 1104, designating the administration of Edessa to Richard of Salerno.

Distraction

Seldom was battle sought as a means to gain territory: the circumstances in which it was a practical strategy were extremely limited and the results of battles could be far from predictable. A more popular strategy was to strike while an adversary was distracted by internal issues or an invasion by a third party; alternatively, a similar situation could be created by attacking along multiple fronts. Raids were often launched during such periods of distraction, while Nūr al-Dīn used them more often than most to attack strongholds.

When Nūr al-Dīn approved Shīrkūh's intervention in Egypt, he recognized that this was not only an opportunity to enhance his wealth and extend his influence, but that it could also weaken the Franks. In 1164, while Amalric moved to counter Shīrkūh in Egypt, Nūr al-Dīn besieged Ḥārim. He had attacked Ḥārim two years earlier but was frustrated by the arrival of a Frankish relief force. Although Amalric was now distracted, a Christian coalition assembled and moved to break the siege. Nūr al-Dīn engaged and defeated this force, in what is known as the battle of Ḥārim, allowing him to take Ḥārim a few days later. Despite the advantage he had gained, Nūr al-Dīn stopped short of attacking Antioch, fearing Byzantine intervention – Bohemond III of Antioch and Constantine Coloman, both Byzantine vassals, were among those captured following the battle but they were quickly ransomed. Word reached Amalric that Ḥārim had fallen while he was besieging Bilbays, a fortified town on the eastern side of the Nile Delta, 790km from Ḥārim (as the crow flies). Learning that Nūr al-Dīn was then moving against Bānyās, the king was compelled to negotiate a truce with Shīrkūh and withdraw from Egypt.

In the aftermath of his victory outside Ḥārim, Nūr al-Dīn must have felt fairly comfortable moving against another Frankish stronghold. He dismissed the Mesopotamian components of his army and, feigning a move against Tiberias, rapidly invested Bānyās. As hoped, the garrison surrendered before Amalric and Humphrey II of Toron, the powerful lord of Bānyās and constable of the kingdom, could complete the more than 900km journey (500km as the crow flies) from Bilbays to Bānyās.

Raymond III of Tripoli was among those captured at the battle of Ḥārim, leaving Amalric regent of the county. When the king was next in Egypt, chasing Shīrkūh up and down the Nile in 1167, Nūr al-Dīn invaded the county of Tripoli and captured a number of strongholds in the Homs–Tripoli gap. It seems he bypassed Crac but that ʿAkkār was briefly taken; the castle was recaptured by the Franks around the end of 1169 or start of 1170. About a month after this campaign in Lebanon, Nūr al-Dīn launched another into Galilee. Using Bānyās as a staging point, he targeted Chastel Neuf, on the opposite side of the Hula Valley. Although it was an impressive stronghold, some members of its garrison may have accompanied Amalric to Egypt and those who remained probably recognized that they stood little chance of holding out with the kingdom's army so far away. Accordingly, the garrison set fire to Chastel Neuf and fled. Nūr al-Dīn similarly recognized the difficulties associated with holding the stronghold upon Amalric's return, leading him to complete the destruction of the castle rather than attempt to repair and then garrison it.

When Nūr al-Dīn died in May 1174, the various parties who scrambled for control of his realm used the preoccupation of others to their advantage. Saladin, who emerged the eventual victor, was aided by the rivalry between Nūr al-Dīn's nephews. Nūr al-Dīn had mediated the succession of Mosul following the death of his brother, Quṭb al-Dīn Mawdūd, in September 1170: he recognized Quṭb al-Dīn's second and preferred son, Sayf al-Dīn Ghāzī II, as ruler of Mosul; granted Sinjār as compensation to Quṭb al-Dīn's eldest son, ʿImād al-Dīn Zankī, namesake of their dynasty's progenitor; and took Raqqa for himself. As Sayf al-Dīn settled into his new position, he would have become increasingly aware that Mosul, not Aleppo, was the traditional seat of Zankid rule – upon Zankī's death, Mosul had gone to his eldest son, Sayf al-Dīn Ghāzī I, Aleppo to his second son, Nūr al-Dīn, and Homs to his third son, Quṭb al-Dīn Mawdūd, who later gained Mosul upon his eldest brother's death in 1149. Accordingly, Sayf al-Dīn was quick to offer support to his young cousin, Nūr al-Dīn's son, al-Ṣāliḥ Ismāʿīl, who had fled from Damascus to Aleppo a few months after his father's death. This, Sayf al-Dīn hoped, would pull northwestern Syria back under Mosuli influence and away from Saladin (then ruler of Egypt), who lost little time extending his influence into western Syria.

After taking control of Damascus in November 1174, Saladin moved quickly against Homs, Hama and Aleppo. He was compelled to lift his siege of Aleppo at the end of January 1175 when Raymond III of Tripoli, who had ransomed himself in early 1174, seized the opportunity to attack Homs – Saladin had taken the town but not the citadel before moving on to Aleppo. Raymond withdrew with Saladin's approach, and this time Saladin remained there until the citadel was captured on 17 March. To the east, Sayf al-Dīn Ghāzī II tasked his brother, ʿIzz al-Dīn Masʿūd, with confronting Saladin; meanwhile, he set out to besiege Sinjār and subdue their older brother, who had declared his support for Saladin. ʿIzz al-Dīn Masʿūd was defeated by Saladin near Hama on 13 April 1175, allowing the latter to briefly renew his siege of Aleppo before a truce was concluded. The defeat of his brother led Sayf al-Dīn Ghāzī II to lift his siege of Sinjār and move to support Aleppo in person, although he too was defeated by Saladin, who had been reinforced, on 22 April 1176 at Tell al-Sulṭān.

While Saladin fought with Nūr al-Dīn's kin, he remained focused on securing control of western Syria. Following his agreement to a truce with Aleppo after defeating 'Izz al-Dīn Mas'ūd in 1175, Saladin besieged Montferrand (Ba'rīn), an *iqṭā'* of one of Nūr al-Dīn's men. In the wake of his victory the following year, he shifted his focus northwards, investing and taking Buzā'a, Manbij and 'Azāz before returning to Aleppo and renewing siege efforts in late June 1176. A month later, a general peace was concluded between Saladin, al-Ṣāliḥ of Aleppo, Sayf al-Dīn Ghāzī II of Mosul, and the rulers of Mardin and Ḥiṣn Kayfā, supporters of Sayf al-Dīn. With his northern front secure, Saladin turned against the Nizārī Assassins, who had recently attempted to kill him while he besieged 'Azāz.

Multidirectional Attacks

By the early 1180s, Saladin had consolidated his position and amassed a degree of power unseen in the region since the arrival of the Franks. Whereas Nūr al-Dīn's opportunistic invasions of Frankish lands in the 1160s were often facilitated by events in Egypt, Saladin was sufficiently powerful to launch a multidirectional attack against the kingdom of Jerusalem in August 1182 with no such outside assistance. The first prong was a naval element: an Egyptian fleet would move up the coast and blockade Beirut from the sea. The second was Saladin's main army, which he kept poised in the Biqā' Valley until the fleet arrived, at which point it would attack Beirut from the landward side. As these forces pressed the city with aggressive attacks, a force from Egypt, the third prong, invaded the kingdom from the south. Unfortunately for Saladin, the southern element was too weak to distract the Franks. Baldwin IV, who had assembled his army at Ṣaffūriyya when news arrived that Saladin was on the march, remained focused on the northern elements, moving to Tyre to coordinate a relief force as soon as Saladin's intentions became clear. Perhaps hoping that he could take the city quite quickly, Saladin had not brought siege engines and instead relied on his sappers and relays of frontal assaults. After three days, having made little headway and with news that a relief force was approaching, Saladin withdrew his army from Beirut and sent the fleet away. A Frankish flotilla arrived shortly after the Muslims had departed, while Baldwin IV, taking no chances, marched the army back to Ṣaffūriyya in case Saladin turned south and struck into Galilee.

Baybars' mastery of logistics and ability to orchestrate multifaceted campaigns, facilitated by the wealth of the Mamlūk treasury, brought things to a whole new level, as seen in his elaborate push against Safed. Baybars left Egypt on 7 May 1266 and arrived at Gaza four days later. From there he arranged for the army of Homs to invade the Homs–Tripoli corridor, where it raided and captured the minor stronghold of Tuban as well as Ḥalba (Castrum Album), 'Arqa and Coliath, destroying the latter three. A part of this force then returned to Homs while the remainder joined Baybars, who had moved to Acre. From Acre, Baybars ordered a portion of his Syrian army to blockade Safed and another to oppose Beaufort, while detachments of the Egyptian army were dispatched to raid the coast around Tyre, Sidon and 'Atlit, and another contingent was sent to attack Montfort. These arrangements prevented the Franks from concentrating or even coordinating their forces, limiting resistance while disguising the Mamlūks' ultimate objective. Baybars remained in front of Acre for

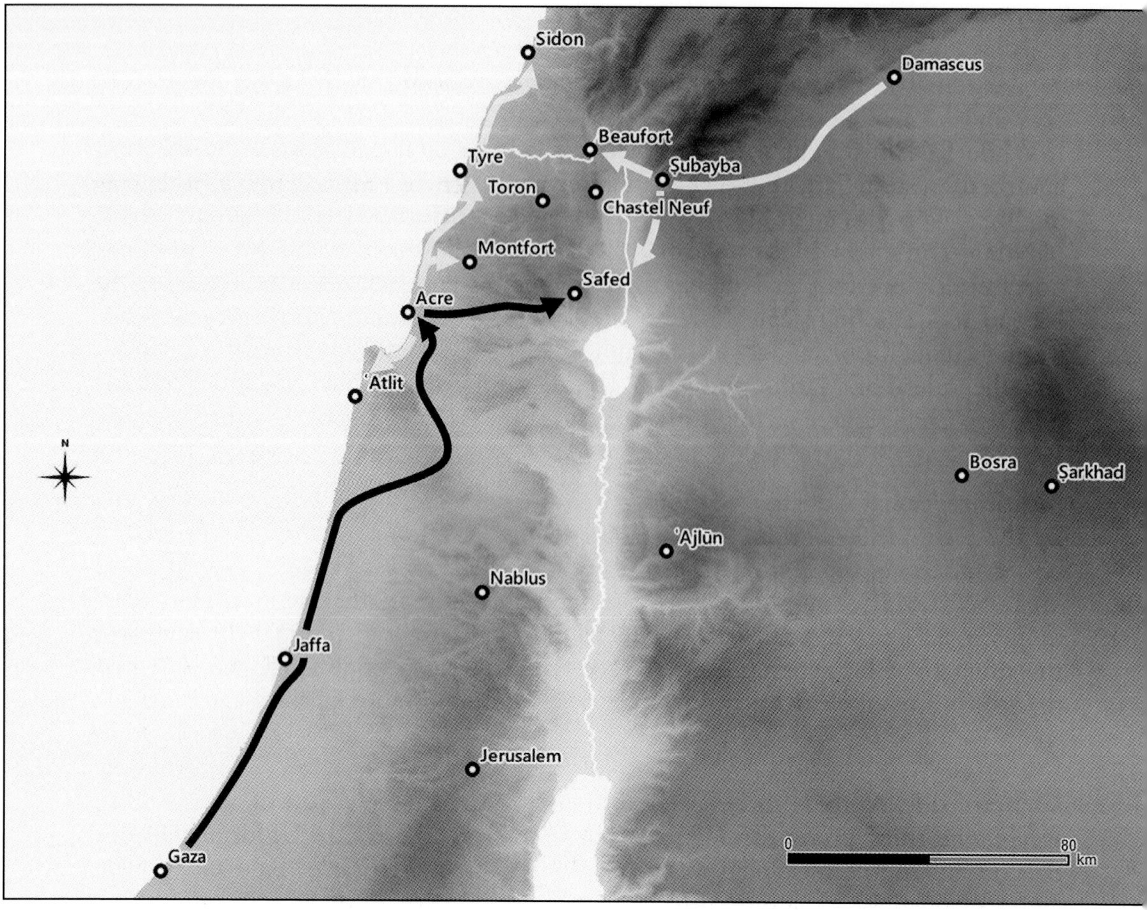

Baybars' campaign against Safed, 1266.

eight days before finally showing his hand. When his raiding parties returned, he moved his army to Safed, where a blockade was already in place. Despite the considerable force brought against it, the mighty Templar castle held out for six weeks.

Baybars similarly divided his forces when moving against Antioch in 1268. Setting out from Homs, he split his army into three groups: one was sent towards Trapessac, another to Qalʿat Simʿān (Church of St Simeon Stylites), and the third he took to Jisr al-Shughr via Apamea, reuniting them around Antioch. By dividing his forces, Baybars allowed his army to move more freely while concealing his ultimate target. Bringing his forces together again, they were able to overwhelm Antioch's defenders, storming the city's walls four days after arriving.

Opportunism

It required considerable resources to launch attacks against distant fronts, as Saladin's failed diversion in 1182 revealed. A more practical if less reliable means of achieving the same end was to take advantage of an alternative distraction. This could include an invasion by another neighbour or even an internal dispute, anything that might weaken the defending power's ability to assemble and dispatch a relief force.

The cave castle of al-Ḥabis Jaldak, perched above the Yarmūk River in the Sawād, was one of the more exposed strongholds in the frontier between the kingdom of Jerusalem and emirate of Damascus, and as such was often attacked during moments of distraction. Ṭughtakīn seized the stronghold in the winter of 1111/12, while the Franks were busy besieging Tyre. It was later retaken by Frankish forces, following the death of Baldwin I, while Ṭughtakīn was preoccupied attempting to coordinate an attack against the Franks with Fāṭimid elements at Ascalon. A more orchestrated diversion contributed to the stronghold's capture in 1182, when it was taken by Saladin's nephew, Farrukhshāh, who led a secondary force against the cave castle during Saladin's invasion of Galilee. Later the same year, while Saladin was away campaigning east of the Euphrates, the Franks launched a raid into Damascene territory, during which they captured the cave castle after a siege of three weeks. Whether the acquisition of al-Ḥabis Jaldak had been an objective of this campaign from the outset or not, Saladin's absence provided the Franks with a significant window of time during which they could besiege the stronghold without fear that a large relief force would suddenly appear to their rear.

In late 1132, Fulk, who had been king for only a few months, found himself occupied in the north, first addressing the regency of Antioch and then confronting an invasion by Sayf al-Dīn Sawār, Zankī's deputy in Aleppo. This preoccupation provided Shams al-Mulūk Ismāʿīl, who had come to power in Damascus that June, with an ideal opportunity to invest Bānyās, a Frankish possession since 1128. The town wall was rapidly undermined and the citadel, which briefly held out following the town's capture, surrendered no more than five days after the start of the siege. When Fulk was again called north in 1137, Damascene forces sacked Nablus, which lacked a town wall. Zankī similarly capitalized on the absence of Joscelin II, who was assisting his Artuqid allies, when he besieged Edessa in 1144. Uncharacteristically, the count of Edessa found himself isolated and without support when he needed it. Fulk had died the previous year, leaving Jerusalem under the rule of his widow, Melisende, who acted as regent for their young son, Baldwin III, and Raymond of Antioch was more interested in extending his influence across Cilicia following the death of the Byzantine emperor John Comnenus the year before.

Whereas Nūr al-Dīn had a hand in controlling events in Egypt through the 1160s, using them to make gains in western Syria, the Franks had benefited from conflicts in Cairo, of which they had no part, a decade earlier. Baldwin III led the army of Jerusalem against Ascalon in January 1153, accompanied by a number of crusaders who had remained in the Levant following the Second Crusade. Relief efforts were hindered when the Fāṭimid vizier, Ibn al-Sallār, was murdered in April, quite likely with the support of Usāma ibn Munqidh, who was at that time in Cairo. The eventual arrival of an Egyptian fleet at Ascalon was not enough to discourage the Franks, who maintained the siege until it was brought to a successful conclusion in August. While the Franks inadvertently benefited from the civil strife in Egypt, Nūr al-Dīn took advantage of the army of Jerusalem's preoccupation to move against Bānyās. Although a portion of the town's garrison was probably with the army at Ascalon, Nūr al-Dīn did not press the siege very hard and withdrew after only a few days – Damascus remained his main objective.

One of the very few offensives launched by the Franks against a Muslim power in the second half of the thirteenth century was led by Prince Edward of England in

1271. Having recently arrived on crusade, the prince took advantage of Baybars' distraction with a Mongol raid against Ḥarrān to attack the small stronghold of Qāqūn, a Mamlūk administrative centre that had once been part of the lordship of Caesarea. Although Baybars believed that the Franks coordinated their attack with the Mongols, the move was probably more opportunistic than collaborative. In any case, this was more an attack or raid than a siege.

Truces

Peace treaties and alliances could be concluded for a number of reasons. For rulers looking to go on the offensive, they were a means to deny a third party an opportune moment to attack while their attention and army were diverted elsewhere. Alternatively, they could be an effective way of preventing a third party from sending relief or assistance to those who were invaded. While the former may have been more common, Muslim rulers turned to the latter with increasing frequency from the late twelfth century when planning campaigns against their Frankish neighbours, who repeatedly showed a willingness to put aside their differences and march to each other's aid.

Peace during this period was something secured between individuals, acting as rulers of specific polities. Accordingly, peace agreements often ended with the death of one of the negotiating parties and, as the kings of Jerusalem and emirs of Aleppo/Damascus came to dominate more than one seat of power, agreements could be limited to certain regions. For example, in the year following the battle of the Field of Blood, Baldwin II of Jerusalem, acting as regent of Antioch, confronted a force led by Īlghāzī; after which, the two men concluded a truce. That winter, Joscelin I of Edessa remained active, raiding Aleppan lands and recovering lost territory. This led Īlghāzī's deputy in Aleppo to appeal to Baldwin, citing their truce. Baldwin, however, was able to claim that his authority, as king of Jerusalem and regent of Antioch, did not extend to the county of Edessa, and thus he had no authority over Joscelin and their truce did not extend to him; the raids continued. Although Joscelin had been Baldwin's vassal while the latter had been count of Edessa, this ended when Baldwin became king of Jerusalem and Joscelin succeeded him as count. Despite the increasing hegemony of the kings of Jerusalem, which became a serious issue of contention during the early reign of Fulk, the county remained an independent principality.

In the same way that the truce between Baldwin and Īlghāzī did not include Edessa, neither did it include the emirate of Shayzar. The small Arab lordship had previously agreed to pay Antioch an annual tribute; however, this lapsed when Roger of Salerno died at the Field of Blood. Antiochene forces thus moved against Shayzar in force, compelling the ruling Banū Munqidh to renew their tribute, for which they were granted a year-long truce.

In 1186, when the monarchy of Jerusalem was particularly weak, Reynald of Châtillon, former prince-regent of Antioch and now lord of Transjordan, went so far as to claim the right to conduct his own peace agreements. Upon his coronation, Guy of Lusignan had renewed a peace that had been in place between Baldwin V and Saladin. When Reynald, Guy's most powerful supporter, subsequently raided a caravan under Saladin's protection, Guy chastised him, but Reynald rebuked the king in turn, declaring 'he [Reynald] was lord of his land, just as he [Guy] was lord of his; and that he [Reynald] had no truce with the Saracens'.[21] Reynald, however, was not the only lord of the kingdom to claim the right to exercise his own foreign policy.

In addition to his own autonomous county, Raymond III of Tripoli held the principality of Galilee, a lordship of the kingdom of Jerusalem, on behalf of his wife, Eschiva Bures, following their marriage in 1174. Unlike Reynald, Raymond was on good terms with Saladin and in open opposition to Guy of Lusignan. In early 1187, Raymond allowed an armed party of the sultan's raiders to pass through his wife's lands, and thus into the kingdom, under the conditions that they withdraw back across the Jordan by nightfall and disturb no property. It was these raiders that encountered and defeated the force of Templars heading from La Fève to Tiberias near the springs of Cresson. Although a small battle took place, the Muslims nevertheless withdrew from Frankish lands before nightfall, keeping to their agreement with Raymond.

Reynald of Châtillon is typically vilified and blamed for bringing about the battle of Hattin, while Raymond III of Tripoli is often presented as a champion of peace. But by allowing raiders to roam his lands, Raymond established the conditions that led to the engagement at the springs of Cresson. It was this that persuaded Saladin to give up his blockade of Kerak, which he had undertaken in response to Reynald's raid on the caravan, to seek a greater prize further north. Although it can be hard to see these events independent of the broader context leading up to the battle of Hattin, both Reynald and Raymond were claiming a considerable degree of baronial autonomy during a period of monarchical weakness.

Although most peace agreements were respected, sometimes opportunities were simply too good to pass up. For example, in the spring of 1110, Mawdūd of Mosul led an army from the Jazīra against Edessa, compelling King Baldwin I to march his army to its relief as soon as he completed his siege of Beirut on 13 May. Mawdūd pulled back with the advance of the Franks, but then struck as they turned to withdraw, ambushing the Frankish army as it re-crossed the Euphrates. Riḍwān of Aleppo evidently thought that this was a greater defeat for the Franks than it turned out to be. Seizing what he believed to be an opportune moment, he broke his truce with Tancred and raided lands in the principality of Antioch. The move backfired. With their peace broken, Tancred besieged and took al-Athārib before demanding a considerable tribute from Riḍwān to renew their truce.

For figures whose lands were particularly exposed, due to the expanse of their realm or strength of their neighbours, tactical peace agreements were particularly valuable. Īlghāzī's acquisition of Aleppo in 1117 forced him to split his focus between the Jazīra and western Syria. In 1121, he ordered his son, Shams al-Dawla, who administered Aleppo on his behalf, to conclude a truce with the Franks according to whatever terms they dictated, ratifying this agreement in person before returning east of the Euphrates. Īlghāzī used this interval to gather his eastern forces and returned to western Syria in June 1122, at which point he besieged Zardanā. While Īlghāzī had orchestrated this peace to buy time, Nūr al-Dīn was the main beneficiary of a later truce he had no part in arranging. Whether coincidental or intended, a two-year peace concluded between Damascus and Jerusalem in the spring of 1149 allowed elements of the Damascene army to join a push by Nūr al-Dīn (then ruler of Aleppo) against the principality of Antioch. The campaign that followed would be distinguished by the battle of Inab and Nūr al-Dīn's acquisition of Ḥārim.

Until it collapsed in the decade following Zankī's capture of Edessa in 1144, the county of Edessa, which straddled the Euphrates, proved a thorn in the side of Muslim rulers who held Aleppo as well as lands in Mesopotamia, notably Īlghāzī, who also held Mardin, and Zankī, whose principal seat of power was Mosul. Travelling via Manbij and the Euphrates crossing at Qalʿat Najm, Mardin and Aleppo are separated by a journey of 400km, regardless of whether the northern or southern route is taken, via Edessa or Ra's al-ʿAyn respectively. From Mosul, the southern route to Aleppo, via Sinjār and either Qalʿat Najm or Raqqa, is almost 600km, slightly shorter than the northern route, via Nisibis, which is better watered but closer to the Frankish sphere of influence.

Even after Frankish rule withdrew west of the Euphrates, Nūr al-Dīn and later Saladin were often compelled to make peace with the Franks before campaigning in the Jazīra or southeastern Anatolia. In May 1155, Nūr al-Dīn negotiated a one-year peace with Antioch and concluded a similar peace with Jerusalem a few months later. Although the latter obliged him to pay a tribute of 8,000 Tyrian dinars, it freed Nūr al-Dīn to campaign against ʿAyntāb and the region that had formerly belonged to the county of Edessa. In the summer of 1175, Saladin similarly made peace with the Franks, allowing him to focus on Aleppo and Sayf al-Dīn Ghāzī II of Mosul. Five years later, Saladin arranged another peace in order to move against Qilij Arslān II of Rūm, assisting Nūr al-Dīn Muḥammad of Ḥiṣn Kayfā, and then campaign against the Armenians.

Saladin's decision not to arrange a peace with the Franks before campaigning in the Jazīra through 1182–83 was significant. As he attempted to strengthen his rule east of the Euphrates, the Franks were almost compelled to strike in his absence, in order to show Saladin that they were still a threat worthy of consideration. Two invasions were launched from the kingdom of Jerusalem: the first was a raid towards Damascus, following which the Franks paused to take al-Ḥabis Jaldak on their return; the second was a more ambitious and complex series of actions. In December 1182, Baldwin IV took the main army and raided towards Damascus, as had been done weeks earlier. Further south, Raymond III of Tripoli led a secondary force against Bosra, which the Franks had not threatened since Nūr al-Dīn had acquired Damascus. The third, and by far the most famous and damaging to Saladin's reputation, was undertaken by Reynald of Châtillon. Having constructed prefabricated boats at Kerak, Reynald arranged for them to be moved overland to Aqaba. From there, raiders preyed on the unfortified ports along the coast of the Red Sea, threatening Mecca and Medina, the holiest sites in Islam. Despite stretching his hegemony across most of the Jazīra and acquiring Aleppo at the end of his campaign, Saladin was unable to effect a blow to the Franks comparable to that which Reynald had dealt his image and perhaps pride. He invaded Galilee but the Franks declined battle, shadowing his force from a series of strong and well-watered positions. The effect Reynald's raid had on Saladin is evident in the focus the sultan subsequently devoted to him, besieging Kerak twice in the twelve months following his withdrawal from Galilee in October 1183. A peace was later concluded between Saladin and the kingdom of Jerusalem following the death of Baldwin IV in March 1185, allowing Saladin to make one more (unsuccessful) attempt to take Mosul. It was the renewal of this peace, following the coronation of Guy of Lusignan in the late summer of 1186, that Reynald later disregarded, contributing to the events leading up to the battle of Hattin.

Although the battle of Hattin transformed the political landscape of the Levant, the utility of truces remained. Saladin crippled the principality of Antioch during the summer of 1188, but he was unable to complete its conquest. At the start of the campaign, Saladin had arranged for his son, al-Ẓāhir Ghāzī, and nephew, Taqī al-Dīn ʿUmar, to move into a position to threaten Antioch, tying down Bohemond III as Saladin led his main army through the county of Tripoli and then north into the principality of Antioch. Reluctant to invest the city of Antioch directly through the winter – his army was already growing restless – Saladin forced Bohemond to agree to a truce. This allowed Saladin to disband most of his army for the winter and freed him to return south to stamp out remaining resistance in Palestine.

By the time Mamlūk authority spread across Syria, the nature of royal power in the kingdom of Jerusalem had changed. The monarchy, often represented by a *bailli* (an administer who acted on behalf of a minor or absentee monarch), negotiated truces that extended only to royal lands, which were concentrated around Acre. This left the kingdom's most powerful lords, including those of Beirut, Jaffa and Tyre, the latter two lordships having passed out of royal control, free or obliged, depending on the circumstances, to secure their own diplomatic arrangements.

When Baybars travelled to Damascus in May 1261, he entertained Frankish emissaries and showed himself willing to secure peace with Acre, Jaffa and Beirut, allowing him to solidify his position and ensuring Mamlūk trade continued to flow through Frankish ports. Five years later, as he arranged his forces around Safed, Baybars received representatives from the lords of Jaffa, Beirut and Tyre, as well as the Assassins, reproaching them all on various pretexts. After taking Safed, he travelled to Damascus, where he received a Hospitaller delegation and tentatively agreed to extend the peace in place with the order. It was not until the following year that the ten-year peace agreements negotiated with the Hospitallers and Tyre were confirmed, by which point Baybars had taken Chastel Neuf and Toron, which had both become parts of the lordship of Tyre, and destroyed the Hospitallers' mill outside Acre. A truce with Beirut was also confirmed around this time, while overtures of peace from Sidon were rejected.

Jaffa was conspicuously left out of the peace agreements confirmed in 1267. The town was by this time isolated and exposed: to the north, Arsūf and Caesarea had been captured in 1265, and the death of John of Jaffa in 1266 left the town without the protection of a peace agreement. The circumstances were thus ideal when, in early 1268, Baybars found himself in Palestine, having mobilized his forces to confront a Mongol attack on Aleppo that failed to materialize. When envoys from Jaffa moved out to greet the Mamlūk army, Baybars had them detained, ordering his forces to launch sudden attacks against the town. The citadel surrendered later the same day.

In a move that has puzzled historians, Baybars agreed to surprisingly generous terms when negotiating a peace with envoys from Acre in April 1272. Once more marching his army through Palestine to confront a Mongol threat to the north, Baybars relinquished a number of estates that the Franks had not held under their previous peace agreement. Baybars' power had increased since that time, so why he felt the need to make these concessions in order to secure his rear is unclear.

Rapid Attack

The main aim of a rapid or surprise attack was to catch the defenders of a stronghold off-guard. By preventing the defenders from preparing themselves sufficiently, attackers hoped to shorten the potential length of a siege, either by overcoming the stronghold's defences relatively quickly or by forcing the defenders to seek terms of surrender before a relief force could be assembled. An example of an attack like this was Baybars' capture of Jaffa in 1268. The Mamlūks' overwhelming superiority was such that the suddenness with which they attacked Jaffa was probably more of a precaution than a necessity, conceived with a desire to avoid the costs of a longer siege. Baybars launched similar, if far less successful, sudden attacks against Acre in 1263, 1267 and 1271. On each occasion, he found the city prepared and his forces had to content themselves with raiding the surrounding gardens. For adversaries on a more equal footing, shortening the period of time that defenders could hold out was one of the easiest ways that attackers could try to avoid the complications associated with the arrival of a relief force.

In 1115, while Baldwin I and the army of Jerusalem were to the north confronting the Seljuk army led by Bursuq ibn Bursuq of Hamadan, an Egyptian force, supported by a fleet, attacked Jaffa. The Fāṭimids attempted to take the town by surprise, rushing its defences with ladders they had brought. Although the attackers managed to burn parts of the town gates, the defenders were able to keep them back from the walls for the most part. Foiled, the besiegers withdrew after a few days, the land force returning to Ascalon while the fleet proceeded to Tyre, which was still under Muslim rule. Another attack was carried out ten days later, but this lasted only a few hours and also failed. In October of the same year, Ṭughtakīn led a similar attack against Rafaniyya, finding greater success. Marching through the night without any baggage, the Muslim army surrounded the town, which had only recently fallen into Frankish hands, and successfully broke in before dawn.

Zankī successfully took Edessa in 1144 after a concerted siege, but his death two years later, while besieging Qalʿat Jaʿbar, provided Joscelin II with an opportunity to reclaim his patrimony. Leading a small force, Joscelin scaled Edessa's walls one night and retook the town, but was unable to gain entrance to the citadel. Nūr al-Dīn, who had inherited Edessa along with Aleppo following Zankī's death, wasted little time in bringing a force to relieve the citadel's garrison. Even with the support of the Armenian population, Joscelin had little chance of holding the town and fled with his force upon Nūr al-Dīn's arrival.

During Saladin's multipronged attack against Beirut in 1182, the main army approached the city by crossing the Lebanon. The rugged path they took over the mountains prevented Saladin from bringing any heavy baggage, but allowed him to appear suddenly from an unlikely direction. Without siege equipment, he was limited to using his miners and frontal attacks, but Saladin's sappers proved unable to repeat

Ibn al- Athīr: Nūr al-Dīn's capture of Munayṭira, *c.*1166

This year Nūr al-Dīn Maḥmūd ibn Zankī conquered the fortress of Munayṭira in Syria, which was in the hands of the Franks. He made no great mobilization, nor assembled all of his forces. He just marched lightly equipped and took them unaware. He knew that, if he assembled his army, the Franks would be on their guard and concentrate their troops. He seized the opportunity, marched to Munayṭira and put it under siege, attacking energetically. He took it by storm and killed or made captive those within and took large amounts of booty. The defenders had felt safe but God's cavalry overwhelmed them suddenly before they were aware. The Franks gathered to repel him only after he had already taken it. Had they known that he was lightly equipped with a small number of troops, they would have hastened against him, but they imagined that he led a large host. After he had taken it, they dispersed and despaired of recovering it.

(Adapted from Ibn al- Athīr, trans. Richards, 2:161.)

the success they had achieved against the far less impressive defences of Jacob's Ford, which they had compromised in less than a week three years earlier. Having achieved little, and with a Frankish relief force approaching, Saladin cut his losses after three days and withdrew.

In 1167, Nūr al-Dīn had made a similar move against Munayṭira, taking advantage of Amalric's absence in Egypt. Leaving his baggage behind, Nūr al-Dīn besieged and took the castle, on the mountain road between Baalbek and the coast, before a Frankish relief force could be assembled. Baybars also employed this tactic in the spring of 1268. After taking Beaufort, he sent detachments out in different directions to conceal his objective, as he often did, leading his main force to Bānyās, where he sent his baggage and siege equipment to Damascus. He then continued on to Baalbek, from where he set out across the mountains to surprise Tripoli. Like Saladin's attack on Beirut, Baybars had little chance against Tripoli's stout urban defences, even with the element of surprise, so avoided a siege of the city and spread his forces through the area, raiding and taking a number of towers and minor cave castles. Baybars repeated this manoeuvre to the north when he set out to attack Margat in January 1270. Leaving his baggage on the eastern side of the Syrian Coastal Mountains, he led a cavalry force towards one of the mountain passes. The season proved to be his undoing. Although an attack would not be expected in the middle of winter, the rains were severe and he was forced to turn back. Undeterred, he made a second attempt about twenty days later but was again forced to turn around after entering the territory of the Nizārī Assassins.

* * *

Far more went into a siege than simply overcoming a stronghold's defences. Although this was the defining part of a siege, success or failure was often determined by more distant elements. No stronghold was designed to hold out indefinitely; each was reliant on the prospect of relief – the least predictable and greatest challenge for besiegers. Avoiding the interference of a relief force could be done in a number of ways, which might include: striking fast, denying the defenders and a potential relief force the chance to prepare themselves; choosing a moment when relief would be weak or slow to assemble; or securing a peace, which might limit the size of a potential relief force and minimize the chances of a counterattack elsewhere. If a relief force arrived, besiegers were typically left with the option to turn and engage it, hoping to defeat it so that they could return to the siege free from this threat, or to cut their losses and withdraw, avoiding the uncertainty of battle.

Chapter Four

Means of Attack: Siege Weapons

Facing a defended stronghold, an attacker had three tactical options: to attempt to overcome the defenders and their fortifications by force; to establish a blockade and wait until the besieged ran out of provisions; or to seek control through negotiations. The third option might include discussions with the stronghold's commander regarding mutually acceptable terms of surrender, or more clandestine talks with a person of lower status, who might be willing to help the besiegers gain entrance in exchange for suitable compensation. Regardless of where a stronghold was located, how large it was or what it looked like, each besieger was faced with this same set of options, and siege strategies more often than not incorporated measures to gain success through two of them, if not all three.

Armies

When examining the tactics and siege methods exhibited by various Frankish and Muslim forces, it is important to keep in mind the context and broader strategic aims of each campaign, as well as the differences between most Frankish and Muslim armies. Very generally, Frankish forces, at least at the highest echelons, were more heavily armoured, giving them an advantage in close-quarter fighting. This influenced the Franks' preference for siege towers during the early twelfth century, which allowed them to bring their forces to a particular point along the top of a wall, compelling the defenders to fight man-to-man. Muslim and Mongol forces, by comparison, tended to be more mobile and more numerous, especially in the thirteenth century, employing proportionally greater numbers of bows. This allowed these forces to commit more men to attacks along multiple fronts, supporting direct actions with showers of arrows.

Franks

The essence of power in Frankish society carried an obligation of combat: boys born into the nobility typically became knights or clergymen – they would fight for their lord or for God. Accordingly, although the knightly class, which fought as heavy cavalry, rarely if ever made up the majority of an army, as a section of society, it was disproportionately represented. This core fighting force was supplemented by sergeants, who fought on horseback but are known to have also fought on foot in some instances. To counter the Muslims' lighter cavalry, and disrupt their horse archers in particular, the Franks made use of their own irregular cavalry, known as turcopoles, who were recruited from local Christian communities or were of mixed Frankish-Syrian ethnicity.

Frankish infantry was raised from among the burgesses and almost certainly included significant numbers of local Christians. As in Europe at the time, the poor and most 'common folk' were typically excluded from the battlefield, due to the cost of weapons and personal equipment – the infantry was far from a body of conscripted peasants. Instead, many of these individuals would have been land owners, some would have been tradesmen, and others labourers. Regardless of their occupation, many would have had previous fighting experience. For men wealthy enough to afford arms, joining the army (a temporary commitment) was a means of helping secure Frankish interests, which in turn benefited their own safety and livelihood. Most who took part, however, would have been drawn by the prospect of wealth – they could expect both pay and plunder, if they survived.

Mercenaries, the private security contractors of their day, made up another part of many armies. They were typically recruited as preformed units, rather than individually, and as such often hailed from a common region and tended to specialize in a certain style of warfare, equipping themselves accordingly. These were individuals who fought primarily for cash, rather than any socio-political incentive. Some, who regarded war as a lucrative profession, came from wealthier elements of the common class, while others were members of the nobility, who saw more profit to be gained by fighting for cash rather than taking their position in the traditional political structure.

Muslims

Turkish armies, which had come to dominate the Near and Middle East with the spread of the Seljuks, were typically more lightly armed than the Franks. They often relied on large numbers of horse archers, who could engage and disengage rapidly, waiting for an opportune moment at which to commit their forces to a close fight. The core of these forces was the *'askar*, a regular force of cavalry that fought for a certain potentate. During the twelfth century, considerable numbers of Turkomans were also employed. These were recruited from regions like Khurasan, where semi-nomadic groups from the Eurasian Steppe, many of whom had only recently or loosely embraced Islam, were migrating into the Middle East. These men were often used as irregular cavalry and fought largely for plunder, making them exceptional raiders but less than ideal siege troops, prone to restlessness when plunder was not forthcoming. Bedouin forces were also recruited by both Egyptian and Syrian figures. Like their Turkoman counterparts, Bedouins often fought as irregular forces and were motivated by prospects of plunder. When the army they joined was defeated, it was not unheard of for Turkoman and Bedouin forces to loot their own side's camp, securing what they could from an otherwise disastrous campaign. Many Bedouin groups were also not opposed to allying with Frankish forces if it served their interests. During certain periods, Muslim armies also benefited from significant numbers of volunteers, who answered the call of jihad. Not unlike European crusaders, most seem to have been motivated foremost by spiritual factors, travelling to take part in the fight against the Franks and then returning to their homes.

By all accounts, Fāṭimid armies were fairly diverse during the twelfth century, employing various units of cavalry and infantry. Like the Seljuks, the Fāṭimids made use of considerable numbers of 'foreigners' recruited from the fringes of their territory. The regiments of Africans from the Sudan and Ethiopia frequently caught the attention of contemporary Frankish historians, while the influence of high-level

Armenian figures led to large numbers of individuals whose ethnic homelands were around the Caucasus. This led Fāṭimid armies to include both Shiite and Sunni forces, as well as regiments of openly Christian Armenians. Fāṭimid forces were so religiously and ethnically diverse because, unlike their Frankish and Turkish neighbours, these 'foreign' elements made up the core of their army.

Although most Muslim powers in the region depended on mamlūks (slave-soldiers) to at least some extent in the twelfth century, these formed a more significant part of the Fāṭimid army than those of contemporary Turks. Through the Ayyūbid period, Muslim rulers became increasingly reliant on bodies of mamlūks, who were bought as children and raised as Muslims to become soldiers in the service of their owner. From the late twelfth century through the thirteenth, these individuals often came from Christian, Cuman and Kipchak populations around the Black Sea. With the ascendancy of the Mamlūk dynasty, mamlūks remained the core of the army, often enjoying higher preference than the free-born sons of other mamlūks.

Action beyond the Walls

Before a besieger attempted to overcome the fortifications of a castle or town, considerable attention might be devoted to developing siege works or overcoming resistance from the defenders who ventured out beyond the stronghold's walls. Almost all sieges involved some kind of effort to impose a blockade or surround the besieged community, even if this involved only scouting the defences for weaknesses or intercepting appeals for aid sent by the garrison. For defenders, keeping an open link to the outside world could be critical to their continued resistance, often leading them to take steps to inhibit the attackers' efforts to cut them off.

If a siege were expected to drag on for a considerable period of time, or it was believed that the defenders would put up a particularly active defence, besieging forces might reinforce their position with a ditch, dug between their camp and the stronghold, to limit the threat posed by sallies. This was done by Tancred at al-Athārib (1110–11), and more famously by the Frankish besiegers of Tyre (1111 and 1124) and Acre (1189–91). At each of the latter three sieges, an additional ditch and defences were excavated beyond the Franks' position to provide protection against field forces to their rear. During the siege of Damietta (1218–19), the crusaders entrenched themselves in a similar manner, providing a degree of protection against the Egyptian forces that attempted to break the siege. Elaborate siege works like these required considerable investments of time and effort, which besiegers rarely appear to have been willing to risk – the costs associated with developing such works left besiegers with more to lose if the siege failed.

Nevertheless, the incentive to build siege works becomes clear when considering the references to the fighting that went on outside some strongholds, especially urban centres, during the early phases of certain sieges. The Franks first encountered this at the siege of Antioch in 1097–98, where the defenders were able to launch effective sallies, and significant engagements appear to have been fought in front of the single landward gate of Tyre in 1124 and 1187. It is perhaps at the numerous 'sieges' of Damascus during the middle decades of the twelfth century that this fighting practice can be seen most clearly. During the Frankish attacks in 1129 and 1148, as well as during the many pushes against the city made by Zankī and Nūr al-Dīn before 1154, at no point did a ladder hit the top of a wall or a sapper begin to undermine a tower. Zankī and Nūr al-Dīn may have shown restraint, hoping to win over the Damascene population they meant to rule and facilitate a smooth transition of power, but this cannot be said of the Frankish campaigns. In the autumn of 1129, the Damascenes' ability to rally and intercept a large Frankish army, led by Baldwin II, who was joined by Pons of Tripoli, Bohemond II of Antioch, Joscelin I of Edessa and Fulk of Anjou (later Fulk of Jerusalem), prevented the Franks from establishing a siege. In 1148, during the Second Crusade, led by Louis VII of France and Conrad III of Germany, the city's defenders again managed to skirmish successfully in the gardens of the city, delaying any formal siege efforts until conflict among the various besieging parties led to the complete collapse of the expedition.

Attacks like these were in essence large coordinated sallies, intended to interfere with the besiegers' ability to organize their siege efforts or to catch them off guard, weakening their strength and compromising their morale. Describing the protracted siege of Ascalon in 1153, Ibn al-Athīr remarked, 'The inhabitants held firm and fought fiercely, some days even fighting outside the city wall. They repulsed the first group of Franks and drove them defeated back to their tents, pursuing them all the way. At that stage the Franks despaired of taking the city.'[22] During the early phase of the siege of Acre in 1189, the numerical weakness of the Franks allowed the defenders to leave the city gates open, facilitating rapid sallies and forcing the Franks to keep a diligent watch lest they be surprised. Acre's defenders were assisted by the presence of Saladin's army, which had arrived only days after the Franks and compelled the besiegers to divide their forces in order to guard against attacks made by the field army. The city's gates remained open from the start of the siege at the end of August until 16 October, when Saladin pulled back his army to al-Kharruba, about 12km from Acre's walls. The Frankish defenders of Jaffa mounted a similar defence in 1192, engaging Saladin's besieging forces beyond the town walls during the first three days of the siege. This disruption may have bought precious time, delaying Saladin's ability to challenge the town's defences and allowing Richard I to arrive just in time to prevent the citadel's capture. Actions like these continued throughout the thirteenth century.

Reminiscent of the manoeuvres executed in 1129 by the defenders of Kafarṭāb and Damascus, Bohemond VI of Antioch-Tripoli intercepted Bertrand of Gibelet (Jubayl) as the latter moved against Tripoli in the late 1250s. Although Bohemond's force was defeated and the prince was wounded, the action was sufficient to discourage a siege.

When Baybars attacked Acre in 1263, he did so with only part of his army, making a surprise appearance before the city one morning. He spent the first day surveying Acre's defences while a contingent began undermining Doc, a fortified mill belonging to the Templars. The following day, Baybars awoke to find Frankish forces deployed in a prepared position outside the city. Although the Franks were eventually pushed back into Acre, they successfully defended its gates during the attacks that followed. This was probably a test of strength and show of force, rather than an earnest effort on the part of Baybars to take the city. The sultan was wary of

Templar of Tyre: digging in against Acre, 1291

The Muslims remained for eight days before Acre, doing nothing besides engaging in the occasional clash between our forces and theirs, in which a few were killed on either side.

At the end of the eight days, they brought up and emplaced their siege engines . . . They set up great barricades and wicker screens, ringing the walls with them the first night, and the second night they moved them further in, and the third night further still, and they brought them so far forward that they came up to the lip of the fosse. Behind these screens the armed men dismounted from their horses, bows in hand. And if you are wondering how they were allowed to draw so near, the answer is that they could not be stopped, as I shall now explain.

These people had their horsemen fully armed, on armoured horses, and they stretched from one side of the city to the other, that is to say, from the beach on one side to the beach on the other. There were more than 15,000 of them, and they worked in four shifts a day, so that no one was overworked. None of our men went out against those who were behind the screens, for if they had, those who were being [the first enemy line] would have defended them and barred the way, and so if it had happened that our men had gone out against them, the men on horseback would have defended them.

So in the end, the Muslims advanced to the edge of the fosse, as I have told you, and the men on horseback each carried four or five *buches** on the necks of their horses, and threw them down behind the screens. And when night came, they put them in front of the screens, and bound a cord on top, and the pile became like a wall that no engine could harm, though some of our medium engines shot and battered at it without effect. The stones merely rebounded into the fosse.

After this, the enemy brought up their *carabohas*, small hand-operated Turkish devices with a high shooting rate which did more damage to our men than the larger engines did, since in the places where the *carabohas* were shooting, no one dared to come out into the open. In front of the *carabohas* they had made the rampart so strong and so high that no one could strike or shoot at those who were shooting. And this situation lasted as long as they were mining . . .

* Bundles of wood and other materials used by besiegers to fortify their siege works.

(Adapted from Templar of Tyre 490–1 [254–5], trans. Crawford, pp. 105–7.)

committing his forces to a potentially lengthy siege with the Mongol threat still looming, but, like his later attacks in 1267 and 1271, he may have hoped to surprise Acre's defenders and took the opportunity to thoroughly raid the surrounding region.

In 1290, Qalāwūn decided to bring the full weight of his army against Acre, but his untimely death meant that it was his son, al-Ashraf Khalīl, who would lead the Mamlūks against the city the following year. The siege saw a considerable period of fighting beyond Acre's walls before siege efforts progressed and the defenders were pushed back into the city. The besiegers then entrenched their positions beyond the town ditch and steadily undermined the city's defences.

Siege Engines

If a besieging army opted for an aggressive strategy, this would often include the use of siege engines. Before discussing what these looked like and how various types were employed, it is important to point out that contemporary descriptions of siege machinery should be viewed critically. Very rarely do independent accounts give similar descriptions of the particular engines used at a certain siege; often, different engines are mentioned by different sources. To complicate matters, some sources had a tendency to include engines they believed 'might' or 'should' have been present at a siege when their information or understanding was incomplete. Most Frankish sources were clerics, typically strangers to the battlefield, and some were not above providing descriptions influenced by classical authors, believing this would give their work greater prestige or credence. In some accounts, regardless of the author's ethnicity, it is possible to discern a learning curve as the author, who might otherwise have little exposure to siege warfare, gained greater insights through the compilation of his history. The initial or continued ignorance of others is often revealed through what are evident additions, containing obvious mistakes or misinterpretations, to the original account they were provided. At times, even the most reliable chroniclers and eyewitnesses with military experience recounted things with tunnel vision, focusing only on their part, that of their patron, or some other aspect during an engagement that they wished to emphasize, doing so at the expense of a more complete picture of events.

Such issues can be seen in the various accounts of Tancred's siege of al-Athārib, which ran from October 1110 to January 1111. Matthew of Edessa reports that the siege involved Tancred camping against the town for a number of days before he took it by assault 'without harming the garrison'. In Damascus, Ibn al-Qalānisī notes that the garrison was spared when the town fell and those who wished to remain were free to do so. Writing from Europe, Albert of Aachen provides perhaps the most detailed account of the siege's progression. He describes the construction of siege engines over a period of days and the digging of a defensive ditch, but the breakthrough came on a Sunday after Christmas when a section of the citadel, battered relentlessly by artillery, supposedly fell and destroyed two towers as it collapsed down the slope. The besiegers were able to approach the damaged defences under the protection of a penthouse, but the rubble prevented them from storming the gap. Before this obstacle could be overcome, the defenders surrendered while favourable terms were still available. In Ibn al-Athīr's account, the town was taken by force, but the focus is an episode of intrigue, in which the defenders planned to tunnel out of the citadel and murder Tancred in his sleep; their plan, however, was betrayed by a young Armenian. Finally, there is Ibn al-'Adim's rendition to consider. Composed in Aleppo in the thirteenth century, it is perhaps the best informed. Like Albert of Aachen, he notes the presence of artillery, but adds the use of a ram, the blows of which were said to have been heard great distances away. In this version of events, Tancred intercepted a pigeon carrying a note from the defenders to Riḍwān of Aleppo, which described the desperate situation within the town. This strengthened Tancred's hand, who was at this point negotiating the town's surrender, or the price of his own withdrawal, with Riḍwān – Tancred rejected a payoff of 20,000 dinars, demanding 30,000 and the release of prisoners. Some kind of an agreement involving a payoff seems to have been concluded between the two princes; but in a final twist, the terms of their arrangement were not met because the defenders threw open the gates of al-Athārib as soon as they received assurances of their safety, suggesting Tancred was simultaneously negotiating directly with the besieged.

Piecing together the various accounts, it seems a breakthrough in the siege occurred when Frankish forces broke into the town by force. Considering their dire position, the defenders, who had withdrawn to the citadel, opted to surrender before this was formally ordered by Riḍwān, for which they received the generous terms noted by Matthew of Edessa, Ibn al-Qalānisī and Albert of Aachen. Although we are left with a fairly clear picture of events, taking any one account on its own can leave a very different impression: something to be considered when we have just one or even two accounts of a given siege.

Rams

The simplest battering weapon was the ram, and a slight modification known as the bore. These engines had been used for millennia before the time of the crusades, but were rarely employed by Latin and Muslim forces in the Near East. Both were essentially a large beam, often capped with a heavy iron head, that was driven against a gate or wall. Rams made use of fairly blunt heads, relying on their weight to deliver a crushing blow, whereas bores used a head that came to a point, focusing the force of each strike. If the beam was light, it could be carried by its operators and swung by hand, otherwise it might be mounted on a cart or some other kind of wheeled framework, allowing it to be rolled back and forth. The most effective rams, however, were typically suspended inside a sheltered framework, allowing the beam to be swung against the masonry or gate ahead of it. This design allowed the operators to work the beam most efficiently and the surrounding structure, often a timber a-frame, could be used as a shelter for both the ram and those propelling it.

The energy of any battering weapon can be expressed by the basic equation for kinetic energy:

$$\textit{kinetic energy} = \frac{1}{2}\,\textit{mass}\,(\textit{velocity})^2$$

Because the beam of a ram could be propelled to only a meagre velocity, whether it was pushed or swung into action, its mass had to be enormous, limiting the use of such engines to situations where there was a relatively easy and flat approach. If a ram was heavy enough and its head sufficiently hard, the percussive force generated by repeated blows would steadily begin to crush the stones struck by the head. Rather than punching a hole in the wall, which was almost certainly much thicker than the head of the ram was long, by breaking up or dislodging a few ashlars, men with picks could begin to pry out these and neighbouring stones, allowing them to then chip away at the core of the wall. Accordingly, it is perhaps best to see rams as mining tools – a means of helping remove outer facing stones.

Although rams were relatively cheap and simple to construct, their cumbersome nature and relative ineffectiveness against sturdy masonry defences meant their use was in decline by the time of the First Crusade. In earlier centuries, rams had been used effectively in Europe against lighter fortifications, often employed against softer sections of defences, such as wooden gates. Fulcher of Chartres and Albert of Aachen include battering rams in the lists of siege engines that they claim were built by the Franks after arriving at Nicaea in 1097. Casual references to the construction of rams can also be found in the slightly later accounts of Guibert of Nogent and Robert the Monk. Critically, Fulcher was the only one of these sources at the siege of Nicaea, and the party that he was travelling with missed most of the siege, arriving only days before it ended. The author of the *Gesta Francorum* and a fellow eyewitness, Raymond of Aguilers, recount that more ambiguous 'machines' were constructed, which appear to have been traction trebuchets and penthouses to shelter miners, rather than rams. Robert the Monk subsequently mentions rams at the sieges of Antioch and Maʿarrat al-Nuʿmān, but these are not supported by any of the other contemporary accounts.

In the late summer of 1099, a ram may have been constructed following the crusaders' arrival at Jerusalem. According to some accounts, this was used to destroy a portion of the outer wall along the north side of the city in the final phase of the siege, allowing the siege tower behind to approach the main wall. Neither Raymond of Aguilers nor the anonymous author of the *Gesta Francorum* mention the ram; however, Albert of Aachen, who composed a detailed account of the First Crusade and the early Latin presence in the Levant without ever leaving Europe, provides a vivid description of its use. Albert's account is followed closely by Ralph of Caen, who would arrive in the East years later. Fulcher of Chartres, who would come to reside in Jerusalem in the following years, but was at this point almost 700km away in Edessa, and Guibert of Nogent, who never left Europe, strangely refer to the use of multiple rams.

The apparent success of the crusaders' ram speaks to the weakness of the outer wall, perhaps no more than an undefended forewall. The butting head would have created a noticeable weak spot: as shockwaves reverberated outwards and the masonry was forced to absorb the energy of each percussive blow, some of the bonds between mortar and stone further from the point of impact would have begun to break as well. Sappers might then have been able to work outwards from this point, driving their picks into the cracks to pull out stones and eventually open and enlarge a breach down to the ground and wide enough for the siege tower to pass through. Despite the weakness of the forewall, it was still necessary to use a very large ram, so great that the crusaders opted to burn it in place rather than attempt to drag it out of the way so the siege tower behind could be pushed up to the main wall.

Twelve years later, the Franks besieged Tyre over the winter of 1111/12. As at Jerusalem, the besiegers focused their strategy on the use of two siege towers. While the Frankish sources make no reference to the use of rams, Ibn al-Qalānisī gives a detailed account of the siege and asserts that rams were key components of the Frankish towers. Two and a half months into the siege, the towers were ready. The smaller of the two was burnt in a sally by the defenders but the larger proved a more menacing threat. A leading sailor from Tripoli, who had some experience in war and happened to be in Tyre during the siege, constructed grappling hooks that were used to grab the head or neck of the large tower's ram as it was swung forward to butt

***Itinerarium*: ram at the siege of Acre, 1190**

They called it a 'ram' because it is pushed backwards and forwards with repeated and frequent blows like a ram, and demolishes walls, no matter how solidly built. The ram was strongly covered all round with iron plates, and when it was finished the archbishop [of Besancon] intended to use it to destroy the wall …

A day was set when they would all attack the wall with the devices they made. The archbishop moved his ram forward to shatter the wall. It was roofed over like a house. Inside it had a long ship's mast, with an iron-covered head. Many hands drove it against the wall, drew it back and aimed it again with even greater force. So with repeated blows they tried to undermine the face of the wall and break it down. As they shook the wall with repeated blows, the roof of the ram kept its operators safe from all danger of attack from above.

The Muslims on the walls defended themselves manfully. They collected a huge heap of old dry wood on top of the machine, which of course they could easily set on fire. At the same time, their stone-throwers were continually hurling enormous boulders at it. At last they dropped Greek fire on top. As it ignited the wood, those inside the machine found the growing heat of the fire unbearable. Realizing that the whole machine was going to be destroyed, they left it and pressed on with the attack using what other devices they could. The Turks kept on tirelessly hurling missiles at the ram, hoping either to crush it with enormous lumps of rock or to burn it with incendiary oil.

(Adapted from *Itinerarium* 1.59, trans. Nicholson, pp. 111–13.)

the wall. People in the city then hauled on the ropes attached to the hooks, pulling the exposed head of the ram upwards until it threatened to topple the whole tower, forcing the Franks to break the ram in order to save the tower. Undeterred, the Franks replaced their broken ram, and those that followed, as this played out a number of times. When the hooks failed, the defenders would drop down two rocks tied together on the exposed neck of the ram, breaking the beam behind its head. But each time the Muslims destroyed a ram, the Franks brought in a new one. Each was 60 cubits (32m) long, with an iron head that weighed 20 pounds, and was hung inside the tower with ropes.

Ibn al-Qalānisī's remarks sound almost instructional, echoing similar thoughts expressed by classical commentators, such as Vitruvius and Procopius, concerning ways of defending against rams. While it may be that it was not uncommon for Frankish siege towers to contain rams, making them unworthy of mention by Frankish authors, there are issues with Ibn al-Qalānisī's account. He claims that the hooks caught the rams as they swung against the wall, but goes on to state that the siege tower was subsequently advanced, at which point it was destroyed when a boom arm, 40 cubits (22m) long, was extended out over the tower to drop incendiaries on it, burning the tower. This, and the large figure he gives for the length of the rams, may reflect a belief that they were being used from a significant distance, perhaps reaching 10–20m from the tower to the town wall. This would leave the necks of the rams unnecessarily exposed and unsupported, and may reveal the author's lack of familiarity with the practical use of such engines. Critically, Ibn al-Qalānisī's home city of Damascus had not been besieged since it was captured by Atsiz ibn Uvaq in the 1070s, at which point he was a young child. He went on to become a leading figure in the Damascene chancery (*dīwān al-rasā'il*), which may have kept him in the city and away from the battlefield until Damascus came under pressure from the Zankids from the 1130s.

Neither Frankish nor Muslim accounts support Ibn al-Qalānisī's remarks regarding the use of rams at Tyre, but they are similar to those found in one of Saladin's letters relating to the brief Sicilian siege of Alexandria in 1174. It states that among the siege engines employed by the besiegers were three siege towers, each equipped with a ram. Frankish accounts of the siege do not mention the rams, leaving it unclear whether Saladin included them to exaggerate the circumstances of the siege, something he was known to do in such letters, or the Franks did not consider the rams noteworthy.

Although references to rams are quite rare and often uncorroborated, it can be said with a fair degree of certainty that at least one ram was used against Acre in 1190 – Muslim and Frankish accounts provide quite similar descriptions of this engine and the attack in which it took part. Among the various crusading contingents that had joined the siege since it had begun in the late summer of 1189, was one led by the archbishop of Besancon, and it was he who commissioned the ram. There is a reference to Count Henry of Champagne building another at the same time, but nothing more is said about this mysterious and probably fictitious second ram. According to Ambroise, a participant of the siege, as well as the slightly later *Itinerarium peregrinorum et gesta regis Ricardi*, composed by another eyewitness who closely followed Ambroise's poetic account, the roof of the ram was solid enough to protect it from rocks dropped from the wall above:

> It was of such rich workmanship that it should not justly nor reasonably fear any creature. It was made as if a house. A great ship's mast, straight and without knots, was in the middle, tipped with iron at both ends. Underneath [the roof of] the ram were those who would strike against the walls, having no fear there.[23]

Unfortunately for the besiegers, it was October by this point and probably many months since it had last rained. This allowed the defenders to burn the ram fairly easily by dropping dry wood on and in front of it, then setting this tinder alight with Greek fire, a naphtha-based flammable liquid resilient to water.

As alluded to above, some historians have suggested that rams might have been so common that contemporary Frankish and European authors regarded their use as obvious. It seems very unlikely, however, that the various sources, who hailed from very different cultural backgrounds, would all have taken this view. Likewise, it is hard to explain why artillery and miners, which were used at many if not most sieges, were considered deserving of regular mention but rams were not. Instead, the seldom appearance of these engines, which are scarce in the twelfth century but even harder to find in the thirteenth, is more likely due to their general inefficacy. It seems the construction of rams was simply not worth the trouble when compared to using sappers alone.

Mining

Mining – more accurately undermining or sapping – was a practice that involved the weakening of the base of a wall, causing the mass of the unsupported masonry above to collapse under its own weight. This was done by excavating a cavity below the foundations of a wall, or by removing its lowest courses, temporarily propping up the structure above with wooden supports. When a sufficient stretch of the targeted wall was completely reliant on these supports, combustibles were placed around them and then set on fire, causing the wall to fall among clouds of smoke and dust. Rather than tunnelling under or even through a wall, which provided only a small passage for a limited number of troops to attack at any one time, undermining created a much larger breach, allowing for a massed frontal attack. Sappers had been used in this way since antiquity, and while both Muslim and European forces had turned to mining at sieges during the Early Middle Ages, this practice is found most often in connection with Byzantine forces in the centuries leading up to the First Crusade.

When considering the period of the crusades, sappers were employed at the very first siege and the very last – those of Nicaea in 1097 and Acre in 1291 – and countless sieges in between. Although mining was practised by all parties, it is often viewed as a Muslim siege tactic. The infrequent use of siege towers and other such large engines by Muslim forces has led to assumptions that they were less technologically savvy or possessed a superior mining tradition; in reality, their apparent partiality for sapping reflected broader tactical preferences. Whereas Frankish forces regarded the siege tower as the best tool of attack in some scenarios, this was ill-suited to most Muslim forces, which were more mobile and may have preferred means of bringing more men into an attack at the same time than was allowed by a siege tower. Likewise, many Muslim armies were from regions where timber was scarce, so developed siege tactics that avoided the need for machines constructed from large trees.

From the opposite perspective, Frankish forces were just as likely to employ sappers at a given siege as were their Muslim counterparts. Between 1097 and 1186, sappers are found at twice as many sieges undertaken by Muslim armies in the Levant than Frankish ones; however, sieges prosecuted by Muslims outnumber those of the Franks by almost exactly 2:1. Similarly, from 1187 to 1291, sieges initiated by Muslim forces outnumber those undertaken by Franks by about 5:1, but so too do references to mining. Accordingly, when considered proportionally, Frankish besiegers were as likely to employ sappers as were their various Muslim neighbours.

When considering the siege of Nicaea, it seems that at least some groups of crusaders arrived in the Near East with sufficient skill to undermine the region's formidable strongholds. Sapping efforts were initiated by the first contingent to arrive and were under way by the time Raymond of St Gilles and the second group showed up. According to Raymond of Aguilers, who accompanied this latter contingent of Provencal forces, as well as the *Gesta Francorum*, composed by another eyewitness, Raymond's sappers went on to successfully bring down the wall of a tower. Unfortunately for the crusaders, this occurred late in the day and the defenders were able to fortify the breach sufficiently to repel an assault the following morning. Albert of Aachen adds two more episodes of mining. In the first, he describes how a 'fox', capable of sheltering twenty men, was commissioned by two lords, one from Lorraine and the other from Swabia, but the structure was improperly built and collapsed, killing those below it. Later in the siege, a Lombard master builder, who was experienced in constructing siege works, offered to build a better shelter that would allow the Franks to take the city. He was promised 15 pounds of the coinage of Chartres and duly oversaw the construction of a penthouse, which had a steeply sloping roof and was large enough to accommodate a number of armed defenders. According to Albert, the master builder and the sappers with him undermined the wall of a tower, leading the defenders to surrender before the breach could be stormed. William of Tyre repeats these anecdotes in his later history. When the accounts are read together, it may be significant that the most successful miners apparently hailed from southern France and Italy, regions with stronger traditions of building with stone than those further north.

Albert's descriptions of mining efforts at Nicaea reveal his clear understanding of this practice; however, many other sources, from various backgrounds, were equally familiar with mining, confirming its popular use. Roger of Antioch's chancellor, Walter, is known to have campaigned at times with the army of Antioch and provides a vivid description of Īlghāzī's sapping efforts against al-Athārib in 1119:

> Since Īlghāzī was unable to take the castle by storm, he sent men from different sides to dig out a cave made underground, and he prepared fuses by grafting together dry pieces of wood so that when they reached the towers and put in that same kindling they would collapse, being supported by posts.[24]

An anonymous Syriac account dating to the thirteenth century, which made use of an earlier source, describes how Roger of Antioch's forces captured 'Azāz the previous year:

> He dug tunnels in the ground under the wall, put beams under it, and then set them on fire. The wall tottered and fell; the Franks leapt in through the breach, took the fort, and slaughtered all the Muslims in it.[25]

A very similar description is provided by Fulcher of Chartres when describing Balak's siege of Kharpūt, which had been seized by the Frankish prisoners Balak had been holding there:

> He immediately ordered the rock on which the castle was situated to be undermined and props to be placed along the tunnel to support the works above. Then he had wood carried in and fire introduced. When the props were burned the excavation suddenly fell in, and the tower which was nearest to the fire collapsed with a loud noise.[26]

Descriptions of tunnelling, rather than undermining, are comparatively rare and lack corroboration. At Shams al-Mulūk's siege of Frankish Bānyās, which began in December 1132, Ibn al-Qalānisī suggests that the Muslim miners, working under cover of vaulted shields, bored through the outer wall. Another rare example can be found in the *Eracles* continuation of William of Tyre's chronicle, where it is stated that the Egyptian forces sent against Ascalon in the spring of 1247 dug under the castle's walls and emerged on the other side.

The problem with tunnelling, and why these accounts warrant a degree of scepticism, is that it takes away the advantage of the besiegers' numerical superiority, as each man emerging from the tunnel would presumably face a far larger number of defenders. When used effectively, tunnelling was instead a means of introducing forces clandestinely, usually with hopes that they would open a gate to allow the army waiting outside to rush in. Ammianus describes how Roman miners, at the siege of Maogamalcha in 363, reached the foundations of the wall, but, rather than expanding the cavity and bringing down the wall, a night attack was launched on multiple fronts, creating a distraction that allowed picked men to emerge from the tunnel during the confusion and open the town gates. It is unclear what influenced the author of this portion of the *Eracles* account, but there is a noticeable trend in Ibn al-Qalānisī's chronicle that indicates his understanding of sapping improved through the following decades of his life.

The most famous description of mining from this period is that provided by Usāma ibn Munqidh, a native of Shayzar. He describes the first time he ventured into a mine, while taking part in Bursuq's siege of Frankish Kafarṭāb in 1115, at which point he was about twenty years old. Here and, about two decades later, at the siege of Masurra (a journey of six days from Mosul), Usāma notes that the miners were from Khurasan. Ibn al-Qalānisī similarly notes that the sappers who helped Shams al-Mulūk capture Bānyās around the end of 1132 were Khurasanian, while those who

Usāma ibn Munqidh: mining at the siege of Kafarṭāb, 1115

I descended into the fosse, with arrows and stones falling on us like rain, and entered the tunnel. I saw there a very clever thing: they had tunnelled from the fosse to the outer defences, and on either side of the tunnel they had set up posts over which stretched a plank to prevent the earth above it from falling in. They extended the tunnel along in this way using timbers right up to the base of the outer defences. Then they tunnelled under the walls of the outer defences, keeping them supported, and reached as far as the foundations of the tower. The tunnel here was narrow, as it was only intended as a way to get to the tower. As soon as they reached the tower, they widened the tunnel along the wall of the tower, supported it on timbers, and, a bit at a time, they started carrying out the pieces of chipped-away stone ...

They then set about cutting up dry wood and stuffing the tunnel with it. Early the next morning they set it ablaze. We had put on our armour and marched to the fosse, under a great shower of stones and arrows, to launch an assault on the citadel once the tower collapsed. As soon as the fire began to do its work, the layers of mortar between the stones of the wall began to fall out, then the wall cracked, the crack widened and the tower fell.

(Adapted from Usāma ibn Munqidh, trans. Cobb, pp. 85–6.)

undermined the defences of Edessa for Zankī in 1144 were from Khurasan and Aleppo. Aleppan miners are also found in the service of Richard I of England at Dārūm in the spring of 1192. Muslim sources assert that these men, who found themselves in the service of the English king, had been defenders of Acre who fell into Frankish hands when the city was captured. Some historians have postulated that these individuals may instead have been among the thirty-five people whom Richard spared when he intercepted a Muslim supply vessel off the coast of Beirut on his way to Acre in 1191.

References like these have led to the conclusion that there was a regional tradition of expertise dealing with stone in the areas of Khurasan and Aleppo. Although certainly possible, this was probably also true of many other regions that would have been represented in large forces like Bursuq's caliphal army. Accordingly, describing miners as Khurasanian, those who hailed from a region more than 2,000km from Damascus, today consisting of northeastern Iran, northern Afghanistan, eastern Tajikistan and Uzbekistan, and Turkmenistan, may simply have been a way of identifying 'Easterners', outsiders to an individual living in western Syria. Ibn al-Qalānisī may have used 'Aleppan' as a similar slur, notably absent in the work of Usāma, who grew up less than 120km from Aleppo and more in its sphere of influence than that of rival Damascus.

Mining required skilled labour, but the regularity with which sappers were employed, by both Frankish and Muslim forces, reveals that experienced sappers were readily available. The speed with which these men could work is also astounding. Al-Bursuqī took Kafarṭāb on 9 May 1125, before moving on to take Zardanā and then besiege 'Azāz. Although it is not stated when the siege of 'Azāz began, al-Bursuqī's sappers reportedly compromised the stronghold's two lines of outer walls before a Frankish relief force arrived under Baldwin II on 22 May. In 1132, catching the Franks off guard, the forces of Shams al-Mulūk of Damascus are supposed to have undermined the defences of Bānyās in less than five days. When Saladin besieged Jaffa in 1192, his miners targeted a section of the town's defences that had recently been slighted, but which had been refortified when the Franks reoccupied the town in 1191. They were able to bring down a section of wall on the third or fifth full day of the siege; however, the defenders were initially able to defend the breach from behind a line of improvised defences. During Baybars' siege of Crac des Chevaliers in 1271, the southwestern corner of the castle's outer defences appears to have been successfully undermined in a period of eight days. At Montfort, the mines opened by Baybars' sappers later that year are still clearly visible to visitors. A large cavity was excavated from the southwestern outer tower in no more than three days, while the exceptionally wide mine dug into the southern wall of the upper castle may have been developed in the eleven days between the fall of the outer defences and surrender of the upper castle.

Despite the extremely hard stone that was used at some castles, miners appear to have worked incredibly efficiently if allowed to toil away unhindered. In this light, it is easy to understand the effort and importance Saladin placed on filling the northern ditch at Kerak in 1183 and 1184, which would have allowed him to set his miners to work against the castle's northern wall. Where such obstacles were not a problem,

Montfort: (*above*) mine in the outer southwestern tower, and (*below*) mine in the southern wall of the upper ward. (*Michael Fulton*)

mining efforts could proceed incredibly quickly. According to William of Tyre, while Baldwin IV was confronting Saladin at Kerak one year, a Damascene force, which raided the villages around Mount Tabor, was able to undermine a tower in just four hours. Similarly, when Baybars encamped outside Acre in April 1263, his sappers undermined a tower, possibly the Templar's fortified mill of Doc, which was defended by four knights and thirty infantrymen, in about thirty-six hours.

The speed at which medieval miners could work is even more impressive when considering that their primary tool was a single-beaked pick, unlike a modern pick-axe, which has two heads or beaks, one tapering to a point and the other splaying into a narrow shovel. Besides providing more options to the user, the second head of a modern pickaxe helps to balance the tool when swung, keeping its centre of mass in line with the shaft and the operator's hands. This helps prevent the tool from twisting with each strike – any twist or roll results in a less efficient and less predictable stroke. These same factors led to the development of the two-headed North American frontier axe, which far outperformed traditional European designs. Although more efficient, two-headed picks required around 30–40 per cent more metal. In an era when tools often stayed in a family through multiple generations, using almost twice as much iron than was minimally necessary was probably regarded as a frivolous expense.

The value of miners and the service they provided was certainly appreciated and at times a bonus was paid as an added incentive. In 1105, Ṭughtakīn reportedly offered 5 dinars for every stone his men pulled from the stronghold Baldwin I had recently erected in the Golan. Richard I of England offered first 2, then 3 and finally 4 bezants to whoever would extract a stone from the tower opposite his position during the siege of Acre in 1191. In 1266, Baybars is said to have offered 100 dinars to each of the men who removed one of the first ten stones from Safed, in addition to the 300 dinars each sapper was paid for his work – almost certainly inflated amounts.

Mining was dangerous. Like a lumberjack felling a tree, determining how a structure would fall once the mine was lit and how large a cavity was needed were considerations that no amount of experience could predict with absolute certainty. Joscelin I of Edessa was seriously wounded, almost buried alive, when a tower made of brick suddenly collapsed while his men were sapping it. In 1108, Jāwulī successfully took Bālis after a siege of five days, but the breach that led to its capture was caused when an undermined tower fell prematurely, killing many of the sappers working below it. In a similar incident in 1184, a number of Saladin's miners working against the small stronghold at Jinīn were killed when it collapsed on them. A group of sappers employed by Philip II, who were working to undermine one of Acre's towers in 1191, found themselves in danger when they lit their mine and the tower above began to lean, threatening to crush them. However, there was more than just the structure above to worry about.

Artillery was commonly used to support mining efforts and, if positioned incorrectly, sappers might be subject to falling projectiles that had hit the defences directly above them. A greater threat was posed by the defenders along the parapet, who were in ideal positions to drop things on top of them. When working at the base of a wall, miners often made use of a penthouse for protection. These timber shelters typically had sloping sides, which deflected stones and other things dropped by the defenders, and perhaps even the odd friendly artillery projectile. To protect the men they sheltered from incendiaries, penthouses were often coated with hides, at times soaked in vinegar, and in rare instances were covered with metal plating. These shelters received various labels, often referred to by animal names used to identify classical engines, including 'tortoise', 'sow' and 'cat'. There seems to have been little consistency in the use of these terms and some were at times used to identify quite different engines, even siege towers in rare examples.

While other siege technologies developed, especially artillery, the basic practice of mining remained the same. Nevertheless, it remained the most physically destructive siege weapon used by any army during this period. It was the pick and the shovel, rather than the ram or trebuchet, that ultimately compromised the fortifications of the most impressive castles and formidable towns, as occurred at Acre in both 1191 and 1291.

Siege Towers

The primary function of a siege tower was to allow a group of besiegers to dominate a section of defences. By elevating a number of attackers above the level of the parapet, defenders lost some of the protection provided by their battlements, exposing them to the arrows and stones cast from the tower. These might also have provided a distraction, drawing the defenders' attention away from other forces who might be trying to undermine or scale nearby walls.

Some siege towers were stationary, typically erected at a distance to provide a vantage point and shooting platform; others were mobile, allowing them to be constructed at a safe distance and then advanced to better dominate the besieged and impair their ability to defend a certain stretch of their defences. The latter were more common and could have a greater impact; however, they were more complicated to build, requiring some kind of carriage, and the ground ahead of them needed to be prepared before they could be moved. A small cluster of rocks, an area of soft ground or a dip in the topography could halt the advance of such a tower or threaten to tip it over. Where the tower was equipped with a bridge, allowing besiegers to access the top of the wall, any ditches or moats would need to be filled and the fill adequately tamped so that the tower could move over it without sinking or tipping. Although these bridging towers have come to be the most iconic, most siege towers built by Frankish and Muslim forces were not used to provide assailing troops access to the besieged parapet.

Medieval siege towers typically had at least three levels. The lowest level contained a staging area and was probably often designed to allow space for men to help push the tower forwards – towers were rarely drawn by draught animals in the Near East. The middle level(s) provided internal support and a sheltered space for water and men preparing to engage in the fight. The top level, reached by internal ladders, was where most of the action took place. It needed to be higher than the top of the besieged wall, allowing the archers and those throwing stones from this level to subject the defenders to plunging fire. Where the tower was designed with a bridge, this was typically at the highest of the middle levels, which would hopefully align with

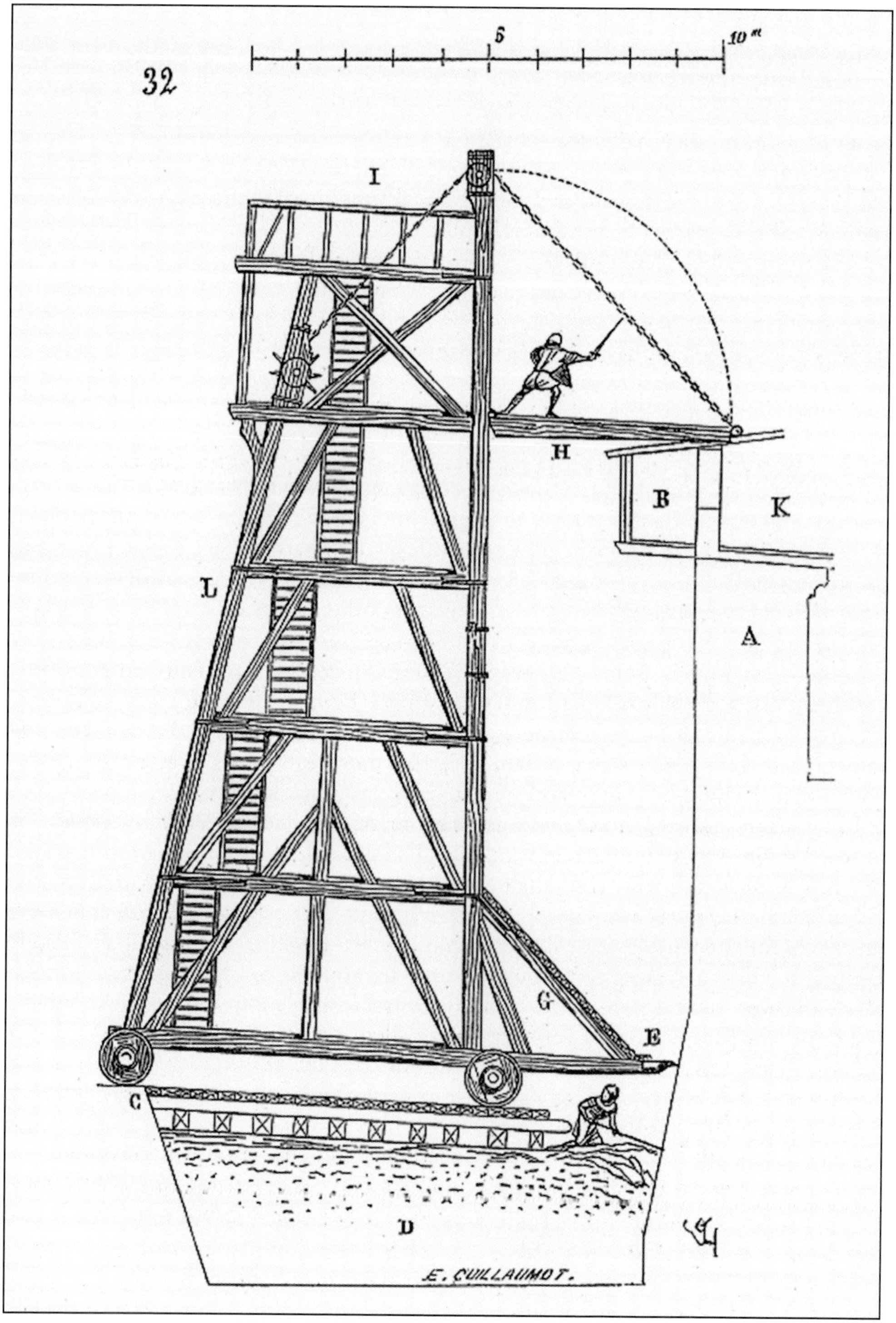

Siege tower (from Viollet-le-Duc).

the parapet, allowing assault forces to enjoy the support of the troops at the highest level, while keeping them out of their way.

Siege towers had been used across Europe and the Near East by the Romans, but they were more commonly employed in Europe than the Middle East during the Early Middle Ages. In the century preceding the First Crusade, Norman forces, some of whom would later take part in the crusade, seem to have used siege towers with particular regularity. In 1091, Robert of Bellême built one for Robert of Normandy at Courcy, and another for the duke at the siege of Bréval the following year. In southern Italy, Norman forces employed siege towers against Trani (1042), Bari (1068–71), and just across the Adriatic at Durazzo (Dyrrachium, mod. Durrës) (1081).

Although appearing less frequently in the Near East, siege towers were used at the sieges of Amorium (ʻAmmūriyya) (830) and Edessa (1070/71), among others. The towers at Amorium may have been quite small, being described as large enough to shelter ten men, while that built for Alp Arslān at Edessa may have been significantly larger, as it was erected on top of ten carts. In both instances, the besiegers were unable to push the towers close to the defenders' walls: at Amorium, one of the towers became stuck in the material that had been used to fill the fosse; at Edessa, Alp Arslān's tower collapsed.

During the First Crusade, siege towers were employed with effect at Maʻarrat al-Nuʻmān in 1098 and Jerusalem the following year. The *Gesta Francorum* and Fulcher of Chartres also mention the construction of 'wooden towers' at the earlier siege of Nicaea. It is possible that the crusaders had begun to build one or more siege towers, which remained incomplete when Nicaea surrendered to the Byzantines, who had made contact with the defenders by sailing across the Ascanian Lake. Alternatively, the original reference may have been included by the author of the *Gesta* to add to the grandeur of the siege, a detail Fulcher later included when compiling his account in the years following the crusade.

In late 1098, Raymond of St Gilles led his forces against Maʻarrat al-Nuʻmān. He ordered the construction of a siege tower and had the section of the town ditch ahead of it filled. Although it was equipped with four wheels and was pushed up almost to the wall, the tower was not used to convey men to the parapet. Instead, it dominated a section of the town's defences, allowing nearby attackers to use ladders to climb up to the top of the wall. The towers at Jerusalem were also designed to command the walls ahead of them, but it is debatable whether they were also designed to transfer men to the opposing parapet – the eyewitnesses are silent on this point.

Two siege towers were constructed during the crusaders' siege of Jerusalem. Raymond of St Gilles commissioned one to the south of the city, where his Provencal forces had established themselves on Mount Zion, and construction of another was ordered by Godfrey of Bouillon to the north of the city, where the remainder of the army was positioned. Albert of Aachen describes the northern tower as having three levels, with the men who pushed it at the bottom, a group of fighters in the middle and Godfrey and his brother Eustace with their men at the top. After a period of intense fighting, planks were pushed out to span the gap between the second level of the tower and the wall, creating a bridge to the parapet. Fulcher of Chartres provides an alternative version, describing how a pair of beams that the defenders had tied to the battlements as additional protection were cut free by men in the tower and used as a makeshift bridge. Planned or improvised, it seems the tower's role as a bridge to the parapet was secondary. Whatever the case may have been, as soon as the first Franks stepped foot on the wall, others used ladders to climb up elsewhere as confusion and panic began to spread among the defenders.

Siege towers were the largest terrestrial engines of war built during this period and they required the finest available timber. Although suitable trees were rare in Palestine and many other regions, small forests of tall and straight trees grew around Beirut and in other pockets through the Lebanon and mountainous regions of what became the principality of Antioch. The significance of building materials was apparent at the siege of Jerusalem in 1099. As fate would have it, a group of Genoese vessels became trapped in Jaffa by a Fāṭimid squadron during the siege. A party of crusaders was sent to collect the sailors and they brought back timber from the Genoese vessels, sinking what remained of the ships. These materials were used to construct Raymond of St Gilles' siege tower to the south of the city. Despite its strength, Raymond's tower was disabled by the defenders' artillery, having been built and brought forward on the restricted plateau outside the Zion Gate.

North of the city, Godfrey's tower was built in a safer position further from the town wall; however, its builders were forced to use materials scavenged from the surrounding countryside. Ironically, this inferior timber permitted Godfrey to build his tower in sections and then move it the better part of a kilometre one night, where

Jerusalem, siege of 1099, final deployments (with topography).

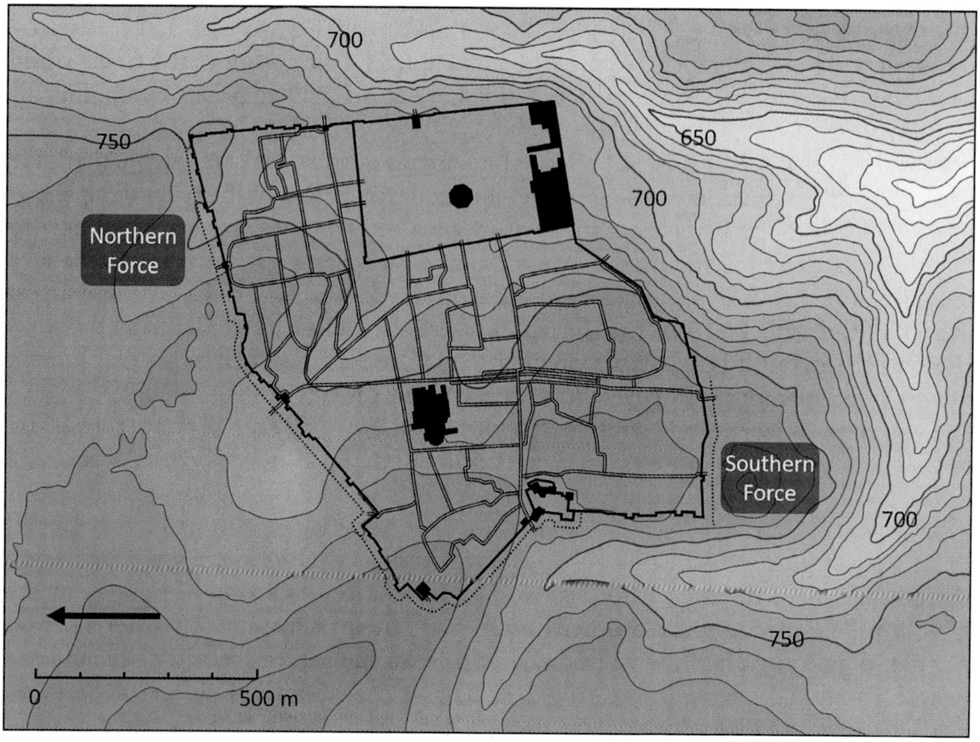

it was reassembled over the course of the following days. This allowed it to oppose a less defended part of the northern wall and forced the defenders to reposition their artillery in the tight urban constraints of the city. Although the tower was shot at for only one day, the final day of the siege (15 July 1099), it was already limping to one side before it reached the wall.

Following the capture of Jerusalem and the crusaders' victory at the battle of Ascalon, Godfrey besieged Arsūf, spending six weeks constructing artillery and two siege towers. Unfortunately for the Franks, one of the siege towers collapsed under the weight of the men trying to use it to reach the besieged parapet. Although the Franks had considerable time to build the tower, their lack of naval support was probably to blame for the tower's shoddy construction. Many Italian sailors would have been accustomed to rigging large beams and their experience might have helped the Franks; however, their real contribution would have been the timber that could be harvested from their ships. The sacrifice of one or more of their vessels was typically a sound investment for the Italian merchants, as they could expect a considerable share of the town and quite lucrative commercial rights in exchange for their support if the siege were successful.

The stripping of ships for materials to construct engines was probably a common practice. The masts of these vessels were particularly useful, ideal for the vertical corner supports around which the rest of the framework of a siege tower was built. Prepared planks from the decks and even hulls could be used to enclose the towers and subdivide their levels. Direct references to the use of masts and oars to build siege towers are found at the sieges of Caesarea (1101), Tyre (1111–12), Ascalon (1153) and Alexandria (1167). It was common practice to beach at least part of a fleet during a siege, providing a natural opportunity to strip materials if they were needed.

At the siege of Ascalon, a naval force of fifteen vessels was commanded by Gerald of Sidon, who was charged with intercepting the Egyptian fleet that was expected to arrive to relieve the city. Baldwin III was compelled to wait until Easter to build a siege tower, at which point he could purchase and impress pilgrim vessels, using their masts and other components for the tower; artillery and penthouses were built with the leftovers. In Egypt, a regime change in April 1153 ended plans to send a relieving field force, although a fleet still managed to break the Frankish naval blockade, extending the siege until August.

The Italians who contributed to sieges along the coast quickly came to appreciate the value of certain building materials. In 1123, a Venetian fleet of crusaders arrived in the Levant with the intention of assisting with the siege of a coastal town. According to Fulcher of Chartres, then living in Jerusalem, it brought 'very long timbers, which when skilfully made into siege machinery by carpenters, could be used for scaling and seizing the high walls of cities' – in other words, wood for building siege towers.[27] This is the only cargo Fulcher mentions. After spending Christmas and then Easter in the Holy Land, the Venetians set out with the army of Jerusalem to besiege Tyre, where two siege towers were built using the materials they had brought. Although the king, Baldwin II, was at that time a captive of Balak in Ḥarrān, the besiegers successfully compelled the surrender of Tyre after a lengthy siege. Timber was brought from an equally exotic, if quite different, source a decade and a half later during the siege of Bānyās.

In 1140, the army of Jerusalem assembled in response to Zankī's aggression against Damascus. In return for mobilizing and compelling Zankī to withdraw from the region, Muʿīn al-Dīn had agreed to help take Bānyās for the Franks – the governor of which had recently rebelled and declared his support for Zankī. The combined army besieged the town for a while before it was decided to send for large beams from a stockpile in Damascus; these were then used by the Franks to construct a siege tower. After the ground ahead of the engine had been levelled, the tower was pushed forwards, allowing the Franks to inflict considerable harm from their vantage point and dominate the defences opposite them. This compelled the garrison to negotiate terms of surrender with Muʿīn al-Dīn, who dutifully turned the town over to the Franks.

In Egypt, the siege tower built to facilitate efforts against Damietta in 1169 was probably constructed using timber brought on board or stripped from Byzantine

William of Tyre: siege tower at the siege of Bānyās, 1140

It finally became evident to the Christians that no advantage could be gained unless they could build a wooden tower, move it close to the walls, and wage war upon the besieged from above. But in all that region no suitable material for such a purpose was to be found. Anar [Muʿīn al-Dīn Unur] therefore dispatched men to Damascus for tall beams of great size which long ago had been set aside especially for such a purpose. He bade them use all possible speed to accomplish their errand and return ...

The messengers sent to Damascus returned without delay. They brought with them immense beams of the necessary size and strength. They were quickly dressed by the carpenters and workmen and put together solidly with iron nails. Soon an engine of great height towered aloft, from whose top the entire city could be surveyed. From this vantage point, arrows and missiles of every sort could be sent, while great stones hurled by hand could also help to keep the defenders back. As soon as the engine was ready, the ground between it and the walls was levelled off, and the machine was attached to the ramparts. There, as it looked down upon the whole city, it seemed as if a tower had been suddenly erected in the very midst of the place.

Now for the first time the situation of the besieged became intolerable; they were driven to the last extremity, for it was impossible to devise any remedy against the downpour of stones and missiles which fell without intermission from the movable tower ...

In addition, they were now debarred from passing back and forth about the ramparts and could not without peril of death carry aid to their comrades who were falling. For the weapons and modes of assault used by those fighting below could be considered little or nothing in comparison with the manifold dangers to which they were exposed from the fighters in the tower. In fact, it seemed to be rather a war with gods than with men.

(Adapted from William of Tyre 15.9–10, trans. Babcock and Krey, 2:108–10.)

ships, or Frankish vessels that had joined the fleet. Five years later, the Sicilian force that attacked Alexandria almost certainly brought specially prepared timber, if not partially assembled engine components. According to a letter that Saladin sent out after the siege, the Sicilians erected three siege towers, complete with rams, which were brought into action the day after they landed. Saladin tended to exaggerate events in such letters – it would have been quite an achievement if the Sicilians had been able to deploy any towers, let alone artillery to support them, given the siege lasted less than a week.

Siege towers are sometimes used to characterize Frankish siege operations. Their use, however, was restricted almost exclusively to engagements along the coast: of the twenty sieges where siege towers were used between the First Crusade and the end of the twelfth century, seventeen were along the shores of the Mediterranean. Unsurprisingly, the use of siege towers declined as the coast fell into Frankish hands: during the century following the arrival of the Franks, two-thirds of sieges featuring siege towers took place in the first fifteen years.

Following the Franks' capture of Ascalon, and with it the entire Palestinian coast, siege towers were not again employed outside Egypt until the Third Crusade. During

Use of siege towers, 1097–1200

Year	Location (*interior*)	No. of towers	Maritime element	Success
1098	*Ma'arrat al-Nu'mān*	1	None	Yes
1099	*Jerusalem*	2	[Genoese]	Yes
1099	Arsūf	2	None	No
1100	Haifa	1	Venetians	Yes
1101	Arsūf	1	Genoese	Yes
1101	Caesarea	1	Genoese	Yes
1101	Jabala	1	None	No
1103	Acre	1	None	No
1108	Sidon	1	Pisans, Genoese, Venetians, Amalfitans	No
1109	Tripoli	1	Genoese	Yes
1110	Beirut	3	Pisans, Genoese	Yes
1110	Sidon	1	Norwegians	Yes
1111–12	Tyre	2	Franks (very small)	No
1124	Tyre	2	Venetians	Yes
1140	*Bānyās*	1	None	Yes
1153	Ascalon	1	Franks, pilgrims	Yes
1167	Alexandria	1	Pisans	Yes
1169	Damietta	1	Byzantines	No
1174	Alexandria	3	Sicilians	No
1190	Acre	3	Italians, crusaders	Yes

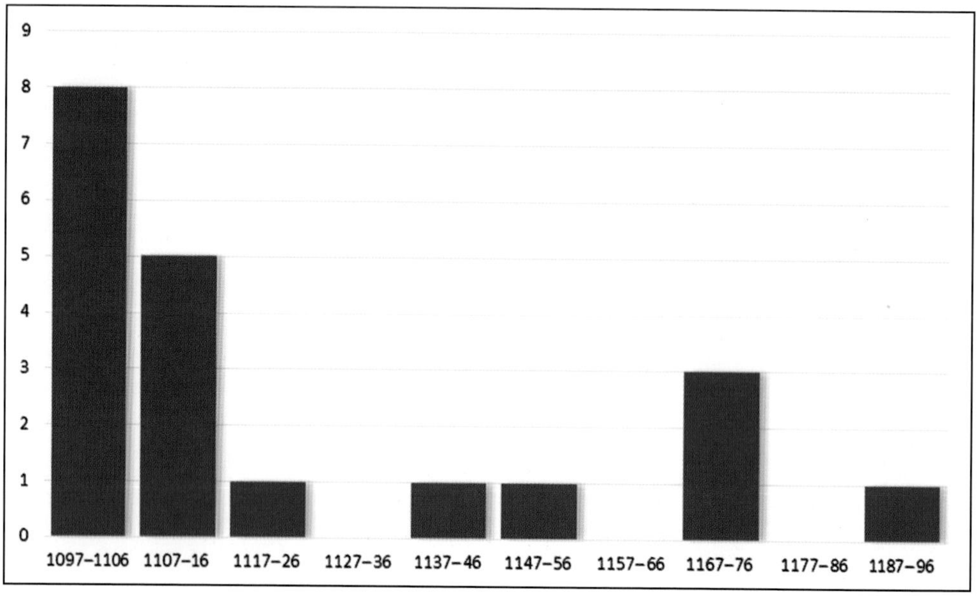

Use of Frankish siege towers by decade.

the lengthy siege of Acre (1189–91), three wheeled siege towers were employed by crusading forces in 1190: one built by Louis III, Landgrave of Thuringia; another by Conrad of Montferrat and the Genoese; and the last by Guy of Lusignan. Revealingly, the wood is described as seasoned or dried, suggesting it had been brought by sea or salvaged from ships, which Muslim sources appear to confirm. Efforts were made to prepare the ground ahead of the towers and measures were taken to fireproof them, which included coating them with hides soaked in vinegar. Despite this, all three towers were eventually burnt. Later in the year, a different kind of elevated platform was used.

With the siege making little headway through the summer of 1190, the Pisan-led fleet that controlled access to Acre by sea made an attempt against the Tower of the Flies, which dominated the entrance to the harbour. At the centre of their plan was a galley with a fortified masthead higher than the tower. It was hoped that Frankish archers in the mast-castle would be able to dominate the tower, perhaps also throwing incendiaries onto the tower's roof, while others would climb up via two large siege ladders raised from accompanying galleys. In another version of events, the mast-castle was equipped with a bridge. By all accounts, the attack was countered by galleys from the city and was finally defeated when the mast-castle was burnt. This was not the first time that a ship had been equipped with what might be described as a fortified crow's nest: in 1108, at the siege of Sidon, the mastheads of some ships were similarly fortified.

What might be more accurately described as a maritime siege tower was built by participants of the Fifth Crusade during the siege of Damietta in 1218. From the end of May, the crusaders, accompanied by a large contingent of the Frankish baronage under King-regent John of Brienne, established themselves on the west side of the

Oliver of Paderborn: attacking Damietta's Tower of the Chain, 1218

We realized that the tower could neither be captured by the blows of petraries or of trebuchets (for this was attempted for many days), nor by bringing the Tower [of the Chain] closer, because of the depth of the river, nor by starvation, because of the surroundings of the city, nor by undermining, because of the roughness of the water flowing about. With the Lord showing us how and providing an architect [Oliver himself], and with the Germans and the Frisians providing supplies and labour, we joined two ships which we bound together sturdily by means of beams and ropes and so prevented (by their closely connected structure) the danger of drifting. We erected four masts and the same number of yards, setting up on the summit a strong fortress joined with poles and a network of fortification. We covered it with skins about its circumference, as protection from the attacks of their machine, and over its top as a defence against the Greek fire. Under the fortress was made a ladder, hung by very strong ropes and stretching out thirty cubits beyond the prow. This task having been successfully completed in a short time, the leaders of the army were invited to see it, so that if anything was lacking that ought to be supplied by material or by human ingenuity, they would point it out.

(Adapted from Oliver of Paderborn 12, trans. Gavigan, pp. 64–5.)

Damietta branch of the Nile, opposite the city and the Tower of the Chain. The tower rose from the water and controlled access up the river with a chain, which ran across the main shipping route between the tower and the city. The crusaders were reliant on supplies arriving by sea, so were obliged to take the tower, and the city, before continuing upriver towards Cairo. One of the best accounts of this siege was penned by Oliver of Paderborn, and it may have been he who devised the means by which the Franks took the tower, although the humble cleric omits any hint of personal involvement in his account of events.

It became apparent that no measure of artillery bombardment would compromise the tower, and a marine attack, involving two ships with siege ladders and another with a fortified masthead, was repulsed. The besiegers then built a more substantial engine. Two ships were joined together and a siege tower built on top of them, using the two masts of each vessel as the corner posts, while their yards provided horizontal structure. On 24 August, the floating tower was moved into place and a bridge was let down, allowing the besiegers to engage the Muslim defenders of the Tower of the Chain. After a bitter fight, the tower's garrison surrendered. The Franks finally crossed the river in early February, enabling them to besiege Damietta's landward defences. No siege towers were employed during this second phase of the siege, which continued until 5 November 1219.

Siege towers were seldom employed during the thirteenth century, but a few were used during the intra-Frankish conflict of the early 1230s. The Lombard (or imperial) party erected a siege tower against Beirut, and their Ibelin adversaries employed two towers when besieging the Cypriot stronghold of Kyrenia. Both were coastal towns and siege efforts probably benefited from naval support. Further inland, Louis IX of

France appears to have constructed two siege towers of a sort in Egypt during the Seventh Crusade.

Although the crusaders who accompanied Louis IX to Egypt were able to take Damietta virtually unopposed in 1249, they stalled and were eventually defeated at Manṣūra, where the Fifth Crusade had collapsed three decades earlier. Manṣūra is about 60km southwest of Damietta, just south of where the Tinnis branch of the Nile diverts to the east, and it was here that the Muslim army waited for the Franks, shielding Cairo, 110km to their rear. In order to confront the Muslims and continue their way south, Louis IX ordered the construction of a causeway across the Tinnis branch of the river. The crusaders approached the task with optimism, having successfully dammed another distributary during their southward march. The earlier dam, however, had been constructed at the point of divergence, allowing the water to flow to the left without any build-up of pressure, but the causeway site was more than a kilometre from where the Tinnis stream left the main Damietta branch of the Nile. Besides the water pressure, there was also the enemy to consider; skirmishers had plagued work on the earlier dam but the crusaders were now faced by the main Egyptian army.

To protect the workers constructing the causeway, Louis commissioned two siege towers. According to John of Joinville, the seneschal of Champagne and a participant of the crusade, these were 'called *chas chastiaus*, because they had two castles [or towers] in front of the cats [or penthouses] and two houses [or covers] behind the castles to protect those on guard from the blows of the engines of the Saracens, who had sixteen engines just across [the river].'[28] Using the towers to command the opposite bank and the shelter provided by the penthouses in front of them, the Franks began constructing their causeway. The Muslims countered this with their artillery and by widening the river opposite the Frankish mole. Their traction trebuchets drove away those guarding the workers, while a counterweight trebuchet threw incendiaries at the towers and penthouses, eventually setting them on fire. Desperate, Louis begged his barons for timber from their ships in order to build a new penthouse, but this too was destroyed by the Muslims' artillery.

Although Louis' towers did not contribute to a siege in the traditional sense, they fulfilled what was essentially the same function: they allowed those at the top level to overlook and dominate their opponents. During one of his campaigns in Egypt, Amalric had built similar structures to secure a bridge he was building over the Nile. Here too, a Muslim force was able to interrupt construction by commanding the far bank. Whereas Louis had the luxury of stripping seasoned and planed timber from ships, Amalric was probably forced to rely primarily on palms.

The relative regularity with which the Franks employed siege towers at significant sieges is in contrast to the infrequency with which they were built by Muslim forces. This was not because Muslim armies lacked the knowledge or skill to do so, or even the materials, as was demonstrated by their ability to furnish such at the siege of Bānyās in 1140. Rather, these cumbersome towers were not as congruent with their style of warfare. Muslim tactics typically involved bringing more men into action than could be conveyed, or supported, by a siege tower.

Ibn al-Athīr notes the construction of siege towers during Sultan Barkyāruq's siege of Isfahan in 1102, and the siege of Mosul, undertaken by his brother, Sultan Muḥammad, which ended when news of Barkyāruq's death arrived in January 1105. In what appears to be a unique example in the Levant, Saladin is said to have employed moveable siege towers against Tyre in 1187. The original reference appears to be that in 'Imād al-Dīn's convoluted versed rendition, subsequently abridged by Ibn al-Athīr and Bahā' al-Dīn. Conspicuously, the towers do not feature in any of the Frankish accounts, suggesting 'Imād al-Dīn included them for dramatic effect or that he meant that these were less impressive shelters, perhaps similar to the one Baybars employed at Caesarea in 1265.

Although Muslim forces rarely built siege towers, they still had to defend against them. To do so often required creativity and ingenuity, especially since no town or castle was attacked with siege towers more than twice in a generation, leaving few opportunities for defenders to learn from previous experience. By comparison, some Franks who fought with the army of Jerusalem in the early twelfth century would have been intimately familiar with their use, having taken part in numerous sieges where such towers had been built.

One of the ways to defend against siege towers was to build counter towers. These were typically temporary wooden structures, erected behind a wall or on top of a tower to reclaim the advantage of elevation. A counter tower was built by the defenders of Durazzo in 1081, which opposed the siege tower advanced by the Norman force led by Robert Giscard and his son, Bohemond. The defenders of Damietta appear to have constructed a similar tower in response to the siege tower built by the Franks in 1169. During the Fourth Crusade, the defenders of Constantinople raised the height of certain towers with a further two or three wooden storeys to confront the ship-born siege ladders of the Venetians in the spring of 1204.

Counter towers provided advantageous positions for archers and others throwing stones and incendiaries, but sometimes more elaborate contraptions were devised, as at the siege of Tyre in 1111–12. According to Fulcher of Chartres, two counter towers were raised inside the town, higher than the Franks' siege towers; however, other accounts suggest that it was an apparatus of a different sort that was responsible for destroying the assailing towers. Albert of Aachen describes the defenders' engine as an exceptionally high tree, raised with ropes, which suspended and then dropped a large wooden ring, covered with an inflammable mixture of materials, onto each of the two siege towers in turn. This roughly fits with Ibn al-Qalānisī's account, which recounts how, after the smaller of the two Frankish towers had been burnt in a sally, a leading sailor from Tripoli erected a baulk on the tower opposite the Frankish siege tower. On top of this solid beam of wood was a second, set horizontally, with a rod of iron at one end and ropes attached at the other, so that it could be rotated with pulleys and a winch like the yard on a mast. The apparatus was used to drop containers of filth and then combustibles on the Franks and their tower, while pots of burning oil were thrown by hand from the town walls. Simpler means were used against the northern siege tower at Jerusalem in 1099. According to Albert of Aachen, a tree trunk, into which nails and hooks were driven, was soaked in incendiaries and thrown over the wall, threatening to burn the base of Godfrey's siege tower until it was extinguished with vinegar.

Ladders and Frontal Attacks

The humble ladder was the oldest and simplest siege weapon, and responsible for the fall of more strongholds than any other. So simple yet functional was the ladder that every two knights were responsible for providing one at the siege of Jerusalem in 1099. Although the first men to break into the city did so from the northern siege tower, the majority who scaled the city's walls, like those at most other sieges, probably did so by ladder. In 1101, impatient Frankish forces besieging Caesarea launched a frontal attack with ladders before their siege tower was complete, taking the city by force.

Most ladders would have been fairly stout wooden constructions, although some were little more than ropes. In 1265, the Mamlūk governor of al-Bīra reported that the Mongols had cast ninety iron pegs, which were attached to ropes to raise the Mongols' ladders. When the siege was broken, the pegs were brought to Baybars as trophies. Only weeks later, Baybars' forces scaled the walls of Caesarea on the opening day of the siege, using iron horse pegs and harnesses. The following year, the Mamlūks climbed the walls of Safed using horse pegs once more, nailing them into the lower parts of the walls. Elsewhere, more preparation was put into the construction of ladders.

Despite the importance of ladders, medieval sources rarely devote much attention to them, focusing instead on the frontal assaults of which they were a pivotal part. These attacks might consist of an all-out push, a general assault launched by all available forces; however, more measured attacks, which were often carried out in relays, were more common. The typical size and composite nature of large Muslim armies, consisting of a number of emirs, each leading a contingent of fighters supported by his *iqṭāʿ*, meant that they were naturally disposed to making attacks in turns. This gave a measure of autonomy and authority to each unit as it made its attack, while allowing others to rest.

In 1137, Zankī encamped his army in the plain below Montferrand, sending his emirs up the rocky slope to attack the castle in turns. Saladin similarly sent portions of his army forwards in rotation during the sieges of Beirut (1182), Tyre (1187) and Bourzey (1188), and presumably many others. When Baybars attacked Acre in 1263, having pushed the Franks back into the city, the Mamlūk emirs attacked the city's gates in turns.

Frankish armies were not that dissimilar; although typically smaller, they were also built around a collection of lords, each bringing a group of fighters that often fought under him. At the siege of Ḥārim in 1177, the Franks settled in to besiege the castle through the winter. According to William of Tyre, once a blockade had been established, the Franks attacked in relays, 'according to custom'.[29] Likewise, during the first phases of the siege of Acre in 1189, the Frankish army was too small to completely blockade the city, so components of the army watched the city gates in rotation. During the Seventh Crusade, Louis IX entrusted the protection of his engines at Manṣūra to his brothers in rotation, while groups of lower-ranking knights received the night shifts in between.

Anonymous Syriac Chronicle: Adana falls to the sword following an attack with ladders, 1137

Adana was full of Jacobite Christians with their metropolitan John of Edessa. When the emperor [Alexius Comnenus] captured it, he left a force to guard it and moved on to Antioch. They rejoiced to be under Greek rule and freed from the severe taxes of the Franks. At dawn on Sunday, while they were quiet and unsuspecting, a Turkish army came upon them, surrounding them like a moat. They began at once a fierce attack like a wind of swords, planting ladders against the walls and swarming up them. When they pushed them down on one side they sprang up on another. The defenders were weakened by the blows of arrows and stones and the great assault that encircled them. They endured in this distress from dawn until midday. God turned his face from them and they were delivered into the hands of the enemy in a way marvellous to tell, incredible to the hearer. A Turk climbed a ladder against the wall and, when he reached the top, the wall was still above him. He gripped a stone projecting from the wall and stood on it. One of the defenders who stood on the wall above him thrust at him with his spear to throw him down. The Turk laid hold of the spear and the man on top pulled it hard to release it from his grip and in this way the Turk was pulled up on to the battlements. He brandished his sword at the man below who gave way before him and went down; fear and trembling took hold of those near and they fled. The Turks were encouraged, climbed up after the pioneer and seized the wall. In a moment it was full of Turks. They went down into the town, opened the gates, and the army entered … They drove out all the people, made the men kneel, and killed them with the sword; they sacked the houses, convents and churches; gathered spoil without end; and took captive boys and girls, whole groups. They took also the metropolitan, priests and young deacons, binding them with ropes and taking them into sad captivity. They destroyed the town, laid it waste, and went to their own land. When the news reached the emperor he sent an army to pursue the Turks, but it did not overtake them as they had seven days' head start. The captives were sold in various places, especially in Malaṭya.

(Adapted from *Anonymous Syriac Chronicle*, trans. Tritton, pp. 276–7.)

These natural divisions within most armies probably facilitated the allocation of other tasks. During the Third Crusade, Acre's defenders were divided into four groups to clear the town ditch, which the Franks were endeavouring to fill: the first went down into the ditch and cut up the material and bodies that choked the fosse; the second carried away the more manageable pieces; the third guarded these workers; the fourth worked the artillery and defended the walls. When besieging the city a century later, al-Ashraf Khalīl similarly divided the tasks of maintaining the attack and guarding the siege works into four shifts. Artillery also seems to have been regularly worked in relays, allowing for a constant barrage if desired. This most famously took place during the crusaders' siege of Lisbon in 1147. John Comnenus may have similarly used shifts of men to operate his artillery at Shayzar in 1138, as Zankī appears to have done at Baalbek in 1139 and Saladin did at Tyre in 1187.

Artillery

Of all the siege weapons employed during the Middle Ages, artillery is perhaps the least understood and most misjudged. The rapid mechanization, digitization and continual advancement of modern technology has led us to praise comparable historical innovations, at times overemphasizing their true impact. Focusing on a selection of sensational anecdotes can lead to the impression that artillery must have been responsible for shortening sieges and inspiring the development of much more sophisticated fortifications; however, when all of the historical and archaeological evidence is considered, and synthesized with a sound appreciation of the governing physics, a different picture emerges. Although artillery was an important siege weapon and trebuchet technology developed considerably through the twelfth and thirteenth centuries, these were far from wonder weapons.

Mechanical stone-throwing engines – artillery – were used throughout the period by all parties. These were not the torsion engines of the classical period, which fell from use during the Early Middle Ages, but rather swing-beam or levered machines, better known by the later term 'trebuchets'. Making use of a beam that rotated around an off-centre axle, these engines operated according to the principle of mechanical advantage: when force was applied at the end of the short arm, the end of the long arm rose at a greater rate, proportional to its greater distance from the axle. By attaching a sling to the end of the long arm, the projectile within could be accelerated at an even faster rate, and thrown at a higher velocity.

The vocabulary used to identify these engines varied. Authors writing in Latin often employed classical terms, such as *tormentum* (pl. *tormenta*) and *manganum* (pl. *mangana*), while *petraria* (pl. *petrariae*), a term first appearing in the Early Middle Ages, appears with increasing frequency through the twelfth century. Often, however, more ambiguous *machinae* are mentioned. Authors may have used certain terms to identify particular types of engine, but there appears to have been little standardization or consistency among sources before the late twelfth or early thirteenth century, at which point various forms of the term 'trebuchet' begin to appear, rendered into Latin as *trebuchetum*. In Arabic sources, the term *manjanīq* (pl. *majānīq*) appears most frequently to identify artillery. Like *manganum*, this was derived from the Greek *manganon*. The term *'arrada* (pl. *'arradat*) was at times used to refer to lighter engines.

The first trebuchets were operated by traction power: a small group of people applied the necessary force by pulling on ropes attached to the end of the short arm. This technology seems to have originated in China and had made it to the eastern Mediterranean by the late sixth century. Both attackers and defenders employed these engines during the First Crusade, confirming that knowledge of this technology had spread throughout the Middle East as well as southern and western Europe by the end of the eleventh century.

Traction trebuchets were light engines, used in an antipersonnel capacity. Although they required more operators than the single person that could work a bow, they harnessed more energy, throwing heavier projectiles with greater force and inflicting more carnage. The lightest engines might be operated by only one or two pullers and a loader; more efficient engines had crews of around a dozen pullers. Due to the finite

Counterweight trebuchet, Cardiff castle. (*Michael Fulton*)

distance that a person can pull a rope in a single tug, the size of these engines was restricted, limiting the number of people that could effectively help operate them. References to engines that made use of crews significantly larger than this, such as the Frankish engine that supposedly required a crew of 600 at the siege of Damietta, are clear exaggerations.

The strengths of the traction trebuchet were its simplicity and potential shooting rate. During the siege of Lisbon, undertaken in 1147 by a contingent of the Second

Traction trebuchet, Caerphilly castle. (*Michael Fulton*)

Crusade on its way to the Holy Land, an eyewitness account states that two traction trebuchets, operated in shifts, were able to shoot 5,000 stones in ten hours. The author almost certainly did not sit and count the stones that were thrown, but the shooting rate of these engines appears to have impressed him. Coincidence or otherwise, trials with reconstructed engines have shown that maintaining a shooting rate of four shots per minute is not unreasonable – maintaining an adequate supply of ammunition is the greater challenge.

Despite what we now recognize as the meagre power of these engines, contemporary descriptions can give the impression that they were significantly more powerful, even capable of destroying walls. It is important to contextualize these remarks, bearing in mind that these were the most powerful ballistic engines until the late twelfth century. At some sieges protection was added to battlements in the form of sacks and mattresses stuffed with soft padding or lengths of wood. This was done at the siege of Jerusalem in 1099 as well as at a number of earlier sieges, such as the Avars' siege of Thessalonica and Byzantines' siege of an unnamed Persian stronghold, both in the late sixth century, and the 'Abbāsids' siege of Amorium in the ninth century.

The counterweight trebuchet was invented or introduced to the area around the late twelfth century. This was essentially an adaption of the existing technology, which saw the pullers replaced by a dead load. No longer limited by the distance a person could pull a rope, these engines could be built as large as the skill of their designers and strengths of their building materials allowed. The sources provide few indications of where this technology was first employed, suggesting there may have been a period of gradual development before the potential advantages were fully appreciated.

In a work on weaponry presented to Saladin around 1180, Marḍī ibn 'Alī al-Ṭarsūsī included the earliest surviving illustration of a counterweight trebuchet. The image, and accompanying description, reveal an early stage of development. The axle was so low that it required a hole to be dug for the counterweight to fall into, while the horizontal starting position of the beam and vertical alignment of the sling, which was

Al-Ṭarsūsī's Persian trebuchet. (*The author*)

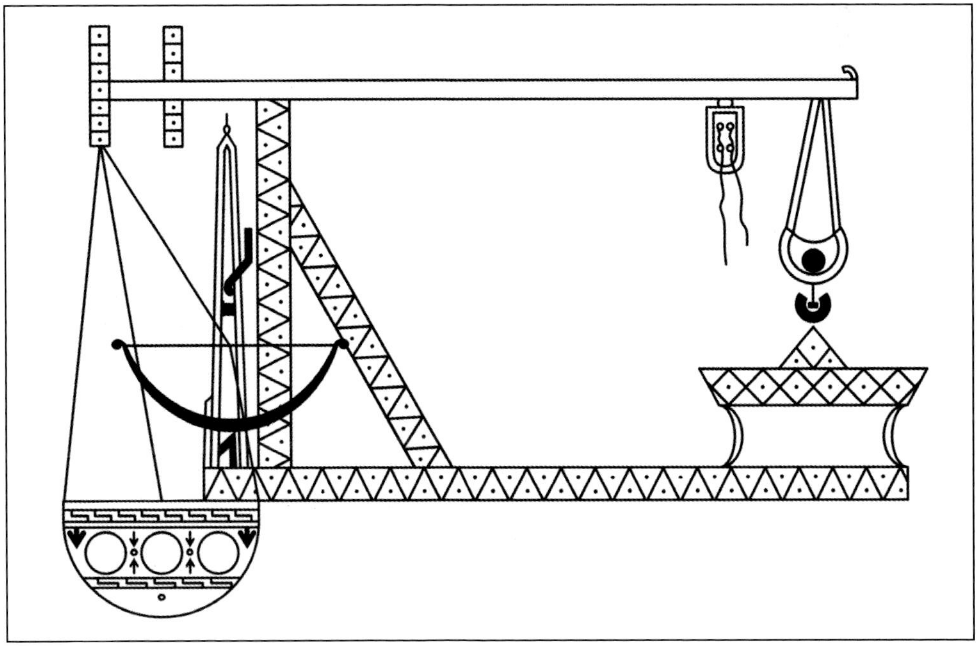

quite short, were better suited to a traction model and would have restricted the potential power and efficiency of the engine. Evidence of artillery damage dating to the 1170s and 1180s confirms the limited power of contemporary engines, whether traction- or counterweight-powered. Although some accounts of the siege of Acre (1189–91) give the impression that the trebuchets employed there were significantly more powerful than those found at earlier sieges, none of the eyewitness sources, men from as far away as England and Persia, suggests there were any differences between the crusaders' artillery and that of the Muslim defenders.

By the Fifth Crusade, the counterweight trebuchet had developed sufficiently to warrant new terminology. It is at the siege of Damietta (1218–19) that the term 'trebuchet' first appears in the Near East. In the following decades, Arabic sources would come to develop terms to distinguish the heaviest, presumably counterweight-powered, type of trebuchet. The *manjanīq maghribī* ('western' or 'north African' trebuchet) is mentioned by contemporary sources at sieges such as Ḥarrān and Edessa (both 1136), often in the singular, while Ibn al-Dawādārī, writing around the early fourteenth century, retrospectively placed engines of this type at the siege of Damietta. A *manjanīq maghribī* was also one of fourteen trebuchets deployed against Homs through the winter of 1248/49; it is distinguished from the others by its power, said to have been able to throw stones weighing 140 *artal* (61kg if using the Egyptian *raṭl*, or an unlikely 259kg if using the Damascene measure).

Less than two decades later, another terminological shift appears to have taken place. At the siege of Caesarea in 1265, the heaviest trebuchets were designated as *maghribī* and *ifranjī* (Frankish). *Maghribī* trebuchets are found at Safed the following year, but references to these engines disappear thereafter. They seem to have been replaced by *ifranjī* trebuchets, which were subsequently used at al-Bīra (1275), Margat (1285), Saone (1287), Tripoli (1289) and Acre (1291). It is possible that there was a sudden technological development, warranting new terminology; however, it seems more likely that the terminology changed independently – a new term came to be applied to the existing technology, which had developed significantly, but gradually, since the old term was first used.

The counterweight trebuchet was probably not the great wall-smashing engine that it is often believed to have been, at least not before the end of the thirteenth century. Despite the significant use of artillery at Acre during the Third Crusade, where it was employed for at least a year, most of the damage to the town's defences was inflicted through mining. Three decades later more powerful engines were evidently used against Damietta, damaging at least one of the town's landward towers. Yet after a bombardment of around six months, no breaches sizeable enough to be stormed had been opened. Even at Acre in 1291, where artillery damaged sections of the city's soft sandstone defences, it was mining that opened the breach that led to the city's capture. Evidence from the sieges of Crac and Montfort (both 1271) reveal that contemporary engines could throw stones of around 70kg, and perhaps even heavier, to distances of about 200m; however, these stones were typically thrown along great arcing trajectories and posed little threat to fortified walls 2–3m thick. Although these were the most powerful ballistic engines of the day, they were nowhere near as destructive as later bombards and siege guns.

The persistent reliance on mining ensured that traction trebuchets, which were ideally suited to support sapping operations, remained in use. Although these seem to have been operated in the shadows of their much larger cousins, their impact would have been felt by defenders. Of the thousands of stones thrown against Arsūf in 1265 (a siege where, unsurprisingly, mining efforts are emphasized by the sources) more than 90 per cent would have come from traction trebuchets.

In addition to the counterweight trebuchet, which he named the Persian *manjanīq*, al-Ṭarsūsī included descriptions of three types of traction trebuchet in his famous treatise. These he named the 'Frankish', 'Arab' and 'Turkish' varieties of *manjanīq*, all of which made use of triangular trestle frameworks, while the light *lu'ab*, which seems to have been a pole-trebuchet that required only one puller, he regarded as sufficiently common that it deserved no description. The proper adjectives used by al-Ṭarsūsī are not found elsewhere, but new terms came into use in the thirteenth century.

The *manjanīq shaytānī* ('satanic trebuchet') is found at a number of sieges from the mid-thirteenth century and was clearly a light traction trebuchet. The *manjanīq qarābughā* was another type of traction trebuchet, often found alongside those of the *shaytānī* variety – *qarābughā* trebuchets were instrumental in protecting the advancing sappers at Acre in 1291. The *manjanīq shaytānī* may have been slightly lighter than the *manjanīq qarābughā*, but it is far from clear what distinguished these two types of engine. The Franks adopted the latter term, if not the technology, by the late

Arsūf (with topography).

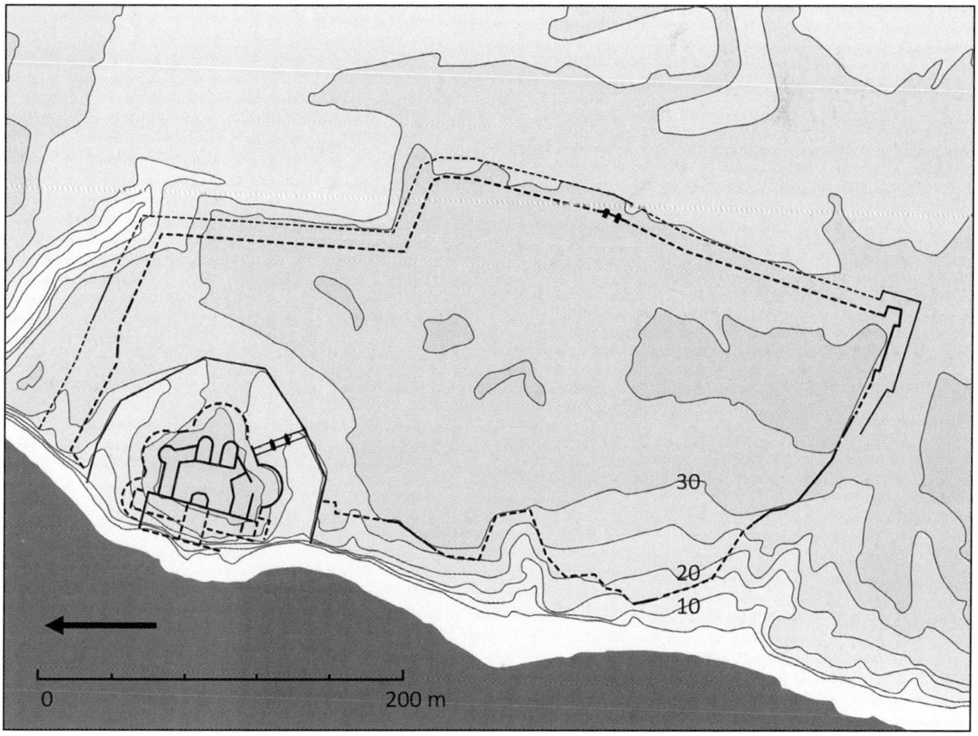

Arsūf: (*above*) the outer southern tower, featuring artillery damage inflicted during the siege of 1265 before the tower was destroyed by the Mamlūk sappers; (*below*) artillery projectiles from the siege. (*Michael Fulton*)

thirteenth century, rendering it as *carabohas* in accounts of the Mamlūk sieges of Tripoli (1289) and Acre (1291).

In addition to the physical effects of artillery, these engines also had an unmeasurable psychological impact during a siege. Both traction and counterweight trebuchets were most often used to target the parapets of walls, both the battlements and the defenders behind them, creating a treacherous environment for defenders. Unfortified structures within a stronghold might also be targeted, adding to the chaos and carnage behind the defensive perimeter. As the level of destruction mounted, organization and communication may have begun to break down, while morale might begin to decline as buildings threatened to collapse and the uncertain danger of incoming projectiles continued. Another terror tactic was the throwing of heads. Both attackers and defenders used their artillery to throw the heads of dead opponents during the First Crusade, but this practice appears to have declined thereafter.

Through most of the twelfth century, Frankish forces appear to have preferred to build their trebuchets on site before each siege. This involved relying on nearby natural sources of timber in western Syria, while wood sourced from ships would have been used to build many employed against the cities of coastal Palestine. As the Franks gained control of the Levantine coast, so too did Frankish naval power come to dominate that of the Fāṭimids and their later successors, denying these forces the same opportunities to source wood from ships. In a rare exception, the Muslim forces besieging Ascalon in 1247 were provided with an abundance of timber, which they used to construct siege machines, when a storm dashed their fleet on some rocks. With the development of the counterweight trebuchet, engines grew larger and there was a greater demand for tall and straight trees. This was highlighted in a letter Baybars sent to Bohemond VI after capturing Antioch, in which he bragged how the Mamlūk army had overrun the region but had preserved the trees suitable for constructing artillery – this resource was now his.

Muslim armies appear to have adopted the practice of storing and transporting artillery at an earlier date than their Frankish neighbours. In 1123, Fāṭimid forces brought artillery with them to Jaffa and by the 1140s there is evidence that artillery was being stored in Damascus. The process through which the Franks began to depend on prefabricated engines was a result of their links with Europe. This appears to have begun with the Italians who helped the Franks conquer the coast: in 1123 the Venetians brought timber to construct the engines that were used against Tyre the following year. In 1174, the Norman-Sicilian force that attacked Alexandria brought prefabricated trebuchets, along with other engines, and Richard I of England built artillery while wintering on Sicily before joining the siege of Acre in 1191. In addition to trebuchets, both of these latter forces also imported ammunition, bringing black stones from Sicily that were harder than the stones found along the southern coast of the Levant.

The practice of storing prefabricated artillery components was well established by the Mamlūk period, but Baybars exploited this to a new degree. A logistical master, he used the cities and large castles of the interior as arsenals. Before besieging Caesarea in 1265, he rode ahead to do some scouting, arranging for timber and stone ammunition to be gathered while he was away. Upon his return, trebuchets of the *maghribī*

Ibn ʿAbd al-Ẓāhir: Baybars prepares artillery, 1265

Baybars went out to reconnoitre Arsūf and Caesarea and when he returned to his royal tent he found that wood for the trebuchets had been brought with the ammunition and supplies by Emir ʿAlam al-Dīn, deputy of the *amīr jāndār*. Baybars summoned the *amīr jāndār*, Emir ʿIzz al-Dīn, and instructed him to set up several trebuchets made from this wood to *maghribī* and *ifranjī* designs. Early before dawn the next day, Baybars went out of his tent to sit in person with the craftsmen, so that they might work their hardest, and on the same day four large trebuchets and some small ones were made. He [also] wrote to the Muslim castles in order to collect [additional] trebuchets and stonecutters, and gave orders to the soldiers to make ladders, assigning to each emir the transportation of a certain number. He then departed for the neighbourhood of ʿUyūn al-Asāwir. At midnight, he ordered the soldiers to put on their arms; and before dawn he mounted and marched on Caesarea, whose people were taken by surprise …

(Adapted from Ibn ʿAbd al-Ẓāhir, trans. al-Khowayter, 2:554–5, 562.)

and *ifranjī* types had been constructed, as well as some smaller ones. When the attack came, the Mamlūks overwhelmed Caesarea's town defences on the first day and the citadel was captured after only a week; it fell so quickly that Baybars was supervising the destruction of its defences by the time engines he had sent for began to arrive from Ṣubayba and Damascus. These prefabricated machines, as well as those that had been built ahead of the siege, were then put to use against Arsūf. The following year, while his army was encamped outside Acre, Baybars had trebuchets constructed in the field once more before moving against Safed, where additional engines from Damascus arrived after the siege had begun. Unlike Caesarea and Arsūf, which were both destroyed, Safed became a regional administrative centre and was integrated into the Mamlūk network of armouries – the engines Baybars had used to take the castle became the first of its new stockpile. Trebuchets from Safed were later among those taken to Beaufort in 1268 and Montfort in 1271.

The engines employed in 1271 against Crac des Chevaliers and ʿAkkār were also probably prefabricated, although this is not explicitly stated. In another of his letters bragging of his success to Bohemond VI, Baybars emphasized the difficulties his army overcame in moving these engines across the rough terrain between Crac and ʿAkkār:

> Count Bohemond … has heard of our arrival at Ḥiṣn ʿAkkār, after leaving Ḥiṣn al-Akrād; how we brought trebuchets there, up the mountains where even birds find it difficult to nest; how when dragging them we endured trials from the mud and rain; how we erected them in places where even ants would slip when they walk there; how we descended into valleys where if the sun were to shine through the clouds it would show no way out except the precipitous mountains …[30]

The network that Baybars developed would be exploited by his successors, ultimately allowing al-Ashraf Khalīl to gather at Acre in 1291 the largest assortment of trebuchets employed in the region during the thirteenth century. The components of one engine allegedly took up 100 carts; the task of moving this machine was so laborious amidst the rains and snow of the winter season that it took a month to move the engine from Crac, a Mamlūk arsenal since 1271, to Acre – a journey that normally took a rider eight days.

Artillery was employed almost as frequently by defenders as it was by besiegers, often being used to target troop concentrations and light siege defences, such as mantlets, as well as other siege machines. The threats posed by both offensive and defensive trebuchets sometimes led to artillery battles, as each side attempted to destroy the other's engines. Siege towers, however, were particularly attractive targets for the operators of defensive trebuchets. During the First Crusade, the artillery deployed by the defenders of Jerusalem successfully disabled Raymond of St Gilles' siege tower and considerable damage was dealt to Godfrey's tower by the time it reached the wall. In 1110, the first siege tower erected by the Frankish besiegers of Beirut was destroyed by stones thrown from the defenders' artillery. The two towers built after this fared better, allowing the besiegers to step from them to the city wall. Later the same year, the Franks appear to have taken particular care when constructing a siege tower at Sidon, cladding it with padding and damp ox-hides as protection against incendiaries.

Over time, siege towers appear to have become more resistant to the stones cast by traction trebuchets, which could be thrown only so hard; however, the pots of inflammable liquids and combustible projectiles tossed by these engines, which would stick to or hook on to siege towers, remained a significant threat. In May 1190, the defenders of Acre struggled in vain to destroy the three siege towers built by the crusaders. In desperation, the task was entrusted to a Damascene man, the son of a cauldron maker, who brewed a special mixture that was then thrown by the defenders' trebuchets against the towers, destroying them each in turn before they reached the city's walls. Larger counterweight trebuchets had a more devastating effect against siege towers, as Louis IX discovered at Manṣūra. The Muslims used traction engines to harass the workers constructing the French king's causeway across the river, but it was a counterweight trebuchet that was brought up to destroy the two towers that the crusaders had built. Rather than stones, this engine used incendiary projectiles to destroy the towers. The stockpiling of these larger machines, making them available to defenders, may have contributed to the declining use of siege towers from the end of the twelfth century.

Unlike heavy counterweight trebuchets, defensive traction engines could be placed on top of town and castle towers, providing them with a good field of view and adding slightly to their range. Counterweight trebuchets were set up on the ground when used in defence; their weight and the dynamic forces unleashed through the shooting sequence posed a threat to most towers they might otherwise be placed upon. Setting them up on the ground also provided these valuable machines with the protection of the curtain wall and saved the trouble of manoeuvring their great components, ammunition and massive counterweights up to the top of a tower. In 1191, during the siege of Acre, a certain defensive trebuchet, dubbed Bad Relation by the Franks, appears to have been set up on the ground behind the town's wall, from where it repeatedly damaged a significant trebuchet erected by Philip II of France, nicknamed

Albert of Aachen: defensive artillery at Jerusalem, 1099

At length the duke [Godfrey] and his men were oppressed and in difficulties from the constant blows of these five mangonels [the defenders had arrayed against them], and they used the strength of the Christians to place the siege tower close to the rampart and walls, so in this way it might withstand the mangonels more safely and, as the mangonels could not be brought into a large space because of the buildings, houses and towers, they were less able to throw and batter the engine. Once the tower had been brought up next to the walls, and the five mangonels could not find a sufficient distance to withdraw from it, a stone loaded and ejected by force from them flew over the too-close engine or sometimes, being too short in flight, fell next to the walls and crushed Saracens.

(Adapted from Albert of Aachen 6.17, trans. Edgington, p. 425.)

Bad Neighbour. In 1291, some of the Franks' largest counterweight trebuchets were deployed in a similar manner; that of the Pisans, which was placed in an open area near the church of San Romano, near the Accursed Tower, may have been quite near to where Bad Relation had been positioned a century earlier.

Ibn ʿAbd al-Ẓāhir provides a detailed account of how artillery was employed by both the Mamlūk besiegers and Frankish defenders of Margat in 1285. Ahead of the siege, Qalāwūn sent out mobilization orders from Egypt, ordering the artillery stored in Damascus to be readied, while arms and provisions were prepared and assigned to various emirs. Marching with the army by this point in time were a number of individuals identified as experts in the art of sieges and blockades. The army moved north, collecting artillery from other strongholds before making a final rapid advance on Margat, proceeding by forced marches to take the defenders off guard. In the opening phase of the siege, the castle was surrounded and the artillery, which was brought up on men's shoulders, was deployed against the castle. Qalāwūn had at his disposal three *ifranjī* trebuchets, three of the *qarābughā* type and four of the *shaytānī* variety. These began to bombard the castle, suppressing the defenders, while sappers started to undermine the castle's walls. The defenders' artillery was destroyed by the *ifranjī* engines, allowing the Mamlūks to advance some of their trebuchets. This turned out to be a mistake: once the Franks repaired their trebuchets, these smashed those the Mamlūks had brought forward and killed some of their operators. The sappers eventually brought down a section of the outer wall and the defenders sued for terms shortly thereafter, fearing the miners had worked their way under additional sections of the castle's defences. Qalāwūn agreed to allow the defenders to go free, provided their property was left behind. The castle then became a regional administrative centre and was incorporated into the Mamlūks' network of armouries – the trebuchets Qalāwūn had just used were deposited in the stronghold. Along with the garrison of fighters entrusted with the castle's defence, a group of men dedicated to the use of artillery was also stationed within.

The engines deployed at Margat were probably as large and powerful as any that would be used in the Levant during the remaining years of the thirteenth century.

Although the archaeological evidence suggests that these machines were capable of throwing large stones considerable distances, the ultimate power of these engines is indicated by the pockmarks they left at Margat – little more than cosmetic blemishes on some of the castle's southfacing basalt walls. Few artillery stones weighing more than about 100kg have been discovered, suggesting references to projectiles significantly larger than this are exaggerations.

Little is known about who designed and built these machines. In an age when basic carpentry skills were a necessary part of life for most men, simply seeing a trebuchet, whether traction- or counterweight-powered, would have allowed most to construct a functioning engine of modest scale. Ideal proportions and dimensions were probably passed along between builders, each refining his machines through a gradual process of trial and error. Although counterweight trebuchets could be directly scaled up – the design of a big engine was no more complicated than that of a small one – greater skill was necessary to move larger components and mitigate the dangers that accompanied any kind of failure, which grew proportionally.

Some Frankish lords seem to have had a certain skill in either designing or overseeing such projects. Robert of Bellême appears to have had a knack for building siege towers, doing so at least twice for Robert of Normandy at the end of the eleventh century, while construction of the siege towers at Jerusalem, the most demanding engines built by the besiegers in 1099, was entrusted to William Embriaco, leader of the Genoese party rescued from Jaffa, and Gaston of Béarn, a lord from the Pyrenees. Later, figures are more closely linked with artillery. In an uncorroborated anecdote, William of Tyre asserts that an Armenian, named Havedic, was summoned to help manage the Franks' artillery during the siege of Tyre in 1124. During the Seventh Crusade, Joscelin of Cornant, an *engingneur*, was responsible for building the artillery and various engines used to support the construction of Louis IX's causeway at Manṣūra. John the Armenian, whom Joinville called 'the king's artillerist', was sent to Damascus to buy horn and glue for crossbows after the crusaders returned to Palestine, suggesting he was responsible for such smaller ballistic weapons.

Who oversaw or designed most of the large siege engines constructed by the Franks and Ayyūbids is unclear. Under Baybars, however, 'Izz al-Dīn Aybak al-Afram, *amīr jāndār*, appears to have been responsible for the sultan's artillery. He was praised by Baybars for overseeing the preparation and use of the Mamlūks' artillery at Caesarea in 1265 and then at Safed the following year. He seems to have been assisted to a degree by a certain 'Alam al-Dīn ('flag of the Faith', a not uncommon *laqab* – an honorific cognomen), identified as *nā'ib amīr jāndār* (deputy to the *amīr jāndār*), who oversaw the gathering of timber and ammunition ahead of the siege of Caesarea. Sayf al-Dīn Balabān al-Zaynī, *amīr 'alam*, brought the trebuchet from Ṣubayba to Caesarea, arriving days after the siege had ended, and it was he who collected the trebuchets that were at Damascus and brought them to Safed the following year. In the lead up to the siege of Acre in 1291, al-Afram was once again called upon, sent ahead to Damascus to prepare the artillery there and orchestrate the assembly of engines deposited in various Syrian strongholds before the main army arrived in Palestine from Egypt.

Siege Forts and Blockades

Besieging forces that were able, or willing, to devote considerable time to a siege might opt to rely on a blockade rather than more active measures. This option was best suited to smaller forces confronting proportionally impressive defences. It was costly to keep a besieging army in the field for a considerable length of time; however, a passive blockade might avoid sacrificing forces unnecessarily while waiting for the defenders to eat their way through their supplies. To be successful, the besiegers had to be well provisioned and face little threat from relief forces, who would be given ample time to assemble and disrupt the siege. The protracted sieges of Kerak (1187–88) and Montreal (1187–89), are clear examples of this. With the army of Jerusalem crushed at Hattin, the fairly small detachments entrusted with reducing these mighty castles had no need to launch frontal attacks, opting instead to simply wear down their defenders.

Siege forts might also be built to strengthen a blockade. These were any fortified structure that helped inhibit communication, disrupt the flow of supplies into the besieged stronghold and impair the defenders' ability to launch sallies. Their use was common in western Europe, especially in Norman spheres of influence. In the three decades leading up to the First Crusade, siege forts had been employed in southern Italy at the sieges of Bari (1068) and Troia (1071), in France at Ste Suzanne (1083), and in England at Rochester (1088) and Bamburgh (1095).

Antioch, town defences and siege forts of the First Crusade (with topography).

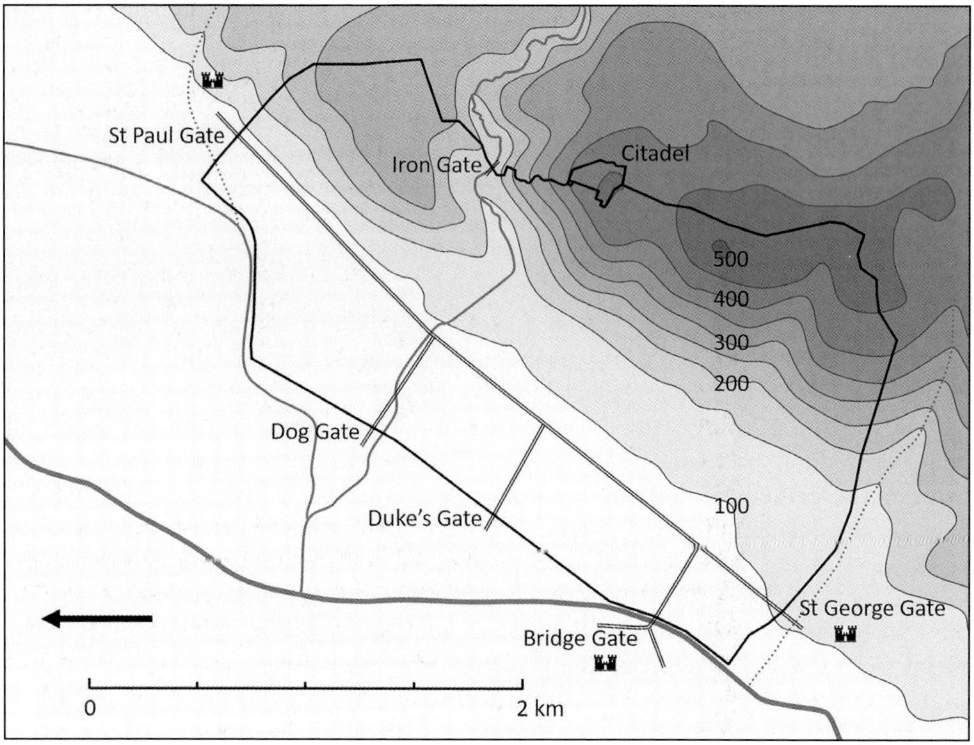

When the contingents of the First Crusade arrived at Antioch in 1097, they recognized that they had little chance of overcoming the city's mighty defences by force. Although there were periods of severe famine during the siege, the crusaders were able to sustain themselves and defeat the relief forces from Damascus, Aleppo and Mosul. To contain the defenders, three siege forts were constructed: Bohemond built the first in late November 1097 to the north of the city, outside the St Paul Gate; Raymond of St Gilles built the second in early March 1098 to the west of the city, near the Muslim cemetery outside the Bridge Gate; and Tancred saw to the third in early April, most likely strengthening a monastery to the south of the city outside the St George Gate. It is perhaps surprising, given the regularity with which siege forts were built in Europe through the late eleventh century and early twelfth, that these were essentially the only ones constructed by the Franks. The shortage of timber and greater threat of significant relief forces may have discouraged their use. Although a number of castles were constructed in the early twelfth century to help impose distant blockades against certain cities, these were often built more than a few kilometres away and were rarely part of active siege operations – an exception was Raymond of St Gilles' castle outside Tripoli.

Naval Support

In his account of Godfrey's siege of Arsūf in 1099, William of Tyre makes a point of highlighting that a critical factor behind the failure of the siege was the Franks' lack of naval support. He returns to this theme when discussing the unsuccessful siege of Acre in 1103 and emphasizes the meagre size of the Frankish 'fleet, such as it was,' employed against Tyre in 1111–12.[31] William was most concerned with the involvement of naval forces because of the assistance they could provide in blockading a coastal town; however, Italian and crusader fleets could also supply provisions, manpower, expertise and building materials.

In the late eleventh century, Egyptian authority along the coast of the Levant had been reliant on its fleet. Following the First Crusade, Fāṭimid naval influence declined as increasing Italian commercial interests saw European vessels come to dominate these waters. This meant that relief by sea for most coastal towns under Fāṭimid control was less reliable, leading ports to the north, including Tripoli and Tyre, to look with increasing focus to Damascus for support. The waters off the coast of the Levant remained under European control for the remainder of the period, providing a vital lifeline for the Latin principalities as Frankish power peaked and then declined.

Blockade and Relief

Acting in conjunction with land forces, a fleet could monitor the maritime approaches to a coastal stronghold and blockade its harbour during a siege. Frankish naval support was often provided by Italian forces, who offered their assistance in exchange for significant commercial rights in the town once it was captured. On some occasions, however, crusaders from northern Europe fulfilled this role: an English fleet that joined the First Crusade assisted with the siege of Antioch and Norwegian naval forces took part in the siege of Sidon in 1110. During the Franks' initial conquest of the coast between the summers of 1099 and 1124, naval elements were present at 68 per cent of these sieges: 85 per cent of those where a considerable fleet was present were successful; two-thirds of those undertaken without significant naval support ended in failure. Although a fleet could offer support, it was rarely sufficient to capture a stronghold on its own. For example, Fāṭimid naval forces attacked but failed to take Jaffa in 1101, 1105, 1123 and 1151.

Naval forces were equally critical to the defence of coastal strongholds. Fāṭimid vessels from Tyre and Sidon brought assistance to Acre when it was besieged by the Franks in 1103; unfortunately for the defenders, no help came by sea the following year when the Franks renewed their siege efforts, contributing to the city's capture. In 1108, the arrival of a Fāṭimid fleet was instrumental in relieving Sidon, defeating the Italian flotilla blockading the city and bringing more defenders; the Franks were finally persuaded to lift the siege when they learned a relief army from Damascus was on its way. Tripoli was less fortunate the following year, falling to its Frankish besiegers while awaiting relief. Unbeknown to the city's garrison, Fāṭimid vessels were headed their way with provisions to last a year – they arrived at Tyre eight days after Tripoli was captured. During the siege of Beirut in 1110, a fleet of nineteen Fāṭimid warships overcame the naval force blockading the city, bringing the defenders supplies and a brief moment of respite before the city eventually fell. Later the same year, the Norwegian fleet assisting with the siege of Sidon successfully prevented the Fāṭimid fleet, anchored at Tyre, from providing assistance to Sidon's defenders.

Symbolic of the changing tide of maritime power, Frankish besiegers imported supplies by sea during their siege of Tyre through the winter of 1111/12. This allowed the Franks to avoid Ṭughtakīn's raiders, who were attempting to distract the besiegers and intercept supplies brought by land. Egyptian influence dipped so low during the following years that the Fāṭimid governor of Tyre was replaced for a period by a Damascene representative, Sayf al-Dīn Masʿūd, who ruled until additional supplies were brought from Egypt. Revealingly, it was Ṭughtakīn, rather than an Egyptian figure, who negotiated the final surrender of the city in 1124. Further south, Ascalon remained a Fāṭimid outpost for another three decades. The construction of the castle at Gaza around 1150 forced the Fāṭimids to rely exclusively on their fleet to send reinforcements and supplies to the town, which, according to William of Tyre, they did diligently four times per year. When Ascalon was besieged in 1153, an Egyptian fleet was able to break through the Frankish blockade, but the town ultimately fell after its landward defences were compromised.

Following the decline of the Fāṭimids, Saladin's siege of Tyre in 1187 was a rare example of a Muslim siege supported by a fleet. In the aftermath of the battle of Hattin, Saladin's army passed by Tyre's mighty defences twice: first as it marched up the coast to Beirut, and then as it moved back down to Ascalon. Only after he had taken Jerusalem did Saladin return to Tyre, making camp on a hill outside the city on 22 November, having paused to wait for his siege engines to arrive and his son, al-Ẓāhir, to join him. The Franks were able to use their fleet to harass the besiegers, shooting them from both the north and south with crossbows as the Muslims advanced along the isthmus between the city and the mainland. Saladin summoned his fleet of galleys from Egypt, which forced the Frankish vessels to seek refuge in

Tyre's harbour, completing the blockade. The size of the Muslim fleet was probably around a dozen vessels; Ibn al-Athīr places the number of galleys at ten, while Ernoul gives the figure of fourteen. Regardless, the siege was eventually broken when the Franks made a successful naval sally on 30 December, seizing five of the Egyptian galleys anchored opposite the harbour. When he saw the engagement, Saladin ordered a frontal attack, but this was countered by a sally led by Hugh of Tiberias. Defeated on both fronts, Saladin sent what remained of his fleet to Beirut. The Franks gave chase, forcing the Muslim sailors to ground their vessels and flee overland. With the blockade no longer in effect, his forces making little progress against the city's formidable defences, and winter weather setting in, Saladin withdrew on 3 January, disbanding most of his army.

Ibn al-Athīr, who owed no personal loyalty to Saladin, summed up the siege fairly condemningly: 'When Saladin saw that the Tyre operation would be a long one, he departed. This was his practice. Whenever a city held firm against him he tired of it and its siege and therefore left it.'[32] To be fair, Saladin's decision was a sound one: his army had been campaigning since the start of the summer, the strength of Tyre's fortifications was renowned and the city was swelling with defenders, refugees who had gathered there as other strongholds fell. Looking ahead, Saladin may also have expected an attack from Europe in response to his capture of Jerusalem. Rather than continue a difficult siege through the winter, Saladin cut his losses and appeased his forces who longed to return home. While his fleet had been bloodied, additional vessels from Egypt would prove instrumental in supporting the defenders of Acre at times through the arduous siege of 1189–91.

Support, Materials and Expertise

A fleet could also facilitate operations by providing logistical support. In 1115, Fāṭimid land and sea forces made a coordinated assault against Jaffa, making a rapid attack and then withdrawing only to strike again ten days later. During this operation, the fleet appears to have transported the ladders and artillery used by the land forces. Decades later, in a final gasp of Fāṭimid aggression against the Franks, a large fleet, said to have included as many as seventy vessels, raided Jaffa and other towns as far north as Tripoli in 1151. Nūr al-Dīn may have hoped to coordinate an attack with the arrival of these raiders, but was preoccupied with his efforts to acquire Damascus.

In the second half of the twelfth century, Christian forces exploited their control of the sea to import siege engines along with large marine forces. The Byzantines appear to have brought siege equipment to Damietta in 1169, much as the Sicilians did when attacking Alexandria in 1174. During the Third Crusade, Richard I of England used his fleet to transport artillery he had commissioned while on Sicily to Acre along with his army. After Acre had been captured, Richard disassembled these engines and stowed them on his ships, allowing him to move them rapidly by sea, as was done when he attacked Dārūm in 1192. This type of manoeuvre would have been appreciated by Baybars, who, despite his aspirations, was never able to outfit a successful fleet.

Although Egypt retained some of its naval traditions, and the Levantine coast gradually fell from Frankish hands, the Mamlūks launched only one significant naval operation between 1260 and 1291: a disastrous attack against Cyprus in 1271 that ended with the fleet wrecked on the rocks around Limassol harbour. Despite this failure, the Mamlūks had little need of a fleet given the dominance of their army. The only real threat they faced came from the Mongols, who had no naval presence in the region. Leaning on the overwhelming strength of their armies, neither Baybars nor Qalāwūn initiated a siege that relied on blockading forces – the Mamlūks intended nearly all of their sieges to be concluded through aggressive action.

As discussed earlier, the involvement of maritime forces might influence what engines were employed at a siege. The arrival of a Genoese squadron and then an English one probably facilitated the construction of the siege forts at Antioch during the First Crusade. Raymond's siege fort was built soon after he and Bohemond set off to escort elements of the latter to the city in March 1098, suggesting they returned with building materials. The following year, it was Raymond who once more championed the expedition to escort the Genoese sailors trapped in Jaffa to Jerusalem, which returned with the timber used to build his siege tower. Over the following decades, similar links can be drawn between the use of significant siege engines and the presence of naval elements.

Some historians have suggested that the frequency with which siege engines were built when Italian elements were present had more to do with the carpentry or engineering skills of the sailors than simply the supplies they brought. The experience of such men handling rigging and manipulating large beams should not be downplayed; however, the early twelfth century was a time when the nobility took an active role in the design of castles and siege engines, while many below this rank would have built their own houses, often using few if any metal fasteners. In such an age, when men would have been far more skilled with an axe than the average person today, the abilities of the rank and file, let alone those with marginally more skill, should not be underestimated. Although some were impressively large, siege engines of this period were structurally simple and the lifting and manoeuvring of large beams into place would have been by far the greatest challenge associated with their construction.

Perhaps the most obvious link between certain nautical traditions and siege engines can be seen at the siege of Lisbon, a sideshow during the Second Crusade. While Louis VII of France and Conrad III of Germany took the overland route via Anatolia, a group of Anglo-Norman and German crusaders made their way east by sea, sailing around the Iberian Peninsula. On their way, this group took Lisbon in 1147 on behalf of Alfonso I of Portugal. During the siege, the Anglo-Normans, who attacked the city from the west while the Germans besieged it from the east, erected two traction trebuchets to support their mining efforts against a section of the western wall, between the Iron Gate and banks of the Tagus River. One of the trebuchets, operated by the knights and their table companions, was set up opposite the Iron Gate, while another, placed near the riverbank, was manned by sailors. Although this supports the theory that sailors had certain talents that were transferrable to the construction and operation of siege engines, this was evidently not a limiting factor, as the knights do not appear to have faced any trouble working their engine.

While the benefits of a fleet are fairly obvious, broader developments led to an increasing reliance on naval transportation. Whereas most participants of the First

Maritime forces at twelfth-century Frankish sieges of coastal Mediterranean towns

Year	Location	Maritime element	Siege tower(s)	Success
1099	Latakia	Pisans	No	No
1099	Arsūf	None	Yes	No
1100	Haifa	Venetians	Yes	Yes
1101	Arsūf	Genoese	Yes	Yes
1101	Caesarea	Genoese	Yes	Yes
1101	Jabala	None	Yes	No
1101–02	Latakia	None	No	Yes
1102	Tortosa	Genoese	No	Yes
1103	Acre	None	Yes	No
1104	Jubayl	Genoese	No	Yes
1104	Acre	Genoese	No	Yes
1108	Sidon	Pisans, Genoese, Venetians, Amalfitans	Yes	No
1109	Tripoli	Genoese	Yes	Yes
1109	Valenia	None	No	Yes
1109	Jabala	Genoese	No	Yes
1110	Beirut	Pisans, Genoese	Yes	Yes
1110	Sidon	Norwegians	Yes	Yes
1111–12	Tyre	Franks (very small)	Yes	No
1124	Tyre	Venetians	Yes	Yes
1153	Ascalon	Franks, pilgrims	Yes	Yes
1167	Alexandria	Pisans	Yes	Yes
1174	Alexandria	Sicilians	Yes	No
1189–91	Acre	Italians, crusaders	Yes	Yes
1192	Dārūm	Crusaders	No	Yes

and Second Crusades had travelled overland, the only contingent to follow this route during the Third Crusade was that led by Emperor Frederick I; all others opted to travel by sea for at least the final leg of the journey, setting sail from southern France or Italy, if not the northern ports of Europe. Subsequent crusading armies would similarly arrive in the East by sea. This was paralleled by events in the Levant: whereas the majority of Frankish forces marched overland when attacking Egypt in the twelfth century, those who joined the Fifth and Seventh Crusades instead travelled by sea.

The Latin principalities along the coast relied on their maritime links to Europe for their economic success and the manpower that sustained them. The county of Edessa and principality of Antioch also profited from alliances with certain Armenians. Although the kingdom of Jerusalem benefited from these links through the accession of the first two counts of Edessa to the throne of Jerusalem, Cilician Armenia was distant and never strong enough to send help as far south as Palestine. Of the four Latin principalities, the county of Edessa was the only one that did not control a significant stretch of the Mediterranean coast, weakening its ties to Europe. Revealingly, the Second Crusade was launched in response to Zankī's capture of Edessa in 1144, but the crusaders quickly reoriented their focus southwards. The decision to attack Damascus has drawn considerable criticism ever since the attack was made in 1148, but Damascus was much closer to the Franks' regional centre of power and a more appealing target for Europeans. By comparison, Edessa was three times as far from the coast, lacked the religious and political significance of Damascus and was controlled by Nūr al-Dīn, who had shown his resolve to retain the city in 1146.

Although the Franks had little use for naval siege forces by the time stronger Muslim powers began to appear in Aleppo and then Damascus in the mid-twelfth century, the importance of the Italian merchant communities remained. They provided the conduit through which trade flowed between Europe and the Near East and were often the ones responsible for ferrying crusaders to and from the Levant. This service became critical as the Franks placed increasing reliance on the support offered by European crusaders in the second half of the twelfth century, something that became a dependence following the battle of Hattin and Saladin's conquests. Although the Franks would look to recover the lands they had once held further inland, the seats and focus of Frankish lordship were already firmly rooted along the coast by the time participants of the Third Crusade set sail for Europe. When Louis IX later thought to fortify a position on the road between Jaffa and Jerusalem in the early 1250s, the local baronage dissuaded him, pointing to the site's distance from the sea and the difficulties associated with resupplying an inland site. Their suggestion that he instead refortify Sidon was accepted – the Franks had become a coastal power.

Deception and Negotiation

A stronghold might be taken through less aggressive means if parties were willing to talk. This could result in a negotiated surrender; alternatively, it might involve deception. In 1098, during the siege of Antioch, Bohemond made contact with an Antiochene within the city, named Firuz, who commanded one of the towers along the southeastern section of the city's walls. Different accounts of the event provide different details, but all accept that Firuz agreed to help Bohemond and a party of men into his tower on the night of 2/3 June 1098. Having gained control of the tower and adjoining walls, the Franks opened a gate and the town was quickly occupied, leaving only the citadel beyond their control twenty-four hours after the operation began. When Nūr al-Dīn finally acquired Damascus fifty-six years later, he had a similar group of betrayers to thank. Other strongholds changed hands through less sensational means.

Treaty

As discussed in Chapter 2, some treaties between Frankish and Muslim parties involved the sharing of territory, others stipulated the transfer of strongholds. Envoys exchanged by Richard I and Saladin through 1191–92 negotiated terms of a peaceful division of Palestine. The final agreement recognized the status quo, including a provision that Ascalon not be fortified in the immediate future, and gave Christian pilgrims access to Jerusalem. More dramatically, al-Kāmil's talks with Frederick II resulted in Jerusalem's peaceful return to Frankish hands in 1229, and negotiations with al-Ṣāliḥ Ismāʿīl during the Barons' Crusade brought Safed, Beaufort and eastern Galilee back under Frankish control in 1240. The results of these negotiations were considerable, but so too were they rare; a large crusading force was present in each case, giving the Franks considerable, if only temporary, leverage. While great potentates might trade castles and territory through treaties, lesser figures could have an equally profound impact on the outcome of individual sieges.

Betrayal

Acts of apparent treachery were typically motivated by prospects of wealth and security. While anyone in a stronghold might be a potential betrayer, chroniclers often identify treacherous figures as members of marginal or minority communities. Firuz, for example, may have been an Armenian convert to Islam, who was motivated to help the crusaders because the ruler of Antioch, Yaghī Siyān, had confiscated his wealth, or simply by Bohemond's promise of a reward. Despite the mixed populations of most cities in the region, examples of Muslims or Christians attempting to help their besieging coreligionists are relatively rare. Members of different ethnic groups of the same religion, who were often able to gain positions of higher power, are more often identified or implicated in acts of betrayal during sieges.

Although some predominantly Christian communities around Antioch and Cilicia used the arrival of the First Crusade to rise up and expel their Muslim garrisons, these episodes are unique to this specific occasion. Reports of treachery or disloyalty, let alone insurrection or rebellion, are extremely rare, casting doubt on the traditional theory that the Franks ruled over a hostile population of locals. Those living on the land appear to have been far more interested in feeding their families than the religious persuasion of the figure who claimed authority over the region, while merchants were often drawn to lucrative markets, regardless of whose flag they were under. Nevertheless, religion was central to polemic arguments and it seems some contemporary authors took advantage of this. In a strange episode recounted by Ibn al-Athīr, the ruler of coastal Jabala, Ibn Ṣulayḥa, conceived a number of plots to divert Frankish attacks in the early twelfth century. In one, he had local Christians reach out to the Franks and promise to help them gain one of the city's towers; the Franks who subsequently climbed up were then cut down one by one as they reached the top of the wall. The episode appears to be a complete fabrication, inspired by events that took place at Antioch a few years earlier, and is suspiciously absent from Ibn al-Qalānisī's account, from which Ibn al-Athīr drew extensively.

The Franks relied quite heavily on the support of local Christians, nowhere more so than in the county of Edessa, but it was members of these communities who were accused most of treachery during sieges of Frankish strongholds. Eastern Christians may have been convenient scapegoats for Latin chroniclers who regarded them with distrust, yet charges of betrayal were not limited to Frankish authors. During

Mawdūd's attack on Edessa in 1112, Eastern Christian accounts describe how a group of Armenians helped a party of Muslims up into their tower. The act of treachery was quickly discovered and Joscelin of Courtenay, who was at that point commanding the city's defence, led an attack that retook the betrayed section of defences.

When dealing with Muslim figures, Kurds are accused of committing acts of betrayal with alarming frequency. When Mawdūd besieged Frankish Turbessel in 1111, Joscelin was able to break the siege by bribing one of the Kurdish emirs. Later, in the 1190s, the Kurdish governor of Jubayl was said to have been bribed by the Franks to hand over the town in the wake of the Third Crusade. Such acts were by no means limited to sieges involving a Christian party: Usāma ibn Munqidh relates a story in which a Kurdish emir led a plot to betray Amida (Āmid) to the Artuqid army besieging the city at the time, and it was a Kurdish emir who was accused of betraying the barbican of Sinjār to Saladin in December 1182, leading to the fall of the city.

Kurdish fighters and emirs, including Saladin and his uncle, Shīrkūh, were an important part of many of the twelfth-century Muslim armies raised in the Jazīra to fight in western Syria; however, the fraction of these armies they accounted for is unclear. Accordingly, determining if Kurds were proportionately responsible for more acts of betrayal than members of other Muslim ethnic groups is hard to say. In all likelihood, there was at least a degree of racial prejudice in some of these accusations, which were launched predominantly by Arab historians. It is also worth noting that Usāma praises various Kurdish figures elsewhere in his work.

When Damascus came under threat from the Zankids in the mid-twelfth century, loyalties were put to the test. During Nūr al-Dīn's blockade of the city in 1154, Mujīr al-Dīn attempted to buy the support of the Franks, reportedly offering them Baalbek in exchange for their help, much as Mu'īn al-Dīn had offered Bānyās to Baldwin III in 1140 when it had been Zankī, Nūr al-Dīn's father, who had threatened the city. Meanwhile, others who looked favourably towards Nūr al-Dīn made different arrangements. Ibn al-Athīr claims it was the town militia that rose up in support of Nūr al-Dīn; however, Ibn al-Qalānisī, a resident of the city at the time, points out that it was a Jewish woman who was responsible for the fall of the city – only after she let down a rope and helped a number of soldiers over the wall did the locals rally and open the city gates.

Damascus was similarly contested at the end of the century, following Saladin's death. When al-'Azīz and al-'Ādil besieged the city in 1196, one of al-Afḍal's emirs betrayed the eastern gate, Bāb Sharqī, to al-'Ādil, forcing al-Afḍal to surrender by the end of the day. Three years later, when al-'Ādil was then in possession of Damascus, al-Afḍal and al-Ẓāhir Ghāzī besieged the city. One of al-Afḍal's emirs, Majd al-Dīn, arranged for the central northern gate, Bāb al-Salām, to be opened for him. Seeking glory for himself, the emir did not tell al-Afḍal or any of the other emirs of his plan. Rushing into the city unsupported, his fairly small force was confronted and cut down as it passed the Umayyad Mosque.

In a very different scenario, the defenders of the Cave of Tyron, a Frankish stronghold in the mountains east of Sidon, were accused of having been bribed by Shīrkūh into surrendering their stronghold in 1165. In what appears to have been a rare example of mass defection, the defenders are said to have fled to Muslim territory afterwards; their leader was the only one who was later apprehended.

Guile

If a besieging army could not persuade any of the defenders to help them, they could try to trick them. One of the ways to do this was by intercepting communications. During the siege of 'Azāz in 1125, a pigeon carrying a letter to the defenders landed in al-Bursuqī's siege camp. The letter had been sent by Baldwin II, who was in Antioch, in response to the garrison's appeal for help, and informed the defenders that a force was preparing to move to their relief. Al-Bursuqī changed the letter to say that no relief was coming, signing the new note with Joscelin of Courtenay's name. Unfortunately for al-Bursuqī, the trick did not work and the garrison stubbornly continued to hold out until a relief force arrived and defeated the besiegers. In 1127, Zankī, who had recently succeeded al-Bursuqī in Mosul, similarly intercepted a pigeon when besieging Nisibis, a possession of Ḥusām al-Dīn Timurtāsh of Mardin. The letter instructed the garrison to hold out for another five days, at which point relief would arrive; however, Zankī altered the note to read twenty days, betting that this was too much to ask of the defenders. The gamble worked and Nisibis was quickly surrendered.

Baybars was also known to engage in deception. When he arrived to besiege Beaufort in 1268, the Frankish defenders sent word of their situation to Acre. The returning messenger was intercepted and a forged letter was sent into the castle to sow discord among the Franks, informing the castellan that he should beware of certain figures under his command. According to Ibn 'Abd al-Ẓāhir, Baybars' secretary and later biographer, Baybars forged another letter when besieging Crac des Chevaliers in 1271. On this occasion, the new letter ordered the castle's commander to surrender the stronghold, which he duly did. Later the same year, during his siege of Montfort, Baybars is said to have shot a pigeon carrying a note from a spy in his army. The message apparently contained little of value as Baybars, taking advantage of a theatrical opportunity, handed the note to the Frankish envoys who were at that time visiting his siege camp, remarking that it was addressed to them. When he set his sights on Cursat in 1275, Baybars had the castellan of the patriarch's castle lured out and detained. Although a letter was sent ordering the garrison to surrender, they refused and held out for seven months. Meanwhile, the castellan joined his father in the dungeons of Damascus, where he died.

One of the more controversial events of the period occurred when Baybars summarily executed the Templar garrison of Safed in 1266. During the siege, he tried to sow discord between the Franks and the Syrian Christians by offering the latter, who accounted for some of the archers and light cavalry in the castle, safe-conduct to leave if they chose. In the negotiations of surrender that followed, the sources offer different accounts of events, obscuring a clear understanding of what actually happened. An agreement of some kind was concluded and the Franks came down from the castle believing they were free to go. A number of explanations are given to explain the massacre that followed. From a Frankish perspective, the Templar of Tyre suggests that the massacre was an act of revenge carried out against the defenders for throwing back a customary gift that they had been offered at the start of the siege. Muslim sources provide a number of explanations, each containing a reason why the agreement of surrender had not been formalized or was otherwise invalid. Whatever the circumstances may have been, Baybars was successful in luring the Frankish defenders out of the castle and securing their arms and wealth before carrying out what was likely an act of more general revenge, perhaps intending it to also serve as an example for others who defied him.

The Nizārī Assassins were masters of infiltration and became famous for the daring high-profile murders carried out by their members. In either 1109 or 1114, a group infiltrated Shayzar while the ruling family was taking in the Christian Easter celebrations, briefly occupying the citadel before they were expelled. About three decades later, they again turned to trickery when taking the castle of Maṣyāf, which was held by a mamlūk of the ruler of Shayzar. On another occasion, they bribed a friend of the gatekeeper of an isolated strongpoint known as Ḥiṣn al-Khurayba ('fortress of the stone heap'). In return for money and an *iqṭā'*, the man visited the castle and, upon gaining entrance, murdered his friend, the gatekeeper, along with the other three occupants of the castle before handing it over to the Assassins.

Attempts to infiltrate a stronghold and take it from the inside were far less likely to work than is presented in the movies and efforts to do so were correspondingly rare. In one such instance, a group of Armenians from Edessa sneaked into Kharpūt in disguise to rescue Baldwin II in 1123. The party successfully killed the jailers and

Maṣyāf. (*monumentsofsyria.com*)

freed the king, who promptly led a takeover of the castle. When news reached Balak, he returned and led a more traditional siege, setting his sappers to work undermining the stronghold while his artillery harassed the defenders. Joscelin I of Edessa, who had been among the Frankish prisoners, had left to get help but was unable to return with a relief force before the mines were lit and the defenders were compelled to surrender the stronghold that had been their prison. In an act of swift revenge, the Armenians and lesser Frankish prisoners were all executed; only Baldwin and a few other high-ranking figures were spared.

On 2 May 1267, Baybars led a disguised force against Acre, carrying captured Templar and Hospitaller banners. The Franks were not fooled as the Mamlūks approached, forcing Baybars to content himself with some fighting beyond the city's walls. He returned and raided around the city two weeks later, remaining in the region for four days while his troops laid waste the surrounding landscape and destroyed Ricordane, the Hospitallers' fortified mill. A few years later, the Mamlūks tried to use the same trick, this time at sea. The fleet sent against Cyprus in 1271 sailed under banners with crosses on them, but they again fooled no one. Although elaborate schemes involving deception or treachery carried the chance of significant rewards, strongholds more often changed hands through negotiations.

Exchange

Negotiations typically preceded any surrender – unconditional submission was rare. In some cases, however, the agreed-upon terms were so generous that they might be more accurately considered a trade. This was a practice most common among senior Muslim figures, a way of weakening a rival or rebellious subordinate while preserving his dignity and mitigating the likelihood that a more deep-seated rivalry would develop. For example, in 1110, Ṭughtakīn gained the surrender of the rebellious governor of Baalbek, following a siege of thirty-five days, by offering him Ṣarkhad in exchange. Although such terms were usually offered or requested after a siege had started, sometimes talks were opened before hostilities began, reducing or even avoiding open conflict between closely associated forces.

As part of Zankī's efforts to consolidate his power in western Syria, he besieged Homs in late 1135. The city's ruler, Khīr Khān, had been an ally, but Zankī had him arrested shortly before siege operations began, compelling him to order the defenders to surrender, which they did not. Although Khīr Khān's sons successfully defended the city, they were so weakened by the affair that they offered Homs to Shihāb al-Dīn Maḥmūd of Damascus in return for Palmyra. In 1146, following Zankī's death, Muʿīn al-Dīn, regent of Damascus, set out to acquire Baalbek. The city was administered by Najm al-Dīn Ayyūb, Saladin's father, who, along with his brother, Shīrkūh, had joined Zankī's service in Mesopotamia and followed him to western Syria, where they went on to serve his son, Nūr al-Dīn. Ayyūb recognized that Nūr al-Dīn was pre-occupied with affairs elsewhere, so quickly surrendered Baalbek in return for a different *iqṭāʿ*. In 1154, after Nūr al-Dīn had established himself and finally gained entrance to Damascus, he benevolently granted Muʿīn al-Dīn a significant *iqṭāʿ*, which included Homs, in exchange for the formal surrender of the citadel of Damascus. The lord of Qalʿat Jaʿbar, Shihāb al-Dīn, was less inclined to give up his mighty castle. Having been captured by the Banū Kilāb and brought before Nūr al-Dīn in 1168, he refused to exchange his castle for another. The mighty stronghold resisted two forces that Nūr al-Dīn sent against it, but eventually the castle was given up in return for Sarūj and al-Mallāḥa, as well as a sum of 20,000 dinars, a lucrative *iqṭāʿ* but one without a significant castle.

The practice of exchanging strongholds remained common throughout the Ayyūbid period. Two years after Saladin's death, ʿIzz al-Dīn Jūrdīk al-Nūrī surrendered Jerusalem to al-Afḍal and al-ʿĀdil, for which he received Bānyās and the surrounding region, including Belvoir and the Golan. A generation later, al-Ṣāliḥ Ismāʿīl and al-Kāmil struggled for control of Damascus following the death of their brother, al-Ashraf, in 1237. Although al-Ṣāliḥ Ismāʿīl initially took control of the city, he was quickly forced to accept Baalbek and Bosra in exchange when confronted by al-Kāmil. In 1239, al-Kāmil's son and successor in Egypt and Damascus, al-ʿĀdil II, became wary of the increasing independence shown by his cousin, al-Jawād Yūnus, to whom the administration of Damascus had been entrusted. When al-Jawād rejected an offer of Alexandria and Montreal as an *iqṭāʿ* in return for relinquishing Damascus, al-ʿĀdil II mobilized his Egyptian forces. This led al-Jawād to offer Damascus to al-Ṣāliḥ Ayyūb, al-ʿĀdil II's brother and to whom al-Kāmil's northeastern lands had passed, for which he would receive Sinjār and Raqqa.

Trading or offering alternative strongholds as a condition of surrender was not unique to the Frankish period. For example, when Malikshāh took Aleppo in 1086, he compensated its dispossessed ruler with the *iqṭāʿ* of Qalʿat Jaʿbar. Nor, it seems, were the Franks excluded from this practice. According to Ibn al-ʿAdim, the Muslim ruler of ʿAzāz offered Tancred his town in exchange for another in 1107 or 1108. Among Frankish parties, however, strongholds rarely changed hands in this manner.

When Frankish fiefs were exchanged, it was typically done when a baron gave up a lesser holding in order to inherit a greater one, or sold off lands he could no longer support. The former was a means through which a prince could prevent any one baron from becoming too powerful: Tancred relinquished the principality of Galilee in order to take up the regency of Antioch, and Philip of Milly surrendered Nablus in return for permission to inherit the lordship of Transjordan. When Frankish nobles were instead downgrading, they typically sold their stronghold, and associated fief, to one of the military orders. This was done by lords great and small who could no longer meet the obligations expected of them, or had no further desire to do so. At large sites, the military orders were occasionally given an interest or partial share from the mid-twelfth century. Humphrey II of Toron famously gave half of Bānyās to the Hospitallers in 1157, Maurice of Transjordan gave the same order property in both Montreal and Kerak in 1152, and defence of Safed appears to have been entrusted to the Templars before the order received outright ownership of the castle in 1168. Julian of Sidon was one of the last barons to hold a major interior castle, selling Beaufort to the Templars only after the Mongol invasion and their raid on Sidon in 1260.

Surrender

The majority of strongholds that fell following a siege did so after some kind of surrender was arranged; instances of towns and castles falling to the sword were comparatively rare but far from unheard of. Town defences were more likely to be captured in this way than citadels, much as the outer defences of a castle were more likely to be taken by force than the keep or another final point of defence. While the defenders of Nicaea negotiated a surrender with the Byzantines before elements of the First Crusade broke into the town, the civic defences of both Antioch and Jerusalem were taken by force, although both citadels held out long enough for those within to negotiate a surrender. During the following decades, the towns of Haifa (1100), Caesarea (1101, 1265), Tortosa (1102), Bālis (1108), Tripoli (1109), Beirut (1110), Hama (1115), Bānyās (1132, 1157), Buzāʿa (1138), Edessa (1144, 1146), Bilbays (1168), Tiberias (1187, 1247), Jaffa (1187), Arsūf (1265), Antioch (1268) and Acre (1291) were among the towns taken by storm, although the citadels of most surrendered on terms, even if these resigned those within to a life of slavery. In a reversal of the norm, when the town of Manbij surrendered in 1176, those in the citadel continued to resist, leading it to be taken by force. The castles of al-Ḥabis Jaldak (1111), Jacob's Ford (1179) and Ascalon (1247) were among those that fell to the sword.

It can be difficult to determine how exactly some sieges ended, as sources were at times provided with contradicting information, and some deliberately presented events to suit certain agendas. For example, Ibn al-Qalānisī reported that Ḥārim fell to the sword in 1157, while William of Tyre wrote that its defenders surrendered, securing both their freedom and property. Despite their differing reports, both men were contemporaries: Ibn al-Qalānisī was in his eighties and living in Damascus, while William of Tyre was in his late twenties. Although the latter was then living in Europe and would not begin to compose his history for another decade, a Syriac account supports his suggestion that the castle surrendered before it could be stormed. Among the events that followed the battle of Hattin, Bahāʾ al-Dīn recorded that many strongholds, including Toron (1187), Bakās (1188) and Bourzey (1188), were taken by storm, which contradicts the accounts of most other Muslim historians, who followed ʿImād al-Dīn's version of events more closely, asserting these places were instead surrendered to Saladin's forces.

There was more at stake than simply possessing the besieged stronghold. If a castle or town fell without an agreement of surrender in place, the customs of war provided no security for the defeated or their property. The longer a siege lasted, the more financing it required: a quick siege could be profitable but a long one costly. Accordingly, both attacking and defending forces had to weigh these considerations. If a stronghold fell quickly by force, there was plenty of plunder to go around, more so since the besieged did not have the opportunity to eat through their provisions. This was the most profitable outcome for the rank and file of a besieging army and a natural incentive. Saladin's troops were reportedly disappointed when the sultan accepted the surrender of Jaffa in 1192, denying the army the opportunity to sack the town. When Mamlūk forces broke into Antioch in 1268, the city was plundered and those who could not flee to the citadel were slaughtered or enslaved. There was so much loot to be taken that it took two days to properly divide it all, during which period the gates were closely guarded to ensure nothing, and no one, escaped.

Unless a besieging commander was in dire need of liquid capital to pay his army or gain their support, which could be expected if a stronghold fell to the sword, a quick surrender was often in his best interests. This limited the disruption to local commerce, from which he now stood to gain, and might mitigate ill-will among the conquered by sparing them the hardships of a lengthy siege. As a siege dragged on, terms typically became less generous: they needed to be liberal enough to persuade the defenders to surrender, but sufficiently harsh to extract enough of a return to compensate the investment that had gone into the siege, a figure that grew with each day the siege ran on. Terms of surrender could range from allowing defenders to leave with only their movable property, to forbidding them from removing any arms or money, to depriving them of any property or even their freedom, reducing them to a state of slavery.

The besieged had the reverse to consider: they were forced to weigh their prospects of holding out and the likelihood of a relief force arriving against what they might be able to extract in return for their surrender. In instances where it was clear that no relief would be coming, strongholds typically fell quite quickly. Garrisons would often make a show of resistance, impressing on the besiegers the potential challenges they could expect to face, but were quick to accept or propose terms before their opponents could invest much time or patience.

While the besieged had only their immediate situation to contemplate, the besiegers also had to judge how much time and effort they were willing to invest in this component of what was naturally a broader campaign, even if ingress and egress from enemy territory were the only other elements. During more complex campaigns, or those that were part of a broader expansionist policy, besiegers were also aware of the message that their terms conveyed to others. By initially offering generous terms, it might be hoped that the defenders of other strongholds would be encouraged to surrender relatively quickly; when resistance was shown, more draconian terms sent an equally clear message.

The multitude of factors to be considered led the terms offered and agreed upon to vary from siege to siege. Some short sieges resulted in harsh terms while some long ones ended with exceptionally generous ones. In this respect, Saladin's campaigns after the battle of Hattin can be quite enlightening. Immediately after the battle, the consequences of his victory were far less obvious than they would later become. His primary interest was to acquire certain key strongpoints deep in Frankish territory as quickly as possible. Foremost among these was Acre, evident in his rush to the coast and the generous terms that he quickly offered, allowing the defenders to freely leave with their possessions. On their part, those who were in the city were probably still dazed from the defeat at Hattin and had little faith in their ability to resist, let alone that they would be quickly relieved. Saladin was happy to offer similar terms through the remainder of 1187 as he pressed his advantage. His strategy was to acquire as many Frankish strongholds as possible before the kingdom could recover and mount any kind of organized resistance, as eventually formed in Tyre, or a significant force of crusaders arrived from Europe.

From a tactical point of view, Saladin may have made a significant error in the autumn of 1187. After joining his forces with those of al-ʿĀdil at Ascalon, the more prudent military decision would have been to attack Tyre, rather than Jerusalem,

Terms of surrender after the battle of Hattin

Surrender	Location	Length (days)	Terms
5 July 1187	Tiberias	3	freedom and property
9 July 1187	Acre	0	freedom and property
26 July 1187	Toron	~14	freedom (or taken by assault)
4 August 1187	Jubayl	<7	(probably freedom and property) release of Guy of Gibelet
6 August 1187	Beirut	8	freedom and property
5 September 1187	Ascalon	13	freedom and property release of Guy of Lusignan
2 October 1187	Jerusalem	15	freedom with ransom
2 December 1187	Chastel Neuf	~150	freedom
22 July 1188	Latakia	2	freedom and property
29 July 1188	Saone	3	freedom with ransom
12 August 1188	al-Shughr	1	freedom
19 August 1188	Sarmīniyya	~6	freedom with ransom
23 August 1188	Bourzey	3	captivity
16 September 1188	Trapessac	14	freedom
26 September 1188	Baghrās	<10	freedom
October/November 1188	Kerak	~560	freedom release of Humphrey IV of Toron
6 December 1188	Safed	~470	freedom
5 January 1189	Belvoir	~500	freedom
April/May 1189	Montreal	~740	freedom
22 April 1190	Beaufort	261	freedom release of Reynald of Sidon

securing the entire coast south of Tripoli and depriving the Franks of a port south of the Lebanon. A crusading army landing at Tripoli or a port further north would be compelled to march south via the narrow coastal road past Beirut, where a small force could halt the advance of a much larger army, or through the Biqāʿ Valley and past Baalbek, a region that had never fallen under Frankish rule. The decision to instead invest Jerusalem was a political one, fitting with the rhetoric of *jihad* that had helped Saladin gain support and legitimacy. Likewise, the harsher terms demanded at the end of the siege, which compelled every Frankish person to pay a ransom in exchange for their freedom (10 dinars/bezants for each man, 5 for a woman and 1 or 2 per child), reflected in part the considerable blood that had been spilt by the Franks in 1099 – Saladin could not be seen to retake the city without a measure of similar brutality. The capture of Jerusalem sent shockwaves through both the Muslim and Christian worlds; however, the period spent besieging the city afforded the defenders of Tyre time to prepare themselves, their numbers swelling with the arrival of those who could afford to pay the cost of their release from Jerusalem. By the time Saladin

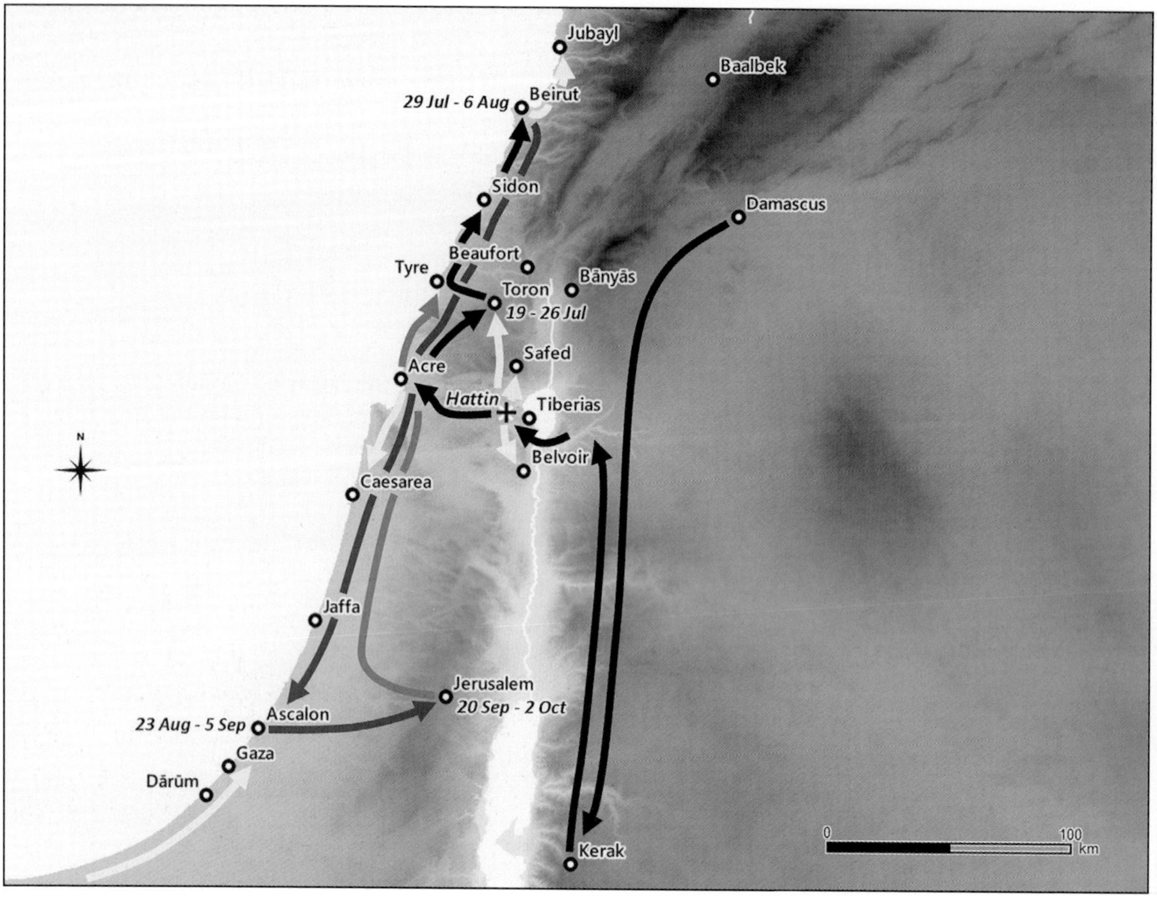

Saladin's campaign in Palestine, 1187.

moved against Tyre, winter had arrived and the defenders exhibited considerable resolve.

During Saladin's campaign through western Syria the following summer, the harshest terms accompanied the shorter sieges. At Bourzey and Saone, and possibly also Sarmīniyya, Muslim forces had captured the larger part of both castles before they were surrendered, suggesting they lacked a sufficient number of defenders. Others, such as the Templar castle of Baghrās, appear to have been more prepared and better defended, demonstrating this before accepting favourable terms reasonably quickly.

Throughout the broader region, the greatest castles were those that held out longest, while some, including Crac and Margat, were simply bypassed. Safed and Belvoir continued to hold out through 1188, as their garrisons may have expected to be the first to receive relief if a significant force were assembled or a group of crusaders suddenly arrived. Only 37km and 55km from the coast respectively, they would have had a reasonable impression of the events going on around them. The defiance shown by the defenders of Montreal and Kerak is harder to explain. Southern Palestine had fallen completely before the end of 1187, leaving these two castles isolated. They may have been lulled into a sense of comfort by the passive blockades imposed by their besiegers or remained hopeful that the situation to the north was less dire than that which we can assume their besiegers were describing to

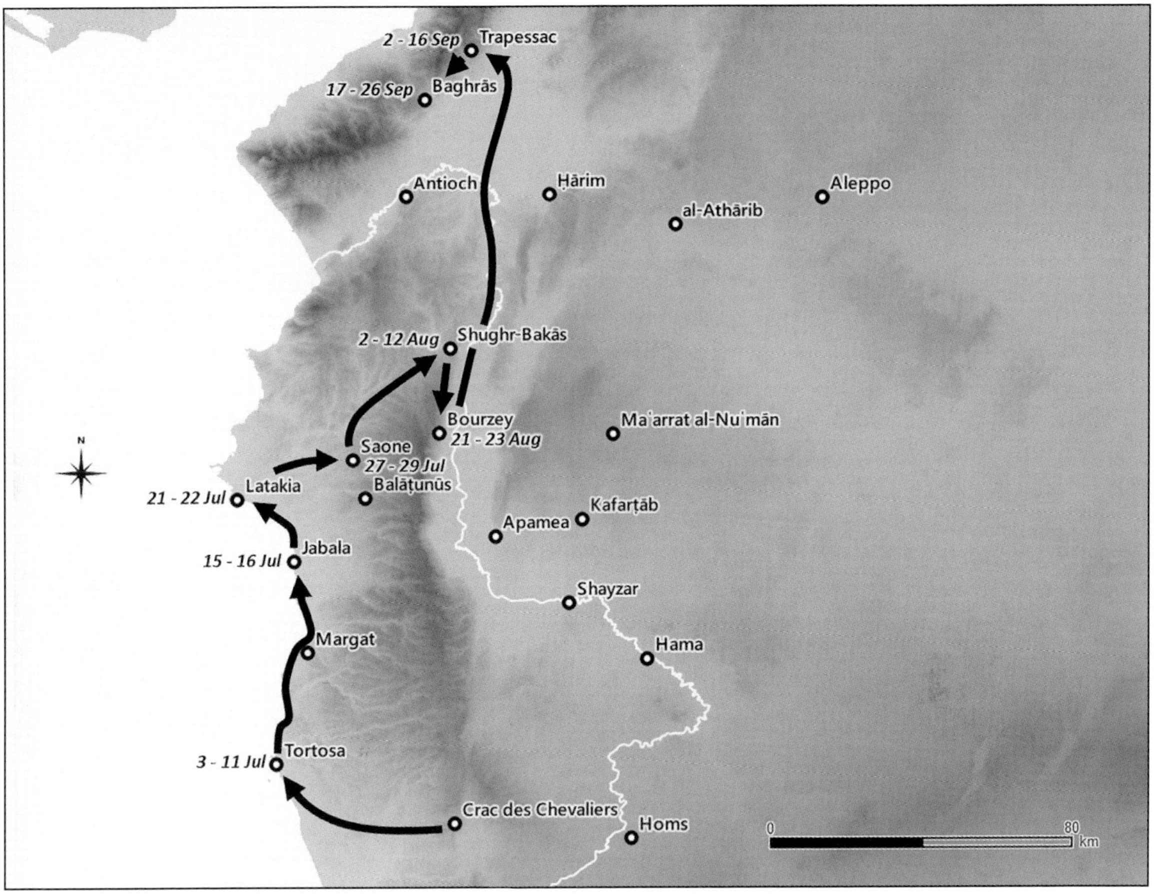

Saladin's campaign in western Syria, 1188.

them. Regardless, after two of the longest sieges of the period, the defenders of both were allowed to return to Frankish lands when they surrendered, testament to their perceived ability to continue resisting and the limited resources that Saladin was willing to devote to their capture.

Perhaps the most ingenious, and certainly most deceitful, defence was that of Beaufort. When Saladin led his army against the castle in April 1189, Reynald of Sidon came out and negotiated a three-month truce, at the end of which he promised to surrender the castle. Muslim accounts assert that Reynald intended to enter Saladin's service, arranging to have a residence in Damascus and a salary, while the three-month grace period was required to collect his family, who were at Tyre. Pragmatically, the three-month truce allowed Saladin to turn his attention elsewhere; his peace with Bohemond III of Antioch ended in May and Frankish opposition was rallying in Tyre. When the three months were up and Saladin returned, it seems he was aware that Reynald had been acting in ill faith, having used the truce to strengthen the castle and gather supplies. Reynald visited Saladin a few days ahead of the deadline to request more time, claiming Conrad of Montferrat had not allowed his family to leave Tyre. When he returned on the due date to ask again he was detained and sent first to Bānyās and then onward to a prison cell in Damascus. Despite the episode of intrigue, the defenders obtained Reynald's release when they finally surrendered in 1190, by which point the Frankish siege of Acre had begun.

The defenders of Kerak had similarly been able to secure not only their own liberty when they capitulated in 1188, but also that of Humphrey IV of Toron, a prisoner since the battle of Hattin.

Eighty years later, the rapid fall of the strongholds around Antioch following Baybars' capture of the city in 1268 is understandable. Unlike Saladin's conquests in the region, when garrisons had offered at least a nominal show of resistance, most strongholds, even those held by the military orders, were abandoned to Baybars without a fight – liberty was not offered to those who compelled the Mamlūks to approach their walls before surrendering. The main difference between the campaigns of 1188 and 1268 was that Antioch had not fallen to Saladin. By comparison, it was the first stronghold that Baybars took upon invading the region, removing the natural hub from which relief forces would most likely be organized, even though Bohemond VI was based in Tripoli by this point. By the end of the spring of 1268, the only remnant of the principality of Antioch in Frankish hands north of Latakia was Cursat, the patriarch's castle, which had surrendered half of its territory to be left alone.

There was little shame in surrendering a stronghold when the odds were almost immeasurably stacked against the garrison, but doing so when confronted by a more modest force, when resistance was judged to be quite possible, was criminal. When Humphrey II of Toron, lord of Bānyās and constable of the kingdom of Jerusalem, accompanied Amalric to Egypt in 1164, he left the defence of Bānyās to one of his knights, Walter of Quesnoy. The rapid fall of the town when it was besieged by Nūr al-Dīn that October led to suspicion that Walter had accepted a bribe, having acted in collusion with a canon named Roger. The accusations of treachery terrified those who were implicated. The following year, the defenders of the Cave of Tyron were believed to have colluded with Shīrkūh when surrendering their stronghold. The castellan was the only one among the defectors to be apprehended, whereupon he was taken to Sidon and hanged. Around the same time, Shīrkūh took the cave castle of al-Ḥabis Jaldak, east of the Jordan. Defence of the cave castle was led by twelve Templars, whom Amalric, upon learning the stronghold had fallen when his relief force reached the Jordan, accused of surrendering too quickly. According to William of Tyre, the king had the twelve Templars hanged. Al-Ḥabis Jaldak had returned to the Franks by 1182, when it was taken by a contingent of Saladin's army led by Farrukhshāh. This time, Fulk of Tiberias, a vassal of Raymond III of Tripoli in his capacity as prince of Galilee, was blamed when it was alleged that the leaders of the castle's garrison, a group of local Syrian Christians whom Fulk had appointed, had been bribed to surrender. Although it is possible that there was treachery in each case, it is not hard to sympathize with the defenders of al-Ḥabis: it was the kingdom's most easterly outpost, nestled claustrophobically into a valley wall, rather than perched on top of a peak where a relief force might be viewed from a distance.

In 1249, Louis IX and elements of the Seventh Crusade fought their way ashore near Damietta. Once they had landed, the Muslim force stationed in the city, which had initially attempted to oppose the crusaders' landing, withdrew. Deserted by the army, many of the city's inhabitants followed. Al-Ṣāliḥ Ayyūb's anger at Damietta's abandonment was not limited to Fakhr al-Dīn, who led the forces that had withdrawn from the city, but included the citizens who had fled, a number of whom he ordered executed; responsibility for Damietta's defence, at least in the eyes of the sultan, seems to have extended to its inhabitants.

Transfer of Knowledge

With so much interaction between the various groups of Muslims and Christians, it is not surprising that their fortifications and siege techniques bear such striking resemblances. Arms and armour, along with the make-up of armies, varied, reflecting different cultural, political and economic factors, but siege engines and techniques were fairly universal. All parties were well acquainted with mining and the various engines and tactics employed by others, so it was enough to see a ram, a siege tower, a trebuchet or a mine to appreciate how it worked and, with a little bit of trial and error, to replicate any superior attributes. The only new engine to be developed during this period was the counterweight trebuchet. The lack of any notice of its sudden appearance and similar absence of any observations that a certain group possessed a particularly impressive artillery tradition suggest that it was employed and developed by various parties as its strengths became apparent. The legendary Greek fire, which gained infamy from the seventh century, had been a particularly fearsome weapon when used at sea. Unlike other siege weapons, its make-up was not immediately identifiable to witnesses. Once a closely guarded secret, a sense of its components had spread with time and a plethora of naphtha-based incendiaries, of varying consistencies, were employed through the twelfth and thirteenth centuries.

Every army would have employed experts and men that we might now call siege engineers; however, there is a risk of placing too much emphasis on the contributions of these individuals, especially in the twelfth century. This was a period when most men would have been able to wield simple carpentry tools with a reasonable degree of comfort, precision and experience, enabling many to provide the labour necessary to build most engines. As time went on, an increasing value was placed on the expertise of those with a proven ability to supervise and design these machines. In the early twelfth century, members of the Frankish baronage are typically found directing the construction of siege towers, while the experience of sailors, accustomed to working with ropes, rigging and long beams, was also clearly valued. If William of Tyre's account of the siege of Tyre is to be believed, the mysterious Havedic is an early example of an identified expert.

In the thirteenth century, experts are more commonly found among the retainers of significant individuals. In the service of Louis IX was John the Armenian, the king's artillery man, so trusted and skilled that he travelled to Damascus following the disastrous Egyptian campaign to procure horn and glue for making crossbows. Also serving the French king was Joscelin of Cornant, who built the crusaders' engines at Manṣūra. Although it is not directly stated, 'Izz al-Dīn al-Afram appears to have had some expertise coordinating Baybars' artillery, as he is regularly commended for his conduct overseeing these engines and their use. His experience did not end there, as he was also charged with repairing certain castles and his position appears to have made him responsible for a number of engineering projects, which included the preparing and maintaining of riverbanks. Although ʿIzz al-Dīn al-Afram appears again ahead of the siege of Acre in 1291, once more making arrangements for the sultan's artillery, the Mamlūks were by this point employing a number of 'siege experts', noted among the forces Qalāwūn had assembled in Egypt before moving against Margat in 1285.

* * *

Besiegers had numerous tools at their disposal. Every siege, like every stronghold, was unique and the weapons that attackers employed reflected this. The siege engines of this period were fairly simple, easily appreciated by those with experience of war, allowing knowledge of any developments to spread quickly. Accordingly, the decision not to employ a certain engine at a given siege can rarely be blamed on ignorance; a plethora of factors from urgency to the availability of materials and local topography all played a part. But engines were only one type of siege weapon. A fleet could play an instrumental role, assisting with a blockade and providing manpower, materials and perhaps even expertise. The emotions of those within could also be manipulated, through offers of reward or compensation, threats or trickery. With so many potential weapons, sieges could end in a variety of ways. While falling to any enemy by the sword was typically the worst scenario for defenders, negotiated surrenders could involve a vast array of terms.

It is hard to say that any of the various parties or powers possessed a superior siege tradition. In the lead-up to the First Crusade, Turkish forces had overrun Arab-ʿAbbāsid strongholds, while Fāṭimid forces overcame the Seljuk defenders of Jerusalem in 1098, as the crusaders took Nicaea, Antioch and finally Jerusalem in turn. Technologically, each group from this point onwards had access to a similar set of tools. The designs of the engines employed by various besiegers inevitably varied; however, the basic assortment of technological and diplomatic options was available to all, if they had the desire and resources to employ them. Each ruler or commander used the weapons and tactics best suited to the nature of his army and the innumerable variables relating to the particular circumstances presented by the targeted stronghold and unique context of each siege. All parties were capable of conducting blockades, launching massed frontal attacks, and employing artillery and miners, but the choice to do so depended on situational factors.

When looking at broader trends, the Franks showed a preference for the use of siege towers in the early twelfth century, particularly when attacking approachable coastal strongholds with the assistance of naval elements. Muslim forces often relied more heavily on waves of frontal attacks, permitted by their typically larger manpower reserves. While the Franks regularly engaged Muslim and fellow Frankish strongholds with similar levels of aggression, some Muslim sieges of coreligionists were more tempered. On some occasions, such as Nūr al-Dīn's 'sieges' of Damascus, this reflected a desire to gain the favour, or at least avoid the hostility, of the local population. Some others were little more than shows of strength, launched to extend or reinforce a ruler's hegemony – in such instances, the neighbouring or rebellious potentate was typically left in command of the besieged stronghold or compensated with one of slightly less significance when a surrender was arranged.

A variety of considerations went into each siege, not least the ultimate objectives of the broader campaign of which the siege was a part. Often these would not only dictate what sites were targeted but also influence the tempo of operations and the tactics that were employed. While each siege was a chess match of sorts between attackers and defenders, there was a larger game afoot that often had a dramatic effect on how specific sieges played out.

Chapter Five

Means of Defence: the Design of Fortifications

Every stronghold was unique. The shape, design and features of each were influenced by the purpose of the structure, the surrounding landscape, the resources of the commissioner and the building traditions of those who constructed it. Although many of the small administrative towers built by Frankish figures in the twelfth century are similar, no two are the same. Larger castles provided more opportunities to incorporate architectural features to further enhance their defensibility. But no matter how strong a castle was, it was always necessary for defenders to make adequate preparations, and often incumbent on them to take action to thwart the attempts of besiegers to gain entrance.

Provisions

Rarely were defences of any design beneficial without defenders, and defenders needed to eat. In the event of a siege or close blockade, defenders would live off non-perishable foodstuffs (including grain) that had been set aside, stored and kept dry in preparation for just such an event. How much was stockpiled depended on estimates of how many defenders there might be and how long a siege might last. In addition to feeding defenders and support personnel, both day-to-day and during sieges, animals also had to be fed. Many large castles accommodated cavalry forces, necessitating huge quantities of fodder for both war horses and service mounts.

Food was important but water was a more immediate concern. Wells were the most reliable sources of fresh water and were reasonably common along the coastal plain. Unlike in Europe, however, wells are rarely found in inland castles, which often crown peaks or ridges high above the water table. A rare and impressive example can be found in the citadel commissioned by Saladin at Cairo: the shaft extends down almost 90m, wrapped by a staircase that winds its way down to the water level.

In some regions, including the Sawād, springs are relatively common and would have provided fresh water for certain strongholds. At Montreal, a tunnel was dug from inside the castle down through the conical hill, upon which the stronghold is perched, to an underground spring below the castle, providing those above with a secure and reliable water source. 'Atlit was surrounded by the sea on three sides, but there were apparently freshwater springs in the castle's fosse, while fresh spring water was used to fill a wet moat around the small stronghold commissioned by Tancred at Baysān. Although most strongholds were built near a water source of some kind, most relied exclusively on cisterns during periods of siege.

In most areas of the Levant, rain rarely fell through the summer months, compelling commissioners to incorporate large cisterns into the plans of their strongholds.

These were designed to collect rain water during the wet winter months and store it through the remainder of the year. The tanks were coated with lime-based hydraulic plaster and were kept as dark as possible, limiting the growth of microbes. Because water was so important, elaborate collection and channelling systems were developed at some castles. At al-Ḥabis, a small Frankish fort on a rocky peak overlooking the basin of ancient Petra, the cistern is the best preserved element of the castle and would have been the most important – today, the region receives less than 200mm of rain each year. For security, and to ensure access, a cistern was constructed or excavated below most keeps, ensuring it would not be thirst that compelled a garrison's ultimate surrender. This was the case at small rural and urban towers, such as Le Destroit, Tarphile (Khirbat al-Manḥata) and Jubayl, as well as at larger castles, including Safed and Montfort.

Cisterns were rarely a stronghold's main water source during periods of peace. Towns developed near natural sources of drinking water and castles were often sited in proximity to some kind of stream – a source of both water and possibly income if the current proved strong enough to power a mill. Taking Montfort as an example, four cisterns have been discovered so far in the upper castle: one below the keep, two under the central range (one of which presumably serviced the castle's kitchen), and one below a large tower at the western end of the upper castle, around which the outer wall of the upper ward was later built. As the castle grew, so too were cisterns

Al-Ḥabis, from the great temple of Petra. (*Michael Fulton*)

Ṣubayba, reservoir. *(photo courtesy of Steve Tibble)*

Saone, cistern. *(monumentsofsyria.com)*

added, as the number of people they were required to support presumably also grew. The tanks were filled by the annual winter rains, which today yield more than 750mm of water. Below the castle, on its northern side, a perennial stream, fed by a number of springs, flowed through Wādī al-Qarn. Although inaccessible during a siege, this was probably the castle's main source of day-to-day water and the power source for a watermill.

At some large castles, including Crac, Kerak and Beaufort, a large open water reservoir, known as a *berquilla*, served as both a defensive obstacle against mining and a working water source, probably used for tasks like watering livestock. While the reservoirs at Kerak and Beaufort were outside the main defences, that at Crac was between the inner and outer walls, fed by an aqueduct that passed through the outer wall.

Walls and Towers

A stronghold's primary line of defence was its walls. Whether these were the walls of a solitary tower or a grand circuit of city walls, they were the main barrier against those trying to gain entrance. At almost all sites in the Levant, both Muslim and Frankish, walls were built of stone. Unlike in Europe, where the majority of defences were still made of wood in the twelfth century, stone was the construction material of choice, due to its availability and the reciprocal shortage of suitable timber, and the existing building traditions oriented around its use in the Near East. Brick was used at some sites along the Euphrates, including Qalʿat Jaʿbar, Raqqa and al-Raḥba, but it was very rarely used in the regions to the west and north more directly affected by the influence of the Franks.

Towers, which had been built along curtain walls since antiquity, were designed and positioned with increasing mindfulness through the twelfth century. These were semi-independent fighting platforms, sometimes stronger and typically taller than neighbouring curtain walls, allowing a tower's defenders to dominate any besiegers who made it to the top of an adjoining stretch of wall. A small doorway, typically lockable from the inside, often provided access from these towers to the tops of the neighbouring walls. At some sites, no such doors were provided, isolating each section of the enceinte should it fall to a besieger, but restricting the defenders' ability to circulate around their defences. Towers that projected from the line of the adjacent walls also allowed archers and slingers on top, as well as any archers shooting from embrasures in the flanks of these towers, to target besiegers near the base of the walls to either side. For this reason, town gates were often flanked by projecting towers. If mural towers were spaced relatively close together, this added firepower could compel besiegers to attack the towers themselves, rather than enter the killing zones between them.

Battlements

At the top of most walls was a parapet and fighting platform. The parapet, or battlements, was a thinner wall rising from the outer edge of the main wall, which was often crenellated – the iconic use of alternating solid merlons and open crenels – to provide protection and facilitate an active defence from the top of the wall. The fighting platform, often a wall-walk, or *chemin de ronde*, allowed defenders to circulate along the top of a stronghold's walls, helping them to move quickly to confront threats as they materialized along different fronts.

By the late twelfth century, some merlons were pierced by embrasures, providing further protection for archers. Early Ayyūbid examples can be found at ʿAjlūn, and every merlon crowning al-ʿĀdil's new citadel at Damascus, dating to the early thirteenth century, appears to have been pierced. The large round donjon at Margat and quadrangular keep of Chastel Blanc, built by the Hospitallers and Templars respectively, are crowned with pierced merlons, while there is evidence that these were used by the Templars along at least some sections of the battlements of Tortosa and ʿAtlit. It is hard to determine how widely crenellations of this style were employed, as the battlements of a stronghold were typically the first part to be slighted or dismantled by stone robbers, leaving relatively few merlons in place today. Sections of surviving battlements at Saone and Jubayl, which predate the earliest known pierced merlons, and the similar solid merlons found at Montfort confirm that this simpler, traditional style was not replaced, but remained in use at some sites through the thirteenth century.

Some towers and walls had a double-level parapet: a lower gallery, servicing embrasures or machicolations, with a traditional open wall-walk and battlements above. This provided space for an additional level of defenders without the costs of adding another level to the tower. In the twelfth century, the Franks employed double-level parapets around the tops of some of Saone's towers and at the central keep of Jubayl. The large circular donjon built by the Hospitallers at Margat, probably dating to the

Crac des Chevaliers, western end of the outer southern defences. (*Courtesy of Denys Pringle*)

early thirteenth century, received similar battlements. Al-ʿĀdil employed this design feature extensively during his fortification efforts in the early thirteenth century and the Mamlūks appear to have shown a similarly strong preference for this style of parapet, famously building such around the outer southern defences at Crac.

Embrasures and Galleries

In order to provide more positions below the top of a wall from which archers could shoot at besiegers, towers and sometimes curtain walls were provided with embrasures – narrow windows that splayed inwards. It was often impractical to extend embrasures through the full thickness of fortified walls, so to give archers a more comfortable and effective space in which to operate, these were often accessed via casemates – vaulted projections of space that typically extended from the inward face of a wall about half way through its thickness. Some casemates were little more than 1m wide, while others were particularly large, such as those in the outer wall of ʿAtlit, each of which might have accommodated two archers. Elsewhere, casemates were not used, as in the four inner corner towers of Belvoir; at the first level of each tower, an exceptionally deep embrasure extended through the entire thickness (3.5m) of each of the tower's four walls. To allow archers to shoot at low targets, such as a person approaching the base of the wall below, the bottoms of some embrasures sloped downwards as they tapered towards the outer plane of the wall, allowing for an opening (or loophole) that extended well below the feet of the archer.

ʿAtlit, outer wall embrasure (after Johns).

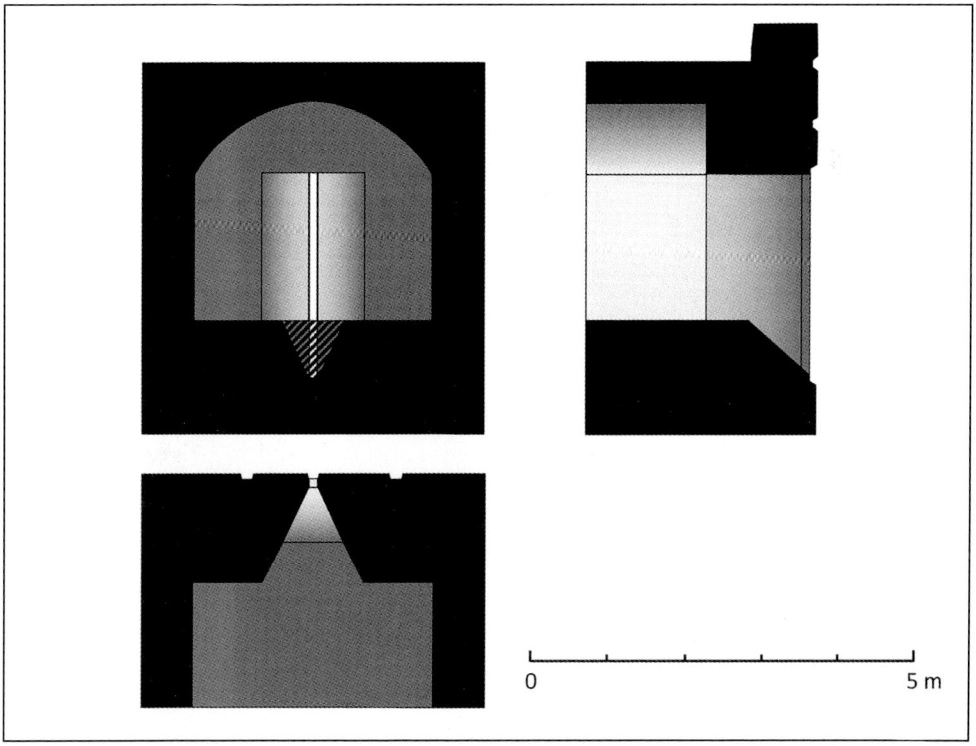

Ṣubayba, casemates and embrasures of the southern rounded tower. *(Michael Fulton)*

During the late twelfth century, it became increasingly fashionable to pierce not only tower walls but also curtain walls with embrasures. The eastern wall of Saone and northern wall of Kerak, the most approachable fronts of both strongholds, were provided with embrasures along their lower levels, while traditional battlements ran along the top of each wall. At both Belvoir and ʿAjlūn, dating to the final third of the twelfth century, vaulted ranges were built against the curtain walls, not unlike those along the northern wall of Kerak. These allowed defenders to access embrasures in the outer walls from internal spaces, while providing a very broad fighting platform for additional defenders on the roof above. A similar system appears to have been employed when al-ʿĀdil rebuilt the citadel of Damascus: he constructed a new line of walls beyond the earlier Seljuk trace, vaulting the space in between to provide a gallery that serviced mural embrasures.

Belvoir, embrasures of one of the inner towers. *(Michael Fulton)*

Belvoir, exterior of one of the embrasures of the inner enclosure. *(Michael Fulton)*

Saone, embrasures along the outer eastern wall. *(Courtesy of Denys Pringle)*

Kerak, line of casemates built by the Mamlūks along the outer western wall. *(Michael Fulton)*

While the embrasures at the citadel of Damascus are spaced fairly evenly, those along the outer walls of Belvoir are not, despite the fairly symmetrical design of the castle. At ʿAjlūn, the southern and eastern walls of the inner castle are provided with a number of embrasures, but when outer ranges were added along both of these fronts (before 1214), it seems embrasures were only provided in the southern wall, suggesting this was regarded as the more vulnerable front. At Qalʿat Ṣadr, also dating to the late twelfth century, embrasures appear to have been placed around most, if not all, sections of the castle's outer wall.

In the early thirteenth century, long stretches of casemates, either open to the air or accessed from galleries or structures built against the curtain wall, became more common. The outer wall of ʿAtlit incorporated a continuous gallery at the upper level, interrupted only by the three outer towers. When the iconic glacis was constructed around the southern and western sides of the upper castle of Crac, a passage was left, creating a mural gallery that serviced more than a dozen embrasures. This was similarly done around the keep at Tortosa, when the Templars added a talus to their earlier tower-turned-keep. At both Ṣubayba and Safed, lines of mural embrasures were incorporated into sections of the castles' outer defences, which date to the early and mid-thirteenth century respectively. Regularly spaced embrasures may also have been provided along the 1km stretch of Caesarea's town walls by at least the time Louis IX had finished strengthening them in the early 1250s. These embrasures

ʿAjlūn, level 2 with exposed sections of level 1 (after Yovitchitch and Johns).

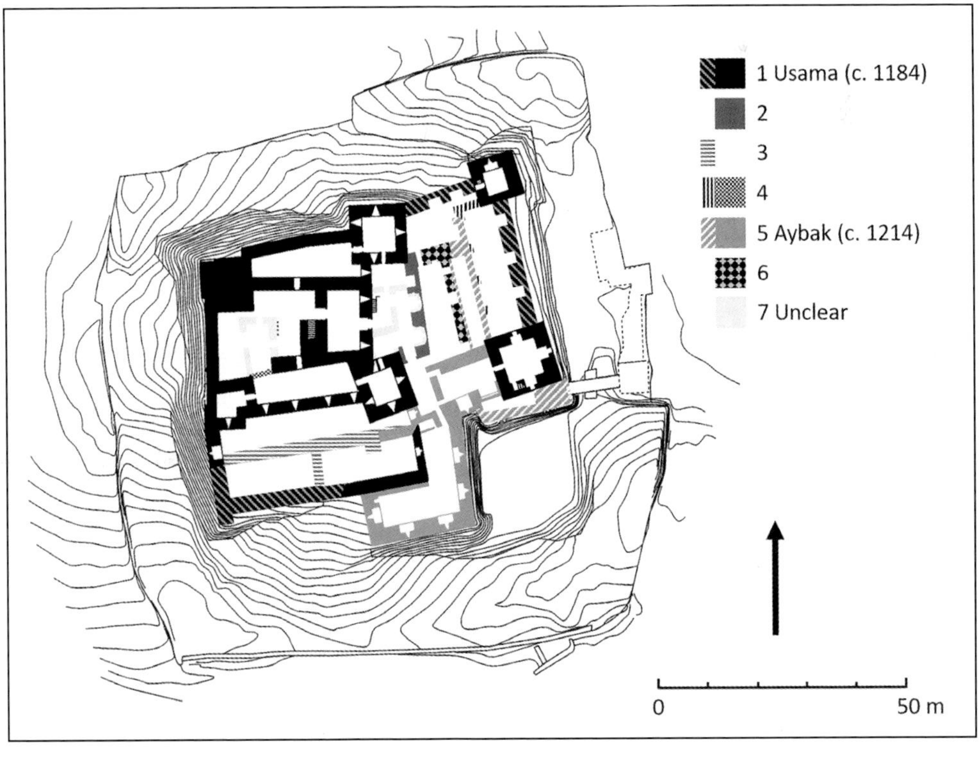

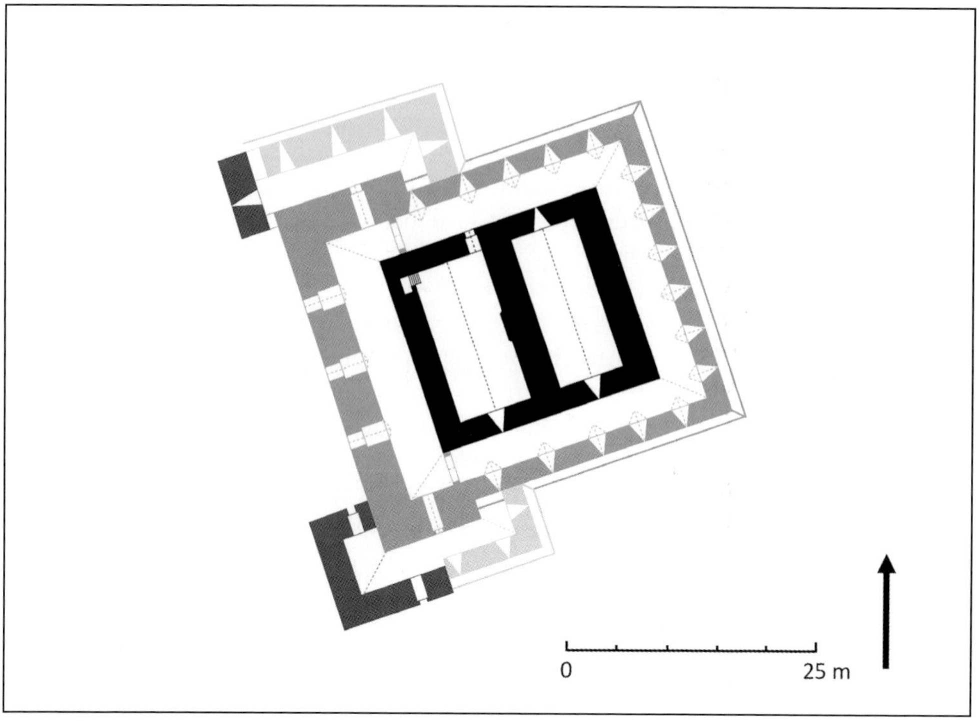

Tortosa, keep (after Pospieszny and Braune).

were arranged at the top of the talus, as was done along the outer defences of Belvoir, while embrasures ran directly through the steep talus of Belvoir's inner defences.

Fosses

One of the simplest ways to provide additional protection to a walled enclosure, whether a tower, a castle or a city, was to add a fosse. Also known as a ditch or moat, these could: completely encircle a stronghold, as was done at ʿAjlūn, Qalʿat Ibn Maʿān and numerous other citadels and towns; surround three sides, if the stronghold had been built at the edge of a plateau, as at Belvoir, Chastel Neuf, Arsūf and many coastal towns; or, cut straight across the most approachable front where a stronghold was naturally defended by the topography on its remaining sides, as can be seen at spur castles like Saone, Montfort, ʿAkkār and Shughr-Bakās, and citadels like those at Caesarea and ʿAtlit, which enjoyed the protection of the sea on three sides.

Regardless of its shape, a fosse served many functions: it increased the relative height of the walls, making frontal attacks and gaining entrance by escalade more difficult; it complicated the use of siege towers and rams, requiring the ditch to be filled before these engines could be pushed up to the walls; and it made the task of mining more difficult. If the fosse were cut into the bedrock, it forced miners either to tunnel into the rock, often at a level significantly below the foundations of the wall above, or to fill the ditch in order to work against the stronghold's masonry fortifications. The rock-cut ditches at Chastel Neuf and Saone are perhaps the most impressive elements of these strongholds, while that at Belvoir was an integral part of its concentric

Chastel Neuf, fosse. (*Michael Fulton*)

Wilbrand of Oldenburg: the castle of Beirut, 1211

[Beirut] is an extremely large city, sited on the sea, having a very pleasant territory. The Saracens, struck with extreme fear of our men and preparing to flee [in 1197], destroyed its walls and withdrew to defend themselves in the city's castle, which is very strong, and was then. However, on approach of the chancellor Conrad, of pious memory, with the whole army of the Germans, so great a fear invaded those sons of iniquity that, fleeing the Teutonic fury, they left behind to our men the undamaged castle with all its contents. It is now owned by a certain John [of Ibelin], a very Christian and vigorous man. And, as has been said, it is a very strong castle. For on one side it is defended by the sea and a high precipice of rock and on the other side it is encompassed by a ditch, walled and so deep that in it we saw many prisoners cast down as in a deep prison. This ditch is overlooked by two strong walls, on which very strong towers have been erected against the assaults of machines, and their large stones are bound together at the joints with large iron bands and hard braces. In one of them, which is being newly built, we saw a very ornate hall.

(Adapted from Wilbrand of Oldenburg, trans. Pringle, p. 65.)

design, and it was the northern ditch at Kerak, between the castle and the town, that ultimately frustrated Saladin's siege efforts in both 1183 and 1184.

A ditch was incorporated into the original planning of many strongholds and, if dug into the bedrock, the stone excavated from the fosse provided plenty of building material. In addition to the ashlars that were often used to face a stronghold's outer

Kerak, northern fosse. (*Michael Fulton*)

walls, a considerable amount of rubble was also needed. Both Frankish and Muslim masons typically constructed fortified walls by building two facing walls of masonry blocks and filling the space between them with a rubble and mortar core. Thus even if the ashlars were sourced from a quarry slightly further from the stronghold, the stone removed from a fosse could be used for the cores of these walls and to build simpler interior structures. Where strongholds were not founded on the natural bedrock, the scarp and counter scarp were often faced with masonry, which helped combat erosion, reducing the frequency at which debris had to be cleared from the fosse, and allowed some with a nearby water source to be flooded. The revetment can still be seen clearly at the coastal strongholds of 'Atlit, Caesarea and Arsūf.

Wet moats were more common along the coast, although still relatively rare in the region, and most appear to have been developed after the Franks arrived in the Levant. Caesarea's impressive town defences were quickly overcome by the Mamlūks in 1265, but the citadel was separated from the remainder of the town by a fosse, filled with sea water, which temporarily halted the advance of the Mamlūk besiegers. The ditches at 'Atlit and Nephin, strongholds that similarly extended out into the sea with ditches that cut them off from the remainder of the mainland, may also have been flooded, or were perhaps floodable. At Damascus, water from the Barada River was diverted in order to flood the fosse of al-'Ādil's new citadel, and attempts may have been made to flood the much longer ditch that encircled the city's town walls. The small castle at Baysān, founded in the early twelfth century, is a rare example of an

Caesarea, defences improved by Louis IX and earlier Roman wall (with topography).

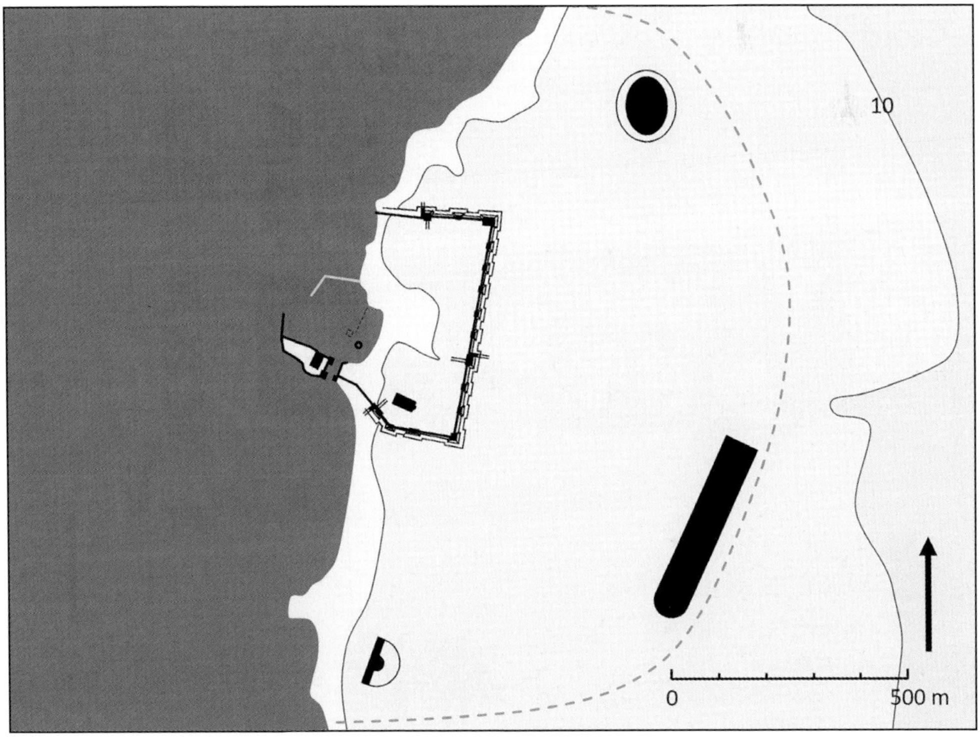

interior castle with a wet moat. Situated southwest of the Sea of Galilee, at the southern edge of the Roman-Byzantine city of Scythopolis, just south of Belvoir, the castle's fosse was lined with hydraulic plaster and flooded by a spring. The small castle complex of Qāqūn, in the plain southeast of Caesarea, is similarly described by one source as a very strong tower 'surrounded with ditches filled with water'.[33]

The advantages of a wet moat were essentially exaggerated at island strongholds. The sea castle at Sidon, developed in at least three stages during the thirteenth century, was never really challenged before it was abandoned in 1291. At Damietta, the Tower of the Chain enjoyed similar protection from the waters of the Nile that flowed around it. The Tower of the Flies, which guarded the harbour of Acre, was less frequently tested but successfully repulsed at least one attack in 1190.

A bridge was usually required to cross a stronghold's ditch. These were often wooden and intended to be temporary – easy to remove or destroy if the stronghold were attacked. This was apparently the case at Kerak, where the confusion and panic of people fleeing to the castle in 1183 led to the collapse of the bridge over the northern fosse. At some sites, a support was left when the rock-cut fosse was excavated, as was done at Saone, where a slender, needle-like pier was left in the eastern ditch, and at Nephin, where a similar, if much lower, example is preserved. Elsewhere, masonry piers might be constructed, the remains of which can still be seen at Arsūf and 'Ajlūn, and in the ditches surrounding the town defences of Edessa, 'Atlit and Caesarea. Although there is some evidence of drawbridges, the surviving architectural

Sidon, sea castle (after Kalayan).

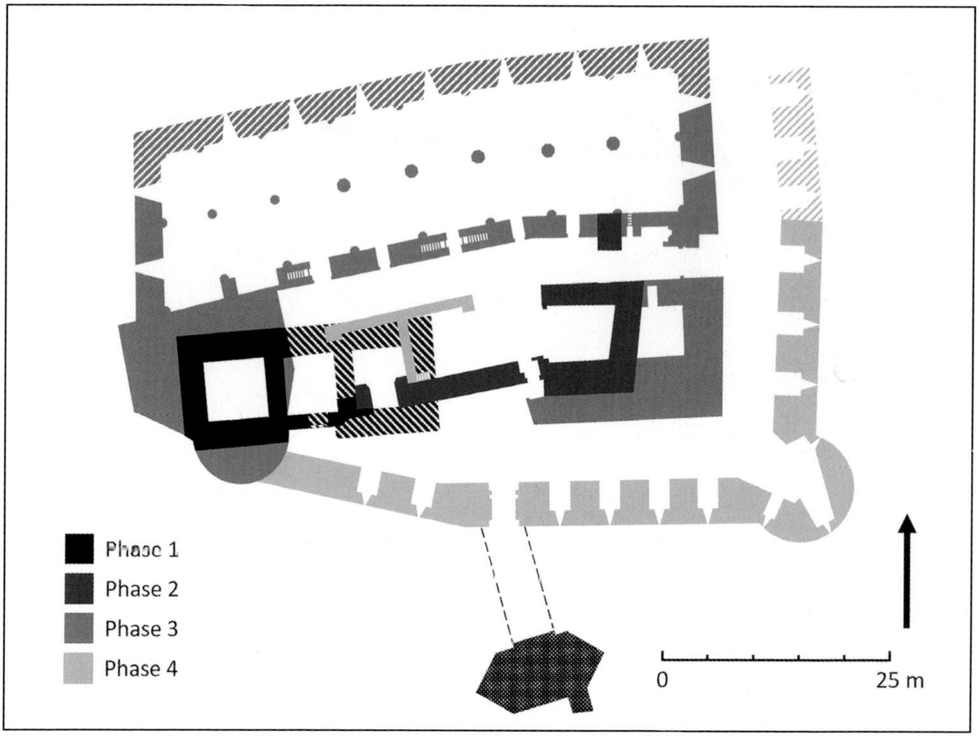

Saone, eastern fosse. *(Courtesy of Denys Pringle)*

evidence suggests these were not particularly popular. One example can be found at the thirteenth-century sea castle at Sidon. When raised, the bridge, which otherwise extended to a pier at the end of a permanent masonry bridge to the mainland, blocked the main gate and left the castle completely surrounded by water.

Visitors to citadels built on tells were often guided along an impressive entrance ramp. These were typically narrow and dominated by the stronghold above, making them deadly killing zones. The iconic ramp leading to the citadel of Aleppo approaches perpendicular to the line of the stronghold's walls, exposing would-be attackers to a long climb out in the open if they chose to use it to cross the ditch. At Qalʿat Najm, the entrance ramp ascends perpendicular to the neighbouring walls but a few metres out from the curtain, leaving a final section to be bridged at the top and allowing the whole approach to be dominated from the walls to the left of anyone climbing the ramp.

Taluses and Glacis

One way to add protection to walls that were fairly easy to approach was to employ a talus: sloping masonry built against or incorporated into the design of the lower section of a wall. These can be found in many Frankish, Ayyūbid and Mamlūk building phases dating to the thirteenth century, although a few earlier examples date to the twelfth century. At some sites, a talus was added to existing walls or towers, as was done at the citadels of Tortosa and Bosra, the castles of ʿAjlūn and Montreal, and the town walls of Caesarea. At others, such as Belvoir and the keep at Montfort, a talus was incorporated into the design of the walls. At Crac des Chevaliers, an exceptionally high talus was incorporated when the inner castle was rebuilt by the Hospitallers following the earthquake of 1202. The sloping masonry appears to begin below the foundations of the wall, climbing up the natural hill, like a glacis, but then continues to rise and joins the wall more than halfway up. The outer stones were cut in such a way as to allow rounded towers to rise seamlessly from the sloping masonry. Following the siege of Margat in 1285, during which the outer southern defences of the castle were undermined, a similar combination of a talus with an integrated rounded tower was built by the Mamlūks.

The primary function of a talus was to dissuade mining. The additional masonry forced the extraction of a greater quantity of stone if the sappers tried to remove the lowest courses, while its mass threatened to collapse a tunnel dug below it, leaving the curtain or tower wall behind standing. Taluses also kept assault forces back from the natural base of a wall, placing them in more exposed positions.

To further secure a stronghold built on a natural or artificial hill, the slope leading up to it might be revetted – forming a glacis – inhibiting any would-be attackers' ability to climb up the hill. Nūr al-Dīn appears to have been responsible for constructing the glacis around the gate at the northern end of the citadel of Shayzar, while others were employed at Qalʿat Najm, Qalʿat Jaʿbar, al-Raḥba and Ṣarkhad. The citadels of Aleppo, Hama and Homs were also provided with glacis by at least the time they were refortified under the Ayyūbids. Frankish strongholds were less frequently built on tells and fewer made use of a glacis; however, that at Kerak is perhaps the most iconic feature of the castle.

Caesarea, talus around the town defences. *(Michael Fulton)*

Shayzar, northern glacis. *(photo courtesy of Denys Pringle)*

Kerak, eastern glacis. (*Michael Fulton*)

Machicolations

Once a besieger made it to the base of a wall, he typically gained a measure of protection. Although archers in projecting towers could still shoot at him from the sides, the defenders directly ahead were less of a threat – those along the parapet would need to lean out over the wall through a crenel to shoot at or drop something on anyone at the base of the wall. Although a talus or glacis might limit the amount of leaning required, this was still a very dangerous position for defenders. What was needed was a safer way for defenders to attack besiegers directly below them. One architectural device that facilitated this was the machicolation.

At their simplest, machicolations could be murder holes: spaces left in a vaulted ceiling through which attackers on the upper level could drop or shoot things at those below. While these were helpful defences for entrance passages, slots were frequently preferred directly in front of gateways, often contained in a recessed arch, ensuring there were no blind spots in which attackers could hide. For exterior walls, corbels were used to build out from the natural plane of the wall, typically at the level of the parapet, leaving spaces between them through which defenders could target anyone at the base of the wall below.

The earliest surviving machicolations date to the eighth century and can be found over the gate of Qaṣr al-Ḥayr al-Sharqī, a fortified Umayyad palace about 95km south of Raqqa and the same distance northeast of Palmyra. As was done here, machicolations were most commonly used to defend gateways through the following centuries. At their simplest, these could be little more than two corbels with a single opening between them, as were employed over each of ʿAtlit's six outer gates, above the gates in the northwestern tower of Montfort's upper ward and the outer northwest gate, and above the entrances of many other towers elsewhere. These often took the form of a box, with masonry rising from the corbels and then returning to the natural plane of the wall at about the height of a person. Larger gates might be defended by such box machicolations with two openings, supported by three corbels, as was done at Qaṣr al-Ḥayr al-Sharqī and those on either side of Cairo's Bāb al-Nasr. Others were dominated by three slots, such as the main outer gate at Margat and those employed along the entrance passage at the citadel of Aleppo. Elsewhere, even longer boxes were used, increasing the number of corbels and openings.

From about the start of the thirteenth century, the use of machicolations increased and the boxes once found almost exclusively over gates were constructed by both Franks and Muslims to defend the bases of walls and towers. Like those built centuries earlier at Qaṣr al-Ḥayr al-Sharqī, box machicolations were used by the Hospitallers around the outer walls of Crac. Surviving examples consist of small projections supported by three corbels, leaving two open spaces between them. Others, built by the Mamlūks following the castle's capture in 1271, make use of between two and five corbels.

Box machicolations similar to those built by the Franks at Crac were constructed around the same time by al-ʿĀdil and al-Ẓāhir Ghāzī, most famously at the citadels of Damascus and Aleppo respectively. These have three or four corbels, while some, which wrap around the corners of certain quadrangular towers, have six or seven. The Tour du Garçon (Burj al-Ṣābi'), built by the Hospitallers to overlook the coastal road

ʿAjlūn, slot machicolation over the inner gate of the outer gateway. (*Michael Fulton*)

Montfort, machicolation over the inner northwestern gate. (*Michael Fulton*)

Montfort, looking down through the machicolation over the outer northwestern gate. *(Michael Fulton)*

Crac des Chevaliers, Mamlūk box machicolations. *(Courtesy of Denys Pringle)*

below Margat, had two two-corbel machicolations along each side of its parapet, aligning with the embrasures at each of the two levels below, and a three-corbel arrangement wrapping around each corner. Many box machicolations that have survived, both Frankish and Muslim, have a small loophole in the outward face, allowing a person inside to see, if not shoot at, what was further away from the base of the wall below.

Under the Mamlūks, continuous stretches of machicolations, rather than boxes, were constructed around the battlements of some strongholds. These were often incorporated into the designs of double-level parapets. The corbels of such an arrangement are still evident along the outer southern defences of Crac. Although this might be considered a superior design, and it would gain particular popularity in southern Europe in the fourteenth and fifteenth centuries, box machicolations remained common in Mamlūk architecture. They were employed when the southern defences of Margat were rebuilt after 1285, at Montreal when a number of towers were rebuilt in the 1290s, and when the Mamlūks rebuilt the citadel of Jerusalem.

Through Columns

Machicolations might help keep attackers away from the foundations of a wall, but there was little that could be done if sappers managed to tunnel into or under the wall. Like a talus, the use of through columns was a defence against mining: classical

Bānyās, through column. (*Michael Fulton*)

Arsūf, through column. (*Michael Fulton*)

granite or marble columns were incorporated into the masonry of walls, aligned through their thickness in order to bond the inner and outer faces with the core. Like medieval rebar, they helped support and spread the weight of a wall, holding up undermined sections that might otherwise collapse.

Columns were frequently used in this way along the coast, as at Alexandria, Ascalon, Caesarea, the sea castle at Sidon and Jubayl, as well as at inland sites such as Cairo, Bānyās, Bosra, Baalbek, Shayzar, Apamea, Diyār Bakr and even Qalāwūn's tower in the centre of Crac's outer southern wall. They were most often employed at sites where there had been a Roman presence, or columns were otherwise readily available. Most surviving examples date to the thirteenth century; however, earlier examples are not uncommon. In addition to thwarting the efforts of miners, through columns added more general strength, providing protection against the effects of earthquakes and at some sites reinforcing areas where structural strain may have been most significant.

Entrances

If attackers were compelled to go through a stronghold's defences, rather than over them, gates could be an attractive place to attack, as these were natural portals in an otherwise solid enclosure. This led to a steady process of developing gateways over the centuries leading up to, during and after the crusades. The size and complexity of gateways were determined by the opposing forces of convenience and security. The day-to-day activities of strongholds encouraged numerous, simple and wide gateways, as these were the main avenues for people and goods entering and exiting the fortified perimeter. The inherent vulnerability of entrances, however, urged the use of only a few narrow gateways with numerous defences.

Large castles and citadels typically had one or two significant entrances, smaller strongholds only one, and larger town defences often had at least one in each cardinal direction. Most town gates were arranged so as to allow the passage of large carts, but this made them more exposed to the approach of rams, penthouses and other siege engines, so were less common at castles. The vulnerability of primary gates led to the development of posterns, which allowed defenders to launch rapid sallies against their attackers without opening the main gates.

The main element of a large gateway was typically a set of wooden leaf doors, which opened inwards. These were fixed in stone sockets at the top and bottom of the doorframe, and secured with a bar or beam that was placed across the doors or slid across from a pocket in the wall on one side. Thirteenth-century Frankish entrances often incorporated a portcullis, the use of which had increased through the twelfth century as fortifications developed. Their use is clearly discernible by the slots found on either side of a gateway, in which the portcullis slid up and down. Although they were less often employed at Muslim strongholds built in the region, three gates at Ṣubayba (those in Ayyūbid towers 3, 8 and 11) incorporated a portcullis. Many entrances, both Frankish and Muslim, also benefited from the security of a slot machicolation, often placed in a recessed arch in front of the main doors.

Compared to larger main gates, posterns were much smaller and lightly guarded, usually reliant on the strength of the surrounding fortifications. These were typically sealed with a single door, opening from one side and secured with a sturdy locking bar. City gates were normally the widest, facilitating the hustle and bustle of trade that sustained the urban community. These were usually positioned between two flanking towers, a tradition long predating the arrival of the Franks, or placed in gate towers, as was the most common arrangement for twelfth- and thirteenth-century castle gates.

The gates of both Frankish and Muslim castles were often smaller than those of comparable European strongholds. Whereas European castles were the primary residences of the nobility, giving them a more palatial quality, castles built in the Levant generally had a more militaristic function – many Frankish and Muslim rulers chose to reside or spend considerable time in the region's cities, entrusting custody of their castles to deputies or castellans. Additionally, the armies that campaigned in the Levant were regularly larger than those operating in Europe at the time.

Bent Entrances and Barbicans

One of the simplest ways to strengthen a gateway was to construct a bent entrance, by placing a second gate, aligned perpendicular to the existing one, in front or behind the first. This created a chokepoint, forcing anyone entering to make a 90 degree turn within an environment controlled by the defenders. While the use of two gates in any alignment provided a killing zone, a bent entrance might disorient attackers and

Caesarea, outer gate of the eastern gateway, featuring a slot machicolation, portcullis groove, lower socket for a leaf door and pocket in the wall for a locking bar. (*Michael Fulton*)

frustrate the use of rams against the inner gate, forcing such cumbersome engines to be rotated and then restricting the space in which they could operate. If the outer gate were placed ahead of the main line of defences, perpendicular to the walls behind, it would be shielded from artillery and besiegers attacking it would be forced to arrange themselves in the shadow of the adjacent curtain wall.

Bent entrances had been employed in the region by the architects of certain Byzantine strongholds and are frequently found at the smaller citadels built in north-western Syria. Earlier Roman-era forts usually had straight entrances flanked by a tower on each side; this design was copied by the planners of the palatial Umayyad 'desert castles', by the Muslim builders of Kafr Lām and Caesarea, where a new set of walls, with straight entrances, was built within the old Roman line of defences, and by the Fāṭimids at Cairo. Straight entrances were similarly preferred in Latin Europe on the eve of the First Crusade. But as fortifications developed, bent entrances came to outnumber straight designs around the end of the twelfth century in the work of Frankish, Armenian and Ayyūbid builders.

Towers were often used to create bent entrances, most commonly by placing an outer gate in one of the tower's flanks and an inner gate in the rear wall. At 'Atlit, a gate was placed in each flank of the three outer towers, and each pair of outer gates then led to a single inner gate at the back of the tower. Similarly, the inner flanks of the towers or protrusions at each end of Kerak's northern wall contained a gate. Bent entrance towers can also be found at Belvoir, Saone, Baghrās, Tortosa, Margat,

Bent entrances.

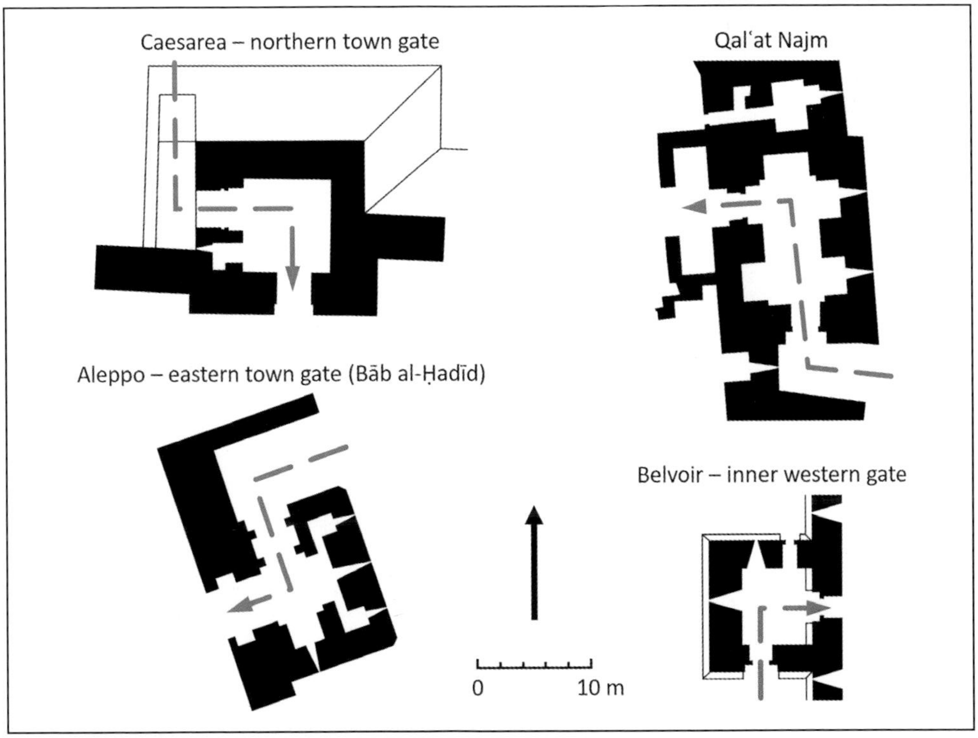

Bourzey, Ḥārim, Safed, Ṣubayba, Crac des Chevaliers, Qalʿat Najm, Apamea, Baalbek and elsewhere. The three town gates of Caesarea were similar bent entrance towers, as were the Zion Gate and Tanners' Gate at Jerusalem, while the addition of a barbican ahead of the northern St Stephen's Gate was only slightly more elaborate. To add further protection, another tower could be placed next to the gate tower on the side of the external entrance, forcing anyone travelling through the gate to pass by the embrasures and defenders of the neighbouring tower. This combined the advantages of a flanked straight gate with those of a bent entrance tower, and was employed at Shughr-Bakās, Bosra, the east gate of the citadel of Damascus and a number of Aleppo's town gates, including Bāb al-Naṣr, Bāb Anṭākiyya, Bāb al-Ḥadīd and the later Bāb Qinnesrīn.

Numerous bent entrances were built under the Ayyūbids at Cairo. Bāb al-Qarāfa is a simple bent entrance tower, while Bāb al-Barqiyya has a slightly more complex entrance portal, commanded by a projecting tower, behind which the gate eventually leads. This system can be found in a more developed form at Bāb al-Jadīd, where a second tower is placed on the other side of the entrance portal, creating a bent entrance flanked by two towers. These are all more sophisticated than the simpler, if typically larger, Fāṭimid gates, such as Bāb al-Naṣr and Bāb al-Futūḥ, which contain a straight entrance portal flanked by two towers.

Longer approaches could be employed to increase the period of time that adversaries were under pressure before they reached a gate. At Ascalon, the northern

Cairo, Bāb al-Barqiyya.

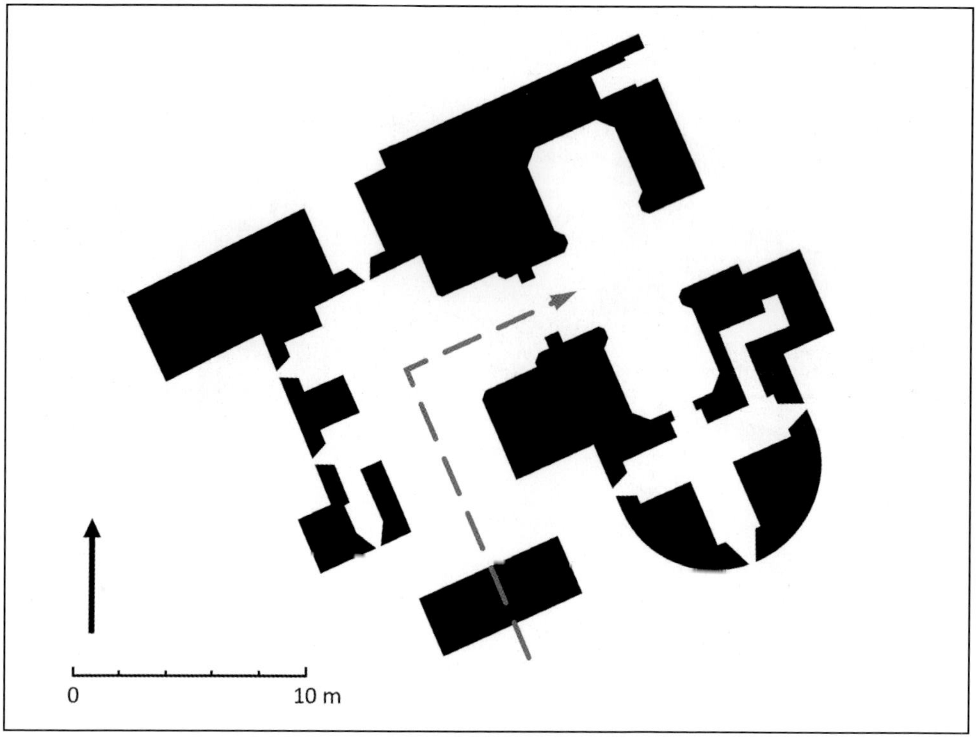

Jaffa Gate was recessed into the town, forcing those who sought entrance to pass first a round tower to the east and then a large quadrangular tower to the west, while another tower dominated the back of this pocket, which led to a bent entrance towards the west. At some sites, the topography could be used, forcing an approach up a predictable route dominated by the stronghold and its defenders, as was often the case at sites built on tells. To further control the progress of intruders, the approach could be enclosed behind an outer gate, creating a barbican, as was done at Qalʿat Ṣadr and Montreal. The Franks strengthened the northern gate of Jerusalem with a barbican, creating a bent entrance in the process, and a similar barbican controlled access to Toron. At ʿAjlūn, a small bent barbican was added beyond the gate of the original quadriburgium and another was built outside the later outer gate in the thirteenth century. The Mamlūks similarly developed the southwest gate of Safed in the second half of the thirteenth century, constructing a barbican that extended north from the original Frankish gate.

The most famous entrances, however, are those at Crac and the citadel of Aleppo. The former, begun by the Hospitallers and developed by the Mamlūks, began and ended with a 90 degree turn, with a 180 degree hairpin in the middle, while the Lion Tower, at the apex of the hairpin, contained another bent entrance that provided access to the space between the inner and outer southern walls. Al-Ẓāhir Ghāzī's contemporary gatehouse at the citadel of Aleppo forced visitors to turn 540 degrees as

ʿAjlūn, outer gate and barbican. (*Michael Fulton*)

ʿAjlūn, inside the outer barbican. *(Courtesy of Fraser Reed)*

Safed, southwestern gate and barbican. (*Michael Fulton*)

Aleppo, citadel gatehouse (after Yovitchitch).

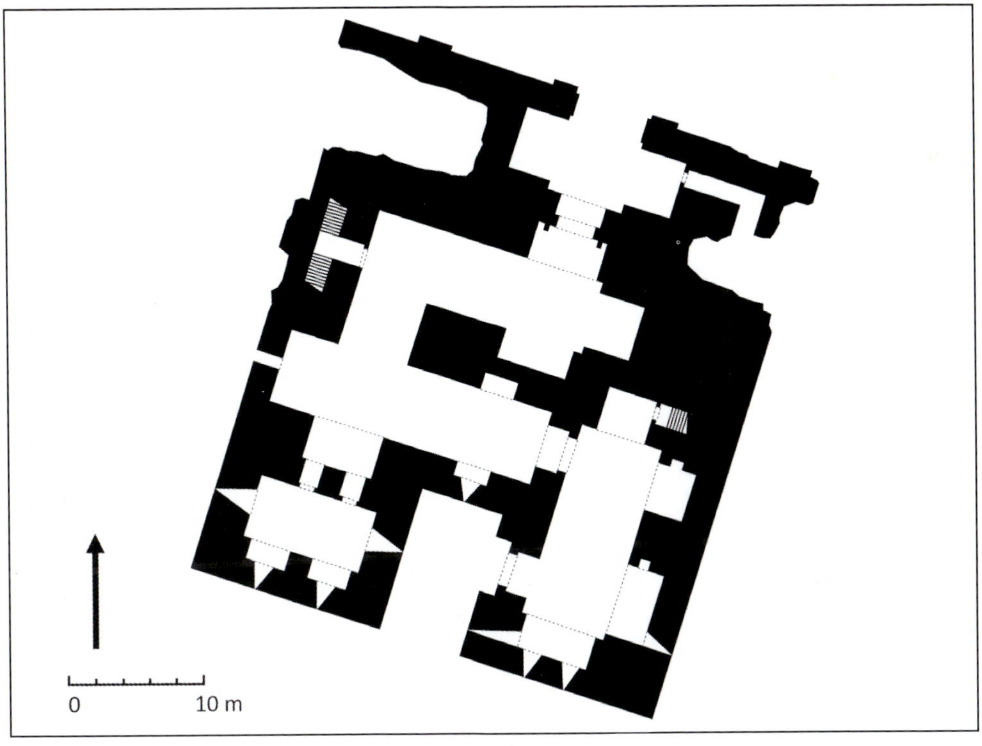

they navigated the serpentine series of 90 degree corners. Designed to resist or detain besiegers as long as possible, most barbicans were provided with embrasures and other defensive elements.

Posterns

While gates kept assailants out, posterns facilitated sallies and helped defenders interrupt the siege activities of their assailants, buying time before relief arrived. If left unobstructed over a sufficient period of time, a reasonably well supplied besieging army could expect to eventually undermine most defences or starve defenders into submission. If a stronghold had only one gate, a single point of ingress and egress, besiegers could concentrate their forces against it, effectively blockading the stronghold without surrounding it. By integrating posterns into the designs of fortifications, builders compelled potential besiegers to extend their lines and spread their forces in order to oppose the threat of a sally from each postern. Unlike gates, posterns were generally large enough for only one person to pass through at a time, ensuring that besiegers could not force their way in during the course of regular siege operations or follow a group of defenders back in after a botched sally.

Posterns can be found in some defences predating the crusades and proved integral at certain early twelfth-century sieges, like that of Mosul in January 1105. Their use, however, increased considerably from about the late twelfth century, as the size of both armies and strongholds grew. Each was positioned to take advantage of the surrounding defences and local topography. At Caesarea, a postern was placed in each of the three landward sides of the city's walls, accessed by a staircase that led down through the wall and talus to a small gate at the bottom of the ditch. The perceived advantage provided by these posterns evidently changed between the final stage of their construction in 1251 and the town's capture in 1265, as those in the eastern and northern walls had been sealed by the time the Mamlūks arrived.

Belvoir was provided with at least five posterns – a sixth may have been located in the destroyed and as yet unexcavated outer northwest tower. Three can be found in the castle's other outer towers, accessed by stairs running down to small gates, tucked into the recesses in the surrounding talus and hidden from view, just above the base of the fosse. The small addition to the east side of the outer northeast tower contains another, and the fifth is located in the lower barbican, which would have facilitated attacks against any force assailing the main gate. The latter two may also have allowed a messenger to escape down the steep eastern slope in times of crisis, as the topography would have made blockading this side of the castle difficult. Collectively these provided numerous points from which the garrison could strike at any besiegers who entered the ditch, forcing their opponents to commit significant forces to guarding each of these points of egress. The larger sally made by the garrison during the winter of 1187/88, however, would have been launched through the main gate. This was a cavalry force that undertook what was effectively a raid during a period of distant blockade – the besiegers being more concerned with relief forces reaching the castle than those in the castle striking out offensively.

While Belvoir's system of posterns was built around principles of opportunity and deception, a different, if equally secretive, approach was taken when the Mamlūks

Caesarea, closed postern in the northern town wall. (*Michael Fulton*)

Belvoir, staircase to the postern in the western mural tower. *(Michael Fulton)*

Belvoir, postern in the outer southwestern tower. (*Michael Fulton*)

developed the western defences of Ṣubayba's outer bailey. When the tower in the middle of the western wall (tower 11) was enlarged, what had been the outer gate in the south flank of the tower was turned into the entrance to a passage that led down a long flight of stairs to a small postern in the north flank of the enlarged Mamlūk tower. Unlike the Ayyūbid gate, the Mamlūk postern is unimposing: a small portal left between the large ashlars and obscured from the outside by a slight rise in the topography before the ground drops away into the surrounding valleys. The staircase behind is quite wide, perhaps twice as wide as those leading to the posterns at Caesarea and Belvoir, with a lofty rather than low ceiling, which would have allowed a significant body of men to gather in this space before exiting the small postern, and possibly in the concealed dip just outside. This would have facilitated sallies that might more accurately be classified as counterattacks.

Before it was rebuilt in the early thirteenth century, Crac des Chevaliers had a single line of walls. The main gate, positioned along the east face of the castle, was flanked by two small towers, and a small postern was located at the north end of the castle. Following the castle's development, the main gate became the final part of the grand entrance ramp and the northern postern became the entrance to the latrine tower – this tower was either a final addition before the great earthquakes of 1202 or the first afterwards. A postern was left in the flank of the latrine tower, which is conspicuously close to the small northern gate that was built when the outer wall

Ṣubayba, postern in tower 11. (*Michael Fulton*)

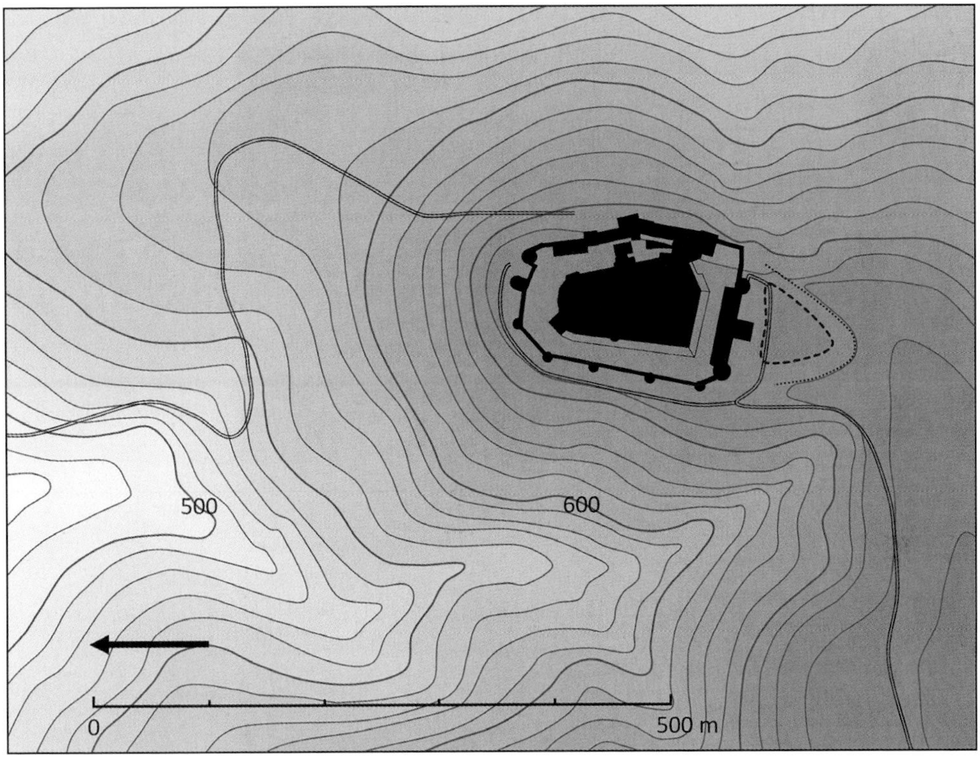

Crac des Chevaliers (with topography).

was added. Flanked by two towers, this outer northern gate was one of two secondary entrances to the Frankish castle; the other was positioned in the flank of the outer southeastern tower, which provided access to the southern outwork via some kind of bridge. Both of these secondary gates, as well as the grand eastern entrance, were developed by the Mamlūks in the immediate aftermath of the siege of 1271. When Qalāwūn's large quadrangular tower was added a decade later, a small postern was incorporated into its flank, accessed through a passage leading through the otherwise solid lower part of the tower.

The expansive defences of Saone were likewise provided with gates at practical points. The main entrance, at the north end of the eastern wall, was accessed from the plateau to the east of the castle. Visitors and assailants who might attack this gate were forced to cross a narrow bridge supported by the needle-like pier that had been left when the great eastern fosse was excavated. The gate itself is flanked by shallow rounded towers and provides access to the various layers of the castle's eastern defences, which acted like an elaborate barbican. A secondary entrance can be found in a simple quadrangular gate tower along the castle's southern side, the outer gate of which can be found in its western flank. The outer western bailey, which encloses the tip of the spur upon which the castle was built, was provided with two gate towers, one leading to the valley on the north side of the castle and the other to the valley on the south side. None of the castle's gates is particularly large.

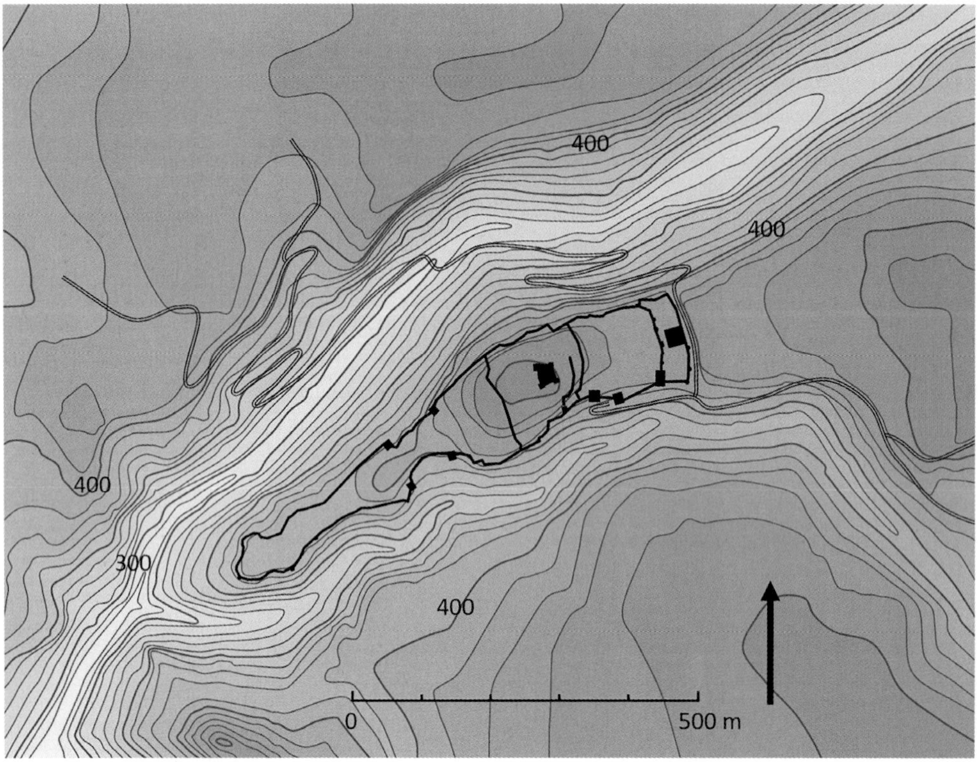

Saone (with topography).

As took place at Belvoir around the start of January 1188, larger sallies, including all those involving cavalry, were launched through main gates, rather than posterns. Such sallies included those undertaken by cavalry forces during the sieges of Arsūf (1265) and Acre (1291), although Acre (and almost certainly also Arsūf) had smaller posterns incorporated into its defences.

The continued use of some posterns in the second half of the thirteenth century and the sealing of others speaks to the particularity of each site and the perceived threats each might be expected to face. Like those that were closed at Caesarea, what appears to have been an Ayyūbid postern in a southern section of curtain at the citadel of Bosra, possibly dating to al-ʿĀdil's early fortification efforts there, was sealed when a talus was added to the southern and eastern sections of the fortified theatre later in the thirteenth century. Evidently it was believed a talus would add more to the defensibility of the site than the existing postern.

Development

An assortment of factors and influences drove the development of this period's fortifications. Although different castles developed in different ways, almost all were the product of ongoing refortification efforts. Where abrupt shifts in the design, scale and style of these structures are evident, as can be seen around the end of the twelfth century and start of the thirteenth, this was typically a reflection of the changing sociopolitical context, rather than a response to the drastic improvement of one or more siege technologies.

Keeps

The keep was a uniquely Frankish defensive element, employed in many regions of Europe. In the Levant, most isolated towers or keeps were built in the kingdom of Jerusalem, where pre-existing defences were comparatively scarce. Rather than a deliberate design feature of a larger stronghold, most keeps began as isolated structures, often administrative towers. Many were surrounded with an outer wall later in the twelfth century, creating early concentric castles, as at Latrun and Belmont (Suba). Although most towers received no outer wall, this was the only addition to many others, while a select few would become the original kernels of much larger castles. To the north, Jubayl, Chastel Blanc and other towers were built and developed in the region around Tripoli, while small Byzantine citadels were often used in lieu of keeps further north. At Saone, the original Byzantine fort remained the centre of the larger castle, which was developed by the Byzantines and then the Franks. The large tower built mid-way along the outer eastern wall is often referred to as the Frankish 'keep'; however, this might better be designated as a donjon (as the term is used here): a particularly strong mural tower akin to those built at certain sites in western Europe from about the late twelfth century.

Quite large towers can also be found in Muslim architecture. These, however, served a different purpose and were often constructed as part of a larger building phase. Al-'Ādil's large towers were some of the biggest built in the early thirteenth

Chastel Blanc. *(Courtesy of Denys Pringle)*

century, but they were often constructed as a series of equally impressive mural towers, no one being central or considerably stronger than the rest. The large circular tower built by the Mamlūks at Safed is perhaps the best example of a Muslim keep. Built within the trace of the Frankish walls, perhaps over an earlier Frankish tower, little remains of this structure. Large Muslim towers were more commonly built along the trace of a curtain, as was done when the outer defences of Ṣubayba, Crac and Montreal were refortified after 1260, 1271 and 1296 respectively. Some of these towers were used as opulent residences, while others were designed with purely military considerations.

Enclosures

For wealthier Frankish patrons, such as the kings of Jerusalem and military orders, the enclosure castle was an alternative to the isolated tower. These were essentially an outer perimeter of walls without a central keep. The three castles built around Ascalon under Fulk were of this type: each was quadrangular with a tower at each corner, one tower being larger than the rest to provide a final position of resistance. Later in the twelfth century, the Hospitallers built Coliath to a roughly square plan, with four corner towers and an additional tower mid-way along three of its walls, with the main gate in the fourth. The order also built Belvoir, which was essentially a small enclosure castle with four corner towers inside a larger one with added mid-wall towers. In the 1170s, elongated enclosure designs were employed at Crac and Jacob's

Twelfth-century quadriburgium enclosure castles.

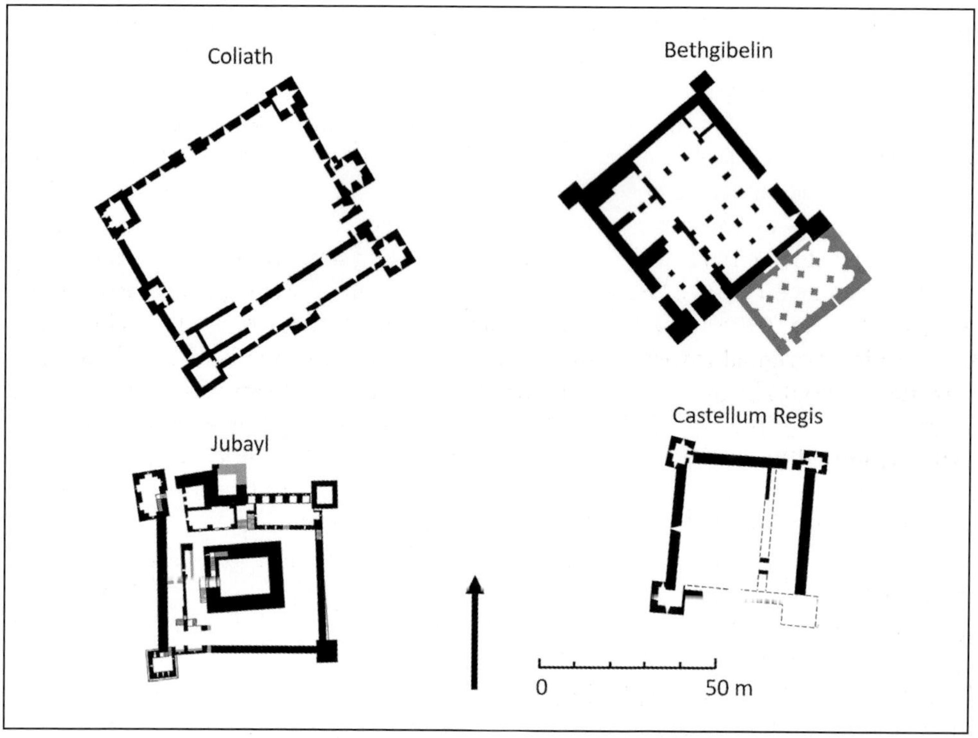

Ford. The former may have had a single tower in the centre of the southern wall and excavations have revealed just one tower in the southeast corner of the latter; neither projected far, if at all, from the adjacent curtain walls. Regardless of their shape, ranges of buildings typically lined the inside of the outer walls of these enclosures, providing internal spaces and a broad fighting platform above. Among the early Ayyūbid strongholds, Qalʿat Ṣadr was built as an irregular enclosure, while the initial phases of ʿAjlūn and Ṣubayba were built to a square plan with a tower at each corner. Unlike many built by the Franks, which had an open courtyard of sorts in the centre, the middles of these Muslim castles tended to be covered.

The square quadriburgium design, adopted by both Frankish and Muslim builders, provided an efficient use of space and was simple to plan and build. The design was inspired, directly or otherwise, by Roman and Byzantine examples, as can be found in the Byzantine remains of Saone and Bourzey. Further south, a more immediate influence may have been certain early Islamic structures, such as Kafr Lām and Māhūz Azdūd, which had been built with Roman-inspired plans long before the First Crusade.

Concentricity

The development of the concentric castle – one built with multiple lines of defences, each enclosing the next – is closely linked with the crusades, although perhaps to an unwarranted degree. The principle of concentricity is often overemphasized, and regarded as some kind of necessary design innovation by historians trying to present linear models of castle development. The addition of an extra line of defences along or around an exposed front was perhaps the easiest and most obvious way of increasing the defensibility of a system of fortifications. Accordingly, most castles with concentric elements were the product of gradual enlargement and refortification; as local rulers accumulated wealth and chose to invest it in a stronghold, they increased the structure's defensibility, but also their prestige and hold over the surrounding region. Although concentricity is often a point of fixation, few castles, with the obvious exception of Belvoir, were designed with truly concentric plans from the outset.

Certain towns in Palestine, including Ascalon, Jerusalem and Tyre, already had a forewall beyond the main curtain by the time of the First Crusade and a number of Frankish towers received outer walls in the twelfth century, as did some larger castles. Rarely, however, were these outer walls built in the same phase as the main line of town walls or original tower – although a central tower, which became a keep once surrounded, could be used as a final point of refuge, most were initially designed to be a first (and only) line of defence. By the time it was captured by Saladin's forces in 1189, Montreal boasted two lines of walls, while some other large castles, including Safed, may also have had multiple lines of walls by this time, although traces of them are hard to identify. In the Syrian Coastal Mountains, many Byzantine citadels, including Saone and Bourzey, became the innermost core of larger strongholds with multiple lines of defences. With the concentration of wealth and power in the early thirteenth century, the means and incentive to add outer walls to the region's most formidable strongholds increased.

A concentric design forced besiegers to commit greater resources if their aim was to undertake an active siege, while providing defenders with multiple opportunities to sustain their defence. The defenders' ability to fall back, regroup and continue fighting as the attackers overcame certain obstacles also provided the defenders with considerable leverage when negotiating terms of surrender, as they could typically do so from a position of reasonable strength, even if they no longer controlled their outer fortifications. This ensured that few concentric castles fell to the sword; similarly, many town defences were taken by force but rarely were citadels captured in this way. Such layered approaches were clearly adopted when the outer walls of 'Atlit, Arsūf and Crac were designed – each closely follows the inner wall, which dominates it from a higher elevation behind.

Beyond adding strength, the construction of an outer wall also created a larger defensible area. For towers, such as Jubayl, Baysān, Chastel Blanc, Chastel Rouge, Le Destroit and many others, the outer wall provided not only an additional line of defence but also protection for important outbuildings, such as stables, and perhaps livestock. The outer walls of many twelfth-century strongholds may have had fairly limited defensive value; often thin and devoid of towers or other defensive elements, they were useful against bandits and small raiding parties, but ineffective against a larger or committed force. This was not the case at Belvoir.

In 1168, the Hospitallers bought an estate from Ivo Velos. Here, on a plateau overlooking the Jordan Valley from the west, the order constructed Belvoir, the region's most symmetrical concentric castle. Designed as essentially a quadriburgium within another, the castle was built in a sequence of phases, but almost certainly to a predetermined plan during a single, continuous construction campaign. The castle's exceptional plan and stout walls reflect its vulnerability – it was easily approached on

Belvoir. *(Courtesy of Michael Eisenberg)*

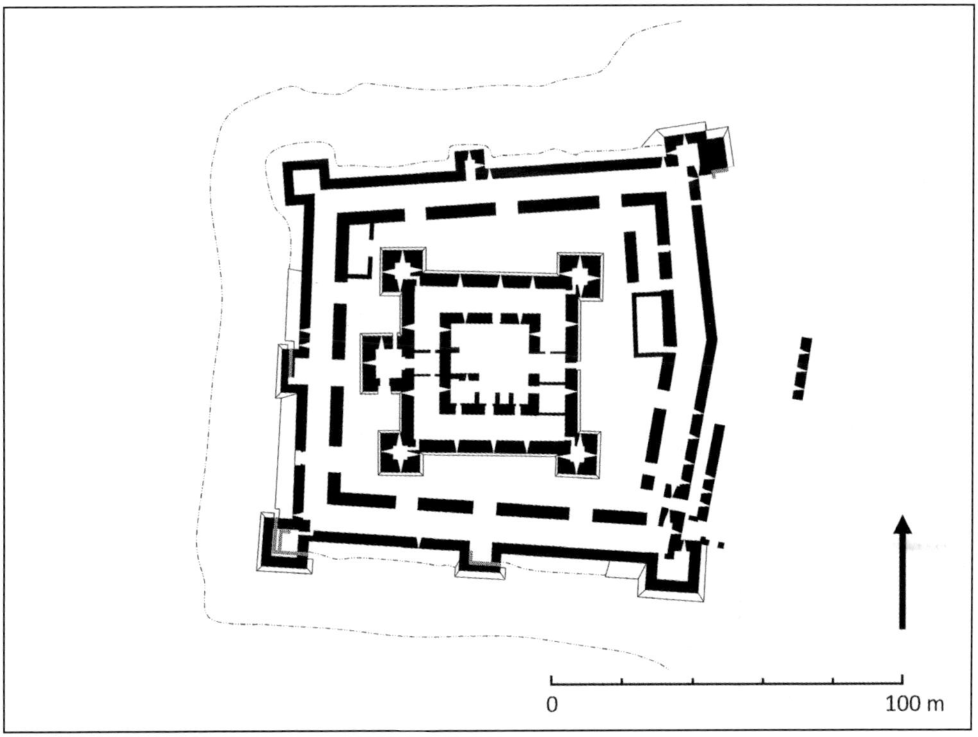

Belvoir (after Biller and Baud).

three sides, leading it to rely on its layered design, rather than the surrounding topography, to a greater extent than any other stronghold of comparable size in the region.

The castle's focus on layered lines of defences and its liberal use of embrasures do not represent a response to the development of any particular siege weapon, but rather to the growing threat posed by Nūr al-Dīn and the manpower reserves that he could commit to an invasion of Frankish territory. Events of the 1170s and early 1180s would demonstrate that contemporary castles, and their designs, were sufficiently strong to resist concerted sieges so long as a Frankish field army was available to offer relief. Belvoir's designers, however, had probably observed the delicacy of this balance in the 1160s, during Amalric's preoccupation with Egypt, and were thus taking steps to reduce the castle's reliance on the arrival of a timely relief force.

With Amalric and the army of Jerusalem in Egypt, Nūr al-Dīn had been able to capitalize on his victory over the northern Franks at the Battle of Ḥārim in 1164, taking Ḥārim and then moving on to take Bānyās before Amalric returned. In 1167, with Amalric once more in Egypt, Nūr al-Dīn struck into Frankish territory first from Hama, taking Ḥalba, Arima and Chastel Blanc before withdrawing, then, after Ramaḍān, he invaded Galilee from Bānyās, occupying Chastel Neuf, which its defenders abandoned. Between these campaigns, rapid attacks by Nūr al-Dīn and Shīrkūh had captured Munayṭira and the cave strongholds of Tyron and al-Ḥabis Jaldak in 1165. Belvoir's plan, conceived or at least settled upon after the campaigns of 1167, was a response to these threats.

The castle's defences worked in three ways: their complexity was an initial deterrent against any attack; their solidity was protection against a sudden surprise attack; and their sophistication was intended to frustrate attackers and prolong siege efforts long enough for relief to arrive. The strength of the castle's various elements is often overshadowed by its exceptional plan. It had a considerable rock-cut ditch on its three approachable sides and a complex entry system that was tucked away along its least accessible front. It was built directly on the bedrock and its walls were uncharacteristically strong, most about 2.5–3.5m thick at the first level and built of the hard local basalt excavated from the fosse. It had numerous posterns, many of which were concealed, and embrasures in the lower level of its inner and outer walls, while more may have once lined the level above, and a crenellated parapet would have crowned its various walls and towers. Belvoir was much more than *just* a concentric castle.

What made Belvoir revolutionary was not only its symmetry, but that its outer walls were probably regarded as its main line of defences. If the outer fortifications fell, the inner structure was designed to provide the defenders with a secure position from which to negotiate favourable terms, rather than attempt to hold out indefinitely. The doors of the inner castle all locked from within the surrounding ranges and towers, rather than the central court; thus, if a gate were forced or the walls scaled, the defenders could continue to hold out even with the very centre of the castle in enemy hands, reducing the chances it would fall to the sword. When the castle was taken in January 1189, Saladin had been forced to undermine the outer barbican, the least assailable section of the castle. Revealingly, as soon as this fell, the defenders quickly sought terms, securing their lives and safe passage to Tyre before the inner structure was attacked. Rather than the plan of Belvoir, which was not copied elsewhere in the Levant, it was the size and strength of the castle's defences that were the real indicators of things to come.

Outworks

Outworks are more often associated with early modern fortifications, but at least two Frankish castles made use of a secondary fortified detachment to strengthen a particularly approachable or exposed front. At Crac des Chevaliers, a triangular outwork, surrounded by a rock-cut ditch and perhaps once crowned with a wooden palisade, was developed ahead of the stronghold's southern front. Although this is generally believed to have been the last element added by the Franks, the spacing of the castle's outer southern towers suggests it was likely planned at the same time as this outer trace of defences. There are striking similarities with the outwork at Château Gaillard, constructed by Richard I of England in the 1190s, but that at Crac is nowhere near as elaborate. When the castle fell to the Mamlūks, focus was removed from the outwork and replaced by Qalāwūn's large quadrangular tower, placed in the centre of the outer southern wall. The outwork's ditch remained a defensive obstacle, but it seems the Mamlūks had no intention of defending it, as the Hospitallers had done during the siege of 1271.

At Beaufort, the Templars built what may have been a more defensible outwork, perhaps more akin to that at Château Gaillard. Often identified as the Templar 'citadel', it was constructed between the order's acquisition of the castle in 1260 and

Crac des Chevaliers, eastern side of the outwork from the outer wall. *(Courtesy of Denys Pringle)*

Baybars' capture of the stronghold in 1268. Very little is known about this defensive feature, as its remains have not yet been exposed by archaeologists. The outwork was probably developed to command the area south of the castle; however, the Templars proved incapable of defending it during the siege of 1268. Opting to evacuate it one night, the Templars gifted the Mamlūk besiegers an ideal position from which to set up some of their artillery, which then bombarded the castle from the shelter of the detached stronghold. Unsurprisingly, the Mamlūks regarded the outwork as a liability and destroyed it after occupying the castle. As at Crac, the Franks' efforts to strengthen an already mighty castle proved to be too little too late in the face of Baybars' dominant Mamlūk forces.

Shift in Design

The construction, expansion and refortification of each stronghold were unique, guided by a particular set of motivations and resources. However, certain trends can be seen in the ways that strongholds developed from the early twelfth century through to the late thirteenth. Notably, many castles and certain citadels became larger and stronger, trends most apparent in those that were built or considerably rebuilt around the start of the thirteenth century. There were two interconnected reasons for this: the nature of the threat that strongholds could expect had changed, and so too had their owners.

The consolidation of western Syria under Nūr al-Dīn, and Saladin's later incorporation of Egypt and much of the Jazīra, meant that far larger forces could be mustered against Frankish castles. These resources may have allowed for the eventual wearing down of the Franks, as appears to have begun in the 1160s and 1170s, and would later take place in the late thirteenth century after the Mamlūks had come to power. But the battle of Hattin changed everything, accelerating the loss of Frankish territory. Frankish rule was effectively preserved for another century thanks to the arrival of the Third Crusade and Saladin's death, which divided Muslim Syria to a degree unseen in five decades.

The old adage that 'the Franks used walls to do the work of men' is most often applied to the twelfth century; however, it more accurately reflects the situation in the thirteenth. The Franks were a small and vulnerable force at the start of the twelfth century, but few sizeable strongholds were built during this period. The growing threats facing the Franks in the late twelfth century are revealed in the investment committed to Belvoir, while Frankish weakness around the start of the thirteenth century is evident in the even greater strongholds that followed, such as 'Atlit, built from 1218, and Crac, rebuilt from 1202.

Whereas small towers and enclosure castles had been common in the twelfth century, nearly all of the castles developed by the Franks in the thirteenth century were much larger and stronger, built on high spurs or small peninsulas that extended into the sea. This was a response not to advancements in siege technologies, but rather to the new sociopolitical environment. The battle of Hattin had curbed the offensive capabilities of the Frankish principalities and thus their ability to disrupt siege activities. With little chance that a large or rapid relief force could be relied upon, Frankish castles had to be able to resist larger forces for longer periods of time. If a stronghold were captured, control of the surrounding region was lost.

Muslim strongholds underwent a concurrent transformation, but this had as much to do with a desire to project authority as it did with increasing defensibility. In the wake of Saladin's death, his successors struggled for control of the Ayyūbid realm, using their strongholds as bases of power against the avarice of their rival relatives, and as projections of their power and legitimacy.

Patrons

The crown was responsible for commissioning many of the larger strongholds built in the kingdom of Jerusalem during the early twelfth century. Most were then entrusted to barons or the military orders, who went on to enlarge them. In the other Frankish principalities, most of the large castles were also held by the baronage and military orders, although the majority were of earlier Byzantine, Armenian, Arab and Kurdish origins. As the military orders inherited and bought lands with increasing regularity from the mid-twelfth century, they were able to put the weight of the resources they acquired in Europe behind the maintenance and development of their strongholds. This became evident following the battle of Hattin: Safed and Belvoir, belonging to the Templars and Hospitallers respectively, held out longer than most other castles in Palestine, and the Templar keep at Tortosa was the only stronghold Saladin besieged but failed to take during his campaign through western Syria in 1188, during which he opted to bypass the Hospitaller castles of Crac and Margat. During the thirteenth century, huge amounts of money were poured into these castles, such that only the military orders were capable of investing. Although most of the orders' castles had been founded in the twelfth century or earlier, some, such as 'Atlit and Montfort, were not built until the thirteenth century.

Most Muslim fortification efforts of the early twelfth century, like those of the Franks, were undertaken organically, parts of piecemeal processes of investment and improvement. After extending his authority across much of western Syria, Nūr al-Dīn commissioned broader fortification campaigns following a series of devastating earthquakes in 1157 and 1170. Beyond his principal power centres, Aleppo and Damascus, his work touched Shayzar, Qal'at Najm, and other secondary strongholds. Although these works appear to have been necessitated by factors beyond Nūr al-Dīn's control, they effectively stamped his mark across his realm. Others took more overt measures to express their authority. Saladin's new citadel at Cairo not only secured his hold over the city, but was a physical manifestation of the regime change he had headed. Following his death, Saladin's heirs undertook similar fortification campaigns, which both entrenched their power and served as outward expressions of their authority. Critically, Muslim power was once more divided, leaving significant rivals vying for influence.

The defences commissioned by Nūr al-Dīn and Saladin are considered fairly traditional, keeping to established forms and scales relative to the more monumental and ostentatious elements chosen by later Ayyūbids. Common motifs or styles were often employed by these latter figures, which served as clear markers of their rule. One of

Cairo, citadel.

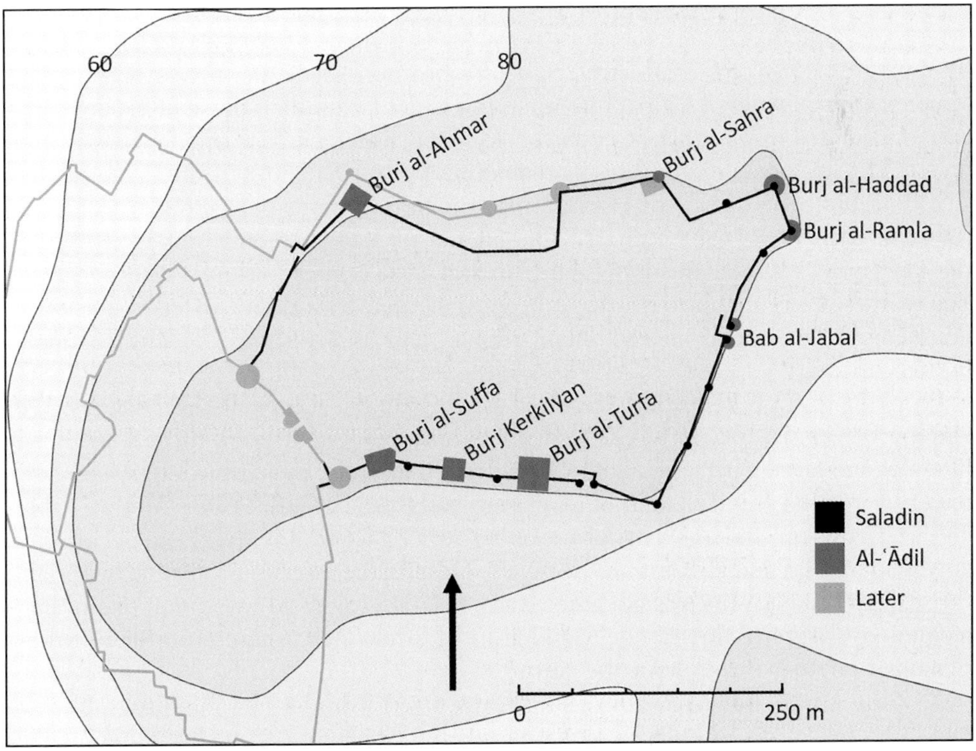

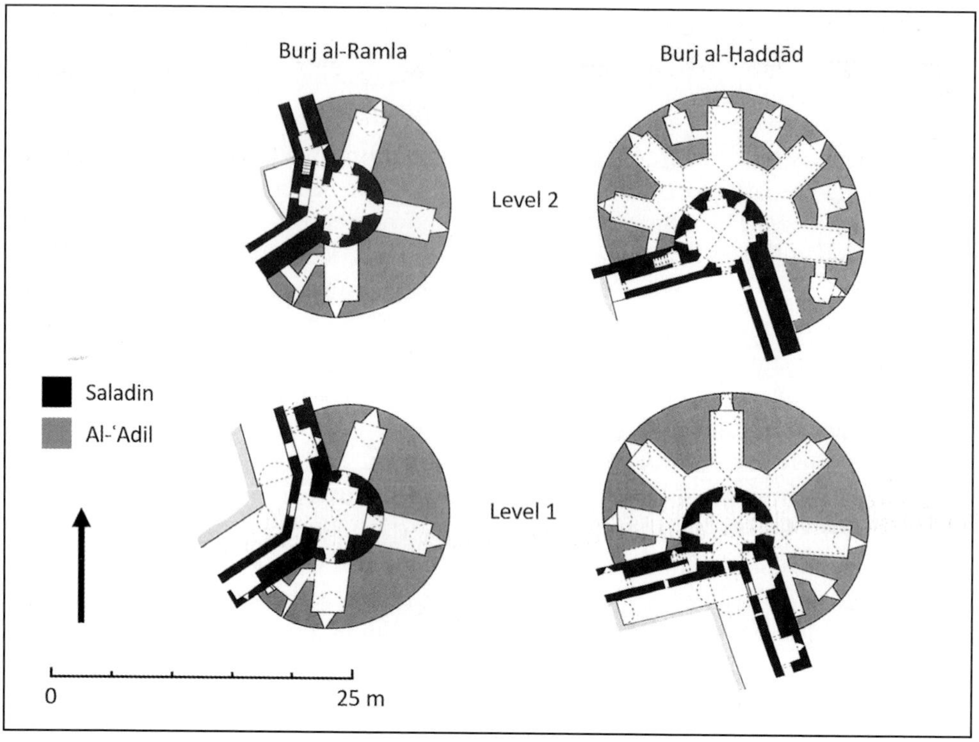

Cairo, citadel towers Burj al-Ramla and Burj al-Ḥaddād (after Creswell).

the building signatures of al-ʿĀdil, Saladin's brother, was scale: the towers he constructed at the citadel of Cairo were up to five times larger than those of his brother – certain rounded towers that he constructed there, which enclose smaller towers built under Saladin, are almost 20m in diameter. Before Saladin's death, al-ʿĀdil had already rebuilt the citadel of Ḥarrān, placing an enormous near-circular polygonal tower at each of its four corners. The citadel of Raqqa, rebuilt under al-ʿĀdil in the 1190s, has a similar quadrangular plan and large corner towers. The exaggerated size of these towers appears to have been motivated by a desire to instil a sense of grandeur in those who viewed them, rather than as a response to any particular military threat.

From the start of the second decade of the thirteenth century, al-ʿĀdil continued to employ enormous towers but settled on a more consistent plan: most were quadrangular and faced with large blocks with drafted margins and rusticated bosses. Such towers were used at the citadels of Damascus and Bosra, as well as atop Mount Tabor, and at Jerusalem and the citadel of Cairo, where work was overseen by his sons al-Muʿaẓẓam ʿĪsā and al-Kāmil respectively. Despite the assertions of some historians, the scale of these towers was not a necessary reaction to the advancement of any siege technology; proof of this can be found at most other sites, where quite small towers remained popular throughout the century.

Al-Ẓāhir Ghāzī, one of Saladin's sons, patronized a similar building programme to that of his uncle, al-ʿĀdil, developing not only the citadel of Aleppo but other citadels

Al-Raḥba. (*monumentsofsyria.com*)

that fell under his influence. Secondary figures, who sought to gain further power and autonomy by leveraging their position between the major Ayyūbid princes, used strongholds in the same way. Al-Mujāhid Shīrkūh II, the grandson of his namesake, had inherited Homs before Saladin's death, and consolidated his position during the struggles that followed by rebuilding the citadel of al-Raḥba in 1207. In 1227, he strengthened the citadel of Homs and around 1230 rebuilt the castle of Shmemis, 4km northwest of Salamiyya, and constructed a new castle on a hill 2km northwest of Palmyra, which replaced the fortified Temple of Bel as the community's citadel. These projects may have encouraged the fortification programme launched by his neighbour, al-Muẓaffar Maḥmūd of Hama, around the same time.

Al-Muẓaffar Maḥmūd was the grandson of Taqī al-Dīn ʿUmar, Saladin's ambitious and capable nephew. He was originally usurped as emir of Hama by his brother, al-Nāṣir Qilij Arslān, upon the death of their father, al-Manṣūr Muḥammad. Although Hama was traditionally in the sphere of Aleppo, their father had supported al-ʿĀdil against al-Ẓāhir Ghāzī, even sending al-Muẓaffar to assist al-Kāmil, al-ʿĀdil's son and successor in Egypt. It was thanks to the later support of al-Kāmil that al-Muẓaffar regained Hama. The shaky and delayed start to his rule probably contributed to al-Muẓaffar's decision to refortify the strongholds of his realm. Around 1232, he reinforced the defences of Hama, rebuilt the citadel of Maʿarrat al-Nuʿmān and strengthened Montferrand.

Under the Mamlūks, Muslim rule was more centralized and many refortification projects reveal clearer attention to military considerations. The ease with which the Mongols seemed to overrun western Syria in 1260 impressed the need to improve certain strongholds. Many castles and citadels had been slighted by the Mongols before they withdrew, providing a natural opportunity to rebuild them. Some sites, such as Ṣubayba, were improved by adding very different elements, including larger quadrangular towers as well as rounded ones. Elsewhere, as at the citadel of Damascus, the defences built by the Ayyūbids were replicated, right down to the masonry style. This site-by-site pragmatism operated in conjunction with a simple policy when it came to captured Frankish strongholds: those along the coast were slighted, so as not to be transformed into bridgeheads from Europe if retaken by crusaders, but significant interior castles were developed and employed as armouries and seats of local power. These great interior castles, including Safed, Beaufort, Crac and Margat, were improved, presumably ensuring they were defensible should another great Mongol invasion materialize.

The designs of Mamlūk towers, like all others, reveal a range of guiding influences. Some, such as the outer southern towers at Crac and Margat, are exceptionally solid, while the expanded southwest tower of Ṣubayba and similarly large tower added to the citadel complex at Baalbek are bristling with embrasures. Others show more apparent domestic functions. Even in those towers designed for quite obvious defensive purposes, the interior can be elegant and the masonry fine, as in the rounded towers at Crac and Ṣubayba. At some sites, efforts were made to match the existing dressing. At Crac, the Mamlūks' smooth masonry blends almost seamlessly with the earlier Hospitaller work, while blocks with rather irregular bosses were used when the

Ṣubayba (after Deschamps and Hartal).

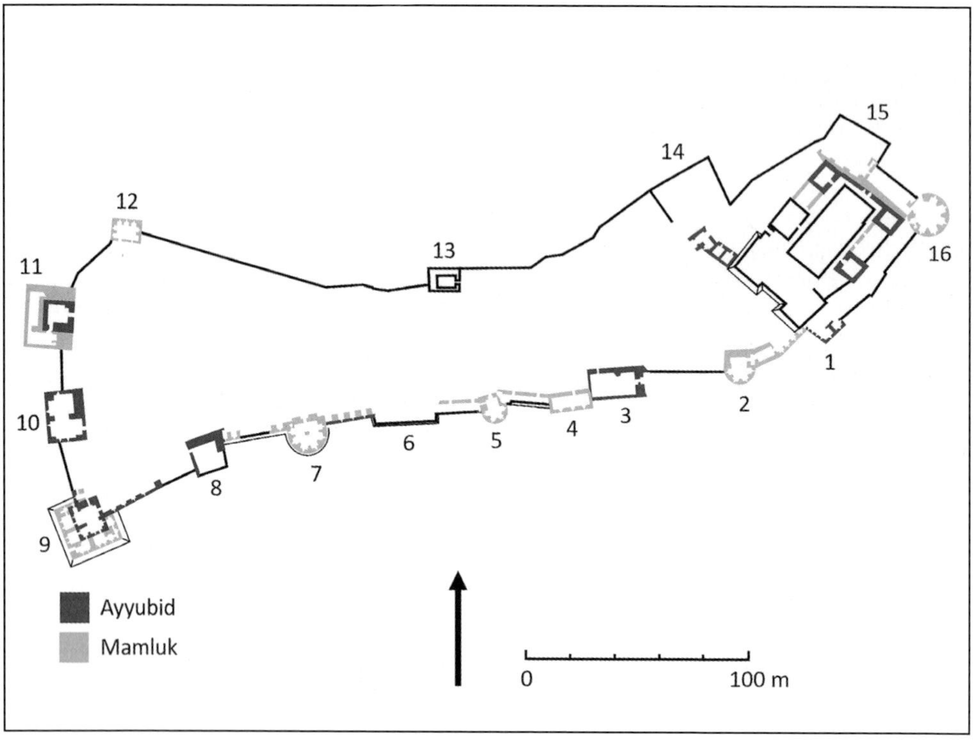

Montreal, inscription on the north tower. (*Michael Fulton*)

southern donjon/palatial tower at Shayzar was expanded, matching the existing Ayyūbid structure.

Perhaps because the authority of the Mamlūk sultan was relatively unchallenged, it is hard to discern many signature styles, as various tower shapes and sizes were employed by both Baybars and Qalāwūn. Instead, the Mamlūks favoured bold inscriptions. The use of inscriptions to dedicate towers and other structures had long-standing precedent in the region, but those of the Mamlūks were often quite brazen, placed in prominent positions so as to leave little doubt in the minds of visitors as to who had commissioned the work. The large tower that now dominates the southern end of Kerak, along with Burj al-Ẓāhir, one of the town's towers, were striped with bold inscriptions, as was done around some of the large towers built at Montreal. At Crac, the rounded towers rebuilt in the 1270s at each end of the castle's outer southern wall display prominent inscriptions below the parapet, as does Qalāwūn's quadrangular tower between them.

Wall Thickness

Thicker walls, perhaps 1m thicker on average, accompanied the appearance of larger castles and towers. Many curtain walls dating to the thirteenth century were no thicker than earlier twelfth-century examples, while the thirteenth-century towers with the thickest walls were typically quite tall or contained vast internal spaces, which required substantial structural support.

The thickness of fortified walls built in the twelfth century ranged from site to site and wall to wall; however, the average thickness was about 2.5m. The walls of Belvoir, built from 1168, are 2.5–3.5m thick, while those of Jacob's Ford, dating to 1178–79, are about 4m thick. These were two of the last castles built in the lead-up to the battle of Hattin, but while impressive, this thickness was not unprecedented. The mid-twelfth-century Frankish 'keep' in the centre of the outer eastern wall at Saone has walls 4.5–5.4m thick. The walls of the keeps at al-Burj (Tantura), Jubayl and Tortosa, all dating to the twelfth century, are 5m, 4m and 3.5–5m thick respectively. As in Europe, it was not uncommon for the walls of such keeps to be thicker than the outer walls subsequently built around them.

Walls built in the thirteenth century were less frequently at the thinner end of the spectrum, rarely less than 2m thick, but neither were they uniformly thicker. Taking Montfort as an example, the walls of the keep, built in the late 1220s, are exceptionally thick, up to 7m in some sections, although a mural passage or gallery is evident. The outer walls of the central domestic range, built behind the keep not long after, are a more modest 2–2.3m thick. The walls of the cistern tower at the west end of the upper castle, which had at least one and perhaps as many as three levels above, are slightly thicker, about 2.8m. Between the central domestic range and the cistern tower, the great hall rested on two barrel vaults and rose another two storeys above. The vaults sprang from a dividing wall 2.5m thick and surviving sections of the southern wall, although unexcavated, indicate the hall rested on outer walls between 3m and 5m thick. A rounded wall, 3.1m thick, encloses the western end of the upper castle, rising from the bedrock further down the spur. At the northern end of this wall stands the inner northwestern gate tower, the walls of which are just 1.1–2m thick,

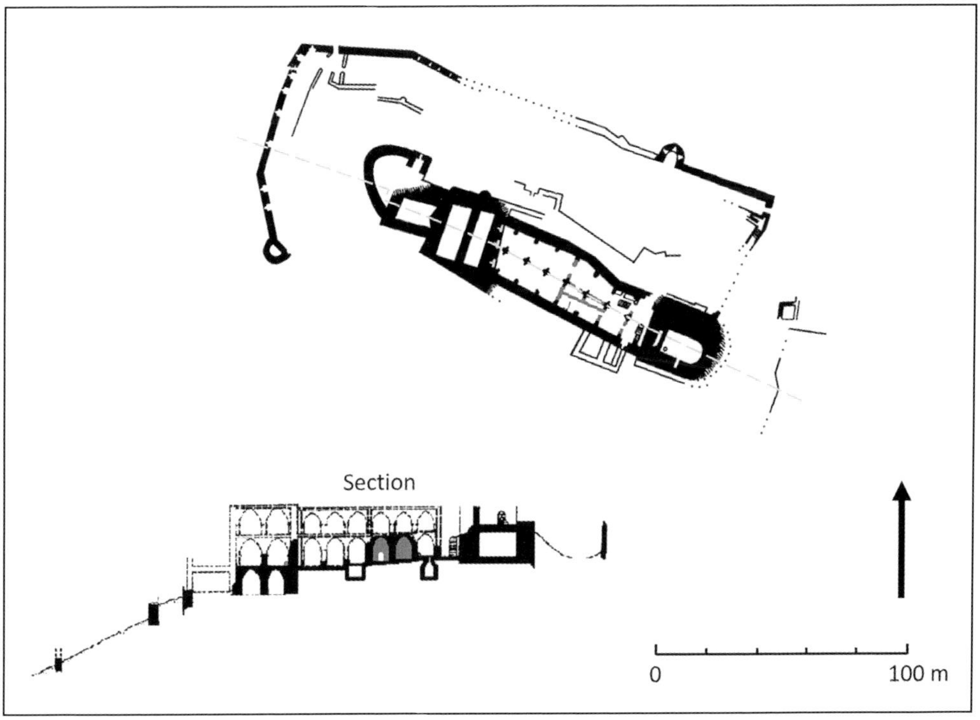

Montfort (after Pringle).

the thinnest wall being the outward north wall. An outer wall enclosed the northern and western sides of the upper castle, running north from the keep at the east end, down the slope and around an outer bailey, rejoining the west end of the upper castle at an unknown spot. The original outer wall was just 1.8m thick and was crowned with a parapet 0.7m thick, with merlons 1–1.5m wide every 0.7m. The Teutonic Knights were in the process of replacing this wall with a new one, only 1.9m thick, when the castle was taken by the Mamlūks. The rebuilding efforts had progressed from west to east, and included a rounded tower with walls similarly 1.9m thick, but had not reached the outer northwest gate when work was interrupted.

Work at Montfort began around 1227 and ended no later than 1271, when the castle was captured and then destroyed by Baybars, leaving a period of no more than forty-five years for the various building phases to have been completed. The thickness of the walls built during this relatively brief window is revealing. While the walls of the keep are exceptionally thick, those of the central range behind it, which would have been exterior walls at one point, are not. Likewise, the walls of the outer bailey are quite thin by thirteenth-century standards. The curved wall at the west end of the upper ward is noticeably thicker, but it was not provided with any embrasures in its lower level(s), suggesting it might postdate the wall of the outer bailey, and that its thickness was influenced by structural requirements, not defensive ones. Likewise, the simple northwestern gate tower at the north end of this wall may also postdate the outer wall. The gate in the north wall of the first level is protected by a machicolation at the third level; however, the tower boasts only a single embrasure, which extends through the north wall of the second level. The apparent effort to rebuild the outer wall is the most revealing: although this new wall is significantly higher, it is hardly thicker, confirming that walls more than 2m thick were not always considered necessary even in the third quarter of the thirteenth century.

Admittedly, Montfort was neither the strongest nor the most sophisticated castle built by the Franks in the thirteenth century; however, it was the principal stronghold of the Teutonic Knights and under near continual development. So why then are some of Montfort's walls so thin, while those of other contemporary castles are so thick? The castle most often associated with thick walls is 'Atlit. Excavations and surveys at 'Atlit were last carried out in the early 1930s and precise measurements of many of its walls have still not been published; nevertheless, the tremendous scale of the castle is immediately apparent.

'Atlit was founded in 1218. Built on a little peninsula, it replaced the small Templar stronghold of Le Destroit, a tower and enclosure complex dating to the twelfth century, about 1km to the northeast. The castle's walls are extremely stout and were built with the soft local *kurkar* (fossilized sand originally washed into the Mediterranean from the Nile), quarried from a ridge less than 1km inland from the coast. The three towers of the outer line of defences have walls about 5m thick at the first level, but the eastern (outer) walls of the second level are only around a third as thick. This

Le Destroit, with 'Atlit in the background. (*Michael Fulton*)

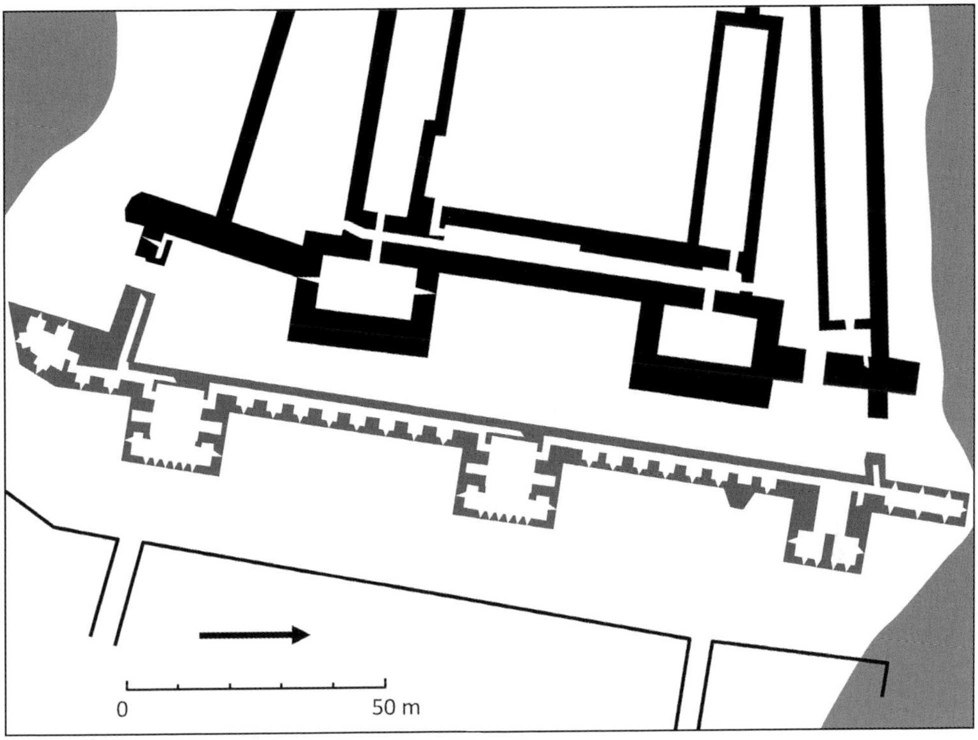

'Atlit, second level of the outer defences, first level of the inner defences (after Johns).

thinning was done to create what was essentially a continuous eastern casemate in the middle and southern towers, each of which serviced six embrasures, and two casemates in the northern tower, each with two embrasures. The curtain walls connecting 'Atlit's three outer towers are about 6m thick, solid at the first level with a gallery above, and an open fighting platform probably ran along the top at the third level. The mural gallery, which halved the thickness of the wall at the second level, provided access to casemates 3m wide, which were spaced less than 3m apart. Behind this line of defences, an inner wall dominated the outer fortifications and was in turn overlooked by two massive towers, more than 34m high with walls more than 5m thick at their bases.

The castle did not impress a young T.E. Lawrence, better known later as Lawrence of Arabia, who remarked, 'The strength of Athlit was brute strength, depending on the defenceless solidity of the inner wall, its impassable height, and the obstacle to mining of a deep sea-level ditch in the sand and rock before the towers. The design is simply unintelligent.'[34] Lawrence's assessment seems overly critical; however, his observations relating to the castle's stoutness are accurate. The extremely thick walls of the outer line's lowest level, its slight talus and use of extremely large ashlars were a defence against undermining. Above, the second level bristled with archers shooting from casemates, while another level of archers was supported along the top of the wall. Massed frontal attacks and sapping were clearly what the designer(s) of this line of defences feared most.

Behind, the two great three-storey towers of the inner wall were aligned between the outer towers, but the surviving east (outer) face of the north tower reveals evidence of few embrasures, suggesting these were quite palatial structures. The third level, which accounted for half the height of each tower, contained opulent rib vaulting, indicating they may have been added in a second building phase. A central pier helped support the vaulting of the second and third levels, but not that of the first below. Left floating, the pillar and all of the weight that it bore from the lofty levels above was supported only by the vaulting of the first level. Accordingly, it seems structural considerations contributed to the incredibly thick walls of these towers – their thickness allowed for their considerable height and magnificent third levels. The scale and grandeur of these towers would no doubt have impressed those within as well as those who viewed them from the outside.

Al-ʿĀdil's building works display a similar preference for the ostentatious. At the citadel of Damascus, the massive mural towers he commissioned contain three levels, each a single open room, supported by walls 3–5m thick. Revealingly, it is the flanks of these towers, at either end of the long axis of the vaulting within, that were often the thickest, not the outer face, which would bear the brunt of an attack.

It seems the evident trend towards the thickening of tower walls was, at least in part, a result of the preference shown by certain early thirteenth-century figures, who possessed deep pockets, for awe-inspiring towers with equally impressive open spaces within. This can also be seen in parts of Europe. For example, as keeps in England and France became larger and taller through the second half of the twelfth century and first half of the thirteenth, so too did their walls become thicker in order to support these increasingly grand structures. Where defensive considerations more clearly contributed to the construction of exceptionally thick walls, as with the outer wall at ʿAtlit, this was typically done to frustrate miners and bring more defenders into the fight to help resist frontal attacks.

Ironically, many of the same principles that guided the designer(s) of ʿAtlit's outer defences, and those of other Frankish castles in the aftermath of the battle of Hattin, can be seen in Mamlūk refortification efforts following the battle of ʿAyn Jālūt, as the threat of another Mongol invasion continued to loom. At Crac, Baybars commissioned a rounded tower at the southwest corner of the outer line of defences, where his miners had broken into the castle in 1271. The chosen design is telling: it has a solid base with a slight batter, creating a small talus, upon which sits a single elevated internal level, consisting of a single room that is arranged in an octagon around a central octagonal pier. A casemate extends into each of the four outward faces of the room, through walls 2.9m thick. This design was both sturdy and accommodated numerous defenders. A similar semi-circular tower, with walls 3.6m thick, was built along the outer southern line of defences at Ṣubayba. It has a solid, battered base and a single internal level, the southern half of which is arranged in a half-octagon while the northern half is rectangular, a shape mirrored by the central pier. Six casemates in the outward faces of the room provide access to embrasures. Another round tower was built at the east end of Ṣubayba, in front of the Ayyūbid citadel. The interior is once more octagonal, although lacking a central pier, and casemates extend into the five outward faces of the walls, which are 3.8m thick.

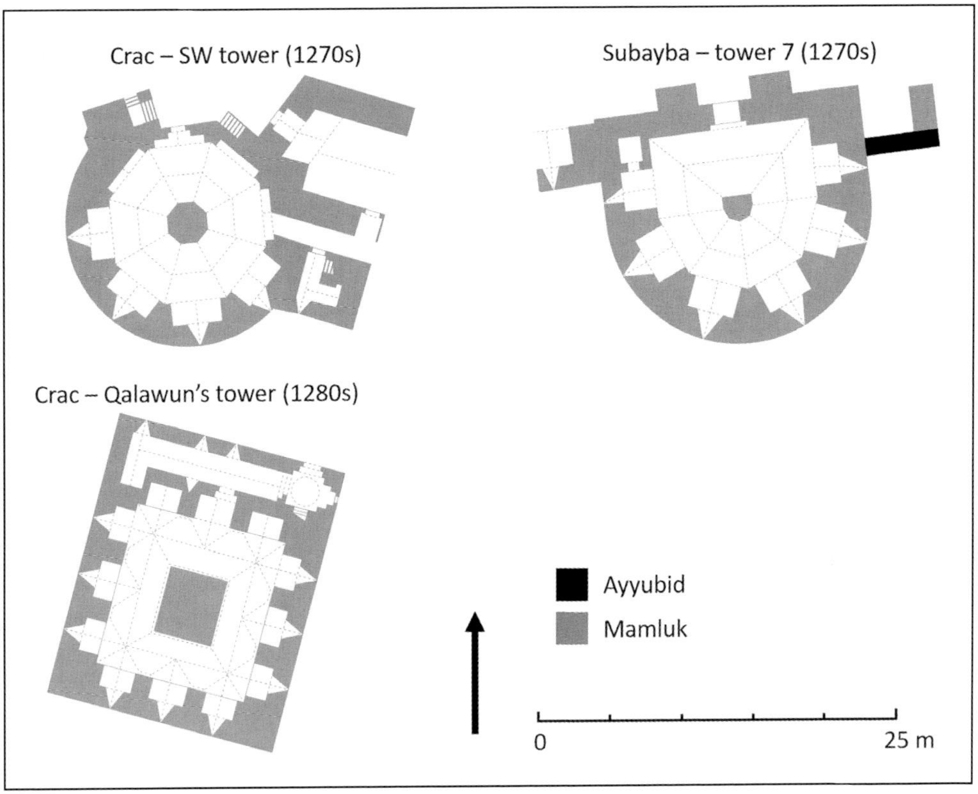

Mamlūk towers with central pillars (after Deschamps and Yovitchitch).

Although the shape of Mamlūk towers varied considerably, these design elements – an emphasis on solidity and providing protected spaces for archers – remained prevalent. Qalāwūn's tower at Crac has a single internal level, at the height of the battlements crowning the adjacent walls. This is essentially a gallery: eight bays of groin vaults wrap around a large central pillar; the seven external bays provide access to nine casemates, servicing three embrasures in each of the tower's outer faces. The same principles can be seen at Montreal, where six large towers were built around existing Frankish ones, each with a sturdy, if not solid base, upon which sat a level liberally provided with embrasures.

The desire to maximize the number of shooting positions within a tower at times overcame the advantages of an otherwise solid lower level. At Baalbek, the large tower built under Qalāwūn at the southeast corner of the Roman Temple of Bacchus is bristling with shooting positions. This philosophy was extended to the wall built around the western and southern sides of the larger temple complex, which had embrasures at two levels, and possibly a double-level parapet above. At Ṣubayba, the first level of the tower built by the Ayyūbids in the southwest corner of the outer bailey (tower 9) had eight embrasures; this increased to fourteen when the tower was enlarged by the Mamlūks, and numerous embrasures are discernible in the surviving masonry above. Below, additional shooting positions were created when two parallel

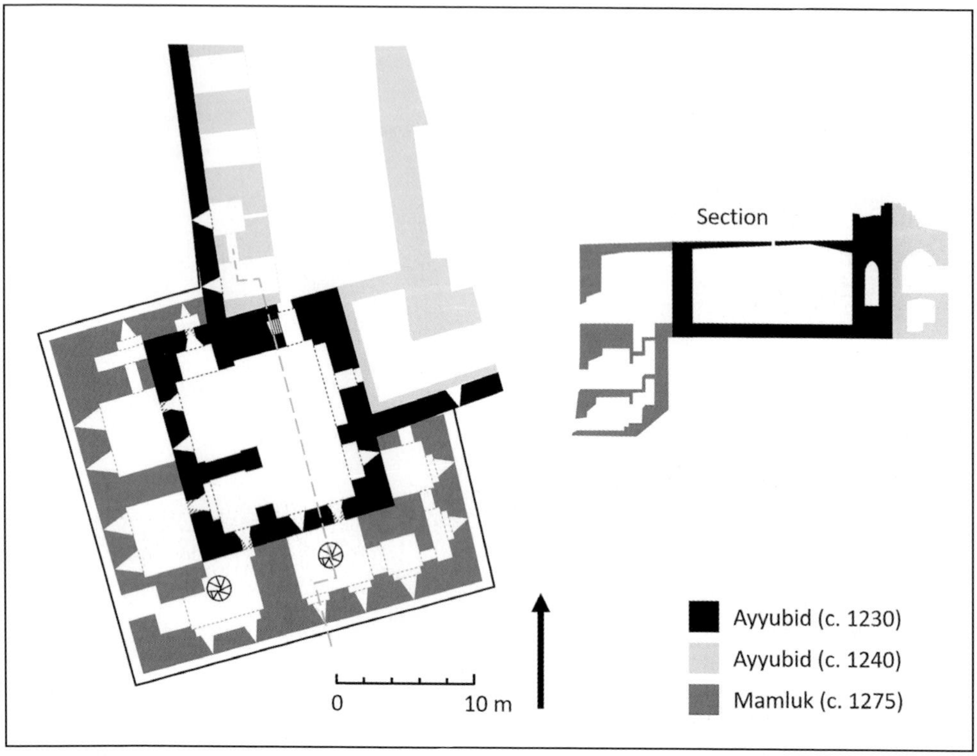

Ṣubayba, outer southwestern tower (after Hartal).

pairs of galleries were incorporated into the sublevels that were built to compensate for the sloping ground around the tower.

From the late twelfth century, the thickness of some curtain walls also increased. Although this balanced the weakening caused by perforating the masonry with embrasures, it seems the main reason behind the thickening of many walls was to provide a broader fighting platform on top, or a mural gallery within, as at 'Atlit. At Ṣubayba, the wall running north from the outer southwestern tower was thickened prior to 1260, creating spacious casemates similar to those at 'Atlit behind earlier embrasures in the original wall. If the goal had been to strengthen these walls, much narrower casemates might have been employed, suggesting the primary objective of this thickening was instead to broaden the wall-walk above. This was also done along the wall leading away from the tower to the east, where the wall was thickened just enough to create springers. These allowed for the construction of a vaulted passage between the wall and the large reservoir behind the tower, which would have supported a broad fighting platform above.

Despite the increasing strength and sophistication of many castles, it can be easy to get carried away emphasizing the importance or prevalence of thick walls. The town walls of Caesarea, developed by Louis IX of France in 1251–52, were taken in less than a day by Baybars' forces in 1265. Weeks later, these same forces, strengthened by the arrival of additional siege equipment, struggled for a month to take the town

Ṣubayba, topmost northeastern shooting chamber of the outer southwestern tower. (*Michael Fulton*)

defences of Arsūf, some exposed sections of which are just 1.2m thick. Although defended by a Hospitaller garrison and boasting walls 3–3.5m thick, the castle surrendered only a few days after the town was captured. Elsewhere there was no progressive thickening of walls. At Beaufort, the thirteenth-century defences added by the Ayyūbids and Mamlūks appear to be no thicker than the walls of the twelfth-century keep (2.5m thick) and the stout enclosing wall to the south (3.6m thick). The twelfth-century town walls of Bānyās are 2.4–2.5m thick, similar to the Ayyūbid curtain walls of Ṣubayba and thinner than the 3.4m-thick Frankish walls of Tiberias built in the twelfth century. For added context, the Lascarid outer wall built around Nicaea in the first quarter of the thirteenth century is about 1.6–2m thick, considerably thinner than the main Roman wall built in the third century, which is upwards of 3.6m thick. All of these pale in comparison to the wall that surrounded Jerusalem around the eighth century BC, exposed sections of which are 6.4–7.2m thick.

Tower Shapes

Since antiquity, many military architects, including Vitruvius, had advocated the use of round or polygonal towers, rather than simpler quadrangular ones. Rounded towers had certain advantages: they were harder to undermine, as they had no vulnerable corners and weight was distributed more evenly; they provided defenders with a more complete field of view, accommodating embrasures in any direction; and they were more effective at deflecting artillery projectiles. They may also have been able to absorb the blows of siege engines more effectively, directing forces towards the centre of the tower, similar to how an arch supports a vertical load. However, rounded towers required more skill to build and the space within could be harder to use efficiently, leading some rounded towers to have rectangular interiors, as can be seen at the inner southwestern tower at Crac, the large 'donjon' at Margat and many of the mural towers built by Saladin at Cairo.

Roman engineers had built both quadrangular and rounded towers in the Levant, as had the Umayyads and early 'Abbāsids, who employed rounded towers at Aqaba (Ayla), Qaṣr Kharana, Qaṣr al-Mshatta, the Roman theatre at Caesarea and Kafr Lām. Polygonal beaked towers were comparatively rare, although Byzantine examples can be found at Ankara, in Anatolia, and further away at Salona. Quadrangular towers were used with increasing frequency under the 'Abbāsids and Fāṭimids, while Byzantine and Armenian builders employed both shapes, although rounded towers have become particularly synonymous with the fortifications of the latter.

At the time of the First Crusade, rectangular stone keeps were becoming popular in some areas of western Europe, although they were still vastly outnumbered by timber castles. The crusaders brought this tradition with them to the Levant, and almost all towers built by the Franks in the twelfth century were quadrangular. The rounded towers along the outer eastern wall of Saone are rare exceptions, suggesting their shape was determined by earlier Byzantine foundations or the influence of Armenian builders.

Rounded towers became more popular in the thirteenth century, although quadrangular towers were constructed at least as frequently by both Frankish and Muslim builders. Under Saladin, quadrangular towers were used at 'Ajlūn, both shapes were used at Qal'at Ṣadr, and numerous rounded towers were employed during the refortification of Cairo. Although al-'Ādil built a number of significant rounded towers, most of those he and his fellow Ayyūbids constructed had quadrangular plans. Under the Mamlūks, no clear preference was shown and often towers of both shapes were used at the same site. Both rounded and rectangular towers were built under Baybars at Ṣubayba, while Qalāwūn added quadrangular towers at Crac and Baalbek, and a rounded tower at Margat. Both rounded and quadrangular plans were also employed when Montreal was refortified in the final years of the century.

Although it is often suggested that the Templars preferred quadrangular towers and the Hospitallers favoured rounded ones, these characterizations do not extend far beyond the orders' most impressive strongholds, which include 'Atlit and Tortosa, Crac and Margat. Regardless of who built them, rural towers and those of smaller secondary castles were typically quadrangular. Although the advantages of rounded towers are often praised by historians, the continued use of quadrangular towers speaks to the limits of these benefits.

Dressing

Fine ashlar masonry, ideally making use of a hard type of stone and finely cut blocks with little room between them, was often considered ideal to confront threats like sapping, as this made it difficult to damage the facing stones or pull them out of place. In practice, the availability of materials and skill, as well as the preferred aesthetic, had a profound influence on what walls eventually looked like. Volcanic types of stone were usually quite hard, but they could be just as difficult to work with. The basalt masonry at Margat is much rougher than that found at Belvoir, while the hard volcanic stone used by Frankish masons at Kerak provides a sharp contrast to the much finer limestone work of the Muslim builders who followed them. Along the Palestinian coast, the local *kurkar* was easy to work with but exceptionally soft, leading to the development of a shelly mortar that was harder and more resilient to the elements than the stone itself. In many regions, limestone was a popular choice. Relatively available, it offered a nice balance: it was fairly hard but also reasonably easy for a skilled stone worker to shape. Together with the thickness of a wall, the type of stone and quality of the masonry are fairly obvious indications of its strength. But what of its dressing – the finish or style of tooling left on the exterior of each stone?

For more than a century, archaeologists have studied the masonry of Frankish and Muslim fortifications with hopes of better understanding who was responsible for which building phases and what styles were preferred by certain figures. Both Frankish and Muslim builders, as well as their Armenian counterparts to the north, regularly made use of ashlars with smoothly drafted margins and raised centres, or bosses, a style which had been employed in the region since at least the Hellenistic period. All parties also used smoothly dressed ashlar, Frankish examples of which are commonly distinguishable by diagonal tooling, traces of a method of shaping stone imported from Europe. Masons' marks, symbols incised on blocks by the men who shaped them, were long thought to be employed only by Frankish masons; however, such marks can also be found at certain Muslim sites, including 'Ajlūn and the citadel of Bosra, in both Ayyūbid and Mamlūk building phases.

A common explanation put forward for the continued use of, and even preference for, bossed masonry was that it was an effective defence against artillery. This, however, was not the case. If these bosses were intended to turn aside or deflect an incoming projectile, the implicit amount of force would be so meagre that even a sustained bombardment could hardly be seen as a threat to walls anywhere from 1.5m to over 4m thick. If the objective were simply to place more material between the point of impact and the rear of the wall, a simpler, and more reliable, solution would have been to avoid shaping a boss at all, leaving as much of the original stone in place and saving the time and effort of tooling the margins. Simply put, building thicker walls would have been a far more effective solution, and a period of prolonged bombardment would naturally create a rough and 'deflective' wall surface.

Bossed masonry was instead employed for practical and aesthetic reasons: such blocks were faster to shape than smooth ashlars and together they produced a rustic yet clean finish. At Jacob's Ford, where walls were erected as quickly as possible, bossed masonry was used on the inner as well as outer faces of the exterior walls, suggesting most blocks were shaped at the quarry to a standard course height and then brought to the castle where they were employed wherever they were needed. The argument of expedience works at some sites but at others the bosses are quite flat and even finely shaped rather than rusticated.

Ayyūbid bosses tended to be quite irregular, except where smooth decorative bosses, resembling horizontal cylinders, were employed. These finer stones are often found embellishing the corners of towers, as at the citadels of Damascus and Bosra. Although Mamlūk masonry varies considerably, at sites such as Kerak and Ṣubayba their work is clearly distinguishable and much finer than that of their predecessors, often employing cleanly cut limestone blocks, either smoothly dressed or with neat, fairly flat bosses. Frankish sites reveal an assortment of boss styles, from the smooth examples at ʿAtlit and Saone to the rougher ones at Belvoir and Tortosa.

Like their dressing, the size of facing stones varied considerably from site to site and building phase to building phase. While colossal stones over 1m in length were employed at ʿAtlit, much smaller blocks, many just 20cm long, were used at Caesarea and Arsūf, similar coastal sites, 22km and 57km to the south respectively, where the same type of stone was used.

Active Defence

As the size of besieging forces grew, allowing attackers to send more men against the defences of a besieged stronghold, the importance of active defensive measures increased. These were often facilitated by architectural elements. Embrasures and crenellated parapets were the simplest, providing protection for archers and other defenders confronting advancing attackers, while posterns permitted rapid or secretive sallies. Regardless of which features were present, a truly active defence meant taking the fight to the besiegers and disrupting, delaying or defeating their attempts to gain entrance.

Sallies

Sallies, attacks launched by defenders against their besiegers, were an integral part of siege warfare: a means through which the besieged could seize the initiative. These were generally small-scale operations, which often targeted a particular group of besiegers or the siege equipment they were employing. Due to the difficulties associated with destroying siege engines from within a stronghold, this task was often delegated to a sally party. The attack that followed was often launched rapidly, a quick strike to catch the besiegers unprepared, allowing them to burn the engine, whether a siege tower, trebuchet or penthouse, and withdraw before additional besieging forces could arrive to support their comrades.

At times, sallies by daring or desperate parties of defenders could have drastic consequences. Effective sallies broke Baldwin II's siege of Bālis in 1122, the Sicilian siege of Alexandria in 1174 and Saladin's siege of Tyre at the end of 1187. Taking pre-emptive measures, a force of defenders disrupted the crusaders who were intent on attacking Mount Tabor in 1217 and a sally from Margat deterred a more concerted Mamlūk siege around 1280. Less conclusively, a sally by the defenders of Aleppo in 1176 compelled the besiegers to content themselves with a blockade, eventually resulting in a truce, while a sally by the defenders of Dieudamor, on the brink of starvation, broke the besiegers' blockade and extended the siege, which ultimately lasted almost a year before it was concluded in 1230. Although typically less decisive than these examples, the impact of sallies was still significant.

Along with the potential benefits, significant risks accompanied each sally, as it would implicitly involve opening a gate and attacking part of a much larger force. In 1101, Tancred's ability to intercept and crush a sally left the defenders of Latakia so weakened that they were compelled to seek peace. According to William of Tyre, Bānyās was captured in 1157 when a party of defenders could not close a gate as they returned from a sally, allowing the besiegers pursuing them to gain entrance to the

Templar of Tyre: a sally during the siege of Acre, 1291

One day our men took counsel and decided to make a general sally on all sides with horse and foot, to burn the *buches*. So my lord the master of the Temple and his men, and Sir John [of Grailly and Sir Otto] of Grandson and other knights went out one night from the Templars' sector (which ran from the seaside to the Gate of St Lazarus), and the master ordered a Provencal, who was viscount of the bourg of Acre, to set fire to the wooden *buches* of the great engine of the sultan. They went out that night, and came up to these *buches*, but the man who was supposed to hurl the Greek fire was afraid when he threw it, and it fell short and landed on the ground where it burned out. The Saracens who were there were all killed, horsemen and footmen. But our men, both brethren and secular knights, went so far in among the tents that their horses got their legs tangled in the tent ropes and went sprawling, whereupon the Saracens slew them. In this way we lost eighteen horsemen that night, both brethren of the Temple and secular knights, though they did capture a number of Saracen shields and bucklers and trumpets and drums. Then my lord and his men turned back towards Acre.

(Adapted from Templar of Tyre 491 [255], trans. Crawford, p. 107.)

town. Later, during the siege of Alexandria in 1167, William asserts that Nūr al-Dīn's forces, led by the 30-year-old Saladin, were reluctant to sally out against their Frankish besiegers, fearing an uprising in their absence by the Egyptian residents of the city, who had no more love for their 'defenders' than for the Franks. Although this highlights another risk associated with conducting sallies, the predominantly Sunni population of Alexandria was probably more sympathetic to the Syrian defenders than William lets on.

Countermining

Few fortifications could deter a determined and experienced group of sappers if they were allowed to go about their work uninterrupted. When sappers chose to tunnel down to the foundations of a stronghold, and the entrances to their tunnels were protected against sallies, defenders had few options but to countermine: to dig their own tunnel, hoping to intercept that of the besiegers. During Saladin's brief siege of Beirut in 1182, his archers aggressively showered the city's defenders with arrows, allowing his miners to begin working undisturbed. By the time Saladin withdrew, after a siege of perhaps only three days, the defenders had already begun to countermine. Nine years later, as the siege of Acre ran into its third year, and the arrival of Philip II of France and Richard I of England tipped the balance in favour of the besiegers, the crusaders launched new sapping initiatives. A tunnel excavated by the defenders intercepted the work of French sappers below the Accursed Tower. The meeting resulted in an agreement that both sides would withdraw and the Muslims sealed their tunnel behind them. Another countermine intercepted Richard's sappers working below a different tower, but the meeting was far less cordial and the defenders, who gained the upper hand in the subterranean fight that ensued, forced the crusaders to abandon their mine.

Fifty years after Saladin's siege of Beirut, John of Beirut led a force to relieve his titular capital, then besieged by imperialist forces. Although too small to break the siege, a part of his force managed to enter the castle and bring much-needed assistance. The defenders then countermined, driving the imperial sappers from their mine and regaining control of the fosse, destroying the defences that the besiegers had set up there. Free from this threat, the defenders maintained their initiative, sallying out against the besiegers and successfully burning a number of their engines.

In 1265, the Frankish defenders of Arsūf gained some short-lived success following the excavation of a countermine during Baybars' siege of the stronghold. Tunnelling out from the castle, they were able to set fire to the brush that the Mamlūks had used to fill the fosse, using casks of fat to make sure the fire took hold and then fanning it with bellows. Just weeks earlier, and with greater success, the defenders of al-Bīra had similarly tunnelled into their fosse, allowing them to burn the material the Mongols had used to fill it. The following year, at the siege of Safed, the Franks again countermined against Baybars' sappers. On this occasion, their tunnel was above that of the besiegers. The Franks dropped into the Muslim tunnel from above and a bitter hand-to-hand fight took place. Although it was a setback for the Mamlūks, this was only one of a number of mines that they had opened and the defenders of Safed, like those of Arsūf, were later compelled to seek terms. At the siege of Acre in 1291, the Franks similarly attempted to countermine against the Mamlūk sappers undermining the Tower of the Countess of Blois, one of a number of sapping parties working against the northeastern section of the city.

Countermining was not typically the first choice of besiegers, as it was dangerous and involved potentially weakening their own defences. If deprived of other options, however, it could be extremely effective.

Payoff

One of the most effective defensive weapons was cash. In the same way that besiegers could entice a garrison to surrender with generous terms or offer its leader an alternative command, defenders could offer the besiegers a payoff in exchange for lifting their siege. During the First Crusade, the ruler of Tripoli persuaded Raymond of St Gilles to give up the siege of 'Arqa in 1099 with a payoff, albeit after the Franks had become discouraged and most were inclined to continue their march towards Jerusalem. Other coastal towns placated the crusaders by opening their markets to them and even offering gifts to encourage them to move on as quickly and peacefully as possible. This remained a popular defensive measure in the decades that followed, particularly in the fractured political landscape of the early twelfth century.

When Raymond of St Gilles returned to the Tripoli region following the disastrous Crusade of 1101, he once more accepted a large payoff. Agreeing not to attack Tripoli for the time being, he left to besiege other towns in the surrounding area. When Baldwin I took a force against Tyre in 1108, he opted not to launch an aggressive siege, in part because he lacked naval support, and eventually accepted a payoff of 7,000 dinars to lead his army away from the city. After taking Beirut in the spring of 1110, Baldwin made a brief appearance before Sidon, departing without attacking the town in exchange for an increase in the city's annual tribute from 2,000 dinars to

6,000. This had probably been a feint, which ended up paying off for the Frankish king: Edessa was then under siege by Mawdūd, suggesting Baldwin had no real intention of besieging Sidon before moving to relieve Edessa. Like the coastal cities, smaller regional powers could secure their autonomy, at least for the time being, and deflect attention with payoffs. The rulers of Shayzar, who commanded a small Arab enclave sandwiched between various larger Frankish and Muslim powers, bought off Tancred for 10,000 dinars in 1109, paid Shams al-Mulūk Ismāʿīl of Damascus to break his siege in 1133, and persuaded the Byzantine emperor John Comnenus, who was receiving little help from his Frankish allies, to lift his siege and depart with a large sum in 1138.

The Franks frequently accepted payoffs to lift sieges around Aleppo. Following the death of Riḍwān in 1113, Aleppo suffered internally for half a decade, allowing the Franks to make considerable gains until Īlghāzī ibn Artuq took control of the city. The Franks pushed their advantage while Īlghāzī consolidated his hold over Aleppo, refusing a payoff to lift their siege of ʿAzāz and then extracting a significant tribute as a condition of a broader peace that was arranged after the town had fallen. Although the balance of power shifted in 1119, in the aftermath of the battle of the Field of Blood, Joscelin I of Edessa was able to besiege Buzāʿa in early 1121. After burning a section of its walls, perhaps indicating they had been undermined, he was bought off and withdrew. After Īlghāzī's death the next year, the Franks launched another series of campaigns into Aleppan territory through 1122, accepting tribute from some regions while rejecting a payoff from Bālis, which turned out to be a mistake when a sally by a group of Turkoman defenders later broke the Frankish siege. In 1123, a combined Frankish force moved to relieve Baldwin II, who had seized the castle of Kharpūt from his jailers. Learning that Balak had retaken the castle while they were still on their way, the Franks turned on Aleppo and raided its suburbs for three or four days, accepting payment to leave according to one source. When control of Aleppo was once more contested in the autumn of 1127, Joscelin took advantage of the situation and appeared in force before the city. Although he probably had no intention of attacking the formidable city directly, his presence was sufficient to encourage a payoff.

Order returned to Aleppo when Zankī took control of the city in 1128. Up to this point, the Franks had taken a share of all Aleppan revenues right up to the city gates, but this would soon change. Zankī quickly went on the offensive, taking al-Athārib and investing Ḥārim, compelling the Franks to offer him half of the town's revenue to end the siege and accept a truce. Suspiciously, Ibn al-Athīr gives a similar account of an attack made by Nūr al-Dīn twenty-seven years later. In 1149, Nūr al-Dīn encamped outside Antioch and opened serious negotiations for the city's surrender; however, he was ultimately forced to settle for a payoff. The same year, Joscelin II, now only titular count of Edessa, bought off the Turkish forces besieging him in Turbessel, benefiting from the leverage provided by the Frankish army marching to his relief under Humphrey II of Toron, constable of the kingdom of Jerusalem.

As the twelfth century progressed, and Nūr al-Dīn continued to consolidate his power, the stakes and payoffs became larger. In late 1168, Amalric accepted a promise of 1,000,000 dinars not to besiege Cairo. Payment, however, was delayed long enough for Shīrkūh to arrive, compelling the Franks to withdraw towards Palestine in January 1169, taking with them only an initial deposit of 100,000 dinars. Nūr al-Dīn died in 1174, prompting the Franks to attack Bānyās. The siege lasted around two weeks before the Franks accepted a payoff of cash and prisoners. By accepting the peace, the Franks also mitigated the risk of a large Mesopotamian or Egyptian army invading western Syria under the pretext of supporting Nūr al-Dīn's young son. In late 1177, with Saladin attending to affairs in Egypt, the crusading Philip of Flanders, accompanied by Raymond III of Tripoli and Bohemond III of Antioch, briefly attacked Hama before investing Ḥārim. The latter siege dragged on for four months through the winter until the Franks were bought off by al-Ṣāliḥ Ismāʿīl ibn Nūr al-Dīn of Aleppo, who then besieged the castle himself. Exhausted, the garrison quickly surrendered.

Payoffs were comparatively rare during the thirteenth century: the Franks were rarely in a position to undertake significant siege operations and it was position rather than cash that mattered most to the various Ayyūbid princes as they struggled for greater power at the expense of their relatives. During the Fifth Crusade, the Franks refused what was probably the largest payoff offered during the period of the crusades. In 1219, during the siege of Damietta, al-Kāmil proposed to return Palestine to the Franks if the crusaders would agree to leave Egypt. Perhaps confident that they could seriously threaten Cairo, or wary that al-Kāmil's offer excluded Kerak and Montreal, the deal was declined. Fear that the Franks might conclude just such an agreement led al-Kāmil's brother, al-Muʿaẓẓam ʿĪsā of Damascus, to slight most of the fortifications west of the Jordan. Much as the Franks had exploited the weakness of the Fāṭimid towns along the coast in the early twelfth century, it was the Franks who found themselves in this position following the rise of the Mamlūks. Although Baybars showed himself willing to negotiate with the Franks, allowing them to buy his good will, he more often sought land than cash and rarely showed himself willing to negotiate terms that involved his withdrawal once hostilities had begun.

* * *

Although different defensive elements and systems came into fashion as the popularity of others declined, the design of each stronghold, rebuilding initiative or repair effort was influenced by a unique set of variables and considerations. Certain similarities and stylistic preferences can be seen among the defences commissioned by particular rulers, but these were incorporated only so far as local conditions and resources, including building materials, cash, skill and manpower, allowed. A variety of architectural elements might be employed, depending on the nature of the threats the stronghold was expected to face, but active defensive measures were often required to counter a more determined adversary.

Defence was, to a degree, an act of desperation, a fight for survival, and there were no guarantees that terms would be offered or honoured by besiegers – Zankī had the defenders of Baalbek executed in 1139, despite having promised them safe-conduct. Fortifications were thus planned pragmatically, if also artistically in some instances.

But sieges, if they ever materialized, were brief periods of time in the history of these structures. Defences were thus also designed around creating spaces intended to fulfil various functions. In the thirteenth century, this led to the construction of thicker walls, as towers were built larger and taller with much greater volumes of open space inside. There was no simple formula that determined the design of fortifications, much as there was none that guided the conduct of sieges.

Chapter Six

Influences and Trends

Siege weapons and the means of defence changed relatively little during the twelfth and thirteenth centuries, yet significant changes to the political environment led to notable developments in the ways that castles were constructed and attacked. The numerical superiority of Muslim armies inspired the construction of larger Frankish castles, made possible by the considerable resources of the military orders and investment by visiting crusaders. Muslim defences also developed, due in large part to the Ayyūbid power struggle and subsequent threat posed by the Mongols to Mamlūk rule in western Syria.

It has long been debated whether the Franks or Muslims possessed a superior building tradition or siege technologies. To support either side, however, arguments have inevitably relied on abstract criteria and the unique nature of each siege has often been neglected. Frankish and Muslim rulers adopted the fortifications, siege engines, fighting styles, etc., best suited to their environmental, political, cultural and social contexts, as well as the skill and resources at their disposal. The considerable variance within these groups of 'Franks' and 'Muslims' speaks to the importance of context, and is enough to cast doubt on the utility of the binary framework that continues to dominate the way the crusades are studied. For example, the Frankish fortifications built in the kingdom of Jerusalem in the early twelfth century looked different from those constructed around the same time in the county of Edessa, and the Muslim armies assembled by al-Afḍal Shāhinshāh in Egypt looked and fought differently from contemporary forces fighting under Īlghāzī's Artuqid banner. When considering the spectrum of traditions and degree of interaction among them, it is natural to question the extent to which various parties were influenced by the practices and technologies of their neighbours.

While it is possible to trace the diffusion of certain architectural features from Europe to the Middle East, and vice versa, it is much harder to judge the effectiveness of the defences, or siege equipment, at any particular siege. Very generally, certain patterns can be seen in the ways that sieges were undertaken through the period; however, the success or failure of most seems to have had more to do with local circumstances and contemporary political realities than the siege traditions or technologies employed by the besiegers.

Fortifications

In the nineteenth century, the famed architect and architectural restorer Eugène Emmanuel Viollet-le-Duc remarked, 'We cannot doubt that the crusades, during which so many memorable sieges were effected, perfected the means of attack, and that consequently important modifications were introduced into the defence of fortified places.'[35] This sentiment has been echoed by countless other historians since, some of whom have looked to the crusades as an almost mythical nexus of technological exchange.

As noted above, there is little evidence to support theories that the Franks or Muslims learned about certain siege technologies through their interactions with each other. Most siege weapons were well known before the start of this period, while the development of the counterweight trebuchet appears to have been undertaken by many parties, regardless of who employed this technology first. The weapons chosen and their method of use reflected the resources and style of warfare suited to the different parties, not superior knowledge or ignorance.

Impetuous suggestions that Europeans 'learned' how to build significant castles as a result of the crusades remain common. At the same time that the Franks were compelled to construct larger and stronger castles in the Levant, made possible by the growing resources of the military orders, so too were European monarchs financing similarly grand structures, facilitated by parallel trends towards increasing monarchical wealth. Ignoring these underlying factors, some have suggested that participants of the Third Crusade found inspiration or gained new knowledge while in the East. Château Gaillard, the mighty castle overlooking the Seine between Rouen and Paris, built by Richard I in 1196–98, is often highlighted, it being suggested that its design was influenced by that of Crac des Chevaliers. The most glaring issue with this suggestion is that Crac, in the 1190s, looked little like it does now, and nothing like Château Gaillard. Furthermore, Richard did not visit Crac, or any other significant inland castle, nor did any known member of his retinue. Saranda Kolones, built in the thirteenth century, probably by the Lusignan rulers of Cyprus, is one of the few castles with a plan clearly copying that of another castle; although only half the size, and provided with rounded and two pentagonal towers, it is a clear copy of Belvoir, down to its numerous posterns. But if Frankish castle plans were not simply copied or imported, what guided their development: were they the natural product of European architectural traditions, or the result of Eastern influences?

The Great Debate: West vs. East

Judgements relating to the superiority of either Frankish or Muslim strongholds are often based on perceptions of influence, particularly those apparent in Frankish castles – were the Franks importing Western building styles or adopting Eastern practices? Emmanuel G. Rey (d. 1916), upon whose work so much later scholarship has been built, pointed to what he interpreted as a mix of traditions evident in the fortifications built by the Franks. After a tour of Frankish castles in 1909, T.E. Lawrence (Lawrence of Arabia, d. 1935) went on to write his undergraduate dissertation on the subject, concluding, 'In dealing with the twelfth century in the East, Arab influences in architecture may be entirely discounted. Beibars seems to have been the first Arab sovereign to build respectable fortresses.'[36] Lawrence had a fairly rudimentary appreciation of the development of these structures; nevertheless, the work was fairly well researched, relying heavily on his own observations, and the challenge he issued – that the architecture of Frankish castles owed little to local innovations and that none was then brought back to Europe – has had a profound impact on subsequent studies.

Later in the twentieth century Robin Fedden (d. 1977) and John Thomson embraced Lawrence's perspective, suggesting that the Frankish building tradition was superior to those of the Byzantines, Armenians, Turks and Arabs. They poetically wrote, 'The Frankish architects built with a two-hundred-years' frenzy, and they built with genius, taste and cunning, leaving the imprint of twelfth- and thirteenth-century France – for theirs was essentially a French venture – strangely and beautifully on the Levant.'[37] These sentiments were echoed a decade and a half later by Israeli scholar Meron Benvenisti. More recently, Carole Hillenbrand has associated Frankish castles with those of the Nizārī Assassins and the Armenians, suggesting these were places of refuge for beleaguered minorities. But she has also asserted that the Franks possessed superior technological skills, characterizing Muslim castles as inferior: 'Crusader castles were built to withstand siege; Muslim castles were not.' So although 'the crusader castles were manifestly superior in design and execution', Muslim rulers and architects had few reasons to borrow from the Frankish arts of fortification.[38]

In opposition to these views, archaeologist and historian of architecture Wolfgang Müller-Wiener (d. 1991), saw local traditions as the most influential, pointing out that most early Frankish strongholds were built prior to the arrival of the Franks or were constructed by local residents using local materials. He suggested that as time progressed, this influence waned and was overshadowed by the 'importation of stylistic elements from Western Europe'.[39] This is particularly true of the region north of the kingdom of Jerusalem.

Rey's fairly centrist position found new breath in T.S.R. Boase (d. 1974), who looked favourably on the Muslim work at sites like Kerak and Ṣubayba, observing that the Franks 'borrowed eclectically from the west and the east, from the present and the past, and they learned from a prolonged and rarely broken experience'. Boase also pushed back against the notion that there were two concurrent Frankish building traditions in the thirteenth century: the Western-influenced 'Hospitaller' style, which was more complicated and favoured smooth masonry and rounded towers, and the Eastern-influenced 'Templar' style, which was more heavily influenced by the Byzantines and made regular use of quadrangular towers and bossed masonry.[40] This was a notion put forward by Rey and picked up on by Lawrence, and it can still be found in many books on 'crusader' castles. What Boase and others have since acknowledged is that although this framework holds up well when looking at a handful of impressive castles, it quickly becomes far less persuasive when a broader range of structures is examined.

Historians Joshua Prawer (d. 1990) and Hugh Kennedy, as well as archaeologist Adrian Boas, have also endorsed this notion of a nexus of interactions and influences. Perhaps the most insightful, although already dated, examination of this debate was made by Denys Pringle, fittingly included when he re-edited Lawrence's thesis in 1988. In the introduction, Pringle emphasizes one of Lawrence's primary insights: that tower-keeps, the most common defensive structures built by the Franks in the kingdom of Jerusalem in the early twelfth century, were imported from Europe. But, to quote Pringle, 'it seems unlikely that any definitive answer to the East-West influences in medieval castle-building will be possible, until Crusader, Armenian, Muslim, Byzantine and, one should add, Italian and perhaps Spanish castles and town defences have been subjected to the same kind of scrutiny that English, Scottish, Welsh and French ones have undergone in the last seventy-five years'.[41] Pringle has since updated this in a study that highlights the contributions of Armenians.

Many nineteenth- and even twentieth-century examinations of crusader castles were plagued by certain biases, often a prejudice that praised a European building tradition or that of the Byzantines. Others have sought to explain the development of Frankish fortifications as conforming to an overly simple model of development, often ignoring regional, topographical, economic and various political influences. As Lawrence wrote, 'To consider the Crusading castles in their chronological order is extremely difficult: they are mainly a series of exceptions to some undiscoverable rule.'[42] Attempts to define that rule have, to date, proven futile.

Keeps and Enclosures

Tower-keeps were one element that the Franks certainly imported. Like their early stone counterparts in Europe, these were centres of local administration and defence. The rural towers built in the Levant typically had two storeys, but, unlike contemporary European examples, the entrance to most was located at the first level (ground floor) rather than the level above. This is indicative of the different threats that these strongholds were expected to face. Towers like these were not strong enough to keep out a large Near Eastern army for an extended period of time, but while an elevated entrance provided protection against the forces of a neighbouring European baron, a ground-floor entrance, which was more convenient, was strong enough to resist the less organized robbers and bandits of Palestine. In both Europe and the Levant, these towers often formed the nuclei of larger castles as defences were gradually developed and expanded over time.

The declining popularity of keeps in Europe during the thirteenth and fourteenth centuries may have been influenced by the designs of certain Frankish strongholds. Dating to the late twelfth century and early thirteenth, a number of large Frankish castles, including Kerak, Belvoir, Crac, Jacob's Ford and 'Atlit, lacked keeps. The shift towards the use of enclosure designs may have been inspired by Eastern traditions, as keeps were not prominent features of contemporary Byzantine, 'Abbāsid or Armenian fortifications. Although less popular, the construction of keeps continued after the battle of Hattin, as at Chastel Blanc and Montfort, while other keeps, like those at Tortosa and Beaufort, became the focal points of much larger castles. What caused the shift towards the construction of enclosures is unclear, but it began with the resources to construct these much larger strongholds – of the examples above, Kerak was the only one commissioned by a baron.

Frankish castles that made use of a quadriburgium design were almost certainly influenced by the layouts of similar Eastern examples, such as the small Byzantine frontier forts in western Syria and larger Muslim strongholds of Kafr Lām and Māhūz Azdūd along the Palestinian coast. This design was particularly popular in the kingdom of Jerusalem during the twelfth century, especially at sites commissioned by the crown, such as Scandelion, Ibelin, Bethgibelin, Blanchegarde, Burj Bardawīl and Castellum Regis. Whether influenced by Frankish strongholds like these or not, the basic rectangular enclosure plan became popular in France around the reign of

Philip II (r. 1180–1223), and a number of castles with this plan were built by Frederick II in Italy. The design gained favour in Britain slightly later, apparently a result of its earlier spread to Savoy; James of St George, the Savoyard master builder, used slight variants of a quadrangular plan when designing castles like Flint, Rhuddlan, Harlech, Conwy and Beaumaris for Edward I in northern Wales. Although it was never completed, Beaumaris replaced Belvoir as what is generally considered to be the most elegantly planned concentric castle. Regardless of whether a keep was present or not, increasing attention was devoted to the development of additional lines of defences in the thirteenth century.

Concentricity

Considerable ink has been dedicated to the topic of concentric defences, their origin, use and development, but the idea of using multiple lines of fortifications was neither dramatic nor new at any point in history, dating back to prehistoric earthworks. Simply adding a ditch ahead of a wall is, by definition, adding a concentric defensive system; however, what is typically meant by this term is the use of an outer line of walls to surround a primary inner circuit. This is exemplified by the famous Theodosian walls of Constantinople, which date to the fifth century. Despite their advantages, concentric defences were expensive, implicitly requiring more than one line of fortifications, so were relatively rare in the centuries leading up to the First Crusade.

The European motte and bailey castle was a quasi-concentric castle: the focal motte, topped with a keep, was often partly surrounded by the outer bailey. Where the bailey secured an approachable front, it might be considered 'concentric'; otherwise, the motte component might be regarded as a donjon or akin to the citadel of a town. At many later 'concentric castles', multiple lines of defences were employed only along fronts that were left exposed by the surrounding geography. This was especially true in the rough region of the northern Levant, where the Franks and Armenians used the topography to their advantage, at times expanding earlier Byzantine outposts but rarely adding a second line of walls along fronts that were naturally inaccessible. To the south, the outer wall at 'Atlit runs only along its eastern front, yet it is often labelled a 'concentric castle', while the famous Theodosian walls at Constantinople similarly stretch along only the western (landward) side of the city.

Securing a vulnerable front with an extra line of defences was a simple way of increasing the defensibility of a stronghold. Truly concentric designs, however, appear most often where the surrounding topography is reasonably level or the castle sits on a conical hill, leaving all sides equally susceptible to attack. Two complete lines of walls can be found at Belvoir and Crac, and may also have encircled Safed and Montreal, but most other large castles had multiple walls along no more than three fronts, as at Arsūf, Montfort, Tortosa, Baghrās and elsewhere. The issue is that the term 'concentric castle' has been abused, leaving it with no clear definition but rather vaguely synonymous with 'significant' or 'strong'.

With few exceptions, truly concentric stone castles were built by the Franks before their European counterparts. While Belvoir is the earliest clear example of a single-phase castle of this type, many other smaller strongholds, such as Baysān, La Fève,

Montreal, from the west. (*Courtesy of APAAME*)

Latrun, Bethgibelin, Jubayl and many smaller towers, were completely encircled by an outer wall by 1187 at the latest. At many of these smaller sites, it seems the outer wall was constructed to create a larger defensible space, rather than a significantly stronger one. At larger sites, starting with Belvoir, defensibility was more clearly the primary motivation. In northwestern Europe, a similar trend towards adding surrounding walls was under way by the late twelfth century, as was the case at Dover, Gisors and many other sites. Gravensteen, built in 1180, and Château Gaillard, built in 1196–98, commissioned by Philip of Alsace and Richard I of England respectively, were perhaps the first stone castles with concentric designs constructed in a single phase in Europe. Philip and Richard had spent significant periods fighting in the Levant before commissioning these castles, but whether the advantages of concentric designs were impressed on them during their time in the East is unclear. Despite both men's links to the Latin East, neither Gravensteen nor Château Gaillard bears any significant resemblance to one of the castles they might have seen while on crusade. This is not unlike the way in which the Franks may have been, subliminally or consciously, influenced by earlier concentric defences they encountered in the region.

One of the European kings most closely associated with concentric defences is Edward I of England, another crusader. Before becoming king, Edward, who arrived in the Holy Land shortly before his thirty-second birthday, spent around 500 days in Acre between May 1271 and September 1272. The city's defences seem to have impressed the prince, who financed a new tower along the outer line of walls near the northeastern salient, and they might have provided the inspiration behind his development of the Tower of London, where he commissioned an outer wall and barbican upon returning to England. This barbican is suspiciously similar to that built around the same time at Goodrich by William of Valence, Edward's half-uncle, who had accompanied Edward on crusade, or his son Aymer, suggesting the same master builder may have directed both projects.

Concentric principles were not employed during all of Edward I's fortification efforts – far from it. During the king's conquest of Wales, Rhuddlan, Harlech and Beaumaris were all designed with an outer wall, while the equally impressive strongholds of Flint, Conwy and Caernarfon were not. None of these castles resembles those he might have seen in the Levant, but reasonably similar templates were to be found in South Wales by this point. Gilbert of Clare commissioned Caerphilly, a concentric castle, in 1268 and work was probably completed under his son and namesake around the time Edward was away on crusade. Less than 80km to the west, Kidwelly was also rebuilt with a concentric plan sometime around the late 1270s; as at Caerphilly, the outer defences surround a quadrangular inner enclosure. By the end of the thirteenth century, a broader movement towards the construction of concentric castles was under way, to which Edward's experiences at Acre contributed.

Despite the increasing popularity of concentric defences, these by no means rendered all others obsolete, nor was it ignorance that led to the continued construction of strongholds without outer walls. Most Muslim castles and citadels were designed with a single line of walls – Ṣubayba is a rare example where a large outer bailey was added around part of the earliest component of the castle. Likewise, many

Edwardian castles.

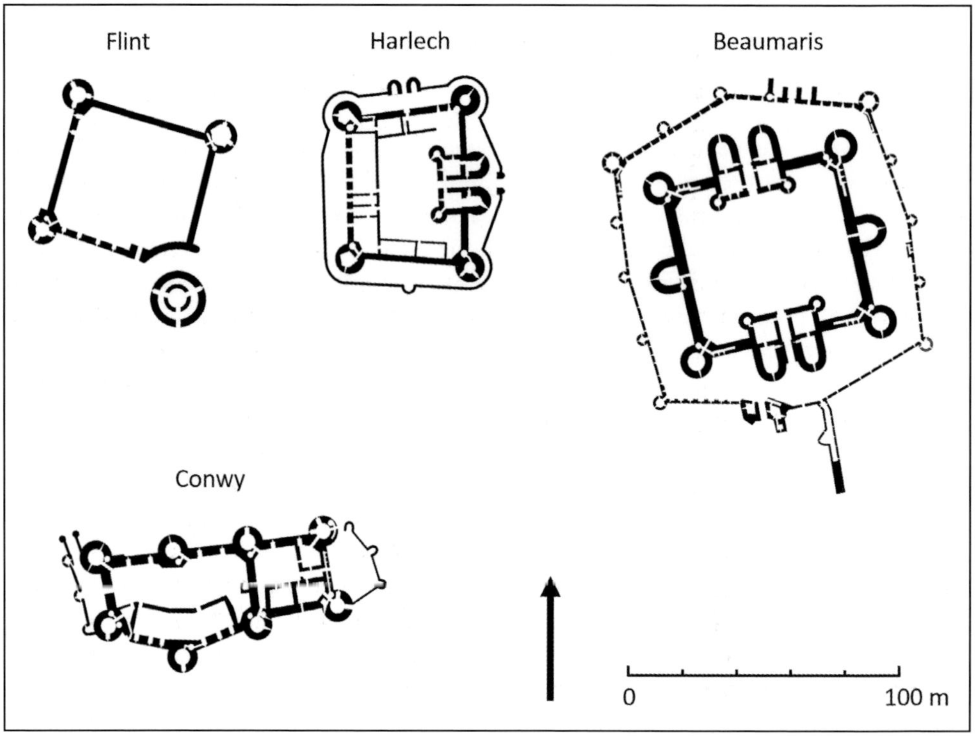

Ṣubayba, upper castle from the outer southwestern tower. (*Michael Fulton*)

of the strongest castles built in Europe during the thirteenth and fourteenth centuries also employed no more than a single line of walls.

Rounded Towers

Rounded towers had been constructed throughout the Roman Empire and continued to be built in the Near East following the Muslim conquests of the seventh century. In Europe and the Frankish Levant, however, they were rarely employed again before the start of the thirteenth century; exceptions include the twelfth-century rounded towers at Saone in the Syrian Coastal Mountains and Châteaudun in France. Rounded towers became more popular in medieval Latin architecture from the time of the Third Crusade, commonly used in the works of the kings of England and France. This design became conspicuously more popular at the same time that larger castles became more common; it seems it was the greater resources of those who financed these projects that led to the use of this slightly more complex tower shape. Regardless of where they were first built by Latin architects, their growing popularity in Europe during the early thirteenth century, particularly in France, probably contributed to their increasingly frequent use in the Levant. In part, this was due to European financing. As Müller-Wiener and many others have noted, European architectural influences are quite clear at most large Frankish castles dating to the thirteenth century.

Machicolations

Machicolations were one of the few elements that can clearly be seen to originate in the East and travel via the Latin principalities to Europe. The earliest examples appear in Umayyad architecture and can be found at some ʿAbbāsid and Fāṭimid sites. Some of the earliest Frankish/European machicolations (discounting simple murder holes, which have an earlier origin) were of a recessed slot or buttress style. These can be found around the top of the keep at Château Gaillard in France, and the earlier northern inner tower of Crac, where they served as latrine chutes rather than defensive elements. Box machicolations, and similar variants that were built out on corbels, were widely used by the Franks from the start of the thirteenth century. These gradually made their way across the Mediterranean and found widespread use in southern Europe in the fourteenth century.

Prior to the introduction of stone machicolations, some European strongholds had employed hoarding, which similarly allowed defenders to cover the walls below them. It was probably advances in artillery technology, to which hoarding was particularly vulnerable, that led to the adoption of machicolations in regions where stone was readily available. In parts of northern Europe, where timber was abundant, there remained a preference for hoarding well into the fourteenth century. Machicolations remained important defensive elements until they were eventually made redundant with the introduction of more effective siege guns in the fifteenth century.

Fort Saint-André (Villeneuve-lès-Avignon), main gate. (*Michael Fulton*)

Embrasures and Battlements

Embrasures were a common feature of Byzantine fortifications in greater Syria. They were seldom employed in Europe before the First Crusade, but became common as fortifications were increasingly built of stone rather than wood. By the mid-twelfth century, Europeans and Franks, as well as their Muslim counterparts, frequently employed embrasures in towers. The use of lines of embrasures, typically accessed by casemates, along stretches of curtain walls appears first in the East, but this quickly spread to Europe. Lines of mural embrasures were employed when Edward I rebuilt the western section of the Tower of London's main wall, and at castles such as Caernarfon and Beaumaris.

The construction of lines of mural casemates and embrasures may have been inspired by the earlier use of double-level battlements. This style of parapet had been employed by the Byzantines prior to the crusades and most twelfth-century Frankish castles that made use of a double-level parapet, such as Jubayl and Saone, were located in regions where Byzantine influence remained significant. From the Levant, the use of double-level battlements also spread to Europe, where they were employed, particularly in the south, from the late thirteenth century.

Taluses

The talus is another feature that may have spread to Europe from the Levant, or may have been developed simultaneously as a response to similar threats. The Frankish glacis at Kerak, talus at Belvoir and Nūr al-Dīn's glacis at the north end of the citadel of Shayzar date to the mid- to late twelfth century, as might some of the revetment on the sides of fortified tells predating Ayyūbid rule. In the early thirteenth century, the outer towers of 'Atlit and keep of Montfort were given battered bases, while a more dramatic glacis was employed when the southern and western fronts of the inner enceinte of Crac was refortified. But perhaps the most iconic talus, that at Caesarea, was added during Louis IX's visit in the 1250s.

In Europe, the keep of Château Gaillard is battered and the western towers of Chinon, also dating to the late twelfth century, were provided with taluses. Battering the bases of towers became a relatively common practice in Europe in the thirteenth and fourteenth centuries. Some, like the tour du Moulin at Chinon, Marten's Tower at Chepstow and the towers of the outer southern gate and those along the wall to the east at Caerphilly, rise from pyramidal bases into round or polygonal towers, a design not found in the Latin East. The inner southern towers built at Crac by the Franks and the outer southern tower at Margat built by the Mamlūks are the closest comparables, but these rounded towers rise from a surrounding glacis, rather than from a base of a different shape.

Portcullises

The portcullis appears to have been a defensive feature imported from Europe, where it was employed sparsely in the twelfth century. Most early examples are found in England, but from about the reign of Philip II of France the portcullis saw increasing use in France, Britain and the Netherlands. This trend extended to the Latin East, where portcullises became more common in the thirteenth century, coinciding with the increasing scale and sophistication of castles. Although employed by the Franks

Chepstow, Marten's Tower and straight eastern entrance. (*Michael Fulton*)

in many of their large strongholds, portcullises were rarely used by neighbouring Muslim rulers, making the presence of portcullis slots at Ṣubayba intriguing.

Staircases

One of the more obvious differences between the strongholds built in the Levant and contemporary fortifications in Europe was the use of spiral staircases. These were common in Europe but so far have been found only at Crac des Chevaliers and Montfort in the Frankish East. They were also used when the Mamlūks expanded the southwestern tower at Ṣubayba, providing access to the two new sub-levels. According to traditional thinking, spiral staircases were designed so that attackers would be forced to ascend or descend in a clockwise direction, permitting defenders to meet them while moving counterclockwise. This allowed a defender to swing a weapon in his right hand across his body, towards the centre of the staircase and any attackers he might meet, while forcing an attacker to resort to an awkward backhand motion. Accordingly, it is possible to postulate the direction from which it was believed attackers were most likely to enter a staircase – would they storm it from the bottom or gain entrance from the top?

Although far from the most celebrated defensive features, the design and placement of staircases were important. If attackers managed to climb up to the top of a wall, they needed a way to get down or were otherwise stuck there; or, if they broke in through a gate or breached a wall, they needed a way to get up to engage the defenders along the parapet. Almost all staircases built by the Franks and Muslims in the Levant were straight and most were constructed within the thickness of tower walls, providing access between the upper and lower levels. A gate often provided access to the adjoining parapet from the upper level of many mural towers. This type of arrangement forced an attacker to gain entrance to the tower in order to change levels.

Vaulting

In addition to having their entrances on different levels, the floors/ceilings of Latin tower-keeps built in Europe and the Levant often differed. In Europe, towers were usually divided by wooden levels, which were cheaper and simpler than stone vaulting. Presumably owing to the general shortage of suitable timber in the Levant, and the local tradition of building with stone, most Frankish towers were built with vaulted ceilings at each level, providing a stone floor for the level above. The regular use of fire as a siege weapon might also have incentivized the use of stone, but this would appear to be a point of encouragement rather than a cause.

Entrances

Despite the common use of bent entrances in the Levant, these never caught on in Europe to the same degree; the majority of European castle and town entrances remained straight. The preference for straight gates in Europe seems to have been influenced by factors of convenience: it was much easier to bring a wagon or ride in ceremony through a straight gate. This was perhaps a greater factor in Europe because these structures remained the primary residences of the nobility, whereas many Frankish nobles in the Levant came to reside along the coast, entrusting their strongholds to castellans or selling them to the military orders.

Trends: Distribution, Success and Duration

The availability of reliable and complete information is the greatest challenge to modelling trends related to the sieges of this period. Despite the number of surviving contemporary accounts, there were probably numerous sieges that went unreported, suggested by the regularity with which sieges, especially smaller ones, are found in some accounts but not others. Contemporaries had a tendency to mention sieges where the side with which they identified was victorious, and more generally to inflate the significance of some successful minor actions and omit or downplay failures. For example, Frankish sources assert that Antioch was besieged by a Mamlūk force in 1262, while Muslim sources unanimously present this as a raid, which resulted in the sack of the port of St Symeon. Similarly, William of Tyre provides a vivid description of Saladin's attack on Beirut in 1182, while contemporary Muslims present this as a far less significant event.

Even when sources agree that a siege took place, the duration of the engagement is rarely stated; in exceptional cases where an exact figure is provided, it is usually found in only one original account. Sieges are more often described as having started in one month and ended in another, or such a rough sense of timing can be deduced by examining surrounding events. Although helpful, this is far from ideal when trying to discern if a siege that began in April and ended in May lasted less than a week or the better part of two months. Sometimes it can be difficult to determine in which year a siege took place, let alone precisely how long it lasted.

With this in mind, some 342 fairly dateable sieges involving parties influenced by the presence of the Franks can be identified between 1097 and 1291 (see pp. 286–99). The region considered stretches from Cilicia across to the drainage basin of the Euphrates north of Raqqa (as far as Sinjār, Ḥiṣn Kayfā, Mayyāfāriqīn, Mardin and Amida, but not as far as Mosul), and down through western Syria, Palestine and Egypt. Although Frankish armies did not penetrate the eastern reaches of the Jazīra, many who came into direct contact with the Franks hailed from this area. Īlghāzī, Zankī, Saladin and certain Ayyūbid princes all divided their attention between affairs in various parts of this broader region. Of these 342 sieges, the outcome of all but one is clear – the exception being Joscelin I's siege of the tower at Tell Aran, during which he was injured and never fully recovered.

Due to the bias and often politically charged vocabulary of contemporary sources, a qualitative judgement is often required to distinguish a 'siege' from an 'attack' and a 'sack' from an immediate or otherwise fairly peaceful surrender. A siege here is considered to be a concerted attack against a fortified position from which determined resistance was offered, at least initially. Accordingly, the siege of Sidon by the Mongols in 1260 might be considered an attack or a sack, yet references to attempts to take the two castles is sufficient to classify it as a siege. Likewise, Nūr al-Dīn's repeated moves against Damascus prior to 1154 might be called sieges by contemporary commentators, but are not considered as such here because his forces did not attack the city's defences or impose an aggressive blockade. An exception has been made in the case of the 'siege' of Damascus in 1148, the climax of the Second Crusade. Although no ladders or projectiles ever touched the city's walls during this event, the scale and significance of the operation are sufficient to warrant the exception and its inclusion.

When considering the principal belligerents of these 342 sieges, 237 (69%) involved Muslim forces, Frankish figures took part in 91 (27%), Byzantine elements were present at 9 (3%), and 13 (4%) were undertaken by the Mongols. On at least two occasions – the siege of Aleppo in 1124–25 and Bānyās in 1140 – Frankish and Muslim besiegers worked cooperatively, while Frankish and Byzantine forces participated alongside each other in at least six sieges, including the siege of Nicaea in 1097, those of John Comnenus' campaign in western Syria in 1138 and the siege of Damietta in 1169. From the opposite perspective, 189 (55%) of these sieges were directed against Muslim strongholds, 144 (42%) targeted Frankish defences and 9 (3%) involved strongholds under Greek or Armenian control. Overall, the success enjoyed by both Frankish and Muslim forces from 1097 to 1260 was almost identical – slightly

Belligerents of sieges.

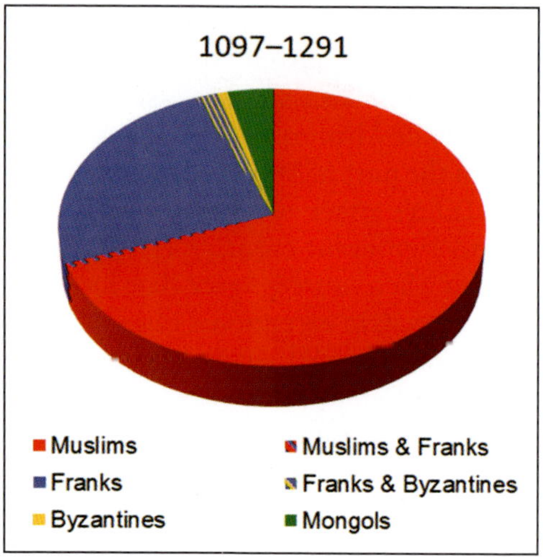

Distribution of sieges, before and after Hattin and Saladin's death

Period	Frankish sieges	Muslim sieges
1097–1187, First Crusade to battle of Hattin	81% (74/91)	59% (141/237)
1187–1291, Battle of Hattin to capture of Acre	19% (17/91)	41% (96/237)
1097–1193, First Crusade to Saladin's death	87% (79/91)	69% (163/237)
1193–1291, Saladin's death to capture of Acre	13% (12/91)	31% (74/237)

better than 62%. During the period that followed, the Franks undertook no sieges against their Muslim neighbours, while the Mamlūks pushed the overall Muslim success rate up to almost 65%.

Two general and very obvious patterns can be seen when looking at the distribution and focus of the period's sieges. First, the frequency of Frankish sieges declined considerably between the twelfth century and the thirteenth: 81% of Frankish sieges took place before the battle of Hattin and just 13% followed the end of the Third Crusade and Richard I's departure from the Holy Land in 1192. By comparison, Muslim sieges were more evenly distributed through the twelfth and thirteenth centuries. Second, the proportion of sieges that were directed against coreligionists rose. Although some Muslim figures might have seen the Franks as their principal adversaries, or at least professed this, most were at least as concerned with Muslim rivals: 45% of Muslim sieges were directed against coreligionists. Although 54% of these took place before Saladin's death, as a proportion of the total number of Muslim sieges these increased from 35% before 1193 to 66% during the following century. In other words, although the overall number of sieges undertaken by Muslim forces against Muslim-controlled strongholds declined slightly, they

Sieges against coreligionists.

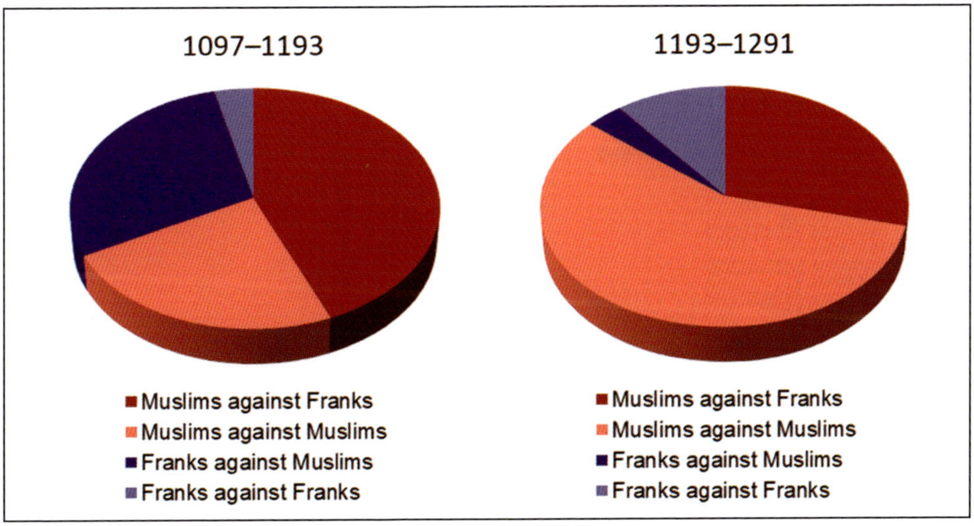

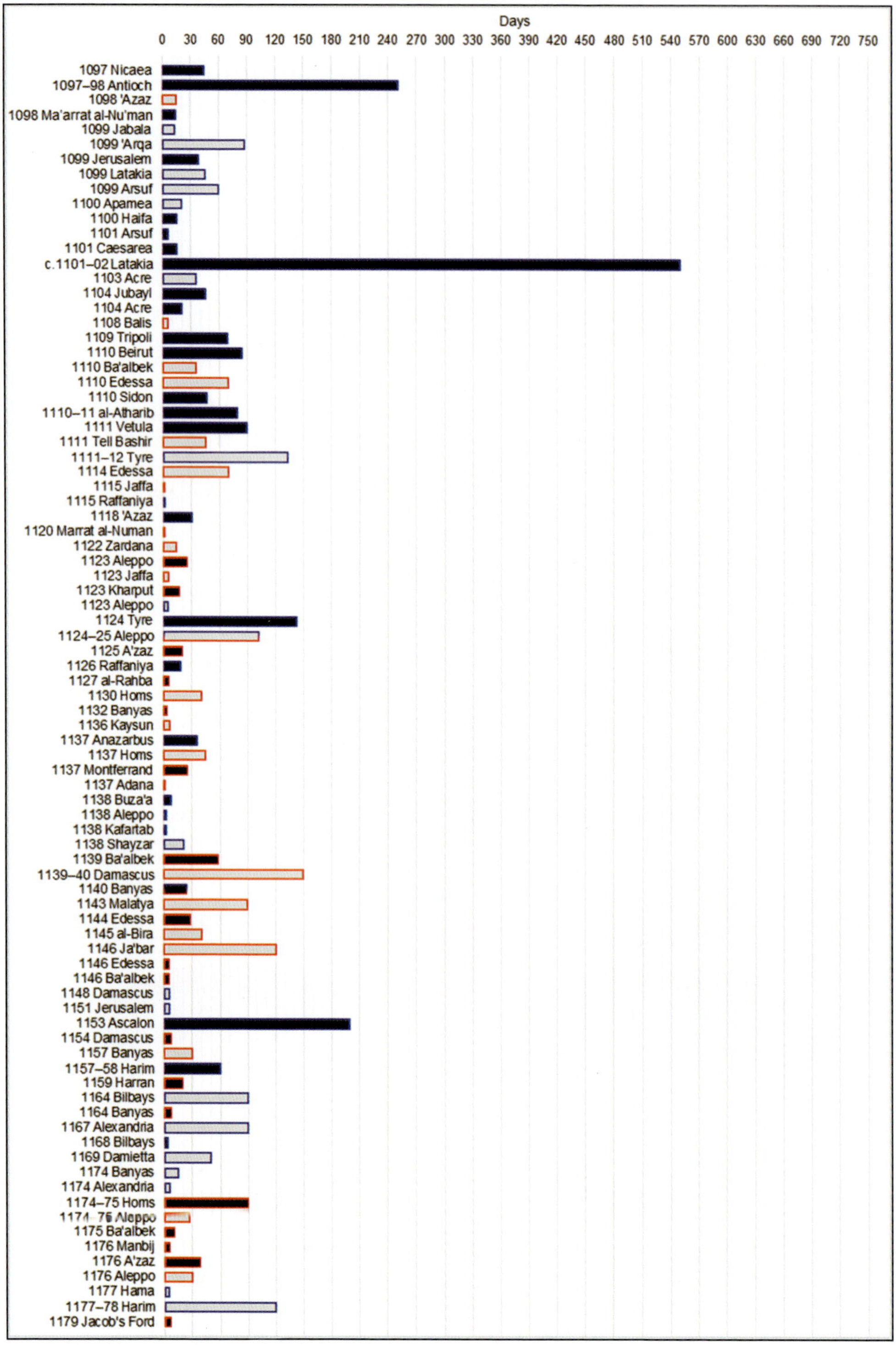

Length of sieges, Frankish/Muslim/Mongol (blue/red/green outline), success/failure (black/grey fill)

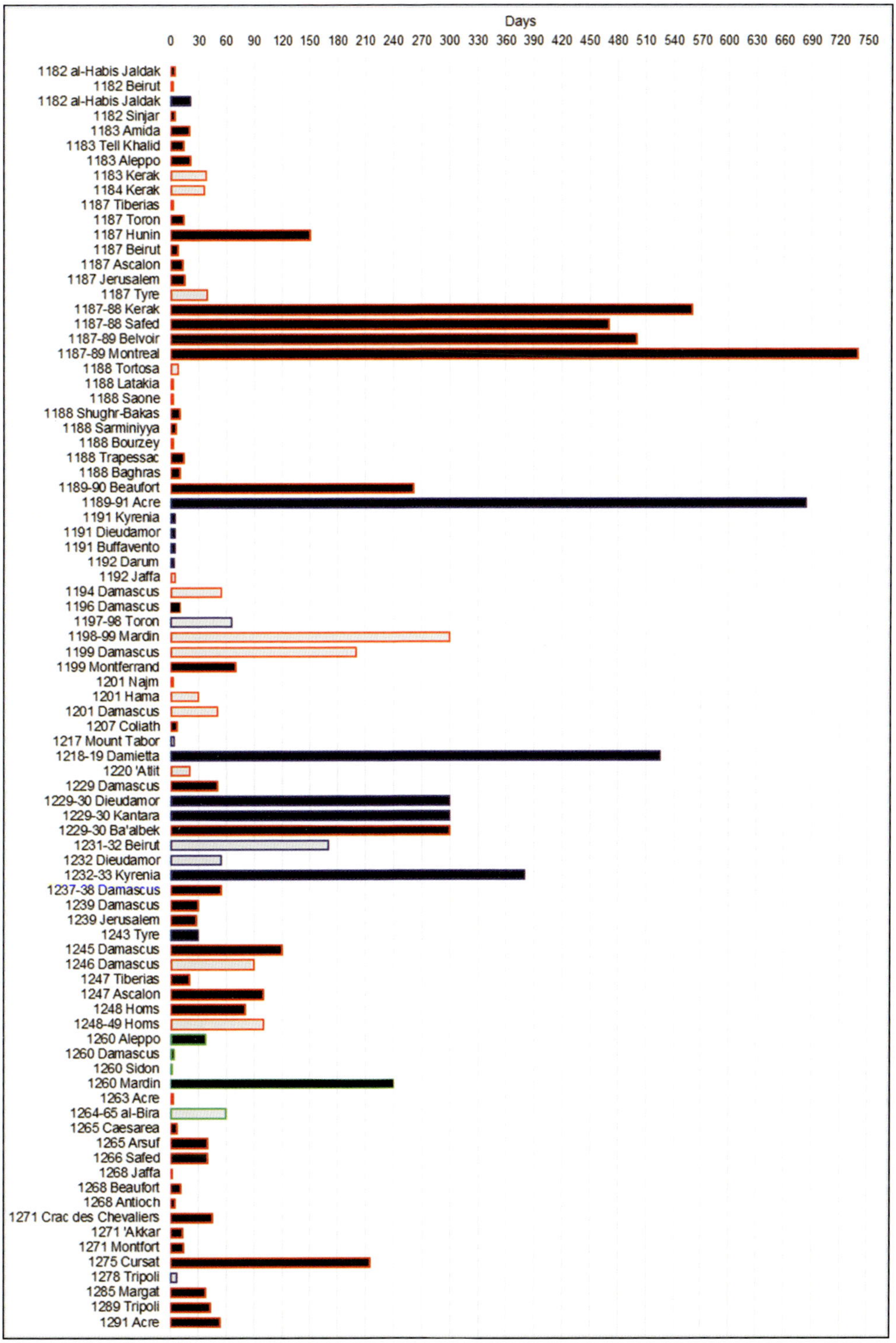
Days
0 30 60 90 120 150 180 210 240 270 300 330 360 390 420 450 480 510 540 570 600 630 660 690 720 750
1182 al-Habis Jaldak
1182 Beirut
1182 al-Habis Jaldak
1182 Sinjar
1183 Amida
1183 Tell Khalid
1183 Aleppo
1183 Kerak
1184 Kerak
1187 Tiberias
1187 Toron
1187 Hunin
1187 Beirut
1187 Ascalon
1187 Jerusalem
1187 Tyre
1187-88 Kerak
1187-88 Safed
1187-89 Belvoir
1187-89 Montreal
1188 Tortosa
1188 Latakia
1188 Saone
1188 Shughr-Bakas
1188 Sarminiyya
1188 Bourzey
1188 Trapessac
1188 Baghras
1189-90 Beaufort
1189-91 Acre
1191 Kyrenia
1191 Dieudamor
1191 Buffavento
1192 Darum
1192 Jaffa
1194 Damascus
1196 Damascus
1197-98 Toron
1198-99 Mardin
1199 Damascus
1199 Montferrand
1201 Najm
1201 Hama
1201 Damascus
1207 Coliath
1217 Mount Tabor
1218-19 Damietta
1220 'Atlit
1229 Damascus
1229-30 Dieudamor
1229-30 Kantara
1229-30 Ba'albek
1231-32 Beirut
1232 Dieudamor
1232-33 Kyrenia
1237-38 Damascus
1239 Damascus
1239 Jerusalem
1243 Tyre
1245 Damascus
1246 Damascus
1247 Tiberias
1247 Ascalon
1248 Homs
1248-49 Homs
1260 Aleppo
1260 Damascus
1260 Sidon
1260 Mardin
1263 Acre
1264-65 al-Bira
1265 Caesarea
1265 Arsuf
1266 Safed
1268 Jaffa
1268 Beaufort
1268 Antioch
1271 Crac des Chevaliers
1271 'Akkar
1271 Montfort
1275 Cursat
1278 Tripoli
1285 Margat
1289 Tripoli
1291 Acre

accounted for two-thirds of Muslim sieges between 1193 and 1291. Frankish sieges are again more dramatically divided in this regard. Aside from Baldwin III's sieges of Mirabel (Majdal Yaba) and Jerusalem, during the brief civil war with his mother, Frankish sieges directed against coreligionists were restricted to Armenian and Byzantine strongholds up to 1193, collectively accounting for just 12% of Frankish sieges during this period. Following the Third Crusade, however, 75% of Frankish siege operations were directed against fellow Franks.

The approximate length of 170 of these 342 sieges can be determined. This is just 50%, and considering that many smaller sieges probably took place that we do not know about, considerable room is left for error. Using the available data, the average siege-length across the entire period was about seventy days. Eight sieges were exceptionally long and lasted more than a year: four accompanied Saladin's conquests in the wake of the battle of Hattin; two were the defining sieges of the Third and Fifth Crusades; the other two were Tancred's extended siege of Latakia in 1101–2 and the Ibelin-Genoese siege of Kyrenia in 1232–33. (The extended blockades of Tripoli, beginning in 1102, renewed in 1104 and lasting until 1109, and that of Ascalon, from 1244 until 1247, have not been included because a concerted or close blockade does not appear to have been maintained throughout.) When examining the complete range of these sieges more closely, it quickly becomes apparent that, like the development of larger and stronger fortifications, patterns in the length and success of sieges were influenced more by dramatic political events than technological advancements or the exceptional capabilities of particular individuals.

Sieges by Generation

During the First Crusade, the Franks engaged in six sieges with discernible lengths. These lasted an average of seventy-four days (two were concluded in just two weeks while the siege of Antioch went on for more than eight months). The Franks enjoyed success at two-thirds of these sieges, their failures coming at ʿArqa, where Raymond of St Gilles bit off slightly more than he could chew, and Jabala, where another group of crusaders abandoned the siege as rumours circulated that a large Muslim force was gathering to attack Raymond's party at ʿArqa. To these can be added Baldwin I of Edessa's successful siege of Sarūj, although it is unclear how long this siege lasted, and Riḍwān's siege of ʿAzāz, which was abandoned less than a month after it began.

Between the crusaders' capture of Jerusalem in 1099 and the point at which Saladin crossed the Jordan ahead of the battle of Hattin in 1187, the length of eighty-seven sieges (42%) can be discerned, lasting an average of forty-three days. Of the larger total number of identifiable sieges during this period, Frankish forces took part in 66 (32%) and Muslim forces in 140 (68%), achieving success on 58% and 60% of occasions respectively. This fairly even picture changes dramatically if the period is broken down.

From August 1099 until 1128, the year Ṭughtakīn died and Zankī acquired Aleppo, Frankish forces engaged in forty-one sieges and Muslim parties in thirty-nine, finding success at 71% and 46% of these respectively. During this period, 31% of Muslim sieges were directed against the strongholds of coreligionists, 67% of which were successful, while just 37% of those directed against Frankish towns and castles ended favourably for the besiegers. It was in the north that Muslim forces found particular difficulties. Ṭughtakīn managed to take Rafaniyya in 1115, but not until Īlghāzī defeated Roger of Antioch at the battle of the Field of Blood in 1119 did the rate of successful sieges in the region increase noticeably, due in part to the effective actions of Balak in the early 1120s.

From 1128 to 1154, the period during which Aleppo was the seat of Zankid power in western Syria, the frequency of Frankish sieges fell, from 1.4 per year between 1099 and 1128 to less than 1 every other year. The Franks' success rate also dipped, dropping to 50%. Meanwhile, Muslim sieges increased from 1.3 per year to almost 2 per year, 63% of which ended successfully. The decline in the number of Frankish sieges was due in part to their earlier conquest of the coast, aside from Ascalon, which removed potential targets. To the north, regency issues persisted in Antioch, with a king of Jerusalem filling this role for around ten of the twenty-six years between 1128 and 1154. Raymond of Poitiers brought strong leadership to the principality between the regencies of Fulk and Baldwin III, but in Aleppo he faced the might of Zankī, who, unlike Riḍwān, could call on resources east of the Euphrates when needed. Muslim sieges of coreligionists rose slightly, to 41% of all Muslim sieges, largely a result of Zankid and Būrid efforts to establish dominance over western Syria.

From 1154, the resources of Aleppo and Damascus came under a single ruler, to which holding Egypt was later added. During the twenty-year period between Nūr al-Dīn's acquisition of Damascus and his death in 1174, the Franks undertook only six sieges (two coincided with Thierry of Flanders' crusade in the late 1150s and four took place during the contest for Egypt in the 1160s). Only two of these (33%) were successful. To make matters worse for the Franks, Nūr al-Dīn's attention also shifted their way. Of the twenty-six sieges prosecuted by or on behalf of Nūr al-Dīn from 1154, only three (12%) were directed against Muslim strongholds (one being the siege of Damascus in 1154), while 68% of all sieges undertaken under his banner were concluded successfully during this period. This figure might have been better had Saladin, who ruled Egypt on Nūr al-Dīn's behalf from 1169, been successful at more than one of the five sieges he initiated in this position.

After Nūr al-Dīn's death in May 1174, Saladin forged an even greater empire, effectively harnessing the resources of Egypt to spread his authority over western Syria and much of the Jazīra. In the thirteen years between Nūr al-Dīn's death and the battle of Hattin (not including the siege of Tiberias, which spanned the battle), Muslim forces conducted twenty-seven sieges, two-thirds of which were successful. Of the twenty-four sieges prior to the summer of 1183, twenty-one targeted Muslim strongholds (seventeen of these were carried out under Saladin's banner). The final siege in this series saw Aleppo fall to Saladin, from which point he devoted his attention to the Franks. Despite his resources, Saladin was successful at only three of the six sieges he undertook against Frankish strongholds prior to the spring of 1187, capturing the incomplete castle at Jacob's Ford (1179), the isolated outpost of al-Ḥabis Jaldak (1182) and the administrative tower at Jinīn (1184). Meanwhile, Latin forces initiated just seven sieges during this period and were successful only once (14%), retaking al-Ḥabis Jaldak in 1182. Among the failed sieges, two corresponded with the crusade of Philip of Flanders and another was the independent Sicilian attack on Alexandria in 1174.

Following Saladin's decisive victory at the battle of Hattin, the three remaining Frankish principalities were pushed to the brink of collapse. From the start of July 1187 to the surrender of Beaufort in April 1190, Saladin orchestrated the sieges of twenty-one strongholds, all Frankish, taking nineteen of them (90%), failing only against Tyre and the Templar tower at Tortosa. Collectively, the average length of these sieges was about 140 days; however, thirteen (62%) were concluded in less than a month, lasting an average of just eight days. The remainder, excluding the siege of Tyre at the end of 1187, which extended for about thirty-nine days, were fairly passive blockades, lasting an average of almost 450 days, or about fifteen months. Meanwhile, the Franks, who were left almost paralysed, could do little in response. The only concerted offensive action during this period was Guy of Lusignan's longshot attack on Acre, which was sustained through the help of the crusaders who streamed into the Holy Land in response to the loss of Jerusalem. The siege eventually ended in a Frankish victory almost 700 days after it had begun. Aside from Richard I's subjugation of Cyprus, the only other sieges prior to the end of the Third Crusade were Richard's siege of Dārūm and Saladin's failed attack on Jaffa. Richard maintained a perfect siege record while on crusade, but this, like Saladin's mixed record, was influenced by the political, economic and social context in which he was operating, not just by his ability and resources.

Although broad trends relating to the frequency and success rate of twelfth-century sieges appear to correspond with the evolving balance of power, siege lengths follow less obvious patterns. From the siege of Nicaea in 1097 to Nūr al-Dīn's capture of Damascus in 1154, the approximate length of 120 sieges can be determined, lasting on average sixty-four days. Nine sieges lasted more than a hundred days (six executed by the Franks, two by Muslim forces, plus the joint siege of Aleppo in 1124–25). Among these, the Franks achieved victory at Antioch (1097–98), Latakia (1101–2), Tyre (1124) and Ascalon (1153), while none of the protracted Muslim sieges ended successfully. At the other end of the spectrum, Frankish and Muslim forces participated in at least thirty-five sieges lasting less than thirty days, sixteen and twenty sieges respectively, including the cooperative siege of Bānyās in 1140, and both found success at about 60% of these.

The length of most sieges remained relatively consistent between August 1099 and June 1187, although the sources reveal little regarding the length of most of Nūr al-Dīn's sieges. Using the available data, there was a slight decrease from fifty-five days between 1099 and 1127, to thirty-eight days from 1128 to 1154, back up to forty-four days between 1155 and 1173, then dipping to twenty-six days from 1174 to June 1187. Although the number of Frankish sieges declined through the twelfth century, the Franks remained willing to commit themselves to lengthy sieges if necessary, especially when joined by significant groups of crusaders. Like Nūr al-Dīn, Saladin appears to have avoided lengthy sieges when possible; most undertaken by his forces lasted no more than about a month and a half. The siege of Homs in 1174–75, which was conducted largely in Saladin's absence, was a rare exception. Most of Saladin's sieges were much shorter, and nearly all resulted in generous terms as he

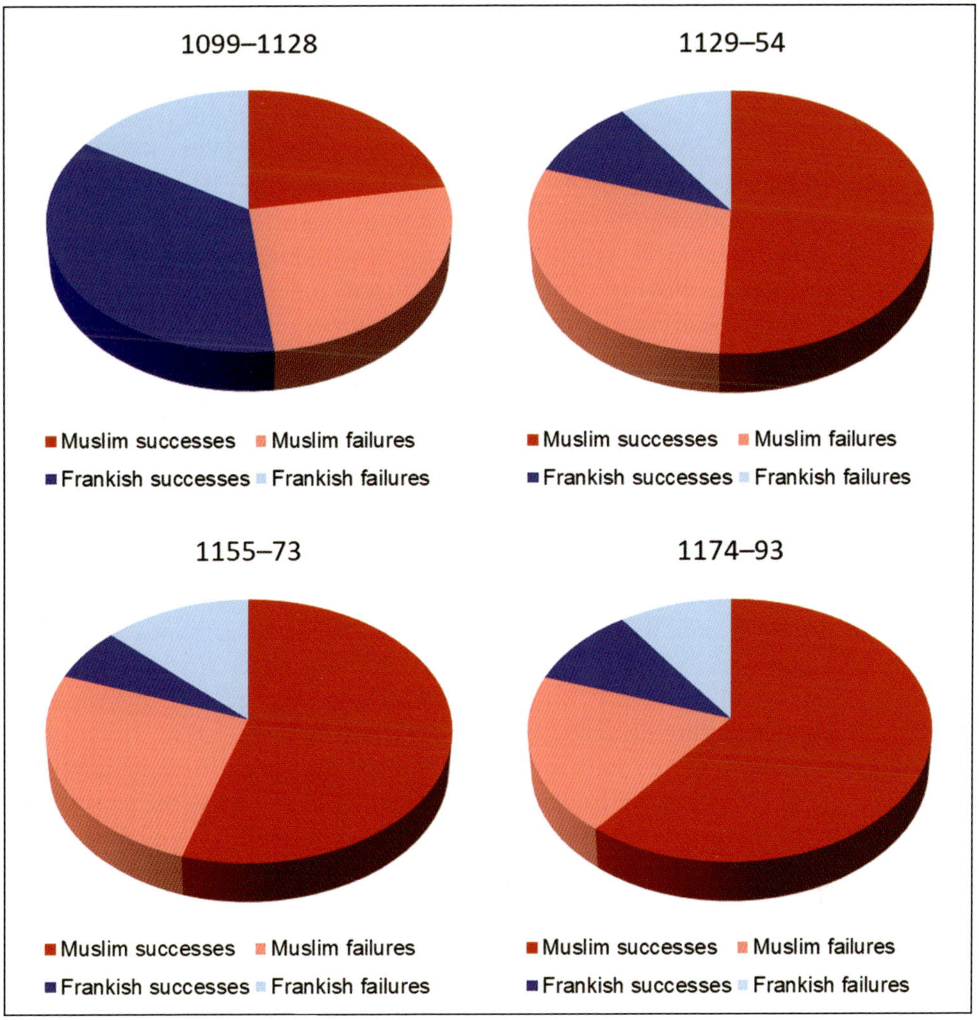

Distribution of twelfth-century sieges.

expanded his hegemony across western Syria during the decade following Nūr al-Dīn's death. The context of the sieges during the six years that followed the battle of Hattin, and their polarized lengths, which were almost all either very short or very long, averaging 135 days, have been dealt with above in the context of negotiated surrenders.

During the post-Saladin Ayyūbid period, siege patterns were relatively consistent, with about 60% of both Frankish and Muslim sieges ending successfully. Taking 1220 as a dividing point, which roughly corresponds with the end of the Fifth Crusade and al-ʻĀdil's death, there were twenty-five Muslim sieges between 1193 and the end of 1220, and an additional thirty before the battle of ʻAyn Jālūt in 1260. In both groups, 60% were directed against fellow Muslims and the same percentage ended successfully. Of the seventy-four total sieges during this broader period, only ten (14%) were undertaken by the Franks: three sieges accompanied the arrival of large forces of crusaders and targeted Muslim strongholds; seven sieges were directed against fellow Franks, five of which were undertaken on Cyprus. These were generally quite long sieges, averaging about 200 days – four continued for more than nine months. Typically happy to leave the Franks to their squabbles along the coast, and fearful of provoking another crusade, Muslim forces besieged Frankish strongholds on only ten occasions during this period, accounting for just 18% of all sieges conducted by Muslim forces in the region. Among the Ayyūbid sieges with determinable lengths, the average was close to three months – this includes three that lasted more than 150 days, while the average length of the remaining eighteen was approximately fifty days.

From 1259, the Mongols' presence was felt in western Syria. Often portrayed as a purely nomadic force with a limited siege tradition, Hülagü's army was successful at eight of the nine clearly distinguishable sieges that it undertook in Syria – the one-day attack on Sidon, often characterized as a raid, saw the sack of the town but failed to bring about the capture of either of its castles. Although the Mongols' numbers were perhaps their greatest siege weapon, they demonstrated their ability to undertake a set-piece siege when investing Aleppo, employing artillery and sappers through the thirty-eight-day operation. But as quickly as the Mongols had swept into Syria, they seemed to disappear, chased out by the Mamlūks. Although they remained a threat, the Mongols showed little ability to take the strongholds occupied by the Mamlūks along their frontier, failing on three separate occasions to take al-Bīra.

Between the battle of 'Ayn Jālūt and the Mamlūks' capture of Acre in 1291, the attack led by Prince Edward of England against Qāqūn in 1271 was the closest that the Franks came to besieging a Muslim stronghold. Two short Templar sieges in 1278, launched against Tripoli and Nephin, both of which failed, were perhaps the only 'sieges' undertaken by Frankish forces during this final period. The episodes of

Distribution of thirteenth-century sieges.

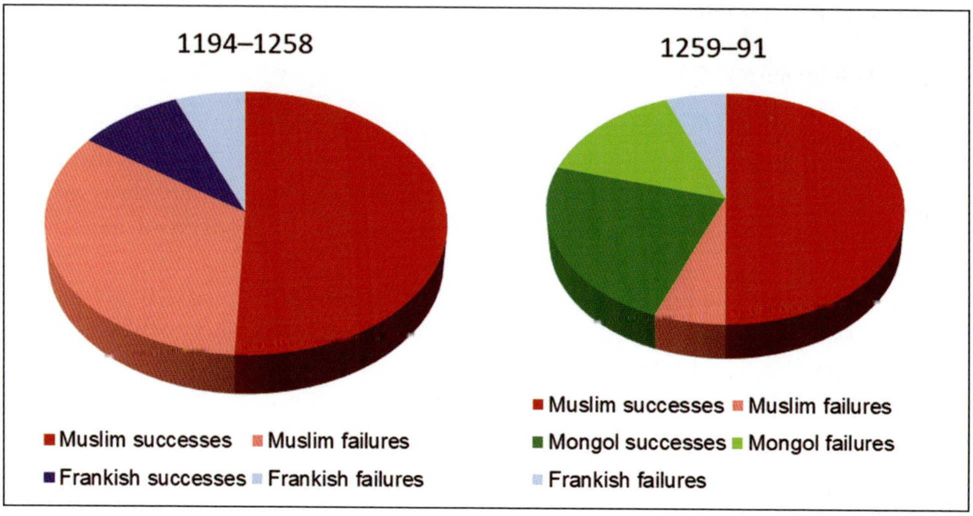

fighting in Acre by Italian factions and the military orders are hard to classify as sieges given the available information, even though siege engines were employed at times as various parties attacked the quarters of their rivals.

The undisputed masters of the region west of the Euphrates during the final four decades of the thirteenth century were the Mamlūks, and their siege record reflects this. Seventeen of their nineteen sieges (89%) were successful: fourteen of fifteen against Frankish strongholds and three of four against fellow Muslims. The two failures appear to have been tests of strength, early efforts by Baybars to size up the defences of Kerak (1261) and Acre (1263). The average duration of the fourteen sieges with discernible lengths was about thirty-eight days, or just twenty-four days if excluding the lengthy siege of Cursat in 1275, which Baybars delegated to subordinates. Testament to the resources that Baybars could bring to bear, Caesarea (1265), Jaffa (1268), Beaufort (1268), Antioch (1268), ʿAkkār (1271) and Montfort (1271) were all taken in two weeks or less. The mighty castles of Arsūf (1265), Safed (1266), Crac (1271) and later Margat (1285) fell between thirty-eight and forty-five days after siege actions began. Tripoli probably fell in a comparable period in 1189, and Acre, the seat of power of the kingdom of Jerusalem since 1191, was taken in fifty-three days.

Length and success rates of sieges by period

Period	Besieger	Sample number	Success rate	Proportion vs. coreligionists	Average length [no. from sample with discernible lengths]	No. over 30 days [% of those with discernible lengths]
First Crusade	Muslims	1	0%	100%	15 days [1]	0 [0%]
(1097–99)	Franks	7	71%	0%	74 days [6]	4 [67%]
First Generations	Muslims	39	46%	31%	28 days [15]	5 [33%]
(1099–1128)	Franks	42	69%	10%	77 days [21]	13 [62%]
Zankid Aleppo	Muslims	49	63%	41%	40 days [16]	7 [44%]
(1128–54)	Franks	12	50%	17%	33 days [8]	1 [12%]
Zankid Damascus	Muslims	25	68%	12%	19 days [3]	0 [0%]
(1154–74)	Franks	6*	33%	0%	59 days [5]	4 [80%]
Age of Saladin	Muslims	27	67%	78%	23 days [15]	4 [27%]
(1174–87)	Franks	7	14%	0%	33 days [5]	1 [20%]
Third Crusade	Muslims	22	86%	0%	135 days [21]	7 [33%]
(1187–92)	Franks	5	100%	60%	141 days [5]	1 [20%]
Ayyūbid Period	Muslims	55	60%	82%	82 days [21]	13 [62%]
(1193–1260)	Franks	10	60%	70%	203 days [9]	7 [78%]
	Mongols	9	89%	0%	71 days [4]	2 [50%]
Early Mamlūk	Muslims	19	89%	21%	38 days [14]	8 [57%]
(1260–91)	Franks	2	0%	100%	n.d. [1]	0 [n.d.]
	Mongols	4	0%	0%	n.d. [1]	1 [n.d.]

*Four of these were led by John Comnenus in 1138: Buzāʿa, Aleppo, Kafarṭāb and Shayzar.

Although they provide a convenient overview of certain trends, analytics like these are no substitute for close analyses of the contexts in which these sieges were undertaken and the plethora of variables that made each unique. While the strength of fortifications and topography might be easy to gauge, numerical strength, experience, morale and even weather could have a far more dramatic effect on a siege than the defences and siege engines that so often draw focus.

Conclusion

The Siege of Acre, 1291

Although there were no 'average' or 'typical' sieges, that of Acre in 1291, the final siege of the period, provides a helpful case study with which to conclude, illustrating the various points that have been addressed above.

During the twelfth century, Acre had become the main port and richest city of the kingdom of Jerusalem. Following Saladin's conquests after the battle of Hattin in 1187, it was recaptured in 1191 and became the kingdom's de facto seat of power thereafter. Jerusalem remained in Muslim hands through most of the thirteenth century, and was never seriously defensible during the periods in which it returned to Frankish rule. Acre was thus the political and economic capital of the kingdom, the centre of power from which the realm was administered. Such an important centre required equally formidable defences.

Acre already possessed impressive fortifications when it was captured by the Franks in 1104 and then by Saladin in 1187. After the city returned to Frankish control, the existing defences were developed and a new line of walls was built around the Montmusard suburb to the north. The city's northern and eastern walls enjoyed the protection of a forewall and ditch beyond, while the sea secured the city's western and southern fronts. The Franks had targeted the northeast salient of the city through most of the protracted siege of 1189–91 and it seems this was still considered to be a particularly vulnerable section of the city's defences in the second half of the thirteenth century. It was here that Edward I's English Tower was constructed, as well as the later Tower of the Countess of Blois, the Tower of the Patriarch and the King's Tower, adding to the security provided by the infamous Accursed Tower. These efforts to strengthen what were already considerable fortifications were to no small degree a response to broader political developments.

In 1290, little remained of the Frankish principalities. Tripoli had fallen the previous year and Frankish rule was restricted to little more than a few strongholds along the coast, including 'Atlit, Acre, Tyre, Sidon, Beirut and Tortosa, the lone remnant of the county of Tripoli. Acre, however, enjoyed peaceful relations with Qalāwūn, the product of a ten-year truce that had been concluded in 1283. This was violated in October, when a group of Italians, who had recently arrived from Europe, killed a number of Muslims in the city. Merchants, who were specifically protected by the peace, were among the dead, giving Qalāwūn a pretext to attack Acre. Although Qalāwūn fell sick around the same time as news of the slayings reached Cairo, he nevertheless pressed on with preparations for a campaign against the Franks.

Qalāwūn had little cause to fear Frankish relief forces interrupting the siege he planned, but Acre was a formidable city and would not fall easily. Orders were sent to

Damascus to prepare artillery and Shams al-Dīn al-Aʿsar was dispatched to Wādī al-Murabbīn, a valley in the Lebanon where ideal trees for the construction of artillery were known to grow. Although challenged by an early and significant snowfall, the trees reached Damascus in late December. Meanwhile, forces stationed in Jinīn were sent to raid around Acre, screening activities to their rear.

Qalāwūn's condition worsened and he died in early November 1290. Undeterred, his son, al-Ashraf Khalīl, set out with the Egyptian army in early March 1291, having sent orders to the administers of Syria and Palestine to gather and send soldiers, sappers, carpenters and masons, along with armour, artillery and other siege equipment. The task of coordinating the transportation of the Syrian artillery and equipment, which was gathering at Damascus, was entrusted to the seasoned veteran ʿIzz al-Dīn Aybak al-Afram, who arrived there around the start of March. Contingents then began moving the engines and supplies to Acre. As the last were leaving, al-Muẓaffar II of Hama arrived. This force brought the great trebuchet from Crac that supposedly took a hundred wagons to transport. These forces were joined at Damascus the next day by others from western Syria under Sayf al-Dīn Balabān al-Ṭabbākhī, and collectively they moved to join those who were already assembling at Acre. To the south, Baybars al-Manṣūrī of Kerak met al-Ashraf at Gaza and together they proceeded north. They reached Acre on about 5 April, a couple of days before the largest Syrian elements arrived from Damascus. The army then surrounded the city's landward approaches, from coast to coast, and as many as ninety-two trebuchets were deployed, fifteen of which were of the *ifranjī* (counterweight) variety.

Those in Acre made their own preparations, readying their artillery, gathering stones and seeing to the city's fortifications. Defence of the town's walls was divided among various parties: the Templars held the northwesternmost section, along the Montmusard suburb, with the Hospitallers to their right; the Teutonic Knights guarded a significant portion of the city's eastern defences; and royal forces and other contingents were responsible for the defence of stretches in between, including the northeastern salient. The defenders reportedly numbered around 700 cavalry and 13,000 infantry, while the Muslim army was said to have been composed of around 200,000, a quarter of which was cavalry – determining the actual size of these forces seems impossible. During the early days of the siege, while the Muslim army continued to prepare itself, Acre's gates remained open and skirmishes took place beyond the town walls.

The besiegers then began to advance their siege works. Working in shifts, the infantry edged closer behind the cover of screens, supported by cavalry to their rear. When they reached the edge of the fosse, they developed a number of positions, fortifying them with improvised defences that were placed in front of the screens at night. These were sufficient to resist the defenders' traction trebuchets, providing a safe place for the besiegers to set up comparable engines, which, along with archers, suppressed the defenders along nearby sections of the parapet. This allowed the Mamlūk sappers to begin working.

Mining efforts were focused against the towers along the outer wall of the northeastern salient. The support provided by nearby archers and artillery frustrated Frankish attempts to inhibit the progress of the sappers. Efforts were made to

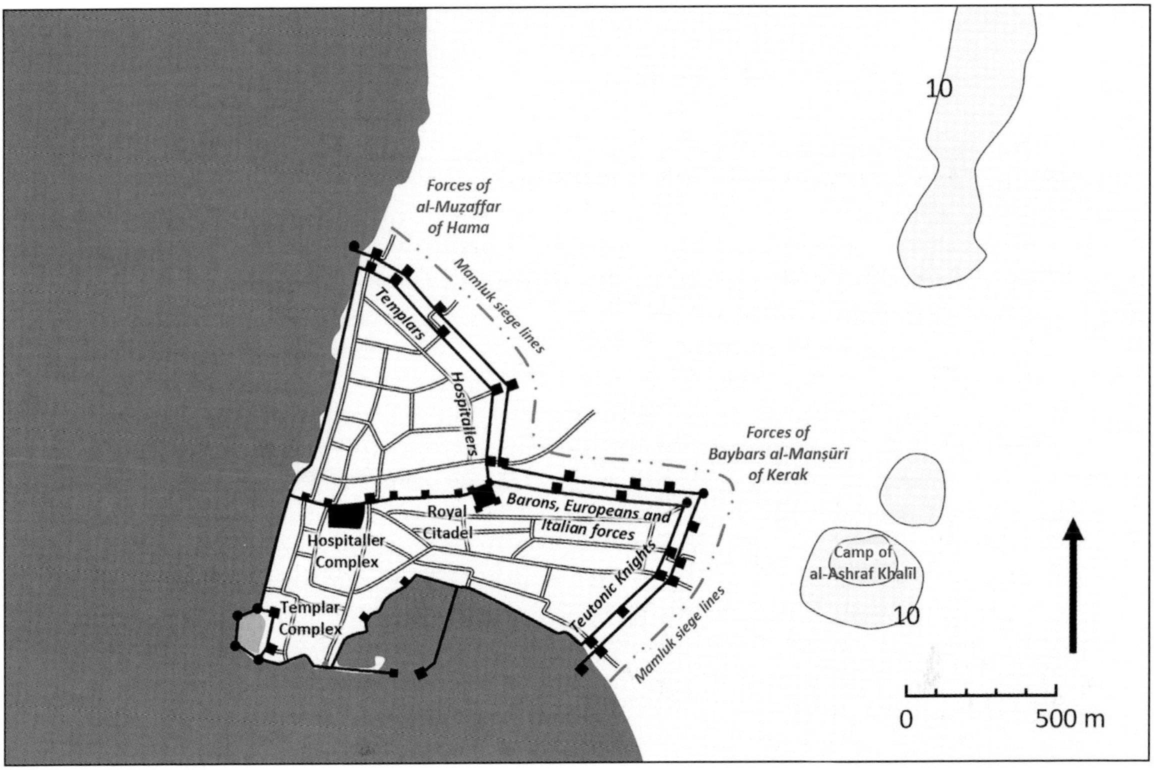

Acre, siege of 1291.

countermine below the Tower of the Countess of Blois and the defenders were eventually forced to set fire to the King's Tower. Besides the miners, the Franks also had to contend with other elements of the Mamlūk army who were working to fill nearby sections of the town ditch, preparing a path for an eventual assault.

Elsewhere, the Templars led a sally one night through one of the gates near the northwestern end of the Montmusard suburb. This brought them up against the army of Hama, which made up the extreme right flank of the Muslim blockading force. The sally was launched to burn the improvised defences around the besiegers' heavy artillery, but the Franks pressed so far that they reached the Muslims' camp, where a number of their horses tripped on tent ropes. This led to the deaths of eighteen of the 300 knights said to have taken part in this action, which proved only marginally successful. Another sally was attempted from the St Anthony Gate, where the Montmusard wall joined the original northern town wall, but the Muslims here were prepared and quickly repulsed the Franks.

Frankish morale was bolstered by the arrival of Henry II of Cyprus on 4 May, bringing a reported 200 knights and 500 infantry. This force was far too small to break the siege, but it did help reinforce the defenders. Not long after, on 8 May, the Franks set fire to the defences around the King's Tower. This came as pressure increased against the northeastern salient, compelling the Franks to send out envoys to al-Ashraf. The delegation offered a tribute if the Mamlūks would lift the siege, but this was not popular with the sultan's emirs nor with the rank and file of the army, who stood to gain little from such an arrangement. Al-Ashraf countered with terms of surrender, offering to allow everyone in the city to leave with whatever they could carry, but this was rejected.

Things were becoming desperate for the defenders. Around the time the Franks attempted to negotiate an end to the siege, the outward face of the King's Tower collapsed, allowing the besiegers to occupy it by nightfall. This led the defenders to bombard the tower with their own artillery in a last effort to keep it out of Muslim hands. A few days later, on Friday, 18 May, al-Ashraf ordered a general assault. To the sound of drums, the attack began just before dawn. The Muslim army advanced in waves: the first carrying large shields, followed by men who threw Greek fire, and then archers and javelin-throwers. Facing assaults along all fronts, the defenders were unable to concentrate their forces at the weakened northeast corner. The Muslims overwhelmed the improvised defences that the Franks had set up behind the King's Tower, allowing them to spread out between the city's inner and outer walls. Some then forced open a postern in the Accursed Tower, while others made for the St Anthony Gate. These latter forces were met by a determined party of Hospitallers, supported by a number of Templars and secular knights, who sought to halt the besiegers outside the gate. This Frankish force steadily gave way as its numbers were worn down. It was here that the master of the Templars and marshal of the Hospitallers were killed, and the master of the Hospitallers was seriously wounded.

With panic spreading through the city, many began to abandon their posts, joining others who had begun to flee towards the harbour, hoping to escape the city by boat. This made it easier for some besiegers to scale the town walls with ladders. Those who had gained entrance through the Accursed Tower found the large counterweight trebuchet of the Pisans close to the nearby Church of St Romano, which they burnt before moving on towards the German quarter in the east part of the city.

With their defences breached and parts of the city burning, most Franks who did not run to the harbour sought refuge in the towers of the Italians and the military orders. All knew the custom of war: no terms had been arranged, no mercy could be expected. King Henry and the wounded master of the Hospitallers were among those who managed to escape by boat, but the number of boats was limited and some became so overloaded that they sank before clearing the harbour. This led many to seek shelter in the Templars' nearby citadel, command of which had fallen to the marshal of the order, Peter of Sevrey. Aside from such citadels and fortified towers, Acre had fallen under Mamlūk control by about noon, and these last bastions of resistance were surrendered or taken by force shortly thereafter.

On 19 May, the day after the main attack, the Templars secured terms for the surrender of their citadel. The gates were opened and a party of perhaps 400 Muslims entered, but some began looting and laying hands on the women who had sought refuge there. This led the Templars to shut the gates and kill those who had entered. Despite this, negotiations resumed – the Franks appreciated the disparity of their situation and al-Ashraf outwardly acknowledged that it was the inappropriate behaviour of his men that had led to their deaths. However, when Peter of Sevrey and a group of fellow Templars came out to arrange another peace, al-Ashraf had them seized and decapitated. Having weakened the defenders, and gained a measure of revenge for the deaths of his men, the sultan then sent in his sappers. By 28 May, the defenders' recognized the inevitability of the citadel's capture and once more agreed to surrender. Wary, al-Ashraf sent in a larger force this time. Unfortunately for all, the structure had been sufficiently undermined that the added weight of the Muslim party that entered to take possession of the stronghold caused the supports in the mines below to buckle. The citadel, or a significant part of it, collapsed, killing the Franks and Muslims within, while one of the towers fell out onto the neighbouring street, killing a large group of Turkish cavalry.

* * *

We still know little about what Acre's defences looked like in 1291. The line of the thirteenth-century town walls was identified in the late twentieth century and ongoing archaeological efforts will hopefully add to our understanding of what were impressive fortifications – some of the last constructed in Palestine by the Franks. Historical sources inform us that there were a number of posterns and we can assume that taluses wrapped along the bases of many towers and walls. Towers, and perhaps some sections of the curtain wall between them, would have been pierced by a number of embrasures, while machicolations were probably incorporated into the battlements above.

To overcome these defences, the besiegers used a range of siege weapons. The most decisive were the groups of sappers who compromised the northeast corner of the city's fortifications. These men enjoyed support provided by archers and others who operated traction trebuchets. Further back, counterweight trebuchets destroyed battlements and weakened the tops of walls, exposing defenders, and caused less discriminate damage behind the defensive perimeter. Assault forces then stormed the breach created by the miners and climbed over the walls using ladders, overwhelming the defenders. The Mamlūks' field forces were numerous enough, and their resolve sufficient, that they had no need to rely on a fleet to complete a blockade of the city. Al-Ashraf showed himself willing to negotiate during the siege, though it was clear that he held the upper hand and nothing less than surrender would be acceptable.

The Mamlūks' success was due in large part to broader strategic factors. Although Henry II of Cyprus brought assistance, this was far from sufficient. It was this lack of a reliable and adequate source of relief that allowed the Mamlūks to overwhelm the Franks. Moving quickly following his father's death, al-Ashraf left no time for a force of crusaders to assemble and interrupt his siege. With the city's capture, he immediately had Acre and its defences destroyed, following established Mamlūk policy – the once mighty administrative centre was left in ruins.

The fall of Acre sent a sobering message to the Franks, who quickly recognized their inability to hold the other strongholds they still possessed. Tyre was evacuated after news arrived of Acre's capture and it was occupied by Mamlūk forces the following day. The Templars at Sidon evacuated the town and withdrew to the sea castle. Hopes of holding the stronghold, loosely besieged by a Mamlūk detachment, gave way when it became clear that support from Cyprus would not be coming, leading the defenders to abandon the castle one night in July. From Sidon, the Mamlūk force moved on to Beirut, which was seized by a ruse. Both strongholds were then dismantled. Further north, the Templars evacuated Tortosa on 3 August, and the mighty castle of ʿAtlit to the south was similarly abandoned. It was this domino effect following the capture of Acre, which led to the end of Latin rule in the Levant, that has led the siege to become synonymous with the conclusion of the crusader period.

List of Sieges

Year[a]	Location[b]	Besieger	Weaponry[c]				Length (days)[d]	Success (Y/N)[e]
			Ram(s)	Siege tower(s)	Artillery	Mining		
1097	Nicaea	First Crusade	×	×	✓	×	44	Y
1097–98	Antioch	First Crusade	×	×	✓	×	250	Y
1098	Sarūj	Baldwin I	×	×	×	×	not known	Y
1098	‘Azāz	Riḍwān	×	×	×	×	<30	N
1098	Ma‘arrat al-Nu‘mān	First Crusade	×	✓	×	✓	14	Y
1099	Jabala	First Crusade	×	×	×	×	13	N
1099	‘Arqa	First Crusade	×	×	✓	✓	88	N
1099	Jerusalem	First Crusade	✓	✓	✓	×	38	Y
1099	Latakia	Bohemond I Pisans	×	×	×	×	>30	N
1099	Arsūf	Godfrey of Bouillon	×	✓	✓	×	~60	N
1100	Apamea	Bohemond					<30	N
1100	Haifa	Tancred Venetians	×	✓	✓	×	15	Y
1101	Sarūj	Suqmān ibn Artuq	×	×	×	×	not known	N
1101	Marash	Bohemond	×	×	×	×	not known	N
1101	Arsūf	Baldwin I Genoese	×	✓	×	×	>3	Y
1101	Caesarea	Baldwin I Genoese	×	✓	✓	×	15	Y
1101	Jabala	Franks	×	✓	×	✓	not known	N
c.1101–2	Latakia	Tancred	×	×	×	×	~550	Y
1102	Tortosa	Raymond of St Gilles Genoese	×	×	×	×	not known	Y
1103	Acre	Baldwin I	×	✓	✓	×	35	N

1104	Jubayl	Raymond of St Gilles	×	×	×	×	<45	Y
		Genoese						
1104	Acre	Baldwin I	×	×	✓	×	20	Y
		Genoese						
1104	Edessa	Jokermish	×	×	×	×	not known	N
1105	Artāḥ	Tancred	×	×	✓	×	not known	Y
1106	Edessa	Qilij Arslān	×	×	×	×	not known	N
1106	Nisibis	Riḍwān	×	×	×	×	<20	N
		Īlghāzī						
1106	Apamea	Tancred	×	×	✓	×	not known	Y
1106	Malaṭya	Qilij Arslān	✓	×	×	×	not known	Y
1106/7	Castrum Arnaldi	Fāṭimids	×	×	✓	×	not known	Y
1108	Sidon	Baldwin I	×	✓	✓	×	not known	N
		Italians						
1108	Bālis	Jāwulī Saqāo	×	×	×	✓	5	Y
1109	‘Arqa	William-Jordan	×	×	×	×	not known	Y
1109 [since 1104]	Tripoli	Bertrand	×	✓	✓	×	69 [~1,850]	Y
		Baldwin I						
		Genoese						
		[Raymond of St Gilles]						
		[William-Jordan]						
1109	Valenia	Tancred	×	×	×	×	not known	Y
1109	Jabala	Tancred	×	×	×	×	<83	Y
1109	Tarsus	Tancred	×	×	×	×	not known	Y
1109	Crac	Tancred	×	×	×	×	not known	Y
1110	Beirut	Baldwin I	×	✓	✓	×	~85	Y
		Genoese						
1110	Baalbek	Ṭughtakīn	×	×	✓	×	35	Y
1110	Edessa	Mawdūd	×	×	×	×	~70	N
1110	Sidon	Baldwin I	×	✓	✓	×	47	Y
		Norwegians						
1110–11	al-Athārib	Tancred	✓	×	✓	×	~80	Y
1111	Zardanā	Tancred	×	×	×	×	not known	Y
1111	Vetula	Tancred	×	×	✓	×	~90	Y

Year[a]	Location[b]	Besieger	Weaponry[c]				Length (days)[d]	Success (Y/N)[e]
			Ram(s)	Siege tower(s)	Artillery	Mining		
1111	Turbessel	Mawdūd	×	×	×	×	45	N
1111–12	Tyre	Baldwin I	✓	✓	✓	×	133	N
1111/12	al-Ḥabis Jaldak	Ṭughtakīn	×	×	×	×	not known	Y
1112	Edessa	Mawdūd	×	×	×	×	not known	N
1114	Edessa	al-Bursuqī	×	×	×	×	~70	N
1115	Crac	al-Bursuqī	×	×	×	×	not known	N
1115	Homs	Īlghāzī	×	×	×	×	not known	N
1115	Hama	Bursuq ibn Bursuq	×	×	×	×	not known	Y
1115	Crac	Bursuq ibn Bursuq	×	×	×	×	not known	N
1115	Kafarṭāb	Bursuq ibn Bursuq	×	×	✓	✓	not known	Y
1115	Jaffa	Fāṭimids	×	×	✓	×	1	N
1115	Rafaniyya	Ṭughtakīn	×	×	×	×	1	Y
c.1115	al-Bīra	Baldwin II of Edessa	×	×	×	×	~365	Y
c.1115	Raban	Baldwin II of Edessa	×	×	×	×	not known	N
1118	al-Ḥabis Jaldak	Franks	×	×	×	×	not known	Y
1118	‘Azāz	Roger of Antioch Leon of Armenia	×	×	×	✓	30	Y
1119	al-Athārib	Īlghāzī	×	×	✓	✓	not known	Y
1119	Zardanā	Īlghāzī	×	×	×	×	not known	Y
1120	Ma‘arrat al-Nu‘mān	Īlghāzī Ṭughtakīn	×	×	×	×	1	N
1121	Jerash	Baldwin II	×	×	×	×	not known	Y
1121	Zardanā	Franks	×	×	×	×	not known	Y
1121	al-Athārib	Baldwin II	×	×	×	×	not known	N
1122	Zardanā	Īlghāzī Balak Ṭughtakīn	×	×	✓	×	14	N
1122	Edessa	Balak	×	×	×	×	not known	N
1122	Bālis	Baldwin II	×	×	✓	×	not known	N

1122	al-Bāra	Baldwin II	×	×	×	×	not known	Y
1123	Homs	Ṭughtakīn	×	×	×	×	not known	N
1123	Gargar	Balak	×	×	×	×	not known	Y
1123	Ḥarrān	Balak	×	×	×	×	not known	Y
1123	al-Bāra	Balak	×	×	×	×	not known	Y
1123	Aleppo	Balak	×	×	×	×	~25	Y
1123	Jaffa	Fāṭimids	×	×	✓	✓	5	N
1123	Kharpūt	Balak	×	×	✓	✓	17	Y
1123	Aleppo	Joscelin I of Edessa	×	×	×	×	4	N
1124	Tyre	William of Bury Pons of Tripoli Venetians	×	✓	✓	×	142	Y
1124	Manbij	Balak	×	×	✓	×	not known	N
1124	Malaṭya	Ghāzī ibn Dānishmand	×	×	×	×	not known	Y
1124–25	Aleppo	Baldwin II Dubays ibn Ṣadaqa	×	×	×	×	102	N
1125	Kafarṭāb	al-Bursuqī	×	×	×	×	not known	Y
1125	Zardanā	al-Bursuqī	×	×	×	×	not known	N
1125	‘Azāz	al-Bursuqī Ṭughtakīn	×	×	✓	✓	<30	N
1126	Rafaniyya	Pons of Tripoli Baldwin II	×	×	✓	×	18	Y
1126	al-Athārib	al-Bursuqī	×	×	×	×	not known	N
1127	al-Raḥba	‘Izz al-Dīn Mas‘ūd	×	×	×	×	<7	Y
1127	Kafarṭāb	Bohemond II	×	×	×	×	not known	Y
1129/30	Ḥārim	Zankī	×	×	×	×	not known	N
1130	Homs	Zankī	×	×	×	×	40	N
1130/31	Tell Aran	Joscelin I	×	×	×	✓	not known	–
1131	Kaysūn	Ghāzī ibn Dānishmand	×	×	×	×	not known	N
1132	Bānyās	Shams al-Mulūk Ismā‘īl	×	×	×	✓	<5	Y
1133	Bālis	Shams al-Mulūk Ismā‘īl	×	×	×	×	not known	Y
1133	Hama	Shams al-Mulūk Ismā‘īl	×	×	×	×	<27	Y
1133	Shayzar	Shams al-Mulūk Ismā‘īl	×	×	×	×	not known	N
1133	Montferrand	Turkomans	×	×	×	×	not known	N

Year[a]	Location[b]	Besieger	Weaponry[c]				Length (days)[d]	Success (Y/N)[e]
			Ram(s)	Siege tower(s)	Artillery	Mining		
1133	Cave of Tyron	Shams al-Mulūk Ismāʿīl	×	×	×	×	not known	Y
1134	Amida	Zankī	×	×	×	×	not known	N
1134	Ṣūr	Zankī	×	×	×	×	not known	Y
1134	Hama	Shams al-Mulūk Ismāʿīl	×	×	×	×	not known	Y
1135	al-Athārib	Zankī	×	×	×	×	<25	Y
1135	Zardanā	Zankī	×	×	×	×	not known	Y
1135	Maʿarrat al-Nuʿmān	Zankī	×	×	×	×	not known	Y
1135	Kafarṭāb	Zankī	×	×	×	×	not known	Y
1136	Kaysūn	Muḥammad ibn Dānishmand	×	×	×	×	6	N
1137	Tarsus	John Comnenus	×	×	×	×	not known	Y
1137	Anazarbus	John Comnenus	×	×	✓	×	35	Y
1137	Antioch	John Comnenus	×	×	✓	×	not known	Y
1137	Homs	Ṣalāḥ al-Dīn al-Yaghīsiyānī (for Zankī) Zankī	×	×	×	×	44	N
1137	Montferrand	Zankī	×	×	✓	×	~25	Y
1137	al-Majdal	Zankī	×	×	×	×	not known	Y
1137	Adana	Turks	×	×	×	×	1	Y
1138	Homs	Zankī	×	×	×	×	not known	Y
1138	Buzāʿa	John Comnenus	×	×	✓	×	7	Y
1138	Aleppo	John Comnenus	×	×	×	×	2	N
1138	Kafarṭāb	John Comnenus	×	×	✓	×	<3	Y
1138	Shayzar	John Comnenus	×	×	✓	×	21	N
1138	Buzāʿa	Zankī	×	×	×	×	not known	Y
1138	al-Athārib	Zankī	×	×	×	×	not known	Y
1138	Edessa	Timurtāsh	×	×	×	×	not known	N
1139	Baalbek	Zankī	×	×	✓	×	58	Y
1139–40	Damascus	Zankī	×	×	×	×	150	N
1140	Bānyās	Muʿīn al-Dīn Unur Fulk	×	✓	✓	×	~24	Y

1143	Malaṭya	Mas'ūd of Iconium	×	×	×	×	~90	N
1144	Wādī Mūsā	Baldwin III	×	×	✓	×	not known	Y
1144	Edessa	Zankī	×	×	✓	✓	28	Y
1145	al-Bīra	Zankī	×	×	×	×	40	N
1146	Ja'bar	Zankī	×	×	×	×	121	N
1146	Edessa	Nūr al-Dīn	×	×	×	✓	5	Y
1146	Baalbek	Mu'īn al-Dīn Unur	×	×	✓	×	<7	Y
1148	Damascus	Second Crusade	×	×	×	×	5	N
1148	Arima	Nūr al-Dīn	×	×	×	✓	not known	Y
1149	Inab	Nūr al-Dīn	×	×	×	×	not known	Y
1149	Ḥārim	Nūr al-Dīn	×	×	×	×	<25	Y
1149	Apamea	Ṣalāḥ al-Dīn al-Yaghīsiyānī (for Nūr al-Dīn) Nūr al-Dīn	×	×	×	×	<26	Y
1149	Ḥārim	Baldwin III	×	×	×	×	not known	N
1149/50	Marash	Mas'ūd of Rūm	×	×	×	×	not known	Y
1150	Turbessel	Mas'ūd of Rūm	×	×	✓	×	not known	N
1150	'Azāz	Nūr al-Dīn	×	×	×	×	not known	Y
1150	Turbessel	Mas'ūd of Rūm	×	×	×	×	not known	N
1151	Turbessel	Nūr al-Dīn	×	×	×	×	not known	Y
1151	Tell Khālid	Nūr al-Dīn	×	×	×	×	not known	Y
1151	Bosra	Nūr al-Dīn	×	×	×	×	not known	N
1152	Mirabel	Baldwin III	×	×	×	×	not known	Y
1152	Jerusalem	Baldwin III	×	×	✓	×	<7	N
1152	Tortosa	Nūr al-Dīn	×	×	×	×	not known	Y
1152	Bosra	Mujīr al-Dīn	×	×	×	×	not known	N
1153	Ascalon	Baldwin III	×	✓	✓	×	199	Y
1153	Bānyās	Nūr al-Dīn	×	×	×	×	not known	N
1154	Damascus	Nūr al-Dīn	×	×	×	×	7	Y
1155	'Ayntāb	Nūr al-Dīn	×	×	×	✓	not known	Y
1157	Bānyās	Nūr al-Dīn	×	×	✓	✓	~30	N
1157	Shayzar	Baldwin III Thierry of Flanders Reynald of Châtillon	×	×	✓	×	not known	N

Year[a]	Location[b]	Besieger	Weaponry[c]				Length (days)[d]	Success (Y/N)[e]
			Ram(s)	Siege tower(s)	Artillery	Mining		
1157–58	Ḥārim	Baldwin III Thierry of Flanders Reynald of Châtillon	×	×	✓	✓	~60	Y
1158	al-Ḥabis Jaldak	Nūr al-Dīn	×	×	×	×	not known	N
1159	Ḥarrān	Nūr al-Dīn	×	×	×	×	~20	Y
1162	Ḥārim	Nūr al-Dīn	×	×	×	×	not known	N
1164	Bilbays	Amalric	×	×	×	×	~90	N
1164	Ḥārim	Nūr al-Dīn	×	×	✓	✓	not known	Y
1164	Bānyās	Nūr al-Dīn	×	×	✓	✓	~7?	Y
1165	Cave of Tyron	Shīrkūh (for Nūr al-Dīn)	×	×	×	×	not known	Y
1165	al-Ḥabis Jaldak	Shīrkūh (for Nūr al-Dīn)	×	×	×	×	not known	Y
*c.*1166	Munayṭira	Nūr al-Dīn	×	×	×	×	not known	Y
1167	Alexandria	Amalric	×	✓	✓	×	~90	N
1167	Ḥalba	Nūr al-Dīn	×	×	×	×	not known	Y
1167	Arima	Nūr al-Dīn	×	×	×	×	not known	Y
1167	Chastel Blanc	Nūr al-Dīn	×	×	×	×	not known	Y
1168	Ja'bar	Fakhr al-Dīn Mas'ūd (for Nūr al-Dīn) Shams al-Dīn Ibn al-Dāya (for Nūr al-Dīn)	×	×	×	×	not known	Y
1168	Bilbays	Amalric	×	×	×	×	3	Y
1169	Damietta	Amalric Andronicus Kontostephanos	×	✓	✓	✓	~50	N
1170	Kerak	Nūr al-Dīn	×	×	✓	×	not known	N
1170	Raqqa	Nūr al-Dīn	×	×	×	×	not known	Y
1170	Sinjār	Nūr al-Dīn	×	×	✓	×	not known	Y
1170	Dārūm	Saladin	×	×	×	✓	not known	N
1170	Gaza	Saladin	×	×	×	×	not known	N
1170	Aqaba	Saladin	×	×	×	×	not known	Y
1171	'Arqa	Nūr al-Dīn	×	×	×	×	not known	Y
1171	Chastel Blanc	Nūr al-Dīn	×	×	×	×	not known	Y

1171	Arima	Nūr al-Dīn	×	×	×	×	not known	Y
1171	Montreal	Saladin	×	×	×	×	not known	N
1173	Kerak	Saladin	×	×	×	×	not known	N
1173	Marash	Nūr al-Dīn	×	×	×	×	not known	Y
1174	Bānyās	Amalric	×	×	×	×	15	N
1174	Alexandria	Sicilians	✓	✓	✓	×	5	N
1174–75	Homs	Saladin	×	×	✓	×	90	Y
1174–75	Hama	Saladin	×	×	×	×	not known	Y
1174–75	Aleppo	Saladin	×	×	×	×	27	N
1175	Baalbek	Saladin	×	×	×	×	<12	Y
1175	Sinjār	Sayf al-Dīn Ghāzī II	×	×	✓	×	<25	N
1175	Montferrand	Saladin	×	×	✓	×	<25	Y
1176	Buzā'a	Saladin	×	×	×	×	not known	Y
1176	Manbij	Saladin	×	×	×	✓	<7	Y
1176	'Azāz	Saladin	×	×	✓	✓	38	Y
1176	Aleppo	Saladin	×	×	×	×	30	N
1176	Maṣyāf	Saladin	×	×	✓	×	not known	N
1177	Hama	Philip of Flanders Raymond III of Tripoli Bohemond III of Antioch	×	×	×	×	4	N
1177–78	Ḥārim	Philip of Flanders Raymond III of Tripoli Bohemond III of Antioch	×	×	✓	×	~120	N
1178	Ḥārim	al-Ṣāliḥ Ismā'īl ibn Nūr al-Dīn	×	×	×	×	not known	Y
1178	Qal'at Ṣadr	Franks (Reynald of Châtillon?)	×	×	×	×	not known	N
1178	Baalbek	Shams al-Dawla Tūrānshāh (for Saladin)	×	×	×	×	not known	Y
1179	Jacob's Ford	Saladin	×	×	×	✓	6	Y
1182	al-Ḥabis Jaldak	Farrukhshāh (for Saladin)	×	×	×	✓	5	Y
1182	Beirut	Saladin	×	×	×	✓	3	N
1182	al-Bīra	Quṭb al-Dīn Ghāzī of Mardin	×	×	×	×	not known	N
1182	Edessa	Saladin	×	×	×	×	not known	Y
1182	Nisibis	Saladin	×	×	×	×	not known	Y
1182	al-Ḥabis Jaldak	Baldwin IV Raymond III of Tripoli	×	×	×	✓	~21	Y

Year[a]	Location[b]	Besieger	Weaponry[c]				Length (days)[d]	Success (Y/N)[e]
			Ram(s)	Siege tower(s)	Artillery	Mining		
1182	Turbessel	ʿImād al-Dīn Zankī II	×	×	×	×	not known	N
1182	Sinjār	Saladin	×	×	×	×	5	Y
1182–83	Aqaba	Reynald of Châtillon	×	×	×	×	not known	N
1183	Amida	Saladin	×	×	✓	✓	~20	Y
1183	Tell Khālid	Saladin	×	×	✓	×	<20	Y
1183	Aleppo	Saladin	×	×	×	×	21	Y
1183	Kerak	Saladin	×	×	✓	×	~38	N
1184	Kerak	Saladin	×	×	✓	×	~36	N
1184	Jinīn	Saladin	×	×	×	✓	not known	Y
1187	Tiberias	Saladin	×	×	×	✓	3	Y
1187	Toron	Taqī al-Dīn (for Saladin) Saladin	×	×	✓	×	~14	Y
1187	Chastel Neuf	for Saladin	×	×	×	×	~150	Y
1187	Beirut	Saladin	×	×	×	×	8	Y
1187	Jaffa	al-ʿĀdil (for Saladin)	×	×	×	×	not known	Y
1187	Ascalon	Saladin	×	×	✓	✓	13	Y
1187	Jerusalem	Saladin	×	×	✓	✓	15	Y
1187	Tyre	Saladin	×	×	✓	✓	39	N
1187–88	Kerak	Saladinal-ʿĀdil (for Saladin) Saʿd al-Dīn Kamshaba (for Saladin)	×	×	×	×	~560	Y
1187–88	Safed	Saladin	×	×	✓	×	~470	Y
1187–89	Belvoir	Sayf al-Dīn (for Saladin) Qaymāz al-Najmī (for Saladin) Saladin	×	×	✓	✓	~500	Y
1187–89	Montreal	al-ʿĀdil (for Saladin) Saʿd al-Dīn Kamshaba (for Saladin)	×	×	×	×	~740	Y
1188	Tortosa	Saladin	×	×	×	×	8	N
1188	Latakia	Saladin	×	×	×	✓	2	Y
1188	Saone	Saladin	×	×	✓	×	3	Y

1188	Shughr-Bakās	Saladin	×	×	✓	×	10	Y
1188	Sarmīniyya	al-Ẓāhir Ghāzī (for Saladin)	×	×	×	×	~6	Y
1188	Bourzey	Saladin	×	×	✓	×	3	Y
1188	Trapessac	Saladin	×	×	✓	✓	14	Y
1188	Baghrās	Saladin	×	×	✓	×	<10	Y
1189–90	Beaufort	Saladin	×	×	×	×	261	Y
1189–91	Acre	Guy of Lusignan Third Crusade	✓	✓	✓	✓	684	Y
1191	Kyrenia	Guy of Lusignan	×	×	×	×	<10	Y
1191	Dieudamor	Guy of Lusignan	×	×	×	×	<10	Y
1191	Buffavento	Richard I Guy of Lusignan	×	×	×	×	<10	Y
1192	Dārūm	Richard I	×	×	✓	✓	4	Y
1192	Jaffa	Saladin	×	×	✓	✓	5	N
1194	Damascus	al-ʿAzīz ʿUthmān	×	×	×	×	54	N
1196	Damascus	al-ʿAzīz ʿUthmān al-ʿĀdil	×	×	×	×	<20	Y
1197	Jaffa	al-ʿĀdil	×	×	×	×	not known	Y
1197–98	Toron	Germans	×	×	×	×	66	N
1198–99	Mardin	al-ʿĀdil	×	×	×	×	~300	N
1199	Damascus	al-Afḍal al-Ẓāhir Ghāzī	×	×	×	✓	200	N
1199	Montferrand	al- Manṣūr Nāṣir al-Dīn	×	×	✓	×	~70	Y
1200	Bānyās	Fakhr al-Dīn (for al-ʿĀdil)	×	×	×	×	not known	Y
1201	Manbij	al-Ẓāhir Ghāzī al-Afḍal	×	×	×	×	<30	Y
1201	Najm	al-Ẓāhir Ghāzī al-Afḍal	×	×	×	×	<4	Y
1201	Apamea	Aleppans (for al-Ẓāhir Ghāzī)	×	×	×	×	not known	Y
1201	Maʿarrat al-Nuʿmān	Aleppans (for al-Ẓāhir Ghāzī)	×	×	×	×	not known	Y
1201	Hama	al-Ẓāhir Ghāzī	×	×	×	×	~30	N
1201	Damascus	al-Ẓāhir Ghāzī al-Afḍal	×	×	×	×	~50	N

Year[a]	Location[b]	Besieger	Weaponry[c]				Length (days)[d]	Success (Y/N)[e]
			Ram(s)	Siege tower(s)	Artillery	Mining		
1203	Mardin	al-Ashraf Mūsā al-ʿĀdil	×	×	×	×	not known	N
1204	Nisibis	Nūr al-Dīn Arslānshāh	×	×	×	×	not known	N
1207	Coliath	al-ʿĀdil	×	×	×	×	<10	Y
1209	Sinjār	al-ʿĀdil	×	×	×	×	not known	N
1209	Nisibis	al-Manṣūr Muḥammad (for al-ʿĀdil) al-Ashraf Mūsā (for al-ʿĀdil)	×	×	×	×	not known	Y
1217	Mount Tabor	Fifth Crusade	×	×	×	×	4	N
1218	Ḥarrān	ʿIzz al-Dīn Kayka'us of Rūm al-Afḍal	×	×	×	×	not known	Y
1218	Edessa	ʿIzz al-Dīn Kayka'us of Rūm al-Afḍal	×	×	×	×	not known	Y
1218	Turbessel	ʿIzz al-Dīn Kayka'us of Rūm al-Afḍal	×	×	×	×	not known	Y
1218	Turbessel	al-Ashraf Mūsā	×	×	×	×	not known	Y
1218	Caesarea	al-Muʿaẓẓam ʿĪsā	×	×	✓	×	not known	Y
1218	ʿAtlit	al-Muʿaẓẓam ʿĪsā	×	×	×	×	not known	N
1218–19	Damietta	Fifth Crusade	×	✓	✓	×	525	Y
1220	ʿAtlit	al-Muʿaẓẓam ʿĪsā	×	×	✓	×	<30	N
1223	Hama	al-Muʿaẓẓam ʿĪsā	×	×	×	×	not known	N
1226	Homs	al-Muʿaẓẓam ʿĪsā	×	×	×	×	not known	N
1226	Kakhtā	ʿAlā' al-Dīn Kayqubād of Rūm	×	×	×	×	not known	Y
1228	Baalbek	al-ʿAzīz ʿUthmān	×	×	×	×	not known	N
1229	Damascus	al-Kāmil al-ʿAzīz ʿUthmān al-Ashraf Mūsā	×	×	×	×	~50	Y
1229	Hama	al-Mujāhid Shīrkūh (for al-Kāmil) Fakhr al-Dīn ʿUmar (for al-Kāmil)	×	×	×	×	not known	Y
1229	Kyrenia	John of Beirut	×	×	×	×	not known	Y

1229–30	Dieudamor	Balian of Ibelin	×	×	×	×	~300	Y
		Baldwin of Ibelin						
		Hugh of Ibelin						
1229–30	Kantara	Anceau of Brie	×	×	✓	×	~300	Y
1229–30	Baalbek	al-Ashraf Mūsā	×	×	×	×	~300	Y
1231–32	Beirut	Imperialists	×	✓	✓	✓	~170	N
1232	Dieudamor	Imperialists	×	×	×	×	~55	N
1232–33	Kyrenia	Ibelin party	×	✓	✓	×	>365	Y
		Genoese						
1232	Amida	al-Kāmil	×	×	✓	×	not known	Y
1234	Kharpūt	‘Alā’ al-Dīn Kayqubād	×	×	✓	×	not known	Y
1236	Edessa	al-Kāmil	×	×	✓	×	not known	Y
1236	Ḥarrān	al-Kāmil	×	×	✓	×	<30	Y
1237–38	Damascus	al-Kāmil	×	×	✓	×	<75	Y
1238	al-Raḥba	al-Ṣāliḥ Ayyūb	×	×	×	×	not known	N
1238	Ḥarrān	Khwārizmians	×	×	×	×	not known	Y
1238	Sinjār	Badr al-Dīn Lu’lu’	×	×	×	×	not known	N
1238	Amida	Ghiyāth al-Dīn Kaykhusraw II of Rūm	×	×	×	×	not known	N
1239	Damascus	al-Ṣāliḥ Ismā‘īl	×	×	×	×	30?	Y
		al-Mujāhid Shīrkūh						
1239	Jerusalem	al-Nāṣir Dā’ūd	×	×	✓	×	27	Y
1240	Beaufort	al-Ṣāliḥ Ismā‘īl	×	×	✓	×	not known	Y
1243	Tyre	Balian of Ibelin	×	×	✓	×	~30?	Y
		Philip of Montfort						
1243	‘Ajlūn	al-Ṣāliḥ Ismā‘īl	×	×	✓	×	not known	N
1245	Damascus	Mu‘īn al-Dīn ibn al-Shaykh (for al-Ṣāliḥ Ayyūb)	×	×	✓	×	~120	Y
1246	Damascus	Khwārizmians	×	×	×	×	~90	N
1246	Kerak	Fakhr al-Dīn Yūsuf (for al-Ṣāliḥ Ayyūb)	×	×	×	×	not known	N
1246	Bosra	Fakhr al-Dīn Yūsuf (for al-Ṣāliḥ Ayyūb)	×	×	×	×	not known	Y
1247	Tiberias	Fakhr al-Dīn Yūsuf (for al-Ṣāliḥ Ayyūb)	×	×	×	×	<40	Y
1247 [since 1244]	Ascalon	Fakhr al-Dīn Yūsuf (for al-Ṣāliḥ Ayyūb)	×	×	✓	✓	~100? [~1,175]	Y
1248	Homs	Shams al-Dīn Lu’lu’ (for al-Nāṣir Yūsuf)	×	×	×	×	~80	Y
		al-Ṣāliḥ Ismā‘īl						

Year[a]	Location[b]	Besieger	Weaponry[c]				Length (days)[d]	Success (Y/N)[e]
			Ram(s)	Siege tower(s)	Artillery	Mining		
1248–49	Homs	Fakhr al-Dīn Yūsuf (for al-Ṣāliḥ Ayyūb)	×	×	✓	×	~100	N
1249	Sidon	Damascenes (for al-Nāṣir Yūsuf)	×	×	×	×	not known	N
1253	Sidon	Damascenes	×	×	×	×	not known	N
1259	al-Bīra	Hülagü	×	×	×	×	not known	Y
1260	Aleppo	Hülagü	×	×	✓	✓	38	Y
1260	Ḥārim	Fakhr al-Dīn Sāqī (for Hülagü)	×	×	×	×	not known	Y
1260	Damascus	Kitbugha (for Hülagü)	×	×	✓	×	<7	Y
1260	Baalbek	Kitbugha (for Hülagü)	×	×	×	×	not known	Y
1260	Cave of Tyron	Shihāb al-Dīn ibn Buḥtur (for Hülagü)	×	×	×	×	not known	Y
1260	ʿAjlūn	Kitbugha (for Hülagü)	×	×	×	×	not known	Y
1260	Sidon	Mongols (for Hülagü)	×	×	×	×	1	N
1260	Mardin	Yashmut (for Hülagü)	×	×	×	×	~240	Y
1261	Kerak	Jamāl al-Dīn al-Muḥammadī (for Baybars)	×	×	×	×	not known	N
1263	Acre	Baybars	×	×	×	×	2	N
1264–65	al-Bīra	Mongols	×	×	✓	✓	~60	N
1265	Caesarea	Baybars	×	×	✓	×	7	Y
1265	Arsūf	Baybars	×	×	✓	✓	40	Y
1266	Safed	Baybars	×	×	✓	✓	40	Y
1266	Amuda	al-Manṣūr Muḥammad II (for Baybars)	×	×	×	×	not known	Y
1267	al-Raḥba	Mongols	×	×	×	×	not known	N
1268	Jaffa	Baybars	×	×	×	×	1	Y
1268	Beaufort	Baybars	×	×	✓	×	11	Y
1268	Antioch	Baybars	×	×	×	×	5	Y
1271	Crac des Chevaliers	Baybars	×	×	✓	✓	45	Y
1271	ʿAkkār	Baybars	×	×	✓	×	13	Y
1271	Montfort	Baybars	×	×	✓	✓	14	Y
1272	al-Bīra	Durbai (for Abagha)	×	×	✓	×	not known	N
1273	Goynuk	Ḥusām al-Dīn al-ʿAyntābī (for Baybars)	×	×	×	×	not known	Y

1275	Cursat	Sayf al-Dīn al-Surūrī (for Baybars) Shihāb al-Dīn Marwān (for Baybars)	×	×	×	×	<215	Y
1275	al-Bīra	Abtai (for Abagha)	×	×	✓	×	not known	N
1278	Tripoli	Templars	×	×	×	×	~7?	N
1278	Nephin	Templars	×	×	×	×	not known	N
1285	Margat	Qalāwūn	×	×	✓	✓	38	Y
1286	Kerak	Ḥusām al-Dīn Ṭuruntay (for Qalāwūn)	×	×	×	×	not known	Y
1286	Saone	Ḥusām al-Dīn Ṭuruntay (for Qalāwūn)	×	×	✓	×	not known	Y
1289	Tripoli	Qalāwūn	×	×	✓	✓	~43	Y
1291	Acre	al-Ashraf	×	×	✓	✓	53	Y

[a] Only instances where attacking forces attempted to gain entrance to a stronghold and defenders attempted to prevent them from doing so have been included. Raids and unopposed sacks have not been included, nor have instances where defenders surrendered before hostilities commenced, nor where strongholds were gained by otherwise peaceful means. This list includes many of the best documented sieges but in no way is meant to include every possible (or plausible) siege that took place during this period.

[b] The selected region stretches from Cilicia in the northwest to the drainage basin of the Euphrates north of Raqqa in the northeast and down to Egypt, roughly the region touched by Frankish influence at its peak. Events along the fringe of this area are given less attention with the withdrawal of Frankish authority – a focus has been placed on sieges involving persons whose policies and actions had a direct influence on events in western Syria or Palestine.

[c] References to ambiguous 'machines' have not been included.

[d] These values should be seen as approximations – conflicting dates are often provided by different sources.

[e] Success is determined by the following criteria: (1) The besieger gained control over all defended areas, including a citadel where present. (2) When terms were arranged that allowed the besieged leader to retain control over his stronghold, the suzerainty of the besieger was acknowledged – receipt of a payoff to break a siege is not considered a 'successful' outcome here, regardless of how this was interpreted at the time.

Rulers and their Reigns

Viziers and Sultans of Egypt, 1099–1291

al-Afḍal Shāhinshāh	1094–1121	Fāṭimid
al-Ma'mūn al-Baṭā'iḥī	1121–25	Fāṭimid
al-Afḍal Kutayfāt	1130–31	Fāṭimid
Abū al-Fatḥ Yānis al-Ḥāfiẓī	1131–32	Fāṭimid
Bahrām	1135–37	Fāṭimid
Riḍwān ibn Walakhshī	1137–39	Fāṭimid
Ibn Maṣāl	1149–50	Fāṭimid
al-'Ādil ibn al-Sallār	1150–53	Fāṭimid
'Abbās ibn Yaḥyā	1153–54	Fāṭimid
al-Ṣāliḥ Ṭalā'i' ibn Ruzzīk	1154–61	Fāṭimid
al-'Ādil Ruzzīk ibn Ṭalā'i'	1161–63	Fāṭimid
Shāwar	1163, 1164–69	Fāṭimid
Ḍirghām	1163–64	Fāṭimid
Asad al-Dīn Shīrkūh	1169	Ayyūbid
Saladin	1169–93	Ayyūbid
al-'Azīz 'Uthmān	1193–98	Ayyūbid
al-Manṣūr Nāṣir al-Dīn	1198–1200	Ayyūbid
al-'Ādil Sayf al-Dīn	1200–18	Ayyūbid
al-Kāmil Muḥammad	1218–38	Ayyūbid
al-'Ādil Sayf al-Dīn II	1238–40	Ayyūbid
al-Ṣāliḥ Ayyūb	1240–49	Ayyūbid
al-Mu'aẓẓam Tūrānshāh	1249–50	Ayyūbid
al-Ashraf Mūsā	1250–52	Ayyūbid
al-Mu'izz al-Dīn Aybak	1250–57	Mamlūk
al-Manṣūr Nūr al-Dīn 'Alī	1257–59	Mamlūk
al-Muẓaffar al-Dīn Quṭuz	1259–60	Mamlūk
al-Zahir Rukn al-Dīn Baybars	1260–77	Mamlūk
al-Sa'īd Nāṣir al-Dīn Baraka	1277–79	Mamlūk
al-Manṣūr Sayf al-Dīn Qalāwūn	1279–90	Mamlūk
al-Ashraf Ṣalāḥ al-Dīn Khalīl	1290–93	

Emirs, Atabegs and Sultans of Damascus, 1099–1260

Duqaq ibn Tutush	1095–1103	Seljuk
Ẓāhir al-Dīn Ṭughtakīn	1103–28	Būrid
Tāj al-Mulūk Būrī	1128–32	Būrid
Shams al-Mulūk Ismā'īl	1132–35	Būrid
Shihāb al-Dīn Maḥmūd	1135–39	Būrid

Jamāl al-Dīn Muḥammad	1139–40	Būrid
Mujīr al-Dīn	1140–54	Būrid
Nūr al-Dīn	1154–74	Zankid
al-Ṣāliḥ Ismā'īl	1174	Zankid
Saladin	1174–93	Ayyūbid
al-Afḍal 'Alī	1193–96	Ayyūbid
al-'Ādil Sayf al-Dīn	1196–18	Ayyūbid
al-Mu'aẓẓam 'Īsā	1218–27	Ayyūbid
al-Nāṣir Dā'ūd	1227–29	Ayyūbid
al-Ashraf Mūsā	1229–37	Ayyūbid
al-Ṣāliḥ Ismā'īl	1237, 1239–45	Ayyūbid
al-Kāmil Muḥammad	1238	Ayyūbid
al-Ṣāliḥ Ayyūb	1238–39, 1245–49	Ayyūbid
al-Mu'aẓẓam Tūrānshāh	1249–50	Ayyūbid
al-Nāṣir Yūsuf	1250–60	Ayyūbid

Mamlūk sultans from 1260

Emirs and Sultans of Aleppo, 1099–1260

Fakhr al-Mulk Riḍwān	1095–1113	Seljuk
Tāj al-Dawla Alp Arslān	1113–14	Seljuk
Sulṭānshāh	1114–17	Seljuk
Najm al-Dīn Īlghāzī	1117–20	Artuqid
Shams al-Dawla Sulaymān	1120–21	Artuqid
Badr al-Dawla Sulaymān	1121–23	Artuqid
Nūr al-Dawla Balak Ghāzī	1123–24	Artuqid
Ḥusām al-Dīn Timurtāsh	1124–25	Artuqid
Āqsunqur al-Bursuqī	1125–26	Seljuk
'Izz al-Dīn Mas'ūd	1126–27	Seljuk
'Imād al-Dīn Zankī	1128–46	Zankid
Nūr al-Dīn	1146–74	Zankid
al-Ṣāliḥ Ismā'īl	1174–81	Zankid
'Izz al-Dīn Mas'ūd	1181–82	Zankid
'Imād al-Dīn Zankī II	1182–83	Zankid
Saladin	1183–93	Ayyūbid
al-Ẓāhir Ghāzī	1193–1216	Ayyūbid
al-'Azīz Muḥammad	1216–36	Ayyūbid
al-Nāṣir Yūsuf	1236–60	Ayyūbid

Mamlūk sultans from 1260

Emirs and Atabegs of Mosul, 1099–1200

Karbughā	1096–1102	Seljuk
Jokermish	1102–6	Seljuk
Jāwulī Saqāo	1107–8	Seljuk
Mawdūd	1108–13	Seljuk
Āqsunqur al-Bursuqī	1114–26	Seljuk

ʿIzz al-Dīn Masʿūd	1126–27	Seljuk
ʿImād al-Dīn Zankī	1127–46	Zankid
Sayf al-Dīn Ghāzī I	1146–49	Zankid
Quṭb al-Dīn Mawdūd	1149–70	Zankid
Sayf al-Dīn Ghāzī II	1170–80	Zankid
ʿIzz al-Dīn Masʿūd	1180–93	Zankid
Nūr al-Dīn Arslānshāh	1193–1211	Zankid

Kings of Jerusalem, 1099–1291

Godfrey (of Bouillon)†	1099–1100
Baldwin I (of Boulogne)†	1100–18
Baldwin II (of Bourcq)†	1118–31
Melisende	1131–52
Fulk (V of Anjou)*†	1131–43
Baldwin III	1143–63
Amalric	1163–74
Baldwin IV	1174–85
Baldwin V	1185–86
Sibylla	1186–90
Guy (of Lusignan)*†	1186–92
Isabella I	1192–1205
Conrad I (of Montferrat)*†	1192
Henry I (of Champagne)*†	1192–97
Aimery (of Cyprus)*†	1197–1205
Maria	1205–12
John I (of Brienne)*†	1210–12
Isabella II	1212–28
Frederick (II of Germany)*†	1225–28
Conrad II (IV of Germany)†	1228–54
Conrad III (II of Sicily, aka Conradin)†	1254–68
Hugh I (III of Cyprus, aka Hugh of Lusignan)	1268–84
John II (I of Cyprus)	1284–85
Henry II (also of Cyprus)	1285–1324

Princes of Antioch, 1099–1268

Bohemond I (of Taranto)†	1098–1111
Bohemond II†	1111–30
Constance	1130–63
Raymond (of Poitiers)*†	1136–49
Reynald (of Châtillon)*†	1153–61
Bohemond III	1163–1201
Bohemond IV	1201–16, 1219–33
Raymond-Roupen	1216–19

*Ruler through his wife. † Born in Europe

Bohemond V 1233–52
Bohemond VI 1252–75

Counts of Tripoli, 1102–1289

Raymond I (of St Gilles)† 1102–5
William-Jordan† 1105–9
Bertrand (of Toulouse)† 1109–12
Pons† 1112–37
Raymond II 1137–52
Raymond III 1152–87
Bohemond IV of Antioch-Tripoli 1187–1233
Bohemond V of Antioch-Tripoli 1233–52
Bohemond VI of Antioch-Tripoli 1252–75
Bohemond VII of Antioch-Tripoli 1275–87
Lucia 1287–90s

Counts of Edessa, 1098–1144

Baldwin I (of Boulogne)† 1098–1100
Baldwin II (of Le Bourcq)† 1100–18
Joscelin I (of Courtenay)† 1119–31
Joscelin II 1131–59
(Joscelin III) .... (1159–1200?)

† Born in Europe

Glossary

Ashlar – A style of masonry that makes use of courses of finely cut stone blocks; alternatively refers to one of such blocks.
Batter – The gradual slope of a wall, often at its base.
Bent entrance – An entrance passage that involves at least one abrupt change of direction, typically a turn of 90° or more.
Boss – A protrusion left in the centre of an ashlar, often framed with finely drafted margins.
Casemate – A small vaulted chamber inserted into the thickness of a wall that provides access to an embrasure.
Castellan – The individual charged by a lord with the defence of a stronghold.
Condominium – A region of land where administration and revenues are shared between two parties.
Corbel – A stone that projects out from a wall and is used to support some kind of architectural element.
Counterscarp – The exterior face or wall of a fosse.
Crenels – The open spaces of a crenellated parapet, between solid merlons.
Curtain wall – The main sections of wall, often running between towers, that make up a stronghold's main line of defences.
Donjon – The principal tower of a stronghold, usually larger than other towers and typically regarded as the final point of refuge for defenders (distinguished here from a *keep*, although often used synonymously).
Dressing – The finish left on the exterior of an ashlar or facing stone.
Embrasure – An arrow slit through the thickness of a wall that splays inwards.
Enceinte – A fortified enclosure.
Fosse – A ditch, either dry or filled with water, surrounding a stronghold or ahead of an approachable front.
Gallery – A passageway running inside or along the inner side of a wall that provides access to embrasures.
Glacis – Typically a revetted slope leading up to a stronghold, although sometimes used as a synonym for talus.
Greek fire – Originally an incendiary liquid developed by the Byzantines in the Early Middle Ages, its composition was a closely guarded secret as it could not be extinguished by water. By the time of the crusades, the term was applied to a wide range of naphtha-based combustibles, the consistency of which varied from liquids to more viscous mud-like pastes.
Hoarding – Temporary wooden shelters, which rested on beams inserted into putlog holes, that were built out beyond the battlements to provide protection for

defenders shooting arrows or dropping stones on targets at the base of the wall below.

Keep – A solitary or central tower, the oldest or only part of a stronghold (distinguished here from a *donjon*, although often used synonymously).

Machicolation – (Box) A small projection built out from the plane of a wall, resting on two or more corbels, between which defenders can shoot at or drop objects on besiegers. (Slot) A narrow opening stretching across the ceiling of a passageway, typically in front of a gate, allowing defenders to shoot at or drop objects on besiegers.

Mamlūk – An individual, born a non-Muslim, bought as a slave in childhood and raised as a Muslim to be a soldier, part of a regiment, loyal to his owner (distinct from the Mamlūk dynasty – established by mamlūks when they seized power in the thirteenth century).

Mantlet – A simple shelter, often movable and made of wood, that was used to provide protection for archers and other siege troops from projectiles shot by the garrison.

Marcher lord – A figure who held a lordship acknowledged to be on the fringe of a principality, and so granted an added degree of autonomy to protect and expand the limits of his realm, and thus that of his overlord. Also known as a marquis (Fr.) or margrave (Ger.).

Merlons – The solid components (or teeth) of a crenellated parapet or battlements.

Moat – *see* **Fosse**.

Penthouse – A shelter or cover, typically used to protect miners or those working to fill a ditch.

Portcullis – A latticed grate, often made or plated with iron, which was raised and lowered in grooves on either side of a passage, used to defend a gateway.

Postern – A small gate in a stronghold from which defenders could launch sallies against their besiegers.

Quadriburgium – A roughly square stronghold with a tower at each corner, some with mural towers between them, particularly popular in the late Roman and early Byzantine periods.

Relief force – An army or body of fighters with the intention of breaking a siege by supplying the defenders, attacking the besiegers, or otherwise compelling the attackers to lift a siege.

Revet – To face with masonry.

Scarp – The interior face or wall of a fosse.

Slight – To destroy or damage so as to leave indefensible.

Spolia – Cut or sculpted stone repurposed or scavenged from an older building and incorporated into a newer one.

Talus – Sloping masonry added to the base of a tower or wall.

Tell – An artificial mound, the product of centuries of occupation as successive generations built on top of earlier remains.

Trebuchet – A machine consisting of a rotating beam, attached to a horizontal axle, that used mechanical advantage to throw stones by harnessing the power of pullers or a counterweight.

Notes

1. Smail, *Crusading Warfare*, p. 206.
2. Rey, *Étude sur les monuments*; Van Berchem and Fatio, *Voyages en Syrie*; Lawrence, *Crusader Castles*.
3. Deschamps, *Les Châteaux des Croisés en Terre-Sainte*.
4. Fedden and Thomson, *Crusader Castles*; Müller-Wiener, *Burgen der Kreuzritter*, trans. Brownjohn as *Castles of the Crusaders*; Kennedy, *Crusader Castles*; Biller et al., *Der Crac des Chevaliers*; Zimmer, Meyer and Boscardin, *Krak des Chevaliers in Syrien*.
5. Faucherre, Mesqui and Prouteau, eds., *La fortification au temps des croisades*; Kennedy, ed., *Muslim Military Architecture in Greater Syria*; Piana, ed., *Burgen und Städte der Kreuzzugszeit*; Yovitchitch, *Forteresses du Proche-Orient*.
6. Johns, *Guide to 'Atlit*.
7. Pringle, *Churches*; idem, *Secular Buildings*.
8. Excavations at Arsūf, which have been ongoing since 1982, were led by the late Israel Roll and continue under Oren Tal. An overview of the finds to 2011 can be found in *The Last Supper at Apollonia*. Under Adrian Boas, surveying began at Montfort in 2006 and annual excavations have taken place since 2011. A fairly comprehensive report, *Montfort*, was published in 2016. Excavations in Syria and at Caesarea were undertaken by a team headed by Nicolas Faucherre and many results have been written up by Jean Mesqui. Excavation reports and much more can be found at http://castellorient.fr/. Work at Belvoir was renewed in 2013 and is currently led by Anne Baud and Jean-Michel Poisson. Excavations at Margat, under the direction of Balázs Major, which began in 2007, have continued despite the current conflict. For an introduction to their efforts, see Major and el-Ajji, 'Al-Marqab Research Project.'
9. Tonghini, *Shayzar I*.
10. Rogers, *Latin Siege Warfare*; Marshall, *Warfare in the Latin East*.
11. Usāma ibn Munqidh, trans. Cobb, p. 115.
12. Fulcher of Chartres 3.37.3–5, ed. Hagenmeyer, pp. 748–9, trans. Ryan, pp. 271–2.
13. Smail, *Crusading Warfare*, p. 61.
14. John of Joinville 446–8, ed. and trans. Monfrin, pp. 218–21, trans. Shaw, pp. 274–5.
15. Niẓām al-Mulk 5.1, trans. Darke, p. 32.
16. Ibn Jubayr, trans. Broadhurst, p. 258.
17. Oliver of Paderborn 6, ed. Hoogeweg p. 169, trans. Gavigan, p. 57.
18. Albert of Aachen 12.21, ed. and trans. Edgington, pp. 856–7.
19. Fulcher of Chartres 3.17.3, ed. Hagenmeyer, p. 663, trans. Ryan, p. 241.
20. Smail, *Crusading Warfare*, p. 106.
21. *Eracles* 23.24, RHC Oc 2, p. 34, ed. Morgan, p. 36.
22. Ibn al-Athīr, trans. Richards, 2:65.
23. Ambroise ll. 3,841–9, ed. Ailes and Barber, p. 62, trans. Ailes, p. 85.
24. Walter the Chancellor, trans. Asbridge and Edgington, p. 146.
25. *Anonymous Syriac Chronicle*, trans. Tritton, p. 85.
26. Fulcher of Chartres 3.26.2, ed. Hagenmeyer, p. 691, trans. Ryan, p. 253.
27. Fulcher of Chartres 3.14.3, ed. Hagenmeyer, pp. 656–7, trans. Ryan, p. 239.
28. John of Joinville 192, ed. and trans. Monfrin, pp. 94–5, trans. Shaw, p. 213.
29. William of Tyre 21.18 (19), ed. Huygens, 2:987, trans. Babcock and Krey, 2:426.
30. Adapted from Ibn 'Abd al-Ẓāhir, trans. al-Khowayter, 2:749. See also Ibn al-Furāt, trans. Lyons and Lyons, 2:148.
31. William of Tyre 11.17, ed. Huygens, 1:521, trans. Babcock and Krey, 1:491.

32. Ibn al-Athīr, trans. Richards, 2:337.
33. Templar of Tyre 381, ed. Minervini, p. 140, trans. p. Crawford, p. 68.
34. Lawrence, *Crusader Castles*, p. 71.
35. Viollet-le-Duc, *Dictionnaire raisonné*, 1:341.
36. Lawrence, *Crusader Castles*, p. 35.
37. Fedden and Thomson, *Crusader Castles*, pp. 11–13.
38. Hillenbrand, *The Crusades*, pp. 467–8.
39. Müller-Wiener, *Burgen der Kreuzritter*, trans. Brownjohn as *Castles of the Crusaders*, p. 8.
40. Boase, 'Military Architecture', pp. 145–51, 156–7, 164.
41. Pringle, in Lawrence, *Crusader Castles*, pp. xxvii–xl.
42. Lawrence, *Crusader Castles*, p. 37.

Select Bibliography by Site

Acre (Arb. ʿAkkā)

(2009) Pringle, *Churches*, 4:1–175.
(1997) Kedar, 'The Outer Walls of Frankish Acre', pp. 157–80.
(1997) Pringle, *Secular Buildings*, no. 5, pp. 15–17.
(1979) Jacoby, 'Crusader Acre in the Thirteenth Century', 1–45.
(1881) Conder and Kitchener, *Survey of Western Palestine*, 1:160–7.
(1871) Rey, *Étude sur les monuments*, pp. 171–2.

ʿAjlūn

(2008) Yovitchitch, 'Die aiyibidisch Burg 'Ağlūn, pp. 110–17.
(2006) Yovitchitch, 'The Tower of Aybak in 'Ajlun Castle', pp. 225–42.
(1931) Johns, 'Medieval 'Ajlun', pp. 21–33.

ʿAkkār (Cr. Gibelacar)

(2000) Fournet and Voisin, 'Le château de Aakkar al-Aatiqa', pp. 149–63.
(1992) Kennedy, *Crusader Castles*, pp. 67–8.
(1973) Deschamps, *La défense du comté de Tripoli et de la principauté d'Antioche*, pp. 307–9.

Aleppo

(2008) Gonnella, 'Die aiyubidische und mamlukische Zitadelle von Aleppo', 139–47.
(2006) Gonnella, 'The Citadel of Aleppo', pp. 165–75.
(2006) Tabbaa, 'Defending Ayyubid Aleppo', 176–83.

Antioch

(1871) Rey, *Étude sur les monuments*, pp. 183–204.

Arima (Arb. al-ʿUrayma)

(1992) Kennedy, *Crusader Castles*, pp. 68–73.
(1973) Deschamps, *La défense du comté de Tripoli et de la principauté d'Antioche*, pp. 313–16.

Arsūf (Cr. Arsur)

(1997) Pringle, *Secular Buildings*, no.19, pp. 20–1.
(1993) Pringle, *Churches*, 1:59–61.
(1882) Conder and Kitchener, *Survey of Western Palestine*, 2:137–44.

Ascalon (Arb. ʿAsqalān)

(1997) Pringle, *Secular Buildings*, no. 20, p. 21.
(1993) Pringle, *Churches*, 1:61–9.
(1984) Pringle, 'Richard I and the Walls of Ascalon', pp. 133–47.
(1883) Conder and Kitchener, *Survey of Western Palestine*, 3:237–47.
(1871) Rey, *Étude sur les monuments*, pp. 205–10.

ʿAtlit (Cr. Castrum Peregrinorum)

(1997) Pringle, *Secular Buildings*, no. 21, pp. 22–3.
(1993) Pringle, *Churches*, 1:69–80.

(1992) Kennedy, *Crusader Castles*, pp. 124–7.
(1947) Johns, *Guide to 'Atlit*.
(1939) Deschamps, *La défense du royaume de Jérusalem*, pp. 24–34.
(1881) Conder and Kitchener, *Survey of Western Palestine*, 1:293–301, 309–10.
(1871) Rey, *Étude sur les monuments*, pp. 93–100.

Baghrās (Cr. Gaston)

(1990) Sinclair, *Eastern Turkey*, 4:266–71.
(1978) Lawrence, 'The Castle of Baghras', pp. 34–83.
(1973) Deschamps, *La défense du comté de Tripoli et de la principauté d'Antioche*, pp. 359–60.

Balāṭunūs

(1973) Deschamps, *La défense du comté de Tripoli et de la principauté d'Antioche*, pp. 339–40.

Bānyās (Cr. Belinas)

(1997) Pringle, *Secular Buildings*, no. 42, p. 30.
(1993) Pringle, *Churches*, 1:108.
(1881) Conder and Kitchener, *Survey of Western Palestine*, 1:109–13.

Baysān (Cr. Bethsan)

(1997) Pringle, *Secular Buildings*, no. 26, p. 25.
(1993) Pringle, *Churches*, 1:93.
(1882) Conder and Kitchener, *Survey of Western Palestine*, 2:101–14.

Beaufort (Arb. Shaqīf Arnūn)

(2008) Yasmine, 'Die Burg Beaufort', pp. 274–84.
(2004) Corvisier, 'Les campagnes de construction', pp. 243–66.
(1997) Pringle, *Secular Buildings*, no. 44, p. 31.
(1993) Pringle, *Churches*, 1:110.
(1992) Kennedy, *Crusader Castles*, pp. 43–5.
(1939) Deschamps, *La défense du royaume de Jérusalem*, pp. 176–208.
(1881) Conder and Kitchener, *Survey of Western Palestine*, 1:128–32.
(1871) Rey, *Étude sur les monuments*, pp. 127–39.

Beirut

(1997) Pringle, *Secular Buildings*, no. 45, p. 32.
(1993) Pringle, *Churches*, 1:111–19.

Belvoir (Arb. Kawkab)

(1997) Pringle, *Secular Buildings*, no. 46, pp. 32–3.
(1993) Pringle, *Churches*, 1:120–2.
(1992) Kennedy, *Crusader Castles*, pp. 59–61.
(1989) Biller, 'Die Johanniterburg Belvoir', pp. 105–36.
(1882) Conder and Kitchener, *Survey of Western Palestine*, 2:117–19.

Bethgibelin (Arb. Bayt Jibrīn)

(2004) Cohen, 'The Fortification of the Fortress of Gybelin', pp. 67–75.
(1997) Pringle, *Secular Buildings*, no. 32, p. 27.
(1993, 2009) Pringle, *Churches*, 1:95–101; 4:250–6.
(1883) Conder and Kitchener, *Survey of Western Palestine*, 3:257–8.

Blanchegarde (Arb. Tell al-Ṣāfī)

(2009) Boas and Maeir, 'The Frankish Castle of Blanche Garde', pp. 1–22.
(1997) Pringle, *Secular Buildings*, no. 194, p. 93.

(1882) Conder and Kitchener, *Survey of Western Palestine*, 2:440.
(1871) Rey, *Étude sur les monuments*, pp. 123–5.

Bosra (Arb. Buṣrā)

(2008) Yovitchitch, 'Bosra', pp. 169–77.
(2004) Yovitchitch, 'La citadelle de Bosra', pp. 205–17.

Bourzey (Arb. Barziyya)

(2008) Michaudel, 'Burzaih', pp. 178–87.
(2004) Mesqui, 'Bourzeÿ', pp. 95–113.
(1992) Kennedy, *Crusader Castles*, pp. 79–84.
(1973) Deschamps, *La défense du comté de Tripoli et de la principauté d'Antioche*, pp. 345–8.

Caesarea (Qaysāriyya)

(2006) Mesqui, 'L'enceinte médiévale de Césarée', pp. 83–94.
(1997) Pringle, *Secular Buildings*, no. 76, pp. 43–5.
(1993) Pringle, *Churches*, 1:166–83.
(1882) Conder and Kitchener, *Survey of Western Palestine*, 2:13–29.
(1871) Rey, *Étude sur les monuments*, pp. 221–7.

Cairo

(2012) Pradines, 'Les murailles du Caire', pp. 1027–63.
(1999) Warner, 'The Fatimid and Ayyubid Eastern Walls', pp. 283–96.
(1952–59) Creswell, Muslim Architecture of Egypt.

Castellum Arnaldi (Arb. Yalu)

(1997) Pringle, *Secular Buildings*, no. 231, pp. 106–7.

Castellum Regis

(2013) Khamisy, 'The History and Architectural Design', pp. 13–51.
(1998) Pringle, *Churches*, 2:30–2
(1997) Pringle, *Secular Buildings*, no. 152, pp. 71–2.
(1881) Conder and Kitchener, *Survey of Western Palestine*, 1:190–1.

Cave of Tyron

(1939) Deschamps, *La défense du royaume de Jérusalem*, pp. 210–20.

Chastel Blanc (Arb. Ṣāfītā)

(2008) Piana, 'Die Templerburg Chastel Blanc'. pp. 293–301.
(1992) Kennedy, *Crusader Castles*, pp. 138–41.
(1973) Deschamps, *La défense du comté de Tripoli et de la principauté d'Antioche*, pp. 249–58.
(1871) Rey, *Étude sur les monuments*, pp. 85–92.

Chastel Neuf (Arb. Hūnīn)

(1997) Pringle, *Secular Buildings*, no. 164, pp. 79–80.
(1992) Kennedy, *Crusader Castles*, pp. 42–3.
(1881) Conder and Kitchener, *Survey of Western Palestine*, 1:123–5.

Chastel Rouge (Arb. Yaḥmur)

(1992) Kennedy, *Crusader Castles*, pp. 73–5.
(1973) Deschamps, *La défense du comté de Tripoli et de la principauté d'Antioche*, pp. 317–19.

Coliath (Arb. al-Qulay'āt)

(1992) Kennedy, *Crusader Castles*, pp. 78–9.
(1973) Deschamps, *La défense du comté de Tripoli et de la principauté d'Antioche*, pp. 311–12.

Crac des Chevaliers (Arb. Ḥiṣn al-Akrād)

(2011) Zimmer, Meyer and Boscardin, *Krak des Chevaliers in Syrien*.
(2006) Biller et al., eds., *Der Crac des Chevaliers*.
(1992) Kennedy, *Crusader Castles*, pp. 145–63.
(1934) Deschamps, *Le Crac des Chevaliers*.
(1871) Rey, *Étude sur les monuments*, pp. 39–67.

Cursat (Arb. al-Quṣayr)

(1992) Kennedy, *Crusader Castles*, p. 84.
(1990) Sinclair, *Eastern Turkey*, 4:261–6.
(1973) Deschamps, *La défense du comté de Tripoli et de la principauté d'Antioche*, pp. 351–7.

Damascus

(2008) Braune, 'Die Stadtbefestigung von Damaskus', pp. 202–10.
(2006) Berthier, 'La citadelle de Damas', pp. 151–64.
(1930) Sauvaget, 'La citadelle de Damas', pp. 59–90.

Damietta

(1993) Pringle, *Churches*, 1:202–3.

Edessa

(1990) Sinclair, *Eastern Turkey*, 4:2–15.

Gaza

(1993) Pringle, *Churches*, 1:208–20.
(1883) Conder and Kitchener, *Survey of Western Palestine*, 3:334–5, 248–51.

al-Ḥabis (Petra)

(1997) Pringle, *Secular Buildings*, no. 97, pp. 49–50.
(1992) Kennedy, *Crusader Castles*, pp. 28–30.

al-Ḥabis Jaldak (Cr. Cava de Suet)

(1997) Pringle, *Secular Buildings*, no. 10, p. 18.
(1992) Kennedy, *Crusader Castles*, pp. 52–4.
(1988) Nicolle, 'Ain al-Habis', pp. 113–40.
(1939) Deschamps, *La défense du royaume de Jérusalem*, pp. 111–15.

Ḥārim (Cr. Harrenc)

(2016) Buck, 'The Castle and Lordship of Harim', pp. 113–31.
(2008) Gelichi, 'Die Burg Ḥārim', pp. 211–20.
(2006) Gelichi, 'The Citadel of Harim', pp. 184–200.
(1973) Deschamps, *La défense du comté de Tripoli et de la principauté d'Antioche*, p. 341.

Ḥarrān

(2004) Hanisch, 'The Works of al-Malik al-'Adil', pp. 165–78.
(1990) Sinclair, *Eastern Turkey*, 4:29–42.
(1951) Lloyd and Brice, 'Harran', pp. 77–111.

Ibelin

(1998) Pringle, *Churches*, 2:379–84.
(1997) Pringle, *Secular Buildings*, no. 235, p. 109.
(1882) Conder and Kitchener, *Survey of Western Palestine*, 2:441–3.

Jacob's Ford (Cr. Chastellet)

(1997) Pringle, *Secular Buildings*, no. 174, p. 85.

Jaffa

(2011) Peilstöcker and Burke, eds., *The History and Archaeology of Jaffa 1*.
(1997) Pringle, *Secular Buildings*, no. 110, p. 52.
(1993) Pringle, *Churches*, 1:264–73.

Jerusalem

(2007) Hawari, Ayyubid Jerusalem.
(1950) Johns, 'The Citadel of Jerusalem', pp. 121–90.

Jubayl (Cr. Gibelet, Anc. Byblos)

(2018) Chaaya, 'Results of the First Season of Excavation', pp. 475–84.
(1992) Kennedy, *Crusader Castles*, pp. 64–6.
(1973) Deschamps, *La défense du comté de Tripoli et de la principauté d'Antioche*, pp. 203–15.
(1871) Rey, *Étude sur les monuments*, pp. 115–21, 217–19.

Kerak (Cr. Petra Deserti)

(2008) Milwrite, The Fortress of the Raven.
(1997) Pringle, *Secular Buildings*, no. 124, pp. 59–60.
(1993) Pringle, *Churches*, 1:286–95.
(1992) Kennedy, *Crusader Castles*, pp. 45–52.
(1939) Deschamps, *La défense du royaume de Jérusalem*, pp. 80–98.

Latrun (Cr. Toron des Chevaliers)

(1998) Pringle, *Churches*, 2:5–9.
(1997) Pringle, *Secular Buildings*, no. 136, pp. 64–5.
(1883) Conder and Kitchener, *Survey of Western Palestine*, 3:15–16, 135.

Maraclea (Arb. Maraqiyya)

(1973) Deschamps, *La défense du comté de Tripoli et de la principauté d'Antioche*, pp. 323–6.

Margat (Arb. Marqab)

(2009) Major and el-Ajji, 'Al-Marqab Research Project', pp. 263–83.
(1992) Kennedy, *Crusader Castles*, pp. 163–79.
(1973) Deschamps, *La défense du comté de Tripoli et de la principauté d'Antioche*, pp. 259–85.
(1871) Rey, *Étude sur les monuments*, pp. 19–38.

Mons Peregrinus (Arb. Sandjīl, Alt. Saint-Gilles)

(2016) Chaaya, 'Les défenses et l'évolution du château Saint-Gilles de Tripoli', pp. 281–312.
(1992) Kennedy, *Crusader Castles*, p. 63.
(1973) Deschamps, *La défense du comté de Tripoli et de la principauté d'Antioche*, pp. 293–5.

Montfort (Arb. al-Qurayn)

(2017) Boas, ed., *Montfort*.
(1998, 2009) Pringle, *Churches*, 2:40–3; 4:271–2.
(1997) Pringle, *Secular Buildings*, no. 156, pp. 73–5.
(1994) Pringle, 'A Thirteenth-Century Hall', pp. 52–81.
(1992) Kennedy, *Crusader Castles*, pp. 128–31.
(1927) Dean, 'The Exploration of a Crusaders' Fortress', pp. 5–46.
(1881) Conder and Kitchener, *Survey of Western Palestine*, 1:186–90.
(1871) Rey, *Étude sur les monuments*, pp. 143–51.

Montreal (Arb. Shawbak)

(2004) Faucherre, 'La forteresse de Shawbak', pp. 43–66.
(1998) Pringle, *Churches*, 2:304–14.
(1997) Pringle, *Secular Buildings*, no. 157, pp. 75–8.
(1992) Kennedy, *Crusader Castles*, pp. 23–4.

Mount Tabor

(1998) Pringle, *Churches*, 2:63–85.
(1976) Battista and Bagatti, La fortezza saracena del Monte Tabor.
(1881) Conder and Kitchener, *Survey of Western Palestine*, 1:388–91.

Nephin (Arb. Anafa)

(1973) Deschamps, *La défense du comté de Tripoli et de la principauté d'Antioche*, pp. 297–301.

Qal'at Ṣadr (Al-Jundī)

(2010) Mouton, *Sadr*.

Raqqa

(2006) Heidemann, 'The Citadel of al-Raqqa', 122–50.
(1985) Al-Khalaf, Murhaf, 'Die 'abbāsidische Stadtmauer von ar-Raqqa/ar-Rāfiqa', 123–31.

Safed (Cr. Saphet)

(2010) Barbé, 'Le château de Safed'.
(2004) Barbé and Damati, 'Le château de Safed', pp. 77–93.
(1998) Pringle, *Churches*, 2:206–9.
(1997) Pringle, *Secular Buildings*, no. 191, pp. 91–2.
(1992) Kennedy, *Crusader Castles*, p. 40.
(1985) Pringle, 'Reconstructing the Castle of Safed', pp. 139–49.
(1965) Huygens, 'Un nouveau text', pp. 355–77.
(1881) Conder and Kitchener, *Survey of Western Palestine*, 1:248–50.

Saone (Arb. Ṣahyūn)

(2008) Mesqui, 'Saône', pp. 356–66.
(1992) Kennedy, *Crusader Castles*, pp. 84–96.
(1973) Deschamps, *La défense du comté de Tripoli et de la principauté d'Antioche*, pp. 217–47.
(1968) Saadé, 'Histoire du château de Saladin', pp. 980–1016.
(1871) Rey, *Étude sur les monuments*, pp. 105–13.

Scandelion (Arb. Iskandarūna)

(1997) Pringle, *Secular Buildings*, no. 106, p. 51.
(1993) Pringle, *Churches*, 1:251.
(1881) Conder and Kitchener, *Survey of Western Palestine*, 1:154, 176.

Shayzar

(2012) Tonghini, *Shayzar I*.

Shughr-Bakās

(1973) Deschamps, *La défense du comté de Tripoli et de la principauté d'Antioche*, pp. 349–50.

Sidon

(1998, 2009) Pringle, *Churches*, 2:317–29; 4:272.
(2008) Piana, 'Die Kreuzfahrerstadt Sidon', 367–83.
(1997) Pringle, *Secular Buildings*, no. 201, pp. 94–5.

(1992) Kennedy, *Crusader Castles*, pp. 121–4.
(1973) Kalayan, 'The Sea Castle of Sidon', pp. 81–90.
(1939) Deschamps, *La défense du royaume de Jérusalem*, pp. 224–33.
(1924) Contenau, 'Deuxième mission archéologique à Sidon', pp. 261–81.
(1871) Rey, *Étude sur les monuments*, pp. 153–9.

Ṣubayba

(2001) Hartal, The al-Subayba (Nimrod) Fortress.
(1989) Ellenblum, 'Who Built Qal'at al-Subayba?' pp. 103–12.
(1881) Conder and Kitchener, *Survey of Western Palestine*, 1:125–8.

Tiberias

(2008) Stepansky, 'Das kreuzfahrerzeitliche Tiberias', pp. 384–95.
(2004) Stepansky, 'The Crusader Castle of Tiberias', pp. 179–81.
(1998) Pringle, *Churches*, 2:351–66.
(1997) Pringle, *Secular Buildings*, no. 222, pp. 101–2.
(1881) Conder and Kitchener, *Survey of Western Palestine*, 1:418–20.

Toron (Arb. Tibnīn)

(2008) Piana, 'Die Burg Toron', pp. 396–407.
(2006) Piana, 'The Crusader Castle of Toron', pp. 173–91.
(1998) Pringle, *Churches*, 2:367–8.
(1997) Pringle, *Secular Buildings*, no. 223, p. 102.
(1992) Kennedy, *Crusader Castles*, pp. 40–2.
(1881) Conder and Kitchener, *Survey of Western Palestine*, 1:133–5.
(1871) Rey, *Étude sur les monuments*, pp. 141–2.

Tortosa (Arb. Ṭarṭūs)

(2008) Piana, 'Die Kreuzfahrerstadt Tortosa', pp. 408–21.
(1992) Kennedy, *Crusader Castles*, pp. 132–8.
(1973) Deschamps, *La défense du comté de Tripoli et de la principauté d'Antioche*, pp. 287–92.
(1871) Rey, *Étude sur les monuments*, pp. 69–83, 211–14.

Tyre

(2009) Pringle, *Churches*, 4:177–230.
(1997) Pringle, *Secular Buildings*, no. 227, pp. 103–4.
(1871) Rey, *Étude sur les monuments*, pp. 167–9.

Wādī Mūsā (Arb. al-Wu'ayra, Cr. Li Vaux Moyses)

(1998, 2009) Pringle, *Churches*, 2:373–7; 4:272.
(1997) Pringle, *Secular Buildings*, no. 230, pp. 105–6.
(1997) Vannini and Tonghini, 'Medieval Petra', pp. 371–84.
(1992) Kennedy, *Crusader Castles*, pp. 25–7.

Baronial Towers and Tower-Forts of the Military Orders

(1998) Pringle, 'Templar Castles between Jaffa and Jerusalem', pp. 89–109.
(1997) Pringle, *Secular Buildings*, passim.
(1994) Pringle, 'Templar Castles on the Road to the Jordan', pp. 148–66.
(1992) Kennedy, *Crusader Castles*, pp. 33–9, 54–9.
(1986) Pringle, *The Red Tower*.

Studies of Fortifications

(2011) Yovitchitch, Forteresses du Proche-Orient.
(1993–2009) Pringle, *Churches*, 2:373–7; 4:272.

(2008) Piana, ed., Burgen und Städte der Kreuzzugszeit.
(2006) Kennedy, ed., Muslim Military Architecture in Greater Syria.
(2004) Faucherre, Mesqui and Prouteau, eds., *La fortification au temps des croisades.*
(1997) Pringle, *Secular Buildings.*
(1995) Pringle, 'Town Defences', pp. 69–121.
(1992) Kennedy, *Crusader Castles.*
(1934–1973) Deschamps, *Les Châteaux des Croisés en Terre-Sainte.*
(1966) Müller-Wiener, *Burgen der Kreuzritter*
(1871) Rey, Étude sur les monuments.

Bibliography

Primary Sources

Abū al-Fidā', *al-Mukhtaṣar fi ta'rīkh al-bashar*

Ed. and trans. (Fr.) as *Résumé des histoire des croisades tiré des annales d'Abou 'l-Fedâ*. RHC Or 1. Paris: Imprimerie Nationale, 1872.

Trans. (Eng.) P.M. Holt. *The Memoirs of a Syrian Prince: Abu'l-Fidā', Sultan of Ḥamāh (672–732/ 1273–1331)*. Wiesbaden: Steiner, 1983.

Abū Shāma, *Kitāb al-Rawḍatayn*

Ed. and trans. (Fr.) as *Livre des deux Jardins*. RHC Or 4–5. Paris: Imprimerie Nationale, 1898–1906.

Albert of Aachen, *Historia Ierosolimitana*

Ed. as *Historia Hierosolymitana*. RHC Oc 4. Paris: Imprimerie Nationale, 1879.

Ed. and trans. (Eng.) Susan B. Edgington. *Historia Ierosolimitana: History of the Journey to Jerusalem*. Oxford: Oxford University Press, 2007.

Chronique d'Amadi

Ed. René de Mas Latrie. In *Chroniques d'Amadi et de Strambaldi*. Vol. 1. Paris: Imprimerie Nationale, 1891.

Trans. (Eng.) Nicholas Coureas and Peter Edbury. *The Chronicle of Amadi*. Nicosia: Cyprus Research Centre, 2015.

Ambroise, *Estoire de la guerre saint*

Ed. Marianne Ailes and Malcolm Barber. *The History of the Holy War: Ambroise's* Estoire de la Guerre Saint. Woodbridge: Boydell, 2003.

Trans. (Eng.) Marianne Ailes. *The History of the Holy War: Ambroise's* Estoire de la Guerre Saint. Ed. Marianne Ailes and Malcolm Barber. Woodbridge: Boydell, 2003.

Anna Comnena, *Alexiad*

Trans. (Eng.) E.R.A. Sewter. *The Alexiad of Anna Comnena*. London: Penguin, 1969.

Annales sancti Rudberti Salisburgenses

Ed. D. Wilhelmus Wattenbach. *Annales Sancti Rudberti Salisburgenses*. MGH SS 9. Hanover, 1851.

Annales de Terre Sainte

Ed. Peter W. Edbury. 'A New Text of the *Annales de Terre Sainte*'. In *In Laudem Hierosolymitani*. Ed. Iris Shagrir, Ronnie Ellenblum and Jonathan Riley-Smith. Aldershot: Ashgate, 2007, pp. 145–61.

Ed. Reinhold Röhricht and Gaston Raynaud. *Annales de Terre Sainte*. Paris: Ernest Leroux, 1884.

Anonymous Syriac Chronicle

Ed. J.-B. Chabot. *Anonymi auctoris chronicon ad annum christi 1234 pertinens*. 2 vols. CSCO Scr. Syri, ser. 3, vols. 14 and 15. Paris, 1916–20.

Part trans. (Eng.) Arthur S. Tritton. 'The First and Second Crusade from an Anonymous Syriac Chronicle'. *Journal of the Royal Asiatic Society* 65 (1933), pp. 69–101, 273–305.

Ansbert, *Historia de expeditione Friderici Imperatoris*

Ed. Anton Chroust. *Quellen zur Geschichte des Kreuzzuges Kaiser Friedrichs I*. MGH SrG NS 5. Berlin, 1928.

Trans. (Eng.) Graham Loud. *The Crusade of Frederick Barbarossa*. Farnham: Ashgate, 2010.

Anselm of Ribemont, *Letters*

Ed. as *Epistyolae Stephani, comitis Carnotensis, atque Anselm de Ribodi Monte*. RHC Oc 3. Paris: Imprimerie Impériale, 1866.

Auctarium Affligemense

Ed. D.L.C. Bethmann. *Auctarium Affligemense*. MGH SS 6. Hanover, 1844.

Auctarium Aquicinense

Ed. D.L.C. Bethmann. *Auctarium Aquicinense*. MGH SS 6. Hanover, 1844.

Aymar the Monk (Haymarus Monachus), *Expeditione Ierosolimitana*

Ed. and trans. (It.) Sascha Falk and Antonio Placanica. *Der 'Rithmus de expeditione Ierosolimitana' des sogenannten Haymarus Monachus Florentinus*. Florence: SISMEL Edizioni del Galluzzo, 2006.

Al-ʿAynī, Badr al-Dīn, *ʿIqd al-jumān*

Ed. and trans. (Fr.) as *Le collier de perles*. RHC Or 2a. Paris: Imprimerie Nationale, 1887.

Bahāʾ al-Dīn Yūsuf ibn Shaddād, *al-Nawādir al-sulṭāniyya wa al-maḥāsin al-Yūsufiyya*

Ed. and trans. (Fr.) as *Anecdotes et beau traits de la vie du sultan Youssof (Salâh ed-Dîn)*. RHC Or 3. Paris: Imprimerie Nationale, 1884.

Trans. (Eng.) D.S. Richards. *The Rare and Excellent History of Saladin*. Aldershot: Ashgate, 2001.

Bar Hebraeus, *Makhtebhânûth Zabhnê*

Ed. and trans. (Eng.) Ernest A. Wallis Budge. *The Chronography of Gregory Abū al-Faraj*. 2 vols. London: Oxford University Press, 1932, reprinted Amsterdam: Philo Press, 1976.

Caffaro and cont., *Annales*

Ed. Luigi Tommaso Belgrano and Cesare Imperiale. In *Annali genovesi di Caffaro e de' suoi continuatori*. 5 vols. SI. Genoa: Istituto Storico Italiano, 1890–1901, Rome: Tipografia del Senato, 1923–29.

Trans. (Eng.) Martin Hall and Jonathan Phillips. In *Caffaro, Genoa and the Twelfth-Century Crusades*. Farnham: Ashgate, 2013.

Caffaro, *De liberatione civitatum orientis*

Ed. Luigi Tommaso Belgrano. In *Annali genovesi di Caffaro e de' suoi continuatori*. Vol. 1. SI. Genoa: Istituto Storico Italiano, 1890.

Trans. (Eng.) Martin Hall and Jonathan Phillips. In *Caffaro, Genoa and the Twelfth-Century Crusades*. Farnham: Ashgate, 2013.

Caffaro, *Ystoria captionis Almarie et Turtuose*

Ed. Luigi Tommaso Belgrano. In *Annali genovesi di Caffaro e de' suoi continuatori*. Vol. 1. SI. Genoa: Istituto Storico Italiano, 1890.

Trans. (Eng.) Martin Hall and Jonathan Phillips. In *Caffaro, Genoa and the Twelfth-Century Crusades*. Farnham: Ashgate, 2013.

Chanson d'Antioche

Trans. (Eng.) Susan B. Edgington and Carol Sweetenham. *The* Chanson d'Antioche*: An Old French Account of the First Crusade*. Farnham: Ashgate, 2011.

De constructione castri Saphet

Ed. R.B.C. Huygens. In 'Un nouveau texte du traité 'De constructione castri Saphet'' *Studi medievali* 3.6 (1965), pp. 355–87.

Trans. (Eng.) Hugh Kennedy. In *Crusader Castles*. Cambridge: Cambridge University Press, 1994, pp. 190–8.

Cronica S Petri Erfordensis moderna

Ed. O. Holder-Egger. *Cronica S. Petri Erfordensis Moderna*. MGH SS 30, pt. 1. Hanover, 1896.

Ekkehard of Aura, *Hierosolymita*

Ed. Heinrich Hagenmeyer. *Hierosolymita*. Tubingen, 1877.

Eracles Continuation of William of Tyre

Ed. as *L'Estoire de Eracles empereur et la conqueste de la terre d'Outremer: c'est la continuation de l'estoire de Guillaime arcevesque de Sur*. RHC Oc 2. Paris: Imprimerie Impériale, 1859.

Part. trans. (Eng.) Janet Shirley. In *Crusader Syria in the Thirteenth Century: The* Rothelin *Continuation of the* History *of William of Tyre with part of the* Eracles *or* Acre *text*. Aldershot: Ashgate, 1999.

Ernoul, *Chronique*

Ed. M.L. de Mas Latrie. *Chronique d'Ernoul et de Bernard le Trésorier*. Paris: SHF, 1871.

Eustathius of Thessalonica, *Capture of Thessalonica*

Ed. and trans. (Eng.) John R. Melville Jones. *Eustathios of Thessaloniki: The Capture of Thessaloniki*. Canberra: Australian Association for Byzantine Studies, 1988.

Evagrius, Scholasticus, *Ecclesiastical History*
Ed. Henri de. Valois. *Evagrii Scholastici epiphaniensis et ex praefectis, Ecclesiasticae histriae, libri sex.* London, 1844.
Trans. (Eng.) as *Evagrius's Ecclesiastical History, From 431 to 594 A.D.* Greek Ecclesiastical Historians of the First Six Centuries of the Christian Era. London: Samuel Bagster, 1846.
Excidium Aconis
Ed. R.B.C. Huygens. As *Excidii Acconis Gestorum Collectio*, in *The Fall of Acre 1291*. CCCM 202. Turnhout: Brepols, 2004.
De expugnatione Lyxbonensi
Ed. and trans. (Eng.) Charles Wendell David. *De Expugnatione Lyxbonensi: The Conquest of Lisbon*. New York: Columbia University Press, 1936.
De expugnatione terrae sanctae per Saladinum
Ed. Joseph Stevenson. *De Expugnatione Terrae Sanctae per Saladinum*. RS 66. London: Longman, 1875.
Part. trans. (Eng.) James Brundage. In *The Crusades: A Documentary History*. Milwaukee, WI: Marquette University Press, 1962, reprinted 1976.
Florence of Worcester, *Chronicon ex chronicis*
Ed. Benjamin Thorpe. *Florentii Wigorniensis Monachi Chronicon ex Chronicis*. 2 vols. London: Sumptibus Societatis, 1848–49.
Trans. (Eng.) Thomas Forester. *The Chronicle of Florence of Worcester with the Two Continuations*. London: Henry G. Bohn, 1854.
Fulcher of Chartres, *Historia Hierosolymitana*
Ed. Heinrich Hagenmeyer. *Historia Hierosolymitana*. Heidelberg: Carl Winter's Universitätsbuchhandlung, 1913.
Trans. (Eng.) Frances Rita Ryan and ed. Harold S. Fink. *A History of the Expedition to Jerusalem, 1095–1127*. Knoxville: The University of Tennessee Press, 1969.
Geoffrey of Villehardouin, *Conquête de Constantinople*
Ed. and trans. (Fr.) M. Natalis de Wailly. *Conquête de Constantinople, avec la continuation de Henri de Valenciennes*. 3rd. ed. Paris: Firmin-Didot, 1882.
Trans. (Eng.) M.R.B. Shaw. In *Chronicles of the Crusades*. London: Penguin, 1963.
Gesta Francorum
Ed. and trans. (Eng.) Rosalind Hill. *The Deeds of the Franks and the other Pilgrims*. Edinburgh: Thomas Nelson & Sons, 1962, reprinted Oxford: Oxford University Press, 1972.
Guibert of Nogent, *Die gesta per Francos*
Ed. R.B.C. Huygens. *Die Gesta per Francos*. CCCM 127a. Turnhout: Brepols, 1996.
Trans. (Eng.) Robert Levine. *The Deeds of God through the Franks*. Woodbridge: Boydell, 1997.
Het'um, *Flos historiarum terre orientis*
Ed. and trans. (Fr.) as *La flor des estoires de la terre d'orient*. RHC Ar 2. Paris: Imprimerie Nationale, 1906.
Historia Nicaena vel Antiochena
Ed. as *Historia Nicaena vel Antiochena*. RHC Oc 5. Paris: Imprimerie Nationale, 1886.
History of the Patriarchs of the Egyptian Church
Ed. and trans. (Eng.) O.H.E. Khs-Burmester, et al. *History of the Patriarchs of the Egyptian Church*. 4 vols. Cairo: Publications de la Sociétés d'Archéologie Copte, Textes et Documents, 1942–74.
Ibn 'Abd al-Ẓāhir, Muḥyī al-Dīn, *al-Rawḍ al-zāhir fi sīrat al-Malik al-Ẓāhir*
Ed. and trans. (Eng.) Abdul Aziz al-Khowayter. *A critical edition of an unknown source for the life of al-Malik al-Ẓāhir Baibars, with introduction, translation, and notes*. SOAS, unpublished PhD thesis, 1960.
Ed. and trans. (Eng.) Syedah Fatima Sadeque. *Baybars I of Egypt*. Dacca: Oxford University Press, 1956.
Ibn al-'Adīm, Kamāl al-Dīn, *Zubdat al-ḥalab*
Ed. and trans. (Eng.) as *Extraits de la Chronique d'Alep*. RHC Or 3. Paris: Imprimerie Nationale, 1884.
Ibn al-'Amīd, al-Makīn, *Kitāb al-majmū' al-mubārak*
Trans. (Fr.) Anne-Marie Eddé and Françoise Micheau. *Chronique des Ayyoubides (602–58/1205–6/1259–60)*. DRHC 16. Paris: L'Académie des Inscriptions et Belles-Lettres, 1994.

Ibn al-Athīr, *al-Kāmil fi al-ta'rīkh*
Trans. (Eng.) D.S. Richards. *The Chronicle of Ibn al-Athīr for the Crusading Period from al-Kamil fi'l-ta'rikh*. 3 vols. Aldershot: Ashgate, 2008.
Ibn al-Azraq, *Ta'rīkh Mayyāfāriqīn wa Āmid*
Trans. (Eng.) Carole Hillenbrand. In *A Muslim Principality in Crusader Times*. Istanbul: Nederlands Historisch-Archeologisch Instituut, 1990.
Ibn al-Furāt, *Ta'rīkh al-duwal wa al-mulūk*
Ed. and trans. (Eng.) U. and M.C. Lyons. *Ayyubids, Mamlukes and Crusaders: Selections from the Tārīkh al-Duwal wa al-Mulūk*. 2 vols. Cambridge: Heffer, 1971.
Ibn Isḥāq, *Sīrat rasūl Allāh*
Trans. (Eng.) A. Guillaume. *The Life of Muhammad*. Oxford: Oxford University Press, 1955, reprinted 2004.
Ibn Jubayr, *Riḥla*
Trans. (Eng.) R.J.C. Broadhurst. *The Travels of Ibn Jubayr*. London, 1952, reprinted New Delhi: Goodword Books, 2001.
Ibn Muyassar, *Akhbār Miṣr*
Ed. and trans. (Fr.) as *Extraits d'Ibn Moyesser*. RHC Or 3. Paris: Imprimerie Nationale, 1884.
Ibn al-Qalānisī, *Dhayl Ta'rīkh Dimashq*
Trans. (Eng.) H.A.R. Gibb. *The Damascus Chronicle of the Crusades*. London: Luzac, 1932, reprinted 1967.
Ibn Shaddād, 'Izz al-Dīn, *al-A'lāq al-khaṭīra fī dhikr umarā' al-Sham wa al-Jazīra*
Trans. (Fr.) Anne-Marie Eddé-Terrasse. *Description de la Syrie du nord*. Damascus: Institut Français de Damas, 1984.
Ibn al-Ṣuqā'ī, *Tālī kitāb wafayāt al-a'yān*
Ed. and trans. (Fr.) Jacqueline Sublet. *Tali kitab wafayat al-a'yan*. Damascus: Institut Français de Damas, 1974.
Ibn Wāṣil, Jamāl al-Dīn Muḥammad, *Mufarrij al-kurūb fi akhbār banī Ayyūb*
Part. trans. (Eng.) Peter Jackson. In *The Seventh Crusade, 1244–1254*. Aldershot: Ashgate, 1988.
'Imād al-Dīn al-Iṣfahānī, *Kitāb al-fatḥ al-qussī fi al-fatḥ al-qudsī*
Trans. (Fr.) Henri Massé. *Conquête de la Syrie et de la Palestine par Saladin*. DRHC 10. Paris: Académie des inscriptions et belles-lettres, 1972.
Itinerarium peregrinorum et gesta regis Ricardi
Ed. William Stubbs. *Itinerarium Peregrinorum et Gesta Regis Ricardi*. RS 38. Vol. 1. London: Longman, 1864.
Trans. (Eng.) Helen J. Nicholson. *Chronicle of the Third Crusade: A Translation of the Itinerarium Peregrinorum et Gesta Regis Ricardi*. Aldershot: Ashgate, 1997.
James of Vitry, *Historia orientalis*
Ed. and trans. (Fr.) Jean Donnadieu. *Histoire orientale / Historia orientalis*. Turnhout: Brepols, 2008.
James of Vitry, *Lettres*
Ed. R.B.C. Huygens. *Lettres de Jacques de Vitry*. Leiden: Brill, 1960.
John of Joinville, *Vie de Saint Louis*
Ed. and trans. (Fr.) Jacques Monfrin. *Vie de Saint Louis*. Paris: Classiques Garnier Multimédia, 1998.
John Kinnamos, *Deeds of John and Manuel Comnenus*
Trans. (Eng.) Charles M. Brand. *Deeds of John and Manuel Comnenus*. New York: Columbia University Press, 1976.
Ludolph of Suchem, *De itinere terrae sanctae liber*
Ed. Ferdinand Deycks. *Ludolphi, rectoris ecclesiae parochialis in Suchem De itinere Terrae sanctae liber*. Stuttgart: Litterarischen Vereins, 1851.
Trans. (Eng.) Aubrey Stewart. *Ludolph von Suchem's Description of the Holy Land and the Way Thither*. London: PPTS, 1895.
Al-Maqrīzī, Aḥmad ibn 'Alī Taqī al-Dīn, *al-Sulūk*
Trans. (Eng.) R.J.C. Broadhurst. *A History of the Ayyūbid Sultans of Egypt*. Library of Classical Arabic Literature 5. Boston: Twayne Publishers, 1980.

Trans. (Fr.) É.M. Quatremère. *Histoire des Sultans mamlouks*. 2 Vols. Paris, 1837–45.
Al-Maqrīzī, Aḥmad ibn ʿAlī Taqī al-Dīn, *Khiṭaṭ*
Trans. (Fr.) Urbain Bouriant and M. Paul Casanova. *Description topographique et historique de l'Égypte*. 4 vols. Mémoires publies par les Membres de la Mission Archéologique Française au Caire 17. Paris: Libraire de la Société Asiatique, 1895–1920.
Marino Sanudo Torsello, *Liber secretorum fidelium crucis*
Ed. J. Bongars. *Liber Secretorum Fidelium Crucis*. Hanover, 1611, reprinted with an introduction by Joshua Prawer, Jerusalem: Massada Press, 1972.
Trans. (Eng.) Peter Lock. *The Book of the Secrets of the Faithful of the Cross – Liber Secretorum Fidelium Crucis*. Farnham: Ashgate, 2011.
Maronite Chronicle
Part trans. (Eng.) Andrew Palmer. 'Extract from the *Maronite Chronicle* (AD 664+)'. In *The Seventh Century in the West-Syrian Chronicles*. Liverpool: Liverpool University Press, 1993, pp. 29–35.
Matthew of Edessa, *Patmowtʿiwn*
Trans. (Eng.) Ara Edmond Dostourian. *The Chronicle of Matthew of Edessa*. Lanham: University Press of America, 1993.
Matthew Paris, *Chronica maiora*
Ed. Henry Richards Luard. *Chronica Majora*. RS 57. 7 vols. London: Longman, 1872–83.
Trans. (Eng.) J.A. Giles. *Matthew Paris's English History: From the Year 1235 to 1273*. 3 vols. London: Henry G. Bohn, 1852–54.
Menkonis Chronicon
Ed. L. Weiland. *Menkonis Chronicon*. MGH SS 23. Leipzig, 1925.
Michael Psellus, *Chronographia*
Trans. (Eng.) E.R.A. Sewter. *Fourteen Byzantine Rulers: The* Chronographia *of Michael Psellus*. Harmondsworth: Penguin, 1966.
Michael the Syrian, *Chronique*
Ed. and trans. (Fr.) Jean B. Chabot. *Chronique de Michel le Syrien, Patriarche Jacobite d'Antioche (1166–1199)*. 4 vols. Paris, 1899–1910.
Ed. and trans. (Fr.) as *La Chronique de Michel le Syrien*. RHC Ar 1. Paris: Imprimerie Impériale, 1869.
Movsēs Dasxuranc'i, *Patmutʿiwn Aluanicʿ*
Trans. (Eng.) C.J.F. Dowsett. *The History of the Caucasian Albanians*. London: Oxford University Press, 1961.
Mufaḍḍal ibn Abī al-Faḍā'il, *al-Nahj al-sadīd wa al-durr al-farīd fīmā baʿda ta'rīkh Ibn al-ʿĀmīd*
Ed. and trans. (Fr.) E. Blochet. *Histoire des Sultans Mamlouks*. 3 fascs. PO 12.3 (1919), pp. 345–550; 14.3 (1920), pp. 375–672; 20.1 (1929), pp. 3–270, reprinted 3 vols. Brepols, 2003.
Nerses Shnorhali, *Voghb Yedesyo*
Ed. and trans. (Fr.) as *Elegie sur la prise d'Edesse*. RHC Ar 1. Paris: Imprimerie Impériale, 1869.
Niketas Choniates, *Historia*
Trans. (Eng.) Harry J. Magoulias. *O City of Byzantium: Annals of Niketas Choniates*. Detroit: Wayne State University Press, 1984.
Oliver of Paderborn, *Historia Damiatina*
Ed. Hermann Hoogeweg. In *Die Schriften des Kölner Domscholasters, späteren Bischofs von Paderborn und Kardinal-Bischofs von S. Sabina*. Tubingen: Litterarischen Verein in Stuttgart, 1894.
Trans. (Eng.) John J. Gavigan. In *Christian Society and the Crusades*. Ed. Edward Peters. Philadelphia: University of Pennsylvania Press, 1971.
Orderic Vitalis, *Historiae ecclesiasticae*
Ed. and trans. (Eng.) Marjorie Chibnall. *The Ecclesiastical History of Orderic Vitalis*. 6 vols. Oxford: Oxford University Press, 1969–80.
Peter Tudebode, *Historia de Hierosolymitano itinere*
Ed. John Hugh Hill and Laurita L. Hill. *Historia de Hierosolymitano Itinere*. DRHC 12. Paris: L'Académie des Inscriptions et Belles-Lettres, 1977.

Trans. (Eng.) John Hugh Hill and Laurita Hill. *Historia de Hierosolymitano Itinere by Peter Tudebode*. Memoirs of the American Philosophical Society 101. Philadelphia: American Philosophical Society, 1974.

Philip of Novara, *Gestes des Chiprois*

Ed. Gaston Raynaud. In *Les Gestes des Chiprois*. Recueil de Chroniques Françaises. Paris: Société de l'Orient Latin, 1887, reprinted Osnabruck: Otto Zeller, 1968.

Trans. (Eng.) John L. La Monte. *The Wars of Frederick II against the Ibelins in Syria and Cyprus*. New York: Columbia University Press, 1936.

Ralph of Caen, *Gesta Tancredi*

Ed. as *Gesta Tancredi*. RHC Oc. 3. Paris: Imprimerie Impériale, 1866.

Trans. (Eng.) Bernard S. Bachrach and David S. Bachrach. *The* Gesta Tancredi *of Ralph of Caen, A History of the Normans on the First Crusade*. Aldershot: Ashgate, 2005.

Ralph of Coggeshall, *Chronicon Anglicanum*

Ed. Joseph Stevenson. *Chronicon Anglicanum*. RS 66. London: Longman, 1875.

Ralph of Diceto, *Ymagines historiarum*

Ed. William Stubbs. In *Opera Historica: The Historical Works of Ralph de Diceto, Dean of London*. RS 68. 2 vols. London: Longman, 1876.

Rashīd al-Dīn Faḍl Allāh, *Ta'rikh-i Ghazani*, in *Jāmi' al-tawārīkh*

Trans. (Eng.) John Andrew Boyle. *The Successors of Genghis Khan*. New York: Columbia University Press, 1971.

Raymond of Aguilers, *Historia Francorum qui ceperunt Iherusalem*

Ed. as *Historia Francorum qui Ceperunt Iherusalem*. RHC Oc. 3. Paris: Imprimerie Impériale, 1866.

Trans. (Eng.) John Hill and Laurita Hill. *Historia Francorum qui Ceperunt Iherusalem*. Philadelphia: The American Philosophical Society, 1968.

Robert the Monk, *Historia Iherosolimitana*

Ed. as *Historia Iherosolimitana*. RHC Oc 3. Paris: Imprimerie Impériale, 1866.

Trans. (Eng.) Carol Sweetenham. *Robert the Monk's History of the Crusade: Historia Iherosolimitana*. Aldershot: Ashgate, 2005.

Robert of Torigni, *Chronique*

Ed. Richard Howlett. In *Chronicles of the Reigns of Stephen, Henry II, and Richard I*. RS 82. Vol. 4. London: Her Majesty's Stationery Office, 1889.

Roger of Howden, *Chronica*

Ed. William Stubbs. *Chronica*. RS. 51. 4 vols. London: Longman, 1868–71.

Trans. (Eng.) Henry T. Riley. *The Annals of Roger de Hoveden: Comprising the History of England and of Other Countries of Europe, from A.D. 732 to A.D. 1201*. 2 vols. London: H. G. Bohn, 1853.

Roger of Wendover, *Flores historiarum*

Ed. Henry Coxe. *Chronica, sive Flores Historiarum: in qua lectionum varietas additionesque, quibus chronicon istud ampliavit et instruxit Matthaeus Parisiensis*. 4 vols. London: Sumptibus Societatis, 1841–44.

Ed. Henry G. Hewlett. *Rogeri de Wendover Liber qui Dicitur Flores Historiarum ab Anno Domini MCLIV. Annoque Henrici Anglorum Regis Secundi Primo / The Flowers of History by Roger de Wendover: From the Year of Our Lord 1154, and the First Year of Henry the Second, King of the English*. RS 84. 3 vols. London: Her Majesty's Stationery Office, 1886–89.

Trans. (Eng.) J.A. Giles. *Roger of Wendover's Flowers of History, comprising the History of England from the descent of the Saxons to A.D. 1235*. 2 vols. London: Henry G. Bohn, 1849.

Rothelin Continuation of William of Tyre

Ed. as *La continuation de Guillaume de Tyre de 1229 a 1261, dite du manuscrit de Rothelin*. RHC Oc 2. Paris: Imprimerie Impériale, 1859.

Trans. (Eng.) Janet Shirley. *Crusader Syria in the Thirteenth Century: The* Rothelin *Continuation of the* History *of William of Tyre with part of the* Eracles *or* Acre *text*. Aldershot: Ashgate, 1999.

Stephen of Blois, *Letters*

Ed. as *Epistyolae Stephani, Comitis Carnotensis, atque Anselm de Ribodi Monte*. RHC Oc 3. Paris: Imprimerie Impériale, 1866.

Al-Ṭabarī, *Ta'rīkh al-rusul wa al-mulūk*

Trans. (Eng.) various. *The History of al-Ṭabarī*. Ed. Ehsan Yar-Shater. 40 vols. Albany: State University Press of New York, 1985–2007.

Al-Ṭarsūsī, Marḍī ibn 'Alī, *Tabṣirat arbāb al-albāb*

Ed. Karen Sader. *Dictionary of Ancient Weapons*. Beirut: Dar Sader, 1998.

Part. ed. and trans. (Fr.) Antoine Boudot-Lamotte. *Contribution à l'étude de l'archerie musulmane*. Damascus: Institut Français de Damas, 1968.

Templar of Tyre, *Gestes des Chiprois*

Ed. Gaston Raynaud. In *Les Gestes des Chiprois*. Recueil de Chroniques Françaises. Paris: Sociétés de l'Orient Latin, 1887, reprinted Osnabruck: Otto Zeller, 1968.

Ed. and trans. (It.) Laura Minervini. *Cronaca del Templare di Tiro (1243–1314)*. Naples: Liguori Editore, 2000.

Trans. (Eng.) Paul Crawford. *The 'Templar of Tyre': Part III of the Deeds of the Cypriots*. Aldershot: Ashgate, 2003.

Thadeus, *Ystoria*

Ed. R.B.C. Huygens. In *The Fall of Acre 1291*. CCCM 202. Turnhout: Brepols, 2004.

Theophylact Simocatta, *History*

Trans. (Eng.) Michael Whitby and Mary Whitby. *The* History *of Theophylact Simocatta*. Oxford: Oxford University Press, 1986.

Al-'Umari, *Masālik al-abṣār*

Trans. (Eng.) D.S. Richards. *Egypt and Syria in the Early Mamluk Period*. Abingdon: Routledge, 2017.

Usāma ibn Munqidh, *Kitāb al-i'tibār*

Trans. (Eng.) Paul M. Cobb. *The Book of Contemplation: Islam and the Crusades*. London: Penguin, 2008.

Vahram, *Chronicle*

Trans. (Eng.) Charles Fried Neumann. *Vahram's Chronicle of the Armenian Kingdom in Cilicia*. London: Oriental Translation Fund, 1831.

Walter the Chancellor, *Bella Antiochena*

Ed. Heinrich Hagenmeyer, *Galterii Cancellarii Bella Antiochena*. Innsbruck: Wagner'schen universitätsbuchhandlung, 1896.

Trans. (Eng.) Thomas S. Asbridge and Susan B. Edgington, *Walter the Chancellor's* The Antiochene Wars. Aldershot: Ashgate, 1999.

Walter of Coventry, *Memoriale*

Ed. William Stubbs. *Memoriale fratris Walteri de Coventria*. RS 58. 2 vols. London: Longman, 1872–73.

Wilbrand of Oldenburg, *Itinerarium terrae sanctae*

Ed. Denys Pringle. In 'Wilbrand of Oldenburg's Journey to Syria, Lesser Armenia, Cyprus, and the Holy Land (1211–1212): A New Edition'. *Crusades* 11 (2012), pp. 109–37.

Trans. (Eng.) Denys Pringle. In *Pilgrimage to Jerusalem and the Holy Land*. Ashgate, 2012.

William of Malmesbury, *De gestis regum Anglorum*

Ed. Thomas Duffy Hardy. *Gesta Regum Anglorum*. 2 vols. London: Sumptibus Societatis, 1840.

Ed. William Stubbs. *De Gestis Regum Anglorum*. RS 90. 2 vols. London: Her Majesty's Stationery Office, 1887–89.

Trans. (Eng.) J.A. Giles. *Chronicle of the Kings of England*. London: George Bell & Sons, 1904.

William of Tripoli, *Tractatus de statu Saracenoroum*

Ed. Hans Prutz. In *Kulturgeschichte der Kreuzzuge*. Berlin: Mittler, 1883.

William of Tyre, *Cronique*

Ed. R.B.C. Huygens. *Cronique*. CCCM 63. 2 vols. London: Brepols, 1986.

Trans. (Eng.) Emily Babcock and A.C. Krey. *A History of Deeds Done Beyond the Sea*. 2 vols. New York: Octagon Books, 1976.

Al-Yūnīnī, Quṭb al-Dīn Mūsā, *Dhayl Mir'āt al-zamān*

Ed. and trans. (Eng.) Li Guo. *Early Mamluk Syrian Historiography: Al-Yūnīnī's* Dhayl Mir'āt al-zamān. 2 vols. Leiden: Brill, 1998.

Ẓahīr al-Dīn Nīshāpūrī, *Saljūq-nāma*
Trans. (Eng.) Kenneth Allin Luther. *The History of the Seljuq Turks*. Ed. C. Edmund Bosworth. Richmond: Routledge, 2001.
Al-Zardkāsh, Ibn Aranbughā, *Kitāb anīq fi al-manājnīq*
Ed. Fuat Sezgin. *Armoury Manuel*. Frankfurt: Institute for the History of Arabic-Islamic Science, 1883.

Edited Collections of Primary Sources

Barber, Malcolm and Keith Bate, eds. *Letters from the East: Crusaders, Pilgrims and Settlers in the 12th–13th Centuries*. Farnham: Ashgate, 2010.
Brundage, James, ed. *The Crusades: A Documentary History*. Milwaukee: Marquette University Press, 1962, reprinted 1976.
Delaville le Roulx, Joseph, ed. *Cartulaire Général de l'ordre des Hospitaliers de S. Jean de Jérusalem (1100–1310)*. 3 vols. Paris: Ernest Leroux, 1894–99.
Eickelman, Dale F. and James Piscatori, eds. *Muslim Travellers: Pilgrimage, Migration, and the Religious Imagination*. Berkeley: University of California Press, 1990.
Gabrieli, Francesco, ed. *Storici arabi delle Crociate*. Turin: Giulio Einaudi, 1957. Trans. (Eng.) E.J. Costello as *Arab Historians of the Crusades*. New York: Dorset Press, 1989.
Hallam, Elizabeth, ed. *Chronicles of the Crusades: Eyewitness Accounts of the Wars Between Christianity and Islam*. London: George Weidenfeld & Nicolson, 1989.
Hoogeweg, Hermann, ed. *Die Schriften des Kölner Domscholasters, späteren Bischofs von Paderborn und Kardinal-Bischofs von S. Sabina*. Tubingen: Litterarischen Verein in Stuttgart, 1894.
Huygens, R.B.C., ed. *The Fall of Acre 1291*. Turnhout: Brepols, 2004.
Jackson, Peter, ed. *The Seventh Crusade, 1244–54: Sources and Documents*. Aldershot: Ashgate, 2007.
Lewis, Bernard, ed. *Islam: From the Prophet Mohammad to the Capture of Constantinople*. 2 vols. Oxford: Oxford University Press, 1974, reprinted 1987.
Luard, Henry Richards, ed. *Annales Monastici*. RS 36. Vol. 3. London: Longman, 1866.
Mayer, Hans. E., ed. *Die Urkunden der lateinischen Könige von Jerusalem*. 4 vols. Hanover: MGH, 2010.
Palmer, Andrew, ed. *The Seventh Century in the West-Syrian Chronicles*. Liverpool: Liverpool University Press, 1993.
Pringle, Denys, ed. *Pilgrimage to Jerusalem and the Holy Land, 1187–1291*. Farnham: Ashgate, 2012.
Prutz, Hans, ed. *Kulturgeschichte der Kreuzzuge*. Berlin: E.S. Mittler und Sohn, 1883.
Röhricht, Reinhold, ed. *Regesta Regni Hierosolymitani*. Innsbruck: Libraria Academica Wagneriana, 1893.
Röhricht, Reinhold, ed. *Regesta Regni Hierosolymitani, Additamentum*. Innsbruck: Libraria Academica Wagneriana, 1904.
Shaw, M.R.B., ed. *Chronicles of the Crusades*. London: Penguin, 1963.
Verci, Giambatista, ed. *Storia degli Ecelini*. 3 vols. Bassano: Stamperia Remondini, 1779.
Wilkinson, John, ed., with Joyce Hill and W.F. Ryan. *Jerusalem Pilgrimage, 1099–1185*. London: The Hakluyt Society, 1988.

Secondary Sources

Amitai, Reuven. 'The Conquest of Arsūf by Baybars: Political and Military Aspects'. *Mamlūk Studies Review* 9.1 (2005), pp. 61–83.
Amitai, Reuven. 'Foot Soldiers, Militiamen and Volunteers'. In *Texts, Documents and Artefacts: Islamic Studies in Honour of D.S. Richards*. Ed. Chase. F. Robinson. Leiden: Brill, 2003.
Amitai, Reuven. 'Mongol Provincial Administration: Syria in 1260 as a Case-study'. In *In Laudem Hierosolymitani*. Ed. Iris Shagrir, Ronnie Ellenblum and Jonathan Riley-Smith. Aldershot: Ashgate, 2007, pp. 117–43.
Amitai, Reuven. *Mongols and Mamluks: The Mamluk-Īlkhānid War, 1260–1281*. Cambridge: Cambridge University Press, 1995.
Amitai, Reuven. 'Notes on the Ayyūbid Inscriptions at al-Ṣubayba (Qal'at Nimrūd)'. *Dumbarton Oaks Papers* 43 (1989), pp. 113–19.

Asbridge, Thomas. *The Crusades: The Authoritative History of the War for the Holy Land*. New York: Harper Collins Publishers, 2010.
Asbridge, Thomas. *The First Crusade: A New History*. Oxford: Oxford University Press, 2004.
Ayalon, David. 'Mamlūk: military slavery in Egypt and Syria'. In Ayalon, David. *Islam and the Abode of War: Military slaves and Islamic adversaries*. Aldershot: Ashgate, 1994, pp. 1–21.
Barbé, Hervé and Emanuel Damati. 'Le château de Safed: sources historiques, problématique et premiers résultats des recherches archéologiques'. In *La fortification au temps des croisades*. Ed. Nicolas Faucherre, Jean Mesqui and Nicolas Prouteau. Rennes: Presses Universitaires des Rennes, 2004, pp. 77–93.
Barber, Malcolm. 'Frontier Warfare in the Latin Kingdom of Jerusalem: The Campaign of Jacob's Ford, 1178–79'. In *The Crusades and Their Sources: Essays Presented to Bernard Hamilton*. Ed. John France and William Zajac. Aldershot: Ashgate, 1998, pp. 9–22.
Bartlett, W.B. *Islam's War against the Crusaders*. Stroud: The History Press, 2008.
Bauden, Frédéric. 'Taqī al-Dīn Aḥmad ibn 'Alī al-Maqrīzī'. In *Medieval Muslim Historians and the Franks of the Levant*. Ed. Alex Mallet. Leiden: Brill, 2015, pp. 161–200.
Beffeyte, Renaud. *Les machines de guerre au Moyen Age*. Rennes: Ouest France, 2008.
Benvenisti, Meron. *The Crusaders in the Holy Land*. New York: The Macmillan Company, 1972.
Berkovich, Ilya. 'The Battle of Forbie and the Second Frankish Kingdom of Jerusalem'. *Journal of Military History* 75 (2011), pp. 9–44.
Berthier, Sophie. 'La Citadelle de Damas: Les apports d'une etude archéologique'. In *Muslim Military Architecture in Greater Syria: From the Coming of Islam to the Ottoman Period*. Ed. Hugh Kennedy. Leiden: Brill, 2006, pp. 151–64.
Biller, Thomas, et al. *Der Crac des Chevaliers: Die Baugeschichte einer Ordensburg der Kreuzfahrerzeit*. Regensburg: Schnell & Steiner, 2006.
Boas, Adrian J. 'Archaeological Evidence for the Mamluk Sieges and Dismantling of Montfort: A Preliminary Discussion'. In *Montfort*. Ed. Adrian Boas. Leiden: Brill, 2017, pp. 41–55.
Boas, Adrian J. 'Archaeological Sources for the History of Palestine: The Frankish Period: A Unique Medieval Society Emerges'. *Near Eastern Archaeology*, 61.3 (September 1998), pp. 138–73.
Boas, Adrian J. *Archaeology of the Military Orders: A Survey of the Urban Centres, Rural Settlement and Castles of the Military Orders in the Latin East (c.1120–1291)*. Abingdon: Routledge, 2006.
Boas, Adrian J. *Crusader Archaeology: The Material Culture of the Latin East*. London: Routledge, 1999.
Boas, Adrian J. 'Interpretation of the Parts'. In *Montfort*. Ed. Adrian Boas. Leiden: Brill, 2017, pp. 102–19.
Boas, Adrian J. *Jerusalem in the Time of the Crusades: Society, Landscape and Art in the Holy City under Frankish Rule*. London: Routledge, 2001.
Boas, Adrian J. 'Stone, Metal, Wood and Worked Bone Finds from the 1926 Expedition'. In *Montfort*. Ed. Adrian Boas. Leiden: Brill, 2017, pp. 195–220.
Boas, Adrian J. and Rabei G. Khamisy. 'Initial Thoughts on the Architectural Development of the Castle. In *Montfort*. Ed. Adrian Boas. Leiden: Brill, 2017, pp. 95–101.
Boase, T.S.R. *Kingdoms and Strongholds of the Crusaders*. London: Thames & Hudson, 1971.
Boase, T.S.R. 'Military Architecture in the Crusader States in Palestine'. In *A History of the Crusades. Vol. 4: The Art and Architecture of the Crusader States*. Ed. Harry W. Hazard. Gen. ed. Kenneth M. Setton. Madison: University of Wisconsin Press, 1977, pp. 140–64.
Bonaparte, Louis-Napoléon. *Études sur le passé et l'avenir de l'artillerie*. 6 vols. Paris: Libraire Militaire de J. Dumaine, 1848–71.
Bosworth, C. Edmund. 'The City of Tarsus and the Arab-Byzantine Frontiers in Early and Middle 'Abbāsid Times'. *Oriens* 33 (1992), pp. 268–86.
Bradbury, Jim. *The Medieval Siege*. Woodbridge: Boydell, 1992.
Braune, Michael. 'Die Stadtbefestigung von Damaskus'. In *Burgen und Städte der Kreuzzugszeit*. Ed. Mathias Piana. Petersburg: Michael Imhof Verlag, 2008, pp. 202–10.
Brown, Robin M. 'Excavations in the 14th Century A.D. Mamluk Palace at Kerak'. *Annual of the Department of Antiquities of Jordan* 33 (1989), pp. 287–304.
Brown, Robin M. 'Summary Report of the 1986 Excavations: Late Islamic Shobak'. *Annual of the Department of Antiquities of Jordan* 32 (1988), pp. 225–46.

Buck, Andrew D. *The Principality of Antioch and its Frontiers in the Twelfth Century*. Woodbridge: Boydell, 2017.

Bylinski, Janusz. 'Exploratory Mission to Shumaymis'. In *Muslim Military Architecture in Greater Syria: From the Coming of Islam to the Ottoman Period*. Ed. Hugh Kennedy. Leiden: Brill, 2006, pp. 243–50.

Bylinski, Janusz 'Three Minor Fortresses in the realm of Ayyubid rulers of Homs in Syria: Shumaimis, Tadmur (Palmyra) and al-Rahba'. In *La fortification au temps des croisades*. Ed. Nicolas Faucherre, Jean Mesqui and Nicolas Prouteau. Rennes: Presses Universitaires des Rennes, 2004, pp. 151–64.

Cahen, Claude. *La Syrie du nord à l'époque des croisades et la principauté franque d'Antioche*. Paris: Geuthner, 1940.

Cahen, Claude. 'Un traité d'armurerie composé pour Saladin'. *Bulletin d'Etudes Orientales* 12 (1947–48), pp. 103–63.

Carver, M.O.H. 'Transition to Islam: Urban Roles in the East and South Mediterranean, Fifth to Tenth Centuries AD'. In *Towns in Transition: Urban Evolution in Late Antiquity and the Early Middle Ages*. Ed. N. Christie and S.T. Loseby. Aldershot: Scolar Press, 1996, pp. 184–212.

Cassas, Louis François, ed. *Voyage pittoresque de la Syrie, de la Phoenicie, de la Palaestine et de la Basse Aegypte*. 3 vols. Paris: Imprimerie de la République, 1800.

Chaaya, Anis. 'Results of the First Season of Excavations at the Medieval Castle of Gbail/Byblos'. In *Proceedings of the 10th International Congress on the Archaeology of the Ancient Near East*. Ed. Barbara Horejs et al. Vol. 2. Wiesbaden: Harrassowitz Verlag, 2018, pp. 475–84.

Chevedden, Paul E. 'Artillery in Late Antiquity: Prelude to the Middle Ages'. In *The Medieval City Under Siege*. Ed. Ivy A. Corfis and Michael Wolfe. Woodbridge: Boydell, 1995, pp. 131–73.

Chevedden, Paul E. 'Artillery of King James I'. In *Iberia and the Mediterranean World of the Middle Ages*. Ed. Larry J. Simon et al. Vol. 2. Leiden: Brill, 1996, pp. 47–94.

Chevedden, Paul E. 'Black Camels and Blazing Bolts: The Bolt-Projecting Trebuchet in the Mamluk Army'. *Mamlūk Studies Review* 8.1 (2004), pp. 227–77.

Chevedden, Paul E. 'Fortifications and the Development of Defensive Planning in the Latin East'. In *The Circle of War in the Middle Ages*. Ed. Donald J. Kagay and L.J. Andrew Villalon. Woodbridge: Boydell, 1999 pp. 33–43.

Chevedden, Paul E. 'The Hybrid Trebuchet: The Halfway Step to the Counterweight Trebuchet'. In *On the Social Origins of Medieval Institutions*. Ed. Donald J. Kagay and Teresa M. Vann. Leiden: Brill, 1998, pp. 179–222.

Chevedden, Paul E. 'The Invention of the Counterweight Trebuchet: A Study in Cultural Diffusion'. *Dumbarton Oaks Papers* 54 (2000), pp. 71–116.

Chevedden, Paul E., et al. 'The Traction Trebuchet: A Triumph of Four Civilizations'. *Viator* 31 (2000), pp. 433–86.

Chevedden, Paul E., et al. 'The Trebuchet: Recent Reconstructions and Computer Simulations Reveal the Operating Principles of the Most Powerful Weapon of its Time'. *Scientific American* 273.1 (July 1995), pp. 66–71.

Christie, Niall. 'Ibn al-Qalānisī'. In *Medieval Muslim Historians and the Franks of the Levant*. Ed. Alex Mallet. Leiden: Brill, 2015, pp. 7–28.

Clermont-Ganneau, Charles. *Archaeological Researches in Palestine During the Years 1873–1874*. Trans. (Eng.) Aubrey Stewart. Vol. 1. London, Published for the Palestine Exploration Fund, 1899.

Cohen, Michael. 'The Fortification of the Fortress of Gybelin'. In *La fortification au temps des croisades*. Ed. Nicolas Faucherre, Jean Mesqui and Nicolas Prouteau. Rennes: Presses Universitaires des Rennes, 2004, pp. 67–75.

Coldstream, Nicola. 'Architects, Advisers and Design at Edward I's Castles in Wales'. *Architectural History* 46 (2003), pp. 19–36.

Conder, C.R. and H.H. Kitchener. *The Survey of Western Palestine: Memoirs of the Topography, Orography, Hydrography, and Archaeology*. Ed. E.H. Palmer and Walter Besant. 3 vols. London: The Committee of the Palestine Exploration Fund, 1881–83.

Contamine, Philippe. *La Guerre au moyen âge*. Paris: Presses Universitaires de France, 1980. Trans. (Eng.) Michael Jones as *War in the Middle Ages*. Oxford: Basil Blackwell, 1984.

Cooper, John P. '"Fear God; Fear the *Bogaze*": The Nile Mouths and the Navigational Landscapes of the Medieval Nile Delta, Egypt'. *Al-Masaq* 24.1 (2012), pp. 53–73.
Corvisier, Christian. 'Les campagnes de construction du château de Beaufort (Qala'at as-Sharqif): une relecture'. In *La fortification au temps des croisades*. Ed. Nicolas Faucherre, Jean Mesqui and Nicolas Prouteau. Rennes: Presses Universitaires des Rennes, 2004, pp. 243–66.
Creswell, K.A.C. 'Fortification in Islam Before A.D. 1250'. *Proceedings of the British Academy*. (1952), pp. 89–125.
Creswell, K.A.C. *The Muslim Architecture of Egypt*. 2 vols. Oxford: Oxford University Press, 1952–59, reprinted New York: Hacker Art Books, 1978.
Dangles, Philippe. 'La refortification d'Afamiyya – Qal'at al-Mudiq sous le sultanat ayyoubide d'Alep (fin XIIe-mi XIIIe siècle)'. In *La fortification au temps des croisades*. Ed. Nicolas Faucherre, Jean Mesqui and Nicolas Prouteau. Rennes: Presses Universitaires des Rennes, 2004, pp. 189–204.
De Meulemeester, Johnny and Denys Pringle. 'Al-'Aqaba Castle, Jordan'. *Château Gaillard* 22 (2006), pp. 97–102.
Dean, Bashford. 'The Exploration of a Crusaders' Fortress (Montfort) in Palestine'. *The Metropolitan Museum of Art Bulletin* 22.9 (September 1927), pp. 5–46.
Dennis, George. 'Byzantine Heavy Artillery: The Helepolis'. *Greek, Roman, and Byzantine Studies* 39 (1998), pp. 99–115.
Deschamps, Paul. *Les Châteaux des Croisés en Terre-Sainte*. 3 vols. Bibliothèque Archéologique et historique 19, 34, 90; (1) *Le Crac des Chevaliers*. Paris: Geuthner, 1934; (2) *La Défense du royaume de Jérusalem*. Paris: Geuthner, 1939; (3) *La Défense du comté de Tripoli et de la Principauté d'Antioche*. Paris: Geuthner, 1973.
Description de l'Égypte. 2nd ed. 37 vols. Paris: C.L.F. Panckoucke, 1821–26.
D'Souza, Andreas. 'The Conquest of 'Akka (690/1291): A Comparative Analysis of Christian and Muslim Sources'. *The Muslim World* 80 (1990), pp. 234–50.
DeVries, Kelly and Robert Douglas Smith. *Medieval Military Technology*. 2nd ed. Toronto: University of Toronto Press, 2012.
Dotti, Francesca. Qal'at Al-Shawbak: An Interpretation on the Basis of the Epigraphic Data. In *ICAANE: Proceedings of the 6th International Congress of the Archaeology of the Ancient Near East*. Vol. 3. Ed. Paolo Matthiae et al. Wiesbaden: Harrassowitz Verlag, 2010, pp. 23–36.
Edbury, Peter W. '*Ernoul*, *Eracles* and the Fifth Crusade'. In *The Fifth Crusade in Context: The Crusading Movement in the Early Thirteenth Century*. Ed. E.J. Mylod et al. Abingdon: Routledge, 2017, pp. 163–74.
Edbury, Peter W. 'The French Translation of William of Tyre's *Historia*: the Manuscript Tradition'. *Crusades* 6 (2007), pp. 69–105.
Edbury, Peter W. *The Kingdom of Cyprus and the Crusades, 1191–1374*. Cambridge: Cambridge University Press, 1991.
Edbury, Peter W. 'Making Sense of the *Annales de Terre Sainte*: Thirteenth-century Vernacular Narratives from the Latin East'. In *Crusader Landscapes in the Medieval Levant: The Archaeology and History of the Latin East*. Ed. Micaela Sinibaldi et al. Cardiff: University of Wales Press, 2016, pp. 403–13.
Eddé, Anne-Marie. 'Kamāl al-Dīn 'Umar Ibn al-'Adīm'. In *Medieval Muslim Historians and the Franks of the Levant*. Ed. Alex Mallet. Leiden: Brill, 2015, pp. 109–35.
Eddé, Anne-Marie. *Saladin*. Paris: Flammarion, 2008. Trans. (Eng.) Jane Marie Todd. *Saladin*. Cambridge: Harvard University Press, 2011.
Edwards, Robert W. *The Fortifications of Armenian Cilicia*. Washington: Dumbarton Oaks Research Library & Collection, 1987.
Elisséeff, Nikita. *Nūr ad-Dīn: Un grand prince musulman de Syrie au temps des Croisades (511–569 h./ 1118–1174)*. 3 vols. Damascus: Institut français de Damas, 1967.
Ellenblum, Ronnie. *Crusader Castles and Modern Histories*. Cambridge: Cambridge University Press, 2007.
Ellenblum, Ronnie. *Frankish Rural Settlement in the Latin Kingdom of Jerusalem*. Cambridge: Cambridge University Press, 1998.
Ellenblum, Ronnie. 'Who Built Qal'at al-Ṣubayba?' *Dumbarton Oaks Papers* 43 (1989), pp. 103–12.
Ellenblum, Ronnie, et al. 'Crusader Castle Torn Apart by Earthquake at Dawn, 20 May 1202'. *Geology* 26.4 (April 1998), pp. 303–6.

Ewart, Gordon and Denys Pringle. 'Dundonald Castle Excavations 1986–93'. *Scottish Archaeological Journal* 26.1–2 (2004).
Faucherre, Nicolas, et al. [*Caesarea, 2007*] *Mission archéologique a Césarée*. Ministère des Affaires Etrangères Français, 2007.
Faucherre, Nicolas, et al. [*Caesarea, 2008*] *Césarée: Fortifications Médiévales*. Ministère des Affaires Etrangères Français, 2008.
Faucherre, Nicolas, et al. [*Caesarea, 2009*] *Caesarea Maritima: Fortifications Médiévales*. Ministère des Affaires Etrangères Français, 2009.
Faucherre, Nicolas, et al. [*Caesarea, 2010*] *Caesarea Maritima: Fortifications Médiévales*. Ministère des Affaires Etrangères Français, 2010.
Faucherre, Nicolas. 'La forteresse de Shawbak (Crac de Montréal), une des premières forteresses Franques sous son corset mamelouk'. In *La fortification au temps des croisades*. Ed. Nicolas Faucherre, Jean Mesqui and Nicolas Prouteau. Rennes: Presses Universitaires des Rennes, 2004, pp. 43–66.
Fedden, Robin and John Thomson. *Crusader Castles*. London: John Murray Publishers, 1957.
Fournet, Thibaud and Jean-Claude Voisin. 'Le Château de Aakkar al-Aatiqa (Nord-Liban)'. *Bulletin d'archéologie et d'architecture libanaises* 4 (2000), pp. 149–63.
France, John. *The Crusades and the Expansion of Catholic Christendom, 1000–1714*. Abingdon: Routledge, 2005.
France, John. 'Fortifications East and West'. In *Muslim Military Architecture in Greater Syria: From the Coming of Islam to the Ottoman Period*. Ed. Hugh Kennedy. Leiden: Brill, 2006, pp. 281–94.
France, John. *Hattin*. Oxford: Oxford University Press, 2015.
France, John. 'Technology and the Success of the First Crusade'. In *War and Society in the Eastern Mediterranean, 7th–15th Centuries*. Ed. Yaacov Lev. Leiden: Brill, 1997, pp. 163–76.
France, John. *Victory in the East: a Military History of the First Crusade*. Cambridge: Cambridge University Press, 1994.
France, John. *Western Warfare in the Age of the Crusades, 1000–1300*. Ithaca: Cornell University Press, 1999.
Freeman, A. Z. 'Wall-Breakers and River-Bridgers: Military Engineers in the Scottish Wars of Edward I'. *Journal of British Studies* 10.2 (May, 1971), pp. 1–16.
Friedman, Yvonne. 'Peacemaking: Perceptions and practices in the medieval Latin East'. In *The Crusades and the Near East*. Ed. Conor Kostick. Abingdon: Routledge, 2011, pp. 229–57.
Fulton, Michael S. 'Anglo-Norman Artillery in Narrative Histories, from the Reign of William I to the Minority of Henry III'. *Journal of Medieval Military History* 14 (2016), pp. 1–31.
Fulton, Michael S. *Artillery in the Era of the Crusades: Siege Warfare and the Development of Trebuchet Technology*. Leiden: Brill, 2018.
Fulton, Michael S. 'Development of Prefabricated Artillery during the Crusades'. *Journal of Medieval Military History* 13 (2015), pp. 51–72.
Fulton, Michael S. 'Diffusion of Artillery Terminology'. *SHARE* 3.1 (2016), pp. 1–27.
Fulton, Michael S. 'The Myth of the Hybrid Trebuchet'. *Viator* 48.2 (2017), pp. 49–70.
Fulton, Michael S. 'A Ridge Too Far: The Siege of Saone/Sahyun in 1188 and Contemporary Trebuchet Technology'. *Crusades* 16 (2017), pp. 33–53.
Gelichi, Sauro. 'Die Burg Ḥārim'. In *Burgen und Städte der Kreuzzugszeit*. Ed. Mathias Piana. Petersburg: Michael Imhof Verlag, 2008, pp. 211–20.
Gelichi, Sauro. 'The Citadel of Ḥārim'. In *Muslim Military Architecture in Greater Syria: From the Coming of Islam to the Ottoman Period*. Ed. Hugh Kennedy. Leiden: Brill, 2006, pp. 184–200.
Genequand, Denis. 'From "desert castle" to medieval town: Qasr al-Hayr al-Sharqi (Syria)'. *Antiquity* 79 (2005), pp. 350–61.
Genequand, Denis. 'Umayyad Castles: The Shift from late Antique Military Architecture to early Islamic Palatial Building'. In *Muslim Military Architecture in Greater Syria: From the Coming of Islam to the Ottoman Period*. Ed. Hugh Kennedy. Leiden: Brill, 2006, pp. 3–25.
Gillmor, Carroll. 'The Introduction of the Traction Trebuchet into the Latin West'. *Viator* 12 (1981), pp. 1–8.

Gonnella, Julia. 'The Citadel of Aleppo: Recent studies'. In *Muslim Military Architecture in Greater Syria: From the Coming of Islam to the Ottoman Period*. Ed. Hugh Kennedy. Leiden: Brill, 2006, pp. 165–75.

Guérin, M. V. *Description géographique, historique et archéologique de la Palestine*. 3 vols. (in 7 parts). Paris: Imprimerie Impériale/Nationale, 1868–80.

Guo, Li. 'Mamluk Historiographic Studies: The State of the Art'. *Mamlūk Studies Review* 1 (1997), pp. 15–43.

Haarmann, Ulrich. 'L'édition de la chronique mamelouke syrienne de Šams ad-Dīn Muḥammad al-Ǧazarī'. *Bulletin d'études orientales* 27 (1974), pp. 195–203.

Hamblin, William. *The Fatimid Army During the Early Crusades*. University of Michigan, unpublished PhD thesis, 1985.

Hamblin, William. 'The Fatimid Navy During the Early Crusades: 1099–1224'. *The American Neptune* 46 (1986), pp. 77–83.

Hamilton, Bernard. 'The Elephant of Christ: Reynald of Châtillon'. *Studies in Church History*, 15 (1978), pp. 97–108.

Hamilton, Bernard. *The Leper King and His Heirs: Baldwin IV and the Crusader Kingdom of Jerusalem*. Cambridge: Cambridge University Press, 2000.

Hanisch, Hanspeter. 'Der Langturm als neuer Turmtypus im aiyūbidischen Wehrbau, dargestellt an einem Linienturm der Zitadelle von Damaskus'. In *Egypt and Syria in the Fatimid, Ayyubid and Mamluk Eras V*. Ed. U. Vermeulen and K. D'Hulster. Leuven: Peeters, 2007, pp. 183–234.

Hanisch, Hanspeter. 'The works of al-Malik al-'Adil in the Citadel of Harrân'. In *La fortification au temps des croisades*. Ed. Nicolas Faucherre, Jean Mesqui and Nicolas Prouteau. Rennes: Presses Universitaires des Rennes, 2004, pp. 165–78.

Hanisch, Hanspeter. 'Die Zitadelle von Damaskus, 14/635 – 1410/1995'. In *Egypt and Syria in the Fatimid, Ayyubid and Mamluk Eras V*. Ed. U. Vermeulen and K. D'Hulster. Leuven: Peeters, 2007, pp. 235–305.

Harper, Richard P. and Denys Pringle. *Belmont Castle: The Excavation of a Crusader Stronghold in the Kingdom of Jerusalem*. Oxford: Oxford University Press, 2000.

Hartal, Moshe. 'Banyas, the Southwestern Tower'. *Hadashot Arkheologiyot* 119 (2007), 16/4/2007.

Hartal, Moshe. *The al-Ṣubayba (Nimrod) Fortress: Towers 11 and 9*. IAA Reports 11. Jerusalem: Israel Antiquities Authority, 2001.

Hartmann-Virnich, Andreas. 'Les portes ayyoubides de la citadelle de Damas: le regard de l'archéologie du bâti'. In *La fortification au temps des croisades*. Ed. Nicolas Faucherre, Jean Mesqui and Nicolas Prouteau. Rennes: Presses Universitaires des Rennes, 2004, pp. 287–311.

Hawari, Mahmoud K. *Ayyubid Jerusalem (1187–1250): An Architectural and Archaeological Study*. Oxford: British Archaeological Reports, 2007.

Heidemann, Stefan. 'The Citadel of al-Raqqa and Fortifications in the Middle Euphrates Area'. In *Muslim Military Architecture in Greater Syria: From the Coming of Islam to the Ottoman Period*. Ed. Hugh Kennedy. Leiden: Brill, 2006, pp. 122–50.

Hill, Donald. 'Trebuchets'. *Viator* 4 (1973), pp. 99–114.

Hillenbrand, Carole. *The Crusades: Islamic Perspectives*. Edinburgh: Edinburgh University Press, 1999.

Hillenbrand, Carole. *A Muslim Principality in Crusader Times*. Istanbul: Nederlands Historisch-Archaeologisch Instituut, 1990.

Hinz, Walther. *Islamische Masse und Gewichte*. Trans. (Eng.) M. Ismail Marcinkowski as *Measures and Weights in the Islamic World*. Kuala Lumpur: International Islamic University of Malaysia, 2003.

Hirschler, Konrad. 'Ibn Wāṣil: An Ayyūbid Perspective on Frankish Lordships and Crusades'. In *Medieval Muslim Historians and the Franks of the Levant*. Ed. Alex Mallet. Leiden: Brill, 2015, pp. 136–60.

Hirschler, Konrad. *Medieval Arabic Historiography: Authors as actors*. London: Routledge, 2006.

Holmes, Urban Tignor. 'Life among the Europeans in Palestine and Syria in the Twelfth and Thirteenth Centuries'. In *A History of the Crusades. Vol. 4: The Art and Architecture of the Crusader States*. Ed. Harry W. Hazard. Gen. ed. Kenneth M. Setton. Madison: University of Wisconsin Press, 1977, pp. 3–35.

Holt, P.M. 'Baybars's Treaty with the Lady of Beirut in 667/1269'. In *Crusade and Settlement*. Ed. Peter W. Edbury. Cardiff: University of Cardiff Press, 1985, pp. 243–5.

Holt, P.M. 'Qalāwūn's Treaty with Acre in 1283'. *English Historical Review* 91 (1976), pp. 802–12.
Humphreys, R. Stephen. *From Saladin to the Mongols: The Ayyubids of Damascus, 1193–1260*. Albany: State University of New York Press, 1977.
Huuri, Kalervo. *Zur Geschichte des mittelalterlichen Geschützwesens aus orientalischen Quellen*. Studia Orientalia 9.3. Helsinki: Druckerei A.G. der Finnischen Literaturgesellschaft, 1941.
Huygens, R.B.C. 'Un nouveau texte du traité "De constructione castri Saphet"'. *Studi medievali* 3.6 (1965), pp. 355–87.
Irwin, Robert. 'The Mamluk Conquest of the County of Tripoli'. In *Crusade and Settlement*. Ed. Peter W. Edbury. Cardiff: University College Cardiff Press, 1985, pp. 246–50.
Irwin, Robert. *The Middle East in the Middle Ages: The Early Mamluk Sultanate 1250–1382*. Beckenham: Croom Helm, 1986.
Irwin, Robert. 'Usamah ibn Munqidh: An Arab-Syrian Gentleman at the Time of the Crusades Reconsidered'. In *The Crusades and Their Sources: Essays Presented to Bernard Hamilton*. Ed. John France and William Zajac. Aldershot: Ashgate, 1998, pp. 71–87.
Jackson, Peter. 'Crisis in the Holy Land in 1260'. *English Historical Review* 95.376 (July 1980), pp. 481–513.
Jacoby, David. 'Crusader Acre in the Thirteenth Century: Urban Layout and Topography'. *Studi medievali* 3.20 (1979), pp. 1–45.
Jacoby, David. 'Montmusard, Suburb of Acre: The First Stage of its Development'. In *Outremer: Studies in the History of the Crusading Kingdom of Jerusalem*. Ed. B.Z. Kedar, et al. Jerusalem: Izhak Ben-Zvi Institute, 1982, pp. 205–17.
Jacoby, David. 'Three Notes on Crusader Acre'. *Zeitschrift des Deutchen Palästina-Vereins* 109.1 (1993), pp. 83–96.
Johns, C.N. 'The Citadel, Jerusalem: A Summary of Work since 1934'. *Quarterly of the Department of Antiquities in Palestine* 14 (1950), pp. 121–90.
Johns, C.N. *Guide to 'Atlit: The Crusader Castle, Town and Surroundings*. Jerusalem: Government of Palestine, Department of Antiquities, 1947, reprinted in *Pilgrims' Castle ('Atlit), David's Tower (Jerusalem) and Qal'at ar-Rabad ('Ajlun): Three Middle Eastern Castles from the Time of the Crusades*. Ed. Denys Pringle. Aldershot: Ashgate, 1997.
Johns, C.N. 'Medieval 'Ajlun'. *Quarterly of the Department of Antiquities in Palestine* 1 (1931), pp. 21–33.
Kalayan, Haroutune. 'The Sea Castle of Sidon'. *Bulletin du Musée de Beyrouth* 26 (1973), pp. 81–90.
Kedar, Benjamin Z. 'The Battle of Hattin Revisited'. In *The Horns of Hattin*. Ed. Benjamin Kedar. (Jerusalem: Yad Izhak Ben-Zvi, 1992), pp. 190–207.
Kedar, Benjamin Z. 'The Outer Walls of Frankish Acre'. *'Atiqot* 31 (1997), pp. 157–80.
Kennedy, Hugh. *Crusader Castles*. Cambridge: Cambridge University Press, 1994.
Khamisy, Rabei G. 'Some Notes on Ayyubid and Mamluk Military Terms'. *Journal of Medieval Military History* 13 (2015), pp. 73–92.
Khamisy, Rabei G. 'The Treaty of 1283 between Sultan Qalāwūn and the Frankish Authorities of Acre: A New Topographical Discussion'. *Israel Excavation Journal* 64.1 (2014), pp. 72–102.
Khamisy, Rabei G. and Michael S. Fulton, 'Manjaniq Qarabugha and Thirteenth-Century Trebuchet Nomenclature'. *Studia Islamica* 111.2 (2016), pp. 179–201.
Khowaiter, Abdul-Aziz. *Baibars the First: His Endeavours and Achievements*. London: Green Mountain Press, 1978.
King, D.J. Cathcart. 'The Taking of Le Krak des Chevaliers in 1271'. *Antiquity* 23.90 (June 1949), pp. 83–92.
King, D.J. Cathcart. 'The Trebuchet and other Siege-Engines'. *Château Gaillard* 9–10 (1982), pp. 457–69.
Köhler, G. *Die Entwickelung des Kriegswesens und der Kriegführung in der Ritterzeit von Mitte des II. Jahrhunderts bis zu den Hussitenkriegen*. 3 vols. Breslau: Wilhelm Koebner, 1887–89.
Lawrence, A.W. 'The Castle of Baghras'. In *The Cilician Kingdom of Armenia*. Ed. T.S.R. Boase. Edinburgh: Scottish Academic Press, 1978, pp. 34–83.
Lawrence, A.W. 'A Skeletal History of Byzantine Fortification'. *The Annual of the British School at Athens* 78 (1983), pp. 171–227.

Lawrence, T.E. *Crusader Castles*. London: Golden Cockerel Press, 1936. Ed. Denys Pringle. *Crusader Castles*. Oxford: Oxford University Press, 1988.

Le Strange, Guy. *Palestine under the Muslims: A Description of Syria and the Holy Land from A.D. 650 to 1500*. Boston: Houghton, Mifflin & Company, 1890.

Leiser, Gary La Viere. 'The Crusader Raid in the Red Sea in 578/1182–83'. *Journal of the American Research Centre in Egypt* 14 (1977), pp. 87–100.

Lev, Yaacov. *Saladin in Egypt*. Leiden: Brill, 1999.

Lewis, Kevin James. *The Counts of Tripoli and Lebanon in the Twelfth Century: Sons of Saint-Gilles*. Abingdon: Routledge, 2017.

Little, Donald P. 'The Fall of 'Akkā in 690/1291: The Muslim Version'. In *Studies in Islamic History and Civilization in Honour of Professor David Ayalon*. Ed. M. Sharon. Jerusalem: Cana, 1986, pp. 159–81.

Little, Donald P. 'Historiography of the Ayyūbid and Mamlūk epochs'. In *The Cambridge History of Egypt, Volume 1: Islamic Egypt, 640–1517*. Ed. Carl F. Petry. Cambridge: Cambridge University Press, 1998, pp. 412–44.

Little, Donald P. *An Introduction to Mamlūk Historiography: An Analysis of Arabic Annalistic and Biographical Sources for the Reign of al-Malik an-Nāṣir Muḥammad ibn Qalā'ūn*. Montreal: McGill-Queen's University Press, 1970.

Lloyd, Seton and William Brice. 'Harran'. *Anatolian Studies* 1 (1951), pp. 77–111.

Lot, F. *L'art militaire et les armées au moyen age en Europe et dans le Proche Orient*. Vol. 1. Paris: Payot, 1946.

Lyons, Malcolm C. and D.E.P. Jackson. *Saladin: The Politics of the Holy War*. Cambridge: Cambridge University Press, 1982.

Maalouf, Amin. *Les croisades vues par les Arabes*. Paris: Jean-Claude Lattès, 1983. Trans. (Eng.) Jon Rothschild as *The Crusades Through Arab Eyes*. London: Al Saqi Books, 1984.

McGeer, Eric. 'Byzantine Siege Warfare in Theory and Practice'. In *The Medieval City Under Siege*. Ed. Ivy A. Corfis and Michael Wolfe. Woodbridge: Boydell, 1995, pp. 123–9.

Major, Balázs and Edmond el-Ajji. 'Al-Marqab Research Project of the Syro-Hungarian Archaeological Mission (a brief report on the activities of 2009)'. *Chronique Archéologique en Syrie* 5 (2011), pp. 263–83.

Mallett, Alex. 'The battle of Inab'. *Journal of Medieval History* 39.1 (2013), pp. 48–60.

Mallett, Alex. 'Sibṭ Ibn al-Jawzī'. In *Medieval Muslim Historians and the Franks of the Levant*. Ed. Alex Mallett. Leiden: Brill, 2015, pp. 84–108.

Mallett, Alex. 'A trip down the Red Sea with Reynald of Châtillon'. *Journal of the Royal Asiatic Society of Great Britain & Ireland* 18.2 (2008), pp. 141–53.

Marino, Luigi, et al. 'The Crusader Settlement in Petra'. *Fortress* 7 (November 1990), pp. 3–13.

Marsden, E.W. *Greek and Roman Artillery: Historical Development*. Oxford: Oxford University Press, 1969.

Marsden, E.W. *Greek and Roman Artillery: Technical Treatises*. Oxford: Oxford University Press, 1971.

Marshall, Christopher. *Warfare in the Latin East, 1192–1291*. Cambridge: Cambridge University Press, 1992.

Mayer, Hans Eberhard. 'The Origins of the Lordships of Ramla and Lydda in the Latin Kingdom of Jerusalem'. *Speculum* 60.3 (July 1985), pp. 537–52.

Mayer, Hans Eberhard. 'Two Unpublished Letters on the Syrian Earthquake of 1202'. In *Medieval and Middle Eastern Studies in Honour of Aziz Suryal Atiya*. Ed. Sami A. Hanna. Leiden: Brill, 1972, pp. 295–310.

Mesqui, Jean. 'La 'barbacane' du Crac des Chevaliers (Syrie) et la signification du terme dans le bassin méditerranéen'. *Bulletin monumental* 176.3 (2018), pp. 215–34.

Mesqui, Jean. 'Bourzeÿ, une forteresse anonyme de l'Oronte'. In *La fortification au temps des croisades*. Ed. Nicolas Faucherre, Jean Mesqui and Nicolas Prouteau. Rennes: Presses Universitaires des Rennes, 2004, pp. 95–133.

Mesqui, Jean. 'L'enceinte médiévale de Césarée'. *Bulletin monumental* 164.1 (2006), pp. 83–94.

Mesqui, Jean and Nicolas Faucherre. 'La fortification des Croisés au temps de Saint Louis au Proche-Orient'. *Bulletin monumental* 164.1 (2006), pp. 5–29.

Michaudel, Benjamin. 'Burzaih'. In *Burgen und Städte der Kreuzzugszeit*. Ed. Mathias Piana. Petersburg: Michael Imhof Verlag, 2008, pp. 178–87.

Michaudel, Benjamin. 'The Development of Islamic Military Architecture during the Ayyubid and Mamluk Reconquest of Frankish Syria'. In *Muslim Military Architecture in Greater Syria: From the Coming of Islam to the Ottoman Period*. Ed. Hugh Kennedy. Leiden: Brill, 2006, pp. 106–21.

Michaudel, Benjamin. 'Les refortifications ayyoubides et mameloukes en Syrie du nord (fin XIIe–début XIVe siècle)'. In *La fortification au temps des croisades*. Ed. Nicolas Faucherre, Jean Mesqui and Nicolas Prouteau. Rennes: Presses Universitaires des Rennes, 2004, pp. 179–88.

Micheau, Françoise. 'Ibn al-Athīr'. In *Medieval Muslim Historians and the Franks of the Levant*. Ed. Alex Mallet. Leiden: Brill, 2015, pp. 52–83.

Milwright, Marcus. *The Fortress of the Raven: Karak in the Middle Islamic Period (1100–1650)*. Leiden: Brill, 2008.

Mokary, Abdalla and Moshe Hartal. 'Tiberias'. *Hadashot Arkheologiyot* 122 (2010), 17/11/2010.

Müller-Wiener, Wolfgang. *Burgen der Kreuzritter*. Munich, Deutscher Kunstverlag, 1966. Trans. (Eng.) J. Maxwell Brownjohn as *Castles of the Crusaders*. London: Thames & Hudson, 1966.

Needham, Joseph. 'China's Trebuchets, Manned and Counterweighted'. In *On Pre-Modern Technology and Science*. Ed. Bert S. Hall and Delno C. West. Malibu: Undena Publications, 1976, pp. 107–45.

Nicolle, David. *Arms and Armour in the Crusading Era, 1050–1350*. 2 vols. White Plains: Kraus International Publications, 1988.

Nicolle, David. 'The Early Trebuchet: Documentary and Archaeological Evidence'. In *La fortification au temps des croisades*. Ed. Nicolas Faucherre, Jean Mesqui and Nicolas Prouteau. Rennes: Presses Universitaires des Rennes, 2004, pp. 269–78.

Northrup, Linda S. *From Slave to Sultan: The Career of al-Manṣūr Qalāwūn and the Consolidation of Mamluk Rule in Egypt and Syria (678–689 A.H./1279–1290 A.D.)*. Stuttgart: Steiner, 1998.

Oman, Sir Charles William Chadwick. *A History of the Art of War: The Middle Ages from the Fourth to the Fourteenth Century*. London: Methuen, 1889.

Omran, Mahmud Said. 'King Amalric and the Siege of Alexandria, 1167'. In *Crusade and Settlement*. Ed. Peter W. Edbury. Cardiff: University of Cardiff Press, 1985, pp. 191–6.

Piana, Mathias. 'The Crusader Castle of Toron: First Results of its Investigation'. *Crusades* 5 (2006), pp. 173–91.

Piana, Mathias. 'Die Kreuzfahrerstadt Tortosa (Ṭarṭūs) in Syrien'. In *Burgen und Städte der Kreuzzugszeit*. Ed. Mathias Piana. Petersburg: Michael Imhof Verlag, 2008, pp. 408–21.

Piana, Mathias. 'Die Templerburg Chastel Blanc (Burǧ aṣ-Ṣāfītā)'. In *Burgen und Städte der Kreuzzugszeit*. Ed. Mathias Piana. Petersburg: Michael Imhof Verlag, 2008, pp. 293–301.

Powell, James M. *Anatomy of a Crusade, 1213–1221*. Philadelphia: University of Pennsylvania Press, 1986.

Prawer, Joshua. *The Crusaders' Kingdom: European Colonialism in the Middle Ages*. London: Phoenix Press, 1972.

Prawer, Joshua. 'The Jerusalem the Crusaders Captured: a Contribution to the Medieval Topography of the City'. In *Crusade and Settlement*. Ed. Peter W. Edbury. Cardiff: University of Cardiff Press, 1985, pp. 1–14.

Pringle, Denys. 'A Castle in the Sand: Mottes in the Crusader East'. *Château Gaillard* 18 (1998), pp. 187–91.

Pringle, Denys. 'The Castle of Ayla (al-'Aqaba) in the Crusader, Ayyubid and Mamluk Periods'. In *Egypt and Syria in the Fatimid, Ayyubid and Mamluk Eras IV*. Ed. U. Vermeulen and J. Van Steenbergen. Leuven: Peeters, 2005, pp. 333–53, reprinted in Pringle, Denys. *Churches, Castles and Landscapes in the Frankish East*. Farnham: Ashgate, 2013.

Pringle, Denys. *The Churches of the Crusader Kingdom of Jerusalem*. 4 vols. Cambridge: Cambridge University Press, 1993–2009.

Pringle, Denys. 'Crusader Castles and Fortifications: The Armenian Connection'. In *La Méditerranée des Arméniens, XIIe–XVe siècle*. Ed. Claude Mutafian. Paris: Geuthner, 2014, pp. 353–72.

Pringle, Denys. 'Edward I, Castle-building and the Tower of the English in Acre'. In *A Fresh Approach: Essays Presented to Colin Platt in Celebration of his Eightieth Birthday, 11 November 2014*. Ed. Clair Donavan. Bristol: Trouser Press, 2014, pp. 48–56.

Pringle, Denys. 'Reconstructing the Castle of Safad'. *Palestine Exploration Quarterly* 117 (1985), pp. 139–49.

Pringle, Denys. *The Red Tower (al-Burj al-Ahmar): Settlement in the Plain of Sharon at the Time of the Crusaders and Mamluks, A.D. 1099–1516*. London: British School of Archaeology in Jerusalem, 1986.

Pringle, Denys. 'Richard I and the Walls of Ascalon'. *Palestine Exploration Quarterly* 116 (1984), pp. 133–47.

Pringle, Denys. *Secular Buildings in the Crusader Kingdom of Jerusalem: An Archaeological Gazetteer*. Cambridge: Cambridge University Press, 1997.

Pringle, Denys. 'Templar Castles between Jaffa and Jerusalem'. *The Military Orders 2: Welfare and Warfare*. Ed. Helen Nicholson. Aldershot: Ashgate, 1998, pp. 89–109.

Pringle, Denys. 'Templar Castles on the Road to the Jordan'. In *The Military Orders: Fighting for the Faith and Caring for the Sick*. Ed. Malcolm Barber. Aldershot: Ashgate, 1994, pp. 148–66.

Pringle, Denys. 'Towers in Crusader Palestine'. *Château Gaillard* 16 (1994), pp. 335–50.

Pringle, Denys. 'Town Defences in the Crusader Kingdom of Jerusalem'. In *The Medieval City Under Siege*. Ed. Ivy A. Corfis and Michael Wolfe. Woodbridge: Boydell, 1995, pp. 69–121.

Prouteau, Nicolas. '"Beneath the Battle?": Miners and Engineers as "Mercenaries" in the Holy Land (XII–XIII siècles)'. In *Mercenaries and Paid Men: The Mercenary Identity in the Middle Ages*. Ed. John France. Leiden: Brill, 2008, pp. 105–17.

Prutz, Hans. *Kulturgeschichte der Kreuzzuge*. Berlin: E.S. Mittler und Sohn, 1883.

Pryor, John and Michael Jeffreys. 'Alexios, Bohemond, and Byzantium's Euphrates Frontier: A Tale of Two Cretans'. *Crusades* 11 (2012), pp. 31–86.

Purton, Peter. *Early Medieval Siege c. 450–1200*. Woodbridge: Boydell, 2009.

Rabbat, Nasser. 'The Militarization of Taste in Medieval Bilād al-Shām'. In *Muslim Military Architecture in Greater Syria: From the Coming of Islam to the Ottoman Period*. Ed. Hugh Kennedy. Leiden: Brill, 2006, pp. 84–105.

Rabie, Hassanein. *The Financial System of Egypt: A.H. 564–741/A.D. 1169–1341*. London: Oxford University Press, 1972.

Raphael, Kate. 'Mighty Towers and Feeble Walls: Ayyubid and Mamluk Fortifications in the Late Twelfth and Early Thirteenth Centuries in the Light of the Decline of Crusader Siege Warfare'. *Crusades* 9 (2010), pp. 147–58.

Raphael, Kate. *Muslim Fortresses in the Levant: Between Crusaders and Mongols*. Abingdon: Routledge, 2011.

Raphael, Kate. 'A Thousand Arrowheads from the Crusader Fortress at Vadum Iacob'. In *In the Hill-Country, and in the Shephelah, and in the Arabah*. Ed. Shay Bar. Jerusalem: Ariel House, 2008, pp. 252–61.

Raphael, Kate and Yotam Tepper. 'The Archaeological Evidence from the Mamluk Siege of Arsuf'. *Mamlūk Studies Review* 9.1 (2005), pp. 85–100.

Rey, E.-G. *Les colonies Franques de Syrie aux XII*^{me} *et XIII*^{me} *siècles*. Paris: Alph. Picard, 1883.

Rey, E.-G. *Étude sur les monuments de l'architecture militaire des croisés en Syrie et dans l'île de Chypre*. Collection de documents inédits sur l'histoire de France. Paris: Imprimerie Nationale, 1871.

Richard, Jean. 'Les causes des victoires mongoles d'après les historiens occidentaux du XIIIe siècle'. *Central Asiatic Journal* 23 (1979), pp. 104–17.

Richard, Jean. *Le comté de Tripoli sous la dynastie Toulousaine (1102–1187)*. Paris: Geuthner, 1945.

Richard, Jean. *Le royaume latin de Jérusalem*. Paris: Presses Universitaires de France, 1953.

Richards, D. S. 'A Consideration of Two Sources for the Life of Saladin'. *Journal of Semitic Studies* 25.1 (1980), pp. 46–65.

Richter-Bernburg, Lutz. ''Imād al-Dīn al-Iṣfahānī'. In *Medieval Muslim Historians and the Franks of the Levant*. Ed. Alex Mallet. Leiden: Brill, 2015, pp. 29–51.

Riley-Smith, Jonathan. *The Crusades: A History*. 2nd ed. New Haven: Yale University Press, 2005.

Rogers, Randall. *Latin Siege Warfare in the Twelfth Century*. Oxford: Oxford University Press, 1992.

Roll, Israel and Oren. 'Introduction: History of the Site, Its Research and Excavations'. In *Apollonia-Arsuf: Final Report of the Excavations, Vol. I: The Persian and Hellenistic Periods*. Ed. Israel Roll and Oren Tal. Tel Aviv: Emery & Claire Yass Publications in Archaeology, 1999, pp. 1–62.

Runciman, Steven. *A History of the Crusades*. 3 vols. Cambridge: Cambridge University Press, 1951–54.

Saadé, Gabriel. 'Histoire du Château de Saladin'. *Studi Medievali* 3.9 (1968), pp. 980–1,016.

Salame-Sarkis, Hassan. 'Chronique archéologique du Liban-Nord'. *Bulletin de Musée de Beyrouth* 2 (1938), pp. 91–8.
Satō, Tsugitaka. *State and Rural Society in Medieval Islam: Sultans, Muqta' and Fallahun*. Leiden: Brill, 1997.
Sauvaget, Jean. 'La citadelle de Damas'. *Syria* 11 (1930), pp. 59–90.
Schneider, Rudolf. *Die Artillerie des Mittelalters*. Berlin: Weidmannsche Buchhandlung, 1910.
Smail, R.C. *Crusading Warfare (1097–1193)*. Cambridge: Cambridge University Press, 1956.
Smith, Caroline. *Crusading in the Age of Joinville*. Aldershot: Ashgate, 2006.
Stager, Lawrence and Douglas Esse. 'Ashkelon, 1985–1986'. *Israel Exploration Journal* 37 (1987), pp. 68–72.
Stepansky, Yosef. 'The Crusader Castle of Tiberias'. *Crusades* 3 (2004), pp. 179–81.
Stepansky, Yosef. 'Das kreuzfahrerzeitliche Tiberias Neue Erkenntnisse'. In *Burgen und Städte der Kreuzzugszeit*. Ed. Mathias Piana. Petersburg: Michael Imhof Verlag, 2008, pp. 384–95.
Stewart, Angus. 'Qal'at al-Rūm / Hṙomgla / Rumkale and the Mamluk Siege of 691AH/1292CE'. In *Muslim Military Architecture in Greater Syria: From the Coming of Islam to the Ottoman Period*. Ed. Hugh Kennedy. Leiden: Brill, 2006, pp. 269–80.
Tabbaa, Yasser. 'Defending Ayyubid Aleppo: The fortifications of al-Ẓāhir Ghāzī (1186–1216)'. In *Muslim Military Architecture in Greater Syria: From the Coming of Islam to the Ottoman Period*. Ed. Hugh Kennedy. Leiden: Brill, 2006, pp. 176–83.
Tal, Oren. 'Apollonia-Arsuf, 2006 and 2009'. *Israel Exploration Journal* 60.1 (2010), pp. 107–14.
Tarver, W.T.S. 'The Traction Trebuchet: A Reconstruction of an Early Medieval Siege Engine'. *Technology and Culture* 36.1 (January 1995), pp. 136–67.
Thompson, A. Hamilton. *Military Architecture in England during the Middle Ages*. London: Oxford University Press, 1912.
Thorau, Peter. 'The Battle of 'Ayn Jālūt: a Re-examination'. In *Crusade and Settlement*. Ed. Peter W. Edbury. Cardiff: University of Cardiff Press, 1985, pp. 236–42.
Thorau, Peter. *Sultan Baibars I. von Ägypten: Ein Beitrag zur Geschichte des Vorderen Orients im 13. Jahrhundert*. Wiesbaden: Ludwig Reichert, 1987. Trans. (Eng.) P.M. Holt as *The Lion of Egypt: Sultan Baybars I & the Near East in the Thirteenth Century*. Harlow: Longman, 1992.
Tibble, Steve. *The Crusader Armies*. New Haven: Yale University Press, 2018.
Tibble, Steve. *Monarchy and Lordships in the Latin Kingdom of Jerusalem, 1099–1291*. Oxford: Oxford University Press, 1989.
Tonghini, Cristina. *Shayzar I: The Fortification of the Citadel*. Leiden: Brill, 2012.
Tsugitaka, Sato. *State and Rural Society in Medieval Islam: Sultans, Muqta's and Fallahun*. Leiden: Brill, 1997.
Vachon, Véronique. 'Les châteaux Ismâ'îliens du Djabal Bahrâ". In *La fortification au temps des croisades*. Ed. Nicolas Faucherre, Jean Mesqui and Nicolas Prouteau. Rennes: Presses Universitaires des Rennes, 2004, pp. 219–41.
Van Berchem, Max and Edmond Fatio. *Voyages en Syrie*. 2 vols. Cairo: L'institut français d'archéologie orientale, 1914–15.
Vannini, Guido and Cristina Tonghini. 'Medieval Petra. The stratigraphic evidence from recent archaeological excavations at al-Wu'ayra'. *Studies in the History and Archaeology of Jordan* 6 (1997), pp. 371–84.
Viollet-le-Duc, Eugene-Emmanuel. *Dictionnaire Raisonne de l'Architecture Française du XI au XVI Siècle*. 10 vols. Paris: Librairies-Imprimeries Réunies, 1860.
Whitcomb, Donald. 'The Walls of early Islamic Ayla: Defence or Symbol?' In *Muslim Military Architecture in Greater Syria: From the Coming of Islam to the Ottoman Period*. Ed. Hugh Kennedy. Leiden: Brill, 2006, pp. 61–74.
White, Lynn Jr. 'The Crusades and the Technological Thrust of the West'. In *War, Technology and Society in the Middle East*. Ed. V.J. Parry and M.E. Yapp. London: Oxford University Press, 1975, pp. 97–112.
White, Lynn Jr. *Medieval Technology and Social Change*. Oxford: Oxford University Press, 1962.
Yasmine, Jean. 'Die Burg Beaufort (Qal'at Šaqif 'Arnūn) – Neue Bauaufnahme, neue Erkenntnisse'. In *Burgen und Städte der Kreuzzugszeit*. Ed. Mathias Piana. Petersburg: Michael Imhof Verlag, 2008, pp. 274–84.

Yovitchitch, Cyril. 'Die aiyubidische Burg 'Ağlūn'. In *Burgen und Städte der Kreuzzugszeit*. Ed. Mathias Piana. Petersburg: Michael Imhof Verlag, 2008, pp. 118–25.

Yovitchitch, Cyril. 'Die Befestigung der Tore Aiyubidischer Burgen – Herausbildung eines Standards'. In *Burgen und Städte der Kreuzzugszeit*. Ed. Mathias Piana. Petersburg: Michael Imhof Verlag, 2008, pp. 110–17.

Yovitchitch, Cyril. 'Bosra: Eine Zitadelle des Fürstentums Damaskus'. In *Burgen und Städte der Kreuzzugszeit*. Ed. Mathias Piana. Petersburg: Michael Imhof Verlag, 2008, pp. 169–77.

Yovitchitch, Cyril. 'La citadelle de Bosra'. In *La fortification au temps des croisades*. Ed. Nicolas Faucherre, Jean Mesqui and Nicolas Prouteau. Rennes: Presses Universitaires des Rennes, 2004, pp. 205–17.

Yovitchitch, Cyril. *Forteresses du Proche-Orient: l'architecture militaire des Ayyoubides*. Paris: Presses de l'Université Paris-Sorbonne, 2011.

Yovitchitch, Cyril. 'The Tower of Aybak in 'Ajlūn Castle: An example of the spread of an architectural concept in early 13th century Ayyubid fortification'. In *Muslim Military Architecture in Greater Syria: From the Coming of Islam to the Ottoman Period*. Ed. Hugh Kennedy. Leiden: Brill, 2006, pp. 225–42.

Zimmer, John, Werner Meyer and Letizia Boscardin. *Krak des Chevaliers in Syrien: Archäologie und Bauforschung 2003 bis 2007*. Braubach: Europäisches Burgeninstitut, 2011.

Index

Alternative names: Cr. (Crusader/European); Arb. (Arabic); Tur. (Turkish); Arm. (Armenian); anc. (ancient); mod. (modern); alt. (alternatively)

Abū Qubays (Cr. Bochebeis) xix, 62, 66, 84
Acre (Arb. ʿAkkā) xx, 3, 5, 7, 9, 19, 21–2, 25, 27, 29, 32, 40, 45, 47, 48–9, 55, 59, 62, 63, 65, 68, 69, 80, 82, 84, 85, 86, 87, 95, 100, 111, 112, 117, 118, 123, 124, 129, 130–1, 135, 136, 137, 140, 142, 143, 149, 150, 154, 155, 160, 161, 163, 164–6, 169, 170, 171, 173, 177, 179, 181, 182, 183, 184, 185, 188, 204, 228, 253, 258, 263, 264, 271, 276, 278, 279, 281–5, 286, 287, 295, 298, 299, 308, Accursed Tower 48, 166, 253, 281, 284
Tower of the Flies 150, 204
Adana xviii 115, 155, 290
al-ʿĀdil Sayf al-Dīn, Ayyūbid sultan of Egypt and Damascus xiii, 22, 23, 50, 53, 54, 55, 56–8, 63, 84, 90, 100, 101, 102, 111, 176, 180, 182, 194, 195, 196, 203, 209, 228, 229, 238, 239, 246, 250, 277, 294, 295, 296, 300, 301
al-ʿĀdil Sayf al-Dīn (II), Ayyūbid sultan of Egypt and Damascus 180, 300
al-Afḍal ʿAlī, Ayyūbid sultan of Damascus 20, 22, 111, 176, 180, 295, 296, 301
al-Afḍal Kutayfāt, Fāṭimid vizier 4, 300
al-Afḍal Shāhinshāh, Fāṭimid vizier 4, 6, 14, 28, 258, 300
Afrabalā (see Forbelet)
al-Afram, ʿIzz al-Dīn Aybak, Mamlūk *amīr jāndār* 26, 102, 164, 167, 187–8, 282
ʿAjlūn xx, xxi, 26, 52–3, 54, 59, 64, 73, 84, 87, 88, 100, 103, 118, 194, 196, 199, 200, 204, 206, 210, 219, 220, 231, 250, 251, 297, 298, 308
ʿAkkā (see Acre)
ʿAkkār (Cr. Gibelacar) xix, xx, 27, 62, 76, 83, 84, 87, 116, 164, 200, 279, 298, 308
ʿAlāʾ al-Dīn Qubruṣ al-Manṣūrī, Mamlūk emir 103
ʿAlam al-Dīn, Mamlūk *nāʾib amīr jāndār* 164, 167
Alamūt 17
Aleppo xii, xiii, xvi, xviii, 3, 4, 6, 7, 8, 9, 10, 11, 15, 16–17, 18, 19, 22, 23–4, 25, 30, 31, 33, 37, 49, 50, 66, 68, 76, 80, 83, 85, 86, 90, 91, 92, 98–9, 102, 108, 109, 112, 113, 116–17, 119, 120, 121, 122, 123, 124, 132, 140, 169, 174, 180, 185, 217, 218, 237, 239, 252, 255, 270, 274, 275, 276, 278, 279, 289, 290, 293, 294, 295, 298, 301, 308
citadel of 24, 57, 206, 209, 219, 221, 238
Alexandretta 67
Alexandria xxiii, 7, 15, 32, 50, 55, 88, 99, 136, 147, 149, 163, 171, 173, 180, 214, 252, 253, 276, 292, 293
Alexius I Comnenus, Byzantine emperor 6–7, 8, 155
Alfonso I, king of Portugal 172
ʿAlī ibn Wafā, leader of the Assassins 113
Alice (of Brittany), countess of Blois 49
Alice of Jerusalem 90
Alp Arslān, Seljuk sultan 5, 6, 49, 145
Amalric, king of Jerusalem 15, 20, 21, 23, 31, 42, 54, 72, 90, 99, 115, 116, 125, 152, 186, 233, 255, 292, 293, 302
Amida (Arb. Āmid) xv, xvi, 7, 9, 176, 270, 290, 294, 297
Amorium (Arb. ʿAmmūriyya) 145, 159
Amuda xviii, 298
Anafa (see Nephin)
Anazarbus xviii, 290
Antioch xviii, 4, 5, 6, 7, 8, 9, 10, 11, 12, 13, 14, 16, 17, 19, 20, 21, 26, 27, 30, 33, 36, 37, 44, 58, 66, 76, 80, 106, 108, 109, 112, 113, 114, 115, 118, 120, 122, 123, 129, 134, 138, 155, 163, 168, 169, 172, 174, 175, 177, 181, 185, 186, 188, 255, 269, 274, 275, 276, 279, 286, 290, 298, 308
Lake of 102
principality of xi, 9, 10–11, 13–14, 17, 19–20, 21, 26–7, 29, 30, 39, 75–6, 80, 81, 82, 84, 90, 94, 97, 115, 119, 120, 121, 122, 123, 146, 173, 180, 186, 275, 302–3
patriarchate of 44, 82, 177, 186
battle of xi
Apamea (Arb. Qalʿat Muḍīq) 11, 16, 17, 18, 84, 113, 118, 185, 215, 218, 286, 287, 291, 295
Aqaba (anc. Ayla) xxii, 35, 36, 53, 54, 55, 73, 95, 122, 250, 292, 294
Arima (Arb. al-ʿUrayma) xix, 31, 62, 76, 85, 233, 291, 292, 293, 308
al-Arish 98
ʿArqa xix, xx, 7, 109, 117, 254, 274, 286, 287, 292
Arsūf (Cr. Arsur) xii, xxi, 26, 36, 44, 58, 68, 87, 93, 96, 102, 123, 147, 149, 161, 162, 164, 169, 173, 181, 200, 203, 204, 214, 228, 232, 249, 252, 254, 262, 279, 286, 298, 308
Arsur (see Arsūf)
Artāḥ xviii, 66, 106, 109, 113, 297

Artuq, Seljuk ruler of Jerusalem 6
family of (for individual members, see elsewhere) 6, 19, 107, 119, 176, 258, 301
Arwād (see Ruad)
Asad al-Dīn Shīrkūh (see Shīrkūh)
Ascalon (Arb. 'Asqalān) xxi, 7, 9, 11, 12, 14, 15, 21, 29, 30, 36, 40, 41, 45, 46, 55, 69, 70, 71, 72, 80, 86, 87, 88, 96, 97, 98, 101, 110, 119, 124, 130, 139, 147, 149, 163, 170, 173, 175, 181, 182, 183, 184, 214, 218–19, 230, 231, 274, 275, 276, 291, 294, 297, 308
battle of xi, 96, 112, 147
al-Ashraf Khalīl, Mamlūk sultan of Egypt and Syria 27, 131, 151, 164, 282, 283, 284, 285, 299, 300
al-Ashraf Mūsā, Ayyūbid ruler of Damascus 90, 180, 296, 301
al-Ashraf Mūsā, Ayyūbid ruler of Homs 24
'Asqalān (see Ascalon)
Assassins 17–18, 43, 52, 66, 84–5, 87, 89, 92, 102, 117, 123, 125, 178, 260
al-Athārib xvi, xviii, 11, 36, 66, 83, 95, 108, 112, 113, 121, 129, 132–3, 138, 185, 255, 287, 288, 289, 290
'Atlit (Cr. Castrum Peregrinorum) xii, xx, xxi, 14, 23, 45, 58, 62, 63, 65, 68, 85, 87, 91, 117, 118, 190, 194, 195, 199, 200, 203, 204, 209, 217, 232, 236, 237, 244–6, 248, 250, 252, 261, 262, 267, 281, 285, 296, 308
Atsiz ibn Uvaq, Seljuk ruler of Damascus 5–6, 7, 136
Aybak, al-Mu'izz al-Dīn, Mamlūk sultan of Egypt 25, 300
Aybak ibn 'Abdullah, 'Izz al-Dīn, Ayyūbid emir 55
Ayyūb, Najm al-Dīn, Zankid emir 50, 179
'Ayn Jālūt, spring of 67
battle of xi, 3, 24, 25, 32, 50, 112, 114, 246, 277, 278
'Ayntāb xvi, 122, 291
'Azāz xvi, xviii, 11, 16, 18, 106, 108, 117, 138, 140, 177, 180, 255, 274, 286, 288, 289, 291, 293
'Azīz al-Dawla Rayḥān al-'Azīzī, Ayyūbid emir 103
al-'Azīz 'Uthmān ibn al-'Ādil, Ayyūbid ruler of Ṣubayba 24, 54, 103, 296
al-'Azīz 'Uthmān ibn Saladin, Ayyūbid ruler of Egypt 22, 176, 295, 300

Baalbek xix, xx, 12, 15, 32, 50, 51, 64, 76, 83, 87, 88, 125, 155, 176, 179, 180, 183, 184, 214, 218, 240, 247, 250, 256, 287, 290, 291, 293, 296, 297, 298
Badr al-Dīn Ibrāhīm al-Hakkārī, Ayyūbid emir 50
Badr al-Jamālī, Fāṭimid vizier 4, 6, 37, 101
Baghdad 5, 18, 23, 30, 69, 98
Baghrās (Cr. Gaston) xviii, 62, 67, 76, 183, 184, 185, 217, 262, 295, 309
Bahrām, Fāṭimid vizier 4, 300
Bahrām, leader of the Assassins 17–18
al-Bakhrā' (anc. Avatha) 35, 36
Baktāsh ibn Tutush 30
Balak Ghāzī ibn Bahrām, Nūr al-Dawla, Artuqid ruler of Aleppo 17, 98, 106, 107, 110, 138, 147, 179, 255, 275, 288, 289, 301
Balāṭunūs xviii, xix, 10, 66, 185, 309
Balduk, ruler of Samosata 106
Baldwin I (of Boulogne), count of Edessa, king of Jerusalem 8, 9, 10, 11, 13, 28, 30, 40, 65, 68, 69, 73, 75, 77, 83, 84, 85, 94, 96, 105–6, 107, 119, 121, 124, 142, 254–5, 274, 286, 287, 288, 302, 303
Baldwin I, lord of Ramla 93
Baldwin II (of Le Bourcq), count of Edessa, king of Jerusalem 9, 10, 13, 14, 30, 31, 44, 59, 64, 73, 78, 89, 92, 93, 94, 98, 106, 107, 108, 110, 113, 114, 115, 120, 130, 140, 147, 177, 178, 179, 252, 255, 288, 289, 302, 303
Baldwin II, lord of Ramla 97
Baldwin III, king of Jerusalem 19, 20, 29, 41, 42, 72, 78, 90, 97, 108, 119, 147, 176, 274, 275, 291, 292, 302
Baldwin IV, king of Jerusalem 14, 21, 23, 29, 41, 48, 78, 97, 114, 117, 122, 123, 142, 293, 302
Baldwin V, king of Jerusalem 21, 120, 302
Baldwin of Ibelin, seneschal of Cyprus 297
Baldwin of Marash 76, 95
Balian of Arsur 44
Balian of Ibelin 44, 97
Balian of Ibelin (the Elder) 70
Balian of Ibelin, lord of Beirut 297
Bālis xv, xvi, xvii, 16, 67, 142, 181, 252, 255, 287, 288, 289
Bamburgh 168
Bānyās (Cr. Belinas) xx, 17, 18, 31, 40, 42, 43, 44, 45, 48, 54, 55, 58, 64, 69, 75, 78, 80, 82, 89, 90, 97, 103, 107–8, 110, 111, 114, 115, 116, 119, 125, 138, 139, 140, 148, 149, 152, 176, 180, 181, 184, 186, 213, 214, 233, 249, 252, 256, 270, 276, 289, 290, 291, 292, 293, 295, 309
al-Bāra xviii, xix, 289
Bari 145, 168
Ba'rīn (see Montferrand)
Barkyāruq, Seljuk sultan 17, 153
Barons' Crusade 25, 46, 98, 175
Barziyya (see Bourzey)
Baybars, al-Zahir Rukn al-Dīn, Mamlūk sultan of Egypt and Syria 18, 25–7, 32, 42, 59, 77, 80, 82, 84–5, 87–8, 91, 93, 101, 102, 103, 111, 117–18, 120, 123–4, 125, 130–1, 140, 142, 153, 154, 163–4, 167, 171–2, 177–8, 179, 186, 187, 235, 242, 243, 246, 248, 250, 254, 256, 279, 298, 299, 300
Baybars al-Manṣūrī, Mamlūk ruler of Kerak 282, 283
Baysān (Cr. Bethsan, anc. Scythopolis) xx, xxi, 40, 53, 64, 114, 190, 203–4, 232, 262, 309
Bayt Jibrīn (see Bethgibelin)
Beaufort (Arb. Shaqīf Arnūn) xii, xx, 21, 26, 32, 40, 42–4, 58, 75, 80, 87, 91, 102, 108, 117, 118,

125, 164, 175, 177, 180, 183, 184, 185, 193, 234, 240, 249, 261, 276, 279, 295, 297, 298, 309
Bedouins 5, 53, 98, 128
Beirut xix, xx, 7, 9, 12, 40, 45, 59, 63, 75, 82, 83, 95, 112, 117, 121, 123, 124–5, 140, 146, 149, 151, 154, 165, 170, 171, 173, 181, 183, 184, 202, 253, 254, 269, 282, 285, 287, 293, 294, 297, 309
Bektut, Mamlūk governor of Ṣubayba 103
Belen Pass (see Syrian Gates)
Belinas (see Bānyās)
Belmont (Arb. Suba) xxi, 86, 229
Belvoir (Arb. Kawkab) xii, xx, xxi, 14, 21, 45, 53, 59, 60, 75, 79, 86, 98, 180, 183, 184, 195, 196, 197, 199, 200, 204, 206, 217, 222, 224, 225, 228, 230, 231, 232–4, 236, 242, 250, 252, 259, 261, 262–3, 267, 294, 309
Benoit of Alignan, bishop of Marseilles 47
Bertrand (of Toulouse), count of Tripoli 13, 31, 69, 287, 303
Bertrand of Gibelet 130
Bethgibelin (Arb. Bayt Jibrīn) xxi, 45, 64, 70–1, 72, 230, 261, 263, 309
Bethlehem xxi, 72
Bethsan (see Baysān)
Bīlīk al-Khaznadār, Badr al-Dīn, Mamlūk ruler of Ṣubayba 101
Bilbays xxiii, 15, 53, 54, 115, 181, 292
al-Bīra xvi, 10, 26, 67, 106, 111, 154, 160, 254, 278, 288, 291, 293, 298, 299
Blanchegarde (Arb. Tell al-Ṣāfī) xxi, 60, 70–1, 72, 86
Bochebeis (see Abū Qubays)
Bohemond I (of Taranto), prince of Antioch 8, 10, 12, 75, 98, 114, 115, 153, 169, 172, 174, 175, 286, 289, 302
Bohemond II, prince of Antioch 20, 13, 90, 93–4, 130, 289, 302
Bohemond III, prince of Antioch 21, 109, 114, 115, 123, 185, 256, 293, 302
Bohemond IV, prince of Antioch and count of Tripoli 302, 304
Bohemond V, prince of Antioch and count of Tripoli 303
Bohemond VI, prince of Antioch and count of Tripoli 24, 32, 130, 163, 164, 186, 303
Bohemond VII, prince of Antioch and count of Tripoli 32, 63, 81, 303
Bosra (Arb. Buṣrā) xx, xxi, 15, 31, 38, 51, 53, 56, 63, 64, 78, 87, 88, 100, 118, 122, 180, 206, 214, 218, 228, 238, 251, 291, 297, 310
Bourzey (Arb. Barziyya) xviii, xix, 10, 37, 58, 62, 66, 154, 181, 183, 184, 185, 218, 231, 295, 310
Bréval 145
Buffavento xxiv, 295
al-Burj (Arb. Tantura) 242
Burj Bardawīl xxi, 261
Burj al-Ṣābi' (see Tour du Garçon)
Bursuq ibn Bursuq, ruler of Hamadan 19, 30, 124, 139, 140
al-Bursuqī, Āqsunqur, ruler of Mosul and Aleppo 18, 19, 32, 84, 85, 108–9, 140, 177, 301
Buṣrā (see Bosra)
Buzā'a xvi, 16, 89, 117, 181, 255, 279, 290, 293
Byblos (see Jubayl)

Caco (see Qāqūn)
Caesarea (Qaysāriyya) xii, xx, xxi, 25, 26, 36, 40, 45, 46, 47, 63, 65, 86, 87, 94, 95, 102, 120, 123, 147, 149, 153, 154, 160, 163–4, 167, 173, 181, 184, 199–200, 203, 204, 206, 207, 214, 216, 217, 218, 222, 223, 225, 228, 248, 250, 252, 267, 279, 286, 296, 298, 310
Cairo xxiii, 3, 9, 14–15, 20, 22, 23, 26, 31, 37, 48, 49, 54, 55, 74, 80, 88, 100, 111, 119, 151, 152, 209, 214, 217, 218, 237, 238, 250, 256, 281, 300, 310
  citadel of 15, 21, 56, 100, 103, 190, 237–8
Casel des Plains (Arb. Yāzūr) 45, 66, 67, 86
Castellum Arnaldi (Arb. Yalu) xxi, 66, 67, 69–70, 72, 86, 287, 310
Castellum Regis (alt. Castellum Novum) xx, 40, 41, 43, 60, 230, 261, 310
Castrum Album (see Ḥalba)
Castrum Peregrinorum (see 'Atlit)
Cava de Suet (see al-Ḥabis Jaldak)
Cave of Tyron xx, 43, 44, 176–7, 186, 290, 292, 298, 310
Chastel Blanc (Arb. Ṣāfīthā) xix, 66, 76, 194, 229, 232, 233, 261, 292, 310
Chastel Neuf (Arb. Hūnīn) xx, 40, 42, 43, 45, 59, 75, 85, 107, 116, 118, 123, 183, 200, 201, 233, 294, 310
Chastel Rouge (Arb. Yaḥmūr) xix, 76, 232, 310
Chastellet (see Jacob's Ford)
Château Gaillard 234, 259, 264, 266, 267
Chilvan Kale (see La Roche de Roussel)
Coliath (Arb. al-Qulay'āt) xix, xx, 76, 117, 230, 296, 310
Conrad I (of Montferrat), king of Jerusalem 21, 23, 44, 150, 185, 302
Conrad II (IV of Germany), king of Jerusalem 23, 302
Conrad III, king of Germany 130, 172
Conrad, archbishop of Mainz 201
Constance, princess of Antioch 90, 302
Constantine Coloman, Byzantine governor of Cilicia 109, 115
Constantinople 5, 7, 8, 12, 28, 153, 262
Courcy 145
Crac des Chevaliers (Arb. Ḥiṣn al-Akrād) xii, xiii, xix, 13, 14, 21, 27, 62, 65, 76, 79, 83, 87, 92, 101, 102, 116, 134, 140, 160, 164–5, 177, 184, 185, 193, 194, 195, 199, 206, 209, 212, 213, 214, 218, 219, 225, 227, 230–1, 232, 234, 235, 236, 240, 242, 246, 247, 250, 259, 261, 262, 266, 267, 268, 279, 282, 287, 288, 298, 311

Cresson, springs of 20, 121
Crusade of 1101 8, 10, 12, 68, 254
Cursat (Arb. al-Quṣayr) xviii, 44, 177, 186, 279, 299, 311

Damascus xii, xx, 3, 6, 7, 9, 12, 15, 16, 17, 18, 19, 20, 22, 25, 26, 29, 30–1, 32, 42, 44, 47, 48, 49, 50–1, 54, 55, 56, 68, 69, 74, 75, 78, 80, 82, 83–4, 87, 94, 99, 100, 102, 109, 111, 112, 113, 116, 118, 119, 120, 121–2, 123, 125, 129–30, 132, 136, 140, 148, 163, 164, 166, 167, 169, 170, 171, 174, 176, 177, 179, 180, 181, 184, 185, 187, 188, 203, 237, 270, 275, 276, 279, 282, 290, 291, 295, 296, 297, 298, 300–1, 311
  citadel of 38, 56, 57, 58, 88, 102, 179, 194, 196, 199, 203, 209, 218, 238, 240, 246, 251
Damietta xxiii, 7, 9, 15, 23, 48, 50, 55, 82, 88, 111, 129, 148, 149, 150–1, 152, 153, 157, 160, 171, 186–7, 204, 256, 270, 292, 296, 311
  Tower of the Chain 15, 151, 204
Dānishmands 28, 98, 115, 289, 290
Darbsāk (see Trapessac)
Dārūm xxi, 40, 54, 64, 72–3, 101, 140, 171, 173, 184, 276, 292, 295
Da'uk (see Doc)
Ḍayfa Khātūn, regent of Aleppo 90
Dieudamor 252, 295, 297
Ḍirghām, Fāṭimid vizier 31, 300
Diyār Bakr 214
Doc (Arb. Da'uk) 48, 59, 130, 142
Dorylaeum, battle of xi
Dubays ibn Ṣadaqa, ruler of al-Ḥilla 30, 98, 289
Duqāq, Seljuk ruler of Damascus 6, 15, 30, 300
Durazzo (anc. Dyrrachium, mod. Durrës) 145, 153

Edessa xv, xvi, 7, 9, 16, 17, 19, 50, 68, 81, 95, 106, 109, 113, 115, 119, 120, 121, 122, 124, 134, 140, 145, 160, 174, 176, 178, 181, 204, 255, 287, 288, 290, 291, 293, 296, 297, 311
  county of 8–10, 13, 17, 19, 30, 39, 75–6, 94, 97, 106, 115, 120, 122, 173–4, 175, 258, 303
Edward I, king of England 25, 48, 119–20, 262, 263–4, 267, 278, 281,
Eighth Crusade 25, 88
Eschiva Bures 32, 121
Eudes of Châteauroux, papal legate 48
Eudes of St Amant, master of the Templars 97
Eustace III, count of Boulogne 145
Eustace Garnier, lord Caesarea and Sidon 75

Fakhr al-Dīn Yūsuf, Ayyūbid emir 187, 297, 298
Fakhr al-Mulk ibn 'Ammār, ruler of Tripoli 68, 69
Farrukhshāh, 'Izz al-Dīn, Ayyūbid emir 186, 119, 293
Field of Blood (Cr. *ager sanguinis*, Arb. Balāṭ), battle of xi, 17, 99, 112, 113, 114, 120, 255, 275
Fifth Crusade 23, 25, 45, 47, 48, 54, 55, 56, 68, 86, 91, 111, 150–1, 152, 160, 173, 256, 274, 277, 296
First Crusade 3, 6, 7–8, 9, 10, 19, 23, 27, 28, 38, 49, 63, 69, 74, 77, 81, 95, 95, 105–6, 134, 137, 145, 149, 156, 163, 165, 168–9, 172–3, 175, 181, 188, 217, 231, 250, 254, 262, 267, 271, 274, 279, 286
Firuz, betrayer of Antioch 174, 175
Forbelet (Arb. Afrabalā) 114
Forbie, battle of xi, 32, 98
Fourth Crusade 55, 84, 153
Frederick I (Barbarossa), Holy Roman Emperor 173
Frederick II, Holy Roman Emperor, king of Jerusalem 23, 29, 45, 46, 54, 84, 175, 262, 302
al-Fūla (see La Fève)
Fulcher of Chartres, lord of Sarūj 107
Fulk, constable of Tiberias 95, 186
Fulk (V of Anjou), king of Jerusalem 13–14, 19, 29, 30, 41, 42, 70, 75, 89, 90, 96–7, 107, 119, 120, 130, 230, 275, 290, 302
Fustat 14–15

Galeran of Le Puiset, lord of Sarūj 10, 98
Gaston (see Baghrās)
Gaston IV, viscount of Béarn 167
Gaza xxi, 45, 46, 64, 70, 71, 72–3, 80, 86, 97, 111, 117, 118, 170, 184, 282, 292, 311
Genghis Khan, Great Khan 23
Genoese 23, 29, 146, 149, 150, 167, 172, 173, 274, 286, 287, 297
Gerald of Sidon 147
Gervais of Bazoches, prince of Galilee 69, 99
Gibelacar (see 'Akkār)
Gibelet (see Jubayl)
Godfrey of Bouillon, protector of Jerusalem 8, 11, 12, 74, 77, 145, 146, 147, 154, 165, 166, 169, 286, 302
Gunther, bishop of Bamberg 65
Guy of Lusignan, king of Jerusalem 21, 22, 32, 91, 111, 120–1, 123, 150, 183, 276, 295, 302
Guy I, lord of Gibelet 183
Guy II, lord of Gibelet 32

al-Ḥabis (Petra) xxii, 191, 311
al-Ḥabis Jaldak (Cr. Cava de Suet) xx, xxi, 77–8, 95, 118–19, 122, 181, 186, 233, 275, 288, 292, 293, 311
Haifa xx, xxi, 47, 85, 149, 173, 181, 286
Hajar Shuglan Pass 76
al-Ḥakim, Fāṭimid caliph 4
Ḥalba (Cr. Castrum Album) 117, 233, 292
Hama xix, 7, 9, 15, 16, 17, 49, 68, 84, 102, 113, 116, 124, 181, 185, 206, 233, 239, 256, 283, 288, 289, 290, 293, 295, 296
Ḥārim (Cr. Harrenc) xviii, 11, 66, 84, 106, 109, 111, 113, 115, 122, 154, 181, 185, 218, 233, 255, 256, 289, 291, 292, 293, 298, 311

battle of 99, 109, 115, 116, 233
Ḥarrān xv, xvi, 7, 9, 16, 50, 98, 120, 147, 160, 238, 289, 292, 296, 297, 311
battle of 114–15
Harrenc (see Ḥārim)
Hattin, battle of xi, 3, 21, 22, 25, 32, 40, 42, 75, 76, 79, 90, 91, 98, 111, 112, 114, 121, 123, 168, 170, 174, 181, 182, 184, 186, 236, 242, 246, 261, 281
terms of surrender following the battle 183
distribution and character of sieges before and after 271, 274–9
Havedic, Armenian artillerist 167, 187
Hebron xxi, 11, 40, 50, 59, 70, 72
Henry I (of Champagne), king of Jerusalem 136, 302
Henry II, king of Cyprus and Jerusalem 49, 283, 284, 285, 302
Henry III, king of England 46
Henry IV, Holy Roman Emperor 29
Hethum I, king of Cilician Armenia 24
Ḥiṣn al-Akrād (see Crac des Chevaliers)
Ḥiṣn Kayfā xv, 117, 122, 270
Ḥiṣn al-Khurayba 178
Ḥiṣn al-Tūfān 84
Homs xix, 7, 9, 12, 15, 16, 17, 22, 24, 27, 49, 50, 51, 62, 66, 68, 76, 83, 84, 109, 112, 116, 117, 118, 160, 179, 185, 206, 239, 276, 288, 289, 290, 293, 296, 297, 298
first battle of 24
second battle of 24, 112
third battle of (see Wādī al-Khazindār)
Hospitallers 14, 21, 22, 23, 29, 44, 45, 48, 53, 59, 60, 66, 68, 70, 75, 76, 84, 85, 91, 92, 93, 98, 99, 102, 123, 179, 180, 194, 206, 209, 219, 230, 232, 234, 236, 240, 249, 250, 260, 282, 284
Hṙomgla (see Qal'at al-Rūm)
Hugh I (III of Cyprus), king of Jerusalem 77, 302
Hugh VIII of Lusignan, count of La Marche 109
Hugh of Caesarea 99
Hugh of Ibelin 297
Hugh of Jaffa 30
Hugh of St Omer, prince of Galilee 42, 69, 75, 77, 83
Hugh of Scandelion 108
Hugh of Tiberias, titular prince of Galilee 171
Hülagü, Il-Khan 23–4, 25, 87, 278, 289
Humphrey II, lord of Toron and constable of the kingdom of Jerusalem 44, 75, 108, 114, 115, 180, 186, 255
Humphrey IV, lord of Toron 96, 183, 186
Hūnīn (see Chastel Neuf)
Ḥusām al-Dīn Lādjīn, Mamlūk sultan of Egypt and Syria 103
Ḥusām al-Dīn Timurtāsh (see Timurtāsh ibn Īlghāzī)

Ibelin xxi, 40, 60, 64, 70–1, 72, 261, 311
family and party of (for individual members, see elsewhere) 23, 70, 151, 274, 297
Ibn al-Muqaddam, Shams al-Din, Ayyūbid emir of Baalbek 50, 113
Ibn al-Sallār, Fāṭimid vizier 119, 300
Ibn Ṣulayḥa, ruler of Jabala 175
Īlghāzī ibn Artuq, Najm al-Dīn, Artuqid ruler of Aleppo 6, 17, 19, 28, 83, 85, 107, 112–13, 120, 121, 122, 138, 255, 258, 270, 275, 287, 288
'Imād al-Dīn Zankī (II), Zankid ruler of Sinjār 116, 294, 301
'Imm xviii, 106, 113
Inab 291
battle of 112, 113, 114, 122
Innocent II, pope 82
Isaac Comnenus, Greek ruler of Cyprus 99
Isabella I, queen of Jerusalem 23, 302
Isabella II, queen of Jerusalem 23, 302
Isfahan 153
Iskandarūna (see Scandelion)
Ismā'īl, leader of the Assassins 18
Ivo Velos, landowner 232
'Izz al-Dīn Aybak al-Afram (see al-Afram)
'Izz al-Dīn Aybak ibn 'Abdullah (see Aybak ibn 'Abdullah)
'Izz al-Dīn Jūrdīk al-Nūrī, Ayyūbid ruler of Jerusalem and Bānyās 180
'Izz al-Dīn Mas'ūd ibn al-Bursuqī, ruler of Aleppo 32–3
'Izz al-Dīn Mas'ūd ibn Quṭb al-Dīn Mawdūd 116, 117
'Izz al-Dīn Usāma, Ayyūbid ruler of 'Ajlūn 53

Jabala xviii, xix, 149, 173, 175, 185, 274, 286, 287
Jacob's Ford (Cr. Chastellet, Arb. Qaṣr al-'Atra) xii, xx, 20, 41, 43, 45, 66, 67, 75, 78–9, 80, 90, 97, 108, 114, 125, 181, 230–1, 242, 251, 261, 275, 293, 312
Jaffa xxi, 7, 9, 29, 30, 40, 45, 47, 48, 66, 67, 69, 70, 72, 82, 86, 87, 89, 90, 96, 112, 118, 123, 124, 130, 140, 146, 163, 167, 170, 171, 172, 174, 181, 184, 276, 279, 288, 289, 294, 295, 298, 312
Jamāl al-Dīn al-Najībī, Mamlūk governor of Syria 80
Janāḥ al-Dawla, ruler of Homs 18
al-Jawād Yūnus, Ayyūbid ruler of Damascus 32, 180
Jāwulī Saqāo, ruler of Mosul 30, 98, 142, 287, 301
Jerash xxi, 53, 59, 64, 73, 78
Jericho xxi, 66, 67, 72
Jerusalem xxi, 3–4, 5, 6, 7, 8, 9, 10, 11, 12, 14, 17, 19, 22, 23, 28, 29, 31, 36, 40, 46, 55, 56, 58, 59, 62, 65, 66, 67, 68, 69–70, 72, 73, 77, 86, 87, 95, 96, 97, 100, 101, 107, 110, 112, 118, 134, 145–7, 149, 153–4, 159, 165, 166, 167, 170, 171, 172, 174, 175, 180, 181, 182–3, 184, 188, 218, 219, 231, 238, 249, 254, 274, 276, 281, 286, 291, 294, 297, 312
kingdom of xi, 9, 11–12, 13, 14, 19, 20, 21, 23, 29, 32, 38–9, 40, 41, 42, 48, 62, 73, 76, 77, 79, 80, 81, 82, 83–4, 90, 91, 94, 96, 108, 113, 114, 117, 118, 119, 120–1, 122, 123, 124, 147, 148,

153, 168, 173–4, 229, 233, 236, 258, 260, 261, 279, 281, 302
  Tower of David 58, 97, 213
Jinīn 142, 275, 282, 294
Jisr al-Shughr 21, 118
John I Tzimiskes, Byzantine emperor 37
John II Comnenus, Byzantine emperor 80, 119, 155, 255, 270, 279, 290
John the Armenian 32, 48, 167, 187
John of Brienne, king of Jerusalem 150, 302
John of Grailly 253
John of Ibelin, lord of Beirut 201, 254, 296
John of Ibelin, lord of Jaffa 82, 123
John of Montfort, lord of Tyre 85
Jokermish, ruler of Mosul 30, 114, 287, 301
Joscelin I (of Courtenay), count of Edessa 9–10, 13, 14, 30, 69, 77, 94, 98, 106, 109, 115, 120, 130, 142, 176, 177, 179, 255, 270, 289, 303
Joscelin II, count of Edessa 95, 98, 99, 119, 124, 255, 303
Joscelin III, titular count of Edessa, seneschal of Jerusalem 14, 17, 40, 97, 109, 303
Joscelin of Cornant, *engingneur* of Louis IX of France 167, 187
Jubayl (Cr. Gibelet, anc. Byblos) xix, xx, 12, 130, 173, 176, 183, 184, 191, 194, 214, 229, 230, 232, 242, 264, 267, 287, 312
Julian of Sidon 44, 180
al-Jundī (see Qalʿat Ṣadr)

Kafr Lām 35, 36, 217, 231, 250, 261
Kafr Salām 65
Kafarṭāb xviii, xix, 94, 130, 139, 140, 185, 279, 288, 289, 290
al-Kahf xix, 66
Kakhtā xvi, 296
al-Kāmil Muḥammad, Ayyūbid sultan of Egypt 15, 46, 86, 90, 111, 175, 180, 238, 239, 256, 296, 297, 300, 301
Kantara xxiv, 297
Karbughā, ruler of Mosul 17, 28, 301
Kawkab (see Belvoir)
Kaysūn xvi, 109, 289, 290
Kerak (Cr. Petra Deserti) xii, xxi, xxii, 9, 12, 20, 21, 22, 24, 40, 42, 44, 50, 54, 55, 58, 64, 73–4, 87, 90, 95, 96, 103, 114, 121, 122, 140, 142, 168, 180, 183, 184–5, 186, 193, 196, 198, 202, 204, 206, 208, 217, 242, 250–1, 256, 260, 261, 267, 279, 282, 292, 293, 294, 297, 298, 299, 312
Kharpūt xv, xvi, 7, 9, 98, 138, 178–9, 255, 289, 297
Khīr Khān, ruler of Homs 179
Khirbat al-Mafjar 34, 35
Khirbat al-Minya 34, 35
Khwārizmians 98, 297
Kitbugha, Mongol general 24, 87, 114, 298
Kurdāna (see Ricordane)
Kurds 13, 20, 50, 51, 76, 100, 176, 236
Kyrenia xxiv, 151, 274, 295, 296, 297

La Fève (Arb. al-Fūla) xx, xxi, 53, 66, 80, 94, 121, 262
La Roche de Roussel (Tur. Chilvan Kale) 76
Lampron xviii, 9, 106
Latakia xviii, xix, 7, 9, 21, 112, 173, 183, 185, 186, 252, 274, 276, 286, 294
Latrun (Cr. Toron des Chevaliers) xxi, 66, 67, 72, 86, 229, 263, 312
Le Destroit xx, xxi, 65, 66, 68, 191, 232, 244
Le Petit Gérin (Arb. Zirʿīn) xx, xxi, 53, 66, 114
Leo II, king of Cilician Armenia 24
Leopold VI, duke of Austria 45
Li Vaux Moyses (see Wādī Mūsā)
Limassol xxiv, 172
Lisbon 155, 157–8, 172
Louis III, Landgrave of Thuringia 150
Louis VII, king of France 130, 172
Louis IX, king of France 25, 26, 29, 32, 47, 48, 84, 87, 88, 151–2, 154, 165, 167, 174, 186, 187, 199, 203, 248, 267
Lydda xxi, 40, 67, 70, 72, 86, 97

Maʿarrat al-Nuʿmān xviii, xix, 7, 11, 16, 36, 94, 134, 145, 149, 185, 239, 286, 288, 290, 295
Maḥmūd Ghāzān, Il-Khan 24
Māhūz Azdūd 35, 36, 231, 261
Majd al-Dīn, Ayyūbid emir 176
Majd al-Dīn al-Ṭawrī, Mamluk governor of Safed 101
al-Majdal xx, 290
Malaicas (Arb. Manīqia) 66
Malaṭya xv, xvi, 7, 9, 155, 287, 289, 291
Malikshāh, Seljuk sultan 6, 29, 49, 180
al-Mallāḥa 180
Mamistra (Arb. al-Maṣṣīṣa) 106, 115
Manbij xvi, 16, 117, 122, 181, 289, 293, 295
Manīqia (see Malaicas)
al-Manṣūr Ibrāhīm, Ayyūbid ruler of Homs 32, 98
al-Manṣūr Muḥammad, Ayyūbid ruler of Hama 102, 239, 296
al-Manṣūr Muḥammad (II), Ayyūbid ruler of Hama 24, 298
Manṣūra xxiii, 111, 152, 154, 165, 167, 187
Manzikert, battle of 5
Maogamalcha 139
Maraclea (Arb. Maraqiyya) xix, 63, 81, 87, 312
Maraqiyya (see Maraclea)
Marash xvi, 106, 276, 291, 293
Mardin xv, 7, 9, 17, 23, 111, 117, 122, 270, 295, 296, 298
Margaret of Tyre 85
Margat (Arb. Marqab) xii, xix, 11, 14, 21, 62, 66, 76, 85, 87, 91, 92, 93, 94, 99, 125, 160, 166–7, 184, 185, 188, 194–5, 206, 209, 213, 217, 236, 240, 250, 252, 267, 279, 299, 312
Marqab (see Margat)
al-Maṣṣīṣa (see Mamistra)
Masurra 139
Maṣyāf xix, 18, 66, 83, 84, 178, 293

Maurice, lord of Transjordan 44, 180
Mawdūd ibn Altūntakīn, ruler of Mosul 18, 19, 121, 176, 255, 287, 288, 301
Mayyāfāriqīn xv, 17, 24, 50, 270
Mecca 28, 54, 55, 85, 122
Medina 54, 55, 122
Melisende, queen of Jerusalem 13, 29, 89–90, 119, 302
Mirabel (Arb. Majdal Yaba) xxi, 40, 86, 274, 291
Möngke, Great Khan 23, 24
Mongols 3, 18, 23–4, 25, 26, 32, 44, 86–7, 88, 111, 114, 120, 123, 124, 127, 131, 154, 172, 180, 239–40, 246, 254, 258, 270, 278, 298
Mons Peregrinus (Arb. Sandjīl, alt. Saint-Gilles) xix, xx, 68, 87, 92, 312
Montferrand (Arb. Ba'rīn) xix, 16, 58, 76, 96–7, 107, 117, 154, 239, 289, 290, 293, 295
Montfort (Arb. al-Qurayn) xii, xx, 14, 27, 43, 45, 46, 60, 61, 65, 87, 117, 118, 140, 141, 160, 164, 177, 191, 193, 194, 200, 206, 209, 211, 212, 237, 242–4, 261, 262, 267, 268, 279, 297, 312
Montgisard, battle of 48, 97, 112
Montreal (Arb. Shawbak) xii, xxii, 12, 21, 40–1, 44, 55, 58, 59–60, 73, 74, 85, 90, 95, 103, 168, 180, 183, 184, 190, 206, 213, 219, 230, 231, 241, 242, 247, 250, 256, 262, 263, 293, 294, 313
Mosul xv, 6, 9, 17, 19, 33, 91, 98, 116, 122, 123, 139, 153, 169, 177, 222, 270, 301–2
Mount Glavianus 59
Mount Tabor xx, xxi, 53, 55–6, 58, 62, 92, 86, 100, 103, 142, 238, 252, 296, 313
al-Mu'aẓẓam 'Īsā, Ayyūbid ruler of Damascus 45, 46–7, 54, 55, 59, 86, 88, 91, 103, 238, 256, 296, 301
al-Mu'aẓẓam Tūrānshāh, Ayyūbid sultan of Egypt and Damascus 25, 88, 300, 301
Mubāriz al-Dīn, Ayyūbid governor of Ṣubayba 103
al-Mughīth 'Umar, Ayyūbid ruler of Kerak 24, 50, 87
Muḥammad, Prophet of Islam 3, 4
Muḥammad, Seljuk sultan 153
Mu'īn al-Dīn Unur, regent of Damascus 31, 63, 148, 176, 179, 290, 291
al-Mu'izz al-Dīn Aybak (see Aybak)
Mujīr al-Dīn, Būrid ruler of Damascus 31, 176, 301, 291
Munayṭira 84, 125, 233, 292
al-Mustarshid, 'Abbāsid caliph 18
al-Muẓaffar Maḥmūd, Ayyūbid ruler of Hama 239
al-Muẓaffar Maḥmūd II, Ayyūbid ruler of Hama 282

Nablus xxi, 7, 9, 32, 40, 53, 74, 118, 119, 180
Najm al-Dīn Ayyūb (see Ayyūb)
al-Nāṣir Dā'ūd, Ayyūbid ruler of Kerak and Damascus 297, 301
al-Nāṣir Qilij Arslān, Ayyūbid ruler of Hama 239
al-Nāṣir Yūsuf, Ayyūbid ruler of Aleppo and Damascus 24, 25, 82, 90, 297, 298, 301
Nazareth 40, 80, 84, 102
Neocaesarea (mod. Niksar) 98
Nephin (Arb. Anafa) xix, xx, 32, 63, 203, 204, 278, 299, 313
Nicaea 3, 7, 8, 134, 137–8, 145, 181, 188, 249, 270, 276, 286
Nicholas of Hanapes, titular patriarch of Jerusalem 49
Nikephoras II Phocas, Byzantine emperor 37
Ninth Crusade 25
Nisibis xv, 122, 177, 287, 293, 296
Nizārīs (see Assassins)
Norwegians 149, 169, 170, 173, 287
Nubia 20
Nūr al-Dīn, Zankid ruler of Aleppo and Damascus 19, 20, 29, 31, 39, 42, 49, 52, 56, 59, 71, 75, 76, 78, 83, 85, 90, 95, 97, 99, 107–8, 109, 113, 115–16, 117, 119, 121–2, 124, 125, 130, 171, 174, 176, 179–80, 186, 188, 206, 233, 235, 237, 253, 255–6, 267, 270, 275, 276, 277, 291, 292, 293, 301
Nūr al-Dīn Muḥammad, Artuqid ruler of Ḥiṣn Kayfā 122

Oshin, Armenian ruler of Lampron 8–9, 106
Otto of Grandson 253

Pagan the Butler, lord of Transjordan 42, 44, 73
Palmyra (Arb. Tadmor) xvii, 16, 36, 38, 64, 179, 209, 239
Peace of God 7
Peasants' Crusade 8
Pelagius, papal legate 48
Peter the Hermit 8
Peter of Sevrey, marshal of the Templars 284
Petra (see al-Ḥabis)
Petra Deserti (see Kerak)
Philip I, count of Flanders 19, 97, 256, 263, 276, 293
Philip I, king of France 29
Philip II, king of France 22, 142, 165, 253, 262, 267
Philip of Milly, lord of Transjordan 74, 180
Philip of Montfort, lord of Tyre 98, 297
Philip Rufus 40
Pisans 23, 29, 149, 150, 166, 173, 284, 286
Pons, count of Tripoli 13, 14, 29, 96–7, 107, 130, 289, 303

Qadmūs xix 18, 66
Qal'at Ibn Ma'ān 200
Qal'at Ja'bar xii, xv, xvi, xvii 16, 30, 52, 67, 98, 99, 124, 179–80, 193, 206, 291, 292
Qal'at Muḍīq (see Apamea)
Qal'at Najm xii, xv, xvi, 16, 52, 67, 122, 206, 217, 218, 237, 295
Qal'at al-Rūm (Cr. Ranculat, Arm. Hřomgla) xvi, 67

Qalʿat Ṣadr (alt. Al-Jundī) xxii, xxiii, 52, 53–4, 55, 102–3, 199, 219, 231, 250, 293, 313
Qalʿat Simʿān (Church of St Simeon Stylites) xvi, xviii, 118
Qalāwūn, al-Manṣūr Sayf al-Dīn, Mamlūk sultan of Egypt and Syria 27, 32, 81, 85, 87, 91, 131, 166, 172, 188, 214, 227, 234, 242, 247, 250, 281, 282, 299, 300
Qāqūn (Cr. Caco) xx, xxi, 25, 120, 204, 278
Qarāqūsh al-Asadī, Bahā' al-Dīn, Ayyūbid emir 21, 50, 100
Qāsim al-Dawla Āqsunqur, Seljuk ruler of Aleppo 37
Qaṣr al-ʿAtra (see Jacob's Ford)
Qaṣr al-Ḥallabāt 34, 35, 36
Qaṣr al-Ḥayr al-Gharbī 35, 36
Qaṣr al-Ḥayr al-Sharqī 35, 36, 209
Qaṣr Kharana 34, 35, 250
Qaṣr al-Mshatta 35, 36, 250
Qaṣr Qasṭal 34, 35
Qaṣr Tuba 35, 36
Qaysāriyya (see Caesarea)
Qilij Arslān, sultan of Rūm 6, 8, 30, 287
Qilij Arslān (II), sultan of Rūm 122
al-Qubba 83
al-Qulayʿāt (see Coliath)
al-Qurayn (see Montfort)
al-Quṣayr (see Cursat)
Quṭb al-Dīn Mawdūd, Zankid ruler of Homs and Mosul 116, 302
Quṭuz, Sayf al-Dīn, Mamlūk sultan of Egypt 25, 300

Raban xvi, 288
Rafaniyya 16, 58, 76, 107, 124, 275, 288, 289
al-Raḥba xvii, 7, 9, 16, 36, 67, 193, 206, 239, 289, 297, 298
Ramla xxi, 11, 40, 65, 67, 70, 72, 80, 84, 86, 93, 96, 97
  second battle of xi, 96
Ranculat (see Qalʿat al-Rūm)
Raqqa xv, xvi, xvii, 7, 9, 16, 36, 67, 112, 116, 122, 180, 193, 209, 238, 270, 292, 299, 313
Ravandal xvi, xviii, 62, 106
Raymond I (of St Gilles), count of Tripoli 8, 12, 13, 30, 68–9, 92, 137, 145, 146, 165, 169, 172, 254, 274, 286, 287, 293, 303
Raymond II, count of Tripoli 14, 18, 31, 76, 303
Raymond III, count of Tripoli 31, 31–2, 53, 97, 108, 109, 114, 116, 121, 122, 186, 256, 303
Raymond of Poitiers, prince of Antioch 19, 113, 119, 275, 302
Raymond Roupen, prince of Antioch 302
Renier Brus, lord of Bānyās 44, 75
Reynald of Châtillon, prince of Antioch and lord of Transjordan 20, 54, 55, 74, 95, 97, 99, 108, 120–1, 122–3, 291, 292, 293, 294, 302
Reynald of Marash 113
Reynald of Sidon 42, 44, 97, 99, 183, 185
Richard I, king of England 22, 45, 73, 99, 130, 140, 142, 163, 171, 175, 234, 253, 259, 263, 271, 276, 295
Richard of Cornwall 46
Richard of Salerno, regent of Edessa 115
Ricordane (Arb. Kurdāna) 48, 59, 179
Riḍwān, Fakhr al-Mulk, Seljuk ruler of Aleppo 6, 16–17, 19, 30, 106, 109, 115, 121, 132–3, 255, 274, 275, 286, 287, 301
Robert I, count of Flanders 7, 19
Robert II, count of Flanders 8, 19
Robert II (Curthose), duke of Normandy 8, 145, 167
Robert of Bellême 145, 167
Robert Giscard 153
Rochester 168
Roger of Salerno, regent of Antioch 13, 17, 30, 83, 85, 112, 113, 120, 138, 275, 288
Romanos IV Diogenes, Byzantine emperor 5
Rosetta 15, 88
Ruad (Arb. Arwād) xix, 63

Saʿd al-Dīn Masʿūd, Ayyūbid emir of Safed 50
Safed (Cr. Saphet) xii, xx, 14, 21, 26, 32, 42, 43, 45, 46–7, 50, 53, 58, 59, 66, 75, 77, 84, 86, 87, 92–3, 97, 98, 101, 102, 103, 108, 117–18, 123, 142, 154, 160, 164, 167, 175, 177, 180, 183, 184, 191, 199, 218, 219, 221, 230, 231, 236, 240, 254, 262, 279, 294, 298, 313
Ṣaffūriyya xx, xxi, 21, 53, 67, 80, 90, 117
Ṣāfīthā (see Chastel Blanc)
Ṣahyūn (see Saone)
al-Saʿīd Ḥasan, Ayyūbid ruler of Ṣubayba 24, 103
Saint-Gilles (see Mons Peregrinus)
St Catherine's Monastery xxii, 95
Ste Suzanne 168
Saladin (al-Nāṣir Ṣalāḥ al-Dīn Yūsuf), Ayyūbid sultan of Egypt and Damascus 3, 15, 16, 18, 20, 21–2, 25, 29, 31, 32, 42, 44, 45, 45, 48, 49, 50, 53, 54, 55, 58, 59, 74, 76, 78, 79, 80, 84, 86, 87, 90–1, 95, 96, 97–8, 99, 100, 101, 103, 107, 111, 113–14, 116–17, 118, 119, 120, 121, 122–3, 124–5, 130, 136, 140, 142, 149, 153, 154, 155, 159, 170–1, 174, 175, 176, 179, 180, 181, 182–5, 186, 190, 202, 231, 234, 235–6, 237–8, 239, 250, 252, 253, 254, 256, 269, 270, 271, 274, 275–7, 279, 281, 292, 293, 294, 295, 300, 301
Salamiyya 16, 239
al-Ṣāliḥ Ayyūb, Ayyūbid sultan of Egypt and Damascus 25, 27, 32, 50, 98, 180, 186–7, 297, 298, 300
al-Ṣāliḥ Ismāʿīl, Ayyūbid ruler of Damascus 32, 47, 98, 175, 180, 297, 301
al-Ṣāliḥ Ismāʿīl ibn Nūr al-Dīn, Zankid ruler of Aleppo 20, 116, 117, 256, 293, 301
Samosata xv, xvi, 106, 109
Sandjīl (see Mons Peregrinus)

Saone (Arb. Ṣahyūn) xviii, xix, 10, 37, 58, 62, 63, 66, 87, 160, 183, 184, 185, 192, 194, 196, 198, 200, 204, 205, 217, 227, 228, 229, 231, 242, 250, 252, 265, 267, 294, 299, 313
Saphet (see Safed)
Saranda Kolones xxiv, 259
Ṣārim al-Dīn Barghash al-ʿĀdilī, Ayyūbid emir 103
Ṣārim al-Dīn Qāymāz al-Kāfirī, Mamlūk emir 102
Ṣarkhad xx, xxi, 15, 31, 51, 88, 118, 179, 206
Sarmada xviii, 66, 112, Pass of 10, 66, 108, 109
Sarmīniyya xvii, xix, 183, 184, 295
Sarūj (mod. Suruç) xv, xvi, 10, 106, 107, 180, 274, 286
Sayf al-Dawla, Ḥamdānid ruler of Aleppo 37
Sayf al-Dīn Balabān al-Ṭabbākhī, Mamlūk emir 282
Sayf al-Dīn Balabān al-Zayni, Mamlūk *amīr ʿalam* 102, 167
Sayf al-Dīn Ghāzī, Zankid ruler of Mosul 19, 116, 302
Sayf al-Dīn Ghāzī (II), Zankid ruler of Mosul 91, 116, 117, 122, 293, 302
Sayf al-Dīn Masʿūd, Būrid governor of Tyre 170
Sayf al-Dīn Sawār, Zankid governor of Aleppo 119
Sayf al-Dīn Ṭaqwī, Mamlūk emir 92
Scandelion (Arb. Iskandarūna) xx, 41, 43, 69, 70, 261, 313
Second Crusade 18, 20, 31, 75, 119, 130, 172, 173, 174, 270, 291
Seljuk, patriarch of the Seljuk dynasty 5
Seventh Crusade 25, 32, 47, 84, 152, 153, 167, 173, 186
Shams al-Dawla Sulaymān, Artuqid governor of Aleppo 121, 301
Shams al-Dīn al-Aʿsar, Mamlūk emir 282
Shams al-Dīn ibn al-Muqaddam, Zankid ruler of Baalbek 113
Shams al-Khalīfa, Fāṭimid governor of Ascalon 30
Shams al-Mulūk Ismāʿīl, Būrid ruler of Damascus 30, 44, 119, 138, 139, 140, 255, 289, 290, 300
Shaqīf Arnūn (see Beaufort)
Shāwar, Fāṭimid vizier 15, 31, 300
Shawbak (see Montreal)
Shayzar xii, xix, 10, 16, 17, 18, 19, 37, 49, 52, 58, 62, 83, 84, 88, 89, 94, 95, 120, 139, 155, 178, 185, 206, 207, 214, 237, 242, 255, 267, 279, 289, 290, 291, 313
Shihāb al-Dīn, ruler of Qalʿat Jaʿbar 179
Shihāb al-Dīn Maḥmūd, Būrid ruler of Damascus 179, 300
Shīrkūh, Asad al-Dīn, Zankid emir and vizier of Egypt xiii, 20, 31, 50, 78, 99, 100, 107–8, 115, 116, 176, 179, 186, 233, 256, 292, 300
Shīrkūh (II), al-Mujāhid, Ayyūbid ruler of Homs 16, 100, 239, 297
Shmemis 16, 88, 239
Shughr-Bakās xviii, xix, 58, 62, 66, 183, 185, 200, 218, 295, 313
Sibylla, queen of Jerusalem 21, 302
Sidon xx, 29–30, 40, 42, 43, 44, 45, 48, 63, 64, 68, 69, 75, 83, 84, 85, 86, 87, 114, 117, 118, 123, 149, 150, 165, 169, 170, 173, 174, 176, 180, 184, 186, 204, 206, 214, 254–5, 270, 278, 281, 285, 287, 298, 313–14
Simon of Montceliard, master of Louis IX's crossbowmen 48
Sinjār xv, 116, 122, 176, 180, 270, 292, 293, 294, 296, 297
Sixth Crusade 23, 45
Stephanie of Milly, lady of Transjordan 74
Ṣubayba xii, xx, 24, 42, 43, 47, 48, 52, 54–5, 56, 58, 61, 87, 88, 101, 102, 103, 118, 164, 167, 192, 196, 199, 215, 218, 225, 226, 230, 231, 240, 246, 247–8, 249, 250, 251, 260, 264, 265, 268, 314
Sulaymān ibn Qutlumush, sultan of Rūm 6
Sunqur al-Ashqar, Mamlūk emir 87
Suqmān ibn Artuq, Artuqid ruler of Ḥiṣn Kayfā 6, 107, 114, 286
Syrian Gates (mod. Belen Pass) 21, 66–7, 76

Tadmor (see Palmyra)
Tāj al-Mulūk Būrī, Būrid ruler of Damascus 18, 300
Tancred, prince of Galilee and regent of Antioch 8, 10, 11, 17, 28, 30, 39, 69, 74, 77, 83, 105–6, 109, 115, 121, 129, 132–3, 169, 180, 190, 252, 255, 274, 286, 287
Taqī al-Dīn ʿUmar, Ayyūbid emir and ruler of Hama 123, 239, 294
Tarphile (Arb. Khirbat al-Manḥata) 191
Tarsus xviii, 7, 9, 106, 115, 290, 287
Ṭarṭūs (see Tortosa)
Tʿatʿul, Armenian ruler of Marash 106
Tell Aran 270, 289
Tell Bāshir (see Turbessel)
Tell Ibn Macher 62
Tell al-Maʿshūqa 69
Tell al-Ṣāfī (see Blanchegarde)
Tell al-Sulṭān 91, 116
Templars 14, 20, 21, 22, 23, 28, 29, 41, 42, 44, 45, 46–7, 48, 59, 62, 63, 65–6, 67, 68, 70, 72, 74, 75, 76, 78, 80, 84, 85, 91, 92–3, 94, 97, 98, 101, 114, 118, 121, 130, 142, 177, 179, 180, 184, 186, 194, 199, 234–5, 236, 244, 250, 253, 260, 278, 282, 283, 284, 285, 299
Teutonic Knights 14, 23, 44, 45, 60, 98, 243, 244, 282
Theobald I (IV of Champagne), king of Navarre 46
Thessalonica 159
Thierry, count of Flanders 19, 78, 275, 291, 292
Third Crusade 3, 14, 19, 22, 45, 46, 73, 84, 86, 101, 111, 149, 155, 160, 171, 173, 174, 176, 236, 259, 265, 271, 274, 276, 279, 295
Tiberias xx, xxi, 9, 11, 20, 21, 32, 53, 69, 74, 77, 78, 86, 97, 114, 115, 121, 181, 183, 184, 249, 275, 294, 297, 314
Tibnīn (see Toron)

Timurtāsh ibn Īlghāzī, Ḥusām al-Dīn, Artuqid ruler of Aleppo and Mardin 177, 290, 301
Tinnis xxiii, 14, 15, 152
Toron (Arb. Tibnīn) xii, xx, 40, 41–2, 69, 75, 76, 77, 82, 86, 108, 114, 118, 123, 181, 183, 184, 219, 294, 295, 314
Toron des Chevaliers (see Latrun)
Toros II, ruler of Cilician Armenia 109
Toros, Greek ruler of Edessa 9
Tortosa (Arb. Ṭarṭūs) xix, 7, 12, 21, 27, 63, 66, 68, 76, 92, 173, 181, 185, 194, 199, 200, 206, 217, 236, 242, 250, 252, 261, 262, 276, 281, 285, 286, 291, 294, 314
Tour du Garçon (Arb. Burj al-Ṣābi') 66, 209, 213
Trani 145
Trapessac (Arb. Darbsāk) xviii, 62, 67, 76, 118, 183, 185, 295
Tripoli xix, xx, 7, 9, 12, 13, 18, 27, 32, 87, 44, 62, 63, 66, 68–9, 76, 81, 83, 92, 107, 109, 112, 114, 116, 117, 125, 130, 134, 149, 153, 160, 163, 169, 170, 171, 173, 181, 183, 186, 229, 254, 274, 278, 279, 281, 287, 299
  county of 9, 12–14, 15, 17, 21, 22, 27, 39, 75, 76, 82, 84, 116, 120, 123, 303
Troia 168
Tuban 117
Ṭughtakīn, Ẓāhir al-Dīn, Būrid ruler of Damascus 15, 17–18, 30, 77, 80, 83, 84, 108, 109, 110–11, 113, 119, 124, 142, 170, 179, 274, 275, 287, 288, 289, 300
Ṭugril-Beg, Seljuk sultan 5
Tūrānshāh, Shams al-Dawla, Ayyūbid emir and ruler of Yemen 50, 293
Turbessel (Arb. Tell Bāshir) xvi, 7, 9, 10, 13, 16, 19, 30, 62, 81, 106, 176, 255, 288, 291, 294, 296
Tutush, Tāj al-Dawla, Seljuk ruler of western Syria 6, 28, 107
Tyre (Arb. Ṣūr) xx, 7, 9, 11, 12, 15, 21, 22, 27, 31, 32, 36, 40, 43, 44, 62, 63, 68, 69, 75, 76, 77, 78, 80, 82, 85, 91, 95, 96, 97, 110–11, 112, 117, 118, 119, 123, 124, 129, 134, 136, 147, 149, 153, 154, 155, 163, 167, 169, 170–1, 173, 182–4, 185, 186, 187, 231, 234, 252, 254, 276, 281, 285, 288, 289, 294, 297, 314

al-'Ullaiqa 102
al-'Urayma (see Arima)
Urban II, pope 6, 7–8, 28

Valenia (mod. Baniyas) 66, 92, 173, 297
Venetians 23, 29, 68, 110, 147, 149, 153, 163, 173, 286, 289
Vetula xviii, xix, 66, 287

Wādī al-Khazindār, battle of 24
Wādī Mūsā (Arb. al-Wu'ayra, Cr. Li Vaux Moyses) xxii, 85, 291, 314
Walter of Caesarea 30
Walter of Quesnoy, knight of Humphrey II of Toron 186
William Embriaco 167
William of Valence 264
William-Jordan, count of Tripoli 13, 109, 287, 303
al-Wu'ayra (see Wādī Mūsā)

Yaghī Siyān, ruler of Antioch 6, 175
Yaḥmūr (see Chastel Rouge)
Yalu (see Castellum Arnaldi)
Yānis, Fāṭimid vizier 4, 300
Yāzūr (see Casel des Plains)
Yemen 20, 50
Yvette, daughter of Baldwin II of Jerusalem 98

al-Ẓāhir Ghāzī, Ayyūbid ruler of Aleppo 22, 50, 90, 100, 111, 123, 170, 176, 209, 219, 238, 239, 295, 301
Zankī, 'Imād al-Dīn, ruler of Mosul and Aleppo 15, 16, 17, 19, 30–1, 37, 44, 68, 76, 85, 95, 96–7, 116, 119, 122, 124, 125, 130, 140, 148, 154, 155, 174, 176, 177, 179, 255, 256, 270, 274, 275, 289, 290, 291, 301, 302
Zardanā xviii, 113, 121, 140, 287, 288, 289, 290
Zir'īn (see Le Petit Gérin)